T͏ ͏k of
͏ oility

Sustainability remains one of the major issues in tourism today. Concerns over climate and environmental change, the fallout from the global economic and financial crisis, and the seeming failure to meeting UN Millennium Development Goals have only reinforced the need for more sustainable approaches to tourism, however they be defined. Given the centrality of sustainability in tourism curricula, policies, research and practice it is therefore appropriate to prepare a state-of-the-art *Handbook* on the relationship between tourism and sustainability.

This timely *Handbook of Tourism and Sustainability* is developed from specifically commissioned original contributions from recognised authors in the field, providing a systematic guide to the current state of knowledge on this area. It is interdisciplinary in coverage and international in scope through its authorship and content. The volume commences with an assessment of tourism's global environmental, e.g. climate, emissions, energy use, biodiversity, water use, land use, and socio-economic effects, e.g. economic impacts, employment and livelihoods, culture. This then provides the context for sections outlining the main theoretical frameworks and constructs that inform tourism and sustainability, management tools and approaches, and the approaches used in different tourism and travel industry sectors. The book concludes by examining emerging and future concerns in tourism and sustainability such as peak-oil, post-carbon tourism, green economy and transition tourism.

This is essential reading for students, researchers and academics interested in the possibilities of sustainable forms of tourism and tourism's contribution to sustainable development. Its assessment of tourism's global impact along with its overviews of sectoral and management approaches will provide a benchmark by which the sustainability of tourism will be measured for years to come.

C. Michael Hall is a Professor in the Department of Management, Marketing and Entrepreneurship, University of Canterbury, New Zealand, and Docent, Department of Geography, University of Oulu, Finland. Co-editor of *Current Issues in Tourism*, he has wide-ranging research interests in tourism, mobility and regional development, food, and environmental history.

Stefan Gössling is a Professor at the Department of Service Management, Lund University and the School of Business and Economics, Linnaeus University, Kalmar, Sweden, and research coordinator at the Western Norway Research Institute's Research Centre for Sustainable Tourism. His research interests include tourism and climate change, tourism and development, mobility studies, renewable energy, low-carbon tourism, as well as climate policy and carbon trading.

Daniel Scott is a Canada Research Chair in Global Change and Tourism in the Department of Geography and Environmental Management, University of Waterloo. His research interests include tourism and climate change, sustainable tourism, protected areas management and climate change, and tourism-recreation climatology.

The Routledge Handbook of Tourism and Sustainability

Edited by C. Michael Hall,
Stefan Gössling and Daniel Scott

LONDON AND NEW YORK

First published 2015
by Routledge
2 Park Square, Milton Park, Abingdon, Oxon OX14 4RN

And by Routledge
711 Third Avenue, New York, NY 10017

First issued in paperback 2017

Routledge is an imprint of the Taylor & Francis Group, an informa business

British Library Cataloguing in Publication Data
A catalogue record for this book is available from the British Library

Library of Congress Cataloging in Publication Data
The Routledge handbook of tourism and sustainability / edited by Stefan Gössling, C. Michael Hall and Daniel Scott.
pages cm
Includes bibliographical references and index.
1. Sustainable tourism. I. Gössling, Stefan, editor of compilation. II. Hall, Colin Michael, editor of compilation. III. Scott, Daniel, editor of compilation. IV. Title: Handbook of tourism and sustainability.
G156.5.S87R68 2015
910.68'4--dc23

Typeset in Bembo
by Saxon Graphics Ltd, Derby

ISBN 13: 978-1-138-07147-6 (pbk)
ISBN 13: 978-0-415-66248-2 (hbk)

Contents

Contents

Contents

Figures

Tables

Contributors

Bas Amelung is an Assistant Professor in the Environmental Systems Analysis Group, Wageningen University, the Netherlands

Susanne Becken is Professor of Sustainable Tourism, Griffith Business School, Griffith University Gold Coast Campus, Queensland, Australia; Director of the Griffith Institute for Tourism, Griffith University and an Adjunct Professor at Lincoln University, New Zealand

Paulina Bohdanowicz-Godfrey is the Senior Sustainability Manager, Engineering Operations EMEA at Hilton Worldwide, Watford, UK

Rob Bongaerts is a lecturer and researcher in the Centre for Sustainable Tourism and Transport, NHTV Breda University of Applied Sciences, Breda, the Netherlands

Helen Briassoulis is a Professor in the Department of Geography, University of the Aegean, Mytilini, Lesvos, Greece

Ralf Buckley holds the International Chair in Ecotourism Research in the Griffith School of Environment, Griffith University Gold Coast Campus, Queensland, Australia

Georgette Leah Burns is an Associate Professor and Head of the Rural Tourism Department at Hólar University College in Iceland, and Head of Tourism Research at the Icelandic Seal Center

Tim Coles is Professor in Management at the University of Exeter, where he is also Director of the Centre for Sport, Leisure and Tourism Research, a centre of excellence for postgraduate and post-doctoral training funded by the Economic and Social Research Council

Janet E. Dickinson is a Senior Lecturer in Leisure & Recreational Studies, Bournemouth University, Poole, UK

Claire Dinan is a Senior Teaching Fellow in the University of Exeter Business School. She was previously sustainable tourism manager for the English Tourism Council and a freelance consultant specialising on sustainable business practices

Rachel Dodds is an Associate Professor in the Ted Rogers School of Hospitality and Tourism Management, Ryerson University, Toronto, Ontario, Canada and Director of the Ted Rogers Institute for Tourism & Hospitality Research

Sara Dolnicar is an ARC Queen Elizabeth II Fellow and Professor, University of Queensland Business School, University of Queensland, Brisbane, Australia

David Duval is an Associate Professor in the Faculty of Business and Economics at the University of Winnipeg and Director of the University of Manitoba Transport Institute, Canada. He is also Honorary Associate Professor in the School of Business, University of Otago, and a Senior Visiting Fellow in the School of Aviation, University of New South Wales, Australia

Eke Eijgelaar is a Researcher and Lecturer in the Centre for Sustainable Tourism and Transport, NHTV Breda University of Applied Sciences, the Netherlands

Emily Fenclova is a Lecturer at the University of New York in Prague, Czech Republic

David A. Fennell is a Professor in the Department of Tourism and Environment, Brock University, St. Catharines, Ontario, Canada and the founding editor-in-chief of the *Journal of Ecotourism*

Viachaslau Filimonau is a Lecturer in Hospitality Management in the School of Tourism, Bournemouth University, Poole, UK

Warwick Frost is an Associate Professor in the Department of Marketing and Tourism and Hospitality, La Trobe Business School, La Trobe University, Victoria, Australia

Brian Garrod is Professor of Tourism Management in the School of Management and Business, Aberystwyth University, Wales, UK

Stefan Gössling is a Professor at the School of Business and Economics at Linnaeus University, Kalmar, and the Department of Service Management, Lund University, both Sweden. He is also the research coordinator of the Research Centre for Sustainable Tourism at the Western Norway Research Institute

Sonya Graci is an Associate Professor, Ted Rogers School of Hospitality and Tourism Management, Ryerson University, Toronto, Canada and Director of Accommodating Green

Rob Hales is a Lecturer in the Department of Tourism, Sport and Hotel Management, Griffith Business School, Gold Coast Campus, Queensland, Australia

C. Michael Hall is a Professor in the Department of Management, Marketing and Entrepreneurship, University of Canterbury, New Zealand; Docent, Department of Geography, University of Oulu, Finland and Visiting Professor in the School of Business and Economics, Linneaus University, Kalmar, Sweden

Stephen Henderson is a Senior Lecturer in the UK Centre for Events Management at Leeds Beckett University, UK

Contributors

Freya Higgins-Desbiolles is a Senior Lecturer in the School of Management, University of South Australia Business School, University of South Australia, Adelaide, South Australia

James Higham is a Professor in the Department of Tourism, University of Otago, New Zealand and Visiting Professor, University of Stavanger, Norway

Erling Holden is Professor in renewable energy at Sogn og Fjordane University College, Department of Engineering and Science, Norway'

Debbie Hopkins is a Postdoctoral Fellow at the Centre for Sustainability, University of Otago, Dunedin, New Zealand

Tazim Jamal is an Associate Professor in the Department of Recreation, Park and Tourism Sciences, Texas A&M University, College Station, Texas, USA

John Jenkins is Professor of Tourism Studies and Chair, Academic Board, Southern Cross University, Lismore, New South Wales, Australia

Jennifer Laing is a Senior Lecturer in the Department of Marketing and Tourism and Hospitality, La Trobe Business School, La Trobe University, Victoria, Australia

Machiel Lamers is an Assistant Professor in the Environmental Policy Group of Wageningen University in the Netherlands

Diem-Trinh Le-Klähn has recently completed a doctorate at the School of Management, the Technical University of Munich, Germany

Kristin Linnerud is a Senior Research Fellow at the CICERO Center for International Climate and Environmental Research, Oslo, Norway

Brent Lovelock is an Associate Professor in the Department of Tourism, University of Otago, Dunedin, New Zealand

Muchazondida Mkono is a Postdoctoral Research Fellow in the University of Queensland Business School, Brisbane, Australia

Susan Moore is a Professor in the School of Veterinary and Life Sciences, Murdoch University, Perth, Western Australia

Gianna Moscardo is a Professor in the College of Business, Law and Governance, James Cook University, Townsville, Queensland, Australia

James Musgrave is a Senior Lecturer in Events Management, Leeds Beckett University, Leeds, UK

David Newsome is an Associate Professor in the School of Veterinary and Life Sciences, Murdoch University, Perth, Western Australia

Jeremy Northcote is a Lecturer in Sociology and Community Development at Murdoch University, Perth, Western Australia

Paul Peeters is an Associate Professor in the Centre for Sustainable Tourism and Transport, NHTV Breda University of Applied Sciences, Breda, The Netherlands

Bruce Prideaux is a Professor in Marketing & Tourism, Faculty of Law, Business & Creative Arts, School of Business, James Cook University, Cairns, Queensland, Australia

Michelle Rutty is a Post-Doctoral Fellow in the Department of Geography and Environmental Management, University of Waterloo, Ontario, Canada

Daniel Scott is a Professor and Canada Research Chair in Global Change and Tourism at the Department of Geography and Environmental Management, University of Waterloo, Ontario, Canada

Melanie Kay Smith is an Associate Professor at BKF University of Applied Sciences, Budapest, Hungary

John Swarbrooke is a Professor in the Department of Food and Tourism Management, Manchester Metropolitan University, Manchester, UK

Rhodri Thomas is a Professor of Tourism and Events Policy and Head of International Centre for Research in Events, Tourism and Hospitality (ICRETH), Leeds Beckett University, Leeds, UK

Dao Truong is a Lecturer in the Department of Tourism and Hospitality, National Economics University, Hanoi, Vietnam

Kyle Powys Whyte is an enrolled member of the Citizen Potawatomi Nation (CPN) in Shawnee, Oklahoma. He is Assistant Professor of philosophy at Michigan State University and affiliated faculty at the Center for the Study of Standards in Society (CS3), the Peace and Justice Studies Specialization, and the American Indian Studies Program

Heather Zeppel is an Associate Professor in the Australian Centre for Sustainable Business and Development, University of Southern Queensland, Queensland, Australia

Piotr Zientara is an Associate Professor in the Department of International Economic Relations, Faculty of Economics, University of Gdansk, Poland

Acronyms

BAU	business as usual
BPM	Balance of Payments Manual
BRICS	Brazil, Russia, India, China and South Africa
CDP	Carbon Disclosure Project
CLIA	Cruise Lines International Association
CO_2	carbon dioxide
CO_2-equivalent	The contribution of greenhouse gases with longlife times (> 100 years) to global warming, made comparable to CO_2
CPR	common pool resources
CSR	corporate social responsibility
DMO	Destination Management/Marketing Organisation
EEDI	Energy Efficiency Design Index
EPA	Environmental Protection Agency
ETC	European Travel Commission
EU	European Union
GFANC	German Federal Agency for Nature Conservation
GGND	Global Green New Deal
GHA	Green Hotel Association
GHG	greenhouse gas
GRI	Global Reporting Initiative
GSTC	Global Sustainable Tourism Criteria
HDI	Human Development Index
IATA	International Aviation Transport Association
IEA	International Energy Agency
IMF	International Monetary Fund
IMO	International Maritime Organization
IPCC	Intergovernmental Panel on Climate Change
ITP	International Tourism Partnership
IUCN	International Union for the Conservation of Nature and Natural Resources
LCA	life cycle assessment
LCEA	life cycle energy analysis
LDC	Less Developed Country
LEED	Leadership in Energy and Environmental Design
LTG	Limits to Growth
mb/d	million barrels per day
MDG	Millennium Development Goal
MRE	material/resource/energy
My	Millions of years
NPS	National Park Service (USA)
OECD	Organisation for Economic Co-operation and Development

PPT	pro-poor tourism
SIDS	Small Island Developing States
STI	Sustainable Tourism Indicators
TC	tourism commons
UDHR	Universal Declaration of Human Rights
UNCTAD	United Nations Conference on Trade and Development
UN DESA	United Nations Development Policy and Analysis Division
UNEP	United Nations Environment Programme
UNESCO	United Nations Educational, Scientific and Cultural Organization
UNFCCC	United Nations Framework Convention on Climate Change
UNWTO	United Nations World Tourism Organization
WCED	World Commission on Environment and Development (Brundtland Commission)
WEF	World Economic Forum
WMO	World Meteorological Organization
WTTC	World Travel and Tourism Council
WWAP	World Water Assessment Programme
WWF	World Wild Fund for Nature

Acknowledgements

Sustainability is one of the most important issues currently facing the tourism sector. Businesses, governments, non-government organisations, destinations and, increasingly, tourists are looking for ways to reduce their environmental impacts, and in some cases their social impacts, while simultaneously continuing to enjoy the economic and experiential benefits that tourism can bring. This book does not provide all the answers for how this may be accomplished. However, what it does do is provide a comprehensive overview of the key concepts and frameworks that underlie how sustainability is understood as well as the different management and sectoral approaches that seek to put the concept into effect. Yet, as noted throughout the book, sustainability has always been a highly contested concept that has led not just to differences in interpretation but also implementation. Arguably such issues are only to worsen in a near-future characterised by climate change, transfer to a low-carbon economy, and biodiversity loss while simultaneously international and domestic tourism are also expected to continue to grow (substantially by most accounts). It may be that green growth is possible but, as the concluding and several other chapters in the book suggest, perhaps it is the growth model itself that is the problem. In the case of tourism the issue is also not one of travel per se, but the fact that there are more people travelling so far and so often. Few destinations appear to have the capacity to say *enough*.

The editors would of course like to thank the authors for their various contributions as well as for their willingness to respond to correspondence at short notice. Undoubtedly, the publishing process of editing was made easier by the support of our publishers. We would all like to extend our sincere thanks to our editor Emma Travis at Routledge and her editorial assistant Philippa Mullins as well as to the rest of the team who have supported us during the project.

Support for collaboration was also provided by the Canada Research Chair program, the Western Norway Research Institute, Nicole Aignier and the Hotel Grüner Baum Merzhausen, and coffee beans from around the world. Finally, on a personal front we would like to thank our partners and families for their love, support and patience: Tonia, Danika and Isabel; Meike and Linnea; and Jody, Cooper and JC.

1

Tourism and sustainability

An introduction

C. Michael Hall, Stefan Gössling and Daniel Scott

Sustainable development 'Development that meets the needs of the present without compromising the ability of future generations to meet their own needs' (World Commission on Environment and Development [WCED] 1987: 49).

Sustainable tourism is a sub-set of sustainable development. Sustainable tourism is a tourism system that encourages qualitative development, with a focus on quality of life and well-being measures, but not aggregate quantitative growth to the detriment of natural capital.

Wicked planning problem A 'Wicked problem' is a phrase originally used in social planning to describe a problem that is difficult or impossible to solve because of incomplete, contradictory and changing requirements that are often difficult to recognise. The term 'wicked' is used to denote resistance to resolution. Moreover, because of complex interdependencies, the effort to solve one aspect of a wicked problem may reveal or create other problems. Climate change has been described as a 'super wicked problem' characterised by (a) lack of time; (b) no central governance authority; (c) those seeking to solve the problem are also causing it; and (d) policies which discount the future irrationally (Levin *et al.* 2012).

Introduction

Although the notion of sustainable development is now integral to tourism, policy and management, the concept has a long history. Indeed, the political and economic debate over the way in which sustainability should be defined, developed and implemented is a reflection of longstanding differences between different members of society over the best use of resources in industrial society. These debates are, in turn, bound up within the wider frameworks of attitudes towards the environment that exist both in contemporary society and, just as importantly, over time (Leiserowitz, Kates & Parris 2005; Dobson 2007). Although environmental issues are now taken for granted as a policy-making concern, it needs to be remembered that the 'age of ecology' is arguably a very recent phenomenon, with the first environmental protection agencies not being established until the late 1960s and early 1970s (Glacken 1967; Worster 1977). That the Earth has firmly entered the Anthropocene – an era that demarks a substantial global impact of humans on planetary environmental systems comparable in scale to those associated with significant perturbations of the geological past – is an even more recent realisation (Crutzen 2002). However, as central as the environment is to notions of sustainability, any understanding of the concept of sustainable development in relation to tourism also needs to chart the interrelationships between environmental, social and economic thought. This first chapter introduces the reader to this volume, its structure and some of the issues that it discusses.

Sustainable development and sustainable tourism

The famous Brundtland definition, that 'sustainable development is development that meets the needs of the present without compromising the ability of future generations to meet their own needs' (World Commission on Environment and Development (WCED) 1987: 49), has come to feature in many tourism textbooks, journal articles and student essays, even though tourism was hardly mentioned in the report. Yet neither sustainable development nor sustainable tourism began with the WCED. Variations of the concepts had been in existence for many years (Worster 1977; Redclift 1987; see Chapter 2). Yet, they are not just abstract academic ideas; they are concepts which trickle down and affect the day-to-day lives of everyone on the planet, even if people never realise it (Mercer 2000).

Sustainability is an 'essentially contested concept' (Gaillie 1955–56); that is, a concept the use and application of which is inherently a matter of dispute. The reason for this is the degree to which the concept is used to refer to a 'balance' or 'wise' use in the way in which natural resources are exploited. The appropriateness of such an approach and the very way in which 'wise use' is defined will depend on the disparate values and ideologies of various stakeholders (Mercer 2000; Runte 2010). However, the history of natural resource management suggests that sustainable development is another term which has emerged in an attempt to reconcile conflicting value positions with regard to the environment and the perception that there is an environmental problem which requires a solution (Saarinen 2006; also see Chapter 2) at one time regional or national in scope, but now recognised as global (see Chapter 3).

Academic adoption of 'sustainable tourism' and 'sustainable development'

As Hall (2011) suggested, the notion of sustainable tourism must be regarded as one of the great success stories of tourism research and knowledge transfer. It has become incorporated into the fabric of tourism discourse in academic, business and governance terms. In addition to a specific academic journal (*Journal of Sustainable Tourism*), there are numerous dedicated texts and readers (e.g. Hall & Lew 1998; Mowforth & Munt 1998; Swarbrooke 1999; Aronsson 2000; Ritchie & Crouch 2003; Weaver 2006; Gössling, Hall & Weaver 2009) as well as a steadily increasing number of academic articles. Table 1.1 illustrates the growing significance of sustainable tourism and sustainable development in tourism as an area of academic interest as evidenced by the number of times the term 'sustainable tourism' has been used in abstracts, keywords or titles in three major databases of academic literature from 1980 to 2013. For reasons of comparison, Table 1.2 illustrates the number of times that 'sustainable development' and 'sustainability' have been used. Both tables show the relative recency of the terms in academic discourse, in great part because of the impact of the WCED (1987) on thinking about resource use and the environment, including with respect to tourism (Bramwell & Lane 1993). In addition, the tables also show that interest in sustainable tourism constitutes only a very small part of the overall sustainable development literature.

Table 1.1 Records of the term 'sustainable tourism' in major academic databases 1980–2013

Year	Within Scopus Keywords cumulative	Within Scopus Keywords	Scopus Abstracts	Within ScienceDirect Keywords	Within ScienceDirect Abstracts	Within ISI/ Web of Science Titles
2013	665	91	130	18	18	39
2012	574	116	128	20	21	41
2011	458	84	108	13	8	30
2010	374	78	120	8	17	38
2009	296	59	70	9	8	36
2008	237	47	74	3	4	35
2007	190	40	56	3	3	16
2006	150	32	53	2	5	19
2005	118	23	40	6	10	13
2004	95	12	30	1	4	14
2003	83	11	30	2	2	6
2002	72	19	33	9	6	14
2001	53	9	25	5	6	11
2000	44	6	24	1	–	14
1999	38	2	16	1	3	6
1998	36	2	9	2	3	6
1997	34	6	13	–	4	17
1996	28	8	7	–	2	11
1995	20	8	7	2	4	8
1994	12	7	7	2	3	4
1993	5	–	3	–	2	2
1992	5	5	8	–	3	2
1991	0	–	–	–	–	–
1990	0	–	1	–	1	1
1989	0	–	2	–	–	–

Table 1.2 Records of the term 'sustainable development' or 'sustainability' in major academic databases 1980–2013

Year	Within Scopus Keywords cumulative	Within Scopus Keywords	Scopus Abstracts	Within ScienceDirect Keywords	Within ScienceDirect Abstracts	Within ISI/ Web of Science Titles
2013	100 888	11 495	10 964	1 033	2 347	1 948
2012	89 393	13 705	10 128	825	1 963	2 098
2011	75 688	11 706	9 887	626	1 485	1 966
2010	63 982	8 101	8 527	482	1 085	1 935
2009	55 881	6 710	7 151	428	989	1 712
2008	49 171	5 537	5 909	355	784	1 326
2007	37 634	6 649	5 152	303	781	1 228
2006	30 985	6 138	4 375	302	690	943
2005	24 847	5 168	3 595	217	523	778
2004	19 679	4 633	2 816	169	375	756
2003	15 046	3 418	2 488	174	424	686
2002	11 628	2 406	1 984	151	380	614
2001	9 222	1 757	1 557	127	326	570
2000	7 465	1 490	1 599	137	363	523
1999	5 975	1 173	1 327	115	253	498

Table 1.2 Records of the term 'sustainable development' or "sustainability" in major academic databases 1980–2013 (continued)

Year	Within Scopus Keywords cumulative	Within Scopus Keywords	Scopus Abstracts	Within ScienceDirect Keywords	Within ScienceDirect Abstracts	Within ISI/ Web of Science Titles
1998	4 802	1 036	1 316	108	225	544
1997	3 766	706	1 168	100	204	508
1996	3 060	668	1 014	68	196	471
1995	2 393	587	737	63	159	408
1994	1 806	480	545	42	126	375
1993	1 326	357	484	6	96	310
1992	969	324	410	4	70	230
1991	645	276	306	5	75	213
1990	369	220	195	1	26	110
1989	149	95	117	0	19	60
1988	54	37	79	0	12	34
1987	17	9	38	1	10	19
1986	8	1	23	1	8	12
1985	7	1	16	0	7	12
1984	6	3	13	0	3	8
1983	3	1	11	1	1	3
1982	2	2	10	1	5	7
1981	0	0	2	0	1	7
1980	0	0	4	0	1	0

Searches undertaken 1 June 2014.

Adoption of 'sustainable tourism' by the public and private sectors

At the same time that sustainable tourism has grown as an area of academic interest, the term been increasingly adopted into tourism policy-making by both the public and private sectors at all levels of governance. For example, the concept of sustainable tourism has been at the forefront of the policy statements of organisations such as the United Nations Environment Programme (UNEP) (2005a, 2005b, 2005c, 2009), United Nations World Tourism Organization (UNWTO) (2007, 2010) and the World Travel and Tourism Council (WTTC) (2003, 2009, 2010), as well as joint exercises between them (e.g. International Task Force on Sustainable Tourism Development 2009; United Nations Environment Programme and the World Tourism Organization 2005; World Travel & Tourism Council, International Federation of Tour Operators, International Hotel & Restaurant Association, & International Council of Cruise Lines 2002). The concept is also mentioned in most national or regional government tourism policies or statements (e.g. Department for Culture, Media and Sport Tourism Division 2005; Hawaii Department of Business, Economic Development and Tourism 2005; Industry Canada, 2006; Ministry of Tourism, Tourism New Zealand, & Tourism Industry Association New Zealand 2007; Department of Resources, Energy and Tourism 2008; South Australian Tourism Commission 2009; USAID 2007) as well as corporate statements (e.g. Tourism Industry Association of Canada 2010; TUI Travel PLC 2010).

Despite the success of the concept of sustainable tourism in academic and policy discourse, tourism's contribution to environmental change, one of the benchmarks of sustainability in terms of the maintenance of 'natural' or 'ecological' capital (Pearce, Barbier & Markandya 1990; WCED 1987), is greater than ever as tourism continues to grow. Table 1.3 provides an outline of international tourism arrivals and forecasts for the period 1950–2030.

Table 1.3 International tourism arrivals and forecasts 1950–2030

Year	World	Africa	Americas	Asia & Pacific	Europe	Middle East
1950	25.3	0.5	7.5	0.2	16.8	0.2
1960	69.3	0.8	16.7	0.9	50.4	0.6
1965	112.9	1.4	23.2	2.1	83.7	2.4
1970	165.8	2.4	42.3	6.2	113.0	1.9
1975	222.3	4.7	50.0	10.2	153.9	3.5
1980	278.1	7.2	62.3	23.0	178.5	7.1
1985	320.1	9.7	65.1	32.9	204.3	8.1
1990	439.5	15.2	92.8	56.2	265.8	9.6
1995	540.6	20.4	109.0	82.4	315.0	13.7
2000	687.0	28.3	128.1	110.5	395.9	24.2
2005	806.8	37.3	133.5	155.4	441.5	39.0
2010	940	49.7	150.7	204.4	474.8	60.3
forecast						
2020	1 360	85	199	355	620	101
2030	1 809	134	248	535	744	149

Source: World Tourism Organization 1997; UN World Tourism Organization 2006, 2012

Gössling (2002) provided the first comprehensive overview of the global environmental consequences of tourism and argued that, from a global perspective, tourism meaningfully contributes to: changes in land cover and land use; energy use; greenhouse gas emissions; biotic exchange and extinction of wild species; exchange and dispersion of diseases; and changes in the perception and understanding of the environment (see also Chapter 3). Gössling's (2002) estimates for 2001 with respect to tourism's contribution to global environmental change (updated in Gössling & Hall (2006)) have been more recently examined by Hall and Lew (2009). They suggest that the contribution of tourism to global change is continuing to grow as a result of increasing numbers of domestic and international tourist trips, greater transport connections between climatically similar regions; increasing energy and water intensity of luxury tourism experiences and consumables (mainly imported food and beverages), as well as increases in distance travelled (Tatem & Hay 2007; Gössling, Peeters & Scott 2008; United Nations World Tourism Organization, United Nations Environment Programme & World Meteorological Organization (UNWTO, UNEP & WMO) 2008; Tatem 2009; Gössling, Hall, Peeters & Scott 2010; Dubois, Peeters, Ceron & Gössling 2011; Scott, Gössling & Hall 2012).

The extent of tourism's contribution to global change is outlined further in Chapter 3. However, to fully understand the interrelationships between tourism and sustainability it is important to look at both conceptual, managerial and policy uses of the term.

The policy problem attributes of sustainable tourism: Implications for approaches

Sustainability is a 'wicked' or meta-policy problem that has led to new institutional arrangements and policy settings at international, national and local scales. Sustainable tourism is a sub-set of this broader policy arena, with its own specific set of institutions and policy actors at various scales, as well as being a sub-set of tourism policy overall (Hall 2011). Sustainability problems may also pose different challenges than other policy problems (e.g. education, taxation, health) because of its attributes (Butler 1991; Dovers 1996; Hall & Lew 1998, 2009; Gössling & Hall 2006; Hall 2008, 2011) including:

- *Temporality* – Natural systems function over timescales that are often vastly greater than those which determine political and policy cycles (i.e. electoral terms) and business cycles and planning (i.e. quarterly reporting and annual shareholder meetings).
- *Spatiality* – Sustainability and environmental problems tend to be cross-boundary in nature and for some types of problems (e.g. climate change, deforestation, and biodiversity loss) global in scale. One of the most significant forms of spatial problem in sustainability is the mismatch between government, regulatory and jurisdictional space, and ecological/environmental boundaries; this greatly complicates the management of certain issues (e.g. watershed and species habitat).
- *Limits* – The concept of sustainability suggests that there are limits to exploitation of natural capital because of its limited capacity for renewal (Kula 1998; see also Chapter 2, this volume).
- *Cumulative* – Most anthropogenic impacts are cumulative rather than discrete.
- *Irreversibility* – Some natural capital or environmental assets cannot be renewed (i.e. a species) or are not easily substituted. In some cases (e.g. soil, groundwater or ozone), the timescale for renewal is well outside the normal parameters of policy and business cycles.
- *Complexity and connectivity* – Sustainability problems are interconnected or interlocking (WCED 1987), meaning that issues such as climate change and biodiversity cannot be easily separated in scientific terms although they often are in policy-making and institutional arrangements. Solutions to environmental sustainability problems, therefore, have salient implications for social and economic policy and vice versa.
- *Ontology* – The terms 'human impact' or 'tourism impact' ontologically positions tourism and tourists as 'outside' the system under analysis, as outside of nature from a realist material ontology of classical empiricism (Hall 2013). This is despite research on global environmental change demonstrating just how deeply entangled tourism is in environmental systems (Gössling & Hall 2006). The emphasis on the moment(s) of impact also assumes a stable natural, social or economic baseline (Hall & Lew 2009). Such an approach is inappropriate for understanding complex and dynamic socio-environmental systems (Head 2008; Hall & Lew 2009), while putting a significant explanatory divide between humans and nature requires the conflation of bundles of variable processes under such headings as 'human', 'climate', 'environment' and 'nature' (Head 2008).
- *Uncertainty* – Some aspects of sustainability are characterised by 'pervasive uncertainty' making it difficult to determine the efficacy, implications and socio-economic impacts of policy measures (Dovers & Handmer 1992).
- *Ethical issues* – Although ethical questions are integral to all policy choices, sustainability is complicated by the centrality of both intra- and inter-generational equity to the concept, as well as the rights of non-human species (see the chapters in the *Theoretical frameworks and concepts in tourism and sustainability* section of this volume for a further discussion of the ethical dimensions of sustainability).

It has long been recognised that the various elements of sustainability affect the capacity of public policy-making to provide effective sustainable tourism outcomes (e.g. Butler 1991; Bramwell & Lane 1993; Wheeler 1993; Hall & Lew 1998). Yet, despite the length of time that the policy problem attributes of sustainability have been recognised, there appears little progress in making the sustainability of tourism more tractable to solution. Several reasons for this can be advanced. It is possible that government policy-making is continually seeking to 'catch up' with the issue of sustainability because environmental change, as well as associated economic, social and political change, is occurring faster than corresponding changes in policy systems. Nevertheless, the increasing contributions of tourism to global and local change clearly highlight the need for appropriate theoretical and management responses and it is to these that we now turn.

Framing tourism and sustainability

The sheer complexity of sustainability issues and sustainable tourism potentially requires a public and private sector response that lies outside of the usual jurisdiction of tourism-specific governance (Hall 2008). This may be an issue of spatial scale, in that a government body may have either limited (or even no) jurisdictional authority over a policy problem, or it may be an issue of means with respect to the existence of operational policy processes, technologies and/ or institutional arrangements. Perhaps the policy and managerial capacity to respond to issues of sustainable tourism may reflect the political acceptability of any solution (i.e. tax increases, greater regulation, concern over travel lifestyle change).

In part, the sections of this book reflect the different levels of response to, and analysis of, issues of sustainable tourism. These issues are illustrated in Table 1.4. The first section introduces the reader to the topic of tourism and sustainability by providing an account of (a) the development of the concept of sustainable development within a tourism context (Chapter 2), and (b) the contribution of tourism to global change (Chapter 3). The second section presents a series of chapters that examine core theoretical frameworks and concepts in tourism and sustainability. The topics discussed in these chapters act as underlying drivers or principles for much of the policy and management thinking that shape day-to-day actions with respect to sustainability. Importantly, these concepts also act as benchmarks by which public and private sector policies and actions are assessed including with respect to their relative worth. Section 3 discusses specific management tools and concepts with respect to tourism and sustainability that are often operationalised within national and regional jurisdictions and at the level of individual agencies, firms and organisations. Section 4 discusses sectoral approaches to tourism and sustainability and examines the different initiatives undertaken in response to the specific challenges faced by individual sectors. The final section of the book examines emerging issues and concepts that overlay the evolving response of the tourism system to sustainable development from a micro- to a macro-level.

The typology presented in Table 1.4 has two main qualifications. First, it is heuristic and approximate with some issues and approaches operating at more than one scale. Moreover, it is important to recognise the high degree of relationality of concepts between different scales. Second, it is designed to apply to the problem set faced by a given polity and is therefore scale-dependent (Dovers 1996). In order to make policy problems more tractable, there has been a tendency to seek to address them via micro-policy means that work within existing policy processes and arrangements. However, the nature of the sustainability problem is such that while policy actions may appear logical or appropriate at the micro-scale, the emergent nature of tourism systems, let alone the inherent complexity of environmental and related change, can mean that such measures may have little effect at the meso- or macro-scales (Dovers 1995; Hall 2011). Indeed, Table 1.3 suggests that the larger the scale, the more the sustainability of tourism is affected by what is occurring outside of the tourism system and, hence, of tourism-specific public- and private-sector actions. Such a situation, if correct, therefore poses particular challenges for destination, regional and sectoral governance and sustainability, which is, by

Table 1.4 The relative scales of approaches to sustainable tourism

Policy problem	Spatial scale	Problem nature	Policy challenge	Examples
Macro-policy (Section 2)	Spatially and temporally diffuse. International or global in scope	Complex and highly uncertain and often connected to other macro-policy issues as part of the meta-policy problem of sustainability. Ill-structured, 'wicked' or 'messy' policy problem	Potentially highly disruptive of natural and socio-economic systems and challenges existing patterns of consumption and production, policy processes and institutional arrangements	Theoretical frameworks and concepts (e.g. precautionary principle, environmental justice, the commons, pro-poor tourism
Meso-policy (Section 3)	Usually addressed within a national, regional or bilateral governance context	Significant problem that is often high on the policy agenda. Moderately structured policy problem	Routine policy management. Does not pose overwhelming threats to existing patterns of production and consumption, policy processes, and/or institutional arrangements	Management tools and concepts (e.g. environmental sustainability indicators and benchmarking, corporate social responsibility, social marketing)
Micro-policy (Section 4)	Spatially and temporally discrete. Usually local or sectoral scale	Not overly complex or uncertain. Well-structured policy problem	Day-to-day policy management. Does not require large resource commitment. Uses existing technology, policy process, and/or institutional arrangements	Sectoral and destination approaches to tourism and sustainability (e.g. events, hotel chains, small business, resort areas)

Sources: Dovers, 1995; Hall, 2008, 2011

definition, constrained by jurisdictional limits as well as the position of the tourism industry within broader governance and policy network contexts. It also possibly suggests that if sustainable tourism policy only focuses on micro-scale solutions, as important as these might be from a tourism destination perspective, then it may be inherently doomed to fail in terms of the larger concerns of sustainable development.

Tourism is undoubtedly a major international industry that is critical to the economic and social well-being of many regions and people. However, it is also a major contributor to global change, hence the central problem of meeting the needs of the present without compromising the needs of future generations. We hope that this volume and the chapters within it help make a contribution to this most important of all the issues facing tourism today.

Key Reading

Crutzen, P. J. (2002). 'Geology of mankind', *Nature*, 415(6867): 23. Paper outlines the concept of the Anthropocene.

World Commission for Environment and Development (WCED) (1987) *Our Common Future. The Brundtland Report*, Oxford: Oxford University Press. Although the WCED report hardly mentions tourism at all, it is nevertheless a cornerstone of sustainable development thought.

An interesting contemporary debate over the direction of the environmental movement/ paradigm is the debate over the 'Death of Environmentalism': www.thebreakthrough.org/ images/Death_of_Environmentalism.pdf

---

References

Aronsson, L. (2000) *The Development of Sustainable Tourism*, London: Continuum.

Bramwell, B. and Lane, B. (1993) 'Sustainable tourism: An evolving global approach', *Journal of Sustainable Tourism*, 1: 1–5.

Butler, R.W. (1991) 'Tourism, environment and sustainable development', *Environmental Conservation*, 18: 201–9.

Crutzen, P. J. (2002) 'Geology of mankind', *Nature,* 415(6867): 23.

Department for Culture, Media and Sport Tourism Division (2005) *National Sustainable Tourism Indicators. Getting it Right: Monitoring Progress towards Sustainable Tourism in England,* London: Department for Culture, Media and Sport Tourism Division.

Department of Resources, Energy and Tourism (2008) *National Long Term Tourism Strategy*, Canberra: Department of Resources, Energy and Tourism.

Dobson, A. (2007) 'Environmental citizenship: Towards sustainable development', *Sustainable Development*, 15(5): 276–85.

Dovers, S. (1995) 'A framework for scaling and framing policy problems in sustainability', *Ecological Economics*, 12: 93–106.

—— (1996) 'Sustainability: Demands on policy', *Journal of Public Policy*, 16: 303–18.

Dovers, S.R. & Handmer, J.W. (1992) 'Uncertainty, sustainability and change', *Global Environmental Change*, 2: 262–76.

Dubois, G., Peeters, P., Ceron, J.P. and Gössling, S. (2011) 'The future tourism mobility of the world population: Emission growth versus climate policy', *Transportation Research Part A: Policy and Practice*, 45: 1031–42.

Gallie, W.B. (1955–56) 'Essentially contested concepts', *Proceedings of the Aristotelian Society* 56, 167–98.

Glacken, C. (1967) *Traces on the Rhodian Shore: Nature and Culture in Western Thought from Ancient Times to the End of the Eighteenth Century*, Berkeley: University of California Press.

Gössling, S. (2002) 'Global environmental consequences of tourism', *Global Environmental Change*, 12: 283–302.

Gössling, S. and Hall, C.M. (eds) (2006) *Tourism and Global Environmental Change*, London: Routledge.

Gössling, S., Hall, C.M. and Weaver, D. (eds) (2009). *Sustainable Tourism Futures: Perspectives on Systems, Rstructuring and Innovations*, New York: Routledge.

Gössling, S., Peeters, P. and Scott, D. (2008) 'Consequences of climate policy for international tourist arrivals in developing countries', *Third World Quarterly*, 29: 873–901.

Gössling, S., Hall, C.M., Peeters, P. and Scott, D. (2010) 'The future of tourism: Can tourism growth and climate policy be reconciled? A climate change mitigation perspective', *Tourism Recreation Research*, 35(2): 119–30.

Hall, C.M. (2008) *Tourism Planning*, 2nd edn, London: Prentice-Hall.

—— (2011) 'Policy learning and policy failure in sustainable tourism governance: From first and second to third order change?' *Journal of Sustainable Tourism*, 19: 649–71.

—— (2013) 'The natural science ontology of environment', in A. Holden and D. Fennell (eds) *The Routledge Handbook of Tourism and the Environment*, Abingdon: Routledge.

Hall, C.M. and Lew, A.A. (eds) (1998) *Sustainable Tourism: A Geographical Perspective*, London: Addison Wesley Longman.

Hall, C.M. and Lew, A.A. (2009) *Understanding and Managing Tourism Impacts: An Integrated Approach*, London: Routledge.

Hawaii Department of Business, Economic Development and Tourism (2005) *Planning for Sustainable Tourism*, Honolulu: Hawaii Department of Business, Economic Development and Tourism.

Head, L. (2008) 'Is the concept of human impacts past its use-by date?' *The Holocene*, 18: 373–77.

Industry Canada (2006) *Building a National Tourism Strategy*, Ottawa: Industry Canada.

International Task Force on Sustainable Tourism Development (2009) *A Three-year Journey for Sustainable Tourism*. Paris: French Ministries of Ecology, Energy, Sustainable Development and the Oceans, UNEP, Sustainable Consumption and Production Marrakech Process.

Kula, E. (1998) *History of Environmental Economic Thought*, London: Routledge.

Leiserowitz, A.A., Kates, R.W. and Parris, T.M. (2005) 'Do global attitudes and behaviors support sustainable development?' *Environment: Science and Policy for Sustainable Development*, 47(9): 22–38.

Levin, K., Cashore, B., Bernstein, S. and Auld, G. (2012) 'Overcoming the tragedy of super wicked problems: Constraining our future selves to ameliorate global climate change', *Policy Sciences*, 45(2): 123–52.

Mercer, D.C. (2000) *A Question of Balance: Natural Resources Conflict Issues in Australia,* 3rd edn, Leichhardt: The Federation Press.

Ministry of Tourism, Tourism New Zealand, and Tourism Industry Association New Zealand (2007) *New Zealand Tourism Strategy 2015*, Wellington: Ministry of Tourism, Tourism New Zealand, and Tourism Industry Association New Zealand.

Mowforth, M. and Munt, I. (1998) *Tourism and Sustainability: Development and New Tourism in the Third World*, London: Routledge.

Pearce, D., Barbier, E. and Markandya, A. (1990) *Sustainable Development: Economics and Environment in the Third World*, London: Earthscan.

Redclift, M. (1987) *Sustainable Development: Exploring the Contradictions*, London: Methuen.

Ritchie, J.B. and Crouch, G.I. (2003) *The Competitive Destination: A Sustainable Tourism Perspective*, Wallingford: CABI.

Runte, A. (2010) *National Parks: The American Experience*, 4th edn, Lanham: Taylor Trade Publishing.

Saarinen, J. (2006) 'Traditions of sustainability in tourism studies', *Annals of Tourism Research*, 33: 1121–40.

Scott, D., Gössling, S. and Hall, C.M. (2012) 'International tourism and climate change', *WIRES Climate Change*, 3(3): 213–32.

South Australian Tourism Commission (2009) *Sustainable Tourism Package*. Available at: www.tourism.sa.gov.au/tourism/SustainableTourismPackage.asp

Swarbrooke, J. (1999) *Sustainable Tourism Management*. Wallingford: CABI.

Tatem, A.J. (2009) 'The worldwide airline network and the dispersal of exotic species: 2007–10', *Ecography*, 32: 94–102.

Tatem, A.J. and Hay, S. (2007) 'Climatic similarity and biological exchange in the worldwide airline transportation network', *Proceedings of the Royal Society B*, 274: 1489–96.

Tourism Industry Association of Canada (2010) *Fast Facts on TIAC's Advocacy Issues: Sustainability*. Available at: www.tiac-aitc.ca/english/advocacy_sustainabletourism.asp

TUI Travel PLC (2010) *Group Sustainable Development Policy*. Available at: www.tuitravelplc.com/tui/pages/sustainabledevelopment/strategysd/policy

United Nations Environment Programme (UNEP) (2005a) *Marketing Sustainable Tourism Products*, Paris: United Nations Environment Programme and Regione Toscana.

—— (2005b) *Integrating Sustainability into Business: An Implementation Guide for Responsible Tourism Coordinators*, Paris: UNEP.

—— (2005c) *Integrating Sustainability into Business: Management Guide for Responsible Tourism Coordinators*, Paris: UNEP.

(2009) *Sustainable Coastal Tourism. An Integrated Planning and Management Approach*, Paris: UNEP.

United Nations Environment Programme and the World Tourism Organization (2005) *Making Tourism More Sustainable: A Guide for Policy Makers*, Paris: UNEP.

United Nations World Tourism Organization (UNWTO) (2006) *International Tourist Arrivals, Tourism Market Trends, 2006 Edition – Annex*, Madrid: UNWTO.

—— (2007). *From Davos to Bali – A Tourism Contribution to the Challenge of Climate Change, Policy Document*, Madrid: UNWTO.

—— (2010) *Sustainable Development of Tourism, Mission Statement*. Available at: www.unep.org

—— (2012) *UNWTO Tourism Highlights, 2012 Edition*, Madrid: UNWTO.

United Nations World Tourism Organization, United Nations Environment Programme, and World Meteorological Organization (2008). *Climate Change and Tourism: Responding to Global Challenges*, Madrid: United Nations World Tourism Organization, United Nations Environment Programme, World Meteorological Organization.

USAID (2007) *Dominica Sustainable Tourism Policy and Marketing Strategy*. Prepared for the Discover Dominica Authority by Chenmonics International. Washington DC: United States Agency for International Development.

Weaver, D.B. (2006) *Sustainable Tourism: Theory and Practice*, Oxford: Butterworth-Heinemann.

Wheeler, B. (1993) 'Sustaining the ego', *Journal of Sustainable Tourism*, 1: 121–29.

World Commission for Environment and Development (WCED) (1987) *Our Common Future: The Brundtland Report*, Oxford: Oxford University Press.

World Travel and Tourism Council (WTTC) (2003) *Blueprint for New Tourism*, London: WTTC.

—— (2009). *Leading the Challenge on Climate Change*, London: WTTC.

—— (2010). *Travel and Tourism Demands 21st Century Thinking for Future Sustainability*, Press Release, 21 April. London: WTTC.

World Travel and Tourism Council, International Federation of Tour Operators, International Hotel and Restaurant Association, and International Council of Cruise Lines (2002). *Industry as a Partner for Sustainable Development*. Developed through a multi-stakeholder process facilitated by UNEP. London: World Travel and Tourism Council, International Hotel and Restaurant Association, International Federation of Tour Operators, International Council of Cruise Lines and United Nations Environment Programme.

World Tourism Organization (WTO) (1997) *Tourism 2020 Vision*, Madrid: WTO.

Worster, D. (1977) *Nature's Economy: A History of Ecological Ideas*, Cambridge: Cambridge University Press.

Part 1

Introductory contexts to tourism and sustainability

2

The evolution of sustainable development and sustainable tourism

C. Michael Hall, Stefan Gössling and Daniel Scott

Romantic movement Intellectual movement that emerged in the late eighteenth century that valued the aesthetic and the spiritual over the material and was extremely significant for the development of ideas regarding the preservation of nature, especially wilderness.

Romantic ecology A term developed by Worster (1977) to describe the reinforcement of the perception of nature and wilderness having spiritual values.

Progressive or Economic conservation movement The mutually interchangeable terms reflected a strand of late nineteenth and early twentieth century conservation thought that represented a 'wise use' and 'balanced' approach to the management of natural resources. From this approach, conservation motives were economic rather than aesthetic in intent, with tourism being a means to leverage economic value from aesthetic properties. In addition, the focus of the movement which provides the intellectual heritage for much contemporary thinking on sustainable development, was on the use of greater technical efficiency to reduce pressures on resources in order to encourage economic growth.

Industrial ecology The study of the flows of materials and energy in industrial and consumer activities, of the effects of these flows on the environment, and of the influences of economic, political, regulatory and social factors on the flow, use and transformation of resources. The concept creates an analogy between biological and industrial food webs. In an industrial ecosystem, waste product by one company should be used as a resource for another.

Ecological economics Is a research field that examines the co-evolution, interdependence and relationality of human economies and natural ecosystems over time and space in order to maintain or enhance natural capital.

Introduction

The study of the appropriate use of the physical environment by humankind serves to chart the history of environmental attitudes and how these are actioned.

Such research can offer profound insights into the manner in which exploitation of the environment occurs, the nature of environmental perceptions, conflicts and behaviours relative to the environment, and the development and analysis of environmental policies. As noted in Chapter 1, sustainability is an 'essentially contested concept' (Gaillie 1955–56). That is, a concept the use and application of which is inherently a matter of dispute. The reason for this is the degree to which the concept of sustainable development is used to refer to a 'balance' or 'wise' use in the way in which natural resources are exploited. The appropriateness of such an approach and the very way in which 'wise use' is defined will depend on the values and ideologies of various stakeholders (Mercer 2000). However, the history of natural resource management suggests that sustainable development, including the sub-concept of sustainable tourism (see Figure 2.1), is one term among several which has emerged in an attempt to reconcile conflicting value positions with regard to the environment. Furthermore, it is argued that the terminology of 'balance' is continuing to evolve, more recently with the notion of the 'green economy' and 'green economic growth' (United Nations Environment Programme (UNEP) 2011) (see Chapter 41). These concepts have already begun to infiltrate the lexicon of tourism.

Yet tourism's relationship to the environment is increasingly problematic. Long held as an economic justification for conservation and use against competing industrial uses it is increasingly recognised that tourism leads to the short- and long-term decline of natural capital at local and global scales (Gössling & Hall 2006; see Chapter 3). The gap between use of the concepts of sustainability and sustainable tourism and empirical reality raises fundamental questions as to the prospects of achieving 'balance' between economic, social and environmental goals entailed in many interpretations of the concept of sustainable development. 'Much tourism growth, as with much economic growth in general, is already uneconomic at the present margin as we currently measure it given that it is leading to a clear running down of natural capital' (Hall 2010: 137). If this is the case, is it really possible to promote economic growth (and potentially long-distance visitor growth) over the long term without damaging the stock of natural capital?

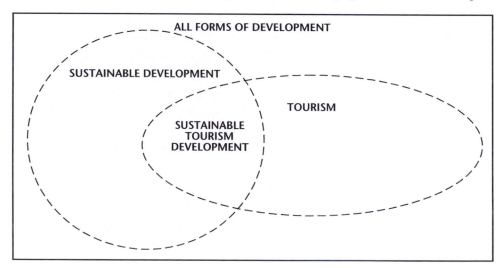

Figure 2.1 Sustainable tourism as a sub-set of sustainable development

This chapter aims to offer an historical overview of the development of the concept of sustainability in relation to tourism. It commences with a discussion of some of the early antecedents of sustainable development, particularly with respect to one of the earliest explicit linkages between tourism and the physical environment in the form of the creation of national parks. In doing so it seeks to emphasise that the contemporary political and economic discourse of sustainable development and growth is the continuation of a debate which has been occurring in industrial society since the latter half of the nineteenth century between what might be broadly described as economic conservationists and Romantic conservationists – together, of course, with those who believe that there are no environmental limits to economic growth. Such historical relationships are significant because they highlight not only continuity in the history of environmental ideas but they also raise significant questions about the likelihood of success in present–day attempts to develop sustainable forms of tourism via greater efficiency.

The Romantic vision: Changing attitudes towards nature in Western society

The relationship of humankind to their environment as well as to each other is not a given. It is socially constructed (Evernden 1992; Castree 2005). Such constructions raise fundamental questions not only about how the environment can actually be understood, but also the various economic and ethical relationships between humans and the environment. Although there were some historical antecedents (Glacken 1967), the development of a positive appreciation toward wild nature in Western society arguably dates to the emergence of the Romantic movement in the late nineteenth century, and was itself a reaction to the emergence of the industrial revolution and the social, economic and environmental changes it had wrought. In the Romantic movement, therefore, lie the first suggestions that there should be limits to the environmental transformations wrought by humankind, and an intellectual legacy towards the environment that lasts to the present day (Hall 1998).

The eighteenth century was an age of classification 'Insects, plants, animals and the races of man were divided into genera, species and sub-species. It was commonly supposed that this would lay bare the Divine Order or rational structure beneath the face of nature...' (Honour 1975: 18). However, the result was 'entirely contrary'. The mechanistic and static conception of nature that characterised the Enlightenment was gradually challenged by one that was organic and dynamic. Romanticism emerged as the result of the decline of old orthodoxies. The physical embodiment of the Enlightenment in the factory movement and mass production in which labour was objectivised and reduced to the status of a commodity was an anathema to the Romantic movement, as was the commodisation of nature (Pepper 1984).

Until the late 1700s the Western ideal of nature was one in which there was an ordered and cultivated landscape in which wild nature was controlled and the boundaries of the wilderness made apparent. For example, the early European settlers in North America found themselves confronted by a harsh, forested environment reminiscent of that of *Beowulf* (Wright 1957). The forests were regarded as being a haven not for the settlers but for 'primitive' Indians, wild animals and beasts (Nash 1963, 1967).

The Puritan attitude towards the forest wilderness set the tone for North American attitudes towards wilderness for the next 200 years and matched attitudes towards the environment by European settlers in the other new worlds of Australia and New Zealand (Hall 1992; Nash 2014). To the Puritans and other early settlers, the 'howling wilderness' was as much a state of mind as a state of fact. The wilderness was not a paradise, it was something to be 'conquered', 'subdued' or 'vanquished'. If the settlers expected to enjoy an idyllic environment then it would only be created through their own toil. It was only in its cultivated state that land acquired any value. The rural idyll was the desired landscape. A notion borne out, for example, in Thomas Jefferson's (1861) emphasis on the moral supremacy of the rural landscape as opposed to the moral degeneracy that could occur in either the towns or the wilderness.

It would be grossly incorrect to characterise Romanticism as a comprehensive manifesto; rather it was an attitude to life that valued the spiritual over the material. As Russell (1946: 653) noted, 'the romantic movement is characterised, as a whole, by the substitution of the aesthetic for utilitarian standards'. Nature, rather than being an object to organise and order, became upheld as a subject in its own right. As John Lorain (1825, in Glacken 1967: 44) wrote: 'the value of animal and vegetable matter is best seen in our lonely forests, where neither art nor ignorance has materially interfered, with the simple but wise economy of nature'.

In the intellectual climate created by the Romantic movement wilderness, and untamed nature, lost much of its repugnance. 'It was not that wilderness was any less solitary, mysterious, and chaotic, but rather in the new intellectual context these qualities were coveted' (Nash 1967: 44). Mountains and wilderness which once were landscapes of fear now became landscapes of awe and admiration (Nicolson 1962; Honour 1975; Tuan 1979). Moreover, in the writings of the Romantics, and more particularly the American transcendentalists such as Emerson and Thoreau, wild nature came to be endowed with a spiritual property, wholeness and wellness (Hall 1998).

In Thoreau's interpretation of the natural world, humankind was a part of nature, not superior to it. Thoreau's romantic ecology represented a revolutionary divergence from the bias against nature in some important strands of Western thought (Worster 1977). Thoreau was concerned with relation, interdependence and continuity; concepts which focused on the holistic structure of nature rather than the reductionist thinking of the day. In this new intellectual climate wilderness became more and more important; the workings of wild nature rather than the works of humanity came to be seen as perfection. It was the notion of the perfection of wild nature that led Thoreau (1968: 11) to exclaim in 1851: 'Let me live where I will, on this side is the city, on that the wilderness, and ever I am leaving the city more and more, and withdrawing into the wilderness.'

The spiritual values identified by Thoreau and the transcendentalists led to the growth of demands to preserve the wilderness. To Thoreau, 'wildness and refinement were not fatal extremes but equally beneficent influences Americans would do well to blend' (Nash 1967: 95). America's future, Thoreau believed, lay in the physical and metaphorical wilderness frontier of the West. 'The West of which I speak is but another name for the Wild; and what I have been preparing to say is, that in Wildness is the preservation of the World' (Thoreau 1968: 11, 12). A dictum that provided an inspiration for the legislative preservation of nature (Hall 1992).

Conserving nature

The transcendentalists provided the intellectual legacy which laid the foundations for the preservation of the natural world and the establishment of a Romantic ecological vision of the environment which survives to the present day. However, one of the main influences in the development of an economic or 'progressive' basis for conservation and a direct legacy for the development of the concept of sustainable development was the publication of George Perkins Marsh's book *Man and Nature; or, Physical Geography as Modified by Human Action* in 1864 (Marsh 1965; also see Lowenthal 1958).

Marsh's book contained two main theses. First, that when nature is left alone it is in harmony. Second, that Mankind impoverishes nature. In an alternative interpretation of *Genesis* 1:28, Marsh (1965: 36) argued that 'the earth was given to him for usufruct alone, not for consumption, still less for profligate waste'. The intention of Marsh was to demonstrate the need to balance man's use of the natural world. Influenced heavily by his observations in Europe, especially by the example of flooding caused by the clearing of forests in the Alps, Marsh identified major economic, as well as romantic, arguments for the preservation of nature.

To Marsh (1968: 14), 'man is everywhere a disturbing agent. Wherever he plants his foot, the harmonies of nature are turned to discords.' The attitude of Marsh to man's effects on nature was summed up in the quotation contained on the original title page of *Man and Nature*: 'Not all the winds, and storms, and earthquakes, and seas, and seasons of the world, have done so much to revolutionize the earth as MAN, the power of an endless life, has done since the day he came forth upon it, and received domain over it' (Marsh 1965: 1). (Marsh's statement can also be regarded as a precursor to the concept of the Anthropocene noted in Chapter 1).

For Marsh a scientific approach to the good husbanding and preservation of natural resources was essential for America's future as elsewhere. Marsh identified America's long-term economic wellbeing as depending upon the maintenance of her renewable natural resources. The impact of Marsh's writings went well beyond America's shores. Marsh's central thesis of the need to restore or maintain the balance of nature that 'man' had disturbed, especially in the forest lands, was well publicised in Australia by leading newspapers such as the Melbourne *Age* and the *Argus*. The *Argus* of 16 October 1865, noted that, 'The conservation of the forest lands, and the extension and improvement of them, concern alike the landholder and the miner, and should occupy the attention of everyone who had leisure and means to become a co-worker with nature' (in Powell 1976: 62). However, recognition of the need for aesthetic or economic conservation of nature were not of themselves sufficient to engage in conservation measures, including the establishment of nature reserves or national parks that restricted economic use of some land areas. The first natural area national reservation to be set aside in the United States was the Arkansas Hot Springs in 1832. 'It was not scenically important, and was reserved to the government' because the springs 'were thought to be valuable in the treatment of certain ailments' (Ise 1961: 13). However, the reservation was not a 'park'; it was reserved for its utility, yet like so many of the national parks that would be established it did have tourism potential.

Tourism, not ecology or what we would now regard as biodiversity conservation, was the driving force behind the creation of the first national parks and conservation reserves (Frost & Hall 2009; Hall & Frost 2009a). For example, Yosemite was ceded to the State of California on 30 June 1864 by President Lincoln as a state park 'for public use, resort, and recreation' (Nash 1963: 7). Tourism gave value to lands that were otherwise useless or worthless in terms of other common forms of economic exploitation, e.g. agriculture, forestry, mining (Hall & Frost 2009b). For example, on introducing congressional legislation in 1864 to grant Mariposa Big Trees and Yosemite Valley to California, Senator John Connes of California assured his colleagues that the lands were 'for all public purposes worthless, but…[they] constitute, perhaps, some of the greatest wonders of the world' (in Runte 1977: 71). Similarly, in the designation of some 2 million acres in northwestern Wyoming as Yellowstone National Park on 1 March 1872, Thomas Hayden, the leader of the geological expedition to the area whose report to Congress proved influential in the declaration of the park, noted the scientific significance of the area and the need for its preservation. However, he also 'assured them that Yellowstone seemed to be worthless for lumbering, mining, settlement or cattle raising' (in Runte 1972: 6). It is notable that the House Committee's report emphasised Hayden's opinions on the economic value of the region and ended with the statement that Yellowstone National Park would take 'nothing away from the value of the public domain' and 'was no pecuniary loss to the Government' (in Runte 1972: 6). Value, instead, came through tourism. It should, therefore, be no surprise that, as with many other early national parks around the world (Hall 1992), support for the establishment of a reserve at Yosemite was also found from the Northern Pacific Railroad Company (Sax 1976) whose lines were routed close to the park.

The rise of progressive conservation

The year 1890 was notable not only for the creation of Yosemite National Park, but also an event that would have far greater impact on the popular consciousness of the United States – the closing of the frontier. The results of the census of 1890 indicated that for the first time centres of population stretched out across the continental United States. This did not mean that vast, empty spaces did not exist, rather it indicated that America was becoming increasingly characterised by industrialisation and urbanisation rather than by the pioneer. For two-and-a-half centuries, 'the frontier had been synonymous with the abundance, opportunity, and distinctiveness of the New World' (Nash 1968: 37). With the close of the frontier, a form of cultural anxiety developed which focused on the need to retain links with the wilderness out of which the American nation had been created (Turner 1893, 1920).

Reaction to the loss of the frontier manifested itself in two ways. First, the rise of progressive conservation in which the finite nature of America's natural resources was recognised (Hays 1957, 1959). Second, the reinforcement of the perception of wilderness having spiritual values for the American people and the consequent rise of what Worster (1977) described as 'Romantic ecology'. The progressive conservation movement represented a 'wise use' approach to the management of natural resources, and its conservation motives were economic rather than aesthetic in intent. Hays (1959) saw three agencies as being the direct product of the movement's focus on greater efficiency in resource use: the Bureau of Reclamation, the National Park Service and the United States Forest Service.

Though the Forest Service was not founded until 1905, momentum for its creation had been building up in the two prior decades. Several bills relating to timber on public land had been introduced from the 1870s onwards, but in 1891, the President was given the power to set aside vast acreages in the public domain as forest reserves (Clarke & McCool 1985). Both preservationists and progressive conservationists saw the *Forests Reserves Act of 1891* as a means to protect wilderness areas. Preservationists led by John Muir wanted these to contain no human activity that would be unsympathetic to the primitive nature of a wilderness area. However, progressive conservationists, led by noted forester Gifford Pinchot and Theodore Roosevelt, wanted forest lands to be managed on a sustained yield basis and were therefore in favour of timber harvesting, the building of dams for water supplies, and selective mining and grazing, all in the name of conservation. In a statement which echoes much of the current debate over sustainability, Gifford Pinchot (1968: 9) stated in 1910 that

> The first great fact about conservation is that it stands for development. There has been a fundamental misconception that conservation means nothing but the husbanding of resources for future generations. There could be no more serious mistake. Conservation does mean provision for the future, but it means also and first of all the recognition of the right of the present generation to the fullest necessary use of all the resources with which this country is so abundantly blessed. Conservation demands the welfare of the country first, and afterward the welfare of the generations to follow.

Initially, there was a reasonable degree of correspondence in the views of Romantic ecologists, such as John Muir, and economic conservationists, such as Pinchot. Muir, for instance, wrote in 1895 that:

> it is impossible in the nature of things to stop at preservation. The forests must be, and will be, not only preserved, but used, and…like perennial fountains…be made to yield a sure harvest of timber, while at the same time all their far-reaching [aesthetic and spiritual] uses may be maintained unimpaired.
>
> *(in Nash 1967: 134–35)*

However, over time a split occurred between the various parties as to how conservation lands should be managed. Pinchot and the progressive conservationists advocated the 'wise' use of natural resources, while the preservationists continued to focus on the aesthetic and spiritual qualities of forest wilderness. As Fernow (1896 in Nash 1967: 137) wrote in *The Forester*, 'the main service, the principal object of the forest has nothing to do with beauty or pleasure. It is not, except incidentally, an object of esthetics, but an object of economics.' Such a viewpoint was anathema to the preservationists. Muir believed that 'government protection should be thrown around every wild grove and forest on the mountains' in order to preserve the 'higher' uses of the wilderness (in Nash 1963: 9). The problem that faced Muir, which exists to the present day, is that the existence of 'undisturbed' wild nature is often incompatible with economically productive forest management, agriculture or mining. Tourism does provide an economic option but, as numbers of visitors grow, so this may also place increased pressure on natural areas.

The creation of the United States Forest Service in 1905, with Pinchot at its head, marked the institutionalisation of progressive conservation in the United States Government (Richardson 1962). Government forestry, and wider involvement in the management of natural resources, in America was founded upon Pinchot's vision of academic forestry 'that is, the scientific management of the timber resource according to the principles of wise use and sustained yield' (in Clarke & McCool 1985: 36) and it is these principles that are the direct antecedents for contemporary dominant discourses of sustainable development and sustainable tourism.

Primitive sustainable tourism? National parks and tourism

It was the aim of the US National Park Service (NPS) to include in the park system all areas which contained 'scenery of supreme and distinctive quality or some natural feature so extraordinary or unique as to be of general interest and importance' (in Buck 1921: 52). However, the mandate of the NPS provided a paradox which lingers to the present day not only in the USA but also throughout the world with respect to national parks (Frost & Hall 2009). The NPS was meant to provide enjoyment for the people and hence attract them to the parks, while simultaneously, they were supposed to keep the parklands in an unimpaired state. Because of the low visitor levels, such a situation was not harmful to the parks in their early days. Indeed, in an effort to promote the national parks cause, the NPS eagerly took up a 'see America first' campaign to encourage tourism.

The value of the national parks to tourism was stressed by the first Director of the National Park Service, Steven Mather, and his assistant, Horace Albright (Shankland 1970; Swain 1970; Sax 1976). Appealing to the utilitarian spirit, Mather often invoked profit motive in relation to the national parks. In 1915, Mather (in Runte 1979: 103) claimed that, 'our national parks are practically lying fallow, and only await proper development to bring them into their own...A hundred thousand people used the national parks last year. A million Americans should play in them every summer.'

Mather and Albright actively encouraged automobile users to visit the national parks by extending and upgrading park roads and supporting the upgrading of highways. The railways also continued their strong support; Lois Hill (in Foresta 1984: 24) of the Great Northern Railroad noting that 'every passenger to the national parks represents practically a net earning'. It is, therefore, not surprising that seventeen western railroad companies contributed to the publication and distribution of a glossy publicity portfolio of the national parks in order to promote tourism activity (Buck 1921). However, it is somewhat ironic that the increased popularity of automobile transport to the parks led to the decline and eventual failure of many park railroads (Runte 1974).

Mather was 'no primitive who wanted to curb mass use', but neither did he want Coney Island-type amusement parks established in the national parks, instead appropriate tourist facilities were regarded as enhancing their appeal (Foresta 1984). Mather's attitude to the national parks is probably best summed up in Secretary Lane's letter of 13 May 1918, in which the administrative policy for the parks was outlined:

> First...national parks must be maintained in absolutely unimpaired form for the use of future generations as well as those of our own time; second...they are set aside for the use, observation, health, and pleasure of the people; and third...the national interest must dictate all decisions affecting public or private enterprise in the parks.
>
> *(Secretary Lane, Letter to Steven Mather 1918, in Ise 1961: 195)*

The principles by which the national parks were managed established the wilderness idea within the national parks – the notion that the parks 'must be maintained in an absolutely unimpaired form'. However, notions of strict wilderness preservation were in many ways at odds with the desire to attract tourism and recreation interests to the parks. The technical efficiency of the economic conservation movement therefore came to be applied to the national parks. Mather and Albright attempted to balance competing visions, 'usually they would allow nuclei of intensive visitor services in the parks, make those nuclei and some of the most spectacular sites...accessible by high-grade roads, and leave the rest of the parkland – most of it – as wilderness' (Foresta 1984: 20).

By the late 1920s, concern for endangered species led the supporters of national parks to recognise that they contained more than just scenery and that protection of plant and animal habitat was an integral part of the nature of environmental conservation (Worster 1977). The natural environment was now evaluated in what Runte (1979: 106) described as 'complete conservation': natural areas were recognised as being able to support a wide range of values: recreation, spiritual renewal, religious experience, health and ecology, a situation synonymous with present-day perceptions of the values of natural areas (Hall 1992).

The first move towards an ecologically based national park was the creation of the Everglades National Park in Florida in 1934. Runte (1979: 108–9) claimed that: 'For the first time a major national park would lack great mountains, deep canyons, and tumbling waterfalls, preservationists accepted the protection of its native plants and animals alone as justification for Everglades National Park.' Runte is correct to note that the park was substantially different from existing national parks in terms of its landscape and ecological characteristics. Yet he is incorrect to assume that its ecology alone was responsible for its preservation. The scenic qualities of the region, so important for tourism, were still an important force behind its creation. As the fact-finding committee of the National Parks Association noted:

> ...even granting the...limitations as to the scenery of parts of the region, there are extensive areas where even the most casual observer can hardly fail to be gripped and inspired by a sense of power and vastness of nature, essentially akin to the feelings inspired by great scenes in our existing National Parks yet arising out of elements so different from these – indeed so wholly unfamiliar to the experience of most visitors to the National Parks – as to have the special force of novelty.
>
> *(Olmsted & Wharton 1932: 143)*

The discussion of the role of tourism in the creation of national parks and the tensions is significant as it highlights that difficulties in managing tourism while conserving the environment are rooted not just in visitor growth but in a philosophy that seeks to use greater technical efficiency to 'conserve' resources and encourage economic growth.

The growth debate

In one sense the debate between the preservationists and economic conservationists in the late nineteenth and early twentieth century United States represented the first challenge to the notion that there were no limits to growth. A challenge that was played out in the creation of national forests and national parks in which tourism came to be an essential element of their establishment and development. Following the closure of the American frontier, economic conservationists came to argue that technical efficiency would provide the basis for the use of the nation's resources; such resources could provide a sustained yield for economic development (Koppes 1987; Bengston 1994; Clawson 2013). Indeed, in the United States and other countries, the depression of the 1930s allowed for even greater intensification of 'wise-use' efficiency approaches in natural resource management, including providing for greater tourist access to parks and reserves via road-building projects (Geisler 1995; Maher 2007; Sirna 2014; Wilson 2014). However, the dominance of such a perspective was assisted by the growing internationalisation of trade, by which local 'shortages' of available cheap resources could be bypassed via imports. In such an economic environment, the true extent of the impact of resource consumption could be hidden via shifting ecological footprints and, in some cases, population pressures offshore. The loss of natural capital in other, sometimes postcolonial, jurisdictions was not to be experienced in the consumption of the industrialised countries, therefore also encouraging the development of some national parks and reserves, because resource pressure had, to a great extent, been shifted. Besides, tourism, it was argued, could provide an alternative means of leveraging economic value even greater than that of alternative land uses (Runte 1977; Hall 1992).

Economic or progressive conservation was the dominant metaphor for natural resource management, including tourism, in the industrialised world for most of the twentieth century. For example, in 1915, the Canadian Commission of Conservation suggested that 'each generation had the right to profit from the interest on nature's capital, but that this capital had to be maintained intact for future generations to use in a similar fashion' (Vaillancourt 1997: 222). Similarly, in 1948, the International Union for the Conservation of Nature and Natural Resources (IUCN) was founded on the premise that both nature and its resources should be protected for the benefit of existing and future generations. Importantly, the IUCN was very much grounded in environmental conservation principles that did not challenge the notion that there are limits to economic growth (Berwick 1969; Curry-Lindahl 1974; Talbot 1983). Such arguments were to come from elsewhere.

The first modern challenges to economic growth emerged in the 1960s. This was also a time of increased awareness of environmental problems (Carson 1962) and the threat of overpopulation (Ehrlich 1968). In this intellectual climate the US think-tank Resources for the Future published *Scarcity and Growth* (Barnett & Morse 1963) which concluded, in a manner that anticipates contemporary discussions of sustainable development, that technological innovation, resource substitution, recovery and discovery of new resources encouraged by the free market system would make Malthusian concerns obsolete. 'A limit may exist, but it can be neither defined nor specified in economic terms...Nature imposes particular scarcities, not an inescapable general scarcity' (Barnett & Morse 1963: 11).

There were few initial doubts about the feasibility or desirability of economic growth, but increasingly, concern began to be expressed about the impact of growth on environmental quality (Jarrett 1966). However, by the end of the decade the work of Boulding (1966) on the economics of 'spaceship earth' and Mishan (1967) on economic growth had started to open up spaces of critique that also contributed to several important strands of research on sustainability. These included works by Ayres and Kneese (1968, 1969) and Odum (1971) that led to the development of industrial ecology; Georgescu-Roegen's (1971) research on entropy, economic processes and energy/matter transformation that served as one of foundations for ecological economics as well as concepts of degrowth, and Daly's (1972, 1974) work on the stationary state economy (Pigou 1943) which developed into steady state economics (Daly 1991). Nevertheless, broader awareness of such work in public debate was raised by the publication of the *Limits to Growth* (LTG) report (Meadows, Meadows, Randers & Behrens 1972).

The benchmark LTG study examined the interaction of global population, industrial production, food production, pollution and natural resource systems. It assumed that population and industrial production were growing exponentially, in a world with absolutely fixed available resources. In each of the scenarios Meadows *et al.* (1972) ran, population collapsed during the twenty-first century due to ever-increasing pollution and food shortages along with other factors such as soil erosion. The study coincided with the first United Nation Conference on the Human Environment (held in Stockholm) as well as broader concerns over the availability and price of oil during the crisis of the early 1970s. However, LTG's main policy recommendation of stabilisation, similar to Daly's (1972) work on steady-state economics, was generally dismissed by politicians. In a foretaste of recent international debates about responsibilities for and limitations on carbon emissions, delegates at the Stockholm conference made it clear that they were not going to accept policies arising from resource limits that would hamper their future development (Beckerman 1972).

The case for there being limits to economic growth as a result of environmental constraints was not helped by its rejection by the vast majority of mainstream economists. For example, Beckerman (1972) suggested:

> ...that the problem of environmental pollution is a simple matter of correcting a minor resource misallocation by means of pollution charges, and that most of the common objections to such a policy can be demolished with the aid of no more economics than that which is the stock-in-trade of any second year economics student....[LTG] was such a brazen, impudent piece of nonsense that nobody could possibly take it seriously so that it would be a waste of time talking about it.
>
> *(Beckerman 1972: 327)*

As Perez-Carmona (2012) noted, again anticipating much of the contemporary debate over response to climate change mitigation, 'The common argumentative line was that technological progress and the market mechanism could prevent scarcity and pollution from constituting a substantial limitation on long-term economic growth' (2012: 91). For example, Cole, Freeman, Jahoda and Pavitt (1973) reran the LTG model under different assumptions and suggested that an annual 2% improvement in technological progress would postpone collapse indefinitely. To do this, the rates of improvement in available resources (through discovery and recycling) and pollution control 'must obviously be competitive with growth rates of population and consumption so that even if the overall growth is rapid, it is also "balanced"' (Cole *et al.* 1973: 119). But, as Lecomber (1975: 42) warned, 'Everything hinges on the rate of technical progress and possibilities of substitution.'

LTG, together with concerns over energy dependency and biodiversity loss, including the 1980 *World Conservation Strategy* (IUCN, UNWP & WWF 1980), helped contribute to the debates on sustainability in the late 1970s and early 1980s (Dryzek 1997). For example, the 1980 'Global 2000 Report to the President' began by stating that:

> If present trends continue, the world in 2000 will be more crowded, more polluted, less stable ecologically, and more vulnerable to disruption than the world we live in now. Serious stresses involving population, resources, and environment are clearly visible ahead. Despite greater material output, the world's people will be poorer in many ways than they are today.
>
> *(Speth 1980: 695)*

The follow-up to the 1972 Stockholm conference was the World Commission on Environment and Development (WCED) established in 1983. Although works on sustainable development had been published before its release, the WCED (1987) report, *Our Common Future* (often referred to by the name of its chairwoman, Mrs Brundtland) undoubtedly set the trajectory of sustainable development discourse to the present-day. As has been discussed elsewhere (Hall 2011), the concept of sustainable development has been extremely successful with respect to its incorporation in public and private sector policy statements, including in tourism (see Chapter 1, this volume). Dryzek (1997) suggests that the report was written in such a way as to ensure that it also received support from business interests. Although the WCED (1987: 44) noted the importance of 'consumption standards within the bounds of the ecological possible and to which all can reasonably aspire' are required as part of achieving greater equity, they nevertheless suggested that although ultimate ecological limits exist, reaching them could be delayed by technological innovation. Importantly for the present discussion they also concluded that 'the international economy must speed up world growth while respecting the environmental constraints' (WCED 1987: 89), primarily by encouraging qualitative economic growth that was less material/resource/energy (MRE) intensive and more equitable, i.e. more decarbonised and dematerialised. This approach lies at the heart of much discussion of green growth to the present (Santarius 2012).

However, the WCED (1987) approach failed to recognise several significant implications of their strategy. First, while dematerialisation may occur at a per unit level, overall industrial expansion continues. Second, becoming more efficient leads to an increase in throughput (input plus output), what is otherwise known as the 'Jevons paradox' or 'rebound effect' (Polimeni, Mayumi, Giampietro & Alcott 2008) (see also Chapter 41). Third, being 'part of an interdependent world economy' (WCED 1987: 51) provided a rationale not only for further liberalisation of the global economy and the reduction of trade barriers by less developed countries (LDCs) but also for already wealthy countries to further pursue economic growth by increasing consumption so as to encourage economic growth in the LDCs. This has also meant the transfer of resource demands from one jurisdiction to another, together with much of the associated externalities. Indeed, the encouragement of economic growth in LDCs via consumption practices of the developed world has become one of the cornerstones of so-called 'pro-poor' tourism (Hall 2007; Schilcher 2007). 'The alternative that poor countries could create their own markets' (Daly 1991: 151), including with respect to tourism, is not one that has been greatly encouraged. However, the benefit of export-led growth as a means for poverty alleviation is moot (Zapata *et al.* 2011; Perez-Carmona 2012). As Simms (2008: 49) observed:

> During the 1980s, for every $100 added to the value of the global economy, around $2.20 found its way to those living below the World Bank's absolute poverty line. During the 1990s, that share shrank to just 60 cents. This inequity in income distribution – more like a flood up than a trickle down – means that for the poor to get slightly less poor, the rich have to get very much richer. It would take around $166 worth of global growth to generate $1 extra for people living on below $1 a day.

A further challenge to economic growth, and one that has become increasingly important in tourism, is climate change. The publication of the Stern Review (Stern 2007) brought the relationship between economic growth and environment back to the forefront of public policy, However, as Jackson (2009: 11) noted: 'it's telling that it took an economist commissioned by a government treasury to alert the world to things climate scientists – most notably the Intergovernmental Panel on Climate Change (IPCC) – had been saying for years.' Nevertheless, despite much of value in the report, 'When Stern published his review in 2006, the global economy already required almost 1.5 planets [worth of resources], yet a discussion on the causality's direction between economic growth and ecological obliteration…was completely absent in Stern's work. Economic growth was Stern's default assumption for the entire globe' (Perez-Carmona 2012: 107). Similarly, economic growth is the default assumption for many of the 'official' statements on sustainable tourism.

In tourism policy terms, sustainability is primarily seen as being 'environmental' and development as 'economic' (and to a lesser extent 'social') and the concept of sustainable tourism or sustainable tourism development aims to mitigate the paradox between them (Saarinen 2006; Hall 2009, 2010). Baeten (2000) argues that, as portrayed via government and supranational institutions, the sustainable development concept suggests that contemporary economic development paradigms are able to cope with environmental crisis without fundamentally affecting existing economic relationships. This approach is conveyed at various scales of governance (e.g. Czech 2008; Hall 2008), but is perhaps most widely accessible in the work of extremely influential organisations in international tourism policy networks such as the World Economic Forum (2009a, 2009b), the UNWTO (2002, 2007a) and the WTTC (2003, 2009). For example, the UNEP and the UNWTO (2005) publication *Making Tourism More Sustainable: Guide for Policy Makers* was described by Eugenio Yunis, UNWTO head of sustainable development of tourism as 'applicable world-wide. It is a "bible" for all decision-makers who are encouraged to be actively involved in the development of an environmentally and socially responsible tourism which creates long term economic benefits for the businesses and destinations' (Yunis 2006: 2). The UNEP and the UNWTO (2005) argue that the concept of sustainable development has evolved since the 1987 Brundtland definition:

Three dimensions or 'pillars' of sustainable development are now recognized and underlined. These are:

- Economic sustainability, which means generating prosperity at different levels of society and addressing the cost effectiveness of all economic activity. Crucially, it is about the viability of enterprises and activities and their ability to be maintained in the long term.
- Social sustainability, which means respecting human rights and equal opportunities for all in society. It requires an equitable distribution of benefits, with a focus on alleviating poverty. There is an emphasis on local communities, maintaining and strengthening their life support systems, recognizing and respecting different cultures and avoiding any form of exploitation.
- Environmental sustainability, which means conserving and managing resources, especially those that are not renewable or are precious in terms of life support. It requires action to minimize pollution of air, land and water, and to conserve biological diversity and natural heritage.

It is important to appreciate that these three pillars are in many ways interdependent and can be both mutually reinforcing or in competition. *Delivering sustainable development means striking a balance between them.*

(UNEP & UNWTO 2005: 9) (our emphasis)

The UNEP and the UNWTO (2005: 71) identified a number of instruments and indicators 'that governments can use to influence the sustainability of tourism' (see also Section 3 of this volume). However, the selection of policy indicators is not a neutral device and instead tends to favour certain instruments and interventions over others (Hall 2011, 2014). 'Imposing the rules of the game, that is to say, the rules used to calculate decisions, by imposing the tools in which these rules are incorporated, is the starting point of relationships of domination' (Callon 1998: 46) not only between institutions, but also of one policy paradigm over another. Similarly, Majone (1989: 116–17) also stressed that 'policy instruments are seldom ideologically neutral… distributionally neutral…[and]…cannot be neatly separated from goals' and instead tend to reflect the values of the policy and wider paradigms within which they are selected. As Majone (1989) suggests:

The choice of policy instruments is not a technical problem that can be safely left to experts. It raises institutional, social, and moral issues that must be clarified….The naive faith of some analysts in the fail-safe properties of certain instruments allegedly capable of lifting the entire regulatory process out of the morass of public debate and compromise can only be explained by the constraining hold on their minds of a model of policymaking in which decisions are, in James Buchanan's words, 'handed down from on high by omniscient beings who cannot err'.

(Majone 1989: 143)

In the case of the UNWTO policy recommendations, as well as those of many other supranational, national and destination governance bodies, one of the longstanding cornerstones of the sustainable tourism policy paradigm is that of 'balance' (Wall 1997; Mercer 2000; Hunter 2002; Hall 2010, 2011). For example, according to the then UNWTO Secretary-General Francesco Frangialli, the UNWTO is 'committed to seek balanced and equitable policies to encourage both responsible energy related consumption as well as anti-poverty operational patterns. This can and must lead to truly sustainable growth within the framework of the Millennium Development Goals' (UNWTO 2007b). Similarly, the Northern Ireland Tourist Board (2009) states that: 'The term Sustainable Tourism…has provided a platform for propelling the importance of a balance between the economic, environmental and socio-cultural aspects of tourism.' The centrality of continued economic growth in conceptualising sustainable tourism is also a theme in much academic writing on the subject. For example, Edgell (2006: 24) states that: 'For sustainable tourism to be successful, long-term policies that balance environmental, social, and economic issues must be fashioned.' His book preface notes that it, 'stresses that positive sustainable tourism development is dependent on forward-looking policies and new management philosophies that seek harmonious relations between local communities, the private sector, not-for-profit organizations, academic institutions, and governments at all levels to develop practices that protect natural, built, and cultural environments *in a way compatible with economic growth*' (2006: xiii) (our emphasis).

Yet the continuing contribution of a growing tourism industry to environmental change (see Chapter 3) raises a clear question as to whether sustainable tourism can actually be achieved via a so-called 'balanced' approach that seeks to continue to promote economic growth. The problem with 'balance' is that, in the long term, environmental capital is being lost along with notions of equity that were also meant to be integral to the WCED's notion of sustainable development. For example, even the highly conservative World Economic Forum (2009a) estimate that CO_2 emissions from tourism (excluding aviation) will grow at 2.5% per year until 2035 with annual increases in carbon emissions from aviation growing at about 2.7%. The International Air Transport Association (2010) forecasts 16 billion air travellers by 2050, although it acknowledges 'Today's jet fuel cannot sustain air transport in the long term. We must find a sustainable alternative and our most promising opportunity is bio fuels, which have the potential to reduce our carbon footprint by up to 80%.' The notion that you can promote international tourism as a means of alleviating poverty while simultaneously reducing tourism's contribution to climate change is also being increasingly criticised (Gössling 2002; Gössling *et al.* 2010; Hall 2010; Dubois *et al.* 2011; Gössling, Scott & Hall 2013). Such observations, together with numerous contributions in the present volume, suggest that there is no simple and predictable relationship between pollution and per capita income so that as incomes or GDP rise, the level of pollution and biodiversity loss declines (the so-called environmental Kuznets curve) (Dietz & Adger 2003; Stern 2004; Mozumder, Berrens & Bohara 2006; Czech 2008; Mills & Waite 2009). Despite repeated attempts to posit sustainable forms of development, including with respect to alternative and sustainable tourisms, the global ecological footprint of humanity continues to grow and run down the stock of the world's natural capital (Figure 2.2). In other words the achievement of sustainable development via economic growth strategies, even if they constitute so-called green growth (UNEP 2011), appears extremely difficult if not impossible. A point to which we shall return in the final section of the book.

Conclusions: Lessons and observations?

A review of the historical antecedents in the sustainable development of natural resources, generates a number of significant insights into the present-day issues which surround sustainability. First, debate over the sustainable development of natural resources in industrialised countries dates from the middle of the nineteenth century and cannot be seen as a new policy issue, at least at the local or national level. What is new is that it has become a global concern, including with respect to tourism (Gössling 2002; Gössling & Hall 2006; and see Chapter 3). Second, tourism has long been a key factor in the justification for environmental conservation.

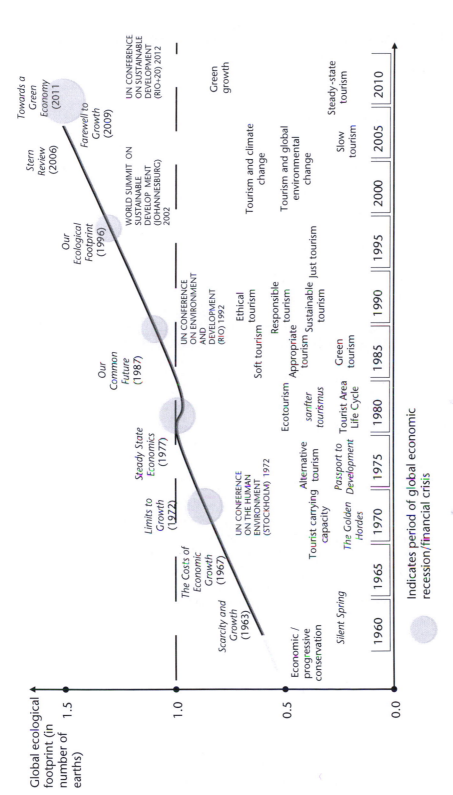

Figure 2.2 Global ecological footprint and the conceptualisation of growth and sustainability (Hall 2013)

Third, there has been no easy middle path in attempting to find a balanced use of natural resources that serves to maintain natural or ecological capital. Political, rather than ecological reality has been the order of the day in promoting economic growth often via the notion of 'balanced' sustainable development, including with respect to sustainable tourism.

Sustainable development, as well as sustainable tourism, has simultaneously come to be understood in terms of both growth and conservation. Yet contemporary discussions on the nature of sustainable development, including those within this book, have their antecedents in the debates that have taken place for well over a century. In the case of tourism, these have been most clearly manifested with respect to the relationship between tourism and protected area systems. The history of national parks, which contained the apparent paradox between visitation and conservation almost from the outset, presents many lessons for understanding the issues of sustainable tourism and sustainable development. Most particularly, the problem of limiting or managing numbers once people have been attracted and when, often, the political rationale for the park is primarily based on visitation. As Hall and Wouters (1994) observed over 20 years ago with respect to tourism in the sub-Antarctic islands, from an ecological perspective, sustainable tourism means conserving the productive basis of the physical environment by preserving the integrity of the biota and ecological processes and producing tourism commodities without degrading other values. Having no form of tourism in the sub-Antarctic islands may well be the most advisable management strategy in terms of ecological integrity; it is also unrealistic. To ensure that natural areas are preserved we must, somewhat paradoxically, seemingly allow people to visit such wild places so that policy makers can be persuaded to maintain their reserve status. Vicarious appreciation through the medium of books and documentaries is important, but it does not seem to be sufficient to create a groundswell of public opinion for preservation or for limiting one's own consumption.

Undoubtedly, the public perception of crisis because of such environmental issues as DDT, deforestation, oil pollution, energy and resource costs, pandemics and climate change, has played a major part in raising the debate over sustainable development. Tourism was, and still is, seen as a mechanism to both conserve the environment and provide for economic development and employment generation, especially as jobs are lost in other sectors as a result of technological change and economic and labour restructuring. However, unlike the nineteenth and early twentieth centuries, the environment is now a global issue that requires both an international response and a global analysis. Finally, unlike the earliest attempts at natural resource conservation, there is also a growing recognition that environmental conservation is ultimately socially constructed and culturally driven and recognition must be given to cultural values, particularly those of indigenous peoples, and broader principles of environmental justice. Nevertheless, the core issues that surround sustainable development, particularly with respect to tourism, still remain. That is the dominance of the economic and political discourse of 'balanced' forms of development, driven by technical efficiencies and innovation, which promote the conservation of the natural environment while simultaneously providing for their exploitation so as to sustain economic growth.

Key Reading

Glacken, C. (1967) *Traces on the Rhodian Shore, Nature and Culture in Western Thought from Ancient Times to the End of the Eighteenth Century*, Berkeley: University of California Press. Glacken's immense work of scholarship provides for a profound understanding of the role of nature in Western societies and its intellectual legacies that last to the present day.

Nash, R. (2014) *Wilderness and the American Mind* (5th ed.), New Haven: Yale University Press. Nash's classic work provides the definitive account of the role of wilderness in the American cultural experience and its export around the world.

Redclift, M. (2005) 'Sustainable development (1987–2005): An oxymoron comes of age', *Sustainable Development*, 13: 212–27. An extremely useful account of the conceptual history of 'sustainable development', from the Brundtland Commission's definition in 1987 to 2005.

Runte, A. (2010) *National Parks: The American Experience* (4th ed.). Lanham: Taylor Trade Publishing. Runte's book provides an excellent discussion on the role of tourism as an economic justification for national park establishment and management.

References

Ayres, R.U. and Kneese, A.V. (1968) 'Pollution and environmental quality', in H.S. Perloff (ed.) *The Quality of Urban Development*, Baltimore: Johns Hopkins University Press.

—— (1969) 'Production, consumption and externalities', *American Economic Review*, 59: 282–97.

Baeten, G. (2000) 'The tragedy of the highway: Empowerment, disempowerment and the politics of sustainability discourses and practices', *European Planning Studies*, 8: 69–86.

Barnett, H. and Morse C. (1963) *Scarcity and Growth: The Economics of Natural Resource Availability*, Baltimore: Johns Hopkins Press.

Beckerman, W. (1972) 'Economists, scientists, and environmental catastrophe', *Oxford Economic Papers*, 24: 327–44.

Bengston, D.N. (1994) 'Changing forest values and ecosystem management', *Society & Natural Resources*, 7: 515–33.

Berwick, E.J.H. (1969) 'The international union for conservation of nature and natural resources: Current activities and situation', *Biological Conservation*, 1(3): 191–99.

Boulding, K.E. (1966) 'The economics of the coming spaceship earth,' in H. Jarrett (ed) *Environmental Quality in a Growing Economy*, Baltimore: John Hopkins University and Resources for the Future.

Buck, P.H. (1921) *The Evolution of the National Park System of the United States*, A Thesis Presented for the Degree of Master of Arts, Ohio State University, June 1921, reprinted 1946 by the United States Department of the Interior, National Park Service, United States Government Printing Office, Washington.

Callon, M. (1998) 'Introduction: The embeddedness of economic markets in economics', in M. Callon (ed) *The Laws of the Markets*, Oxford: Blackwell.

Carson, R. (1962 [2002]) *Silent Spring*, New York: Houghton Mifflin Harcourt.

Castree, N. (2005) *Nature*, London: Routledge.

Clarke, J.N. and McCool, D. (1985) *Staking Out the Terrain: Power Differentials Among Natural Resource Management Agencies*, Albany: State University of New York Press.

Clawson, M. (2013) *The Federal Lands Revisited*. New York: RFF Press.

Cole, H.D.S., Freeman, C., Jahoda, M. and Pavitt, K.L.R. (eds) (1973) *Thinking About the Future: A Critique of the Limits to Growth*, London: Chatto and Windus.

Curry-Lindahl, K. (1974) 'The conservation story in Africa during the 1960s', *Biological Conservation*, 6: 170–78.

Czech, B. (2008) 'Prospects for reconciling the conflict between economic growth and biodiversity conservation with technological progress', *Conservation Biology*, 22: 1389–98.

Daly, H.E. (1972) 'In defense of a steady-state economy,' *American Journal of Agricultural Economics*, 54: 945–54.

—— (1974) 'The economics of the steady state', *The American Economic Review*, 64(2): 15–21.

—— (1991) *Steady-State Economics* (2nd ed.), Washington DC: Island Press.

Dietz, S. and Adger, W.N. (2003) 'Economic growth, biodiversity loss and conservation effort', *Journal of Environmental Management*, 68: 23–35.

Dryzek, J.S. (1997) *The Politics of the Earth*, New York: Oxford University Press.

Dubois, G., Peeters, P., Ceron, J-P. and Gössling, S. (2011) 'The future tourism mobility of the world population: Emission growth versus climate policy', *Transportation Research Part A: Policy and Practice*, 45: 1031–42.

Edgell Sr., D.L. (2006) *Managing Sustainable Tourism – A Legacy for the Future*, Binghampton: Haworth Press.

Ehrlich, P. (1968) *The Population Bomb*, New York: Ballantine Books.

Evernden, N. (1992) *The Social Creation of Nature*, Baltimore: John Hopkins University Press.

Foresta, R.A. (1984) *America's National Parks and Their Keepers*, Washington DC: Resources for the Future.

Frost, W. and Hall, C.M. (2009) 'American invention to international concept: the spread and evolution of national parks', in W. Frost and C.M. Hall (eds) *Tourism and National Parks: International Perspectives on Development, Histories and Change*, London: Routledge.

Gallie, W.B. (1955–56) 'Essentially contested concepts', *Proceedings of the Aristotelian Society*, 56: 167–98.

Geisler, C.C. (1995) 'Land and poverty in the United States: Insights and oversights', *Land Economics*, 71: 16–34.

Georgescu-Roegen, N. (1971) *The Entropy Law and the Economic Process*, Cambridge MA: Harvard University Press.

Glacken, C. (1967) *Traces on the Rhodian Shore: Nature and Culture in Western Thought from Ancient Times to the End of the Eighteenth Century*, Berkeley: University of California Press.

Gössling, S. (2002) 'Global environmental consequences of tourism', *Global Environmental Change*, 12: 283–302.

Gössling, S. and Hall, C.M. (eds) (2006) *Tourism and Global Environmental Change*, London: Routledge.

Gössling, S., Hall, C.M., Peeters, P. and Scott, D. (2010) 'The future of tourism: Can tourism growth and climate policy be reconciled? A climate change mitigation perspective', *Tourism Recreation Research*, 35(2): 119–30.

Gössling, S., Scott, D. and Hall, C.M. (2013) 'Challenges of tourism in a low-carbon economy', *WIRES Climate Change*, 4(6): 525–38.

Hall, C.M. (1992) *Wasteland to World Heritage: Preserving Australia's Wilderness*, Carlton: Melbourne University Press.

—— (1998) 'Historical antecedents of sustainable development and ecotourism: New labels on old bottles?' in C.M. Hall & A. Lew (eds) *Sustainable Tourism Development: Geographical Perspectives*, London: Addison-Wesley Longman.

—— (2007) 'Pro-poor tourism: Do "tourism exchanges benefit primarily the countries of the South"?' *Current Issues in Tourism*, 10: 111–18.

—— (2008) *Tourism Planning*, Harlow: Pearson.

—— (2009) 'Degrowing tourism: Décroissance, sustainable consumption and steady-state tourism', *Anatolia*, 20: 46–61.

—— (2010) 'Changing paradigms and global change: From sustainable to steady-state tourism', *Tourism Recreation Research*, 35(2): 131–45.

—— (2011) 'Policy learning and policy failure in sustainable tourism governance: From first and second to third order change?' *Journal of Sustainable Tourism*, 19: 649–71.

—— (2013) 'Green growth and tourism for a sustainable future: 'We just need to put the right policies in place', or, the lunatics have taken over the asylum', presented at *International Critical Tourism Studies Conference V*, Sarajevo, Bosnia & Herzegovina, 26 June.

—— (2014) *Tourism and Social Marketing*, Abingdon: Routledge.

Hall, C.M. and Frost, W. (2009a) 'Introduction: The making of the national park concept', in W. Frost and C.M. Hall (eds) *Tourism and National Parks: International Perspectives on Development, Histories and Change*, London: Routledge.

—— (2009b) 'National parks and the 'Worthless Lands Hypothesis' revisited', in W. Frost and C.M. Hall (eds) *Tourism and National Parks: International Perspectives on Development, Histories and Change*, London: Routledge.

Hall, C.M. and Wouters, M.M. (1994) 'Managing nature tourism in the Sub-Antarctic islands', *Annals of Tourism Research*, 21: 355–74.

Hays, S.P. (1957) *The Response to Industrialism, 1885–1914*, Chicago: University of Chicago Press.

—— (1959) *Conservation and the Gospel of Efficiency: The Progressive Conservation Movement 1890–1920*, Cambridge, MA: Harvard University Press.

Honour, H. (1975) *The New Golden Land: European Images of America from the Discoverers to the Present Times*, New York: Pantheon Books.

Hunter, C. (2002) 'Aspects of the sustainable tourism debate from a natural resources perspective', in R. Harris, T. Griffin and P. Williams (eds) *Sustainable Tourism: A Global Perspective*, Oxford. Butterworth-Heinemann.

International Air Transport Association (2010) *Four Cornerstones of Change – IATA Launches Vision 2050*. IATA Press Release No.24, 7 June.

Ise, J. (1961) *Our National Park Policy: A Critical History*, Baltimore: Published for Resources for the Future by John Hopkins Press.

IUCN, UNEP, and WWF (1980) *World Conservation Strategy*, Gland: IUCN.

Jackson, T. (2009) *Prosperity Without Growth*, London: Earthscan.

Jarrett, H. (ed.) (1966) *Environmental Quality in a Growing Economy*, Baltimore: John Hopkins University and Resources for the Future

Jefferson, T. (1861) *Notes on the State of Virginia*, New York: Harper and Row.

Koppes, C.R. (1987) 'Efficiency/equity/esthetics: Towards a reinterpretation of American conservation', *Environmental History Review*, 11: 127–46.

Lecomber, R. (1975) *Economic Growth Versus the Environment*, London: Macmillan.

Lowenthal, D. (1958) *George Perkins Marsh: Versatile Vermonter*, New York: Columbia University Press.

Maher, N.M. (2007) *Nature's New Deal: The Civilian Conservation Corps and the Roots of the American Environmental Movement*, New York: Oxford University Press.

Majone, G. (1989) *Evidence, Argument and Persuasion in the Policy Process*, New Haven: Yale University Press.

Marsh, G.P. (1965) *Man and Nature; or, Physical Geography as Modified by Human Action*, orig. 1864, ed. D. Lowenthal, Cambridge: The Belknap Press of Harvard University Press.

—— (1968) 'Man's responsibility for the land', in R. Nash (ed.) *The American Environment, Readings in the History of Conservation*, Reading: Addison–Wesley Publishing.

Meadows, D.H., Meadows, D.L., Randers, J. and Behrens, W.W. (1972) *Limits to Growth: A Report for the Club of Rome's Project on the Predicament of Mankind*. New York: Universe Books.

Mercer, D.C. (2000) *A Question of Balance: Natural Resources Conflict Issues in Australia* (3rd ed.), Leichhardt: The Federation Press.

Mills, J.H. and Waite, T.A. (2009) 'Economic prosperity, biodiversity conservation, and the environmental Kuznets curve', *Ecological Economics*, 68: 2087–95.

Mishan, E.J. (1967) *The Costs of Economic Growth*, London: Staples Press.

Mozumder, P., Berrens, R.P. and Bohara, A.K. (2006) 'Is there an environmental Kuznets curve for the risk of biodiversity loss?' *The Journal of Developing Areas*, 39: 175–90.

Nash, R. (1963) 'The American wilderness in historical perspective', *Journal of Forest History*, 6(4): 2–13.

—— (1967) *Wilderness and the American Mind*, New Haven: Yale University Press.

Nash, R. (ed.) (1968) *The American Environment: Readings in the History of Conservation*, Reading, MA: Addison-Wesley Publishing.

Nash, R. (2014) *Wilderness and the American Mind* (5th ed.), New Haven: Yale University Press.

Nicholson, M.H. (1962) *Mountain Gloom and Mountain Glory*, New York: Norton.

Northern Ireland Tourist Board (2009) *Sustainable Tourism*, Belfast: Northern Ireland Tourism Board.

Odum, H.T. (1971) *Environment, Power and Society*. New York: Wiley.

Olmsted, F.L. and Wharton, W.P. (1932) 'The Florida Everglades: Where the mangrove forests meet the storm waves of a thousand miles of water', *American Forests*, 38(March): 142–47, 192.

Pepper, D. (1984) *The Roots of Modern Environmentalism*, London: Croom Helm.

Perez-Carmona, A. (2012) 'Growth: A discussion of the margins of economic and ecological thought,' in L. Meuleman (ed.) *Transgovernance: Advancing Sustainable Governance*, Dortrecht: Springer.

Pigou, A.C. (1943) 'The classical stationary state,' *The Economic Journal*, 53: 343–51.

Pinchot, G. (1968) 'Ends and means', in R. Nash (ed.) *The American Environment: Readings in the History of Conservation*, Reading, MA: Addison-Wesley.

Polimeni, J.M., Mayumi, K., Giampietro, M. and Alcott, B. (2008) *The Jevons Paradox and the Myth of Resource Efficiency Improvements*, London: Earthscan.

Powell, J.M. (1976) *Conservation and Resource Management in Australia 1788–1914, Guardians, Improvers and Profit: An Introductory Survey*, Melbourne: Oxford University Press.

Richardson, E.R. (1962) *The Politics of Conservation: Crusades and Controversies 1897–1913*, Berkeley: University of California Press.

Runte, A. (1972) 'Yellowstone: It's useless, so why not a park', *National Parks and Conservation Magazine*, 46(March): 4–7.

—— (1974) 'Pragmatic alliance: Western railroads and the national parks', *National Parks and Conservation Magazine*, 48(April): 14–21.

—— (1977) 'The national park idea: Origins and paradox of the American experience', *Journal of Forest History*, 21(2): 64–75.

—— (1979) *National Parks: The American Experience*, Lincoln: University of Nebraska Press.

Russell, B. (1946) *A History of Western Philosophy*, London: Unwin.

Saarinen, J. (2006). 'Traditions of sustainability in tourism studies', *Annals of Tourism Research*, 33(4), 1121–40.

Santarius, T. (2012) *Green Growth Unravelled – How Rebound Effects Baffle Sustainability Targets When the Economy Keeps Growing*, Berlin: Wuppertal Institute for Climate, Environment and Energy.

Sax, J.L. (1976) 'America's national parks: Their principles, purposes and prospects', *Natural History*, 85(8): 57–88.

Schilcher, D. (2007) 'Growth versus equity: The continuum of pro-poor tourism and neoliberal governance', *Current Issues in Tourism*, 10(2–3): 166–93.

Shankland, R. (1970) *Steve Mather of the National Parks* (3rd ed.), New York: Alfred A. Knopf.

Simms, A. (2008) 'The poverty myth,' *New Scientist*, 200(2678): 49.

Sirna, A. (2014) 'Reconciling competing visions in New Deal parks: Natural conservation, historic preservation, and recreational development', *George Wright Forum*, 31(1): 63–68.

Speth, G. (1980) 'The Global 2000 Report to the President,' *Boston College Environmental Affairs Law Review*, 8: 695–703.

Stern, D.I. (2004) 'The rise and fall of the environmental Kuznets curve', *World Development*, 32: 1419–39.

Stern, N. (2007) *The Economics of Climate Change: The Stern Review*, Cambridge: Cambridge University Press.

Swain, D.C. (1970) *Wilderness Defender: Horace M. Albright and Conservation*, Chicago: University of Chicago Press.

Talbot, L. M. (1983) 'IUCN in retrospect and prospect', *Environmental Conservation*, 10(1): 5–11.

Thoreau, H.D. (1968) *Walden*, Everyman's Library, London: Dent.

Tuan, Y–F. (1979) *Landscapes of Fear*, New York: Pantheon.

Turner, F.J. (1893) *The Significance of the Frontier in American History*, El Paso: Academic Reprints.

—— (1920) *The Frontier in American History*, New York: Henry Holt.

United Nations Environment Programme (UNEP) (2011) *Towards a Green Economy: Pathways to Sustainable Development and Poverty Eradication*, Nairobi: UNEP.

United Nations Environment Programme and the World Tourism Organization (2005) *Making Tourism More Sustainable: A Guide for Policy Makers*, Paris: UNEP.

United Nations World Tourism Organization (UNWTO) (2002) *Tourism and Poverty Alleviation*, Madrid: World Tourism Organization.

—— (2007a) *From Davos to Bali – A Tourism Contribution to the Challenge of Climate Change*, Policy Document, Madrid: UNWTO.

—— (2007b) *Tourism Will Contribute to Solutions for Global Climate Change and Poverty Challenges*, Press release, UNWTO Press and Communications Department, 8 March, Berlin/Madrid.

Vaillancourt, J. (1997) 'Sustainable development: A sociologist's view of the definition, origins and implications of the concept', in M.D. Mehta and E. Ouellet (eds) *Environmental Sociology: Theory and Practice*, York: Captus Press.

Wall, G. (1997) 'Sustainable tourism – unsustainable development', in S. Wahab and J. Pigram (eds) *Tourism, Development and Growth*, London: Routledge.

Wilson, B.B. (2014) 'Before the "triple bottom line" New Deal defense housing as proto-sustainability', *Journal of Planning History*, doi:10.1177/1538513214529404

World Commission for Environment and Development (WCED) (1987) *Our Common Future. The Brundtland Report*, Oxford: Oxford University Press.

World Economic Forum (WEF) (2009a) *Towards a Low Carbon Travel & Tourism Sector*. Davos: WEF.

—— (2009b) *The Travel & Tourism Competitiveness Report 2009: Managing in a Time of Turbulence*, Davos: WEF.

World Travel and Tourism Council (WTTC) (2003) *Blueprint for New Tourism*, London: WTTC.

—— (2009) *Leading the Challenge on Climate Change*, London: WTTC.

Worster, D. (1977) *Nature's Economy: A History of Ecological Ideas*, Cambridge: Cambridge University Press.

Wright, D. (trans.) (1957) *Beowulf*, Harmondsworth: Penguin.

Yunis, E. (2006) '12 aims of a sustainable tourism', presentation at *EcoTrans European Network for Sustainable Tourism Development. Making Tourism More Sustainable – helpful instruments and examples of good practice in Europe*. 3 February 2006, Reisepavillon Fairgrounds, Hanover/Germany. Retrieved from www.ecotrans.org/docs/1_hamele_Yunis_intro_aims.pdf

Zapata, M.J., Hall, C.M., Lindo, P. and Vanderschaeghen, M. (2011) 'Can community-based tourism contribute to development and poverty alleviation?' *Current Issues in Tourism*, 14: 725–49.

3

The global effects and impacts of tourism

An overview

Michelle Rutty, Stefan Gössling, Daniel Scott and C. Michael Hall

---

Human Development Index A composite index that combines indicators of health (i.e., life expectancy at birth), educational attainment (i.e., mean years of schooling, expected years of schooling), and living standards (i.e., gross national income per capita) in order to measure human well-being.

Introduction

The global impacts of tourism are garnering increased societal attention. Climate change, coastal urbanization, biodiversity loss, fossil fuel consumption, disease transmission, and cultural commoditization, are among the more contentious tourism issues permeating the media. However, until relatively recently, the positive economic impacts of tourism were the primary focus, with far less emphasis on the environmental and social consequences. Throughout the 1960s, tourism was generally viewed optimistically because of its contribution to economic development (e.g. employment, investment, income, balance of payments, tax revenues) (Mathieson & Wall 1982). Concern regarding the negative impacts of tourism only emerged as a significant issue in the 1970s and 1980s (De Kadt 1979; Hall & Page 2006). It was during this time that broader public concern over the impact of natural resource management began to grow, with the passage of the first environmental impact legislation (i.e. *United States National Environmental Policy Act* enacted in 1969) and the creation of national environmental protection agencies (e.g. the United States Environmental Protection Agency (EPA) established in 1970) (Hall & Lew 2009).

In the seminal work of Mathieson and Wall (1982), a review of the tourism impact literature available at that time highlighted the substantial environmental and social risks and costs that tourism posed. This recognition prompted a reorientation of tourism research towards a more balanced perspective, with studies critically examining both the positive and negative implications of tourism. In their updated book, Wall and Mathieson (2006: 5) note that 'as tourism has grown in volume and diversity, the consequences of tourism have become increasingly complex and contradictory'. This is also attributable to the influential insights provided by the 1987 Brundtland Report, which formally introduced the concept of sustainable development to a wider audience (WCED 1987). By taking sustainability into account, impact studies are approached with consideration for the interrelationship between economic, social and environmental impact types, rather than focusing on environmental impacts – the original focus of the Brundtland Report – in isolation. There is now a wealth of literature on sustainable tourism development, with sustainable tourism a major focus of impact research (Wall & Mathieson 2006; Hall & Lew 2009; see also Chapter 1).

Unlike tourism-related impact assessments, which focus on a particular project, event or facility, impact studies are concerned with the broader aspects of change, including the factors that lead to change. Importantly, impact studies aim to provide an account of the bigger picture with respect to tourism and its relationship to economic, environmental and sociocultural change over time (Hall & Lew 2009). An inherent challenge with impact studies is trying to disentangle changes that are attributable to pre-existing processes versus changes induced by tourism. Consequently, the scope and accuracy of research results become constrained (Wall & Mathieson 2006). Few impact studies attempt a comprehensive examination, but rather focus on a particular activity or destination. Impact results subsequently become isolated from the broader tourism phenomena of which they are a part, limiting the narrative at the larger global level (Hall & Lew 2009).

This chapter looks at the macro-scale, global environmental footprint of tourism and the global impact of tourism on development, using conventional economic indicators (e.g. GDP, employment), as well as broader indicators of human well-being and societal development (e.g. Human Development Index). This is done through an examination of what is widely regarded as the three dimensions of sustainable tourism: economic, environmental and sociocultural. While tourism impacts are rarely, if ever, just an issue of one of these dimensions, most impact studies focus primarily on one of these three types of impacts (Hall & Lew 2009). Therefore the organization of this chapter echoes the dominant approach in the current literature.

Economic

International tourism has grown rapidly over the past 60 years. It has become one of the largest global economic sectors and a significant contributor to many national and local economies (Coles & Hall 2008). However, one of the difficulties in assessing the economic impacts of tourism is that it is not a standard industrial classification and is therefore subject to different interpretations with respect to contributing sectors in different international and national jurisdictions (Hall & Coles 2008; Hall & Lew 2009).

The growth of international tourist arrivals has been virtually continuous; from 25 million in 1950, to 278 million in 1980, 528 million in 1995, and exceeding the 1 billion mark for the first time ever in 2012 with 1,035 million international tourists (UNWTO 2013). Just over half of all international tourist arrivals (52% or 536 million arrivals in 2012) travel for holidays, recreation and types of leisure, followed by 27% to visit friends and relatives (VFR), religious regions/pilgrimages or health/treatment, and 14% of trips are for business and professional purposes (the remaining 7% not specified) (UNWTO 2013). Although international tourism is usually the primary policy focus because of its business and trade dimensions (Coles & Hall 2008), the vast majority of tourism is domestic in nature and is estimated to have accounted for 6 billion arrivals in 2012 (UNWTO 2013).

International tourism receipts achieved a new record in 2012 of US$1,075 billion worldwide (UNWTO 2013). According to the UNWTO (2013), in 2012, tourism generated an estimated 9% of world's Gross Domestic Product (GDP) (direct, indirect and induced), and contributed to one in 11 jobs globally. Tourism also accounted for 6% of the world's exports (US$1.3 trillion) (UNWTO 2013) or 30% of the world's export of commercial services (UNWTO 2012). However, UNCTAD and WTO statistics provide a slightly different picture of its contribution to the global economy. According to UNCTAD, WTO and IMF statistics (see Table 3.1), in 2012, the export of travel services accounted for 25.1% of total global trade in commercial services and 4.91% of total trade in goods and services. This figure is reasonably similar to that of 1980. However, it represents a decline from 1995 when travel exports accounted for 32.79% of global trade in commercial services and 6.32% of total trade in goods and services. Such figures also raise questions about the often made statement about tourism being the 'world's fastest growing industry' as well as the relative values of tourism as a development mechanism. Nevertheless, this does not deny the economic importance of tourism. Tourism is one of five top export earners in over 150 countries, while in 60 countries it is the number one export sector (UNCTAD 2010; UNWTO & UNEP 2011). It is also the main source of foreign exchange for one-third of developing countries and one-half of less developed countries (LDCs) (UNWTO & UNEP 2011) (see Tables 3.2 and 3.3).

Table 3.1 Travel service exports as proportion of total trade in goods and services and total trade in commercial services 1980–2012

Year	Travel service exports as % of total trade in goods & services	Travel service exports as % of total trade in commercial services
1980	4.36%	26.16%
1985	5.03%	28.21%
1990	6.16%	31.66%
1995	6.32%	32.79%
2000	5.99%	31.30%
2005	5.41%	27.26%
2010	4.99%	24.43%
2012	4.91%	25.10%

Sources:
Contributions are derived from UNCTAD, WTO and ITC secretariats' calculations of international exports and imports, based on: IMF, Balance of Payments Statistics; Eurostat, online database; UN/DESA/Statistics Division, Service Trade Statistical Database; OECD, OECD.Stat; other international and national sources. See http://unctad.org/en/pages/Statistics.aspx or WTO statistical database: http://stat.wto.org/Home/WSDBHome.aspx?Language=E

Notes:
Exports and imports of goods and services are credits and debits of goods and services as reported in the current account of the balance of payments.

Goods include general merchandise, goods used for processing other goods, and non-monetary gold. In order for a transaction to be recorded under 'goods', a change of ownership from/to a resident of a local country to/from a non-resident in a foreign country has to take place.

Services are defined as the economic output of intangible commodities that may be produced, transferred and consumed at the same time. However, services cover a heterogeneous range of intangible products and activities that are difficult to capture within a single definition and are sometimes hard to separate from goods. Services are outputs produced to order, and they typically include changes in the condition of the consumers realized through the activities of the producers at the demand of customers. Ownership rights over services cannot be established. By the time production of a service is completed, it must have been provided to a consumer. International trade covers transactions between residents and non-residents of an economy.

Travel: Includes goods and services acquired from an economy by non-resident travellers during visits shorter than one year.

For detailed explanations, refer to IMF (1993, 2002, 2009).

Table 3.2 Travel as an export activity 2000–2011

Country grouping	Billions of dollars				As % of total services			
	2000	2005	2010	2011	2000	2005	2010	2011
World	479.4	694.6	950.5	1,067.4	31.5	27.1	24.8	25.2
Least developed countries	2.5	4.8	9.8	11.3	35.9	41.3	44.1	44.0
Developing economies	130.3	213.6	362.4	411.4	37.1	33.9	31.9	32.5
Developing economies excluding China	114.1	184.3	316.6	362.9	35.6	33.2	32.8	33.5
Developing economies: Africa	14.5	28.8	42.2	40.5	43.7	48.2	46.6	44.1
Developing economies: America	31.6	42.9	55.8	58.8	51.2	48.7	41.9	39.6
Developing economies: Asia	83.9	140.5	262.9	310.4	32.9	29.4	28.9	30.4
Developing economies: Oceania	0.3	1.4	1.5	1.7	33.4	45.9	45.6	46.1
Transition economies	8.4	20.5	29.5	35.8	34.8	35.6	28.6	29.6
Developed economies	340.7	460.5	558.5	620.2	29.7	24.5	21.5	21.7
Developed economies: America	111.5	119.9	151.9	166.8	33.9	27.7	24.3	24.6
Developed economies: Asia	8.6	9.5	18.0	15.9	10.0	7.8	10.9	9.2
Developed economies: Europe	209.0	309.0	354.9	400.6	29.6	24.1	20.3	20.6
Developed economies: Oceania	11.6	22.1	34.7	36.9	47.6	55.6	61.1	59.7

Source: Adapted from UNCTAD (2012)

Table 3.3 The importance of tourism for developing economies

Region	Visitor spending as a % of GDP (2009 or most recent available)			
	> 50%	25–50%	10–24%	5–9%
Eastern Africa	–	Seychelles	Mauritius, Zimbabwe	United Republic of Tanzania, Madagascar, Comoros, Eritrea, Kenya
Middle Africa	–	–	Sao Tome and Principe	–
Western Africa	–	Cape Verde	Gambia	Ghana
Northern Africa	–	–	Morocco	Tunisia, Egypt
Southern Africa	–	–	–	Namibia, Botswana
Eastern Asia	China, Macao SAR	–	Bahrain	Mongolia; China, Hong Kong SAR
Western Asia	–	–	Lebanon, Jordan	Syrian Arab Republic
Southern Asia	–	Maldives	–	–
Southeast Asia	–	–	Cambodia	Thailand, Singapore
Central America	–	–	Belize	Costa Rica, Panama, El Salvador, Honduras
South America	–	–	–	Suriname
Caribbean	Anguilla	Aruba, Turks and Caicos Islands, Saint Lucia, Antigua and Barbuda, Bahamas, Barbados	Saint Kitts and Nevis, Saint Vincent and the Grenadines, Grenada, Dominica, Cayman Islands, Jamaica, Montserrat, Dominican Republic	–
Oceania	Palau, Cook Islands	Vanuatu	Samoa, Fiji, French Polynesia	Micronesia (Federated States of), Tonga, New Caledonia

Source: Derived from UNCTAD (2008) and UNWTO (2011)

Classifying countries based on their level of development (i.e. developed, developing, LDCs, emerging economies) is not grounded in theory or based on a universally accepted benchmark (Nielsen 2011). In the absence of a general classification system, membership in the Organisation for Economic Co-operation and Development (OECD) is sometimes used as the main criterion for developed country status. For the UN, the country classification system is based on the Human Development Index (HDI), which is a composite index of three indices that measure a country's achievement in longevity (i.e. life expectancy at birth), education (actual and expected years of schooling) and income (Gross National Income per capita). Developed countries are those in the top quartile of the HDI distribution, with the bottom three quartiles considered developing countries (Nielsen 2011). The UN also classifies some countries as LDCs, which are defined as 'low-income countries suffering from structural impediments to sustainable development' (UN DESA 2013). This classification is based on GNI per capita, Human Assets Index (percentage of population undernourished, mortality rate for children aged five years or under, gross secondary school enrolment ratio, adult literacy rate), and the Economic Vulnerability Index (an exposure index and shock index that consists of seven indicators: 1) population size, 2) remoteness, 3) merchandise export concentration, 4) share of agriculture, forestry and fisheries in gross domestic product, 5) homelessness owing to natural disasters, 6) instability of agricultural production, and 7) instability of exports of goods and services). The threshold for inclusion as an LDC is determined by the index number corresponding to the third quartile in the distribution of results for the reference group of all developing countries (i.e. if the reference group consists of 60 countries, there will be 45 countries below the threshold and meet inclusion criterion). Emerging economies are countries considered to be in a transitional phase, with social and/or economic activity in the process of rapid growth and industrialization (Nielsen 2011).

While the majority of international tourism currently occurs in developed countries, the UNWTO has reported that between 1995 and 2007, international tourism in emerging and developing markets grew at twice the rate of industrialized countries (UNWTO 2007). International tourism in developing countries also expanded by 6% as a whole between 1996 and 2006, by 9% for LDCs and by 8% for other low and lower-middle income economies (UNWTO 2008). Growth between 2000 and 2009 was also most marked in emerging economies (58.8%), with their overall global market share growing from 38.1% in 2000 to 46.9% in 2009 (UNEP 2011). UNWTO (2012) expects international arrivals to almost double from 940 million in 2010 to 1.8 billion by 2030 (an average increase of 3.3% per year). Most of this international tourism growth is forecast to come from the emerging economies and the Asia-Pacific region; by 2030 it is estimated that 57% of international arrivals will be in what are currently classified as emerging economies (UNWTO 2011, 2012) (see Chapter 1, Table 1.3).

The significant role of tourism in many developing economies is highlighted in Tables 3.2 and 3.3. Table 3.2 indicates that although travel as an export activity has continued to grow between 2000 and 2011, its relative proportion of total global export of services has declined during this period, particularly as the result of the growth of ICT. In developing economies, the relative proportion of total export services has declined since 2000 levels (-4.6%), with regional declines noted in the developing economies of Asia (-2.5%), and particularly in America (-11.6%). Declines from 2000 levels are also evident in transition economies (-5.2%), as well as in developed economies (-8%), including substantial decreases in America (-9.3%) and Europe (-9%). One exception is in the developed economies of Oceania, whereby tourism's relative importance in service exports has increased substantially since 2000 (+12.1%). Such regional differences are also reflected in Table 3.3, which outlines the importance of tourism to different developing economies. Tourism is especially important to island states in the

Caribbean, Eastern Africa, and Oceania. For example, in the Caribbean, visitor spending contributes between 10–50% of the GDP for 14 countries in the region, and more than 50% of GDP in Anguilla. It should also be noted that the vast majority of global tourism is domestic rather than international in nature and may not be fully captured in these statistics (UNWTO-UNEP-WMO 2008). The overall economic importance of tourism in contributing to particular economies may therefore be much greater.

Given the ongoing growth of international tourism in developing countries, it is perhaps not surprising that tourism is increasingly supported by many development agencies and organizations, such as the UNWTO and the UNEP, as an important component in national employment generation and poverty reduction strategies. International tourism is also recognized as an important sector by policy makers in developing economies within the context of the perceived need to sustain international competitiveness (Crouch & Ritchie 2012; Hall 2013). Although the relative long-term value of an open economy to many countries is increasingly being questioned, especially post the economic and financial crises of 2008–12 (Scheyvens 2007). Nevertheless, many policy makers have come to regard tourism as an avenue to achieve competitive economic specialization (Komlev & Encontre 2004) and improve foreign exchange flows (Kasahara 2004). It is along these lines that the UNWTO, World Travel and Tourism Council (WTTC), and international development organizations strongly promote international tourism as a means to achieve both poverty reduction and advancement on the UN Millennium Development Goals (Gössling 2009) This position has been similarly advocated by other international bodies such as the World Economic Forum (WEF) (2009a, 2009b), as well as the international development cooperation sector, including, for example, the Asian Development Bank, British Department for International Development, Canadian International Development Agency, German Gesellschaft für Technische Zusammenarbeit, Inter-American Development Bank, Swedish Agency for International Development Cooperation, and United States Agency for International Development (Hawkins & Mann 2007; Saarinen *et al.* 2009). As stated by the UNWTO (2005: 3), 'tourism development, if properly developed and supported, can indeed be a "quick-win" in overcoming the economic and social conditions that prevail in LDCs and in accelerating their integration into the world economy'. More recently, as part of its green economy strategy, the UNEP (2011: 424) has been advocating the potential poverty reduction benefits of tourism, indicating that 'when tourism-related income grows with a substantial reorientation in favour of the poor, poverty can be reduced'. Significantly, tourism can also have an important enabling function and support international transport and business connections, which can then be utilized to export other products and services.

The UNWTO (2006: 1) outlines several reasons why tourism makes an 'especially suitable economic development sector for LDCs':

- Tourism is consumed at the point of production; the tourist has to go to the destination and spend his/her money there, opening an opportunity for local businesses of all sorts, and allowing local communities to benefit through the informal economy, by selling goods and services directly to visitors;
- Most LDCs have a comparative advantage in tourism over developed countries;
- Tourism is a more diverse industry than many others. It has the potential to support other economic activities, both through providing flexible, part-time jobs that can complement other livelihood options, and through creating income throughout a complex supply chain of goods and services;

- Tourism is labour intensive, which is particularly important in tackling poverty. It also provides a wide range of different employment opportunities especially for women and young people – from the highly skilled to the unskilled – and it usually requires relatively little training;
- It creates opportunities for many small and micro entrepreneurs, either in the formal or informal economy; it is an industry in which start–up costs and barriers to entry are generally low or can easily be lowered;
- Tourism provides not only material benefits for the poor but also cultural pride. It creates greater awareness of the natural environment and its economic value, a sense of ownership and reduced vulnerability through diversification of income sources;
- The infrastructure required by tourism, such as transport and communications, water supply and sanitation, public security, and health services, can also benefit poor communities.

However, international tourism as a development strategy to achieve welfare equity and poverty reduction has long been substantially criticized (e.g. De Kadt 1979; Chok *et al.* 2007; Hall 2007; Telfer & Sharpley 2008; Hall & Lew 2009; Truong *et al.* 2014; see also Truong this volume). There may be limited opportunities for many developing countries and regions to benefit from international tourism, with the supposed comparative advantage of LDCs unevenly distributed (Blake *et al.* 2008). Moreover, the economic advantages accompanying with international tourism development may not be as pronounced as anticipated due to profit repatriation by foreign investors, the nature of local economic networks and structures, relatively low wages, underemployment because of seasonal demand, and the replacement of existing economic activity in some tourism resort areas (e.g. Chok *et al.* 2007). A detailed study by Wieranga (2008: 133) of the benefits of tourism as a means of poverty reduction, often termed pro–poor tourism (PPT), concluded, 'all in all, PPT is more of a livelihood supplement than a poverty solution, and poverty elimination through ethnic tourism is the exception rather than the rule'. This is supported by Blake's (2008) study of Kenya, Tanzania and Uganda, which found that compared to other export sectors, hotels and restaurants, and in particular the transport industry, provide below–average shares of income to poor households. As such, 'these results paint a fairly poor picture of the ability of tourism to alleviate poverty' (Blake 2008: 511), a result of tourism's tendency to be disproportionally beneficial to the already wealthy (Schilcher 2007; Blake *et al.* 2008). This may consequently reinforce existing inequalities (Scheyvens & Momsen 2008). As shown in the case of Thailand, 'the expansion of foreign tourism demand creates general equilibrium effects that undermine profitability in tradable sectors (such as agriculture) from which the poor derive a substantial fraction of their income' (Wattanakuljarus & Coxhead 2008: 929).

In addition to contrary evidence for tourism being a decisive mechanism of poverty reduction and alleviation, tourism also negatively contributes to resource consumption (Gössling 2002; Hall 2010c) and global environmental change (Gössling & Hall 2006b; Scott *et al.* 2012). For example, Hall (2010c) observed that the estimated economic losses with respect to climate change in the developing world are already greater than the level of international tourism expenditure in the 49 least-developed countries. This led him to conclude that 'Tourism may contribute to poverty alleviation but the benefits of tourism need to be weighed up against all its costs, including the effects of climate change' (Hall 2010c: 135).

Despite sustainable tourism being at the forefront of policy statements within supranational institutions, national governments, industry associations and tourism operators, the more that is published on sustainable tourism, the less sustainable it appears to be (Hall 2011a; see also Chapter 1). The sustainability of tourism as a development mechanism is increasingly questioned for two primary reasons. First, while tourism has been promoted by some in the development community since the late 1960s, the mid- to long-term relative contribution of tourism projects to development strategies remains poorly evaluated (Hawkins & Mann 2007). Rather than critically assessing the consequences of tourism-related development strategies, international development agencies and other international bodies have placed greater emphasis on advocating tourism and initiating projects (Gössling, Haglund et al. 2009; Zapata et al. 2011). Second, and in which the first reason is potentially embedded, the paradigmatic and institutional context of tourism and sustainable development often makes it difficult for some policy actors to recognize 'other' policy alternatives and priorities (Hall 2011a).

Environmental

Tourism is a human activity that is both dependent on natural resources and contributes to the their depletion. This interrelationship can be direct or indirect, and while all tourism activities may inevitably be local, they add up to phenomena of global significance (Gössling 2002; Gössling & Hall 2006a). Tourism plays an important role in the consumption of energy and the generation of greenhouse gas (GHG) emissions, exerting pressure on global water sources, impacting land use and change, as well as contributing to biodiversity loss and unsustainable food consumption. In 2007, it has been estimated that tourism's global environmental impacts resulted in energy consumption of 18,586 PJ and emissions of 1461 Mt CO_2 for transport, accommodation and activities, as well as contributing to 0.6–0.7% in land cover change, and an estimated 3.5–5.5% of global species loss (Hall 2011a). Global freshwater consumption by the tourism sector is estimated to account for less than 1% of fresh water, but overall, the water use for infrastructure construction, fuel, and food production is considerably larger (Gössling et al. 2012). In terms of food consumption, tourists eat an estimated 75 billion meals per annum, which is a relatively small share of global food use, yet significant in terms of the higher-order foodstuffs used (Gössling et al. 2011; Gössling & Hall 2013). Tourism's role in global resource consumption is detailed below, while underscoring the notion that the sector is likely to increasingly compete for scarce resources.

Energy use and emissions

The tourism sector depends on fossil fuels and other sources of energy, thereby contributing to the global emissions of various GHGs, particularly carbon dioxide (CO_2), as well as methane (CH_4), nitrous oxides (NOx), hydrofluorocarbons (HFCs), perfluorocarbons (PFCs) and sulphur hexafluoride (SF_6). Tourism-related energy use and emissions include all domestic and international leisure and business travel, and have thus far been calculated for three major subsectors: transport to and from the destination; accommodation; and activities at destinations. An estimate by two independent analyses found that for these three subsectors, tourism contributed approximately 5% to global anthropogenic emissions of CO_2 in 2005, corresponding to 1,304 Mt CO_2 (see Table 3.4) (UNWTO-UNEP-WMO 2008; WEF 2009a). In terms of energy use, this equates to 435 Mt of fuel, or about 17,500 PJ of energy, at an assumed conservative average of 3 kg CO_2 per 1 kg of fuel (Defra 2013).

As outlined in Table 3.4, most CO_2 emissions from tourism are associated with transportation. Aviation emits the largest share at 515 Mt CO_2 or 40% of tourism's overall carbon footprint. While aviation's share of global emissions of CO_2 (i.e. 26,400 Mt CO_2) may seem small, most of these emissions are generated by the 'hyper-mobile' (Gössling, Ceron et al. 2009), the less than 2–3% of the world's population that participate in international aviation on an annual basis

Table 3.4 Distribution of emissions from tourism by sub-sector

	2005		2035*	
Sub–sectors	CO₂(Mt)	%	CO₂(Mt)	%
Air transport	515	40%	1,631	53%
Car transport	420	32%	456	15%
Other transport	45	3%	37	1%
Accommodation	274	21%	739	24%
Activities	48	4%	195	6%
Total	1,307	100%	3,059	100%
Total world (IPCC 2007)	26,400			
Tourism contribution		5%		

*Assumes business as usual (BAU)

Source: UNWTO-UNEP-WMO (2008)

(Peeters *et al.* 2007). Car transportation emits 420 Mt CO_2, accounting for 32% of the sector's carbon footprint, followed by accommodation (274 Mt CO_2 or 21%), and activities at the destination (48 Mt CO_2 or 4%) (UNWTO-UNEP-WMO 2008). Cruise ships are included in 'other transport' with an estimated 19.17 Mt CO_2, accounting for 1.5% of global tourism emissions (De Bruijn *et al.* 2010). Importantly, these calculations represent energy throughput and do not include the impact of short-lived GHGs (Scott *et al.* 2010). A more accurate assessment of tourism's contribution to global warming can be made on the basis of radiative forcing (RF) (i.e. the contribution to warming of long- and short-lived GHGs in a given past year). With RF considered, Scott *et al.* (2010) estimated that tourism contributed 5.2–12.5% of all anthropogenic forcing in 2005, with a best estimate of approximately 8%. A more comprehensive analysis would also need to include food and beverages, infrastructure construction and maintenance, as well as tourist retail and services. This assessment should be based on a lifecycle perspective, taking into account the energy embodied in the goods and services consumed in tourism (Gössling 2013).

While tourism's emissions are already considerable, this contribution is expected to grow significantly in both absolute terms and proportionately, as other economic sectors achieve emission reduction targets (legislated or voluntary). As previously noted, tourism is projected to grow at an average of 3.3% per year until 2030 (UNWTO 2012), resulting in large energy use and emissions trajectories (Gössling 2013). Several tourism trends are expected to increase emissions, including the growth in the number of people travelling for employment, business, leisure, education and health services; continuing declines in the real cost of travel; increases in per capita disposable incomes leading to a growing number of trips made per capita; and growth in the average length of trips made, a function of the greater speed of the transport modes used (Scott *et al.* 2012). Based on a business–as–usual (BAU) growth scenario to 2035, which considers changes in travel frequency, length of stay, travel distance and technological efficiency gains, CO_2 emissions from tourism are projected to grow approximately 135% by 2035 compared with 2005 levels, totalling 3.059 Gt CO_2 (UNWTO-UNEP-WMO 2008). These estimates are very similar to the WEF (2009a) projection for tourism emissions growth of 3.164 Gt CO_2 by 2035 (Table 3.5). Most of this growth will be associated with air transportation, with emissions anticipated to increase in the order of 290–670% by 2050 (IEA 2009; Gössling *et al.* 2013). These projections also align with projections from aviation organizations and aircraft producers that the global fleet of aircraft will double between 2011 and 2031 (Boeing 2011; Airbus 2012).

Table 3.5 Tourism sector emissions and mitigation targets

Year	Emission estimates and BAU projections (CO₂)			Mitigation targets	
	UNWTO-UNEP (2008)	WEF (2009a)	WTTC (2009) *	5% allocation of overall GHG emissions to tourism **
2005	1.304 Gt	1.476 Gt	–	
2020	2.181 Gt	2.319 Gt	0.978 Gt	1.254 Gt
2035	3.059 Gt	3.164 Gt	0.652 Gt	0.940 Gt

*** Pathway that limits global average temperature increase to below 2°C; assuming CO_2 continues to representing approximately 57% (IPCC 2007) of the median estimate of 44 Gt CO_2-e total GHG emissions in 2020 and 2035 (Rogeli 2011) and the tourism sector continues to represent approximately 5% of global CO_2 emissions (UNWTO-UNEP-WMO 2008; WEF 2009a) over the same time frame (Gössling *et al.* 2013).

It is important to note that none of these future emissions projections for the tourism sector account for either the rebound effects (i.e. the behavioural or other systemic responses to the introduction of new technologies that stimulate resource consumption) (Jenkins *et al.* 2011; Santarius 2012) or the gains in energy efficiencies over the period to 2035, which may be significantly lower than expected (Hall *et al.* 2013). Hence, these projections are in stark contrast to mitigation targets, as for instance presented by WTTC (2009) (see Table 3.5). With other major emitting sectors (e.g. manufacturing, energy supply, housing) looking to stabilize or reduce emissions over the next 30 years in many regions of the world, if travel and tourism remain on a BAU pathway, the sector will become an increasingly important source of global GHG emissions (Gössling *et al.* 2010; Hall 2011a). In a recent review by Gössling (2013), these findings for global tourism have been confirmed on a national scale, with emissions from tourism in 22 countries, including several OECD nations, assessed on the basis of Kyoto Protocol guidelines for national GHG inventories (i.e. a calculation excluding international bunker fuels from shipping/aviation). The study found that tourism contributes the equivalent of 4% (Suriname) to 150% (Turks and Caicos) of national emissions, with Small Island Developing States (SIDS) often having economies that are much more energy intense than suggested by Kyoto-based assessments, with tourism dwarfing energy use in all other sectors.

Importantly, other national assessments have underscored the low carbon-efficiency of tourism as an economic sector. In the Netherlands, the carbon-efficiency of the Dutch economy is approximately 0.3 kg CO_2 per Euro, which is more than three times lower than the tourism average at 1 kg CO_2 per Euro (de Bruijn *et al.* 2010). In Switzerland, tourism is the fourth most emission-intense sector (of 22 sectors; Perch-Nielsen *et al.* 2010) and the fifth most emission-intense sector in Australia (of 17 sectors; Dwyer *et al.* 2010). In Sweden, tourism accounted for 11% of national emissions in 2001, which is expected to increase 5% by 2020 (Gössling & Hall 2008). The UK Department of Transport (2007) project that the 9% contribution of aviation to total UK emissions in 2005 (taking radiative forcing into account) will grow to approximately 15% in 2020 and to 29% in 2050. Similarly, the Australian government's energy white paper estimates that air transport will more than quadruple by 2050 (Department of Resources, Energy and Tourism 2012).

The use of energy and subsequent emissions within the tourism sector leads to various conclusions. First, tourism is more energy intense than other economic sectors, and hence more vulnerable to changes in the cost of energy and fossil fuels. Second, this vulnerability is likely to intensify given both tourism's growth and the mounting competition over increasingly scarce fossil fuel resources. Third, if efforts to reduce absolute global emissions of GHG are to be achieved, the cost of CO_2 emissions due to market-based measures (taxes, duties) will become increasingly relevant for tourism. Together, both fuel cost developments and climate policy may affect the global tourism system in a way that would imply changing travel patterns.

Fresh water

Tourism is heavily reliant on the availability of fresh water. Tourists consume fresh water directly, including consumption for hygienic purposes (e.g., for showers and toilets), as well as when engaging in a wide range of activities (e.g., spas, saunas, wellness areas, swimming pools). Tourists also consume fresh water in the form of irrigated hotel gardens and golf courses, as well as supporting infrastructure development (e.g. accommodation), and indirectly in food and fuel (Pigram 1995; Gössling 2001; Hoekstra & Hung 2002; Worldwatch Institute 2004; Chapagain & Hoekstra 2008; Gössling *et al.* 2012). Though people also consume water while at home, there is strong evidence that tourism increases overall water consumption (Gössling *et al.* 2012). On average, water use by tourism stays below 5% of domestic water use, but there are several countries where tourism is a major factor in both water consumption and security (e.g. Caribbean, China, southeast Asia, Mediterranean) (see Table 3.6). Such high levels of consumption, in addition to pollution, population growth, and climate change, have placed increased pressure on freshwater sources (WWAP 2012). Given the global growth in tourism, as well as declining water resources in some regions, changes in the availability or quality of water resources can have negative impacts on tourism, requiring careful attention to account for water usage patterns within the sector.

For accommodation, water consumption ranges from 84 to 2,000 L per tourist per day, or up to 3,423 L per bedroom per day have been reported (Gössling *et al.* 2012). Higher standard accommodation tends to consume more litres of water per tourist, due to the amenities provided. For example, high consumption of water is linked to hotels that provide spas and have multiple large swimming pools (Bohdanowicz & Martinac 2007), as well as hotels with on-site sport and health centres. The quality of textiles within a hotel also increases water consumption as it increases the weight of laundry items (e.g. very large towels at spa facilities). On a global average, it has been suggested that an international tourist consumes 300 L per day in direct water use (Gössling *et al.* 2012).

Table 3.6 Important tourism regions facing water security threat

Region	Tourism importance (% GDP)	Water security threat	Tourism > 5% of domestic water use
Caribbean	High	High	Barbados
Mediterranean	High	Low-High	8 countries
Southeast Asia	Medium-High	High	Thailand, Indonesia
New Zealand & SW Australia	High	Low	no
East Africa	High	High	unknown
West Coast USA	High	Low	no
Coastal zone Brazil	Medium	Low-High	no
Indian subcontinent	Low	High	India
China	Low	High	no

Source: Derived from Vörösmarty *et al.* (2000) and Gössling *et al.* (2012)

Various tourist activities add to freshwater use. An often cited example is golf (Rodriguez Diaz et al. 2007). While the consumption of water at golf courses varies considerably based on soil, climate and size, a standard golf course may have an annual consumption of 80,000 m³ to 100,000 m³ in the North of France and 150,000 m³ to 200,000 m³ in Southern France (Baillon & Ceron 1991; Ceron & Kovacs 1993). Much higher values are reported in dry and warm climates, such that an 18-hole golf course in a Mediterranean sand dune system uses 0.5 to 1 million m³ of fresh water per year (van der Meulen & Salman 1996). Snowmaking for ski resorts is also highly water intensive. Based on a literature review by Rixen et al. (2011), the water consumption for the production of 1 m³ of snow ranges between 200 and 500 L of water (or between 600,000 and 1,500,000 L for 1 ha with 30cm of artificial snow). A case study by Badré et al. (2009) concluded that to produce man-made snow, water consumption in a ski resort in France was 19 million m³ in 2007, of which approximately 70% was run-off. Large conventions or events and attractions infrastructure can also add to freshwater demand (e.g. Meyer & Chaffee 1997; Zaizen et al. 2000; Sebake & Gibberd 2008). In a study of the Millennium Dome in London, each of the six million visitors in 2000 used approximately 22 L of water; 55% was consumed by the flushing of toilets and urinals, 32% for cleaning and canteen use, and 13% for hand washing (Hills et al. 2002).

While there are limited studies that examine water use within the lifecycle of tourism infrastructure, research suggests a high level of water consumption. Roselló-Batie et al. (2010) found that building construction is responsible for 17% of global water consumption. A life-cycle analysis of three hotels in the Balearic Islands accounted for approximately 5% of the total mass of the construction materials. Moreover, after water, concrete is the most consumed material in the world (Low 2005), with Van Oss and Padovani (2003) estimating that global water consumption for cement hydration is approximately 1 billion m³ of water annually. Tourism's contribution to this is likely to be significant, given that the major end uses of concrete are residential buildings (31%), highways and roads (26%) and industrial and commercial buildings (18%), with increasing second home ownership being a significant driver of the growing demand for building materials (Low 2005).

Water use is also interlinked with energy as it is required for the production of water (e.g. pumping, transport, treatment, desalination) and energy (e.g. thermoelectric cooling, hydropower, minerals extraction and mining, fuel production, emission controls). Fuel production is particularly water-intensive, with 18 L of water required to produce 1 L of gasoline (Worldwatch Institute 2004). Given that air travel entails an average energy consumption of 4.1 L of fuel per passenger for every 100 km (UNWTO-UNEP-WMO 2008), the average international air-based tourist trip over 7,600 km (return distance) would consequently lead to the consumption of 5,600 L (Gössling et al. 2012). This is equivalent to the direct water use associated with a stay in a higher-standard resort hotel over a 14-day period (at 400 L per tourist per day).

Biofuels are increasingly advocated for having the greatest potential as a sustainable fuel for air transport, but this will also increase water use. For instance, UNESCO (2009: 11) reports that 44 km³ or 2% of all irrigation water is already allocated to biofuel production. Should all current national biofuel policies and plans be realized, an additional 180 km³ of irrigation water will be needed. Other fuel alternatives, including bioethanol from sugarcane, corn, sugar beet, wheat and sorghum, tripled water use between 2000 and 2007, with the production of biodiesel from oil- and tree-seeds (e.g. rapeseed, sunflower, soybean, palm oil, coconut, jatropha) leading to an 11-fold increase in water use during the same time period. The production of 1 L of liquid biofuels currently takes a global average of 2,500 L of water. The European Union, the United States and Brazil consume most of these biofuels, including 23% of maize production in the US (ethanol production) or 47% of vegetable oil produced in the EU (biodiesel) – and necessitating higher imports of vegetable oil to meet domestic consumption needs. Yet, biodiesel accounts for only 3% of fuel use in the EU thus far (UNESCO 2009).

Food consumption also requires a considerable amount of water. Pending local climate, crop or livestock varieties and agricultural practices, it can take between 400 to 2,000 L of water to produce 1 kg of wheat or 1,000 to 20,000 L of water to produce 1 kg of meat (UNESCO 2009; Gössling & Hall 2013). Based on these figures, it is estimated that daily water requirements to support human diets range from 2,000 to 5,000 L of water per person per day, with an estimate of 1 L of water for 1 kcal of food. Within a tourism context, tourists may be responsible for greater share of higher-order, protein-rich foods, while also requiring additional energy for transport by air over large distances. Both of these contribute to a larger water footprint (Gössling *et al.* 2010). As such, a 14-day holiday may involve water use for food exceeding 70 m^3 of water.

As shown in Table 3.7 indirect water use is likely to be more relevant than direct uses, with fuel use and food consumption constituting particularly high levels of water use. Overall water consumption also varies considerably on an individual basis, depending on hotel standard, distance to the destination, as well as the type and amount of food consumed (Table 3.7). These results would indicate that water management in tourism should look beyond direct water use, and examine more closely 'sustainable' solutions currently seen as promising to solve energy-related problems, such as the greater use of biofuels in global transport, but which will increase global water use.

With the continued growth in tourism and the trend towards higher-standard accommodation and more water-intense activities, pressure on water is bound to increase in many destinations, particularly in regions with a high level of water security threat (e.g. the Caribbean, China, southeast Asia, the Mediterranean) (Table 3.6) (Vörösmarty *et al.* 2000). Tourism may lead to possible competition with other users, which can be further exacerbated by a decrease in freshwater availability. Consequently, the development of tourism may become less viable, or perhaps even unfeasible, for many areas of the world as a result of rising costs associated with fresh water or declining water quality. Impacts will ultimately depend on several factors, including the relative scarcity of fresh water in existing and potential tourism destinations, competition with other economic sectors such as agriculture or biofuels, and the structure of the tourist industry (e.g. small guesthouses vs. large resort hotels), and concomitant low or high daily water use per guest. Regional conflicts over water use have already been reported (Mutiga *et al.* 2010; Deyà Tortella & Tirado 2011), and are projected to increase in the future due to increasing demand and a declining supply (Gössling *et al.* 2012; International Tourism

Table 3.7 Water use categories and estimated use per tourist per day

Water use category – direct	Litres per tourist per day
Accommodation	84–2,000
Activities	10–30
Water use category – indirect	Litres per tourist per day
Fossil fuels	750 (per 1,000 km)
Biofuels	2,500 (per L)
Food	2,000–500,000
Total per tourist per day	2,000–7,500

Source: Derived from Gössling *et al.* (2012)

Partnership 2013). Pollution, population growth and climate change are creating further pressure on freshwater resources (WWAP 2012), to the extent that water issues are no longer discussed solely on a local or national basis, but also on a global scale (Hoekstra & Mekonnen 2012). To adapt to future water situations and mitigate its use, the tourism industry needs to engage in strategic and integrated water management. This includes measuring water consumption, taking measures to reduce and recycle water, invest in new water-conserving technologies, and educate tourists and staff, amongst others. Most of these measures may also lead to positive economic gains, but as with other environmental resource-related measures, strong policies are needed to ensure their proper and successful implementation (Gössling *et al.* 2012).

Land use and change

The use and conversion of the Earth's lands 'represents the most substantial human alteration of the Earth system' as it has a profound impact on global ecosystems and 'interacts strongly with most other components of global environmental change' (Vitousek *et al.* 1997: 494). Not only has some 50% of the Earth's surface been transformed; nearly all land is in some way affected by human-induced processes (Turner *et al.* 2007). Tourism is no exception, with the use and conversion of land central for this sector. In 1999, it was estimated that leisure-related land use amounted to approximately 515,000 km^2, representing 0.34% of the Earth's terrestrial surface or 0.5% of its biologically productive area (Gössling 2002). Since 2000, approximately 27,000 km^2 or 4% of the total global sale of land has been for tourism purposes (Anseeuw *et al.* 2012). While the construction of accommodation establishments may be the primary direct use of land for tourism, a multitude of other direct uses are also present. Examples include airports, roads, railways, paths, trails, pedestrian walks, shopping areas, parking, campsites, vacation homes, golf courses, marinas, ski areas and indirect land use for food production, burying grounds for solid wastes, lands to treat waste waters, and industrial areas required for the production of infrastructure (e.g. computers, TVs, beds). Hence, the land surfaces affected by tourism are considerably larger than the directly built area alone.

UNWTO identifies over 80 categories of accommodation, which includes hotels, hostels, motels, pensions, bed and breakfast, self-catering accommodation, and holiday villages. These are responsible for most of the direct land alteration linked to tourism. Depending on the accommodation category, land use per bed can vary between 30 m^2 to 100 m^2 at ground level. For example, reported average land use per bed in hotels and youth hostels are 30 m^2, followed by 50 m^2 for rented and self-catering accommodation, as well as for camping and caravan sites (per site), and 100 m^2 for holiday villas (Grenon & Batisse 1989, cited in GFANC 1997). In a survey by Lüthje and Lindstädt (1994), the average size of holiday villages was 41 ha. However, since the mid-1990s, there has been a strong trend towards larger holiday villages, and land use per bed has been found to increase (Strasdas 1992).

Given the comparably cheap lands available in tropical regions, land use for tourism may be particularly extensive in these regions, leading to the construction of relatively large hotels. In the Kiwengwa area of Unguja Island (Tanzania), a survey of the land use for five resort hotels indicated that an average of 284 m^2 of land was used per bed (Dahlin & Stridh 1996, Gössling 2001). Land use also increases with the standard of the hotel. For example, the five-star Lemuria Resort in the Seychelles, spans an area of 110 ha (including the golf course), which amounts to over 4,580 m^2 per bed (Gössling *et al.* 2002). Conversely, up-market hotels in cities are comparably smaller in area as a result of the high value of prime urban sites. They are often functional blocks with relatively limited areas available for gardens, forecourts and swimming pools (cf. Jim 2000).

Global land use for tourism is substantial. Worldwide accommodation is estimated to use approximately 1,450 km^2 of land, with an additional 500,000 km^2 used for traffic infrastructure that supports tourism (e.g. airports, roads, railways) (Gössling 2002). Tourism activities also require high land acquisition, with golf courses estimated to cover 13,500 km^2 of global land surfaces alone (Gössling *et al.* 2002). However, these figures are likely to be extremely conservative given the growth in accommodation, traffic infrastructure and golf courses since Gössling's (2002) study (Hall 2011a). For example, Wiles (2013) suggested that golfing establishments take up around 2,700 km^2 in England alone, a figure that constitutes approximately 2% of England's total land area. As noted, assessments on land use and change for tourism remain somewhat limited. An important consideration with respect to indirect tourism land use is the growth and development of biofuels. With the increase in advocacy for biofuels as a sustainable fuel alternative, an increase in land use would be needed to allow crops to be grown for its production (e.g. sugarcane, corn, soybean). The indirect impact of the ecological footprint of tourism land use can also be quite high, particularly in coastal areas due to pressures on biodiversity (Hall 2006, 2010a). On a positive note, the surface area covered by protected recreational areas has increased over time as a result of tourism, especially ecotourism, likely an important economic factor behind this development (Frost & Hall 2009; Buckley 2010). For example, the UN List of Protected Areas has increased from 2.4 million km^2 in 1962, to 18.8 million km^2 in 2003, and protected areas that have recreation as the primary management function (i.e. National Parks and Protected Land-/Seascapes), represent approximately 29% of total protected areas (Chape *et al.* 2003). Yet, these protected areas are often of low biological diversity and their conversion will not have interfered with the acquisition of (frequently high-biodiversity) coastal areas for tourism development (Hall 2010a). To date, conflicts regarding land use for tourism appear regionally restricted, although it may be possible that conflicts are widespread, but not reported upon due to the complexity of land use conflicts and their often small-scale nature.

Biodiversity

Tourism is often dependent on opportunities to observe, see or collect flora and fauna, and to visit specific landscapes, landscape elements, habitats or ecosystems. The rate of species extinction and biodiversity loss during the Anthropocene of 100 to 1,000 times more than natural (Mace *et al.* 2005; Rockström *et al.* 2009) should therefore be of significant concern for the tourism industry, especially given the significance of charismatic fauna and flora (Hall *et al.* 2011). Over the past four decades, biodiversity has experienced a continual decline, as evidenced by various indicators, including the Living Planet Index (mean population trends of vertebrates) and the Red List Index (extinction risk of mammals, birds, amphibians, and corals). Pressure indicators, such as the ecological footprint, have also increased (Butchart *et al.* 2010). While the impact of tourism on biodiversity may be difficult to both specify and quantify (Hall 2010a, b, c; 2011b), direct impacts can result from land use (habitat) change, introduction of diseases, the exchange of species, or locally relevant impacts related to disturbances, collection or purchases of species by tourists (Gössling 2002; Hall 2010a, d).

Although tourism may enhance awareness for preserving and protecting species and ecosystems, the sector may not be a net contributor to biodiversity conservation (Hall 2010a, d), rather, it can be responsible for altering the landscapes and ecosystems of entire regions (Gössling 1999; Buckley 2010). Landscape change is reported as the most important driver of biodiversity loss (Mace *et al.* 2005). The direct use of land for tourism (e.g. construction of accommodation) can lead to the introduction of plant species that are alien to the local ecosystem. Infrastructure to support tourist mobility (i.e. airports, roads, bridges) can also fragment or destroy habitats (Gössling 2002). Such land use changes are also interlinked with tourism urbanization, with disturbance or loss of biodiversity in coastal and alpine areas, as well as wetland and dune conversion, of specific concern (see Table 3.8) (Serra *et al.* 2008; UNWTO 2010).

Human mobility also significantly contributes to biotic exchange on a large and global scale, while simultaneously contributing to the dispersion of diseases and the extinction of wild species. For instance, cruise ships can transport organisms over long distances. In the North American Great Lakes, one-third of the 130 non-native species were introduced by ships (Wilson 1997). Since the seventeenth century, invasive alien species have contributed to nearly 40% of all animal extinctions for which the cause is known, while as of 2000, it was estimated that approximately 480,000 species had been accidentally or deliberately introduced by humans into locations that lie beyond the natural limits of their geographic range (Hall & Baird 2013). However, the overall scale and importance of tourism-related biotic exchange remains relatively unknown, with assessments on the size of this exchange difficult to evaluate (Gössling 2002; Hall & Baird 2013).

Tourism also contributes to the extinction of species through disturbance, collection, and purchase (Hunter & Green 1995; Orams 1998). Trade in souvenirs of biological origin, including shells, corals, shark teeth and other parts of marine species, are popular in many coastal areas of tropical countries and have been identified as a driving force in ecosystem degradation (e.g. Poulsen 1995). A survey of tourists in Zanzibar (Tanzania) found, for instance, that 46% collected or purchased shells (equivalent of 13 tonnes per year), to be exported back home as a souvenir (Gössling *et al.* 2004).

Indirect impacts on biodiversity are also relevant. Plants and animals suffer from increased levels of emissions of various pollutants through leisure-related transport as, for example, described for the National Park Bayerischer Wald in Germany (Brüggemann 1997). Tourism is also a significant contributor to GHG emissions, with climate change playing a dominant role in the extinction of species this century (Mace *et al.* 2005). Hall (2010a) conservatively estimates that tourism is responsible for 3.5–5.5% of species loss based on the relationship between energy use and biodiversity, with this figure to increase in the future should climate change scenarios be considered.

Table 3.8 Important tourism regions facing biodiversity threat

Region	Tourism importance (% GDP)	Regional biodiversity hotspot
Caribbean	High	Caribbean
Mediterranean	High	Mediterranean Basin
Southeast Asia	Medium–High	Sundaland, Wallacea, Philippines & Indo-Burma
New Zealand & SW Australia	High	New Zealand and South West Australia
East Africa	High	Eastern Arc Mountains and Coastal Forests of Tanzania and Kenya
West Coast USA	High	California Floristic Province
Coastal zone Brazil	Medium	Atlantic Forest Region
Indian subcontinent	Low	Western Ghats and Sri Lanka
China	Low	Mountains of South-Central China

Sources: Derived from Christ *et al.* (2003); UNCTAD (2008); Vörösmarty *et al.* (2000)

Food consumption

Due to the central role of food in hospitality and travel, food consumption has both direct and indirect links to tourism impacts (Gössling *et al.* 2011; Hall & Gössling 2013). In 2005, there were close to 25 billion tourist days (UNWTO-UNEP-WMO 2008); at an average of three meals per tourist per day, approximately 75 billion meals per year, or 200 million meals per day, were consumed by tourists. Foodservice providers prepare the majority of these meals, which has considerable relevance for sustainability. As an example, a board initiative by the Scandic hotel chain to purchase only organic and fairly traded coffee affected 20 million cups of coffee annually served to hotel guests (Gössling *et al.* 2011). Hotels consequently have considerable power over food production. Through local (regional) or organic food-purchasing policies, tourism can directly influence sustainable food production. However, when food purchases are made entirely with a focus on the lowest per-unit costs, pressure on food producers increases, leading to the globalization of food production, which Vos (2000) argues, is the primary obstacle to sustainable food production.

Food production has a wide range of sustainability implications. This includes land conversion and the associated loss of biodiversity and ecosystems (Lawton & May 1995; Pimm *et al.* 1995; Vitousek *et al.* 1997); changes in global biogeochemical processes, such as nitrogen and phosporus cycles (Vitousek *et al.* 1997); water consumption (Chapagain & Hoekstra 2007, 2008; Hoekstra & Chapagain 2007); the use of substances potentially harmful to human health, such as pesticides, herbicides and fungicides (Koutros *et al.* 2008); and the foodservice sector's contribution to global GHG emissions relating to agriculture, food processing, transport, the preparation of meals, and waste (Gössling & Hall 2013). Tourism is also a factor in the consumption of 'problematic' foods, such as giant shrimps leading to the deforestation of mangrove ecosystems (Gössling *et al.* 2012). As such, food is an important category, though other than energy or water use, its impacts are more distributed and relevant for a greater number of impact categories.

Depending on the nature of backward linkages and supply chains the relationships of food production and tourism can have both positive and negative contributions for sustainability (Telfer & Wall 1996; Hall & Gössling 2013). In some developing country destinations there may be considerable scope in replacing imports of food by ship and air with locally grown foodstuffs (Gössling 2013). However, such initiatives may require the development of new food policies, particularly in those countries where tourism is currently impacting other export sectors (e.g. Tanzania, Uganda and Kenya) (Blake 2008). Even more broadly, food policies can have significant importance for the overall structure and development of global food production. Nevertheless, sustainable food provisions can have considerable appeal to tourists. Food is the one area where regional or organic purchases constitute added value to guests, with indications that interest in sustainable, high-quality and 'locally distinctive' foods is increasing among tourists (Cohen & Avieli 2004; du Rand & Heath 2006; Hall & Gössling 2013).

Sociocultural

According to Wolf (1977: 3), sociocultural impacts can be summarized as 'people impacts'; it is the impacts experienced by host communities as a result of the direct and indirect relationships with tourists. More specifically, it refers to the manner in which tourism effects changes in collective and individual systems, behaviour patterns, community structures, lifestyle, and the quality of life (Hall & Lew 2009). A rapidly growing body of literature has emerged that examines the sociocultural impact of tourism. In contrast with the economic impact of tourism, the sociocultural impact is often portrayed as negative in the literature. Studies are increasingly questioning whether or not tourism development brings benefits to the host communities. Jafari (2001) concludes that the output of sociocultural research within tourism illuminates one of two platforms; advocacy or controversy. The advocacy platform includes positive impacts such as the spread of international peace and understanding, the preservation of heritage and culture, a reduction in religious, racial and language barriers, and enhanced appreciation for one's own culture. The controversy platform highlights negative impacts, including trends of xenophobia, prostitution, increased crime, breakdowns in family structure, and the commercialization of arts, crafts and cultural traditions. A further dimension that is also significant when considering the benefits of tourism are the (often) low wages paid to some workers in the tourism and hospitality sector; in some cases these may be below that of a living wage (Hightower 2002).

Wall and Mathieson (2006) describe the sociocultural impacts literature for tourism as largely negative and summarize such research findings to fall within five general impacts: (1) overcrowding of infrastructures, accommodation, services and facilities as tourists increasingly share with locals; (2) explosive situations by way of demonstration effect due to the display of prosperity by tourists amidst less-wealthy/impoverished host destination; (3) spread of undesirable activities (e.g. prostitution, gambling, crime); (4) non-locals are employed for managerial and professional occupations, which hold greater responsibility and pay higher wages, compared to the occupations open to local community members; (5) gradual erosion of indigenous language and culture as host communities increasingly adopt the language of tourists. The authors note that while sociocultural changes in many areas are coincident with tourism growth, it is unclear whether these negative impacts can all be attributable to tourism. Much of this research tends to adopt a narrow focus (e.g. a case study in a specific country) or concentrates on a limited number of sociocultural effects (Hall & Lew 2009). This is partly attributable to what Marsh (1975: 19) and Dana (1999: 60) describe as the 'incremental intangible costs', which are the inherently difficult social and cultural effects that are hard to measure and may be overlooked until major, irreversible changes in society occur (Wall & Mathieson 2006). Sociocultural impacts are highly dependent on local conditions, as well as the types of tourist development being analyzsed. Generally, the more rapid and larger tourism developments tend to generate more impact than the slower, more organic and smaller-scale developments (Hall & Lew 2009). Nevertheless, the sociocultural impact of tourism is difficult to unpack from the broader processes of global economic, political and social change.

Measurable factors and associated social indicators that contribute to the social well-being and quality of life for host communities include economic security, employment, health, personal safety, housing conditions, physical environment, and recreational opportunities (Hall & Lew 2009). Many of these factors have been evaluated using the Human Development Index (HDI). As noted above, the HDI combines indicators of health (i.e. life expectancy at birth), educational attainment (i.e. mean years of schooling, expected years of schooling) and living standards (i.e. gross national income per capita) into a composite index to measure human well-being. As shown in Figure 3.1 the HDI improves for Small Island Developing States (SIDS) as the contribution of travel and tourism to national GDP increases. An increased HDI for LDCs is also shown in Figure 3.2, as the contribution of travel and tourism to national GDP increases. Figures 3.3 and 3.4 also indicate that HDI improves for both SIDS and LDCs as the total contribution of travel and tourism to employment increases. These figures suggest that on a national and global scale, tourism can have a positive sociocultural impact that can improve the well-being of hosts. Importantly, these figures capture only international tourism with the possibility of even greater improvements in human development should domestic tourism be considered.

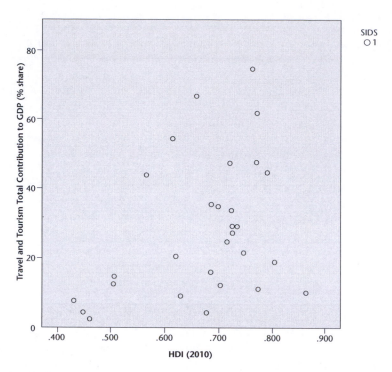

Figure 3.1 Relationship between tourism's contribution to GDP and the HDI for SIDS

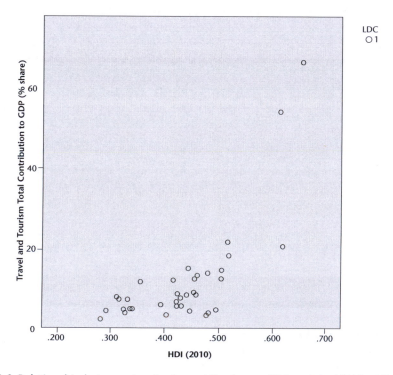

Figure 3.2 Relationship between tourism's contribution to GDP and the HDI for LDCs

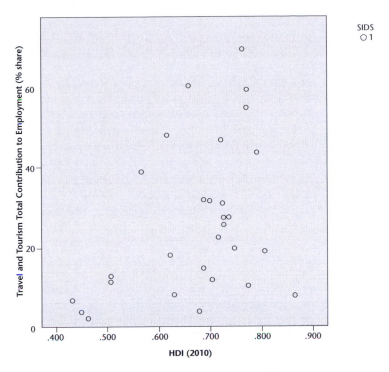

Figure 3.3 Relationship between tourism's contribution to employment and the HDI for SIDS

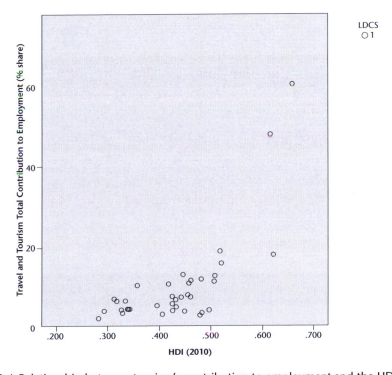

Figure 3.4 Relationship between tourism's contribution to employment and the HDI for LDCs

Conclusion

Tourism is a significant factor in resource use, global environmental and social change. While social and cultural changes are more difficult to assess and change, resource use intensities might serve as a new metric to compare the relative impact of various forms of tourism. Results as presented in this chapter have shown that there are many interlinkages between tourism's sub-sectors, such as food production's relevance for freshwater consumption. These need to be considered to adequately understand tourism's impacts and interaction with resource scarcity. It is also important to note that different forms of tourism affect resource use differently. Table 3.9 provides values for tourism's resource intensities for energy and emissions, fresh water, land use and food consumption, indicating that there exist vast differences, depending on the tourist and tourism product consumed. Values can serve as global benchmarks and potentially help develop such products that lead to low-intensity consumption, and consequently a de-materialization of the global tourism system. However, as discussed, there are many reasons why tourism is currently becoming more energy, freshwater, land and food intense on a per trip/arrival/guest night basis, and changes in the tourism system would be required in order to reverse this trend.

Table 3.9 Resource use intensities in global tourism

Aspect	Range of estimates	Global average	Reference
Energy			
per guest night	1.4–3,717 MJ	n.a.	Gössling 2010
per activity/tourist	7–1,300 MJ per activity	n.a.	Becken 2001
Emissions			
per trip (domestic and international)	0.2–9.00 t CO_2	0.25 t CO_2	UNWTO-UNEP-WMO 2008; Eijgelaar et al. 2010
per international arrival (air transport)	0.37–1.83 t CO_2	n.a.	Gössling et al. 2013
per night (accommodation)	0.1–260 kg CO_2	16 kg CO_2/night	Gössling 2002, 2010
Fresh water			
direct (accommodation)	87–2,000 L/day/tourist	300 L/day/tourist	Gössling et al. 2011
indirect (fuels, food)	2,000–5,000 L/day/tourist	n.a.	Gössling et al. 2011
Land use			
direct, per bed	30–34,580 m²/bed	40 m²/bed	Gössling 2002

Source: OECD 2013

Yet, there is very limited evidence that restricting resource use would have a fundamental impact on the global tourism system (see also UNEP 2011). Tourism is flexible and adjustable, as many case studies have shown (e.g. Gössling 2010; Scott *et al.* 2012). A new perspective of 'scarcity' could help to increase efficiencies and reduce wastage, which will usually translate directly into resource and economic savings, while maintaining the capacity to engage in tourist trips. Tourism has, for decades, been built on the availability of cheap natural resources such as water and energy, and resource limitations have only very recently been considered by a small share of decision makers in tourism. To develop an understanding of preservation for tourism's own sustainable future is thus likely to have negligible negative, and in most cases, even positive effects. Better education on these benefits is needed throughout tourism value chains. Where greater resource use efficiencies are combined with tourism's positive economic potential, there are many options for the sector to contribute to global economic development.

To achieve greater resource efficiencies, green investment structures, and cross-sectoral synergies, UNEP (2011) suggests in its green economy approach that 'sustainability drivers' be considered. These include, for energy, increased costs and carbon surcharges; government incentives; eco-labels; as well as regulations/legislation on energy efficiency. For water, price structures reflecting water scarcity and responsible water management. For biodiversity, regulation regarding sensitive ecosystems, as well as national policies attracting revenue through tourism for protecting critical biological habitat. Implementing these sustainability drivers will, however, be a major political challenge.

Key Reading

www.waterfootprint.org – Website of the Water Footprint Network's global water database.

http://footprintnetwork.org – Website of the global footprint network. Provides for assessments of global, national and individual consumption in terms of ecological footprints.

www.millenniumassessment.org/en/index.html – Website provides free access to the Millennium Ecosystem Assessment (MEA). The MEA assessed the consequences of ecosystem change for human well-being. From 2001 to 2005, the MEA involved the work of more than a thousand experts worldwide. Their findings provide a state-of-the-art scientific appraisal and benchmark of the condition of the world's ecosystems and the services they provide.

Intergovernmental Panel on Climate Change (IPCC): https://www.ipcc.ch/index.htm – The leading scientific body on climate change that provides state-of-the-art syntheses of our understanding of climate change and associated adaptation, mitigation and vulnerability.

References

Airbus (2012) *Global Market Forecast 2012–2031*. Available from: www.airbus.com/company/market/forecast (accessed 23 November 2012).

Anseeuw, W., Wily, L.A., Cotula, L. and Taylor, M. (2012) *Land Rights and the Rush for Land: Findings of the Global Commercial Pressures on Land Research Project*. Rome: The International Land Coalition.

Badré, M., Prime, J. and Ribière, G. (2009) *Neige de culture: Etat des lieux et impacts environnementaux. Note socio-economique*. Paris: Conseil Général de l'Environnement et du Développement Durable.

Baillon, J. and Ceron, J. (1991) *L'essor du golf*. Grenoble: Presses Universitaires de Grenoble.

Becken, S. (2001) *Energy consumption of tourist attractions and activities in New Zealand: summary report of a survey*. Lincoln: Landcare Research and Lincoln University.

Blake, A. (2008) 'Tourism and income distribution in East Africa', *International Journal of Tourism Research*, 10: 511–24.

Blake, A., Arbache, J.S., Sinclair, M.T. and Teles, V. (2008) 'Tourism and poverty relief', *Annals of Tourism Research*, 35: 107–26.

Boeing (2011) *Current Market Outlook 2012–2031*. Available at: www.boeing.com/commercial/cmo (accessed 23 October 2012).

Bohdanowicz, P. and Martinac, I. (2007) 'Determinants and benchmarking of resource consumption in hotels – case study of Hilton International and Scandic in Europe', *Energy and Buildings,* 39: 82–95.

Brüggemann, J. (1997) 'Nationalpark Bayerischer Wald', in L. Ellenberg, B. Beier and M. Scholz (eds) *Ökotourismus: Reisen zwischen Ökonomie und Ökologie*. Heidelberg: Springer.

Michelle Rutty *et al.*

Buckley, R. (2010) *Conservation Tourism*. Wallingford: CABI.

Butchart, S.H.M., Walpole, M., Collen, B., van Strien, A., Scharlemann, J.P.W., Almond, R.E.A., Baillie, J.E.M., Bomhard, B., Brown, C., Bruno, J., Carpenter, K.E., Carr, G.M., Chanson, J., Chenery, A.M., Csirke, J., Davidson, N.C., Dentener, F., Foster, M., Galli, A., Galloway, J.N., Genovesi, P., Gregory, R.D., Hockings, M., Kapos, V., Lamarque, J-F., Leverington, F., Loh, J., McGeoch, M.A., McRae, L., Minasyan, A., Morcillo, M.H., Oldfield, T.E.E., Pauly, D., Quader, S., Revenga, C., Sauer, J.R., Skolnik, B., Spear, D., Stanwell-Smith, D., Stuart, S.N., Symes, A., Tierney, M., Tyrrell, T.D., Vié, J-C. and Watson, R. (2010) 'Global biodiversity: Indicators of recent declines', *Science,* 328(5982): 1164–68.

Ceron, J. and Kovacs, J.C. (1993) *Golf et environnement: un aperçu des principaux problèmes. Le golf et le respect de l'environnement*. Les Arcs: Fédération française de golf.

Chapagain, A.K. and Hoekstra, A.Y. (2007) 'The water footprint of coffee and tea consumption in the Netherlands', *Ecological Economics*, 64(1): 109–18.

—— (2008) 'The global component of freshwater demand and supply: An assessment of virtual water flows between nations as a result of trade in agricultural and industrial products', *Water International,* 33(1): 19–32.

Chape, S., Blyth, S., Fish, L., Fox, P. and Spalding, M. (eds) (2003) *2003 United Nations List of Protected Areas*. Gland and Cambridge: IUCN & UNEP-WCMC.

Chok, S., Macbeth, J. and Warren, C. (2007) 'Tourism as a tool for poverty alleviation: A critical analysis of "pro-poor tourism" and implications for sustainability', *Current Issues in Tourism*, 10: 144–65.

Christ, C., Hillel, O., Matus, S. and Sweeting, J. (2003) *Tourism and Biodiversity: Mapping Tourism's Global Footprint*. Washington DC: Conservation International & UNEP.

Cohen, E. and Avieli, N. (2004) 'Food in tourism: Attraction and impediment', *Annals of Tourism Research*, 31: 755–78.

Coles, T. and Hall, C.M. (eds) (2008) *Tourism and International Business*. London: Routledge.

Crouch, G.I. and Ritchie, J.R.B. (eds) (2012) *Competitiveness and Tourism*. Cheltenham: Edward Elgar Publishing.

Dahlin, P. and Stridh, P. (1996) *Huts or Hotels? A Minor Field Study on Land Management Within the Tourism Sector in Zanzibar*. Examensarbete 22. Royal Institute of Technology, Division of Real Estate Planning and Land Law: Stockholm

Dana, L.P. (1999) 'The social cost of tourism. A case study of IOS', *The Cornell Hotel and Restaurant Administration Quarterly*, 40(4): 60–64.

de Bruijn, K., Dirven, R., Eijgelaar, E. and Peeters, P. (2010) *Travelling Large in 2008. The carbon footprint of Dutch holidaymakers in 2008 and the development since 2002*. Available at: www.cstt.nl/userdata/documents/nhtv-cstt_travellinglargein2010_lowres.pdf (Accessed 4 September 2013).

Defra (2013) '2012 Guidelines to Defra/DECC's GHG Conversion Factors For Company Reporting, Defra. Available at: www.defra.gov.uk/publications/fi les/pb13773-ghg-conversion-factors-2012.pdf (accessed 2 April 2013)

De Kadt, E. (ed.) (1979) *Tourism – Passport to Development?* Oxford: Oxford University Press.

Department of Resources, Energy and Tourism (2012) *Energy White Paper 2012, Australia's Energy Transformation*. Canberra: Department of Resources, Energy and Tourism.

Department of Transport (2007) *Air Passenger Demand and CO$_2$ Forecasts*. London: Department of Transport.

Deyà Tortella, B. and Tirado, D. (2011) 'Hotel water consumption at a seasonal mass tourist destination: The case of the island of Mallorca', *Journal of Environmental Management*, 92: 2568–79.

du Rand, G.E. and Heath, E. (2006) 'Towards a framework for food tourism as an element of destination marketing', *Current Issues in Tourism*, 9: 206–34.

Dwyer, L., Forsyth, P., Spurr, R. and Hoque, S. (2010) 'Estimating the carbon footprint of Australian tourism', *Journal of Sustainable Tourism,* 15: 1–18.

Eijgelaar, E., Thaper, C. and Peeters, P. (2010) 'Antarctic cruise tourism: the paradoxes of ambassadorship, "last chance tourism" and greenhouse gas emissions', *Journal of Sustainable Tourism*, 18: 337–354.

Frost, W. and Hall, C.M. (eds) (2009) *Tourism and National Parks: International Perspectives on Development, Histories and Change*. London: Routledge.

German Federal Agency for Nature Conservation (GFANC) (ed.) (1997) *Biodiversity and Tourism: Conflicts on the World's Seacoasts and Strategies for Their Solution*. Berlin: Springer-Verlag.

Gössling, S. (1999) 'Ecotourism – a means to safeguard biodiversity and ecosystem functions?', *Ecological Economics, 29:* 303–20.

—— (2001) 'The consequences of tourism for sustainable water use on a tropical island: Zanzibar, Tanzania,' *Journal of Environmental Management*, 61(2): 179–91.

—— (2002) 'Global environmental consequences of tourism', *Global Environmental Change*, 12: 283–302.

—— (2009) 'Carbon neutral destinations: A conceptual analysis', *Journal of Sustainable Tourism*, 17: 17–37.

—— (2010) *Carbon Management in Tourism: Mitigating the Impacts on Climate Change*. London: Routledge.

—— (2013) 'National emissions from tourism: An overlooked policy challenge?', *Energy Policy*, 59: 433–42.

Gössling, S. and Hall, C.M. (eds) (2006a) *Tourism and Global Environmental Change*. London: Routledge.

Gössling, S. and Hall, C.M. (2006b) 'Uncertainties in predicting tourist flows under scenarios of climate change', *Climatic Change*, 79(3–4): 163–73.

—— (2008) 'Swedish tourism and climate change mitigation: An emerging conflict?', *Scandinavian Journal of Hospitality and Tourism*, 8(2): 141–58.

—— (2013) 'Sustainable culinary systems: An introduction', in C.M. Hall and S. Gössling (eds) *Sustainable Culinary Systems: Local Foods, Innovation, and Tourism & Hospitality*. Abingdon: Routledge.

Gössling, S., Kunkel, T., Schumacher, K. and Zilger, M. (2004) 'Use of molluscs, fish and other marine taxa by tourism in Zanzibar, Tanzania', *Biodiversity & Conservation*, 13(12): 2623–39.

Gössling, S., Ceron, J-P., Dubios, G. and Hall, C.M. (2009) 'Hypermobile travellers', in S. Gössling and P. Upham (eds) *Climate Change and Aviation*. London: Earthscan.

Gössling, S., Haglund, L., Kallgren, H., Revahl, M. and Hultman, J. (2009) 'Swedish air travellers and voluntary carbon offsets: Towards the co-creation of environmental value?', *Current Issues in Tourism*, 12: 1–19.

Gössling, S., Hall, C.M., Peeters, P. and Scott, D. (2010) 'The future of tourism: a climate change mitigation perspective', *Tourism Recreation Research*, 35(2): 119–130.

Gössling, S., Garrod, B., Aall, C., Hille, J. and Peeters, P. (2011) 'Food management in tourism. Reducing tourism's carbon "foodprint"', *Tourism Management*, 32: 534–43.

Gössling, S., Peeters, P., Hall, C.M., Dubois, G., Ceron, J.P., Lehmann, L. and Scott, D. (2012) 'Tourism and water use: Supply, demand, and security, an international review', *Tourism Management*, 33: 1–15.

Gössling, S., Scott, D. and Hall, C.M. (2013) 'Challenges of tourism in a low-carbon economy', *WIRES Climate Change*, 4(6): 525–38.

Hall, C.M. (2006) 'Tourism urbanisation and global environmental change', in S. Gössling and C.M. Hall (eds) *Tourism and Global Environmental Change: Ecological, Social, Economic and Political Interrelationships*. Abingdon: Routledge.

—— (2007) 'Pro-poor tourism: Do "tourism exchanges benefit primarily the countries of the South"?' *Current Issues in Tourism*, 10: 111–18.

—— (2010a) 'Implementation of the convention on biological diversity guidelines on biodiversity and tourism development', *Journal of Heritage Tourism*, 5(4): 267–84.

—— (2010b) 'An island biogeographical approach to island tourism and biodiversity: An exploratory study of the Caribbean and Pacific Islands', *Asia Pacific Journal of Tourism Research*, 15(3): 383–99.

—— (2010c) 'Changing paradigms and global change: From sustainable to steady-state tourism', *Tourism Recreation Research*, 35(2): 131–45.

—— (2010d) 'Tourism and biodiversity: More significant than climate change?' *Journal of Heritage Tourism*, 5: 253–66.

—— (2011a) 'Policy learning and policy failure in sustainable tourism governance: From first and second to third order change?' *Journal of Sustainable Tourism*, 19: 649–71.

—— (2011b) 'Biosecurity, tourism and mobility: Institutional arrangements for managing biological invasions', *Journal of Policy Research in Tourism, Leisure and Events*, 3(3): 256–80.

—— (2013) 'A review of "Competitiveness and tourism",' *Journal of Sustainable Tourism*, DOI:10.1080/09669582.2013.820886.

Hall, C.M. and Baird, T. (2013) 'Ecotourism, biological invasions and biosecurity', in R. Ballantyne and J. Packer (eds) *The International Handbook of Ecotourism*. Aldershot: Ashgate.

Hall, C.M. and Coles, T. (2008) 'Introduction: Tourism and international business – tourism as international business', in T. Coles and C.M. Hall (eds) *International Business and Tourism: Global Issues, Contemporary Interactions*. London: Routledge.

Hall, C.M. and Gössling, S. (eds) (2013) *Sustainable Culinary Systems: Local Foods, Innovation, and Tourism & Hospitality*. Abingdon: Routledge.

Hall, C.M. and Lew, A. (2009) *Understanding and Managing Tourism Impacts: An Integrated Approach*. London: Routledge.

Hall, C.M. and Page, S.J. (2006) *Geography of Tourism and Recreation,* 3rd edn, London: Routledge.

Hall, C.M. and Saarinen, J. (2010) 'Geotourism and climate change: Paradoxes and promises of geotourism in polar regions', *Téoros*, 29(2): 77–86.

Hall, C.M., James, M. and Baird, T. (2011) 'Forests and trees as charismatic mega-flora: Implications for heritage tourism and conservation', *Journal of Heritage Tourism*, 6: 309–23.

Hall, C.M., Scott, D. and Gössling, S. (2013) 'The primacy of climate change for sustainable international tourism', *Sustainable Development*, 21(2): 112–21.

Hawkins, D.E. and Mann, S. (2007) 'The World Bank's role in tourism development', *Annals of Tourism Research*, 34: 348–63.

Hightower, J. (2002) 'Campaign for a living wage', *Journal of Public Health Policy*, 23(3): 265–67.

Hills, S., Birks, R. and McKenzie, B. (2002) 'The Millennium Dome "watercycle" experiment: To evaluate water efficiency and customer perception at a recycling scheme for 6 million visitors', *Water Science and Technology,* 46(6–7): 233–40.

Hoekstra, A.Y. and Chapagain, A.K. (2007) 'Water footprints of nations: Water use by people as a function of their consumption pattern', *Water Resources Management*, 21(1): 35–48.

Hoekstra, A.Y. and Hung, P.Q. (2002) 'Virtual water trade: A quantification of virtual water flows between nations in relation to international crop trade', *Value of Water Research Report Series No.11.* Delft: UNESCO-IHE.

Hoekstra, A.Y. and Mekonnen, M.M. (2012) 'The water footprint of humanity', *Proceedings of the National Academy of Sciences,* 109(9): 3232–37.

Hunter, C. and Green, H. (1995) *Tourism and the Environment: A Sustainable Relationship?* London: Routledge.

International Energy Agency (IEA) (2009) *Transport, Energy and CO_2: Moving Towards Sustainability.* Paris: International Energy Agency.

International Monetary Fund (IMF) (1993) *Balance of Payments Manual*, 5th edn [BPM5]. Washington DC: IMF.

IMF (2002) *Manual on Statistics of International Trade in Services* [MSITS]. Washington DC: IMF.

—— (2009) *Balance of Payments Manual*, 6th edn [BPM6]. Washington DC: IMF.

Intergovernmental Panel on Climate Change (2007) *Contribution of Working Group I to the Fourth Assessment Report 2007: The physical science basis.* Cambridge: Cambridge University Press.

International Tourism Partnership (2013) *Water Risk Assessment.* Stockholm International Water Institute (SIWI).

Jafari, J. (2001) 'The scientification of tourism', in V.L. Smith and M. Brent (eds) *Hosts and Guests Revisited.* New York: Cognizant Communications.

Jenkins, J., Nordhaus T. and Shellenberger M. (2011) *Energy Emergence: Rebound and Backfire as Emergent Phenomena.* Oakland: Breakthrough Institute.

Jim, C.Y. (2000) 'Environmental changes associated with mass urban tourism and nature tourism development in Hong Kong', *The Environmentalist*, 20: 233–47.

Kasahara, S. (2004) *The Flying Geese Paradigm: A Critical Study of Its Application to East Asian Regional Development*, UNCTAD discussion papers. New York: UNCTAD.

Komlev, L. and Encontre, P. (2004) 'Least developed, landlocked and island developing countries', in *Beyond Conventional Wisdom in Development Policy: An Intellectual History of UNCTAD 1964–2004.* UNCTAD/EDM/2004/4. New York: UNCTAD.

Koutros, S., Lynch, C.F., Ma, X., Lee, W.J., Hoppin, J.A., Christensen, C.H., Andreotti, G., Freeman, L.B., Rusiecki, J.A., Hou, L., Sandler, D.P. and Alavanja, M.C.R. (2008) 'Heterocyclic aromatic amine pesticide use and human cancer risk: Results from the US Agricultural Health Study', *International Journal of Cancer*, 124(5): 1206–12.

Lawton, J.H. and May, R.M. (1995) *Extinction Rates.* Oxford: Oxford University Press.

Low, M-S. (2005). *Material Flow Analysis of Concrete in the United States*, Unpublished Master of Science in Building Technology thesis, Massachusetts Institute of Technology.

Lüthje, K. and Lindstädt, B. (1994). *Freizeit-und Ferienzentren. Umfang und regionale Verteilung.* Materialien zur Raumentwicklung, Heft 66. Bonn: Bundesforschungsanstalt für Landeskunde und Raumordnung.

Mace, G., Masundire, H. and Baillie, J. (2005) 'Biodiversity', in R. Hassan, R. Scholes and N. Ash (eds) *Ecosystems and Human Well-being: Current State and Trends, Volume 1.* Washington DC: Island Press.

Marsh, J.S. (1975) 'Tourism and development: The East African case', *Alternatives*, 5(1): 15–22.

Mathieson, A.R. and Wall, G. (1982) *Tourism: Economic, Physical and Social Impacts.* Harlow: Longman.

Meyer, A. and Chaffee, C. (1997) 'Life-cycle analysis for design of the Sydney Olympic Stadium', *Renewable Energy*, 10: 169–72.

Mutiga, J.K., Mavengano, S.T., Zhongbo, S., Woldai, T. and Becht, R. (2010) 'Water allocation as a planning tool to minimise water use conflicts in the upper Ewaso Ng'iro North Basin, Kenya', *Water Resources Management*, 24: 3939–59.

Nielsen, L. (2011) *Classification of Countries Based on Their Level of Development: How It Is Done and How It Could Be Done*, IMF Working Paper WP/11/31. Washington DC: IMF.

Orams, M. (1998) *Marine Tourism: Development, Impacts and Management*. London: Routledge.

Organisation for Economic Co-operation and Development (OECD) (2013) 'Effective policies for growth', in *Progress Report, Annex 2, Competing Demands for Scarce Resources: A Discussion Paper*. Paris: OECD.

Peeters, P., Szimba, E. and Duijnisveld, M. (2007) 'Major environmental impacts of European tourist transport', *Journal of Transport Geography*, 15: 83–93.

Perch-Nielsen, S., Sesartic, A. and Stucki, M. (2010) The greenhouse gas intensity of the tourism sector: The case of Switzerland, *Environmental Science & Policy*, 13: 131–40.

Pigram, J.J.J. (1995) 'Resource constraints on tourism: Water resources and sustainability', in R.W. Butler and D. Pearce (eds) *Change in Tourism: People, Places, Processes*. London: Routledge.

Pimm, S.L., Russell, G.J., Gittleman, J.L. and Brooks, T.M. (1995) 'The future of biodiversity', *Science*, 269(5222): 347–50.

Poulsen, A.L. (1995) 'Coral reef gastropods—a sustainable resource?' *Pacific Conservation Biology*, 2: 142–45.

Rixen, C., Teich, M., Lardelli, C., Gallati, D., Pohl, M., Puutz, M. and Bebi, P. (2011) 'Winter tourism and climate change in the alps: An assessment of resource consumption, snow reliability, and future snowmaking potential', *Mountain Research and Development*, 31: 229–36.

Rockström, J., Steffen, W., Noone, K., Persson, Å., Chapin, F.S., Lambin, E.F., Lenton, T.M., Scheffer, M., Folke, C., Schellnhuber, H.J., Nykvist, B., de Wit, C.A., Hughes, T., van der Leeuw, S., Rodhe, H., Sörlin, S., Snyder, P.K., Costanza, R., Svedin, U., Falkenmark, M., Karlberg, L., Corell, R.W., Fabry, V.J., Hansen, J., Walker, B., Liverman, D., Richardson, K., Crutzen, P. and Foley, J.A. (2009) 'A safe operating space for humanity', *Nature*, 461(7263): 472–75.

Rodriguez Diaz, J.A., Knox, J.W. and Weatherhead, E.K. (2007) 'Competing demands for irrigation water: Golf and agriculture in Spain', *Irrigation and Drainage*, 56: 541–49.

Rogelj, J., Hare, W., Lowe, J., van Vuuren, D.P., Riahi, K., Matthews, B., Hanaoka, T., Jiang, K., and Meinshausen, M. (2011) 'Emission pathways consistent with a 2°C global temperature limit', *Nature Climate Change*, 1: 413–418.

Roselló-Batie, B., Molá, A., Cladera, A. and Martinez, V. (2010) 'Energy use, CO_2 emissions and waste throughout the life cycle of a sample of hotels in the Balearic Islands', *Energy and Buildings*, 42: 547–58.

Saarinen, J., Becker, F., Manwa, H. and Wilson, D. (eds) (2009) *Sustainable Tourism in Southern Africa: Local Communities and Natural Resources in Transition*. Bristol: Channel View Publications.

Santarius, T. (2012) *How Rebound Effects Baffle Sustainability Targets When the Economy Keeps Growing*. Berlin: Heinrich Böll Foundation.

Scheyvens, R. (2007) 'Exploring the tourism-poverty nexus', *Current Issues in Tourism*, 10: 231–54.

Scheyvens, R. and Momsen, J. (2008) 'Tourism and poverty reduction: Issues for small island states', *Tourism Geographies*, 10: 22–41.

Schilcher, D. (2007) 'Growth versus equity: The continuum of pro-poor tourism and neoliberal governance', *Current Issues in Tourism*, 10: 166–93.

Scott, D., Peeters, P. and Gössling, S. (2010) 'Can tourism deliver its "aspirational" emission reduction targets?', *Journal of Sustainable Tourism*, 18: 393–408.

Scott, D., Gössling, S. and Hall, C.M. (2012) *Tourism and Climate Change: Impacts, Adaptation and Mitigation*. London: Routledge.

Sebake, T.N. and Gibberd, J.T. (2008) 'Assessing the sustainability performance of the 2010 FIFA World Cup stadia using the sustainable building assessment tool (SBAT) for stadia', in *5th Post Graduate Conference on Construction Industry Development*, Bloemfontein, South Africa, 16–18 March 2008. Available at: http://researchspace.csir.co.za/dspace/handle/10204/3238

Serra, P., Pons, X. and Saurí, D. (2008) 'Land-cover and land-use change in a Mediterranean landscape: A spatial analysis of driving forces integrating biophysical and human factors', *Applied Geography*, 28(3): 189–209.

Strasdas, W. (1992) *Ferienzentren der zweiten Generation. Ökologische, soziale und ökonomische Auswirkungen.* Studie im Auftrag der Bundesministers für Umwelt, Naturschutz und Reaktorsicherheit. Berlin: Bundesministerium für Umwelt, Naturschutz und Reaktorsicherheit.

Telfer, D. and Sharpley, R. (2008) *Tourism and Development in the Developing World.* London: Routledge.

Telfer, D.J. and Wall, G. (1996) 'Linkages between tourism and food production', *Annals of Tourism Research*, 23(3): 635–53.

Truong, V.D., Hall, C.M. and Garry, T. (2014) 'Tourism and poverty alleviation: Perceptions and experiences of poor people in Sapa, Vietnam', *Journal of Sustainable Tourism*, DOI: 10.1080/09669582.2013.871019.

Turner, B.L., Lambin, E.F. and Reenberg, A. (2007) 'The emergence of land change science for global environmental change and sustainability', *Proceedings of the National Academy of Sciences,* 104(52): 20666–71.

United Nations Conference on Trade and Development (UNCTAD) (2010) *The Contribution of Tourism to Trade and Development.* Note by the UNCTAD Secretariat, TD/b/C.I/8. Geneva: UNCTAD.

UNCTAD (2008) *Human Development Report 2007/8. Fighting Climate Change: Human Solidarity in a Divided World.* Geneva: UNCTAD.

—— (2012) *UNCTAD Handbook of Statistics 2012.* New York & Geneva: UN.

United Nations Development Policy and Analysis Division (UN DESA) (2013) *LDC Information: The Criteria for Identifying Least Developed Countries.* New York: UN DESA. Available at: www.un.org/en/development/desa/policy/cdp/ldc/ldc_criteria.shtml

United Nations Environment Programme (UNEP) (2011) *Towards a Green Economy: Pathways to Sustainable Development and Poverty Eradication.* Geneva & Nairobi: UNEP.

United Nations Educational, Scientific and Cultural Organization (UNESCO) (2009) *United Nations World Water Development Report 3: Water in a Changing World.* Paris: UNESCO.

United Nations World Tourism Organization (UNWTO) (2005) *Tourism Market Trends: World Overview and Tourism Topics 2004 Edition.* Madrid: UNWTO.

UNWTO (2006) *Tourism and Least Developed Countries: A Sustainable Opportunity to Reduce Poverty.* Madrid: UNWTO.

—— (2007) *Tourism Will Contribute to Solutions for Global Climate Change and Poverty Challenges.* Press release, UNWTO Press and Communications Department. Berlin/Madrid: UNWTO.

—— (2008) *Emerging Tourism Markets – The Coming Economic Boom.* Press Release, 24 June 2008. Madrid: UNWTO.

—— (2010) *World Tourism Organization Statement Regarding Mitigation of Greenhouse Gas Emissions from Air Passenger Transport.* Madrid: UNWTO

—— (2011) *Tourism Towards 2030: Global Overview.* UNWTO General Assembly, 19th Session, Gyeongju, Republic of Korea, 10 October 2011, Madrid: UNWTO

—— (2012) *UNWTO Tourism Highlights. 2012 Edition.* Madrid: UNWTO.

—— (2013) *UNWTO Tourism Highlights, 2013 Edition.* Madrid: UNWTO

UNWTO and UNEP (2011) 'Tourism: Investing in the green economy', in *UNEP Towards a Green Economy.* Geneva: UNEP: Geneva.

UNWTO, UNEP, World Meteorological Organization (WMO) (2008) 'Davos Declaration', in *Climate Change and Tourism: Responding to Global Challenges.* Madrid: UNWTO; Paris: UNEP; Geneva: WMO.

Van der Meulen, F. and Salman, A.H.P.M. (1996) 'Management of Mediterranean coastal dunes', *Ocean and Coastal Management,* 30(2–3): 177–95.

van Oss, H.G. and Padovani, A.C. (2003) 'Cement manufacture and the environment. Part II: Environmental challenges and opportunities', *Journal of Industrial Ecology*, 7(1): 93–126.

Vitousek, P.M., Mooney, H.A., Lubchenco, J. and Melillo, J.M. (1997) 'Human domination of Earth's ecosystems', *Science,* 277(5325): 494–99.

Vos, E. (2000) 'EU food safety regulation in the aftermath of the BSE crisis', *Journal of Consumer Policy*, 23(3): 227–55.

Vörösmarty, C.J., Green, P., Salisbury, J. and Lammers, R.B. (2000) 'Global water resources: Vulnerability from climate change and population growth', *Science,* 289: 284–88.

Wall, G. and Mathieson, A. (2006) *Tourism: Change, Impacts and Opportunities.* Harlow: Pearson Education.

Wattanakuljarus, A. and Coxhead, I. (2008) 'Is tourism-based development good for the poor? A general equilibrium analysis for Thailand', *Journal of Policy Modelling*, 30: 929–55.

Wieranga, P. (2008) Assessing pro-poor tourism principles in practice: Ethnic tourism in Northern Thailand and Lao PDR. Unpublished thesis, University of Northern British Columbia.

Wiles, C. (2013) Golf and gaff. *Inside Housing.co.uk News, Views and Jobs in Social Housing*, 5 November. Available at: www.insidehousing.co.uk/home/blogs/golf-and-gaff/6529332.blog (accessed 10 December 2013).

Wilson, M.E. (1997) 'Population movements and emerging diseases', *Journal of Travel Medicine,* 4: 183–86.

Wolf, C.P. (1977) 'Social impact assessment: the state of the art updated', *SIA Newsletter,* 29: 3–23.

World Commission on Environment and Development (WCED) (1987) *Our Common Future* (Brundtland Report). Oxford: Oxford University Press.

World Economic Forum (WEF) (2009a) *Towards a Low Carbon Travel & Tourism Sector*. Davos: WEF.

WEF (2009b) *The Travel and Tourism Competitiveness Report 2009: Managing in a Time of Turbulence*. Davos: WEF.

World Travel and Tourism Council (WTTC) (2009) *Leading the challenge*. London: WTTC.

Worldwatch Institute (2004) *Rising Impacts of Water Use*. Washington DC: Worldwatch Institute. Available at: www.worldwatch.org/topics/consumption/sow/trendsfacts/2004/03/03 (accessed 4 September 2013).

World Water Assessment Programme (WWAP) (2012) *The United Nations World Water Development Report 4: Managing Water under Uncertainty and Risk*. Paris: UNESCO.

Zapata, M.J., Hall, C.M., Lindo, P. and Vanderschaeghen, M. (2011) 'Can community-based tourism contribute to development and poverty alleviation?' *Current Issues in Tourism*, 14: 725–49.

Zaizen, M., Urakawa, T., Matsumoto, Y. and Takai, H. (2000) 'The collection of rainwater from dome stadiums in Japan', *Urban Water*, 1: 355–59.

Part 2

Theoretical frameworks and concepts in tourism and sustainability

4

Tourism and the precautionary principle in theory and practice

David A. Fennell

Precautionary principle A culturally framed concept that takes its cue from changing social conceptions about the appropriate roles of science, economics, ethics, politics, and the law in proactive environmental protection and management (O'Riordan & Cameron 1994: 12).

Principle 15 of the Rio Earth Summit Principle 15 advocates for the use of precaution in attempts to protect the environment from threats of serious or irreversible damage.

The paradox of tourism Economic gain is sought at the expense of the natural world and local identity (traditional cultures).

Scientific uncertainty Cases where there is incomplete science or knowledge on the effects of certain agents or actions on the environment and people.

Duty of care Places the onus of proof on those who are in a position to institute change. These agents have a duty that ought to extend beyond their own interests, to understand and communicate potential risks and detrimental consequences to present and future generations.

Introduction

Over the past 60 years the tourism industry has been marked by change, innovation, and development. Increased foreign revenue, higher levels of income and employment, as well as greater public sector revenues, have been attractive forces catalysing governments to develop new destinations (Archer 1996). Unfortunately, such growth has often been conceived as short-term financial gain, without due regard for long-term environmental or socio–cultural implications. Hence, the paradox of tourism has been revealed: economic gain at the expense of the natural world and local identity and traditional cultures. In recognising these problems, there has been a sustained call for better planning and management within the tourism industry, at all levels (Inskeep 1991).

One planning instrument which has received considerable attention is the precautionary principle; a concept which has provided guidance on debates regarding health and safety, as well as environmental and resource management issues. 'Precaution' is often applied in circumstances where chemicals have potentially toxic or bio-accumulative effects, and where usage could lead to serious physical harm on humans or the environment. It has thus become an increasingly powerful mechanism for environmental groups to amass political and public support. Intuitively, precaution appeals to our sense of controlling risks and detrimental outcomes, designed to address scientific uncertainty in areas where failure to act may lead to future harm or disaster (Kaiser 1997). Just like sustainable development, precaution puts the onus on the present population to address current actions which may incite potential risks and detrimental consequences for future generations. However, although examined in detail in the aforementioned fields, it has still received little attention in the realm of tourism. With this in mind, the aim of this paper is to: (i) provide a brief review of literature on the precautionary principle, (ii) explore the fundamental concepts which underlie the precautionary principle, and (iii) discuss its applicability to tourism.

THE PRECAUTIONARY PRINCIPLE

O'Riordan and Cameron (1994: 12) define the precautionary principle as 'a culturally framed concept that takes its cue from changing social conceptions about the appropriate roles of science, economics, ethics, politics and the law in pro-active environmental protection and management'. In this regard, precaution has been extended to include six basic concepts, including (i) preventative anticipation, (ii) safeguarding ecological space, (iii) restraint adopted is not unduly costly, (iv) duty of care, or onus of proof on those who propose change, (v) promotion of the cause of intrinsic natural rights, and (vi) paying for past ecological debt. More concisely, precaution is grounded in the need for a 'premium on a cautious and conservative approach to human interventions in environmental sectors that are: (a) usually short on scientific understanding, and (b) usually susceptible to significant injury, especially irreversible injury' (Myers 1993: 74). VanderZwaag (1994: 7) writes that there are a number of core elements associated with the precautionary principle, including:

- a willingness to take action (or no action) in advance of formal scientific proof;
- cost effectiveness of action, that is, some consideration of proportionality of costs;
- providing ecological margins of error;
- intrinsic value of non-human entities;
- a shift in the onus of proof to those who propose change;
- concern with future generations;
- paying for ecological debts through strict/absolute liability regimes.

The precautionary principle was conceived in Germany (*Vorsorgeprinzip,* meaning precautionary principle) during the 1970s for the purpose of exercising foresight in matters of environmental policy and resource protection (see Boehmer-Christiansen 1994). It was introduced internationally in 1984 at the First International Conference on Protection of the North Sea (Tickner & Raffensberger 1998). Since then, the principle has been extended into national and international environmental policy by more than 40 countries, and is now affirmed in many international treaties and laws, e.g. 1990 Bergen Declaration; 1992 Rio Declaration; 1992 Maastricht Treaty on European Union; The Convention on International Trade in Endangered Species of Wild Flora and Fauna (Freestone & Hey 1996; Rogers, Sinden & De Lacy 1997;

Dickson 1999; Ellis 2000; Tapper 2001). In 1992, the precautionary principle was incorporated in the Earth Summit in Rio de Janeiro. Principle 15 states that:

> In order to protect the environment, the precautionary approach shall be widely applied by States according to their capabilities. Where there are threats of serious or irreversible damage, lack of full scientific certainty shall not be used as a reason for postponing cost-effective measures to prevent environmental degradation.
>
> *(Van Dyke 1996: 10)*

Responding to this document, VanderZwaag (1999) feels that phrases such as 'according to their capabilities' are wide open to interpretation. He also questions how threats are to be determined; the role of scientific assessments; who will make such determinations; and to what extent economic costs should be weighed against environmental benefits. There is also the question of how principles are refined into practice in much the same way as decision makers have grappled with how to operationalise the principles of sustainable development.

Precaution appears to have more support in Europe, where it forms the basis of environmental law and policy in several European states (e.g. the United Kingdom, Denmark, and Sweden). In North America, Canada has a long-standing history of implementing the precautionary approach in science-based programmes of health, safety, and natural resources protection (Government of Canada 2001a). For example, discussions on the value of precaution have been taken up with regard to oceans policy. Canada's *Oceans Act* now requires the Minister of Fisheries and Oceans to develop an oceans management strategy based on (i) sustainable development, (ii) integrated management, and (iii) the precautionary approach (as cited in VanderZwaag, 1999). Although the Canadian government does not consider the precautionary principle to be a rule of customary international law, there may be sufficient state practice to allow a good argument for the principle's induction into international law (Government of Canada 2001b). In the United States, Tickner and Raffensberger (1998) note that the precautionary principle is a relatively new concept, although the general principle of precaution underpins much legislation.

Tourism and precaution

Tourism has consistently been shown to have an impact on air and water quality, erode soil, create noise pollution, expand the built environment, increase transport networks, disrupt species behaviour in any number of ways, and dislocate human communities – socially, politically, and economically. There are myriad examples where tourism has been instituted in an ad hoc fashion, and with little regard to appropriate socio-ecological planning. A classic example of poor development is Cancun, Mexico, where ineffective sewage management has polluted beaches, natural habitat has been reduced, economic benefits are unevenly distributed, changes in lifestyles and tradition have occured, and increased competition for resources exists (see Daltabuit & Pi-Sunyer 1990).

The numerous ecological impacts stemming from tourism are likely to increase in number and intensity as domestic and international travel increases. The World Tourism Organization's *Tourism 2020 Vision* forecast predicts that twenty-first century travellers will go farther and farther, and that by 2020, one out of every three trips will be a long-haul journey to another region of the world (WTO 2001). Such future tourist activities are forecasted to be most intense in 'unspoilt' natural areas and remoter places, taking people to the most ecologically fragile parts of the earth (Holden 2000; Martin 2000).

Tourism development, especially when it occurs in regions unaccustomed to the industry (e.g. Antarctica), holds many uncertainties and unknown impacts. Many of these areas are particularly sensitive to change – physically distinctive areas that are extremely vulnerable to increased human impact and environmental change due to tourism. DeFur and Kaszuba (2002) consider the precautionary principle to be an invaluable tool when policy makers are forced to make decisions with little or no experience or history to draw from. Thus, the precautionary principle may be most applicable in these areas of new tourism development – situations in which it may be especially difficult to predict and prove the full range of consequences. Adhering to the sustainability philosophy, the precautionary principle could be proactive in assessing impacts accruing from tourism while acknowledging the uncertainty inherent in these systems, instead of trying to modify systems to cope with resulting impacts as they occur.

Hall (1995) and Faulkner (1998) argue that conventional Newtonian/Cartesian approaches to tourism research are more in step with studying relatively stable systems, resulting in an inadequate understanding of the dynamics of change and chaotic phases of tourism development. In contrast to these traditional reductionist approaches to research on tourism destination development, Russell and Faulkner (1999) suggest that chaos and complexity theories provide a sound alternative perspective in recognising that systems are innately complex (i.e. non-linear), unstable, and dynamic/life-like. Tourism is an integrated system in which many elements are linked (e.g. environment protection, economic viability), thus changes in one element affect other elements (Swarbrooke 1999). In line with these theories, the precautionary principle also acknowledges the possibility of change, instability, and uncertainty in systems.

There is still a dearth of literature on tourism and the precautionary principle. Many texts mention the concept, but most do so only in passing or as it relates to some broader concept like sustainability. Tribe *et al.* (2000) mention the precautionary principle as a guiding principle to effective policy development, along with conservation of resources, improvement of environmental quality, preventing environmental damage, the 'polluter pays' principle, and incentive-based policies. Kirstges (1995) also mentions it as one of several principles that should be followed by tour operators. Kirstges observes that there should be an environmental audit for all tourism developments that cause negative impacts. (See also Jennings (2003), in the context of sport and adventure tourism; Thorsby (2009), in the context of cultural heritage; Butler (2011), in the context of island tourism; and Soleimanpour (2012), in reference to environmental law and nature-based tourism.)

Two areas in tourism research that have focused on the precautionary principle include cetaceans and Antarctica/Arctic. In the former case, scholars have advocated the precautionary principle for the better management of whale and dolphin tourism. In the absence of solid data on the real effects of boat noise and other related disturbances on cetaceans, a precautionary approach is suggested (see Garrod & Fennell 2004; Lusseau, Slooten & Currey 2006; Martinez & Orams 2011). In regard to the latter, scholars argue that better management techniques, including the precautionary principle, are needed to regulate tourism activities in Arctic and Antarctic regions (see Scott 2001; Bastmeijer & Roura 2004; Stewart & Draper 2006).

One of the most noteworthy applications of the precautionary principle and tourism is by Gössling (2001) in his work on sustainable water use in Zanzibar. He observes that tourism development has placed a significant level of pressure on the water resources of Zanzibar, including the lowering of the groundwater table, deteriorating water quality, and saltwater intrusion. Gössling recommends a precautionary approach, where water consumption would be reduced to 200 litres of water per bed space as compared to daily average consumption levels of 2000 litres. Hall (2011) has used the precautionary principle in detail with reference to the management of tourism-related biological invasions, and Holden (1999) argues that the precautionary principle has a role to play in policies designed to limit the effects of downhill skiing at Cairngorm.

Precaution also appears to be frequently cited in tourism policy documents of various organisations. For example, The Wilderness Society (1999) of Australia, in their *Tourism in Natural Areas Policy* document, makes reference to precaution, under Policy 2:

> 2. Provision of visitor access to natural areas must not compromise or infringe on the environmental qualities of the area, or the normal and desired routine of local communities. It will be determined largely by the visitor carrying capacity of an area or the limits of acceptable change. Where difficulties are encountered in determining visitor carrying capacity, the precautionary principle should apply.

The World Wild Fund for Nature (2002), in their tourism principles and aims, also makes reference to the precautionary principle, as follows:

> WWF will promote in particular the precautionary principle; the polluter pays principle; economic instruments; minimum standards; and environmentally sound technologies, especially in sustainable means of travel to reduce fuel consumption and pollution emissions.

> • work with the tourism industry, governments and others to support the development of national and regional sustainable tourism policies.

The World Wild Fund for Nature (2001) believes that action must be taken to reduce and, where possible, eliminate negative impacts on natural resources and processes. These actions include limiting tourism-related pollution so as not to exceed ecological carrying capacity (i.e. the robustness of habitats and their ability to replenish extracted resources), including waste assimilation processes. Tourism-related pollution and exploitation must, therefore, be carefully controlled and regulated, and the precautionary approach should be considered a fundamental principle in tourism development.

The British Columbia Wilderness Tourism Association (2001), in their *Draft Code of Practices for BC's Wilderness Tourism Operators*, makes the following reference to the precautionary principle, as the last of 22 statements: 'Follow the ideal of the precautionary principle: When in doubt – Don't!' Finally, the Convention on Biological Diversity (CBD) (2001) has established *International Guidelines for Sustainable Tourism*, for the purpose of assisting stakeholders at all levels in sustainable management. The report indicates that the act of decision making 'should be a transparent and accountable process to approve or refuse a proposal, and it should always apply the precautionary principle' (CBD 2001: 21).

Given that none of these environmentally based organisations fully articulate the conceptual basis of the precautionary principle suggests that there is either a tacit understanding of precaution, or perhaps a lack of understanding of how it might be infused in tourism decision making. One could argue that principles such as low impact, sustainability, local control, and responsibility are implicit applications of the precautionary principle. In reality, however, what is needed is a more explicit understanding of how it applies in a tourism context. As such, the potential for integrating precaution into tourism planning has yet to be examined.

However, in the context of urban planning and development, Counsell (1999) found that proponents of a weak sustainable development see the precautionary principle as an obstacle and threat to urban planning and development, while those who maintain a strong sustainable development perspective view it as necessary. Howie (2003) argues that the precautionary principle has been criticised because it is thought to counter the spirit of entrepreneurialism, under the belief that risk is often good for business. In a study of town planning in five regions of England and Wales, Counsell found that respondents (various community stakeholders involved in planning) were divided over the use of the precautionary principle, with many suggesting that it has been misapplied, while others consider that it has no place in planning. The author attributes this to the notion that engaging with socio-economic themes and principles related to sustainable development pose many problems in a transition towards sustainable development. Counsell concludes by observing that, in a planning context, the precautionary principle has a role to play in safeguarding areas that are inviolable, for ensuring that the overall quality of the environment is maintained.

The aforementioned regard for assets and integrity holds true for communities in general. For example, Rogers, Sinden, and De Lacy (1997) identify a number of cases where local people have been willing to spend time and money defending their natural environments from damage from large developments, because they recognise that the benefits they receive far outweigh the costs of defence. Such attempts provide further credence to the notion that communities need not sit idly waiting for others to decide their fate. This means that for tourism to be truly representative of a broad number of stakeholder groups, the natural environment included, many hard questions need to be addressed in regards to appropriate tourism planning, development, and management, and how precaution may guide better decision making. Some of these questions include:

- What in the community will be sacrificed for tourism development?
- What are the anticipated direct and indirect social, economic, and ecological impacts?
- Who inside and outside the community has been consulted, over what period of time?
- Who will be compensated for loss and how? Is the possibility for loss built into the proposal?
- What is the political and industry receptivity to the precautionary principle?
- How can precaution be built into these existing structures or visa versa?
- How can scientific data be more accessible to the public?
- Who has the knowledge to effectively plan with the interests of the community in mind?

Many of these questions can be addressed through the precautionary decision–making framework initially proposed at the Wingspread Conference attended by scientists, academics, policy makers, and environmental advocates (adapted here from Tickner & Raffensberger 1998). Proposed steps for incorporating the precautionary principle for better tourism industry decision making include:

- *Define the general duty to take precautionary action.* This involves the adoption of a corporate or industry-wide duty to take precautionary action in the face of scientific uncertainty where there is a threat to human health or the environment. The concept of human health could be expanded to include an assessment of how tourism developments have impacts on the ecology and customs of local communities.
- *Set aggressive goals/vision for achieving sustainability (backcasting).* This step involves the establishment of clear and measurable goals from which to drive innovative best practices within the tourism industry.
- *Assume responsibility for demonstrating the safety of products and processes.* Tourism industry stakeholders involved in the planning, development, and management of the tourism industry must demonstrate the safety of their operations before engaging in such activities.

- *Create criteria for decision making under uncertainty*. Indicators of sustainability and other such tools will need to be employed for the purpose of determining how to assess and what type of evidence to weigh in assessing impacts.
- *Use tools for implementing precautionary, preventative approaches*. There are numerous tools for carrying out precautionary policies related to the provision of services (e.g. environmental management systems).
- *Use the 'polluter pays' principle*. Offending parties must pay the costs of the damage they cause. One mechanism is assurance bonding. Companies are required to pay a premium before undertaking a project, which is based on the worst potential damage that might occur from development. If no damage occurs, the bond is returned to the developer.
- *Develop a scheme to systematically evaluate alternative activities, technologies, chemicals, etc*. In order to prevent an impact while creating another, developers must be careful that the substitutes they may use are not more harmful than the original product. This becomes especially salient in a tourism context where tourism developments have life cycles of many years.
- *Assume a duty to monitor, understand, investigate, inform, and act*. Tourism businesses have an ongoing obligation to investigate and understand their potential impacts. This calls for more science to understand how developments impact people, sites, communities, and regions. Companies should be responsible for periodic assessments and audits of their initiatives, over the long term.
- *Employ participative corporate decision making*. Just as many perspectives enrich decision making within a firm, tourism industry development decisions must be open to those who are often affected by the initiative. This means involvement by the development firm, governments, community members, and so on.

Conclusion

There is general consensus pointing to the fact that precaution is a tool that is here to stay (VanderZwaag 1999). The breadth of discussion on precaution and its inclusion as a principle in many international conventions, serves notice that it holds potential in standing up to the many uncertainties which exist in human–environment relationships. However, like sustainability, there appears to be a void between what industry, environmentalists, and governments want.

It is understandable that the precautionary principle has led to a backlash from industry, because it accentuates the process of pulling back the reins on unfettered growth (Howie 2003). So, while no caution is dangerous, too much caution may be equally counterproductive. Opponents suggested that there is a fear that, if taken too far in the other direction, science will have no role to play in qualifying the usefulness of certain products (see Cohen 2001). Scientific proof has thus become a burden and a barrier in the protection of the environment and people. At the same time, however, there must be the realisation that market forces, left unchecked, cannot run economies. Slowly, and with little respect for time (time to ask the right questions, to follow process, and to consider impacts over longer periods), there has been a steady erosion of a market culture, which is no longer respectful of the rule of law. As such, corporate actions have a significant effect on quality of life, particularly on LDCs (O'Riordan & Cameron 1994).

Tourism has been criticised for failing to adopt practices aimed at achieving sustainability (Swarbrooke 1999; McCool & Moisey 2001), even though there are several different mechanisms at hand to meet these challenges, including regulations, codes of conduct, action plans, and so on. In relation to these others mechanisms, the precautionary principle is underrepresented in the literature and in practice. Precaution holds promise as a planning tool that actualises the imperative of sustainability, effectively managing tourism in a more proactive, future-focused manner and acknowledging the uncertainty inherent in tourism–related development and activities. Since tourism development is continuously stretching into less populated and more pristine environments, science is often unable to provide data or causal links connecting action to harm in these new, unique areas. Thus, the precautionary principle can be employed as a decision-making tool within tourism development for the purpose of safeguarding natural environments and securing human wellbeing. The proposed framework discussed earlier for incorporating the precautionary principle into better decision making for the tourism industry illustrates the relevance and potential applicability of the principle.

One of the main drawbacks of the precautionary approach is that it does not directly offer explanations about how it should be applied. Who will implement? How will they implement? What level of expertise is required to implement? This final question is especially important. After all, one need only look at the legacy of tourism to question process and end. What passes for 'highly trained' and 'expert' has, too often, reduced complex systems or entities into individual pieces for the purpose of making decisions, without any effort to ask essential questions about the whole. In the absence of definitive expertise, politicians must still make decisions. They cannot sit idle, thus leaving themselves open to criticism about not being active enough in policy making, spending, and research and development. There comes a time for action, even though there is danger about the implications of such action. To politicians, it may be better to suffer criticism at a later date – when they may not be in power – than to suffer it at a time when they are attempting to consolidate authority and popularity.

Another constraint to the implementation of precaution is that a precise definition is far from clear, even though it has acquired the standing of a political/moral norm (Kaiser 1997). Thus, increased attention should be paid to what the precautionary principle actually means to tourism, and in particular, how it can be operationalised. Furthermore, the use of the precautionary principle for regulatory purposes is highly controversial. Some stakeholders express trepidation in the misuse or abuse of the precautionary principle, as evidenced by the extensive recent debate on the concept. Certain groups feel that it could be applied to perceived risks for which there is no firm scientific foundation. Many European industries view the precautionary principle less as an acceptable risk management approach, and more as a tool for the more radical environment and health advocates (EEA 2001).

This suggests that we may never be able to fully understand and control the impact that tourism developments have on social and ecological systems. There will be cases where the best way – or perhaps the only way forward, is by adopting a precautionary position. However, the adoption of such will no doubt be contentious in view of the interests of a broad array of different stakeholders – what they stand to gain and lose in the balance.

Key Reading

- Bastmeijer, K. and Roura, R. (2004) 'Regulating Antarctic tourism and the precautionary principle', *The American Journal of International Law*, 98: 763–81.
- O'Riordan, T. and Cameron, J. (1994) 'The history and contemporary significance of the precautionary principle', In T. O'Riordan and J. Cameron, *Interpreting the Precautionary Principle*, London: Earthscan, 12–30.
- Rogers, M.F., Sinden, J.A. and De Lacy, T. (1997) 'The precautionary principle for environmental management: A defensive-expenditure application', *Journal of Environmental Management*, 51: 343–60.
- Scott, S.V. (2001) 'How cautious is precautious? Antarctic tourism and the precautionary principle', *International and Comparative Law Quarterly*, 50: 963–71.
- Tickner, J. and Raffensberger, C. (1998) 'The precautionary principle: A framework for sustainable business decision-making', *Environmental Policy*, 5(4): 75–82.

References

Archer, B. (1996) 'Sustainable tourism – do economists really care?', *Progress in Tourism and Hospitality Research*, 2: 217–22.

Bastmeijer, K. and Roura, R. (2004) 'Regulating Antarctic tourism and the precautionary principle', *The American Journal of International Law*, 98: 763–81.

Boehmer-Christiansen, S. (1994) 'The precautionary principle in Germany – enabling Government', in T. O'Riordan and J. Cameron (eds) *Interpreting the Precautionary Principle*, London: Earthscan.

British Columbia Wilderness Tourism Association (2001) *Draft Code of Practices for BC's Wilderness Tourism Operators*. Available at: www.wilderness-tourism.bc.ca/code.html (accessed 22 January 2010).

Butler, R.W. (2011) 'Sustainable tourism in high-latitude islands: Shetland Islands', in J. Carlsen and R.W. Butler (eds) *Island Tourism: Sustainable Perspectives*, Wallingford: CABI.

Cohen, B.R. (2001) 'The safety Nazis', *American Spectator*, 34: 16.

Convention on Biological Diversity (CBD), United Nations Environment Programme (UNEP) (2001) *Biological Diversity and Tourism: International Guidelines for Sustainable Tourism*. Available at: www.biodv.org/programmes/socio-eco/tourism/guidelines.asp (accessed 6 April 2010).

Counsell, D. (1999) 'Sustainable development and structure plans in England and Wales: Operationalizing the themes and principles', *Journal of Environmental Planning and Management*, 42: 45–61.

Daltabuit, M. and Pi-Sunyer, O. (1990) 'Tourism development in Quintana Roo, Mexico', *Cultural Survival Quarterly*, 14: 9–13.

deFur, P. and Kaszuba, M. (2002) 'Implementing the precautionary principle', *The Science of the Total Environment*, 288: 155–65.

Dickson, B. (1999) 'The precautionary principle in CITES: A critical assessment', *Natural Resources Journal*, 39: 211–28.

Ellis, J. (2000) 'The precautionary principle: From paradigm to rule of law', *International Law*, 2: 127–29.

European Environment Agency (2001) Late lessons from early warnings: the precautionary principle 1896-2000', Environmental Issue Report No. 22. Luxembourg: Office for Official Publications of the European Communities.

Faulkner, B. (1998) 'Introduction', in E. Laws, B. Faulkner and G. Moscardo (eds) *Embracing and Managing Change in Tourism: International Case Studies*. London: Routledge.

Freestone, D. and Hey, E. (1996) 'Origins and development of the precautionary principle', in D. Freestone and E. Hey (eds) *The Precautionary Principle and Environmental Law: The Challenge of Implementation*. The Hague: Kluwer Law International.

Garrod, B. and Fennell, D.A. (2004) 'A content analysis of whalewatching codes of conduct', *Annals of Tourism Research*, 31: 201–12.

David A. Fennell

Gössling, S. (2001) 'The consequences of tourism for sustainable water use on a tropical island: Zanzibar, Tanzania', *Journal of Environmental Management,* 61: 179–91.

Government of Canada (2001a) *A Canadian Perspective on the Precautionary Approach/Principle Proposed Guiding Principles.* Available at: www.ncr.dfo.ca/cppa/HTML/booklet_e.htm (accessed 13 January 2012).

—— (2001b) *A Canadian Perspective on the Precautionary Principle/Approach.* Available at: www.ncr.dfo.ca/cppa/HTML/Pamphlet_e.htm (accessed 13 January 2012).

Hall, C.M. (1995) 'In search of common ground: Reflections on sustainability and complexity and process in the tourism system – a discussion between C. Michael Hall and Richard W. Butler', *Journal of Sustainable Tourism,* 3: 99–105.

—— (2011) 'Biosecurity, tourism and mobility: Institutional arrangements for managing tourism-related biological invasions', *Journal of Policy Research in Tourism, Leisure & Events,* 3: 256–80.

Holden, A. (1999) 'High impact tourism: A suitable component of sustainable policy? The case of downhill skiing development at Cairngorm, Scotland', *Journal of Sustainable Tourism,* 7: 97–107.

—— (2000) *Environment and Tourism,* London: Routledge.

Howie, F. (2003) *Managing the Tourist Destination,* London: Thomson.

Inskeep, E. (1991) *Tourism Planning: An Integrated and Sustainable Development Approach,* New York: Wiley and Sons.

Jennings, G. (2003) 'Marine tourism', in S. Hudson (ed.) *Sport and Adventure Tourism,* New York: Haworth Hospitality Press.

Kaiser, M. (1997) 'The precautionary principle and its implications for science', *Foundations of Science,* 2: 201–5.

Kirstges, T. (1995) *Sanfter Tourismus,* 2nd edn, Munich: Oldenbourg Verlag.

Lusseau, D., Slooten, L. and Currey, R. (2006) 'Unsustainable dolphin-watching tourism in Fiordland, New Zealand', *Tourism in Marine Environments,* 3: 173–78.

Martin, A. (2000) 'Making tourism sustainable', *UNESCO Sources,* 120: 10–12.

Martinez, E. and Orams, M. (2011) 'Kia angi puku to hoe I te wai: Ocean noise and tourism', *Tourism in Marine Environments,* 7: 191–202.

McCool, S.F. and Moisey, R.N. (eds) (2001) *Tourism, Recreation and Sustainability: Linking Culture and the Environment,* New York: CABI Publishing.

Myers, N. (1993) 'Biodiversity and the precautionary principle, *Ambio,* 22: 74–79.

O'Riordan, T. and Cameron, J. (1994) 'The history and contemporary significance of the precautionary principle', in T. O'Riordan and J. Cameron (eds) *Interpreting the Precautionary Principle,* London: Earthscan.

Rogers, M.F., Sinden, J.A. and De Lacy, T. (1997) 'The precautionary principle for environmental management: A defensive-expenditure application', *Journal of Environmental Management,* 51: 343–60.

Russell, R. and Faulkner, B. (1999) 'Movers and shakers: Chaos makers in tourism development', *Tourism Management,* 20: 411–23.

Scott, S.V. (2001) 'How cautious is precautious? Antarctic tourism and the precautionary principle', *International and Comparative Law Quarterly,* 50: 963–71.

Soleimanpour, H. (2012) 'Legal implications for nature-based tourism', in J.A. Seba (ed.) *Ecotourism and Sustainable Tourism: New Perspectives and Studies,* Oakville: Apple Academic Press.

Stewart, E.J. and Draper, D. (2006) 'Sustainable cruise tourism in Arctic Canada: An integrated coastal management approach', *Tourism in Marine Environments,* 3: 77–88.

Swarbrooke, J. (1999) *Sustainable Tourism Management,* Wallingford: CABI Publishing.

Tapper, R. (2001) Tourism and socio-economic development: UK tour operators' business approaches in the context of the new international agenda', *International Journal of Tourism Research,* 3: 351–66.

The Wilderness Society (1999) *Tourism in Natural Areas Policy.* Available at: www.wilderness.org.au/tourism-natural-areas-policy (accessed 17 December 2012).

Thorsby, D. (2009), Tourism, heritage and cultural sustainability: three 'golden rules', in Girard, L.F. and Nijkamp, P. (eds.), Cultural Tourism and Sustainable Local Development, Aldershot: Ashgate, pp 13-29.

Tickner, J. and Raffensberger, C. (1998) 'The precautionary principle: A framework for sustainable business decision-making', *Environmental Policy,* 5: 75–82.

Tribe, J., Font, X., Griffiths, N., Vickery, R. and Yale, K. (2000) *Environmental Management for Rural Tourism and Recreation,* London: Cassell.

VanderZwaag, D. (1994) *CEPA and the Precautionary Principle/Approach*, Hull, Quebec: Minister of Supply and Services.

—— (1999) 'The precautionary principle in environmental law and policy: Elusive rhetoric and first embraces', *Journal of Environmental Law and Practice*, 8: 355–75.

Van Dyke, J.M. (1996) 'The Rio principles and our responsibilities of ocean stewardship', *Ocean & Coastal Management*, 31: 1–23.

World Tourism Organization (WTO) (2001) *Tourism 2020 Vision – Global Forecast and Profiles of Market Segments*, Madrid: World Tourism Organization.

World Wild Fund for Nature (2001) *Position Statement on Tourism*. Available at: www.panda.org/resources/publications/sustainability/tourism/tourpp.doc (accessed 17 December 2012).

—— (2002) *Tourism*. Available at: www.Panda.org/resources/pub…s/sustainability/tourism/will.html (accessed 17 December 2012).

5

Sustainable yield

An integrated approach to tourism management

Jeremy Northcote

Yield Refers to a return on effort in some form; that is, an activity is seen to "yield" a certain quantity of produce. In research, yield is applied in two ways: as the level of produce (what shall be referred to here as production yield), and as the financial returns on investment (what shall be referred to as financial yield).

Sustainability Can be understood in two ways in yield analysis: first, as the means for sustaining yield levels over the long term (which shall be referred to as "sustained yield" in order to avoid terminological confusion); second, as a concern for ensuring that yield levels do not negatively impact on the ecosystem.

Introduction

Tourism is all too often seen as a "growth" industry that is presented as a savior of economic stagnation and decline. Since the 1980s, however, the discourse of sustainability has entered the frame, such that the notion of limitless growth has been replaced by a sensitivity regarding environmental and social impacts. However, as something of a latecomer to tourism conceptualization, sustainability is still approached as something of a niche area, which is set apart from the financial/economic analysis that remains the bedrock of tourism research and industry focus. This two-pronged approach has been somewhat disjointed: environmental impacts tend to be considered separately to financial/economic ones with the result that tourism planning tends to remain one-dimensional. This is where sustainable yield comes in.

Sustainable yield integrates financial/economic analysis with environmental and socio-cultural analysis, so the two aspects are not only considered alongside one another, but are directly related to one another as part of an integrated decision framework to determine which visitors, how many, to target, and in what ways. Sustainable yield is both a research field and a strategic management tool; it therefore bridges the gap between theory and practice.

Sustainable tourism yield is, however, still an emerging concept. Research on sustainable yield thus far – principally carried out by Australian and New Zealand researchers – is still in its early stages. An overview of the key aspects of sustainable yield research in tourism is the central task of the present chapter.

What is yield?

The concept of "yield" refers to a return on effort in some form, such that an activity is seen to "yield" a certain quantity of produce. In research, yield is applied in two ways: as the level of produce (referred to here as "production yield"), and as the financial returns on investment ("financial yield"). Both approaches to yield are relevant to tourism analysis, and both approaches are important for understanding the emerging concept of tourism sustainable yield. For this reason, it will be necessary to outline the key features of production and financial yield before the sustainable yield concept is explored in more detail. The yield dimensions that will be outlined are shown in Figure 5.1.

Production yield

Yield analysis centers on maximizing production or extraction using the most efficient means available. In agriculture, it might concern strategies to produce high-yield crop varieties through genetic engineering, fertilization techniques, soil quality and so on (e.g. van Wart *et al.* 2013). In mining and hydrology, production yield is in the form of energy resources and water extracted (e.g. McFarlane *et al.* 2012). In fisheries, yield refers to the number of fish harvested (e.g. Ranta and Lindström 1989). Similarly, in tourism, the production yield of interest is the number of visitors that destinations attempt to attract ("catch" if you will) through destination marketing. In this respect, tourism can be conceptualized as a "production process" whereby "physical and human resources constitute the input…and the output is then formed by arrivals, bed-nights, value added, employment, customer satisfaction, etc." (Cracolici *et al.* 2008: 326). Yield refers to the output, although its measurement depends on an understanding of the input as well, being basically the output subtracted by the input.

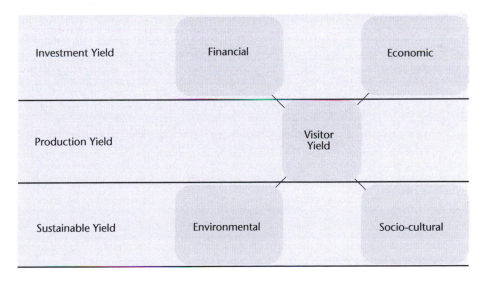

Figure 5.1 Yield dimensions

A focus on yield at the production level is fundamentally a matter of quantity. In simple terms, yield is the amount of produce extracted, generated or harvested, which in the case of tourism refers to visitor numbers. A measure of quality can also be added to the concept, so that yield can refer to the quantity of a material produced of a sufficient grade (e.g. the amount of premium iron ore mined). To the extent that a value is placed on visitors (most often in financial or economic terms), this introduces a quality dimension, not just quantity. In other words, the objective for most tourism destinations is not to increase the number of visitors per se, but to increase the expenditure of visitors, which leads to the concept of financial and economic yields.

Investment yield

Investment yield has financial revenue and economic growth as its primary focus. One might talk about the financial yield from a particular investment, which in basic terms is the return minus the amount invested (i.e. profit and loss). For tourism operators, financial yield is the key focus for their activities. Financial return concerns various aspects: the expenditure of visitors; the duration of their spending (e.g. length of stay); and the costs of servicing those visitors (Dwyer *et al.* 2007b).

Financial yield management is centered on the convergence of supply and demand, with supply referring to the capacity to service visitors, and demand referring to the number of visitors (i.e. visitor yield) requiring those services. Yield management is mostly centered on maximizing financial revenue through profit-making activities. It might involve, for example, offering last-minute reduced rates for unoccupied rooms in hotels (Brotherton & Mooney 1992; Kimes 1999, 2002), an airline offering discounted seats (Beloboba 1989; Belobaba & Wilson 1997; Botimer 1996; Brumelle & McGill 1993; Johns 2000; Smith, Leimkuhler & Darrow 1992), restaurants (Kimes 1999), or a theme park offering reduced tickets (Heo & Lee 2009). Such strategies are particularly important for enterprises that are subject to fluctuating demand and fixed capacity (i.e. supply) to meet that demand, and also where the product or service offered is "perishable" (Okumus 2004) (e.g. a seat that will be "wasted" if not filled).

The focus on financial yield shifts attention to the market value of visitors. Much like a high yield of a resource like grain may not be compatible with a financial yield if, for example, the market price of grain plummets, so too in tourism might a high yield of visitors for, say, a major sporting event (like the Olympic Games or World Cup) be incompatible with a financial yield if the costs of staging that event outweigh visitor expenditure and other forms of revenue (Humphreys & Prokopowicz 2007). The ability to track, segment and forecast demand is important to yield management strategies (Scott & Breakey 2007).

An extension of financial yield is economic yield, which refers to the costs and benefits across sectors, and which include economic aspects such as employment and industry multiplier effects. Economic yield in tourism has been the focus of work by Dwyer *et al.* (e.g. Dwyer & Forsyth 1997, 2008; Dwyer & Thomas 2012), who have devised various methods for measuring and predicting economic yield, particularly making use of Computable General Equilibrium models, Tourism Satellite Accounts and visitor surveys.

Sustained vs. sustainable yield

Sustainability can be understood in two ways in yield analysis: first, as the means for sustaining yield levels over the long term (referred to as "sustained yield" to avoid terminological confusion); second, as a concern for ensuring that yield levels do not negatively impact on the ecosystem (for which the term "sustainable yield" is reserved in this discussion). The distinction between these two concepts is not well understood in the sustainability literature, which has resulted in considerable confusion and has led sustained yield to be treated synonymously with sustainable yield.

Sustained yield

The realization that extraction of most renewable resources cannot be maintained over the long term if limits are not placed on their utilization has led to an interest in sustained yields. For example, overfishing can lead to the collapse of fish populations which do not have the time or population size to effectively reproduce; fishing yield therefore reduces over the long term. Deforestation, fertilization and irrigation to increase crop yields can lead to soil erosion, salinization, water scarcity and other forms of environmental degradation that can ultimately reduce crop yield. Therefore, it is often necessary to place limits on production yields to allow time for the resource base to sufficiently regenerate.

The main focus of sustained yield is to ensure that the resource base for production is not degraded over the long term. In the case of renewable resources such as water, the interest is to regulate rates of extraction to allow sufficient time for the resource to renew. The ideal limit for the extraction of renewable resources is referred to as the "optimum sustainable yield" (or what should be renamed "optimum sustained yield"). This is generally lower than the "maximum sustainable yield" (which should be renamed "maximum sustained yield"), which is the postulated "tipping point" that leads to a collapse of the resource base altogether (e.g. the collapse of a fish species through overfishing). In tourism, the maximum sustained yield is synonymous with the concept of "tourism carrying capacity," which is the limit of visitor numbers that particular destinations can "carry" before decline occurs to the physical environment and/or user satisfaction (Seidl & Tisdell 1999). To the extent that the decline relates to impacts on the environment, it is a matter of sustainable yield (discussed in the next section). To the extent that the decline relates to visitor numbers (mostly by way of impacts on visitor experience through overcrowding) it is a matter of sustained yield. The difference in the way carrying capacity can refer to either ecological or population limits is noted by Seidl and Tisdell (1999).

One of the key issues has been whether objective tipping points exist or whether there are just degrees of decline that come to be defined as unacceptable (Lindberg et al. 1997). McCool and Lime (2001) prefer the concept of "limits of acceptable change." Such an approach emphasizes the optimum sustained yield over the notion of a maximum sustained yield.

Although sustained yield is often focused on the management of renewable resources to ensure they have enough time to replenish and sustain production, the management of non-renewable resources can also be of relevance. The utilization rate of energy resources, for example, might need to vary to take account of changing commodity prices and minimize production costs.

The concept of sustained yield is narrowly focused on impacts concerned with sustaining the production area in question, not on the impact on the wider environment (except in cases where degradation of the wider environment affects yield). Sustained yield is not, strictly speaking, a holistic concept; hence it is not necessarily compatible with ecological sustainability.

Sustained visitor yield is the management of various resources and infrastructure to ensure that long-term visitor rates are maintained. For example, the use of resources (such as water and energy) is a concern in terms of sustaining visitor yields only insofar as it limits the capacity of destinations to service visitors. The state of the physical environment (e.g. flora, fauna and terrain) is relevant only insofar as environmental damage degrades the visitor experience and hence impacts on visitor yield. For example, Reynolds and Braithwaite (1997) draw attention to the importance of considering environmental impacts in visitor yield management techniques, making the case that maximizing capacity in boat tours should not be just about profits and visitor satisfaction, but also long-term impacts on the environment that are important for maintaining visitor satisfaction (and hence a means of sustaining visitor yield).

Similarly, sustained financial yield is based on the notion that: "for the output of an economy to be sustainable it must generate sufficient income to meet all costs of production and make investment such that at least a constant stock of capital is maintained" (Becken & Simmons 2008: 421). In terms of sustaining financial yields from visitors, resource use is merely a cost that impacts on profitability or, in economic terms, threatens to rob other industries (such as agriculture) of their required resource inputs.

Sustainable yield

"Sustainable yield," in contrast to sustained yield, is fundamentally concerned with the way production and financial yields impact on the surrounding environment and community (Becken & Butcher 2004). It accords with Butler's definition of sustainable tourism as:

> Tourism which is developed and maintained in an area in such a manner, and at such a scale, that it remains viable over an indefinite period and does not degrade or alter the environment in which it exists to such a degree that it prohibits the successful development and well being of other activities and process.
>
> *(1993: 28–29)*

From a sustainable yield perspective, the management of non-renewable resources receives as much priority as renewable resources, as the interest is not on managing the resource base for the purpose of sustaining particular yields, but on managing the ecosystem in the interests of environmental stewardship. For example, the use of coal-generated electricity, or gas and petroleum-based fuels (whether through visitor transportation, or through transportation of the goods and services that visitors use), receives as much attention as the renewable resources that tourism relies on, as it is concerned with the wellbeing of the environment in terms of global warming, not just with tourism (which is not to deny that global warming would not have long-term effects on tourism). Resource use, wastes and other impacts are studied right down the tourism supply chain (Rodríguez-Díaz & Rodríguez-Espino 2008). The emphasis is placed on the minimal use of resources (referred to elsewhere as "eco-efficiency"; Gössling et al. 2005).

The socio–cultural dimension is also part of the sustainable yield dimension (Northcote & Macbeth 2006; Lundie et al. 2007; Dwyer et al. 2007a), although it is the least-conceptualized dimension. Socio–cultural yield includes the socio–cultural benefits of tourism, not just negative socio–cultural impacts. Some of these benefits are by-products of economic benefits such as higher employment and improved infrastructure, but they may also be more direct, such as the "local pride" that develops from town beautification and heritage preservation, or the lifestyle benefits brought about by the addition of recreational facilities. Some impacts can be beneficial or detrimental depending on one's point of view (e.g. growth in property prices that might benefit existing home-owners, but not those renting, thus widening the gap between rich and poor). Incorporating the points of view of different stakeholders is a challenge to yield modeling, and will be discussed later.

While there has been a great deal of research on determining the capacity of destinations to accommodate a certain number of visitors, the benefit of reorienting these sorts of approaches to sustainable visitor yield research relates to the explicit integrative emphasis of the yield concept. An illustration of sustainable yield analysis applied at the national level will underline this key advantage.

Case Study

Sustainable yield

Lundie *et al.* (2007) integrate economic yield and environmental concerns in their tourism yield model, noting that the ideal tourist segment is one where economic benefits are maximized and environmental impacts are minimized. Focusing on selected niche visitor markets in Australia, they take visitor expenditure and length of stay as the key variables. Their findings with respect to Japanese honeymooners and backpackers (see Table 5.1) will be used to demonstrate their method of sustainable yield assessment.

Table 5.1 Mean expenditure per visitor

Visitor segment	Japanese honeymooners	Backpackers
Spend per night (AU$)	214	76
Length of stay (nights)	5.6	66.5
Total spend (AU$)	1,198	5,028

Source: Lundie *et al.* 2007

Lundie *et al.* (2007) found that Japanese honeymooners have a high level of mean expenditure per day (AU$214) in contrast to backpackers (AU$76). Yet, backpackers have a much longer duration of stay (66.5 days) than Japanese honeymooners (5.6 days), so the overall financial contribution of backpackers (AU$5,028) is considerably higher than Japanese honeymooners (AU$1,198).

Lundie *et al.* (2007) also provide the breakdown for expenditure areas, which is important for examining economic yields across sectors. Although they do not develop economic measures, Dwyer *et al.* (2007b) used the same set of data to determine gross operating surplus (GOS) and employment generation using a computable general equilibrium (CGE) model. Their modeling (see Table 5.2) shows Japanese honeymooners contribute AU$97.45 per trip into the economy or AU$17.46 per night and create 4.56 jobs per $million spent, while backpackers contribute AU$389.81 per trip or AU$5.86 per night and create 6.08 jobs per $million spent. It should also be kept in mind that backpackers often seek out employment themselves, and therefore contribute economically through their labor.

Table 5.2 Mean economic yield per visitor

Visitor segment	Japanese honeymooners	Backpackers
No. jobs/AU$ million spent	4.56	6.08
GVA/visitor night	$27.76	$10.09
GOS/visitor night	$17.46	$5.86
Net benefit/visitor night	$22.23	$6.66

Source: Dwyer *et al.* 2007b

Jeremy Northcote

The environmental impacts were calculated for direct and indirect use of primary energy, greenhouse gas emissions (CO_2 and equivalents), water usage and visitors' "environmental footprint" which measures the theoretical area of productive land that would be disturbed as a result of the resources, impacts and wastes associated with supporting visitor activities and consumption (Lenzen and Murray 2001). The problem of distinguishing impacts between different sectors and incorporating both direct and indirect effects pertains to quantifying environmental impacts, and is where input-output models may prove useful, as Lundie et al. (2007) suggest.

It can be seen (from Table 5.3) that Japanese honeymooners had the highest environmental impact per visitor night stayed (2.2 GJ of energy use, 18 kL of water use, 448 kg of CO_2–eq. and 213 ha of land disturbance, compared to 0.7 GJ of energy, 7 kL of water, 143 kg of CO_2 and 44 ha for backpackers), but backpackers had the highest environmental impacts overall by virtue of their long length of stay (48 GJ of energy, 0.5 ML of water, 9.5 tonnes of CO_2–eq. and 2.9 ha of land disturbance compared to 12.1 GJ of energy, 0.1 ML of water, 2.5 tonnes of CO_2–eq. and 1.2 ha of land disturbance for Japanese honeymooners).

Table 5.3 Mean environmental impacts per visitor

Visitor segment	Japanese honeymooners	Backpackers
Per visitor night		
Energy	2.2 GJ	0.7 GJ
Water use	18 kL	7 kL
Greenhouse gas emissions	448 kg CO_2-eq.	143 kg CO_2-eq.
Ecological footprint	213 ha	53 ha
Per visitor trip		
Energy	12.1 GJ	48 GJ
Water use	0.1 ML	0.5 ML
Greenhouse gas emissions	2.5 t CO_2-eq.	9.5 t CO_2-eq.
Ecological footprint	1.2 ha	2.9 ha
Per $ spent		
Energy	10.1 MJ	9.4 MJ
Water use	0.08 kL	0.09 kL
Greenhouse gas emissions	2.1 kg CO_2-eq.	1.9 kg CO_2-eq.
Ecological footprint	9.9 m^2	5.7 m^2

Source: Lundie et al. 2007

Yield analysis becomes particularly useful when combining the financial and environmental results. In terms of environmental impact per dollar spent, Japanese honeymooners and backpackers come out as more or less even (10.1 MJ of energy, 0.08 kL of water, 2.1 CO_2–eq. and 9.9 m^2 of land disturbance for Japanese honeymooners compared to 9.4 MJ of energy, 0.09 kL of water, 1.9 CO_2–eq. and 5.7 m^2 of land disturbance). The only measure where there is substantial difference is with land requirements where the impact of Japanese honeymooners is deemed to be greater. However, because Japanese honeymooners tend to restrict their visits more to built-up destinations than natural areas, the environmental impact profile for each segment may be quite different. Also, as Dwyer et al. (2007a) point out, the environmental impacts across all sectors, not just tourism, are also important to know.

Yield trade-offs

The particular yield quality that tourism planners wish to emphasize is a key factor in yield management techniques using these sorts of findings. The manner in which financial yield, economic yield, environmental impacts and socio-cultural impacts are considered alongside one another opens the way for considering trade-offs in sustainable yield management. If it is the case, for example, that economic decline has emerged as a serious issue in a destination, then economic yield may take priority over environmental impacts. Northcote and Macbeth (2006) emphasize that the consideration of trade-offs always involves values, so it is necessary to consider the prevailing "philosophies" that characterize tourism planning and the political climate (including the concerns of various interest groups) that shape them.

It is also the case that planning/management authorities have a range of options on how to best implement a sustainable yield management strategy. Sustainable yield management involves the manipulation of certain key yield variables, including length of stay (which can be manipulated through pricing), capacity (such as accommodation and transportation), services provided (including activities catered for) and destination marketing. For example, it is obvious that the development of yield profiles (i.e. segmenting) for visitor types can be very useful for tourism planning, assuming of course, that operators and destinations have the flexibility to attract different visitor segments (Dwyer *et al.* 2007b). Although Lundie *et al.* (2007) consider impact per visitor night as the key measure of sustainable value, tourism planners interested in alleviating environmental impact through destination marketing would probably consider overall length of stay as the key measure. Alternatively, if they feel confident that they can regulate visitor behavior or alleviate environmental impact through on-site management, then limiting the length of stay may not be of much concern.

In this respect it needs to be emphasized when developing sustainable yield profiles of visitors that impacts are not merely a matter of visitor behavior, but perhaps more importantly, an outcome of visitor management strategies and policies (Forsyth & Dwyer 1995). These strategies and policies need to be considered in the context of destination characteristics such as existing infrastructure and ecological vulnerabilities. With the right sorts of infrastructure and services in place, it may be possible for destinations to limit the ecological impact of visitors who might otherwise leave a strong environmental footprint. It is also the case, as Dwyer and Thomas (2012) note, that tourism's links with other sectors vary between destinations; some are more reliant on imported resources than others, hence varying in their degree of economic "leakage."

For this reason, Northcote and Macbeth (2006) emphasize destination-level yield analyses rather than generic profiling. It also leads them to pay attention to destinations as systems where the different aspects that define the quality of visitor yield are interrelated.

A systems approach

Northcote and Macbeth (2006) have sought to develop a systems model to integrate production, investment and sustainable yields in tourism in ways that take account of the particular characteristics of destinations and the needs of destination managers in an interrelated manner. Proposing the integrated tourism yield (ITY) framework, Northcote and Macbeth demonstrate its utility through a hypothetical application to a small island destination (Rottnest Island) close to a major population center (Perth, Western Australia).

The first step of the ITY approach is to apportion weightings to each yield dimension within a yield prioritization matrix, which employs a simple 5-step scale (Figure 5.2). The matrix involves: (1) determining the current level of emphasis on yield dimensions; (2) determining what level of emphasis is required to maintain the level of yield necessary to ensure sustainability at the destination; and (3) determining the ideal level of yield desired (i.e. potential yield). These prioritizations are based on analysis of current, required and potential yield returns in each of the dimensions. For example, financial yield (Figure 5.3) is determined at AU$2.7 million when costs for staffing, administration, depreciation, facilities and other costs are deducted from gross revenue.

Environmental impacts are then assessed (Figure 5.4), and it is determined, for example, that the substantive vegetation cover for the destination needs to be raised from 25% to 50% to combat serious erosion.

Together with other conservation programs, it is estimated that another AU$2 million in revenue is needed to fund those targets (through measures such as tree-planting and protective fencing), so an additional revenue of AU$2 million is added to the "required yield" on the financial yield matrix. This leads them to consider ways of raising visitor numbers, pricing or

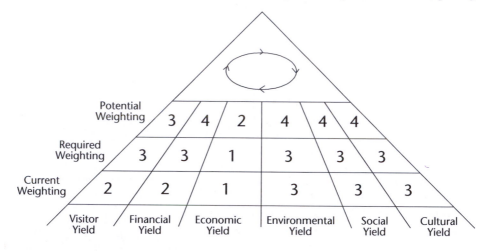

Figure 5.2 Integrated tourism yield framework

Source: Northcote & Macbeth, 2006

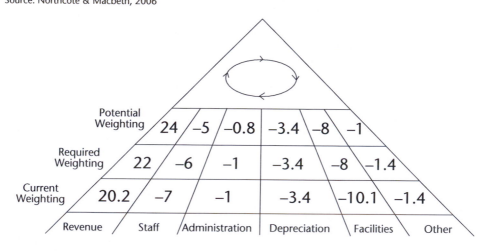

Figure 5.3 Financial Yield Matrix (in AU$)

Source: Northcote & Macbeth, 2006

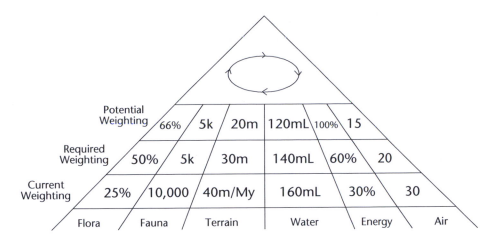

Figure 5.4 Environmental yield matrix

Source: Northcote & Macbeth, 2006

alternative sources of revenue to meet those financial requirements (which, in turn, may have additional environmental impacts, which then need to be factored in).

It can be seen how the ITY framework incorporates a systems understanding into its yield estimates and does not involve reducing non-financial dimensions to monetary costs. The application of the "balanced scorecard" approach to sustainable planning (Vila *et al.* 2010) also has similarities with Northcote and Macbeth's (2006) ITY approach.

As an example of the systems perspective underlying the ITY framework, destinations that rely on visitor revenue to fund their environmental management programs will tend to place a higher premium on high-spending visitors than destinations that do not. In destinations where the environment is a key attraction for visitors, conservation efforts will, in turn, contribute to sustaining visitor yield and, consequently, ongoing financial returns, such that the relationship between visitor revenue and environmental conservation is one of mutual dependence.

The cross-sector impacts can also be factored into economic yield analysis, so that, for example, energy resource use for the tourism industry is seen to have an impact on the available energy resources for other industries and vice versa. The development of an agricultural industry in a particular region may impact on water availability for tourism (e.g. draining away waterways used for recreational activities). Conversely, the exclusion of certain areas as natural parks for visitor use may limit the agricultural land available. This "replacement" value and inter-sector impact is something that the ITY framework seeks to incorporate in its economic dimension.

A systems approach to tourism yield views "sustained yield" and "sustainable yield" as closely related. Because tourism is situated in a web of interdependent relationships with other sectors and the wider environment, the sustained yield of tourism depends on maintaining a certain balance within the system. Although trade-offs are possible where some parts of the system are emphasized over others, this must be done in an holistic way to ensure that the system as a whole is not degraded. So, for example, activities might be directed at increasing the level of financial yield over the long term to cover rising maintenance costs which, in turn, are important for maintaining a positive visitor experience and, hence, growth in visitor numbers. Conversely, a destination might seek to reduce visitor numbers as a way of reducing environmental impacts, but might need to sustain financial yield to fund its environmental management initiatives. This might result in switching target markets from, say, backpackers and families to more exclusive holidaymakers, replacing the hostel and cabins with a resort. However, such a switch might have an unacceptable social impact.

Of course, the options available for attracting a certain type of visitor are not unlimited for most destinations, such that some destinations might be stuck with particular market segments given the range of attractions available. There may also be equity reasons for ensuring that destinations remain open to families rather than becoming exclusive. This will, of course, differ from destination to destination. Understanding the scope for catering to different types of visitors, given constraints in the resource base, is therefore necessary for realistic yield targets.

Sustainable yield measures

A key point to keep in mind is that the results are only as useful as the data and measures employed in arriving at yield estimates, working on the "rubbish-in/rubbish-out" principle (Northcote & Macbeth, 2006). Hence, the standard array of issues surrounding the robustness of visitor statistics, visitor surveys and economic reporting apply, but issues around distinguishing sector-specific impacts, direct-indirect impacts and other complexities involved in modeling input-output and various impacts also become evident. Each country has various strengths and weaknesses in terms of the quality of data available. Hopefully, with more awareness of the value of yield research, governments will pay more attention to strengthening the data resources available to researchers.

The social dimension of visitor impacts continues to present special challenges in sustainable yield assessment. It is absent in the research undertaken by Lundie *et al.* (2007). Dwyer *et al.* (2007a) consider employment generated as a social impact, although it may be better to consider employment as an economic impact instead. For Dwyer *et al.* (2007a), the main challenge is in providing a monetary value for social impacts. Some social impacts (e.g. socio–economic inequalities) can readily be valued in monetary terms (Dwyer & Thomas 2011). It is more difficult to attach a monetary value to other kinds of social impacts.

Certainly, there is scope for putting a nominal price on intangible goods using a "user–pay" framework. Methods such as contingent valuation (or willingness to pay) models or choice models are able to place hypothetical values on a range of yield types (Bhandari & Heshmati 2010; Choi *et al.* 2010). Such methods, however, are accompanied by their own set of difficulties. In particular, the attempt to place an economic value on such intangible qualities like "cultural value" is fraught with problems of commensurability. Also, while a price might be placed on carbon, does it really reflect the value of carbon reduction in averting a potential environmental catastrophe? What price is paid as a result of the commodification of native cultures through the emergence of souvenir industries to support tourism, or conversely, the value of preserving traditions that without tourism may fade into oblivion?

Northcote and Macbeth (2006) suggest that the measurement of tourism yield can be mostly done using existing impact modeling approaches that do not rely on monetary values. Instead, they propose moving in the opposite direction and converting financial and economic monetary values to ratings so that each yield dimension can be appropriately compared. The means for measuring yield levels are selected by the assessors and can be undertaken using standard forms of analysis, such as financial accounting, economic analysis (input-output, general equilibrium), social impact assessments and environmental impact assessments. Their ITY rating framework can readily combine quantitative and qualitative measures.

Conclusion

There has yet to be a widespread application of sustainable yield models in tourism research, perhaps due to two main factors: (1) the relatively recent development of the concept; and (2) the time, effort and expense of gathering data required to undertake yield analysis. However, given the benefits of integrating various quality dimensions when identifying target markets in a more systematic manner, the interest in sustainable tourism yield analysis as an overarching approach to tourism research, planning and management has immense potential.

Sustainable tourism yield analysis certainly offers a more coherent approach to tourism that combines a range of financial, economic, social and environmental interests than previous approaches, and also bridges the divide between tourism analysis and tourism planning in a way that most previous approaches have struggled to do. It will be interesting to see the new sorts of models and measures that emerge as more research is carried out in this area, including the reorientation of input–output models and impact assessment frameworks to sustainable yield frameworks.

An important point to note about sustainable yield is Scott and Breakey's (2007) observation that the types of qualities of interest to stakeholders may vary considerably between operators (who are principally interested in financial yield) and regional and national bodies (where economic and sustainable yield tend to take on greater importance). However, as noted by Northcote and Macbeth (2006), exchanging views on desired yield parameters between different stakeholders represents a potential mutual learning opportunity if handled sensitively. This underscores their point that sustainable yield analysis in tourism is as much a basis for engagement and visioning as it is about measuring and forecasting. It has the potential to build social capital within, and between, planning/managing authorities – a form of yield in itself. Integrating cultural values, political interests and sustainability philosophies constitutes another interesting avenue of research for further developing the sustainable yield concept.

Key Reading

Dwyer L., Deery, M., Fredline, E. and Jago, L. (2007) 'Corporate responsibility as essential to sustainable tourism yield', *Tourism Review International*, 11(2): 155–66.

Lundie, S., Dwyer, L. and Forsyth, P. (2007) 'Environmental-economic measures of tourism yield', *Journal of Sustainable Tourism*, 15(5): 503–19.

Northcote, J. and Macbeth, J. (2006) 'Conceptualizing yield: Sustainable tourism management', *Annals of Tourism Research*, 33(1): 199–220.

References

Becken, S. and Butcher, G. (2004) *Economic Yield Associated with Different Types of Tourists – a Pilot Analysis*. Discussion Paper.

Becken, S., and Simmons, D. (2008) 'Using the concept of yield to assess the sustainability of different tourist types', *Ecological Economics*, 67: 420–29.

Belobaba, P. (1989) 'Yield management, overbooking, and pricing', *Operations Research*, 37(2): 183–97.

Belobaba, P. and Wilson, J. (1997) 'Impacts of yield management in competitive airline markets', *Journal of Air Transport Management*, 3(1): 3–9.

Bhandari, A. and Heshmati, A. (2010) 'Willingness to pay for biodiversity conservation', *Journal of Travel and Tourism Marketing*, 27(6): 612–23.

Botimer, T.C. (1996) 'Efficiency considerations in airline pricing and yield management', *Transportation Research*, 30(4): 307–17.

Brotherton, B. and Mooney, S. (1992) 'Yield management – progress and prospects', *International Journal of Hospitality Management*, 11(1): 23–32.

Brumelle, S. and McGill, J. (1993) 'Airline seat allocation with multiple nested fare classes', *Operations Research*, 41(1): 127–37.

Butler, R.W. (1993) 'Tourism – an evolutionary perspective', in J.G. Nelson, R.W. Butler and G. Wall (ed) *Tourism and Sustainable Development: Monitoring, Planning, and Managing*, Waterloo, Ontario: University of Waterloo.

Choi, A., Ritchie, B., Papendrea, F. and Bennett, J. (2010) 'Economic valuation of cultural heritage sites: a choice modelling approach', *Tourism Management*, 31(2): 213–20.

Cracolici, M. F., Nijkamp, P. and Rietveld, P. (2008) 'Assessment of tourism competitiveness by analysing destination efficiency', *Tourism Economics*, 14(2), 325-342.

Dwyer, L. and Forsyth, P. (1997) 'Measuring the benefits and yield from foreign tourism,' *International Journal of Social Economics*, 24(1–3): 223–36.

—— (2008) 'Economic measures of tourism yield: What markets to target?', *International Journal of Tourism Research*, 10: 155–68.

Dwyer, L. and Thomas, F. (2012) 'Tourism yield measures for Cambodia', *Current Issues in Tourism*, 15(4): 303–28.

Dwyer, L., Deery, M., Fredline, E. and Jago, L. (2007a) 'Corporate responsibility as essential to sustainable tourism yield', *Tourism Review International*, 11(2): 155–66.

Dwyer, L., Forsyth, P., Fredline, L., Jago, L., Deery, M. and Lundi, S. (2007b) 'Yield measures for Australia's special interest inbound tourism markets', *Tourism Economics*, 13(3): 421–40.

Forsyth, P. and Dwyer, L. (1995) *The Yield from Inbound Tourism*. Occasional Paper No.3. Commonwealth Department of Tourism, Canberra.

Gössling, S., Peeters, P., Ceron, J.P., Dubois, G., Patterson, T. and Richardson, R. (2005) 'The eco-efficiency of tourism,' *Ecological Economics*, 54(4): 417–34.

Heo, C.Y. and Lee, S. (2009) 'Application of revenue management practices to the theme park industry', *International Journal of Hospitality Management*, 28(3): 446–53.

Humphreys, B.R. and Prokopowicz, S. (2007) 'Assessing the impact of sports mega-events in transition economies: Euro 2012 in Poland and Ukraine', *International Journal of Sport Management and Marketing*, 2(5/6): 496–509.

Johns, N. (2000) 'Computerised yield management systems: Lessons from the airline industry', in A. Ingold, U. McMahon-Beattie and I. Yeoman (eds) *Yield Management Strategies for the Service Industries*, London: Continuum.

Kimes, S. (1999) 'Implementing restaurant revenue management', *Cornell Hotel and Restaurant Administration Quarterly*, 40(3): 6–21.

—— (2002) 'Perceived fairness of yield management', *Cornell Hotel and Restaurant Administration Quarterly*, 21(1): 21–30.

Lenzen, M. and Murray, S.A. (2001) 'A modified ecological footprint method and its application to Australia', *Ecological Economics*, 37(2): 229–55.

Lindberg, K., McCool, S. and Stankey, G. (1997) 'Rethinking carrying capacity,' *Annals of Tourism Research*, 24: 461–65.

Lundie, S., Dwyer, L. and Forsyth, P. (2007) 'Environmental-economic measures of tourism yield', *Journal of Sustainable Tourism*, 15(5): 503–19.

McCool, S. and Lime, D. (2001) 'Tourism carrying capacity: Tempting fantasy or useful reality?' *Journal of Sustainable Tourism*, 9: 372–88.

McFarlane, D., Stone, R., Martens, S., Thomas, J., Silberstein, R., Ali, R. and Hodgson, G. (2012) 'Climate change impacts on water yields and demands in south-western Australia', *Journal of Hydrology*, 475: 488–98.

Northcote, J. and Macbeth, J. (2006) 'Conceptualizing yield: Sustainable tourism management', *Annals of Tourism Research*, 33(1): 199–220.

Okumus, F. (2004) 'Implementation of yield management practices in service organisations: Empirical findings from a major hotel group', *The Service Industries Journal*, 24(6): 65–89.

Ranta, E. and Lindström, K. (1989) 'Prediction of lake-specific fish yield', *Fisheries Research*, 8: 113–28.

Reynolds, P.C. and Braithwaite R.W. (1997) 'Whose yield is it anyway? Compromise options for sustainable boat tour ventures', *International Journal of Contemporary Hospitality Management*, 9(2): 70–74.

Rodríguez-Díaz, M. and Rodríguez-Espino, T.F. (2008) 'A model of strategic evaluation of a tourism destination based on internal and relational capabilities', *Journal of Travel Research*, 46: 368–80.

Scott, N. and Breakey, N. (2007) 'Yield applied to destination management – an inefficient analogy?' *Tourism Economics*, 13(3): 441–45.

Seidl, J. and Tisdell, C.A. (1999) 'Carrying capacity reconsidered: From Malthus' population theory to cultural carrying capacity', *Ecological Economics*, 31: 395–408.

Smith, B., Leimkuhler, J. and Darrow, R. (1992) 'Yield management at American Airlines', *Interfaces*, 22(1): 8–31.

van Wart, J., Kersebaum, K.C., Peng, S., Milner, M. and Cassman, K.G. (2013) 'A protocol for estimating crop yield potential at regional to national scales', *Field Crops Research*, 143: 34–43.

Vila, M., Costa, G. and Rovira, X. (2010) 'The creation and use of scorecards in tourism planning: A Spanish example', *Tourism Management*, 31(2): 232–39.

6

Tourism and common pool resources

Helen Briassoulis

Common pool resources (CPRs) Natural and human resources characterized by non-excludability and subtractability.

Subtractability The consumption of one individual reduces the quantity of a good available to other individuals.

Nonexcludability It is physically impossible or socially unacceptable to exclude any individual from using a good.

Tourism commons The collection of natural, manmade and socio-cultural resources of host areas and their surrounding regions that are purposefully or inadvertently used *in common* by tourist and non-tourist activities.

Adaptive tourism governance Multi-level, participatory processes of sustainably managing collective affairs under uncertainty in complex tourism social-ecological systems.

"The common interest makes people live together, because it makes them live well"

Aristotle, Politics, Book 3, passage 6

Introduction: tourism and resources

Tourism is a complex of intertwined activities; namely, travel to, from and within a destination, accommodation, sightseeing, entertainment and use of general and specialized services (Briassoulis 2002). Besides tourists, visitors and locals variously participate in these activities that are spatio-temporally diffuse, extending from the local to the global level over varying time periods, and thus, difficult to delimit in space and in time.

A wide array of diverse natural, manmade and socio–cultural, local and supra-local resources (a) provide inputs to and (b) serve as sinks of the wastes of a heterogeneous mix of tourism and non-tourism-related activities, the negative resource impacts of which ultimately affect the quantity and the quality of the tourist product. Most resources are indivisible and difficult to strictly define in space and time. *Almost inescapably*, they are used *in common by* tourist and non-tourist activities; thus, they are "common pool resources" (CPRs) (i.e. resources for which exclusion of users is difficult or impossible and use by one user reduces the amount available for other users (Bromley 1991; Ostrom 1990)). In the context of tourism studies, Briassoulis (2002) named them "tourism commons" (TC).

Complex, place- and time-specific, cross-level relationships develop between tourism and CPRs as tourist destinations constantly self-organize to adapt to environmental and socio-economic change. They depend on the distinct form and evolutionary trajectory of tourism development, the non-tourist activities present, the characteristics of the CPRs involved and the kind of collective action taken to manage them. Eventually, these relationships determine the composition and quality of the tourist product and the degree of achievement of sustainable tourism at a destination and beyond. Sustainable tourism denotes a dynamic process of tourism development that promotes the economic well-being, preserves the natural and socio-cultural capital, achieves intra- and inter-generational justice, and secures the self-sufficiency of host areas while satisfying the material and immaterial needs of tourists (Briassoulis 2002; UNEP & UNWTO 2005).

This chapter provides a concise discussion of the main issues concerning the relationship between tourism and CPRs drawing on the literature on sustainable tourism development, common pool resources, complex systems and tourism governance. The next section defines the CPRs and their main features, details the tourism commons and presents the main threats facing them. The governance of the tourism commons is discussed in the third section. A summary of the current state of research and of future research needs conclude the chapter. A case study illustrates selected points discussed.

Common pool resources in tourism

The CPR discourse is rooted in the theory of public goods in public economics (Samuelson 1954). Public goods are indivisible goods of infinite supply. Indivisibility implies that (a) they cannot be partitioned in units for sale in the market (hence, the private sector has no incentive to provide them); and (b) it may be physically impossible or socially unacceptable to exclude any individual from using them; *nonexcludability* implies that once they are provided for one individual they are available to all. Infinite supply implies *nonsubtractability* and *nonrivalry* in their use; the consumption of one individual does not reduce the quantity of the good available to other individuals; hence, their use is not rivalrous.

> CPRs are natural human resources characterized by *nonexcludability* in their use and *subtractability* because their quantity is finite for specified time periods. This implies *rivalry and competition in their use among potential users* (Bromley 1991; Ostrom 1990). Conventional CPRs are the atmosphere, water resources, oceans, fisheries, ecosystems, forests, wildlife, landscapes, and grazing systems, among others. Non-conventional CPRs include transport systems, ports, urban areas, the Internet, the electro-magnetic spectrum, genetic data, traditional transmission (cultural commons), intellectual resources, socio-economic costs and benefits, and budgets, among others.
>
> *(Briassoulis 2002)*

Ostrom (1990) has distinguished three types of CPR users: owners (ownership rights), appropriators (use rights) and consumers (utilization rights). In terms of ownership, CPRs can be under any of four main property regimes: public, private, common property and open access (no regime) (Bromley 1991; Ostrom 1990).

> The role of CPRs in tourism has been addressed mostly in the context of the broader discourse on sustainable tourism development (Bramwell & Lane 2011). The pertinent theoretical and empirical literature is limited and focuses on selected issues. The tourism commons (TC) can be defined as the collection of natural, manmade and socio-cultural resources in host areas and their surrounding regions which are implicated in tourism; thus, they are purposefully or inadvertently used *in common* by tourist and non-tourist activities. In this sense, they are components of, or even coincide with, the tourist product.
>
> *(Briassoulis 2002)*

The elements of the TC belong to four broad categories: the broader landscape, natural, socio-cultural and manmade resources. Table 6.1 offers a non-exhaustive list of these elements. It schematically presents the tourism commons and their principal relationship with tourist and non-tourist activities – providing input to human activities and receiving their unwanted byproducts.

The first row of Table 6.1 shows a distinct class of the TC, the "background tourist elements" (BTEs) that cut across the first three categories of resources. They comprise the natural, socio-cultural, and manmade attractions of tourist areas that usually constitute the main reason for visiting a destination (Jafari 1982). The contemporary trends and forms of tourism suggest that the BTEs are dynamic elements of the TC whose importance and role varies with environmental and socio-economic change.

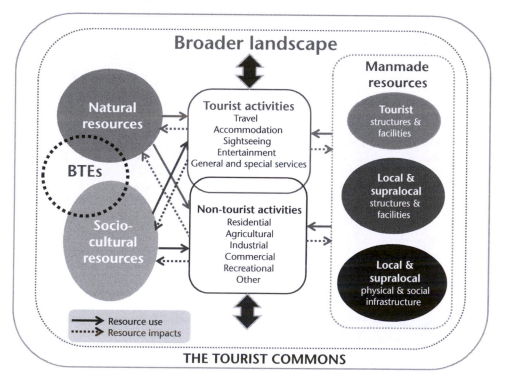

Figure 6.1 The tourism commons

Table 6.1 The elements of the tourism commons

Broader landscape	Natural resources	Socio-cultural resources	Man made resources
Background tourist elements (BTEs)			
The broader landscape	Air, atmosphere	Tangible	Tourist infrastructure (structures and
Vistas, panoramas	Climate, sunshine	Archaeological, historical, traditional	facilities)
Townscape/cityscape	Water Bodies	and modern artifacts; such as:	Various types of accommodation:
Rural landscape	Oceans, seas	Monuments, buildings, settlements,	Hotels
Seascapes	Coasts, beaches	neighborhoods, churches,	Villas
Smellscapes	Lakes	monasteries, cemeteries, etc.	Tourist villages
Soundscapes	Rivers, deltas	Intangible	Camps
	Geomorphological forms	Genius loci	Special accommodation (eco-villages,
	Ecosystems	Traditions	agrotourist accommodation, etc.)
	Forests	Local culture/events	Specialized facilities:
	Meadows	Local/traditional cuisine	Ski centers
	Mountains		Spas
	Geological forms		Golf courses
	Wildlife		Marinas
			Local and supralocal physical and
			social infrastructure
			Transportation, energy,
			communication, water supply,
			sewage, garbage collection, etc.
			networks
			Health, education, financial and
			recreation facilities
			Ancillary facilities (gas stations, car
			rentals, etc.)
			Local and supralocal structures and
			facilities
			Housing, commercial, recreational,
			industrial facilities

The broader landscape refers to the total landscape of a destination and its surroundings as both BTEs and tourist facilities are not isolated elements in space. They constitute and are constituted by their broader regions where agricultural, residential, commercial, recreational, industrial, and other activities – most of them predating tourism development – are taking place. The broader landscape, comprising both tangible and intangible elements, is the "container" of all resources, integrates the tourist experience and regulates the psychological satisfaction of tourists (Briassoulis 2002; Healy 1994). It represents an important input to tourism and, simultaneously, an important locational factor for activities such as residential second homes, and others.

The multi-activity, multi-sectoral, fragmented and spatio-temporally diffuse character of tourism and the multi-dimensionality of the tourist product inadvertently draw the elements of the TC into dynamically interacting and evolving place- and time-specific combinations (Briassoulis 2002). Numerous and diverse tourist and non-tourist user groups from various spatial levels subject them to multiple, overlapping, potentially conflicting and volatile uses under various institutional arrangements. The tourism commons are complex CPRs (Selsky & Memon 2000) like the tourism socio-ecological systems of which they are part (McDonald 2009). The characteristic features of the TC that are presented below draw on their axiomatic definition and complex nature.

- *Nonexcludability and subtractability.* These are the principal defining features of the tourism commons. It is not easy or feasible to exclude tourists or other users from using the TC. Moreover, as soon as the conditions of the TC improve (e.g. bathing water) for a class of tourists this improvement is shared by all users. Because the TC are not infinite in general, use by one or a small portion of tourists diminishes the quantity (of the same quality) available to other tourists and other users in general. This applies to resources that are relatively abundant such as air, water and scenery.
- *Heterogeneity and variety.* The tourism commons are inherently heterogeneous in several respects. They comprise diverse resources. Their elements are both material (tangible) and immaterial (intangible) and they are subject to multiple consumptive and nonconsumptive uses (Steins & Edwards 1999).

Different elements of the TC are under one of four principal property regimes: private, public, common and open access (no regime) both before and after tourism development (Briassoulis 2002; Healy 1994). Some elements are pure public goods. The combination of these regimes is highly variable and dynamic because they are place and time specific. The public and private actors involved have different ownership and use rights (Ostrom 1990). Certain elements of the TC rights do not exist in general such as rights over the use of vistas, sunsets, etc. The heterogeneity of the TC renders the characteristic CPR "appropriation problem" (Ostrom 1990) (i.e. which user group has use rights over a given resource) even more important.

The tourism commons may be formally (*de jure*) designated in space and time (e.g. controlled-use beaches, hiking paths, camping sites, parking lots) or they may comprise *de facto* informal commons. Similarly, their use and change may be subject to planned, formal arrangements and interventions or to unplanned, autonomous and spontaneous decisions and actions. Consequently, different managers and management systems are involved with different concerns regarding their use and protection. In particular, external users – tourists and tourist entrepreneurs – use local resources interfering with existing rules of use and management and influencing the status and value of the TC (Briassoulis 2002). The institutional heterogeneity of the TC is of paramount importance from the point of view of their governance.

The use of the TC exhibits significant socio–cultural heterogeneity and variety because it is mediated by different socio–cultural value systems – those of the locals, tourists, and tourist entrepreneurs. Hence, their utilization and valuation is more socio–culturally differentiated than in cases of simpler CPRs used by fewer or a single socio–cultural user group (e.g., grazing commons). This is especially important for those elements (miscellaneous facilities, roads, etc.) that are controlled by non-tourist interests and poses problems of coordination among users for efficient resource management (Briassoulis 2002).

- *Spatio-temporal variability*. The different elements of the TC that combine in the course of tourist activities have broad, highly variable, spatial and temporal reach (size), fluid boundaries and intermingle within space and over time as tourists move to, from and around destinations. They range from single spots to localities up to global commons (e.g. the oceans) and from single instances to short-duration and long-lasting "episodes".
- *Asymmetry, simultaneity and unpredictability of use*. The heterogeneity and spatio-temporal variability of the TC result in asymmetric and uneven use over space and time that is difficult to predict and poses planning and management challenges (coordination, conflict resolution, eliminating inefficiencies) especially where tourism is an economic "monoculture".

The tourism commons are used *simultaneously* as inputs to tourist and non-tourist activities by both tourists and locals in the tourist and the off-tourist season *and* as sinks of the unwanted products of these activities. Therefore, tourism may not only destroy the resources upon which it depends but also non-tourist activities as well unless appropriate planning and enforcement are exercised to continuously manage the unpredictable outcomes of planned or spontaneous change in the TC.

These characteristic features importantly explain the threats that the TC face. *Overuse* is an umbrella term that encompasses two interrelated categories of threats – excessive resource use and negative resource impacts – that originate in various tourist and non-tourist activities (Figure 6.1). Overuse may be direct, indirect or induced and produces environmental "bads" that are CPRs too (Clapp & Meyer 2000). Overuse reduces and/or harms the quantity and quality of the TC, thus, jeopardizing the achievement of sustainable tourism at destinations (Briassoulis 2002; Healy 1994).

Excessive resource use leads to *resource depletion, resource congestion* and *capacity problems* but also to *negative resource impacts*. Depletion (i.e. reduction of the available quantity of resources (of a given quality)) threatens water and land resources, forests, fauna, flora, biodiversity, etc. in tourist destinations and potentially reduces the range of present and future tourist and non-tourist development options that rely on these resources or renders their exploitation costly and ineffective.

Resource congestion and capacity problems result from excessive resource use that may not necessarily affect the quality of the resource, at least permanently. BTEs of high visitation frequency and physical and social infrastructure experience these problems. Local infrastructure, originally designed to serve the local population and temporary visitors, faces capacity problems as tourism develops because demand exceeds the originally planned supply. The result is bad maintenance, inadequate or low quality servicing and dissatisfaction of tourists and locals.

Tourist facilities experience over- and under-capacity problems that incur economic, environmental and social costs to tourism and to the host area generally. Overcapacity occurs in the tourist season when these facilities may be used by non-tourist activities too. Undercapacity occurs in the off-tourist season of low to null demand.

The *negative environmental and resource impacts of tourism* have been extensively covered in the literature (Briassoulis 2000). The negative impacts of non-tourist activities, especially on the broader landscape, that are more pronounced and severe in heterogeneous tourist areas, and indeed, may outweigh those caused by tourism, are less studied and relatively neglected.

The environmental, resource and socio-cultural impacts of tourist and non-tourist activities are difficult to disentangle and analyze. Nevertheless, the fact remains that all activities are affected by these impacts through the negative and positive feedback mechanisms at work in complex tourism commons. Negative feedback preserves the original "balance" of the tourism system. Positive feedback amplifies small "disturbances" (e.g. a new hotel, new road access to a destination) and generate path dependencies that may lock the host socio-ecological system into undesirable states where the TC suffer from depletion, congestion, overcapacity and deterioration (McDonald 2009). In the case of negative impacts, tourism receives lower quality resources (e.g. polluted air and water, spoiled landscapes), host areas offer lower quality product, lose their appeal to tourists and other users, and may suffer revenue and job losses due to competition from other destinations. Similarly, non-tourist activities have to cope with environmental inputs of reduced quality and increased abatement costs (Briassoulis 2002).

The overuse threats owe to the intrinsic features of the TC as well as to external and contextual factors. The heterogeneity and variety of the TC engender numerous and diverse tourist and non-tourist related sources of potential threats which are difficult to contain given the *nonexcludability* of users who *simultaneously* use *and* negatively affect the TC.

External factors encompass the volatility of tourist and non-tourist demand and broader socio-economic, technological and cultural changes. Variable and volatile demand implies unpredictable, unevenly distributed and differential impacts on the elements of the TC that generate considerable uncertainty regarding their management. Socio-economic and other changes modify and shift in space and time the pressures on the TC, relieving some places and burdening some others.

Contextual factors concern the host geographical, historical and political setting and circumstances. They include demographic, socio-economic and institutional structure and dynamics, decision making, policy and planning, especially implementation and enforcement, culture, resource management tradition, value systems and environmental awareness of locals and tourists, general and tourism-related power relationships, cross-scale relationships (Briassoulis 2002). The composition and property status of the TC involved are of critical importance. "Open access" resources are prone to free-riding that generates resource overuse and deterioration (Healy 1994).

The aggregate effect of these factors is the often insurmountable difficulties in coping with the threats facing the tourism commons as a whole or their individual elements. Healy (1994) suggested that overuse results from free-riding and produces "lack of investment incentive" in protecting the TC. The more comprehensive approach taken here suggests that a broader constellation of factors underlie the lack of investment incentive which should be considered in the deliberations on governing the tourism commons.

Governing the tourism commons

Governance refers to dynamic political processes whereby state and non-state actors, from various spatial/organizational levels, set collective goals and select specific structures, mechanisms and instruments of coordination to steer society towards achieving them (Briassoulis 2008). Models of governance reflect theories specifying *who* should be involved (politics), *how* – through which structures and processes (polity), and *which* instruments should be employed (policy) to steer society towards desirable goals (Martens 2007; Hall 2011). Different models of governance are associated with different *modes of governance* (i.e. alternative mechanisms to achieve coordination) defined along the same dimensions. The four principal models of governance: states, markets, associations and communities correspond to three main modes of governance: hierarchy (command and control), competition (market) and communication (participatory) (Hall 2011; Briassoulis 2008).

In reality, different modes of governance co-exist and intermingle. *Fuzzy governance* describes situations characterized by unclear definition of the roles and responsibilities of various actors, "new" modes of governance emphasizing participation, communication, collaboration, networking and multi-level governance, the adoption of more competitive modes of governance, and the establishment of partnerships among public, private, voluntary and community sectors (Briassoulis 2008).

The governance of the commons has been the focus of important research in the last decades, the landmark work being Ostrom's "Governing the Commons" (1990). The original pursuit of public vs. private and of appropriate common property regimes questions, were soon replaced by the quest for collective action institutional arrangements to safeguard the commons. The theoretical and empirical literature almost unanimously concurs on the appropriateness of communicative/participatory modes of governance and of adaptive governance in particular. Adaptive governance, exemplified by adaptive co-management, concerns flexible community-based resource management systems, tailored to specific places and situations. Polycentric institutional arrangements among nested quasi-autonomous decision-making units operating at multiple scales (multi-level governance), preferably complemented by modest overlaps in authority and capability, balance centralized and decentralized control and favor dynamic, self-organized processes of learning-by-doing. Under particular conditions, adaptive governance may better handle uncertainty and change in socio-ecological systems than traditional governance approaches (Martens 2007; Folke *et al.* 2005).

The interest in tourism governance is relatively recent, although the tourism literature has long been dealing with tourism and resources management, policy and planning that belong to the tourism governance discourse (Bramwell & Lane 2011). The governance of CPRs at destination regions has been tackled in research on protected areas and ecotourism (Moore & Rodger 2010; Bramwell & Lane 2011; Healy 2006). Collaboration, partnerships, community-based and adaptive co-management are recommended optimal arrangements for sustainable tourism and CPR management.

Governing the tourism commons is far from easy given their heterogeneity and the threats they face. The overarching goal is to promote sustainable tourism at destination regions. Two specific objectives are to address the threats identified and to provide incentives for using the TC sustainably. Suitable governance systems to achieve these goals should respect the particular features and the importance of the different elements of the TC for sustainable development in specific tourism socio-economic and political contexts.

The heterogeneity and interdependence of the TC dictates the adoption of an adaptive governance framework to accommodate, network and coordinate the governance systems of their individual elements and of the tourist and non-tourist activities on a focal level (e.g., community, local, regional) and across levels. Furthermore, a common property resource regime framework is essential to advance integration and coordination of the diverse property regimes; to internalize new uses into existing commons; to manage transitions between regimes; to provide adequate flexibility to renegotiate resource use, if necessary, to adapt to changes in demand and socio-economic conditions and to avoid adverse impacts associated with overexploitation and inter-user conflicts (Briassoulis 2002).

State and non-state actors from various levels should be included – resource owners and users, tourism and non-tourism producers, consumers (tourists, locals, visitors) and third-sector parties. Locals, as stewards of the CPRs and direct recipients of changes in their status, should receive priority in decision making. Participatory structures and processes, such as collaborations and partnerships, are essential to the development of bonds and networks among diverse user groups across levels for mutual benefit and social equity (Bramwell & Lane 2000). More importantly, they should frame the establishment of collective behavior rules (rights and duties) and resource allocation principles in host areas and offer the requisite authority to legitimize and protect local and nonlocal resource owners, appropriators and users.

A variety of instruments are necessary to control access to and use of the TC according to their sensitivity to human pressures and to create incentives for users to invest in their maintenance and enhancement. These include administrative/organizational (e.g. zoning), legislative, economic (e.g. resource pricing, user fees), voluntary (e.g. labeling, pacts, etc.), education and awareness-raising but also physical and technological instruments. The establishment of *platforms for resource use negotiation* has been proposed for complex natural resource management problems (Steins & Edwards 1999) as it is the case of the tourism commons.

The success of participatory governance approaches hinges on important prerequisites (enabling conditions, design principles *sensu* Ostrom) with regard to: (a) resource characteristics, (b) resource user characteristics, (c) relationships between resource and resource user characteristics, (d) institutional arrangements, (e) relationships between resources and institutional arrangements and (f) external factors (Moore & Rodger 2010; Ostrom *et al.* 2002; Agrawal 2001, 2002; Ostrom 1990). The available empirical evidence suggests that these approaches are successful when (a) resource systems are small, with clearly defined boundaries, predictable and resources are not mobile; (b) a few, clearly defined user groups are involved who share common values, rules of resource use and perception of CPR management as well as of their interdependencies in jointly solving problems, leaders are present, social capital is well developed, and poverty levels are low; (c) users live close to and depend on the CPRs, demand is low and changes slowly, and they enjoy equitable distribution of costs and benefits; (d) the rules of resource use are simple and understandable, enforcement is easy, low-cost conflict resolution is feasible and accountability systems are in place; common property systems are mostly desirable as well as conversion of all "open access" to common property resources (Bromley 1991); and (e) the institutional arrangements of resource use must match the resource replenishment rate. Favorable external factors include: low cost technologies to exclude users, compatible adaptation time to new technologies, a low level of articulation with global markets, relative local autonomy, external assistance to compensate locals, and hierarchical levels of use and other rights (Moore & Rodger 2010; Ostrom 1990; Agrawal 2001; Steins & Edwards 1999). The real world diversity of the TC suggests that the feasibility of any one or combinations of property regimes can be assessed only for concrete cases.

Finally, the success of any governance approach requires the recognition of the whole repertoire and integrity of the TC as presented here and the education of all users to heighten their awareness of their 'common interest' in governing sustainably. This will inevitably include the development of a culture of cooperation and a conservation and environmental ethic that holds the key for the ultimate sustainability of the TC (Holden 2005).

Case Study

Commons management and ecotourism in the Amazon

The study of Infierno, a Native Peruvian Amazon Community and biodiversity hotspot, illustrates the heterogeneity and variety of users and uses, the threats facing and the governance of the tourism commons (Stronza 2010). Based on longitudinal ethnographic data (1996–2008), it explores the pros and cons of a joint venture ecotourism project, a form of participatory/adaptive governance.

Infierno, a poor, isolated community, encompasses 9,558 hectares on either side of the Tambopata River. The Peruvian government titled it indigenous territory in 1976. The land is communally owned by ~150 families (~500 people) of diverse cultural backgrounds who share legal tenure and title (use rights) to 10,000 hectares of forested land. In 1996, the community entered a 20-year joint venture with a private company to establish the ecotourism lodge Posada Amazonas.

The tourism commons. Infierno's oxbow lakes and portion of the Tambopata River are important shared resources, representing critical habitat for a variety of local needs (agriculture, fishing, transportation of goods and people, washing, bathing) and vital habitat for countless plant and animal species used for subsistence, hunting, commercial exploitation *and* ecotourism; the highly endangered giant otters as well as caimans and wading birds are particularly valuable for ecotourism.

The ecotourist lodge was built in a 2,000 hectare reserve – that was expanded to 3,000 hectares following the ecotourism venture decision – where locals had maintained a forest garden of medicinal plants and trees, and built a center for traditional healing and the revitalization of cultural heritage. The reserve is a protected commons; hunting, timber harvesting and farming are prohibited.

Threats. This long-established community is threatened by the advent of tourism and the construction of the Inter-Oceanic Highway as new settlers claim its territory to undertake commercial activities (logging, gold mining, ranching, coca cultivation, wildlife trafficking).

Governance. A community-based, co-management scheme was adopted. State and non-state actors – the local community, the government, international aid agencies and conservation organizations, environmental NGOs, and others – jointly manage the commons. Nonlocals support investment, provide training in conservation, leadership, micro-enterprise and handicrafts and co-manage the commons (e.g. establish codes of conduct for wildlife).

Pros of the scheme. The economic returns from ecotourism (employment and income) provided direct incentives for the locals to co-manage their commons. The benefits were strengthened organization, new skills, clearly established and upheld rules, collective planning and expanded networks of support from outside actors. Community membership is collectively determined (i.e. rules governing inclusion/exclusion of members) and access to and use of the commons, thus containing the subtractability of the commons while safeguarding the community against present and future threats.

Cons of the scheme. The direct economic returns enable expanded individual production and extraction. An individual entrepreneurship spirit threatens to debilitate traditional social relations and institutions. A conservation ethic fosters dualistic thinking – places where resources are used vs. where they are preserved. These constitute endogenous threats to the continued management of the commons stemming from the ecotourism venture.

Current state of research and future research needs

The wise management of CPRs in pursuing any activity is of fundamental importance for the achievement of sustainable development. Tourism could be no exception. In fact, the protection of the CPRs is an integral element of sustainable tourism.

The current state of research on the relationship of tourism to CPRs – the tourism commons – is at a relatively early stage. Some aspects of this relationship have been addressed directly in case studies of nature-based tourism and ecotourism in protected areas. However, the treatment of the TC and their governance remains indirect, limited to particular geographic areas, and partial owing mainly to their narrow definition. The focus of most pertinent work is on tourist attractions, in particular natural resources and landscapes, as the dominant view equates the CPRs with the natural environment. Landscapes are treated rather vaguely, the emphasis being mostly on their visual and material elements. The broader geographical, socio-economic and historical context and dynamics of host areas is little touched upon. Tourists are prioritized over all other potential users. Overall, the literature has addressed selected forms of tourism and selected elements of the TC, usually in isolation from other elements on the same and across levels.

Future research is confronted with a rich repertoire of theoretical, methodological and empirical subjects. All elements of the TC should be explored (Figure 6.1), not individually but in their context-specific combinations. The definition of tourist attraction *sensu* Jafari (1982) has to open up to new elements and activities brought about by socio-economic and technological change. The intangible elements of the TC, the associated threats and their relationships with the tangible elements demand greater attention. Common "bads" (eyesores, polluters, etc.), a special case of CPRs, should be studied also because they subtly influence the tourist product.

The rich variety of types and forms of tourism should be analyzed together with the related CPRs to support effective governance in host areas. The study of urban and rural tourism commons should be prioritized given the rapid development of tourism in these highly heterogeneous settings. Moreover, studies of the TC should better integrate the role of locals and non-tourist actors, from all spatial levels, and of non-tourist activities because they often produce more serious changes to the commons than does tourism.

The dynamics of the TC deserves closer examination because numerous forces contribute to their formation and change in contemporary turbulent environments. Of particular interest are the *de facto* TC that emerges from a gradual assertion of rights on resources by tourism-related interests. More case studies of the broad worldwide variety of the TC should be undertaken.

The institutional arrangements employed in various geographic settings and tourism situations for the governance of the TC should receive particular attention. The effectiveness of variants of adaptive governance should be systematically assessed from the perspective of promoting sustainable tourism. The contribution of ethics in general and of environmental ethics in particular may be best studied in this context.

Lastly, research on the tourism commons should be integrated with sustainable tourism research as the two are inseparable. The latter cannot be meaningfully examined without explicitly acknowledging the former. What is more crucial, however, is that integrated research adopts the complexity paradigm to meaningfully analyze tourism development that invariably involves diverse users and resources, multiple uses in dynamic environments shaped by environmental and socio-economic forces operating at multiple spatial and temporal scales.

Key Reading

Briassoulis, H. (2002) 'Sustainable tourism and the question of the commons', *Annals of Tourism Research*, 19: 1065–85.

Healy, R.G. (1994) 'The "common pool" problem in tourism landscapes', *Annals of Tourism Research*, 21: 596–611.

Holden, A. (2005) 'Achieving a sustainable relationship between common pool resources and tourism: The role of environmental ethics', *Journal of Sustainable Tourism*, 13: 339–52.

Ostrom, E. (1990) *Governing the Commons: The Evolution of Institutions of Collective Action*, Cambridge, MA: Cambridge University Press.

References

Agrawal, A. (2001) 'Common property institutions and sustainable governance of resources', *World Development*, 29: 1649–72.

—— (2002) 'Common resources and institutional sustainability', in E. Ostrom, T. Dietz, N. Dolsak, P. Stern, S. Stonich and E. Weber (eds) *The Drama of the Commons, Committee on the Human Dimensions of Global Change*, Washington DC: National Academy Press.

Aristotle (1993) *Politics*, Athens: Odysseas Chatzopoulos Publications (in Greek).

Bramwell, B. and Lane, B. (eds) (2000) *Tourism Collaboration and Partnerships: Politics, Practice and Sustainability*, Clevedon: Channel View Publications.

—— (2011) *Tourism Governance: Critical Perspectives on Governance and Sustainability*, London: Routledge.

Briassoulis, H. (2000) 'Tourism and the environment', in H. Briassoulis and J. van der Straaten (eds) *Tourism and the Environment: Regional, Economic, Cultural and Policy Issues*, Dordrecht: Kluwer Academic Publishers

—— (2002) 'Sustainable tourism and the question of the commons', *Annals of Tourism Research*, 19: 1065–85.

—— (2008) *Governing Desertification in Mediterranean Europe: The Challenge of EPI from the International to the National Level*, EPIGOV Paper No. 38, Berlin: Ecologic.

Bromley, D.W. (1991) *Environment and Economy*, Cambridge, MA: Blackwell Publishers.

Clapp, T.L. and Meyer, P.B. (2000) *Managing the Urban Commons: Applying Common Property Frameworks to Urban Environmental Quality*, paper presented at the 8th IASCP Conference, Bloomington, Indiana, May–June 2000.

Folke, C., Hahn, T., Olsson P. and Norberg, J. (2005) 'Adaptive governance of social-ecological systems', *Annual Review of Environment and Resources*, 30: 441–73.

Hall, C.M. (2011) 'A typology of governance and its implications for tourism policy analysis', *Journal of Sustainable Tourism*, 19: 437–57.

Healy, R.G. (1994) 'The "Common Pool" Problem in Tourism Landscapes', *Annals of Tourism Research*, 21: 596–611.

—— (2006) 'The commons problem and Canada's Niagara Falls', *Annals of Tourism Research*, 33: 525–44.

Holden, A. (2005) 'Achieving a sustainable relationship between common pool resources and tourism: The role of environmental ethics', *Journal of Sustainable Tourism*, 13: 339–52.

Jafari, J. (1982) 'The tourism market basket of goods and services', in T.V. Singh, J. Kaur and P.D. Singh (eds) *Studies in Tourism Wildlife Parks Conservation*, New Delhi: Metropolitan Book.

Martens, K. (2007) 'Actors in a fuzzy governance environment', in G. de Roo and G. Porter (eds) *Fuzzy Planning*, Aldershot: Ashgate.

McDonald, J.R. (2009) 'Complexity science: An alternative world view for understanding sustainable tourism development', *Journal of Sustainable Tourism*, 17: 455–71

Moore, S.A., and Rodger, K. (2010) 'Wildlife tourism as a common pool resource issue: Enabling conditions for sustainability governance', *Journal of Sustainable Tourism*, 18: 831–44

Ostrom, E. (1990) *Governing the Commons: The Evolution of Institutions of Collective Action*, Cambridge, MA: Cambridge University Press.

Ostrom, E., Dietz, T., Dolsak, N., Stern, P., Stonich, S. and Weber, E. (eds) (2002) *The Drama of the Commons*, Committee on the Human Dimensions of Global Change. Washington DC: National Academy Press.

Samuelson, P. (1954) 'The pure theory of public expenditure', *Review of Economics and Statistics* 36: 387–89.

Selsky, J.W. and Memon, P.A. (2000) *Emergent Commons: Local Responses in Complex CPR Systems,* paper presented at the 8th IASCP Conference, Bloomington, Indiana, May –June 2000.

Steins, N.A. and Edwards V.M. (1999) 'Platforms for collective action in multiple-use common-pool resources', *Agriculture and Human Values,* 16: 241–55.

Stronza, A.L. (2010) 'Commons management and ecotourism: Ethnographic evidence from the Amazon', *International Journal of the Commons*, 4: 56–77.

United Nations Enviornment Programme (UNEP) and United Nations World Tourism Organization (UNWTO) (2005) *Making Tourism More Sustainable – A Guide for Policy Makers*. Available at: www.earthprint.com/productfocus.php?id=DTI/0592/PA (accessed 30 January 2013).

7

Tourism and human rights

Freya Higgins-Desbiolles and Kyle Powys Whyte

Human rights are rights inherent to all human beings.

Neoliberalism An extreme political-economic philosophy whose advocates support economic liberalization, free trade, marketization, privatization, deregulation, and reducing the size of the public sector to enable the private sector to take on a more active role in the economy including activities that had formally been the role of the state.

NGOs Non-government organizations.

Universal Declaration on the Rights of Indigenous Peoples (2007) The rights enumerated include the right to self-determination, the right to free, prior and informed consent and participation in decision-making and the right to cultural and intellectual property.

Introduction

Sustainability has become a key concern since its articulation in the Brundtland Report of 1987. Originally, sustainability had a strong environmental focus, particularly from the 1993 Rio Earth Summit on Environment and Development. More recently, social concerns have come to the fore with new campaigns for corporate social responsibility and triple bottom–line reporting (examining the economic, environmental and social impacts of business). However, the social concerns in tourism are often limited. Sustainability discourse has not offered a more macro perspective on the social impacts of tourism. Higgins-Desbiolles and Blanchard have argued that "we must consider tourism in the context of human rights and social justice" (2010: 45). A human rights perspective gives us this more macro approach and is essential for thinking meaningfully about sustainability.

Human rights emerged following the world wars of the twentieth century and are most fully articulated in the Universal Declaration of Human Rights of 1948 (UDHR), the International Covenant on Civil and Political Rights and the International Covenant on Economic, Social and Cultural Rights. Recognition of human rights is a relatively recent phenomenon and the meaning of the term is not uncontested, but most broadly "human rights are rights inherent to all human beings" (United Nations Human Rights n.d.). One articulation claims "at their core, human rights are tools for empowering and providing security to individuals" (Gibney 2003: 5). In the UDHR, rights are essential to life (right to life, security), human development (right to education, work) and a more intangible well-being (the right to freedom of association, to freely participate in the cultural life of the community, to enjoy the arts). One might not anticipate a "right to tourism" in the UDHR, but arguably it is. An implicit right to tourism may be found in Art. 13, s 2 which states "everyone has the right to leave any country, including his [sic] own, and to return to his [sic] country" and in Art. 24 which claims "everyone has the right to rest and leisure, including reasonable limitation of working hours and periodic holidays with pay."

Intuitively we might expect a possible hierarchy where some rights are more essential than others, but it is important to note that the United Nations asserts that all rights in the UDHR "…are all interrelated, interdependent and indivisible" (United Nations Human Rights n.d.). Despite this clear declaration of indivisibility, economic, social and cultural rights were left to languish as political and civil rights were emphasized in the Cold War contest between East and West. With decolonization in the 1960s, there was hope that Art. 28, with its promise of a "social and international order in which the [UDHR] rights and freedoms…could be fully realized," would result in a "new international economic order" capable of addressing the inequity and injustice between North and South. However, with the hegemony of neoliberalism from the 1980s, economic, social and culture rights hold little traction:

> Notions of citizenship have been reconfigured as the values, norms and language of market rationality become embedded. This has clear implications for many social and economic rights as they are no longer the responsibility of the state but have become commodities available for purchase by individual citizens in the marketplace
>
> *(Gideon 2006: 1280).*

It is in such a context that any discussions of tourism and human rights must be situated. In fact, it could be argued that discourses on tourism were undergoing similar dynamics. Prior to the advent of neoliberalism, there was a stream of tourism analysis which focused on the social capacities of tourism. But Higgins-Desbiolles has argued that now "the mantra that tourism is an 'industry' that is subject only to the rules of the marketplace has been repeated so frequently that to think otherwise is almost viewed as non-sensical" (Higgins-Desbiolles 2006: 1195).

Neoliberal practices pressure communities to enter the market economy on unfair and unsustainable terms. Communities are faced with intolerable choices between ecological integrity, social and community well-being and the need for economic growth as their subsistence capabilities are daily undermined with entry into the global marketplace. Tourism is presented as the best development option for many communities in this scenario, but a host of human rights issues often follow, including dispossession, displacement, commodification of culture, and pollution of all types. Neoliberalism's insistence on unfettered growth is unsustainable, and corporatized tourism plays a significant role; violation of the human rights of the people in the places incorporated is not an unfortunate side effect, but a direct result of neoliberal ideology.

We will survey the key issues associated with the intersection of tourism and human rights and analyze tourism's significance in the attainment of more sustainable futures.

Tourism as a violator of human rights

Both non-government organizations (NGOs) and academia have made it clear that tourism is frequently responsible for human rights violations. While tourism is often touted as a more benign economic development option than industrial production, mining or logging, it in fact brings with it numerous negative impacts that result in the violation of the basic human rights of the local population. The most advanced work on human rights issues in tourism has come from the NGO sector (see Table 7.1).

First and foremost is the displacement and dispossession of local people in places of touristic development. Mowforth and Munt (2003), for example, note that

> of all the problems experienced by local communities facing tourism development schemes, the most harrowing involve accounts of people being displaced. Such events normally reflect the distribution of power around the activity of tourism and highlight the powerlessness of many local communities.
>
> *(Mowforth & Munt 2003: 236–37)*

Tourism is particularly guilty of causing dispossession because of the tourism industry's insatiable appetite for attractive environments which need to be free of the unattractive poor so that tourists can enjoy their holidays undisturbed. Perhaps the worst instance most recently documented is the dispossession that followed in the wake of the 2004 Asian tsunami when some coastal communities were prevented from returning to their homes ostensibly for their future safety but in fact for coastal resort development, as alleged by the NGO Tourism Concern (2005).

Tourism also contributes to many other human rights violations, including violation of workers' rights, over-exploitation of vital resources, pollution of all kinds, commodification and damage of cultural treasures, abuse of vulnerable populations including women and children, particularly through sex tourism, and violations of the right to self-determination and free, prior and informed consent. One of the most extreme examples, exposed in 2008, is the case of the Kayan people's struggle to break out of Thailand's "human zoo" as tourists come to see their women with their "long necks." As one tourism operator claimed "It is the No. 1 attraction in this area. It's why tourists come here" (The Age 2008). As NGO EQUATIONS (2008: 5) states "tourism behaves as if it has nothing to do with the contexts and realities of the places it locates itself in…[and leaves] a trail of human rights violations that tourism brochures, promoters and policy-makers refuse to face up to."

The tourism industry debated how far it should go in its observance of human rights imperatives with the "Boycott Burma" campaign that was initiated when the military government declared 1996 the "Visit Myanmar (Burma) Year." This was closely followed by Aung San Suu Kyi's plea for visitors to stay away until democracy was restored (Mowforth & Munt 2003: 289–93). The debate saw industry leaders Tony and Maureen Wheeler of Lonely Planet Publications pitted against the NGOs Burma Campaign UK and Tourism Concern about the continued production of the Lonely Planet travel guidebook to Burma (Mowforth & Munt 2003). But the issue involved travel agencies, consumers and activists around the world as the effectiveness and ethics of a travel boycott were debated (with Intrepid Travel deciding to stop tours as a result). This was a complex debate, but essentially it highlighted that human rights issues are pertinent to tourism and it also introduced the idea that tourists could be facilitators of respect for human rights as tools of "citizen diplomacy" (Hudson 2007).

Table 7.1 Some indicative NGOs concerned with human rights issues in tourism

NGO	Geographic focus	Focus of work
Ecumenical Coalition on Tourism (defunct 2012)	International – based in Chiang Mai, Thailand	Advocacy for developing nation communities and their rights
Tourism Concern	Developing countries where UK public travels – UK based	Works to ensure tourism always benefits the local people – focus on educating government, industry and travellers
TEN (Tourism European/Ecumenical Network)	Umbrella organization of 12 European NGOs	Effects of tourism on people in developing countries
Arkbeitskreis Tourismus & Entwicklung (AKTE)	Developing countries – based in Switzerland	Impacts of tourism on developing countries
ECPAT (End Child Prostitution)	International – based in Bangkok (there are affiliated national chapters in various countries)	Opposing all forms of sexual exploitation of children (including through tourism)
Tourism Concern Gambia	The Gambia	Advocates tourism that benefits the local people of the Gambia
Fair Trade in Tourism in South Africa	South Africa	Encourages the tourism industry to adopt fair trade principles in tourism and respect human rights
Global Exchange – Reality Tours	International – based in USA	Using reality tours for human rights education and activism
Alternative Tourism Group of Palestine	Palestine	Offers critical insights into the history, culture and politics of Palestine and its complex relationship with Israel through justice tours
Responsible Tourism Network (defunct 2006)	Australia	Fostered responsible tourism awareness in tourism industry and tourists
Community Aid Abroad Tours (defunct 2006)	Developing countries – Australian based	Offered responsible tour experiences for creating sustainable development opportunities for partner communities
EQUATIONS	India	Offers research, campaign and advocacy on the social, cultural, economic and environmental impact of tourism on local communities
Kerala Tourism Watch	Kerala, India	Responds to the threats posed by exploitative tourism practices in Kerala that damage people's livelihood and cause negative impacts that the Government is unable to control
Tourism Interventions & Monitoring Team (TIM-Team)	International – based in Bangkok	An independent research and monitoring initiative to provide information and to engage in campaigns for social and ecological justice in tourism and development
International Porter Protection Group	International	Advocating rights of porters to adequate pay and working conditions

Tourism, human rights and NGOs

The most advanced work on addressing human rights issues in tourism has come from the NGO sector. This is due to the fact that many NGOs have either sprung from the grassroots campaigns on tourism (e.g. EQUATIONS) or have worked closely with grassroots communities facing damage from tourism (e.g. Tourism Concern). Here we offer a brief survey of this contribution.

NGO activism has been present since at least the 1980s and has laid the foundations for a human rights approach to tourism which has yet to be taken up. For instance, European NGOs issued the Wijgmaal-Louvain Declaration in 1984 declaring tourism should be measured by its contribution to "just, participatory and sustainable societies."

More recently, NGOs have offered important publications on human rights and tourism. For instance, Tourism Concern's *Putting Tourism to Rights* (2009) outlined the ways in which tourism violates the human rights of host communities. The organization also developed a briefing document calling for "a human rights approach in tourism" which offered specific recommendations for the UN Human Rights Council, the UN World Tourism Organization (UNWTO), the European Union, governments of tourist sending and receiving countries, tourism and hospitality agencies, NGOs and tourists (Tourism Watch-EED n.d.).

In 2011, six NGOs called on the UNWTO to enable poor communities negatively affected by tourism to have full access to UNWTO processes as a means to address human rights violations in tourism development (Tourism Watch 2011). Currently, the UNWTO is much more accessible to large tourism transnationals who are able to afford its membership fees and access its processes. (As Bianchi (n.d.) noted "the UNWTO is one of the few UN agencies that essentially represents an industry.")

Another intervention by NGOs has tackled the injustice and human rights violations that are set to arise from human-induced global climate change. Seven tourism NGOs issued a declaration entitled "Last call to Durban – beyond numbers: A call for social, economic and climate justice in tourism" in 2011 in conjunction with the global Climate Change Conference convened in Durban, South Africa ("Last call to Durban" 2011). In this six-page document, these NGOs directly challenged the tourism industry's position of opposing a mandatory reduction in aviation's greenhouse emissions, arguing tourism's vital contribution to poverty alleviation in developing countries. These NGOs argued this was a strategy for the industry to protect its own business interests. Demonstrating that developing countries actually receive little of the benefits of tourism while potentially suffering grave consequences from climate change, these NGOs sought binding regulations of emissions from international transport and the creation of funds for impact mitigation. They advocated "a people-centred and human rights-based approach" to these issues ("Last call to Durban" 2011).

However, it is important to note that not all communities suffering human rights abuses through tourism have equal access to NGOs and their advocacy capacities (Bob 2002). Despite their positive record on human rights in tourism, it would be a mistake to view all work by NGOs as positive and supportive of community rights – some NGOs can have a patronizing, even neo-colonial, approach. It is also evident from our research that there is a potential rift between northern and southern NGOs as their constituencies, backgrounds and contexts mean that they can disagree significantly on agenda setting.

Academic insights

Academic analysis of human rights in the tourism field is minimal. Smith and Duffy (2003) outlined debates on human rights and commented briefly on their relevance to the tourism domain. One key debate concerns whether human rights are problematic because they are based on "a particularly bourgeois conception of that isolated, autonomous and propertied individual so central to capitalist enterprise" (Smith & Duffy 2003: 81). Regarding tourism, this conception also supports neoliberal tourism development.

Higgins-Desbiolles and Blanchard (2010) reviewed the more sensitive niches of alternative tourism that are alleged to contribute to better social impacts of tourism, including peace through tourism, pro-poor tourism and social tourism. They found that, due to the structural injustices and inequalities of tourism under a neoliberal paradigm, tourism proves inadequate to meeting social and welfare objectives and they suggest that only "justice tourism" can transform tourism's capacity to meet human needs through tourism.

Cole and Eriksson (2010) have made arguably the most focused exposition on tourism and human rights in the tourism literature to date. However, their examination was limited to talking about human rights issues arising from tourists originating from the developed countries and using the facilitation of the transnational corporations (TNCs) to enjoy cheap travel to developing countries. They argued that this form of travel is based on exploitative and extractive practices which bring such human rights violations as abuse of labor, resource exploitation and dispossession (Cole & Eriksson 2010). These authors also acknowledged that while human rights enforcement is typically the remit of the state, weak governance, together with corporate power, results in poor enforcement in reality. They chose to present "a business case for human rights considerations" arguing that new consumer movements for ethical consumption meant business must now engage with social and environmental responsibility and respect human rights (Cole & Eriksson 2010: 120–21).

These last two chapters point to very different approaches. The work by Cole and Eriksson (2010) suggests working with the tourism industry to reform it while the work of Higgins-Desbiolles and Blanchard (2010) identifies a possible segment of tourism that represents a paradigm shift toward tourism grounded in justice and human rights instead of neoliberal aspirations.

Indigenous rights and tourism

Many indigenous peoples have suffered from tourism. For instance, EQUATIONS, a campaigning NGO based in India, has long advocated for the rights of the indigenous peoples of India, the Adivasis (e.g. EQUATIONS 2007). They identified the heart of the issue:

> The significance of their [adivasi] sustainable subsistence economy in the midst of a profit-oriented economy is not recognised in the political discourse. Rather, the negative stereotyping of the sustainable subsistence economy of adivasi societies is based on the wrong premise that the production of surplus is more progressive than the social reproduction in co-existence with nature.
>
> *(EQUATIONS 2007: 27)*

Johnston's (2006) book *Is the Sacred for Sale?* critiqued the rhetoric that ecotourism goals are more symbiotic with indigenous interests. The problems she identified included a corporatized form of ecotourism where lucrative profits are sought, the neo-colonial nature of international fora like the Convention on Biological Diversity where indigenous communities are pressured into ecotourism for international conservation goals, the exploitation of our market system where indigenous cultures provide "local colour" for a voracious cultural-ecotourism industry, and the inappropriate development models which work to assimilate indigenous peoples into an alien and detrimental system (Johnston 2006). Powys Whyte (2010) offered an analysis of indigenous tourism which suggested "even when the intentions behind the practices are caring, love, concern for humanity," exploitation may result in the absence of direct and "meaningful participation" and "expression of difference" by the local community in the tourism planning process (Powys Whyte 2010: 87–89). Johnston's work similarly demanded self-determination for indigenous communities and cautioned on the consequences if we allow the non-indigenous paradigm of development to continue.

This right to self-determination is reinforced with the new indigenous rights regime brought by the Universal Declaration on the Rights of Indigenous Peoples which in 2007 was endorsed by an overwhelming majority of the world's nations. This brings a special rights agenda that should impact the conduct of tourism and help shield indigenous peoples from some of the worst exploitation and damages of tourism. The rights enumerated include the right to self-determination, the right to free, prior and informed consent and participation in decision-making and the right to cultural and intellectual property.

There have also been gatherings of indigenous peoples in recent decades and interventions in tourism and development that have reinforced wider initiatives resisting neoliberalism. For instance, the *Kimberley Declaration* from the International Indigenous Peoples Summit on Sustainable Development in 2002 declared:

> Indigenous Peoples, our lands and territories are not objects of tourism development. We have rights and responsibilities towards our lands and territories. We are responsible to defend our lands, territories and indigenous peoples against tourism exploitation by governments, development agencies, private enterprises, NGOs, and individuals…we urge governments to recognize, accept, support and invest in pastoralism and hunting-gathering as viable and sustainable economic systems.
>
> *(Kimberley Declaration 2002)*

Other communities that adhere to collective rights have similar difficulties. This is well illustrated by the Gullah people's experiences in the United States (see case study).

Case Study

The Gullah people of the USA and tourism dispossession

The Gullah Islands are located on the eastern coast of the US spanning from North Carolina to Florida. They are home to a unique African-American history and culture. The Gullah people are descendants of the African slaves brought to the islands to harvest rice and indigo. After the Civil War, although freed African-Americans were promised land grants, widespread Southern white resistance meant this was poorly implemented. However, some Gullah descendants were able to purchase land in the area, even that they had previously cultivated as slaves. Because the Gullah Islands were not considered favorable for agricultural cultivation, the Gullah people were left in their relatively autonomous communities for almost a century.

The Gullah has a communal system of land ownership called heirs' property. Property is not willed, but rather shared collectively through an informal arrangement where every descendant shares ownership of the land. Prior to the arrival of wealthy northerners in search of a vacation destination, this system of ownership caused little conflict and the Gullah was able to survive.

In the 1950s "the outside world discovered the islands and started paying millions to own them" (Williams 1993). While it is usually more difficult to acquire large plots of land from multiple owners, it has proved possible for the Gullah to lose their land through tactics where one claimant agrees to sell and this forces a partition. Gullah who actually reside on their lands find themselves unable to obtain loans on this form of title and so cannot buy out the claimants forcing the partition. Partition proceedings often lead to a public auction of the land, which allows developers to acquire it at minimal cost, far below the actual value of the land but much higher than the residents can afford.

Once these developers have entered their community and acquired land near theirs, the Gullah became vulnerable. Golf courses, retirement communities, shopping centers and leisure developments raise the price of land; this subsequently results in an increase in taxes, which is beyond the level of affordability for residents who have survived on subsistence farming and fishing for 100 years or more. The result has been extensive land loss.

As tourism expanded worldwide due to decreasing travel costs in the 1950s, a bridge was built linking Hilton Head Island to the mainland. This brought an influx of tourists, retirees and new residents to the lands of the Gullah community, even on islands without bridges (Williams 1993). Hilton Head serves as a good example of what has occurred in all but a few of the islands since that period. There are very few Gullah on Hilton Head; many left to find better work; others have sold or were forced to sell their property. Few markers in the region indicate the rich African-American history that exists there; instead gates have emerged everywhere to protect the communities of newcomers (Williams 1993).

Adapted from: Abiosseh Davis (2009) *Preserving Gullah Land Rights in the Wake of Tourism Expansion*, Center of Concern, Washington, DC. Available at: www.coc.org/files/Gullah%20 Land%20Righs_Abiosseh_Davis.pdf (accessed 22 March 2013).

Copyright © 2009, Center of Concern. Used with permission.

The impact of neoliberalism

Understanding the impact of tourism on human rights in communities receiving tourists is not possible without contextualization in the dynamics of an economy driven by neoliberal principles. Current neoliberal economics presses developing countries into the market system as a precondition of gaining access to funds and support from international financial institutions. Tourism enters this equation as one of the areas of competitive advantage that developing countries hold, because of their exotic cultures and "untouched" environment. The tourism approach adopted under neoliberal ideology is one that puts "tourism first" rather than "development first" (Burns 1999). The "tourism first" approach is "wholly framed by the development and advancement of the industry with national development as its [possible] byproduct" (Burns 1999: 336); its focus is developing airports, hotels and resorts – growing the tourism sector with little thought for the local community. Their rights are left to the government to protect. But these very governments are acquiescent as their country is absorbed into the global market economy of the terms of neoliberal diktats. These include ending protectionism of the home economy, opening up to foreign investments and freeing up regulatory environments.

Harvey (2005) has identified a key aspect of neoliberalism as capitalist accumulation by dispossession. People are forced from subsistence living; they are required to give up lucrative land and become the "disposable workers" of neoliberal economics as the Western model of development requires. Locals are forced into low paid, insecure, seasonal tourism jobs as their subsistence capabilities are undermined. People are also dispossessed as desirable land is made available for tourism development, including the coasts, CBDs, areas of natural beauty and conservation. Simultaneously legislation is watered down as neoliberalism guts governmental regulatory powers and the capacity for taxation. Particularly damaging is the reduction in workers' rights and the weakening of environmental protection mechanisms. These dynamics are not limited to the developing world; all communities are now so many beggars at the door of the market.

In summary, instead of serving their people, governments become agents of capital. Because in our current system, human rights enforcement depends on the state, we find a wholly inadequate protection system. This is why NGOs have stepped into this vacuum to advocate for impacted peoples, but their capacities are limited. In such a context, people become commodity labor and environments become commodified tourism resources. As a result, we are facing impending social and environmental crises because this system is wholly unsustainable (Sklair 2002; Harvey 2005). This is a catalyst to a global struggle for the future and tourism is in the fray.

Tourism, human rights and global transformations

Numerous analysts have argued the contemporary era features a contestation over what form globalization should take (e.g. Sklair 2002; Harvey 2005). Falk argued conceptualizations of human rights are at the center (2002: 69–70) and identified a "globalization from above" which is pushed by the neoliberal forces of the USA, international organizations such as the World Trade Organization and the World Bank, and is supported by mainstream international human rights bodies such as Amnesty International, and which discusses human rights in terms of civil and political rights. This is countered by a "globalization from below" which offers a "subaltern discourse on human rights…which insist upon a broader conception of human rights, extending to, if not focusing upon, economic, social, and cultural concerns" (Falk 2002: 69).

In tourism, there is a phenomenon of human rights education through tourism which could be viewed as part of this "subaltern" movement. The best example of this is the human rights NGO Global Exchange (GX) and its use of "reality tours" for "human rights education, citizen diplomacy, fostering just relationships and solidarity activism" (Higgins-Desbiolles 2010: 201). GX claims: "Global Exchange Reality Tours has a vision that meaningful, socially responsible travel can and does, change the world. By offering experiential educational tours, Reality Tours has connected people to issues, issues to movements, and movements to social change" (GX n.d).

In fact, tourism NGOs have participated in the larger struggle against the injustice of neoliberalism in gatherings like the World Social Forum (WSF). As Higgins-Desbiolles reported:

> protest at a global level has…emerged at the WSF convened in Mumbai, India, in 2004. At this meeting, tourism was put on the agenda of the WSF for the first time as a Global

Summit on Tourism was held. The theme was "Who really benefits from tourism?" The summit issued a call to "democratise tourism". One NGO participant, the ECOT called for a tourism that is "pro-people". Attendees at the meeting released a statement of concern, which voiced similar concerns to the opponents of capitalist globalisation, and formed a Tourism Interventions Group.

(Higgins-Desbiolles 2008: 357)

The most recent WSF was convened in Tunisia in March 2013 and representatives of tourism NGOs from around the world again met to ensure that tourism is recognized as a human rights and justice issue in such global fora and is treated as seriously as other issues confronting the global community.

Conclusion

Analyses of human rights issues in tourism have previously tended to focus on specific issues such as sex tourism or human rights abuses in one location. This analysis suggests that in order to understand the human rights effects of tourism, it is important to take a structural view. In terms of tourism, we would argue that the key issue is consent. In tourism discourse, the local population is designated the "host community" but this is a serious misnomer because it implies a consent to host which is often not the case; it is often governments and tourism business interests which bring in the tourists without the consent of the local populations who must live with the consequences. This is a key outcome of the dynamics of neoliberalism and the corporatized tourism that accompanies it; this is also the cornerstone of human rights abuse in tourism.

To date, tourism discourse has been centered on the needs of the tourists and the interests of the industry. A human rights perspective would require us to shift to a "host" community-centered approach. This is justified by the fact that tourists already have a home to retreat to when the locals do not. It is the locals who know their place best and its carrying capacity, it is they who must live with the consequences of their choices and it is they who have the real right to host visitors. Neoliberalism has diverted us from these foundations by usurping the rights of the local people for an elite minority to expropriate and benefit from their human and ecological resources. The human rights perspective that we offer here provides a path towards sustainability. We would argue that tourism could be turned on its head if such an approach were adopted.

In closing, it is appropriate to return to the UDHR. Article 25(1) states: "everyone has a right to a standard of well-being of himself [sic] and of his [sic] family, including food, clothing, housing and medical care and necessary social services, and the right to security in the event of unemployment, sickness, disability, widowhood, old age or other lack of livelihood in circumstances beyond his control." Article 28 declares: "Everyone is entitled to a social and international order in which the rights and freedoms set forth in this Declaration can be fully realized." We need to return to these words and envision a more just order than the market order we currently accept. Human rights are not to be bought by consumers in the marketplace, but are instead the bonds of our international community. Humanizing tourism through respect for human rights is our part to play in creating a just and sustainable international order.

Key Reading:

- Cole, S. and Eriksson, J. (2010) 'Tourism and human rights', in S. Cole and N. Morgan (eds) *Tourism and Inequality: Problems and Prospects*, Wallingford, UK: CABI.
- EQUATIONS (2008) *Who Really Benefits from Tourism?* Bangalore: EQUATIONS.
- Higgins-Desbiolles, F. and Blanchard, L. (2010) 'Challenging peace through tourism: Placing tourism in the context of human rights, justice & peace', in O. Moufakkir and I. Kelly (eds) *Tourism Progress and Peace*, Wallingford: CABI.
- Johnston, A. (2006) *Is the scared for sale? Tourism and Indigenous peoples*, London: Earthscan.
- Tourism Concern (2009) *Putting tourism to rights: A challenge to human rights abuses in the tourism industry*, London: Tourism Concern.

References

The Age (2008, 12 January) *Burma's Long-Neck Women Struggle to Break Out of Thailand's "Human Zoo"*. Available at: www.theage.com.au/articles/2008/01/11/1199988589409.html (accessed 22 March 2013).

Bianchi, R. (n.d.) *Interview with Ecoclub*. Available at: http://ecoclub.com/articles/interviews/702-raoul-bianchi (accessed 23 March 2013).

Bob, C. (2002) 'Globalisation and the social construction of human rights campaigns', in A. Brysk (ed.) *Globalization and Human Rights*, Berkeley: University of California Press.

Burns, P. (1999) 'Paradoxes in planning: Tourism elitism or brutalism?', *Annals of Tourism Research*, 26: 329–48.

Cole, S. and Eriksson, J. (2010) 'Tourism and human rights', in S. Cole and N. Morgan (eds) *Tourism and Inequality: Problems and Prospects*, Wallingford, UK: CABI.

Falk, R. (2002) 'Interpreting the interaction of global markets and human rights', in A. Brysk (ed.) *Globalization and Human Rights*, Berkeley: University of California Press.

EQUATIONS (2007) *This is Our Homeland: A Collection of Essays on the Betrayal of Adivasi Rights in India*, Bangalore: EQUATIONS.

—— (2008) *Who Really Benefits from Tourism?* Bangalore: EQUATIONS.

Gibney, M.J. (2003) 'Introduction', in M.J. Gibney (ed.) *Globalizing Rights*, Oxford: Oxford University Press.

Gideon, J. (2006) 'Accessing economic and social rights under neoliberalism: Gender and rights in Chile', *Third World Quarterly*, 27: 1269–83.

Global Exchange (n.d.) *Reality Tours*. Available at: www.globalexchange.org/tours/ (accessed 6 March 2013).

Harvey, D. (2005) *A Brief History of Neoliberalism*, Oxford: Oxford University Press.

Higgins-Desbiolles, F. (2006) 'More than an "industry": The forgotten power of tourism as a social force', *Tourism Management*, 27: 1192–1208.

—— (2008) 'Justice tourism and alternative globalisation', *Journal of Sustainable Tourism*, 16: 345–64.

—— (2010) 'Justifying tourism: Justice through tourism', in S. Cole and N. Morgan (eds) *Tourism and Inequality: Problems and Prospects*, Wallingford: CABI.

Higgins-Desbiolles, F. and Blanchard, L. (2010) 'Challenging peace through tourism: Placing tourism in the context of human rights, justice & peace', in O. Moufakkir and I. Kelly (eds) *Tourism Progress and Peace*, Wallingford: CABI.

Hudson, S. (2007) 'To go or not to go? Ethical perspectives on tourism in an "outpost of tyranny"', *Journal of Business Ethics*, 76: 385–96.

Johnston, A. (2006) *Is the Sacred for Sale? Tourism and Indigenous Peoples*, London: Earthscan.

Kimberley Declaration (2002) *International Indigenous Peoples Summit on Sustainable Development*. Available at: www.tebtebba.org/index.php/all-resources/category/17-rio-10-world-summit-on-sustainable-development (accessed 22 March 2013).

Last call to Durban (2011) "Last call to Durban" Available at: www.fairtourismsa.org.za/mediareleases/LAST%20CALL%20TO%20DURBAN_COP%2017_position%20paper_climate%20justice_tourism.pdf (accessed 22 March 2013).

Mowforth, M. and Munt, I. (2003) *Tourism and Sustainability: New Tourism in the Third World,* 2nd edn, London: Routledge.

Sklair, L. (2002) *Globalization: Capitalism and its Alternatives,* Oxford: Blackwell.

Smith, M. and Duffy, R. (2003) *The Ethics of Tourism Development,* London: Routledge.

Tourism Concern (2005) *Post-tsunami Reconstruction and Tourism: A Second Disaster?* London: Tourism Concern. Available at: www.naomiklein.org/files/resources/pdfs/tourism-concern-tsunami-report.pdf (accessed 22 March 2013).

—— (2009) *Putting Tourism to Rights: A Challenge to Human Rights Abuses in the Tourism Industry,* London: Tourism Concern.

Tourism Watch (2011) *Campaigning Groups Urge UNWTO to Open its Doors.* Available at: www.tourism-watch.de/en/content/campaigning-groups-urge-unwto-open-its-doors (accessed 22 March 2013).

Tourism Watch–EED (n.d.) *Putting Tourism to Rights: A Call for a Human Rights Approach in Tourism.* Available at: www.tourism-watch.de/files/eed_tourism_human_rights_shortversion_2011_en.pdf (accessed 22 March 2013).

United Nations Human Rights (n.d.) *What Are Human Rights?* Available at: www.ohchr.org/EN/Issues/Pages/WhatareHumanRights.aspx (accessed 11 March 2013).

Whyte, K.P. (2010) 'An environmental justice framework for indigenous tourism', *Environmental Philosophy,* 7: 75–92.

Williams, P. (1993) 'Gullah: A vanishing culture', *Charlotte Observer,* 7 February 1993.

8

Ethics in tourism

Georgette Leah Burns

Ethics comes from the Greek word "ethos" and is concerned with answering the question of how to act in order to do good (Fennell 2009: 212).

Utilitarianism, concerned with achieving the greatest happiness for the greatest number, is a moral theory developed in the late eighteenth century (Mill 1863; Bentham 1948). Discussions on the rights and wrongs of tourism are most commonly based in utilitarian arguments (Smith 2009: 621).

Instrumentalism is based on the concept of an extrinsic value and states that the value of an object or animal is determined by its use to humans. It is the opposite to the concept of an intrinsic value, which states that an object or animal has value in and of itself (i.e. the value is independent of its use to humans).

Anthropocentrism, or a human-centered approach, is the dominant ideological justification for most ethical approaches to tourism.

Ecocentrism shifts ethical focus to the environment, and ecosystems and non-humans contained within it. Humans are recognized as a part of, rather than central to, the wider system.

Introduction

The wafer thin air is numbingly cold, the sky is crystal clear and the scenery is stunningly beautiful. Your boots crunch against the snow as you close your eyes against its blinding glare. Following a line of trekkers up the side of Mt Everest you pass another dead body, and walk on...

Ethical considerations in tourism are a potential minefield: simultaneously explaining why understanding them is crucial and why many stakeholders might wish to avoid confronting them. Ethical issues are, however, increasingly a focus in many academic disciplines and applied practices, and tourism is no exception. In a large and multifaceted field such as tourism, ethics are, or should be, integral to aspects of it. Yet, as Macbeth (2006: 963) notes, "dominant paradigms in tourism development and theory do not acknowledge ethics and values." He attributes this to the dominance of a positivistic scientific paradigm that upholds "the myth of objectivity" (Macbeth 2006: 963). Fennell (2009: 211) expresses surprise at the marginal willingness of researchers to explore ethics in tourism. That this needs to change becomes increasingly more obvious as the tourism community recognizes that tourism cannot be free of ethics (Smith 2009: 619).

This chapter provides a review of research on ethics in tourism, commencing with a brief outline of the history of scholarly engagement with ethics in the field of tourism studies. It is not possible, nor is it the intention, to cover all types of ethical dilemmas in all types of tourism. Instead, a focus on the broad categories of mass versus responsible tourism serves to elucidate some of the major issues relevant to this topic. The chapter concludes by highlighting key current areas of research focus at the interface of ethics and tourism.

Definitions and basic complexities

"Ethics" comes from the Greek word "ethos" and is concerned with answering the question "what should one do in order to be good?" (Fennell 2009: 212; 2006: 54). As the prescriber of human conduct and laws (Holmes 1992), ethics establish rules for distinguishing between conduct that is right and wrong, and its links with morality enable both individuals and groups to establish a shared basis for appropriate action (Miller 1991). As a key constitutive part of any society that helps to structure patterns of shared behavior (Smith & Duffy 2003: 32), ethics are vital because they function to hold society together (Durkheim 1968, 1993). They differ within and between cultures and are a key aspect of any individual reasoning.

The field of tourism ethics is almost impenetrably muddy, and there are many reasons for this. First, ethics are complex. They represent only one of a multitude of possible ways of ascribing value, they are abstract, and in different contexts, different ethics may dominate making what constitutes an ethical relationship inherently difficult to define. Second, tourism is complex. It is a large and multifaceted industry containing many divergent stakeholders, a wide diversity of situations, and encompassing many heterogeneous practices and purposes. Consequently, the relationship between ethics and tourism is extraordinarily complex (Smith 2009: 614).

An ethical value, of "evaluating the moral worth of a thing, action or person" (Smith & Duffy 2003: 9), is just one of many different ways we have of valuing the things that are important, or not important, to us. For example, we can also prioritize something for its perceived aesthetic, economic, or religious value. These values are not discrete, they overlap, interrelate and an ethical value is often hard to conceptually separate from others.

Ethical values are vital to everyday lives, yet are less tangible, less measurable, and more abstract than economic values (Smith & Duffy 2003: 5). They lack clarity and objectivity (Hultsman 1995: 554) and, unlike the objects of tourism, ethics cannot be commoditized. Thus, as Smith (2009: 626) notes, there are "few definitive answers in ethics." This contributes significantly to their complexity.

The field of tourism ethics is additionally complicated because each distinct situation will often contain many different and conflicting ethical concerns. Choosing which to prioritize may be unclear. Putting aside the difficulties of multitude, single ethical problems are frequently ambiguous, open to debate along cultural (among many other) lines; thus it is often not possible to find solutions that are uncontested (Bauman 1993). Despite this, ethics are often treated as though they can provide formulae enabling a definitive determination of right or wrong. As Smith (2009: 626) cautions, this is a "fundamental mistake."

Involvement in tourism clearly generates many ethical quandaries (Smith 2009: 615) and, while some of these will become apparent in the examples used in this chapter, the aim is not to examine, or even acknowledge, them all. Instead, having established that the philosophical field of ethics is complicated and the relationship between tourism and ethics extraordinarily complex, the chapter focuses on how research has approached studies about tourism and ethics.

History of scholarly engagement with ethics

Tourism has been responsible for profound socio-economic changes to many communities around the world. In situations where the host and guest cultures differ substantially, this can, and has, led to conflicts over different perceptions of values. It comes as no surprise then that many researchers have focused on these changes in their ethical investigations into tourism.

Ethics were given limited attention in tourism studies until the 1990s (Holden 2003). In 1993, Lea traced the history of environment and development ethics, noting a lack of tourism in this domain. In 1995, Hultsman's literature survey found that the discussion of ethical issues was increasing in frequency, but more likely to be present in journals and conference proceedings than in textbooks. This trend has persisted, with authors such as Fennell (2006) and Smith and Duffy (2003) being notable exceptions. Is it still the case that many texts (e.g. Hall & Lew 2009, and Telfer & Sharpley 2008) focus on impacts rather than ethics?

Fennell's recent review of the field of tourism and ethics notes a "tendency of tourism researchers to examine impacts as the traditional root of ethical issues in tourism" (2006: 1). This is evidenced in the work of Smith and Duffy (2003: 14), for example, who state "the ethical issues that arise in many, if not most, cases of tourism development are closely connected to the socioeconomic effects that development has on the 'host' community."

Not surprisingly, given the initial domination of tourism by Western interests, tourism scholars have most frequently drawn upon Western theories of ethics. The potential contribution of other research approaches and ways of knowing are yet to have a noticeable influence on the field. Western ethics traditionally focused almost exclusively on human relationships, though this began to change in the 1960s as world focus on environmental issues and sustainability grew (e.g. Carson 1962; see also Chapter 1).

Different types of tourism elicit different ethical concerns. Sex tourism raises concerns about the physical wellbeing and exploitation of workers in this industry. This is one example of where ethical considerations overlap with human rights (the focus of Chapter 7). A recent trend toward marketing destinations as "last chance tourism" (Lemelin et al. 2010, Lemelin, Dawson & Stewart 2012) raises concerns about the potential for increased damage to fragile environments (Dawson et al. 2011). It is not possible to focus on all the potential permutations of ethics in tourism research here. Instead, I discuss the study of ethics in regards to the two – very broad – categories of "mass" versus "responsible" tourism as a way of highlighting issues amongst two theoretically polar opposite types. This dichotomy persists in the literature. I follow this with a discussion of some current pivotal works in the field which enables us to see how it has moved on from an early, yet long-lasting, focus on the ethics of impacts.

Ethics and mass tourism

Tourism is essentially an egotistical and hedonistic pursuit, and the much maligned "mass tourism" began in an era when ethical considerations, beyond the satisfaction of the tourist, did not take center stage. Most definitions of tourism from the 1980s and early 1990s have in common the consensus that tourism involves temporarily and voluntarily visiting a place away from home (e.g. Przeclawski 1993: 11; Smith 1989), with tourist motivations based on desire for leisure, notions of escapism and the perceived need for a "break" from daily life (e.g. Lanfant 1993: 75). Defined this way, the tourist is fundamentally concerned with seeking pleasure; pausing to contemplate the ethical issues of their actions may reduce that pleasure.

Traditionally for many, then, there was no concern for the effects on the environment or on different cultures or even of the sustainability of their actions. This initially suited well the purposes of an economically driven industry. Thus, tourists and proponents of the industry were, and in some cases still are, unlikely to willingly engage with an ethics of care.

For many Third World, and so-called "developing" countries, tourism was embraced, perhaps most strongly between the 1960s and the 1980s, as a form of development and optimistically viewed as an answer to their financial problems (Lynn 1992). Tourism seemed a natural and logical path to economic development because it placed an economic value on everything – it commodified and commercialized people, animals, landscapes, cultures and artifacts.

It was under this unspoken (un)ethical, but widely publicized, economic approach that tourism moved in the late 1950s and early 1960s to something done by the masses rather than by the elite few. In its heyday, this led to the types of tourism now known as mass tourism – when infrastructure struggled to keep up with demand in popular tourist destinations and international chains of hotels opened up in more and more destinations. However, scholars soon began to question this growth on many fronts.

A binary separation, based on the notion of classifying tourism as either fundamentally positive or negative (Burns 2004) or as either a "godsend" or an "evil" (Crick 1988: 88), frequently appeared in the 1970s and 1980s literature on mass tourism. A "pro-tourist position", MacCannell (1976: 162) argued, was held by those who saw tourism exclusively as a way of making money, in contrast to the "anti-tourist position" held by those who questioned the value of touristic development for the local people. Observing that economic benefits from tourism often did not reach the host community in large quantities or lead to widespread positive social changes, authors such as Turner and Ash (1975), Mathieson and Wall (1982), and Lea (1988) claimed that, when the industry is not managed by local community members, tourism becomes a form of imperialism. While not writing specially about "ethics," authors such as these began to question the moral grounds upon which tourism development was based. Ultimately, mass tourism came under heavy criticism for being culturally insensitive and damaging to both indigenous communities and the local environment. The demand for alternative forms of tourism was born.

Ethics and responsible tourism

The scholarly move away from a focus solely on the economic positives of tourism to consider social negatives led authors to write of exploitation, commercialization, commodification and consumerism (e.g. Greenwood 1989). This focused debate on social over economic issues as interest grew in forms of tourism that were considered more socially and culturally responsible, better meeting the needs of the host community. The concept of pro-poor tourism, for example, first coined in 1999, explores the use of tourism to assist with poverty reduction (Ashley & Goodwin 2007) thus attempting to combine both social and economic benefits.

Concern with tourism impacts on the environment was a later consideration and paralleled a wider spread interest in ethics. Holden, for example, noted a conservation ethic was emerging (2003) and much needed (2005) but that rationale for it remained limited. This can be linked to the traditionally anthropocentric focus of tourism business and scholarship.

Alternatives to mass tourism are collectively called many things: responsible tourism (Lea 1993), just tourism (Hultsman 1995), and New Moral Tourism (Butcher 2003). Butcher (2003) refers to ecotourism, sustainable tourism, and responsible tourism as the New Moral Tourism because these concepts are associated with the idea that these are more morally aware and responsible forms of tourism. They "define their practices and purposes in contrast to what they regard as the socially and environmentally damaging aspects of mass tourism" and represent a structural response to consumer pressure (Smith 2009: 615).

As previously stated, ethics are inextricably linked with all tourism. However, they are particularly pertinent to sustainable tourism, which tends to place itself on higher moral ground than other forms (Lansing & Vries 2007). Literature on sustainable tourism, like literature on ethics in tourism, barely existed prior to 1990 (Weaver 2012). We might understandably expect ethics to feature in the sustainable tourism literature, especially in the more recent work, but it remains absent from or is given only cursory comment in many texts (e.g. Mowforth & Munt 2009).

Ethics and ecotourism

A type of tourism that highlights ethical issues of a more environmental, rather than humanistic, imperative is ecotourism. Perhaps because of this connection with the environment, or because of the more recent rise of ecotourism as a phenomenon, ethics appears as a more persistent theme in the ecotourism literature (e.g. Malloy & Fennell 1998; Honey 1999; Fennell 2007) than in literature on other tourism forms. Indeed, the topic of ethics has been viewed by some as so crucial to the ideology of ecotourism that it should distinguish itself from other forms of tourism by being based on principled values and ethics (Fennell 2004). Other authors, however, argue that it is unrealistic to define ecotourism in ethical terms (Buckley 2005: 129).

Buckley (2005: 129) asked "Can one be an unethical ecotourist?" The subsequent wealth of literature on the abuse and misuse of the ecotourism label, particularly in marketing, leans so strongly towards a "yes" that the question no longer seems necessary. Ecotourists can, and are, capably of being unethical. The real question is, should they be? If they are unethical, are they still really an ecotourist? Responding to Buckley (2005), Malloy (2009: 70) argues that "ecotourist must be defined in terms of its ontological ethical nature" and therefore "a 'genuine' ecotourist cannot be ethical." Following this, ecotourism projects not sufficiently informed by environmental ethics are easily transformed into a form of mass tourism (Smith 2009: 626), and the need for consensus and regulation becomes apparent.

Ethical codes for the tourism industry

The World Tourism Organization Network (WTO) developed a Tourism Bill of Rights and Tourist Code in 1985 that, mirroring popular definitions of tourism from around that time, focused on tourist rights to leisure, rest and freedom to travel. Coinciding with a moral turn in tourism (Caton 2012), scholars in the following decade began to comment on the need for a code of ethics in tourism.

Krohn and Ahmed (1992), for example, argued for the need to develop an ethical code for international tourism services and D'Amore (1993) suggested that such a code should incorporate guidelines for both socially and environmentally responsible tourism. This was a sign of the increasing recognition of environmental considerations creeping in to scholarly debate about tourism in the 1990s.

In 1998, Malloy and Fennell carried out a content analysis of forty separate codes of ethics in the tourism industry, joining the call for a more global and comprehensive code (Fennell & Malloy 1999). The calls were answered by the World Tourism Organization's (WTO) 1999 adoption of a Global Code of Ethics for Tourism. The code contains ten non-legally binding articles designed to guide tourism development:

- Article 1: Tourism's contribution to mutual understanding and respect between peoples and societies.
- Article 2: Tourism as a vehicle for individual and collective fulfillment.
- Article 3: Tourism, a factor of sustainable development.
- Article 4: Tourism, a user of the cultural heritage of mankind and contributor to its enhancement.
- Article 5: Tourism, a beneficial activity for host countries and communities.
- Article 6: Obligations of stakeholders in tourism development.
- Article 7: Right to tourism.
- Article 8: Liberty of tourist movements.
- Article 9: Rights of the workers and entrepreneurs in the tourism industry.
- Article 10: Implementation of the principles of the Global Code of Ethics for Tourism.

The code stands as a valuable reference guide, but is not legally binding. A notable absence, in its recognition of rights accorded to various stakeholders such as workers, tourists and hosts, is consideration of non-human species and the environment. In this way its approach is anthropocentric, mirroring the dominant ideological justifications for most ethical approaches to tourism study and practice. Given current directions in tourist demands and tourism marketing of new experiences, as well as recent scholarly endeavors, it is perhaps time the code was revisited.

Current directions

In the last decade, scholarship around the topic of ethics in tourism appears to have increased significantly and branched into more areas of tourism. Jafari's four platforms of tourism, devised in 1990 and revised in 2001, for example, were the object of scrutiny by Macbeth in 2006 who suggested adding a fifth platform on sustainable development and a sixth on ethics. As Macbeth (2006: 963) noted:

> one of the rising challenges in the 21st century will be to find an ethical stance that facilitates tourism scholarship moving beyond the paradigm of objectivity and frontier thinking in order to contribute to a more thoughtful, reflexive, and sustainable platform.

While a particular stance may not yet have been found, there is certainly increasing research around such an ideal. The *Journal of Ecotourism*, for example, published a special edition on ethics in 2011 and in 2012, *Tourism Recreation Research* introduced a series of papers on tourism and animal ethics (e.g. Fennell 2012), which were described as a "somewhat obscure though significant theme" (2012: 157).

Tourist interest in the fields of nature-based, and particularly wildlife, tourism will hopefully ensure that the consideration of animals in tourism ethics becomes less obscure. Increasing scholarship in this field is evidenced by a chapter on "Animals and Tourism" in a new text by

Lovelock and Lovelock (2013) and a proposal to reframe wildlife tourism management to align with more ecocentric values by Burns, Macbeth and Moore (2011).

Despite branching out in new directions, issues relating to the ethics of tourism and development have not gone away. Feighery (2011) laments the scholarly neglect of "consulting ethics" within tourism studies, describing how the role of tourism scholars as consultants in development processes is fraught with complex and competing interests that the scholar needs to negotiate through ethically informed decisions.

The following boxed case study offers a practical example of many of the complexities theorized in this chapter and clearly follows the historical pattern of the rise of ethics in tourism.

Case Study

Human–Wildlife Interactions on Fraser Island

Fraser Island in south-east Queensland attracts approximately 500,000 visitors per year (Alexander 2009). World Heritage listed in 1992 for its Outstanding Universal Value, the island is home to over 350 species of birds, 48 species of mammals and approximately 200 residents. Managing the ethical issues between and within the numerous stakeholder groups (see Burns & Howard 2003) at this destination demonstrates many of the ethical complexities of tourism, but I will focus here on just one and that is the ethical responsibilities of tourism to the non-human world it commodifies.

World Heritage listing highlights the unique features of a location and invariably results in increased visitor numbers. On Fraser Island, visitors are the leading threat to these heritage values. In the pursuit of tourism in this fragile environment, four-wheel drive vehicles are driven over sand dunes and wildlife is regularly shot to prevent it from harming people. What is right and what is wrong in this situation? Different stakeholders hold differing opinions and perspectives. Some think it is right to kill wildlife if it threatens the safety of people. Others do not.

Particular controversy exists over the interactions between dingoes and tourists. Once treated as pets by some residents and offered food by some tourists, habituation of this wildlife species has been blamed for increasing negative interactions in which people are bitten and dingoes are subsequently shot. The dingoes are just one of many tourist attractions on the island, famous for being the world's largest sand island, a popular fishing destination and heavily marketed to both domestic and international travelers.

Should managers prioritize protection of the tourists or conservation of the dingoes (Burns 2009)? If we argue it is wrong to kill the dingoes, do we not also have an ethical responsibility to protect the people? Does tourism have an ethical responsibility to assist with the conservation of the species it commercializes?

An extrinsic and anthropocentric ethic currently dominates the management strategies practiced on Fraser Island over the more intrinsic and ecocentric ethic suggested by the location's World Heritage listing (Burns, Macbeth & Moore 2011). This manifests in the construction of fences to exclude dingoes from popular tourist areas as well as the lethal control of those classified as potentially hazardous to human safety. The practical, and ethical, challenge lies in keeping both people and dingoes safe from harm; thus the case study highlights the ethical complexities of managing the sustainability of wildlife (here as the tourism product) and the sustainability of the tourism market.

Conclusion

Ethical considerations are an essential part of tourism being sustainable (Smith & Duffy 2003) and "At the heart of ethics in tourism is a concern about our environment and future generations" (Moufakkir 2012: 20). However, the argument has been raised that tourism scholars have not been tackling the centrality of ethics effectively (Macbeth 2006; Burns, Macbeth & Moore 2011). There is a "pressing need for a more profound ethical analysis of tourism practices" (Smith 2009: 615) and this requires "an ethically reflexive scholarship" (Macbeth 2006: 963).

That the very core of tourism is based on individual pursuit for personal satisfaction means that tourism has long proceeded under the guise of an instrumental approach. That is, the industry is based on valuing its product, be that people, landscapes or artifacts, by its use to the tourist. Viewed in this way, any chance of recognizing an intrinsic value, of the subject having a value in and of itself that is independent from its use to tourists, is impoverished. This may have assisted the lengthy uptake of ethical issues in tourism. As Kant (1785) argued, an ethical relationship needs to be based in the recognition of intrinsic over instrumental value. The historically widespread lack of such recognition led Smith (2009: 614) to question whether tourism is inherently unethical and argue that "tourism ethics are important because they make us mindful of the importance of resisting a wordview which would reduce everything to economic objects, commodities to be bought and sold" (Smith 2009: 629).

For the vast majority of tourism stakeholders, ethical considerations are not as personally confronting as stepping over a dead body on the way to achieving your goal. Although more subtle for most, often by virtue of the fact that any deaths (such as those of dingoes) are more hidden, ethics are nevertheless a pervasive element of all tourism activities; scholarly recognition of, and engagement with, this concept is crucial. Twenty years ago Lea (1993) predicted "tourism ethics in general and environmental ethics in particular will become an important subdiscipline within tourism studies in the new future." He was right.

Key Reading

Fennell, D.A. (2006) *Tourism Ethics*, Clevedon: Channel View Publications.

Smith, M. (2009) 'Ethical perspectives: Exploring the ethical landscape of tourism', in T. Jamal and M. Robinson (eds) *The SAGE Handbook of Tourism Studies*, London: Sage.

Smith, M. and Duffy, R. (2003) *The Ethics of Tourism Development*, London: Routledge.

Macbeth, J. (2006) 'Towards an ethics platform for tourism', *Annals of Tourism Research*, 32: 962–84.

Lovelock, B. and Lovelock, K.M. (2013) *The Ethics of Tourism: Critical and Applied Perspectives*, New York: Routledge.

References

Alexander, N. (2009) 'Concerns heightening for Fraser Island dingoes', *Science Alert*. Available at: www.sciencealert.com.au/features/20091910–20025.html

Ashley, C. and Goodwin, H. (2007) '"Pro poor tourism": What's gone right and what's gone wrong?' *ODI Opinion Paper*, 80.

Bauman, Z. (1993) *Post-modern Ethics*, Oxford: Blackwell.

Bentham, J. (1948) "A fragment on government", in W. Harrison (ed.) *A Fragment on Government and an Introduction to the Principles of Moral and Legislation*, Oxford: Blackwell.

Buckley, R. (2005) 'In search of the Narwhal: Ethical dilemmas in ecotourism', *Journal of Ecotourism*, 4: 129–34.

Burns, G.L. (2004) 'Anthropology and tourism: Past contributions and future theoretical challenges', *Anthropological Forum*, 14: 5–22.

—— (2009) 'Managing wildlife for people or people for wildlife? A case study of dingoes and tourism on Fraser Island, Queensland, Australia' in, J. Hill and T. Gale (eds) *Ecotourism and Environmental Sustainability: Principles and Practice*, Cheltenham: Ashgate.

Burns, G.L. and Howard, P. (2003) 'When wildlife tourism goes wrong: A case study of stakeholder and management issues regarding dingoes on Fraser Island, Australia', *Tourism Management*, 24: 699–712.

Burns, G.L., Macbeth, J. and Moore, S. (2011) 'Should dingoes die? Principles for engaging ecocentric ethics in wildlife tourism management', *Journal of Ecotourism*, 10: 179–96.

Butcher, J. (2003) *The Moralisation of Tourism: Sun, Sand…and Saving the World?* London: Routledge.

Carson, R. (1962) *Silent Spring*, Boston: Houghton Mifflin Co.

Caton, K. (2012) 'Taking the moral turn in tourism studies', *Annals of Tourism Research*, 39: 1906–28.

Crick, M. (1988) 'Sun, sex, sights, savings and servility: Representations of international tourism in the social sciences', *Criticism, Heresy and Interpretation*, 1: 37–65.

D'Amore, L.J. (1993) 'A code of ethics and guidelines for socially and environmentally responsible tourism', *Journal of Travel Research*, 32: 64.

Dawson, J., Johnston, M.J., Stewart, E.J., Lemieux, C.J., Lemelin, R.H., Maher, P.T. and Grimwood, B.S.R. (2011) 'Ethical considerations of last chance tourism', *Journal of Ecotourism*, 10: 250–65.

Durkheim, E. (1968) *The Elementary Forms of the Religious Life*, London: George Allen and Unwin.

—— (1993) *Ethics and the Sociology of Morals*, New York: Prometheus.

Feighery, W.G. (2011) 'Consulting ethics', *Annals of Tourism Research*, 38: 1031–50.

Fennell, D.A. (2004) 'Deep ecotourism: Seeking theoretical and practical reverence', in T.V. Singh (ed.) *New Horizons in Tourism: Strange Experiences and Stranger Practices*, Wallingford: CABI Publishing.

—— (2006) *Tourism Ethics*, Clevedon: Channel View Publications.

—— (2007) *Ecotourism*, 3rd edn, Oxford: Routledge.

—— (2009) 'Ethics and tourism', in J. Tribe (ed.) *Philosophical Issues in Tourism*, Bristol: Channel View Publications.

—— (2012) 'Tourism and animal rights', *Tourism Recreation Research*, 37: 157–66.

Fennell, D.A. and Malloy, D.C. (1999) 'Measuring the ethical nature of tourism operators', *Annals of Tourism Research*, 26: 928–43.

Greenwood, D.J. (1989) 'Culture by the pound: An anthropological perspective on tourism as cultural commoditization', in V. Smith (ed.) *Hosts and Guests: The Anthropology of Tourism*, 2nd edn, Philadelphia: University of Pennsylvania Press.

Hall, C.M. and Lew, A.A. (2009) *Understanding and Managing Tourism Impacts: An Integrated Approach*, New York: Routledge.

Holden, A. (2003) 'In need of new environmental ethics for tourism?', *Annals of Tourism Research*, 30: 94–108.

—— (2005) *Tourism Studies and the Social Sciences*, New York: Routledge.

Holmes, R. (1992) 'Challenges in environmental ethics', in D. Cooper and J. Palmer (eds) *Environment in Question: Ethics and Global Issues*, London: Routledge.

Honey, M. (1999) *Ecotourism and Sustainable Development: Who Owns Paradise?* Washington DC: Island Press.

Hultsman, J. (1995) 'Just tourism: An ethical framework', *Annals of Tourism Research*, 22: 553–67.

Jafari, J. (1990) 'The basis of tourism education', *The Journal of Tourism Studies*, 1: 33–41.

—— (2001) 'The scientification of tourism', in V. Smith and M. Brent (eds) *Hosts and Guests Revisited: Tourism Issues of the 21st Century*, Elmsford: Cognizant Communications.

Kant, I. (1785) *The Groundwork of the Metaphysics of Morals*. Translated by M. Gregor (ed.) (1998) Cambridge: Cambridge University Press.

Krohn, F.B. and Ahmed, Z.U. (1992) 'The need for developing an ethical code for the marketing of international tourism services', *Journal of Professional Services Marketing*, 8: 189–200.

Lanfant, M.-F. (1993) 'Methodological and conceptual issues raised by the study of international tourism: A test for sociology', in D.G. Pearce and R.W. Butler (eds) *Tourism Research: Critiques and Challenges*, London: Routledge.

Lansing, P. and Vries, P. (2007) 'Sustainable tourism: Ethical alternative or marketing ploy?', *Journal of Business Ethics*, 72: 77–85.

Lea, J. (1988) *Tourism and Development in the Third World,* London: Routledge.

—— (1993) 'Tourism development ethics in the third world', *Annals of Tourism Research,* 20: 701–15.

Lemelin, H., Dawson, J., Stewart, E. J., Maher, P. and Lueck, M. (2010) 'Last-chance tourism: The boom, doom, and gloom of visiting vanishing destinations', *Current Issues in Tourism*, 13(5), 477–493.

Lemelin, R.H., Dawson, J. and Stewart, E. (eds) (2012) *Last Chance Tourism*, London: Taylor and Francis.

Lovelock, B. and Lovelock, K.M. (2013) *The Ethics of Tourism: Critical and Applied Perspectives*, New York: Routledge.

Lynn, W. (1992) 'Tourism in the people's interest', *Community Development Journal*, 27: 371–77.

Macbeth, J. (2006) 'Towards an ethics platform for tourism', *Annals of Tourism Research*, 32: 962–84.

MacCannell, D. (1976) *The Tourist: A New Theory of the Leisure Class*, New York: Shocken.

Malloy, D.C. (2009) 'Can one be an unethical tourist? A response to R. Buckley's "In search of the Narwhal"', *Journal of Ecotourism*, 8: 70–73.

Malloy, D.C. and Fennell, D.A. (1998) 'Ecotourism and ethics: Moral development and organisational cultures', *Journal of Travel Research*, 26: 47–56.

Mathieson, A. and Wall, G. (1982) *Tourism: Economic, Physical and Social Impacts*, Honolulu: University of Hawai'i Press.

Mill, J.S. (1863) *Utilitarianism* (7th edn, 1879), London: Longman.

Miller, A.S. (1991) *Gaia Connections: An Introduction to Ecology, Ecoethics, and Economics,* New York: Rowman and Littlefield Publishers.

Moufakkir, O. (2012) 'Of ethics, leisure and tourism: The "serious fun of doing tourism"', in O. Moufakkir and P. Burns (eds) *Controversies in Tourism*, CABI International.

Mowforth, M. and Munt, I. (2009) *Tourism and Sustainability: Development, Globalization and New Tourism in the Third World*, 3rd edn, New York: Routledge.

Przeclawski, K. (1993) 'Tourism as a subject of interdisciplinary research', in D.G. Pearce and R.W. Butler (eds) *Tourism Research: Critiques and Challenges*, London: Routledge.

Smith, M. (2009) 'Ethical perspectives: Exploring the ethical landscape of tourism', in T. Jamal and M. Robinson (eds) *The SAGE Handbook of Tourism Studies*, London: Sage Publications Ltd.

Smith, M. and Duffy, R. (2003) *The Ethics of Tourism Development*, London: Routledge.

Smith, V.L. (1989) 'Introduction', in V. Smith (ed.) *Hosts and Guests: The Anthropology of Tourism*, 2nd edn, Philadelphia: University of Pennsylvania Press.

Telfer, D.J. and Sharpley, R. (2008) *Tourism and Development in the Developing World,* New York: Routledge.

Turner, L. and Ash, J. (1975) *The Golden Hordes: International Tourism and the Pleasure Periphery*, London: Constable.

Weaver, D. (2012) 'Towards sustainable mass tourism: Paradigm shift or paradigm nudge?' in T.V. Singh (ed.) *Critical Debates in Tourism*, Bristol: Channel View Publications.

World Tourism Organization (1999) Global Code of Ethics for Tourism. Available at : http://ethics.unwto.org/en/content/global-code-ethics-tourism

9

Pro-poor tourism

Reflections on past research and directions for the future

Dao Truong

Pro-poor tourism The use of tourism as a means of poverty alleviation and reduction.

Poverty alleviation/Poverty reduction The use of specific economic development strategies as a means of income and employment generation in areas and communities with high levels of poverty.

Content analysis A research technique that systematically, objectively and quantitatively analyses message characteristics.

Introduction

Poverty alleviation is an important task in many countries. At the 2000 Millennium Summit, the United Nations (UN) adopted the Millennium Development Goals (MDGs), where the first goal is to halve the number of poor people by 2015. According to a UN report, in developing countries the proportion of people living on less than US$1.25/day fell from 47% in 1990 to 24% in 2008. The World Bank (WB) estimates that the global poverty rate at US$1.25/day fell in 2010 to less than half its 1990 value, meaning that the first target of the MDGs will have been achieved before 2015. However, it also suggests that about one billion people worldwide will still be living on less than US$1.25/day in 2015 (UN 2012).

As one of the fastest-growing industries, tourism has been perceived as an important contributor to economic growth and poverty alleviation (UN World Tourism Organization (UNWTO), 2011). The policy debate over the tourism–poverty nexus led to the emergence of the PPT concept in 1999 which aims to 'increase the net benefits for the poor from tourism' and ensures that 'tourism growth contributes to poverty reduction' (Ashley, Roe, & Goodwin 2001: viii). The UNWTO adopted the PPT concept, endorsing the Sustainable Tourism–Eliminating Poverty Initiative in 2003, and regarded poverty alleviation as a 'natural extension' of its concern for harnessing tourism's pivotal role in sustainable development (UNWTO 2011). The UNWTO also considered 2007 a critical year where tourism was consolidated as a key agent in the anti-poverty front and a primary tool for sustainable development (UNWTO 2007).

That poverty alleviation is placed at the centre of the tourism agenda not only reflects significant changes in the UNWTO's stance as a UN specialised agency but also indicates its increased perception of the importance of poverty alleviation to sustainable tourism and sustainable development overall. Although the notion of sustainable tourism and its parental concept of sustainable development may be interpreted differently (Butler 1999), it is acknowledged that sustainability can only be achieved when each component or dimension embraced is attained individually and jointly (Kirchgeorg & Winn 2006). Meanwhile, poverty is detrimental to economic viability, social equity, and environmental integrity as it contributes to widening income gaps and increasing social unrest. The daily struggle for survival also tends to result in environmental degradation, particularly within the tourism context where many important resources are associated with sites of conservation significance such as national parks and nature reserves. That said, poverty is a barrier to sustainable tourism and the call to improve tourism's contributions to poverty alleviation serves the goal of sustainable development at large.

Although the PPT concept was not coined until 1999, the pro-poor potential of tourism had been discussed in academic articles published before 1985. De Kadt (1979) indicated that tourism brings about jobs, backward linkages with agriculture and other sectors, and provides opportunities, particularly for young people and women. It also improves the quality of life for poor people through funding basic facilities, education and training. However, the contribution of tourism to poverty alleviation remains debatable (Pleumarom 2012) although quantifiable evidence has been documented (Mitchell 2012) and pathways highlighted through which the benefits of tourism can be maximised for poor people (Mitchell & Ashley 2010). Several reviews have also indicated important gaps (Goodwin 2009; Zeng & Ryan 2012) and critiques directed at the theoretical foundations of PPT (Harrison 2008). Although these are useful reviews and critiques, none of them has assessed the theoretical and methodological bases of PPT research. This raises the need for a systematic evaluation of the extant PPT literature if guidance is to be sought for future research. Indeed, reviewing past research not only provides an overview of the progress achieved in a particular field but also identifies gaps and extends prior studies (Creswell 2009). In addition, evaluating previous research efforts reveals the theoretical awareness, methodological sophistication, and the direction of research in a field of study (Hesse-Biber 2010; Krippendorff 2004).

Therefore, this chapter seeks to examine the development of PPT research over a 15-year period, from 1999 to 2013. Drawing upon a content analysis (CA) of published journal articles, it seeks to answer the following questions: How many journal articles on PPT have been published? Which country or region has attracted most attention? What are the theoretical frameworks and research methods used by tourism scholars? What is the potential for the future development of PPT research?

Methodology

Refereed journal articles were analysed since they are considered essential communication channels for researchers (Creswell 2009; Xiao & Smith 2006). The author browsed each issue of tourism journals chosen on the basis of McKercher, Law, and Lam's (2006) study. Google Scholar and Scopus databases were also used. Article titles were first investigated. In many cases, these titles suggested that they dealt specifically with PPT. In other cases, the author examined their abstracts, key words, and full length to ensure that relevant articles were retrieved. The searches continued up to the end of April 2013.

The chosen articles were then investigated using the CA method, among the most important research techniques in the social sciences (Krippendorff 2004) and particularly in tourism studies (Nunkoo, Smith, & Ramkissoon 2013; Xiao & Smith 2006; Hall & Valentin 2005). Each article was read through, with particular attention being given to its theoretical underpinnings, data gathering and processing methods, and discussions of research findings. An article was considered 'atheoretical' if it was not framed around a specific theoretical framework. It was regarded as 'theoretical' if it explicitly utilised at least one theory. Theory is a 'body of logistically interconnected propositions which provides an interpretative basis for understanding phenomena' (Dann, Nash, & Pearce 1988: 4). The theoretical awareness of a study can be assessed in terms of the criteria of understanding, prediction and falsifiability. While these criteria are subject to debate, they may be considered important to the evaluation of progress in the realm of theory (Dann *et al.* 1988). An article was deemed 'qualitative' if it used qualitative methods to collect, analyse and present data (e.g. observation, interview, NVivo). In contrast, it was considered 'quantitative' if it utilised quantitative methods (e.g. survey, experiment, SPSS). A 'mixed methods' label was attached if both qualitative and quantitative methods were combined. In addition, an article was considered a review if it dealt with untested hypotheses and/or propositions and reviewed the PPT literature (Nunkoo *et al.* 2013).

Findings

Number of articles published

Up to the end of April 2013, 142 academic articles were retrieved. A further examination resulted in the exclusion of 20 articles. Therefore, 122 articles were analysed for this chapter. These articles are divided into three main periods, each of which is five years long (see Figure 9.1). The last period only covers up to the end of April 2013 as noted.

In the first period, only six articles were published with a poverty focus since PPT was then very new to tourism researchers. Most early PPT papers were released by the PPT Partnership in the form of working papers. The number of PPT articles increased seven–fold between 2004 and 2008 (42 articles). From 2009 to 2013, 74 articles were published with a PPT focus: 2012 accounted for 32.4% (24 articles), followed by 2011 with 23 articles (31%). This confirms that more tourism scholars are interested in PPT research. It also suggests that PPT research has not reached a point of academic saturation. Twenty articles were published in *Current Issues in Tourism*, followed by *Development South Africa* (13), *Journal of Sustainable Tourism* (11), *Tourism*

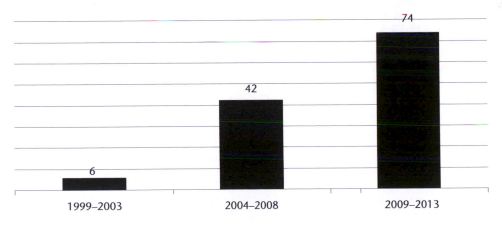

Figure 9.1 Growth of PPT articles

Planning & Development (11) and *Asia Pacific Journal of Tourism Research* (8). Both *Annals of Tourism Research* (ATR) and *Tourism Management* (TM) published only eight articles (four each) with an explicit focus on PPT over the examined period. Although they are among the oldest and the highest ranked in the tourism field (McKercher *et al.* 2006), they are not specifically dedicated to PPT. ATR is driven by theoretical constructs, while TM is concerned with planning and management issues. Other journals (e.g. *Current Issues in Tourism*), although they emerged much later, embrace various aspects of tourism, including poverty alleviation. Indeed, these journals have featured PPT in their special issues, which are not found in both ATR and TM.

PPT research by region

Of the 122 articles examined, 101 were case studies of tourist destinations (86 single case studies and 15 multiple case studies). Two articles discussed the WB's role in promoting PPT (Ferguson 2011; Hawkins & Mann 2007). The remaining 19 articles were general discussions of PPT and, as noted, reviewed previous PPT research. The number of case studies increased across regions over time. This is perhaps because tourism is a place-specific activity and hence a destination-focused industry. Case study is thus among the predominant approaches to tourism research, including research on tourism policy (Scott 2011) and residents' attitudes towards tourism (Nunkoo *et al.* 2013). Africa was the case study site for over half of the total articles considered, followed by Asia and the Pacific (see Table 9.1). Of the 15 multiple case studies, only one (Thomas 2013) covered two countries (Laos and Mali) in two different regions (Asia and Africa). Therefore, each country was considered to constitute half of the article.

That Africa attracted a substantial amount of PPT research can be ascribed to several reasons. First, Africa is home to the largest number of people worldwide, where 47% of the total population lives on less than US$1.25 a day (UN 2012). Second, it was a focus of projects undertaken by the PPT Partnership until this organisation was closed. Third, Africa was the WB's second highest fund beneficiary, both in terms of project numbers and total values (Hawkins & Mann 2007). As the WB has recently resumed its tourism focus, Africa is still the top prioritised beneficiary as indicated by the number of ongoing tourism projects (Messerli 2011). Fourth, a significant shift has been seen among African governments where poverty reduction policies have attached importance to the tourism sector and new tourism strategies have placed a greater focus on poverty alleviation (Ashley & Goodwin 2007). Among African countries considered, South Africa was much researched with nearly 40% (23) of the articles being published on the region.

The amount of PPT research on the Asia–Pacific region is less than half of that on the African region, although it is much larger than that on American and European regions. China comes first with six articles, followed by Laos (4), Vietnam (2), Thailand (2), Fiji (2) and Vanuatu (2).

Table 9.1 Geographic distribution of PPT research

Period	1999–2003	2004–2008	2009–2013	No. of articles	%
Africa	4	14	41.5	59.5	58.9
Asia-Pacific	0	9	15.5	24.5	24.2
Americas	0	6	7	13	12.9
Europe	1	1	2	4	4.0
Total	5	30	66	101	100

This finding reinforces the observation of other scholars (Scott 2011; Truong 2013) that little research attention has been given to Southeast Asian countries, where 17% of the total population lives in poverty (UN 2012). Surprisingly, far fewer studies (4.3%) have examined PPT in Europe and the Americas. While absolute poverty (i.e. lack of food) often occurs in less-developed countries, relative poverty is found in developed societies; this is sometimes termed 'urban poverty' (Sachs 2005). Although tourism has been perceived as a tool for poverty alleviation in developing countries, it is unclear if the same can be said in the context of developed nations.

Use of theories and models

Of the 122 articles considered, 44 clearly referred to theory and model use, while the remaining 78 did not explicitly report using a specific theoretical framework or model (see Table 9.2). This suggests that PPT research is lacking rigorous theoretical foundations.

Table 9.2 Theories, models and frameworks underpinning PPT research

	Freq.	%
Atheoretical	78	63.9
Theoretical[ab]	44	36.1
Value chain analysis framework	8	17.8
General equilibrium model	4	8.9
(Neo)Liberalism	4	8.9
Corporate social responsibility	3	6.7
Social accounting matrix	3	6.7
(Socio)Political theory	3	6.7
Actor-network theory	2	4.4
Participatory development approach	2	4.4
Social capital theory	2	4.4
Feminist theory	2	4.4
Community corporate joint-venture model	1	2.2
Mobilisation developmentalism	1	2.2
Anti-poverty model	1	2.2
Globalisation theory	1	2.2
Structuration and institutional theory	1	2.2
Emotional intelligence theory	1	2.2
Supply curve theory	1	2.2
Rapid rural appraisal model	1	2.2
Positive psychology theory	1	2.2
Tourism policy-making model	1	2.2
Tourist area lifecycle model	1	2.2
Social exchange theory	1	2.2

[a] Only explicitly reported theories, models and frameworks were counted
[b] Zapata et al. (2011) combined the lifecycle model and actor-network theory

Of the 44 articles that clearly stated theory and model use, only one (2.3%) was published between 1999 and 2003. This number increased to 13 (29.5%) from 2004 to 2008 and 30 (68.2%) between 2009 and 2013. This finding suggests that researchers increasingly use theories and frameworks in their PPT studies. Theoretical triangulation was only found in Zapata *et al.*'s (2011) study where the lifecycle and actor–network theories were combined. The value chain and sustainable livelihood approach is being used more frequently in recent PPT research (Lapeyre 2011; Mitchell 2012). This was considered a partial convergence of the (neo)liberal, critical and alternative approaches to tourism development that were perceived to place a strong focus on privatisation and market development (Hummel & van der Dium 2012) and hence were critiqued by some scholars (Hall 2007; Pleumarom 2012; Scheyvens 2007; Schilcher 2007). The adoption of this approach may also be construed as a response to the demand for more holistic measures that are capable of embracing various pro-poor effects of tourism on host communities.

Table 9.2 suggests that theories and frameworks used in PPT research are characterised by low frequencies but are diverse in origin. Some theories originated from economics (e.g. supply curve theory), psychology (e.g. positive psychology), while others emerged from political sciences (e.g. socio-political theory), or sociology (e.g. globalisation theory). Although some are widely recognised theories, others appear to represent an approach, a model, or a framework rather than a theory as defined earlier in this chapter (e.g. value chain analysis). Corporate social responsibility, for instance, is not a theory in itself. Rather, it is considered an approach or orientation. However, its theoretical underpinnings are rooted in marketing theory. It was originally referred to in Kotler's 1967 *Marketing Management* as societal marketing, by which Kotler meant socially responsible marketing, which is now known as corporate social responsibility. Similarly, while coined a *theory*, actor–network theory is perhaps more an approach or orientation than a theory (Law 2009). Synthesising or criticising theories, frameworks, and models used in (pro-poor) tourism research is thus a challenge. This indicates both the multidisciplinary (Pearce D. 2012), post-disciplinary (Coles *et al.* 2006) and indisciplinary (Tribe 1997) nature of (pro-poor) tourism as a field of study.

Theories and models underpinning PPT studies are not only diverse in origin but also in usage. This is largely due to the diversity of the disciplines from which these theories and models have emerged and their relevance to the objective of specific PPT studies. For instance, the actor–network theory was used to trace the ordering of and relationships between people and organisations in tourism development (van der Dium & Caalders 2008). Meanwhile, Pearce (P., 2012) drew on the positive psychology theory to examine tourists' written reactions to the poverty situation in tourist destinations. Erskine and Meyer (2012) emphasised the importance of the structuration theory in discussing the roles of tourism as a means of poverty alleviation. While it is recognised that theories and models provide a useful framework for research studies (Pearce, D. 2012), in the context of PPT research questions may be raised as to why studies that did not explicitly report theory and model use outweighed those that were theoretically informed. This leads to difficulties in identifying common theories or models that effectively guide PPT research.

Research methods used in PPT studies

The selected PPT articles were also examined for their use of research methods, data gathering and analytical techniques. Of the 122 articles considered, three were reviews, 86 were qualitative in nature, 15 used quantitative methods to collect and analyse data, and the remaining 18 applied a mixed methods approach. Although quantitative methods were used in 33 articles (15

+ 18), only 21 instances of quantitative statistical techniques were recorded (see Table 9.3). This is because a number of quantitative articles did not explicitly state the use of quantitative statistical techniques while multiple quantitative statistical techniques were reported in others. SPSS and social accounting matrices were used more frequently than others. Desk review, focus groups, interviews, and observations were extensively used in qualitative articles where data was often coded by themes determined by the researchers. The popularity of these qualitative methods confirms that the interpretive paradigm has dominated research on PPT. This is similar to studies on tourism policy (Scott 2011) but is in contrast to research on residents' attitudes towards tourism where quantitative methods have prevailed (Nunkoo et al. 2013).

Table 9.4 indicates that all articles published between 1999 and 2003 were qualitative in nature. This is understandable as the PPT concept was new at the time and articles on the subject primarily discussed its conceptual and definitional issues. In the five years that followed, quantitative methods were used in 16.7% of all PPT articles published, although qualitative methods were still dominant. The mixed methods approach was adopted by 7.1% of all PPT articles published in this period. The use of the mixed methods approach witnessed a three-fold increase in the period 2009–2013 as compared to the preceding period, while a slight decline was found in both qualitative and quantitative methods.

Table 9.3 Types of research and analytical techniques used in PPT studies

	No. of articles (n = 122)	%
Reviews	3	2.5
Qualitative	86	70.5
Quantitative	15	12.3
Mixed methods	18	14.7
Quantitative data analysis techniques (n = 21)		
Applied general equilibrium and social marketing matrix	5	23.8
SPSS	5	23.8
Descriptive statistics	2	9.5
t-test	2	9.5
chi-square	2	9.5
Factor analysis	1	4.8
Satellite accounting	1	4.8
Geographically weighted regression	1	4.8
Co-integration	1	4.8
Analytical hierarchy process modelling	1	4.8

Table 9.4 Use of research methods over time

	Qualitative (n = 86)		Quantitative (n = 15)		Mixed (n = 18)	
	Freq.	%	Freq.	%	Freq.	%
1999–2003	6	100	0	0	0	0
2004–2008	32	76.2	7	16.7	3	7.1
2009–2013	48	67.6	8	11.3	15	21.1

Overall, Table 9.4 indicates that qualitative articles dominated across all the periods examined. It also suggests that researchers attach increased importance to both quantitative and mixed methods approaches. The evidence demonstrates the methodological evolution of PPT research from purely descriptive and conceptual discourse towards a greater focus on data quantification. It also proves that the challenge of providing quantifiable pro-poor impacts of tourism has been increasingly perceived by tourism scholars.

Future research

Several areas have emerged from this chapter that may hold important potential for future research. As indicated above, a majority of PPT research was qualitative. The PPT literature is lacking measures that quantify tourism's pro-poor impacts. This is a challenge for two main reasons. First, tourism is a destination-based activity, hence its impacts vary by destination. As a result, there is possibly no 'one-size-fits-all' measure that can be applied in all host communities. Second, tourism is a complex industry that involves many others. It is difficult to separate the actual contributions of tourism from those of other industries. Therefore, without appropriate quantitative measures, even after the first target of the MDGs has been achieved as mentioned previously, little is known of the contribution made by the tourism sector to attaining that target and to sustainable development overall. This suggests that Goodwin's (2009) call for quantifiable evidence of tourism's pro-poor impact remains valid for further PPT studies. In addition, further research is also possible to examine how theories and models are used to guide PPT studies. It may then be possible to identify common theories or models that are effective in informing the design, implementation and evaluation of PPT studies.

Of the 101 articles dealing with case studies, 86 were single case studies. Only 15 articles were multiple case studies. PPT research has proliferated in the African context, while little attention has been given to less-developed countries in Asia and First World countries. It is thus difficult to make cross-comparisons of the pro-poor effects of tourism since each case study differs in terms of aims, objectives, and methods used. Even when comparisons were made, they tended to focus on the impacts of PPT on the same community before and after interventions. Comparisons of the pro-poor impacts of tourism between a target community and a (untargeted) community are lacking. Therefore, questions may be raised as to the difference in income, employment and/or living standards between the community that receives PPT interventions and the community that is not the target beneficiary of such interventions. For this reason, research into the pro-poor effects of tourism between a target community and a (untargeted) community may help to provide clearer evidence of the roles of tourism as a means of poverty alleviation.

The chosen 122 articles analysed PPT at various scales. Twenty-four examined PPT from a macro perspective, where policy implications were indicated (Bowden 2005; Schilcher 2007). Sixty-four articles considered PPT from a micro perspective with references to income distribution, employment, capacity building, or discrimination (Akyeampong, 2011; Koutra & Edwards 2012). PPT was also studied at corporate level (Lapeyre 2011; Spenceley & Goodwin 2007). However, few PPT studies considered the voice of poor people impacted by tourism (Holden, Sonne, & Novelli 2011). Indeed, Pleumarom (2012) argues that PPT discourses and initiatives are of very little value if the perceptions and opinions of poor people are not duly considered. Research indicates that poor people often perceive poverty differently from academics and policy-makers. For example, people in Laos and Vietnam tend to define poverty as a lack of rice (Harrison & Schipani, 2007; Truong, Hall, & Garry 2014), while the poor in Ghana perceive poverty as a lack of income and/or opportunity (Holden *et al.* 2011). Johnston

(2007) suggests that some indigenous peoples think of themselves as being poor only when they lose their land, are displaced and relocated due to tourism development. Even in such cases, they are not necessarily poor in spiritual terms. The evidence suggests that poverty is multidimensional, complex, and different by context. The difficulty in addressing the poverty issue within the tourism context is compounded by the destination nature of tourism itself. It is for this reason that Max-Neef, a Chilean economist, called for a 'barefoot' approach to poverty alleviation, that is, only through the experiences of poor people that poverty measures can be identified effectively (Democracy Now! 2010). The same can be said of PPT research: it is only by giving a voice to poor people that meaningful approaches to alleviating poverty through tourism become clearer and are more likely to succeed.

Allowing poor people to raise their voice may also help to gain insights into the root causes of poverty. Research indicates that poverty can be ascribed to external (e.g. structural barriers, market constraints) (Begovic, Matkovic, Mijatovic, & Popovic, 2007) and/or internal (e.g. poor people's behaviours) factors (Amsden 2012; Moore 2012). Yet the causes of poverty have been generally neglected in the PPT literature (Pleumarom 2012). Instead of questioning whether tourism can be an appropriate measure for poverty alleviation, the majority of tourism scholars tend to focus on how tourism can alleviate poverty. This is perilous because, instead of understanding poverty and benefiting poor people, some organisations may adopt PPT to promote market growth and privatisation (Scheyvens 2007; Schilcher 2007). Powerful stakeholders may take advantage of PPT to serve their own interests (Chok, Macbeth & Warren, 2007). For example, in the southern Indian state of Kerala, a Responsible Tourism Initiative was launched by the local authority in partnership with the Indian section of the International Centre for Responsible Tourism. In 2006, the WTTC chose the initiative as one of the nominees for the Tourism for Tomorrow Awards. This led to a street demonstration organised by local people and civil society organisations, who claimed that Kerala was not a model of sustainable, responsible or pro-poor tourism of any international standard, but instead served the interests of the local authority and the private sector (Pleumarom 2012). In the small Amazonian town of Nazareth that joins Colombia, Brazil and Peru, local guards armed with traditional sticks stand at the town entrance to prohibit tourists from entering the town. The argument is that, despite the growth of tourism, only meagre benefits have trickled down to the poor indigenous people. Most tourism profits have instead accrued to private travel agencies (Muse 2011).

Although the tourism–poverty nexus has been examined from differing perspectives as discussed above, a dearth of research has explored how tourists would react towards the poverty situation in host destinations and thus what they would do to contribute to lifting poor people out of poverty (Pearce P. 2012). Pearce (P., 2012) suggests that tourists' emotional reaction may generate meaningful behaviours including willingness to spend time on directly assisting poor people and pro-poor projects, purchasing and promoting of products and services produced by poor communities. Further research into tourists' perceptions of poverty and actions towards poverty alleviation may, therefore, be an interesting theme and may contribute to building a larger and more holistic body of knowledge with respect to tourism and poverty alleviation. In short, all the noted areas provide meaningful themes for future research.

Case Study

Pro-poor tourism: The case of Sapa, Vietnam

Sapa is located in the mountainous province of Lao Cai. It is home to the Hoang Lien Son mountain range that includes the Fansipan peak. Administratively, Sapa consists of Sapa town and 17 communes. In terms of ethnicity, apart from Kinh people (lowland Vietnamese), Sapa is home to some poor ethnic minority groups. Due to its natural beauty and traditional ethnic cultures, Sapa is among the most popular tourist attractions in Vietnam. However, it still has substantial levels of poverty.

In 2009, Sapa was chosen as a project site of the *Northern Highlands Trail* project. Specific project interventions include public-private partnership, policy support, product creation, and market demand promotion. Important outcomes include the establishment of a handicraft market in Ta Phin village and the improved capacity of the private and public sectors. About 1,153 ethnic households are providing tourism services, 71 of which are homestay owners. Sixty per cent of local tour guides are ethnic minority women.

Interviews and observations conducted by the author indicated that most local people are rice farmers and handicraft sellers. Of the 20 poor people interviewed, 19 stated that tourism had benefited the rich and the tour operators. While some respondents in Ta Phin village could participate in project meetings, those in Lao Chai and Ta Van villages could not. Local women often chase tourists to sell handicrafts, resulting in discomfort for tourists and conflict between sellers. The handicraft market in Ta Phin was abandoned because it was located at the edge of the village where very few tourists visited. Because of aggressive sellers, tour operators and hotels no longer send their guests to Ta Phin. Although local people do not consider tourism a means of poverty alleviation, they all wish to become homestay owners or tour guides, suggesting that they regard tourism as the only alternative livelihood outside rice farming. Although they may be a potential workforce for tourism, they may place considerable pressure on tourism as they lack professional skills and work experiences, particularly the handicraft sellers. While an appropriate approach is needed to involve more local poor people in tourism and allow them to voice their opinions and expectations, alternative livelihoods other than tourism are required. Measures should also be taken to stop handicraft sellers from chasing tourists. These issues require an insightful understanding of local poor people and what they need, want and prioritise in their everyday life.

Source: This case study draws on SNV's *Case study Asia* (retrieved May 2012, from www.snvworld.org), and Truong *et al.* (2014).

Conclusion

This chapter has attempted to analyse the content of 122 refereed journal articles on PPT published from 1999 to 2013. It has indicated that PPT has attracted increased attention of tourism researchers as evidenced by the growing number of academic articles published on the topic. A considerable number of PPT studies have focused on African countries, while less research attention has been paid to those in Asia and, more specifically, Southeast Asia. Less research has been carried out in developed nations. PPT research has evolved from conceptual discourse towards a greater emphasis on theoretical and methodological bases. Although qualitative methods have prevailed in PPT research, both quantitative and mixed methods approaches are gaining prominence. It is predicted that more PPT research based on quantitative and mixed methods will be published in the future. Therefore, tourism's pro-poor impact may be demonstrated by quantifiable data, which may then help to indicate more clearly the contributions of tourism to sustainable development overall.

Despite the potential contribution this chapter may make to the PPT literature and to sustainable tourism research, its limitations should be acknowledged. This chapter was limited to refereed journal articles published in English. Books, project reports, and working papers were not examined. Therefore, other reviews may be conducted on these documents and on the PPT literature published in other languages. It is also possible that this chapter omitted several valuable articles due to restricted subscriptions. In addition, the identification of theories, frameworks and/or models underpinning a journal article (Table 9.2) may be subject to debate given the blurred boundary between these concepts in tourism research (Pearce D. 2012). The determination of what is a framework and/or a model is thus a challenge. This challenge is compounded by the nature of tourism research itself that attracts scholars from a wide range of majors and disciplines. Furthermore, the inclusion or exclusion of articles that may have pro-poor implications in a discussion that is otherwise primarily focused on ecotourism or community-based tourism may explain the (conceptual) ambiguity of and the interrelationships between various forms of tourism. It may also explain why reviewing the PPT literature may become a daunting task and thus a debate over its actual size. Further research is warranted.

Key Reading

Goodwin, H. (2009) 'Reflections on 10 years of pro-poor tourism', *Journal of Policy Research in Tourism, Leisure and Events,* 1(1): 90–94.

Harrison, D. (2008) 'Pro-poor tourism: A critique', *Third World Quarterly,* 29(5): 851–68.

Pleumarom, A. (2012) *The Politics of Tourism, Poverty Alleviation and Sustainable Development.* Penang: Third World Network.

Scheyvens, R. (2007) 'Exploring the tourism-poverty nexus', *Current Issues in Tourism,* 10(2–3): 231–54.

Schilcher, D. (2007) 'Growth versus equity: The continuum of pro-poor tourism and neoliberal governance', *Current Issues in Tourism,* 10(2–3): 166–93.

References

Akyeampong, O.A. (2011) 'Pro-poor tourism: Residents' expectations, experiences and perceptions in the Kakum National Park area of Ghana', *Journal of Sustainable Tourism,* 19: 197–213.

Amsden, A.H. (2012) 'Grass roots war on poverty', *World Economic Review,* 1(1): 114–31.

Ashley, C. and Goodwin, H. (2007) *'Pro-poor Tourism': What's Gone Right and What's Gone Wrong?* London: Overseas Development Institute.

Ashley, C., Roe, D. and Goodwin, H. (2001) *Pro-poor Tourism Strategies: Making Tourism Work for the Poor.* London: Pro-poor Tourism Partnership.

Begovic, B., Matkovic, G., Mijatovic, B. and Popovic, B. (2007) *From Poverty to Prosperity: Free Market Based Solution.* Belgrade: Centre for Liberal-Democratic Studies.

Bowden, J. (2005) 'Pro-poor tourism and the Chinese experience', *Asia Pacific Journal of Tourism Research,* 10: 379–98.

Butler, R. (1999) 'Sustainable tourism: A state-of-the-art review', *Tourism Geographies,* 1: 7–25.

Chok, S., Macbeth, J. and Warren, C. (2007) 'Tourism as a tool for poverty alleviation: A critical analysis of PPT and implications for sustainability', *Current Issues in Tourism*, 10: 144–65.

Coles, T., Hall, C.M. and Duval, D. (2006) 'Tourism and post-disciplinary inquiry', *Current Issues in Tourism*, 9(4–5): 293–319.

Creswell, J.W. (2009) *Research Design: Qualitative, Quantitative, and Mixed Methods Approaches* (3rd ed.). Thousand Oaks: Sage.

Dann, G., Nash, D. and Pearce, P. (1988) 'Methodology in tourism research', *Annals of Tourism Research*, 15: 1–28.

De Kadt, E. (1979) 'Social planning for tourism in the developing countries', *Annals of Tourism Research*, January/March: 36–48.

Democracy Now! (2010) *Chilean Economist Manfred Max-Neef on Barefoot Economics, Poverty and Why the US is Becoming an 'Underdeveloping Nation'*. Transcript of an interview with Manfred Max-Neef on 26 Nov. Retrieved from www.democracynow.org.

Erskine, L.M. and Meyer, D. (2012) 'Influenced and influential: The role of tour operators and development organisations in tourism and poverty reduction in Ecuador', *Journal of Sustainable Tourism*, 20: 339–57.

Ferguson, L. (2011) 'Promoting gender equality and empowering women? Tourism and the third Millennium Development Goal', *Current Issues in Tourism*, 14: 235–49.

Goodwin, H. (2009) 'Reflections on 10 years of pro-poor tourism', *Journal of Policy Research in Tourism, Leisure and Events*, 1: 90–94.

Hall, C.M. (2007) 'Pro-poor tourism: Do tourism exchanges benefit primarily the countries of the South?' *Current Issues in Tourism*, 10: 111–18.

Hall, C.M. and Valentin, A. (2005) 'Content analysis', in P. Burns, C. Palmer, and B. Ritchie (eds) *Tourism Research Methods: Integrating Theory with Practice*, Wallingford: CABI.

Harrison, D. (2008) 'Pro-poor tourism: A critique', *Third World Quarterly*, 29: 851–68.

Harrison, D. and Schipani, S. (2007) 'Lao tourism and poverty alleviation: Community-based tourism and the private sector', *Current Issues in Tourism*, 10: 194–230.

Hawkins, D.E. and Mann, S. (2007) 'The World Bank's role in tourism development', *Annals of Tourism Research*, 34: 348–63.

Hesse-Biber, S.N. (2010) *Mixed Methods Research: Merging Theory with Practice*. London: The Guilford Press.

Holden, A., Sonne, J. and Novelli, M. (2011) 'Tourism and poverty reduction: An interpretation by the poor of Elmina, Ghana', *Tourism Planning & Development*, 8: 317–34.

Hummel, J. and van der Dium, R. (2012) 'Tourism and development at work: 15 years of tourism and poverty alleviation within the SNV Netherlands Development Organisation', *Journal of Sustainable Tourism*, 20: 319–38.

Johnston, A.M. (2007) *Is the Sacred for Sale? Tourism and Indigenous Peoples* (2nd ed.). London: Earthscan.

Kirchgeorg, M. and Winn, M.I. (2006) 'Sustainability marketing for the poorest of the poor', *Business Strategy and the Environment*, 15: 171–84.

Kotler, P. (1967) *Marketing Management: Analysis, Planning, and Control*. London: Prentice Hall.

Koutra, C. and Edwards, J. (2012) 'Capacity building through socially responsible tourism development: A Ghanaian case study', *Journal of Travel Research*, 51: 779–92.

Krippendorff, K. (2004) *Content Analysis: An Introduction to Its Methodology* (2nd ed.), Thousand Oaks: Sage.

Lapeyre, R. (2011) 'The Grootberg lodge partners in Namibia: Towards poverty alleviation and empowerment for long-term sustainability?' *Current Issues in Tourism*, 14: 221–34.

Law, J. (2009) 'Actor network theory and material semiotics', in B. Turner (ed.) *The New Blackwell Companion to Social Theory*. Malden: Blackwell.

McKercher, B., Law, R. and Lam, T. (2006) 'Rating tourism and hospitality journals', *Tourism Management*, 27: 1235–52.

Messerli, H.R. (2011) 'Transformation through tourism: Harnessing tourism as a development tool for improved livelihoods', *Tourism Planning & Development*, 8(3): 335–37.

Mitchell, J. (2012) 'Value chain approaches to assessing the impact of tourism on low-income households in developing countries', *Journal of Sustainable Tourism*, 20: 457–75.

Mitchell, J. and Ashley, C. (2010) *Tourism and Poverty Reduction: Pathways to Prosperity*. London: ODI & Earthscan.

Moore, S. (2012) *Instead of Being Disgusted by Poverty, We Are Disgusted by Poor People Themselves*. Retrieved February 2012, from www.guardian.co.uk.

Muse, T. (2011) *Amazon Town Bans Tourists*. Retrieved December 2012, from www.guardian.co.uk.

Nunkoo, R., Smith, S.L.J. and Ramkissoon, H. (2013) 'Residents' attitudes to tourism: A longitudinal study of 140 articles from 1984 to 2010', *Journal of Sustainable Tourism*, 21: 5–25.

Pearce, D. (2012) *Frameworks for Tourism Research*. Wallingford: CABI.

Pearce, P. (2012) 'Tourists' written reactions to poverty in Southern Africa', *Journal of Travel Research*, 51(2): 154–65.

Pleumarom, A. (2012) *The Politics of Tourism, Poverty Alleviation and Sustainable Development*. Penang: Third World Network.

Sachs, J.D. (2005) *The End of Poverty: Economic Possibilities for Our Time*. New York: The Penguin Press.

Scheyvens, R. (2007) 'Exploring the tourism–poverty nexus', *Current Issues in Tourism*, 10: 231–54.

Schilcher, D. (2007) 'Growth versus equity: The continuum of pro-poor tourism and neoliberal governance', *Current Issues in Tourism*, 10: 166–93.

Scott, N. (2011) *Tourism Policy: A Strategic Review*. Contemporary Tourism Reviews. Oxford: Goodfellow Publishers.

Spenceley, A. and Goodwin, H. (2007) 'Nature-based tourism and poverty alleviation: Impacts of private sector and parastatal enterprises in and around Kruger National Park, South Africa', *Current Issues in Tourism*, 10: 255–77.

Thomas, F. (2013) 'Addressing the measurement of tourism in terms of poverty reduction: Tourism value chain analysis in Lao PDR and Mali', *International Journal of Tourism Research*, DOI: 10.1002/jtr.1930.

Tribe, J. (1997) 'The indiscipline of tourism', *Annals of Tourism Research*, 24: 638–57.

Truong, V.D. (2013) 'Tourism policy development in Vietnam: A pro-poor perspective', *Journal of Policy Research in Tourism, Leisure and Events*, 5(1): 28–45.

Truong, V.D., Hall, C.M. and Garry, T. (2014) 'Tourism and poverty alleviation: Perceptions and experiences of poor people in Sapa, Vietnam', *Journal of Sustainable Tourism*, DOI: 10.1080/09669582.2013.871019.

United Nations (UN) (2012) *The Millennium Development Goals Report 2012*. New York: UN.

United Nations World Tourism Organisation (UNWTO) (2007) *Increase Tourism to Fight Poverty – New Year Message from UNWTO*. Madrid: UNWTO.

—— (2011) *Policy and Practice for Global Tourism*. Madrid: UNWTO.

Van der Dium, V.R. and Caalders, J. (2008) 'Tourism chains and pro-poor tourism development: An actor-network analysis of a pilot project in Costa Rica', *Current Issues in Tourism*, 11: 109–25.

Xiao, H. and Smith, S. (2006) 'The making of tourism research: Insights from a social sciences journal', *Annals of Tourism Research*, 3: 490–507.

Zapata, M.J., Hall, C.M., Lindo, P. and Vanderschaeghen, M. (2011) 'Can community-based tourism contribute to development and poverty alleviation?' *Current Issues in Tourism*, 14: 725–49

Zeng, B. and Ryan, C. (2012) 'Assisting the poor in China through tourism development: A review of research', *Tourism Management*, 33: 239–48.

10

Environmentally sustainable tourists?

Sara Dolnicar

> **Environmentally friendly tourists/sustainable tourists/green tourists/biocentric tourists** Definitions vary, but such tourists are believed to cause less or wish to cause less environmental harm when on vacation.
>
> **Market segment** A group of consumers who have something in common, for example, they all behave in pro-environmental ways when they are on vacation.
>
> **Publicly visible specific commitment** A way shown to increase pro-environmental behavior in the tourism context. Tourists wear a badge which shows that they have committed to undertaking a very specific pro-environmental action during their vacation.
>
> **Enabling infrastructure** Infrastructure provided at the tourism destination or at the tourism business that allows tourist who wish to behave in an environmentally friendly way to do so.

Introduction

Many years ago I developed a keen interest in sustainable tourism. Being an idealist, I wanted to believe that tourists exist who are intrinsically environmentally friendly and who will make an extra effort to enjoy their vacation while still protecting the environment. Being a marketer, I knew that it is common for tourism destinations and tourism businesses to identify target markets and proactively pursue them. Combining these two facts made it appear as if the solution to sustainable tourism was really not that complicated: find and understand intrinsically environmentally friendly tourists, select them as a target segment and develop a marketing plan to attract them (Dolnicar 2006). No need for market regulation, no need for capacity restrictions, no need for any attempts to educate tourists upon arrival at the destination. Easily fixed, I thought (somewhat naively). Unfortunately, at least four reasons stand in the way of the above solution.

It remains unclear whether an environmentally friendly tourist exists

Despite the fact that environmentally sustainable tourists (referred to also as environmentally friendly tourists, sustainable tourists, ecotourists, green tourists, biocentric tourists; see also Chapter 2) have been the subject of extensive research, there is little compelling evidence that they actually exist, neither is there agreement on the potential market size of this segment or characteristics of members of the segment. To some extent this is due to the fact that every study attempting to profile tourists has operationalized them in a different way, as demonstrated recently by Dolnicar, Juvan and Yanamandram (2013). For example, about a third of studies investigate visitors to parks and protected areas (e.g. Hvenegaard & Dearden 1998; Kerstetter, Hou & Lin 2004; Ryan, Hughes & Chirgwin 2000), one-fifth investigate visitors to well-known eco-destinations (e.g. Ballantine & Eagles 1994; Palacio & McCool 1997) and one-fifth investigate tourists who stay in eco-lodges (e.g. Weaver & Lawton 2002). While it is likely that tourists who wish to cause the smallest possible environmental damage at the destination will visit parks and protected areas and may be more likely to choose eco-destinations and sleep in eco-lodges, the reverse conclusion is not necessarily true: not everyone who visits a park, not everyone who travels to an eco-destination, not everyone who sleeps in an eco-lodge, is an environmentally sustainable tourist.

The profiles of environmentally friendly tourists developed in a large number of empirical studies in the past therefore do not necessarily profile truly environmentally sustainable tourists and they vary greatly, as pointed out by Tao, Eagles and Smith (2004) and Dolnicar, Crouch and Long (2008). As a consequence, firm conclusions about who environmentally sustainable tourists actually are cannot be derived. If one attempted to paint a picture of the average environmentally sustainable tourist based on the literature this person would be middle aged, half highly educated, half not, slightly environmentally concerned, slightly environmentally aware, slightly willing to forgo comfort and adventure seeking, and slightly female. Clearly, such a profile is not particularly useful for a destination manager or the manager of a tourism business as a basis for targeting this segment.

Possibly the most promising approach to understanding who the more environmentally sustainable tourists involve approaching them in a context which can be reasonably assumed to be indicative of them being committed to the protection of the environment. One way of doing this, which has been shown to discriminate effectively between people who behave in an environmentally friendly way and those who do not (Olli, Grendstad & Wollebaek 2001) is to recruit as study participants members of environmental protection organizations. This approach was taken, for example, by Eagles (1992) who reports on data collected from members of two Canadian associations whose mission is environmental conservation, finding that respondents have distinctly different travel motivations patterns than other Canadian tourists, specifically they are more motivated by wilderness, parks and rural areas, and water and mountains. They are more physically active, seek adventure and are keen to meet other people who share their interests. A similar approach was taken by Meric and Hunt (1998); again, members of environmental organizations were targeted with an invitation to participate in this study. In this case, however, the focus was on nature tourism, so also camping travelers and members of nature organizations were included thus broadening the scope from purely environmentally sustainable tourism to ecotourism in the broader sense of the meaning.

The body of work studying people known to be committed to environmental protection results in a somewhat clearer picture of who environmentally sustainable tourists might be. However, as raised by Blamey (1997), research investigating environmentally sustainable tourists can be either intentions or outcome based. It appears that the body of work to date is highly biased towards intentions. There is very little, if any, firm evidence of environmentally sustainable tourists actually behaving in an environmentally sustainable manner in the vacation context.

People's behavior changes with context

People behave differently in different situations in life. A number of researchers have suggested that people tend to reduce their level of environmentally friendly behavior when on vacation. For example, McKercher (1993: 12) states that on vacation: "mass tourists tend to exhibit atypical behaviours […]. It must be remembered that tourists are seeking an escape from their everyday existence. While on vacation, they do not want to be burdened with the concerns of the normal world."

Empirical support for this notion was provided by Dolnicar and Grün (2009) who show that tourists will generally reduce their engagement in environmentally friendly behaviors when moving from the home environment to the vacation environment. The key reasons provided by tourists to explain why this change in behavior occurs include aspects that cannot be changed, such as people's feeling that they deserve a break from their everyday efforts when on vacation, but also reasons that could be addressed by policy makers and the tourism industry, including that tourists do not feel as responsible for the destination as they do for their home, they feel that their behavior at home has more of a long-term impact, that they have available in their home environment the infrastructure required to behave in an environmentally friendly way, whereas they do not at the destination and that environmental action at home has the potential to save them money, such as water and energy costs. Similar conclusions have emerged from a qualitative study conducted in the UK: people felt entitled to enjoy their holidays without worrying about the environment and were not willing to change their behavior as tourists to protect the environment at their destination, arguing that environmental protection is the government's responsibility (Miller, Rathouse, Scarles, Holmes & Tribe 2010).

Despite these discouraging findings, it may still be possible that at least a small, very committed group of people exist who assess the impact of each behavior they undertake with respect to its environmental impact. In the context of tourism some evidence for this is provided by Mair (2011), concluding that about 10 per cent of conference travelers engage in carbon offsetting. While this gives some hope, it also leads to the next problem, a question my PhD student, Emil Juvan, asked me: if a person who is absolutely committed to produce the lowest possible environmental footprint with respect to every behavior, including vacation behavior, are they actually in a position to choose the vacation with the lowest environmental footprint?

Even "dark green" tourists cannot make a fully informed vacation choice

Extremely environmentally concerned people may choose not to travel at all and to spend their work-free days at home. From an environmental point of view, this is an excellent decision; from a tourism point of view, it is disastrous. If the tourism industry genuinely wishes to cater to tourists who are interested in keeping their vacation-induced carbon footprint as low as possible, tourists must be provided with tools that allow them to assess the comparative environmental cost of alternative vacation options. Such tools are currently not readily available.

Tourists can use online carbon calculators, but only a few of them allow the calculation of the complete footprint for a vacation. Those that do, lead to different results, making it difficult for a user to feel that they generate credible data (Juvan & Dolnicar 2014). Similarly, there are a wide range of certification labels on the market indicating the environmental sustainability of a trip, but it is not obvious to consumers which criteria are used to award certifications. The lack of reliable information about the environmental cost of any given vacation invites the less honorable tourism providers to engage in green wash, further reducing the credibility of information provided to the marketplace on the environmental consequences of a vacation offer.

A similar argument was made by Moisander (2007) who argues that the burden of environmentally friendly consumption is too heavy for most consumers. Moisander (2007) identifies at least four barriers to environmentally friendly consumption in the broader, non-tourism context: (1) expert knowledge is required to assess the extent of negative environmental effects of different behaviors, (2) consumers have to have the ability and skill-set to search for information and make the assessment, (3) contradictory information makes it difficult to actually determine which source to trust and, to complicate matters even further, (4) green wash has increased consumer skepticism about statements of environmental sustainability on products. Moisander (2007: 406) refers to this mix of problems as the "perplexity of environmental information." This term is illustrative of how a person motivated to do the right thing must feel after attempting to do so: utterly perplexed, probably frustrated and in all likelihood only the most persistent of environmentally sustainably consumers will persist with considering environmental impacts when making a consumer choice or planning a vacation.

If tourists don't demand it, the tourism industry does not offer it

As McKercher (1993: 9) stated, tourism: "is a private sector dominated industry, with investment decisions being based predominantly on profit maximization." This aim leaves little space for idealism. A number of empirical studies have demonstrated that environmental sustainability is typically not prioritized by tourism businesses because it stands in the way of profit maximization. For example, a study of residents' attitudes towards tourism, conservation, growth and change in the Spey Valley in Scotland conducted by Getz (1994) reveals that about 80 per cent of respondents, both in 1978 and 1992 agree or strongly agree with the statement that "We must protect wildlife even at the expense of some development." At the same time, about half of the respondents in both samples agree or strongly agree with the statement that "More skiing facilities would not hurt the Cairngorms too much" and between 56 per cent (in 1978) and 74 per cent (in 1992) agree or strongly agree with the statement that "Nature reserves are here for people to use and more access should be provided to them." While residents display good environmental intentions, the high level of support for additional development does not reflect these intentions.

Barry and Ladkin's (1997) study of small tourism business owners in East Sussex similarly showed that, while they were predominantly in favor of sustainable tourism practices, a key barrier to their implementation was cost. Particular concerns were raised in relation to legislated sustainability policies which would increase cost to a point where marginal businesses may not be able to survive. Similar concerns were raised about additional time that may be required to implement sustainable practices with small business owners stating that they could not afford to spend more time away from their business. Barry and Ladkin's (1997) results are largely confirmed in a study conducted by Knowles et al. (1999). The three key conclusions resulting from their survey study of hotel managers are that (1) most hotels stated that they undertook some kind of environmental action, but that (2) there is a clear gap between theory and practice with "widespread awareness of environmental issues among hoteliers" which is "not always translated into action" (p. 263) and that (3) environmental action is motivated primarily by financial benefits or strategic fit. The key role of financial benefits in encouraging pro-environmental action and the key role of additional resource requirement in discouraging pro-environmental action have been confirmed in a number of studies (including Carlsen, Getz

& Ali-Knight 2001; Garay & Font 2012; Hobson & Essex 2001; van Haastert & de Grosbois 2010; Vernon, Essex, Pinder & Curry 2003).

Hope for the future

Despite the fact that the quest for the substantially sized and economically attractive market segment of environmentally friendly tourists has been unsuccessful, there is still hope for environmentally sustainable tourism. However, harvesting these opportunities will require effort (not necessarily financial) and commitment from different stakeholders to implement. Approaches that have particular potential include traditional ones, such as government regulation, which will need to be implemented in a more committed way, but also possible new avenues such as:

1   Providing infrastructure at the tourist destination which enables tourists who wish to maintain their high level of environmentally friendly everyway behaviors while on vacation to actually engage in those behaviors. Examples include making available separate garbage bins or bicycles for travel around the destination. A more radical approach, tested by Christopher Warren, who runs a highly environmentally sustainable small accommodation business in regional Australia, is to offer visitors a free transfer to a connecting train or coach service and then a free loan of a car during their stay. From the carbon audit of their business, they had identified that petrol consumption by both the business and guests was by far the biggest source of CO_2, so this service helped to reduce the impact of visitors.

2   Providing infrastructure to small tourism businesses to make it easy and viable to engage in environmental practices. An example illustrating what a difference infrastructure makes is provided by Radwan, Jones and Minoli (2012) in the context of the adoption of solid waste management practices in small hotels in the UK. An example of how a small accommodation business in Australia (Crystal Creek Meadows, Kangaroo Valley, New South Wales) provides the necessary infrastructure and calls for active participation from their visitors is provided in the box case; key infrastructure is italicized.

How we minimize our environmental impacts...and with your help make a difference

Recycling

- We promote recycling, reused cardboard for mulching and select items with minimal packaging.

How you can help: *There is a bin for recyclable items in your cottage*, when you leave you can place items in the correct waste bins.

Food Waste

- We have managed to cut landfill waste by 66% in three years. One of the ways we have achieved this is by feeding food scraps to the chickens.

How you can help: Keep your *food scraps in the bucket provided* and feed the chooks; they'll love you for it!

Plastic Waste

- We support Kangaroo Valley's Plastic Bag Free Zone and have a voluntary ban on plastic water bottles.

How you can help: *Buy our refillable water bottles and borrow our shopping bags.*

Water

- Harvest rainwater for our cottages. Collect storm water for property irrigation.

How you can help: Be mindful of water use, especially during times of drought.

Electricity

- Consumption has been cut. Our 5 kW solar farm provides one-third of our needs, the purchased balance is 100% Accredited Green Energy.

How you can help: use natural ventilation (we have designed the cottages so you enjoy the breeze of fresh clean air), use the key tags, turn off outside lights at night, *note the Centmetre (a fun device that shows energy use and cost in real time)*, turn off things you don't require.

Firewood

Firewood from environmentally sustainable forests is a magnificent resource, cleaner and more efficient than electricity…and renewable. Visit our firewood plantation which is also a conservation area for wildlife.

- How you can help: read your wood fire guide that explains how to light your romantic cosy fire efficiently, *collect some kindling* together as you enjoy a walk on the property.

Gas

We use instant hot water systems so there is no energy waste in keeping water storage hot.

- How you can help: don't run the hot water unnecessarily.

Vehicles

- We keep vehicle use to a minimum (buying locally), use E10 fuel.

How you can help*: take advantage of our free rail and bus transfers from Berry;* make the journey to us part of your holiday. Guests can *borrow our bikes* (its fun and you might get to see more), for longer journeys *borrow our car* (conditions apply).

Chemicals

Although not a certified organic farm, Crystal Creek Meadows has a minimal chemical use policy. So you will see some weeds in the garden but also butterflies, bees and birds. Our cottages are cleaned with eco friendly products using native essential oils.

- How you can help: tell us what interesting insects, birds and animals you saw during your walk as we are monitoring the results of low/no chemical use on the land. Enjoy the chemical-free fresh scent in your cottage.

Biodiversity

Free range meat, salmon from Australian fish farms and priority given to organic and local produce. Our aromatherapy range promotes the medicinal values of plants.

- How you can help: select items on local menus and markets that contain local, organic ingredients. Purchase souvenirs made from local sustainable natural materials, or items that are antiques or second hand. Enjoy the scent of the aromatherapy plants on your walks around the property.

Conservation

60% of our property is devoted to conservation through the rehabilitation of wetlands and perennial streams.

- How you can help: Guests can plant trees on our property for $3.50 or enjoy a day in the garden with Christopher and family with some conservation work (kids love to take part and travel in the trailer!).

Every little bit makes a difference. Thank you to all our guests for their participation.

Source: http://www.crystalcreekmeadows.com.au/green-credentials, reproduced with permission of Christopher Warren.

3 Focusing on environmentally friendly kinds of tourism. It is well understood that certain aspects of a vacation come at a higher environmental cost (see, for example, Gössling *et al.* 2005). Therefore, if a tourism destination has the option, it could choose to focus on offering tourism products which have a smaller global environmental footprint, such as short haul city travel (Dolnicar, Laesser & Matus 2010).

4 Harvesting the opportunity of change of context, if managed well, could bear the potential of positive behavioral change. An example of how that can occur in the context of people moving their primary place of residence was provided by Bamberg (2006). Bamberg demonstrated that when people relocate an intervention can have significant impact on their behavior. In the case of Bamberg's study, people who had recently moved had been given a free public transport ticket and a recommended itinerary for the travel required. The recipients increased their use of public transport. The explanation offered by the

author is that the interaction of the change in environment and the intervention (free ticket and itinerary recommendation) caused the effect. This situation is similar to that in the tourism context: people relocate temporarily and have to establish new routines, new ways of traveling around the destination, new ways of disposing of garbage etc. This time of re-establishing routines could offer an invaluable opportunity to modify behavior, for example, by providing a free ticket for public transport or a discount voucher for a market selling locally grown produce etc.

5   Tapping into fundamental mechanisms of human nature and effectively "tricking" tourists into behaving in a more environmentally sustainable manner. A recent empirical study demonstrates how this can be done quite simply and how effective it is: Baca-Motes, Brown, Gneezy, Keenan and Nelson (2013) used cognitive dissonance theory as the mechanism to tap into. They conducted an experiment where they asked random hotel visitors at the hotel check-in to commit, at different levels, to reusing their towels. The highest level of commitment was symbolized by a pin which tagged them as environmentally sustainable in a way that was visible to every other guest in the hotel. In the control group of this experiment 57 per cent of participants hung the towel for reuse at least once, in the highest specific commitment group the percentage was 73 per cent.

6   And there is even still hope for a segmentation approach targeting environmentally sustainable tourists. But, as opposed to the idealistic view presented at the beginning of this chapter, this is likely to be a very small niche segment of people who are absolutely committed to environmental conservation. It is probably not easy to find these people, but some of them are likely to be members of social groups and associations with the mission of environmental protection. Participating in such a group is a good predictor of pro-environmental behavior (Olli, Grendstad & Wollebaek 2001) and could provide tourism marketers with access to this niche market. Another advantage of this approach is that members of this niche segment are very likely to be immune to any shallow attempt of green wash. They are likely, instead, to have a good understanding of what makes a vacation environmentally friendly and will therefore be able to see through attempts of convincing them otherwise using, for example, certification symbols of unknown origin.

Conclusions

There is no doubt that the environmental sustainability of tourism activity matters, both at a local and at a global level. It has also become clear that trusting in tourists' intrinsic motivation to behave in an environmentally friendly manner when on vacation is unlikely to be a successful strategy. There is no mass market or substantially sized market segment of environmentally friendly tourists. While there is some indication that a small – probably extremely small – niche segment of people exists who are passionate about the protection of the environment and assess every behavior, including that on vacation, in view of the environmental cost associated with it, this segment is not large enough to enable the global tourism industry to survive and grow. Nevertheless, this niche segment can be harvested by some destinations; they would probably have to totally commit to being genuinely and all-encompassingly environmentally sustainable to cater for this segment. It may be possible to reach parts of this segment through environmental groups. While this may not provide access to the entire market, it still makes this niche segment actionable and tapping into those who are organized in groups first and then relying on word of mouth may be a successful strategy.

Given that the niche segment discussed above is very small and requires a very specific tourism offer, catering for it is unlikely to make a huge impact on the environmental sustainability of the global tourism industry. Other approaches are needed. Of the traditional approaches, industry self-regulation is not a promising strategy given that the tourism industry is primarily interested in survival and profit. Educating tourists is not a promising strategy either. Given that tourists come to a tourist destination to relax and let their hair down, they are unlikely to represent a captive audience for environmental lectures which will prevent them from having a real break from their everyday life. Government regulation remains an option, if governments are willing to commit to imposing restrictions with serious environmental impacts and, optimally, bear the cost at least for small businesses which may genuinely not be able to afford compliance with strict, new regulations relating to environmental practices. Government interventions that would assist in environmental sustainability could also involve the provision of infrastructure required for some operational aspects which affect the environment, such as solid waste management.

In addition, a number of new demand-side approaches could be investigated, which do not assume the existence of a mass segment of environmentally friendly tourists driven by their intrinsic motivation to protect the environment. Rather, such approaches would involve harvesting opportunities, such as the fact that a vacation is effectively a temporary relocation and that new routines are established. Routine behavior displayed at home cannot be replicated exactly, so the key is to intervene in the establishment phase of vacation routines in an attempt to increase environmentally friendly behavioral options. For example, offering hotel guests free bicycles for moving around the destination as soon as they check into the hotel may prevent them from either considering or investigating other travel options. A second mechanism proven to be highly effective is towel reuse, but this is applicable in other contexts to make tourists commit – if possible in a publicly visible way – to very specific behaviors during their vacation which reduce the negative environmental impact on the vacation.

Key Reading

Baca-Motes, K., Brown, A., Gneezy, A., Keenan, E.A. and Nelson, L.D. (2013) 'Commitment and behavior change: Evidence from the field', *Journal of Consumer Research,* 39: 1070–84.

Blamey, R.K. (1997) 'Ecotourism: The search for an operational definition', *Journal of Sustainable Tourism,* 5: 109–30.

Dolnicar, S. and Grün, B. (2009) 'Environmentally friendly behavior – can heterogeneity among individuals and contexts/environments be harvested for improved sustainable management?', *Environment and Behavior,* 41: 693–714.

Moisander, J. (2007) 'Motivational complexity of green consumerism', *International Journal of Consumer Studies,* 31: 404–9.

Olli, E., Grendstad, G. and Wollebaek, D. (2001) 'Correlates of environmental behaviours: Bringing back social context', *Environment and Behaviour,* 33: 181–208.

References

Baca-Motes, K., Brown, A., Gneezy, A., Keenan, E.A. and Nelson, L.D. (2013) 'Commitment and behavior change: Evidence from the field', *Journal of Consumer Research.* 39: 1070–84.

Ballantine, J.L. and Eagles, P.F. (1994) 'Defining Canadian ecotourists', *Journal of Sustainable Tourism,* 2: 210–14.

Bamberg, S. (2006) 'Is a residential relocation a good opportunity to change people's travel behavior? Results from a theory driven intervention study', *Environment and Behavior*, 38: 820–40.

Barry, S. and Ladkin, A. (1997) 'Sustainable tourism: A regional perspective', *Tourism Management*, 18: 433–40.

Blamey, R.K. (1997) 'Ecotourism: The search for an operational definition', *Journal of Sustainable Tourism*, 5: 109–30.

Carlsen, J., Getz, D. and Ali-Knight, J. (2001) 'The environmental attitudes and practices of family businesses in the rural tourism and hospitality sectors', *Journal of Sustainable Tourism*, 9: 281–97.

Dolnicar, S. (2006) 'Nature-conserving tourists: The need for a broader perspective', *Anatolia*, 17: 235–56.

Dolnicar, S. and Grün, B. (2009) 'Environmentally friendly behavior – can heterogeneity among individuals and contexts/environments be harvested for improved sustainable management?', *Environment and Behavior*, 41: 693–714.

Dolnicar, S., Crouch, G.I. and Long, P. (2008) 'Environmentally friendly tourists: What do we really know about them?', *Journal of Sustainable Tourism*, 16: 197–210.

Dolnicar, S., Laesser, C. and Matus, K. (2010) 'Short haul city travel is truly environmentally sustainable tourism management,' *Tourism Management*, 31: 505–12.

Dolnicar, S., Juvan, E. and Yanamandram, V. (2013) 'Ecotourists – Who are they and what should we really call them?' in R. Ballantyne and J. Packer (eds) *International Handbook on Ecotourism*, Cheltenham: Edward Elgar.

Eagles, P.F. (1992) 'The travel motivations of Canadian ecotourists,' *Journal of Travel Research*, 31: 3–7.

Garay, L. and Font, X. (2012) 'Doing good to do well? Corporate social responsibility reasons, practices and impacts in small and medium accommodation enterprises', *International Journal of Hospitality Management*, 31: 329–37.

Getz, D. (1994) 'Residents' attitudes towards tourism – a longitudinal study in Spey Valley, Scotland', *Tourism Management*, 15: 247–58.

Gössling, S., Peeters, P., Ceron, J., Dubois, G., Patterson, T. and Richardson, R. (2005) 'The eco-efficiency of tourism', *Ecological Economics*, 54: 417–34.

Hobson, K. and Essex, S. (2001) 'Sustainable tourism: A view from accommodation businesses', *Service Industries Journal*, 21: 133–46.

Hvenegaard, G.T. and Dearden, P. (1998) 'Ecotourism versus tourism in a Thai National Park', *Annals of Tourism Research*, 25: 700–20.

Juvan, E. and Dolnicar, S. (2014) 'Can tourists easily choose a low carbon footprint vacation?', *Journal of Sustainable Tourism*, 22: 175–94.

Kerstetter, D.L., Hou, J.S. and Lin, C.H. (2004) 'Profiling Taiwanese ecotourists using a behavioral approach', *Tourism Management*, 25: 491–98.

Knowles, T., Macmillan, S., Palmer, J., Grabowski, P. and Hashimoto, A. (1999) 'The development of environmental initiatives in tourism: Responses from the London hotel sector', *International Journal of Tourism Research*, 1: 255–65.

Mair, J. (2011) 'Exploring air travellers' voluntary carbon-offsetting behaviour', *Journal of Sustainable Tourism*, 19: 215–30.

McKercher, B. (1993) 'Some fundamental truths about tourism: Understanding tourism's social and environmental impacts', *Journal of Sustainable Tourism*, 1: 6–16.

Meric, H.J. and Hunt, J. (1998) 'Ecotourists' motivational and demographic characteristics: A case of North Carolina travellers', *Journal of Travel Research*, 36: 57–61.

Miller, G., Rathouse, K., Scarles, C., Holmes, K. and Tribe, J. (2010) 'Public understanding of sustainable tourism', *Annals of Tourism Research*, 37: 627–45.

Moisander, J. (2007) 'Motivational complexity of green consumerism', *International Journal of Consumer Studies*, 31: 404–9.

Olli, E., Grendstad, G. and Wollebaek, D. (2001) 'Correlates of environmental behaviours: Bringing back social context', *Environment and Behaviour*, 33: 181–208.

Palacio, V. and McCool, S.F. (1997) 'Identifying ecotourists in Belize through benefit segmentation: A preliminary analysis', *Journal of Sustainable Tourism*, 5: 234–43.

Radwan, H.R.I., Jones, E. and Minoli, D. (2012) 'Solid waste management in small hotels: A comparison of green and non-green small hotels in Wales', *Journal of Sustainable Tourism*, 20: 533–50.

Ryan, C., Hughes, K. and Chirgwin, S. (2000) 'The gaze, spectacle and ecotourism', *Annals of Tourism Research*, 27: 148–63.

Tao, C.-H., Eagles, P.F. and Smith, S.L. (2004) 'Implications of alternative definitions of ecotourists', *Tourism Analysis*, 9: 1–13.

van Haastert, M. and de Grosbois, D. (2010) 'Environmental initiatives in bed and breakfast establishments in Canada: Scope and major challenges with implementation,' *Tourism and Hospitality, Planning and Development*, 7: 179–93.

Vernon, J., Essex, S., Pinder, D. and Curry, K. (2003) 'The "greening" of tourism micro-businesses: Outcomes of focus group investigations in South East Cornwall', *Business Strategy and the Environment*, 12: 49–69.

Weaver, D.B. and Lawton, L.J. (2002) 'Overnight ecotourist market segmentation in the Gold Coast Hinterland of Australia', *Journal of Travel Research*, 40: 270–80.

11

Environmental justice and tourism

Rob Hales and Tazim Jamal

Distributive justice This principle is concerned with how goods and benefits are distributed between the members of a society. The key issue here is equitable (which is not the same as equal) distribution of goods and benefits.

Procedural justice At the heart of procedural justice lies fair and just participation of individuals and groups in the socio-political processes through which environmental decisions are made.

Environmental discrimination The practices and results of environmental policies that create disproportionately adverse impacts on minority groups or marginalized communities, diverse populations, women or lower income groups. "Environmental racism" is used when environmental discrimination applies to minority ethnic groups and people of color.

Environmental equity This refers to the fair distribution of environmental benefits, advantages and disadvantages across social groups and populations. Whilst examining root causes and seeking solutions to inequity has always been the principal agenda, this has expanded to more complex and pluralistic conceptions of environmental justice beyond maldistributions and benefits sharing.

Climate justice This refers to the disproportionate vulnerability and adaptive capacity of individuals and communities as a result of climate change. The disadvantaged and poor are a key concern, as are people from less developed countries who have contributed less per capita to global climate change.

Introduction

Despite a rich and growing literature on environmental justice, there is a paucity of research on this subject area in tourism studies (Bramwell & Lane 2008). Social justice issues such as sex tourism and injustices related to exploitation of local cultural rituals are being addressed (see Cole & Morgan 2010). Far less is understood of injustices related to tourism and the distribution and use of ecological resources, especially with respect to the disproportionate impacts of environmental risks and harms on marginalized populations and people of color. The environmental justice literature has expanded the conception of social justice, as Schlosberg (2013: 51) puts it, "into a whole new realm of inequity, misrecognition, and exclusion – that of environmental disadvantage." The concept has expanded from the early influential movements around environmental racism in the USA to embrace pluralistic conceptualizations and diverse communities across the globe.

This chapter situates environmental justice and tourism within this local–global movement. Following a brief history of the environmental justice movement, some key justice-related concepts are presented and discussed, using tourism-related examples as much as possible. Two increasingly important twenty-first century issues, climate change and climate justice, are then addressed. A short case study follows that illustrates some of the issues and concepts discussed thus far. The chapter closes with a forward look at the emerging paradigm of tourism and environmental justice.

Environmental justice and the environment movement

The environmental justice movement gathered momentum with rising awareness and unrest over unfair practices and adverse impacts of development on disadvantaged people, low income earners and minority communities in western societies (Cole & Foster 2000). Waste facility siting was an early issue in the United States, with the first charge of discrimination in waste facility siting under civil rights law taking place in the late 1970s (Bullard 2001). Another defining moment was the summer of 1982 in North Carolina, USA, when the state decided to construct a toxic waste landfill in Warren County, against the wishes of its predominantly black, poor and rural residents (Faber 1998). The story raised international awareness and helped to set the stage for activists fighting environmental injustices related to people of color. The insertion of "justice" into the environmental movement brought attention to minority communities, low-income and poor, ethnic and racial groups and individuals who are exposed to environmental risks brought about by development, and who suffer the consequences of those risks, but have not benefited from the regulation of development in ways that the general population have (Schlosberg 1999). Pursuant to his seminal work *Dumping in Dixie: Race, Class and Environmental Quality* (Bullard 1990), Robert Bullard forwarded an environmental justice principle that "all people and communities are entitled to equal protection of environmental and public health laws and regulations" (Schweitzer 1999 cited in Mohai *et al.* 2009). The US Environmental Protection Agency (EPA) subsequently elaborated this as:

> The fair treatment and meaningful involvement of all people regardless of race, color, national origin, or income with respect to the development, implementation, and enforcement of environmental laws, regulations, and policies. Fair treatment means that no population, due to policy or economic disempowerment, is forced to bear a disproportionate share of the negative human health or environmental impacts of pollution or environmental consequences resulting from industrial, municipal, and commercial operations or the execution of federal, state, local and tribal programs and policies.
>
> *(cited in Mohai et al. 2009)*

Environmental injustices thus tend to occur when individuals or groups are not in a position to effectively respond to environmental harms and risks because of factors such as socio-economic disadvantage, class, race, lack of mobility in housing, plus education levels (Bowen 2002;

Briggs, Abellan & Fecht 2008; Cutter 1995; Mohai & Bryant 1992). The environmental justice movement in the United States rose to address issues related to environmental racism and discrimination in development, environmental policy making, laws and regulatory practices. Its source for action was located within social justice and civil rights movements (Bullard, Warren & Johnson 2005), and women played a significant role (see Di Chiro 1992). Gathering momentum, it expanded to include civil rights and anti-toxic movements, indigenous rights, labor, occupational health and safety movements, and food movements (see Schlosberg 2013). With this came a more collective and unified awareness at a national level, which resulted in greater national regulation in the United States to manage environmental inequalities such as the impacts of pollution and other hazards on disadvantaged communities (Faber 1998). Differences between this movement and the environmental movement (which was made up predominantly of affluent whites with higher education degrees focused on campaigns such as species and biodiversity conservation) were evident—the environmental justice movement focused on the intersection of the environment and social justice issues (Pezzullo 2007).

While the environmental justice literature has traditionally focused on injustices related to disadvantaged populations, people of color and the poor being exposed to environmental harms and hazards such as exposure to toxic waste and industrial pollution due to inequitable environmental policy applications, a number of new trajectories have arisen recently. As Schlosberg (2013) notes, the trend of environmental justice in both theory and practice has expanded into new spaces, and across many boundaries, bringing into focus the examination of issues such as the global nature of environmental injustices, postcolonial environmental justice issues in numerous postcolonial countries, global waste management and disposal issues. A greater emphasis is also evident on issues relevant to rural, natural-resource-dependent communities and residents of the global south (Schroeder 2008). A growing body of research has emerged with respect to inferior access to environmental benefits (e.g. fresh water, clean air, open space) for some diverse, ethnic populations (i.e. environmental inequity; Byrne et al. 2009; Floyd & Johnson 2002).

The shift in environmental justice has paralleled changes in environmental sustainability agendas in both the developing and developed nations. Schlosberg (2013) notes that environmental justice is turning much more specifically to the local experience of increasing vulnerability to climate change. With Hurricane Katrina, for instance, the "link between ecological stability and community functioning – or climate instability and social disadvantage – became clear" (Schlosberg 2013: 47). There has consequently been a shift from local issues of environmental justice to the globalization of environmental issues and the need for international cooperation and regulation to curtail negative socio-environmental impacts that may arise from related dependency-oriented economic development (Burac 2005) and greenhouse gas emissions (Mohai, Pellow & Roberts 2009).

However, Getches and Pellow (2002) caution against conflating evolving environmental justice discourses with the environmental movement, as "it is the additional factor of group disadvantage that merits the heightened attention of the environmental justice movement. Thus, the claims of poor people and of people of color, including tribal communities, are uniquely issues of environmental justice" (Getches & Pellow 2002: 17 cited in Schroeder 2008). Addressing these issues required attention to not only issues of environmental discrimination, racism, equity and distributive justice, but also issues of procedural justice and voice for disadvantaged individuals, communities and populations. These concepts are summarized below and examined from a tourism perspective.

Key environmental justice concepts and issues in tourism

Distributive justice and environmental equity

Distributive justice is concerned with how social and economic goods are distributed between the members of a society. A key issue here is *equitable* distribution of environmental goods and benefits (noting that equitable does not mean equal). *Environmental equity* refers to the fair distribution of environmental benefits, advantages and disadvantages across social groups and populations. The Brundtland Commission's notion of "sustainable development" attempts to incorporate this in terms of intra- and inter-generational equity in development among present and future generations (World Commission on Environment 1987). Distributive justice in the environmental justice context has focused on issues such as water scarcity and water quality, environmental degradation, unequal distribution of resources and unequal access to natural resources (Bullard 1983; Bullard & Johnson 2000; Mohai & Bryant 1992). The state is often considered responsible for the way in which the social and economic goods are distributed (Bojer 2003).

Water consumption and resource conflicts between tourists and residents have been well documented (Holden 2000; Salem 1995; Stonich 1998). Tourists can use considerably more water than residents—up to 15 times the rate of daily use by residents (Gössling *et al.* 2010). Another important line of research relates to inequities related to tourist waste and pollution, but fewer studies have examined related health-related injustices. The impact of sewerage waste has been examined (e.g. in the Caribbean) where high tourist demand has resulted in pollution levels that were deemed a public health hazard for both the local population and the local ecosystem (Grandoit 2005). A political ecology study by Stonich (1998) showed that resident islanders in the Honduras frequently became ill from contaminated drinking water caused by waste from tourism development. Consumption of the island's finite water supply by tourists raised issues of both cost and sustainable access to clean water; the inequities were exacerbated by higher quality hotels being equipped with purification systems that provided safe drinking water to their wealthy inbound visitors, which the poorer islanders could not afford (Stonich 1998).

A growing pool of research also exists on issues of access, exclusion and displacement through tourism development. Studies reveal how coastal resort development has occurred in conjunction with policies that privilege private-sector development (McCool & Moisey 2001; Nicholson-Lord 1993; Wilson 1997). Relocation because of an increase in land prices and the cost of living has denied local residents recreation and leisure that tourists can now enjoy (see Geisler & Lesoalo 2000). A rich body of research has also explored issues of location and access in relation to urban parks, where distance is seen to negatively affect access by lower socio-economic classes (Byrne & Wolch 2009; Byrne, Wolch & Zhang 2009). Studies on the distribution of tourism and recreational sites in the United States revealed ease of access by white collar workers, but more restricted opportunities for blue collar workers who were more likely to be located further away and had limited transportation options (Floyd & Johnson 2002; Porter & Tarrant 2001; Zhang, Tarrant & Green 2008).

Indigenous people have been greatly affected by the creation of parks and protected areas and, despite co-management efforts, there are still considerable inequities and dissatisfaction by local inhabitants (Colchester 2004; Disko 2010; Krueger 2009). A number of studies have explored how conservation interests, and land tenure changes in relation to parks and protected areas can differentially impact certain groups (e.g. Schroeder 2008; Alcorn & Royo 2007). Economic leakage and disproportionate distribution of the economic benefits of environmental resources towards external, multinational interests have been documented (Fennell & Dowling

2003), while pro-poor tourism proponents argue that there should be a greater flow of economic benefits from tourism development to poor residents in the destination (Meyer 2010; Schilcher 2007). *Economic equity* thus addresses the equitable distribution of economic benefits (and costs) from environmental resources among its stakeholders.

The pro-poor tourism approach is not without its critics, as issues of empowerment and self-determination in relation to distributive justice and procedural justice tend to prevail (Scheyvens 2012). Livelihoods and cultural survival may be at stake where local and traditional ways of life are being threatened. For instance, in Nepal, firewood has been depleted as it is used by the tourism trekking industry. This has resulted in increased hardship for local Nepali communities, especially those located further from popular touring routes who are unable to derive any benefit from trekking (Nepal 2000).

Environmental justice and gender was brought to international attention by the Chipko Movement, where local women aggressively protested environmental injustice in India in the 1970s (Taylor 2011). Surprisingly, gender and environmental justice has received limited attention in the tourism literature given the emphasis on the positive role of tourism in decreasing inequality and injustice (Ferguson 2011). This is even more surprising when injustice and gender has been examined at length at the societal level (Di Chiro 1992). Social justice and related environmental issues examined within tourism include sex tourism (Jefferys 1999; Williams 2012), reproductive tourism (Aitchison 2005) and employment and development studies (Ferguson 2011). Richter (1995) concluded that if women were to fill upper management roles in the private and public sector of tourism, *just* decisions over such issues such as health, social welfare and the environment might be more prevalent. Table 11.1 offers examples of research related to environmental equity in tourism (see also Lee & Jamal 2008).

Environmental racism and environmental discrimination

Early research on environmental racism in the United States showed that income and race were strong determinants: low income and minorities were exposed to greater risks than the general population (Bullard 2000); lower socio-economic groups were less likely to benefit from resource access and development policies (Porter & Tarrant 2001). Environmental justice has evolved over the years from discriminatory social practices rooted in environmental racism to a global phenomenon addressing racism as well as discriminatory environmental practices affecting diverse, low-income, marginalized groups and populations at societal and community levels (Bullard & Wright 1990; Mohai & Bryant 1992). *Environmental discrimination*, more broadly, refers to the disproportionate (intentional or unintentional) impact of environmental policy and rules on individuals (gender is one issue here), populations or communities of minority groups or races, low income and the poor.

There is strong evidence of environmental racism related to outdoor recreation and parks in the United States of America—controversy notwithstanding (see Tarrant & Cordell 1999; Taylor 2011). Porter and Tarrant (2001) examined whether inequalities exist for certain socio-economic and ethnic groups with respect to the distribution of federally managed tourism sites in Southern Appalachia. They found that there was a negative relationship between income, occupation and the location of a number of federal tourist sites. Low income, ethnic minorities and the poor are especially vulnerable, even more so if they face unfair discrimination due to historical or structural conditions (e.g. by dominant groups in a postcolonial or post–civil war context). Research recommendations include the adoption of rules and regulations, the enforcement of existing laws and regulations, as well as changes in philosophies and attitudes, to eliminate environmental racism (Newton 1996).

Table 11.1 Environmental equity issues in tourism

Realm of equity issue	Specific issues	Examples of research studies
Waste and pollution	Water pollution, air quality and waste management inequities resulting from over-exploitation by tourism	Jenner & Smith (1992), Stonich (1998), Ukayli & Husain (1988), Holden (2000), Pezzullo (2007), Meletis & Campbell (2009)
Issues of access, exclusion and displacement	Distribution and location of tourism and recreational sites	Floyd & Johnson (2002), Porter & Tarrant (2001), Byrne & Wolch (2009)
		Byrne, Wolch & Zhang (2009), Zebich-Knos (2008), Zhang, et al. (2008)
	Land use change—freehold or park creation and conversion. Impacts on indigenous people	McCool & Stankey (2001), Nicholson-Lord (1993)
		Wilson (1997), Akama (1999), Geisler & Lesoalo (2000), Akama & Camargo (2011)
	Gender, environmental justice and tourism	Ferguson (2011), Tucker (2012)
Inequitable distribution of costs and benefits	Water consumption and resource conflicts between tourists and residents	Draper (1997), Gössling (2001), Holden (2000), Salem (1995), Stonich (1998)
	Human rights and antipoaching programs vs. land entitlement claims	Schroeder (2008), Alcorn & Royo (2007)
	Economic equity	Fennell (2003), Weaver (1998), Schroeder (2008)
	Deforestation and sustainable livelihoods	Nepal (2000)
Public health and environmental health	Tourism development and environmental health plus human health	Grandoit (2005), Stonich (1998)

Neocolonial effects from tourism can further exacerbate environmental inequalities. Torres and Momsen (2005), for instance, illustrate the hardships of impoverished workers in Cancun, a popular resort destination that lies at the northern end of the Riviera Maya, Mexico. There are huge disparities between the tourist zones and the impoverished town periphery where shanty townships and squatter colonies are inhabited by a huge proportion of Cancun's low-paid, unskilled laborers, migrants and the poorest—a continuum ranging from extreme luxury to abject poverty and a complete absence of basic services. Beach access for local residents is also highly restricted. The minority Mayan population bears the consequences of both historically embedded racism as well as neocolonialism in the guise of mass tourism in Cancun and the Riviera Maya (Jamal & Camargo 2014). Similar examples such as Carlisle (2010) support an argument for broadening the study of environmental justice to encompass not only places of everyday life, but also the historical context and the transnational geopolitical context in which tourism and development-related socio-environmental injustices to the poor might be embedded.

The various articles in Baver and Lynch (2005) add a further layer of complexity. Using a political ecology lens in the study of Caribbean populations and tourism, these studies show tourism-related environmental discrimination (e.g. Burac 2005), as well as environmental risks and harms stemming from other sources such as industrial pollution that were endangering public health among the working poor (Pizzini 2006). Unpacking these interrelated issues requires close attention to processes and approaches to development, planning and policy making that address not only racial inequalities in relation to tourism, but also the *cumulative* environmental-social effects of various forms of development and growth (including tourism) on diverse and disadvantaged populations, including women and the working poor.

Procedural justice

Integral to enabling distributive justice is *procedural justice*, the socio-political processes through which environmental decisions, rules, regulations and policies are enacted within and between societies. Participation by individuals and societal groups within the system lies at the heart of procedural justice. The influential political theorist, John Rawls (2001) forwarded a concept of justice that is based on individual freedom (liberty) as well as the fair and equitable distribution of goods and benefits of development. The ability of people to freely influence decision making related to environmental policy, planning and regulation is essential (see case study below, related to free prior consent), and a punitive system is commonly relied on for reinforcing justice-related principles.

Two appropriate norms for procedural justice are, therefore, "fair compensation" and "participative justice" as summarized by Whyte (2010): "'Fair compensation' requires that environmental tourism practices generate fair exchanges of good, bad, and risks; 'participative justice' requires that all agents who stand to benefit or be harmed have the opportunity to give their informed consent." Examples of procedural injustices can be seen in Stonich's (1998) political ecology study of international tourism in Honduras, where local residents bore the brunt of inequitable use and appropriation of finite water resources by tourism industry stakeholders—nor did they have the means to alter these inequalities.

Participative justice is integral not only to enable a formal opportunity to address discriminatory or race-related harms or risks, but also to having *meaningful* participation (i.e. in accordance with a community member or group's social circumstances and cultural terms (Whyte 2010)). Using an environmental justice approach to examine the solid waste impact of ecotourism in Tortuguero, Costa Rica (renowned for its turtle conservation and ecotourism programs),

157

Meletis and Campbell (2009: 743) observed that local residents used the language of justice to describe the waste crisis: "They saw the lodges and other powerful tourism actors as greatly benefiting from tourism to Tortuguero, while residents were bearing heavy costs related to its increasing waste burden." Leakage of tourism profits is high, foreign ownership is dominant, and there is no local bank to capture deposits or facilitate local investment; job positions are mostly menial. The residents recognized the village's dependency on tourism, and perceived the reluctance of the local government, the Park, and the lodges to contribute to local waste management to be unfair and unjust because "their community remains marginalized, without the resources and support required to manage the negative environmental impacts that its members must live with but did not necessarily consent to" (Meletis & Campbell 2009: 772). Willingness by local or state authorities to provide mechanisms for consent or direct resident participation in this economically marginalized community was not evident.

"How can the benefits of nature's bounty—captured by small, rural communities involving common pool resources—be best distributed among their residents?" Following this question, McCool (2012: 1) notes the need for governance systems that can effectively manage common pool resources and services, where access and regulation are particularly challenging with respect to conservation and use. Mohai *et al.* (2009) discuss the growth of transnational social movement organizations and networks concerned with environmental justice and human rights issues focused on a range of government and industrial sectors. But the most important components of that movement, as they explain, are the domestic local, regional and national organizations in the various nations and communities. "Together, the numerous local grassroots organizations and their collaborating global networks produce and maintain a transnational public sphere" (Mohai *et al.* 2009: 423–24). In the context of tourism and ecotourism, the "transnational public sphere" includes global tourism organizations like the United Nations World Tourism Organization, numerous environmental NGOs and active civil society organizations like Ecumenical Coalition on Tourism (ECOT), Tourism Concern and Equitable Tourism Options (better known as EQUATIONS), as well as approaches like the Pro-Poor Tourism Partnership (see Higgins-Desbiolles *et al.* 2013).

Opportunities for coalition building and the participation of local, indigenous and traditional knowledge is especially important in conservation projects driven by dominant narratives of science and by conservation organizations (see Tsosie 2007; Whyte 2010). Schroeder's (2008) political economy study of wildlife management in Tanzania illustrates how Tanzanian wildlife authorities chose to pursue revenue sharing via rural development projects that were limited in addressing community concerns and bore little connection to the costs borne by communities in wildlife management areas that served tourist markets.

Climate justice

Tourism contributes 5% of the world's greenhouse gas emissions but this is projected to double in 25 years unless low-carbon, resource-efficient policies are enacted (OECD-UNEP 2011). Although small in comparison to other sector contributions, it is significant as the unfettered growth of tourism, lack of progressive action on climate change mitigation in the tourism sector, dependency on export earnings through tourism, and the high impact of climate change on developing countries, may contribute significantly to climate change injustices (Scott & Becken 2010; Scott, Peeters & Gössling 2010; Thomas & Twyman 2005; see also Chapter 3). The burden is greater for developing countries due to lack of adaptive capacity and ability to cope with the risks and costs of climate change (Posner & Sunstein 2007). However, it should be noted that the cumulative total emissions are higher from developing countries compared to developed countries. Increased tourism in developing countries (and their trade with developed countries) will most likely tend to increase their greenhouse gas emissions (Heil & Selden 2001).

There are three realms of injustices related to climate change and tourism: (i) on a global scale in terms of nation states experiencing the injustice of climate change; (ii) within countries where climate change disproportionately impacts local populations; and (iii) as experienced by many communities of indigenous people around the globe. Climate change adaptation strategies for a large proportion of indigenous people living in remote areas often emphasize removing and re-situating their communities (Nyong, Adesina & Osman 2007). Considering that many exist on the periphery of the economic system and that their contributions to greenhouse gas emissions are minimal, the burden placed on these communities are great and they are more vulnerable because climate change directly impacts on their relationship with their traditional homelands (United Nations University 2008).

One challenge of climate justice for disadvantaged people in developed countries, as well as for marginalized people in developing countries and for impacted indigenous communities, is to address distributive justice issues through legislative, regulatory and policy mechanisms—enacting procedural justice to coordinate, regulate and enable equity (Adger 2001). A self-determination approach enacting the rights and sovereignty of indigenous people is a key element here (Tsosie 2009), and participative justice is vital (Whyte 2010). Moreover, a conception of rights is needed that is not based on a compensatory tort-based system to redress the harms of climate change as this does not factor traditional association to homelands (Tsosie 2007).

Case Study

Indigenous consultation, Cape York Peninsula

This case illustrates how difficult it is to ensure the just treatment of indigenous people in the face of development that uses tourism as a significant justification. At issue is the potential World Heritage nomination of parts of Cape York Peninsula in northern Australia. The nomination process is still progressing at the time of writing with ongoing negotiations with traditional owners and other stakeholders. It is the intention of the Australian Government to submit a nomination in 2013.

The land use context of Cape York Peninsula is complex and contested (Holmes 2011). There are over 100 Traditional Owner clan groups on Cape York Peninsula, located within 17 indigenous communities and represented by 11 Shire Councils. The Cape York Land Council is the peak representative body that represents indigenous people in their land rights claims and other indigenous matters. To date, over 70 Land Trusts and Prescribed Body Corporate organizations have been established. The Aboriginal and Torres Strait Islander people make up over 60% of the total population of 18,000 people. Aboriginal people's language, dance, song, art and customs are still very much alive and practiced, and vary from community to community.

The Queensland Government and the Australian Federal Government have indicated the importance of the consent of the indigenous people and have stated that a nomination will not proceed without the consent of Traditional Owners (Australian Government 2013). However, UNESCO does not include free, prior, informed consent as a criterion for indigenous agreement to World Heritage nominations (Disko 2010), despite lobbying by indigenous representative groups worldwide. Prevailing issues relate to sovereignty and to operationalizing the principles of free, prior, informed, consent (Hales *et al.* 2013). Consent is needed from a range of sources, including individual members of affected communities, representative traditional owners of each homeland to be included in the potential nomination, and representative organizations that collectively negotiate with the state (the proponent of the World Heritage nomination process). These are problems of procedural justice.

The next layer to consider is tourism, as it is purported to be a major benefit of the nomination. Economic modeling conducted by Chester and Drimwal (2012) indicates that benefits for the period 2011 to 2031 could be AUD$13–30 million if state investment were to occur. To date, there is little evidence that the World Heritage definition has increased economic development in Australia, and it is unlikely to do so in the Cape York case (Buckley 2002; Chester & Drimwal 2012).

For tourism to be of benefit "the management regime needs to engage the local community, management staff [should] be permanently based in the region, and it involves establishing long term programs which train, employ and empower indigenous and local community staff" (Chester & Drimwal 2012: 118). Whyte's (2010) framework for indigenous tourism may offer helpful guidance for distributive and procedural justice here: it involves fair compensation through agreements; participative justice through forums for meaningful representations; and an ethic of coalition development as opposed to mutually advantageous exploitation. However, the problems of gaining consent detailed above, and the lack of UNESCO guideline, suggest that benefits from investment in tourism development may be uncertain, and less than adequate participative justice may result for the indigenous peoples involved.

The way forward

Environmental justice has evolved from locally situated issues of maldistribution and benefit sharing to a global-level concept and movement. It has shifted from seeking solutions to environmental inequities (i.e. distributive justice), particularly as related to discrimination and racism, to more pluralistic concepts of environmental justice. In its latest incarnation, as Schlosberg (2013: 51) observes, environmental justice "is now also about the material relationships between human disadvantage and vulnerability and the condition of the environment and natural world in which that experience is immersed." This expanding body of research in environmental justice has much to offer to tourism studies.

The small, evolving, base of tourism-related research appears to reflect this expanded notion well (see Higgins-Desbiolles *et al.* 2013). Political ecology and political economy, as well as participatory action research, offer useful theoretical and methodological directions to understanding issues around environmental equity and distributive justice (Stonich 1998; Schroeder 2008). The chapter offered examples related to access, exclusion, displacement, pollution, waste and public health. Research on the political ecology of consumption also offers promise for extending the analysis of tourism and associated impacts to tourists (Meletis & Campbell 2009; see Torres & Momsen 2005 for a geographical approach). Challenging ethical imperatives arise in notions of "just sustainability" (Bramwell & Lane 2008), and the "Just Destination" (Jamal & Camargo, 2014).

Climate change and climate justice agendas will continue to raise awareness of participative justice and procedural justice with respect to marginalized communities and diverse populations, including women, low income, indigenous and ethnic minorities. Issues such as prioritizing self-determination within free, prior, informed, consent to ensure the intent of the United Nations Declaration on the Rights of Indigenous Peoples, reflect these priorities (Hales *et al.* 2013). The compilation of articles in Baver and Lynch (2005) illustrates the importance of addressing the geopolitical landscape of neocolonial and postcolonial issues, as well as academic-community collaborations that bring in alternative research perspectives and the voices of the "other." A critical sustainability agenda awaits tourism and environmental justice in bridging the "North–South" gap in research and practice.

Key Reading

Schroeder, R. (2008) 'Environmental justice and the market: The politics of sharing wildlife revenues in Tanzania', *Society and Natural Resources*, 21: 583–96.

Meletis, Z. and Campbell, L. (2009) 'Benevolent and benign? Using environmental justice to investigate waste-related impacts of ecotourism in destination communities', *Antipode*, 41: 741–80.

Whyte, K. (2010) 'An environmental justice framework for indigenous tourism', *Journal of Environmental Philosophy*, 7: 75–92.

Higgins-Desbiolles, F., Whyte, K. and Tedmanson, D. (2013) 'Tourism and environmental justice', in D. Dustin and K. Schwab (eds) *Just Leisure: Things That We Believe In*, Illinois: Sagamore Publishing.

Cole, S. and Morgan, N. (eds) (2010) *Tourism and Inequality: Problems and Prospects*, Oxford: CAB International.

References

Adger, W. (2001) 'Scales of governance and environmental justice for adaptation and mitigation of climate change', *Journal of International Development*, 13: 921–31.

Aitchison, C. (2005) 'Feminist and gender perspectives in tourism studies: The social-cultural nexus of critical and cultural theories', *Tourist Studies*, 5: 207–24.

Akama, J. and Camargo, C. (2011) 'Wildlife conservation, safari tourism and the role of certification in Kenya', in T. Jamal and D. Dredge (eds) *Special Issue on Certification and Indicators, Tourism Recreation Research*, 36: 281–91.

Alcorn, J. and Royo, A. (2007) 'Conservation's engagement with human rights: "Traction," "slippage," "or avoidance"', *Policy Matters*, 15: 115–39.

Australian Government (2013) *A World Heritage Nomination for Cape York Peninsula*. Available at: www.environment.gov.au/heritage/about/world/cape-york/nomination.html (accessed 1 April 2013).

Baver, S. and Lynch, B. (eds) (2005) *Beyond Sun and Sand: Caribbean Environmentalisms*, New Jersey: Rutgers University Press.

Bojer, H. (2003) *Distributional Justice: Theory and Measurement*, London: Routledge.

Bowen, W. (2002) 'An analytical review of environmental justice research: What do we really know?' *Environmental Management*, 29: 3–15.

Bramwell, B. and Lane, B. (2008) 'Priorities in sustainable tourism research', *Journal of Sustainable Tourism*, 6: 1–4.

Briggs, D., Abellan, J. and Fecht, D. (2008) 'Environmental inequity in England: Small area associations between socio-economic status and environmental pollution', *Social Science & Medicine*, 67: 1612–29.

Buckley, R. (2002) *World Heritage Icon Value: Contribution of World Heritage Branding to Nature Tourism*, Canberra: Australian Heritage Commission.

Bullard, R.D. (1983) 'Solid waste sites and the Black Houston community', *Sociological Inquiry*, 53(Spring): 273–88.

Bullard, R.D. (1990). 'Ecological inequities and the New South: Black communities under siege', *Journal of Ethnic Studies*, 17(Winter), 101–115.

Bullard, R.D. (2000) *Dumping in Dixie: Race, class, and environmental quality* (3rd ed.). Boulder, CO: Westview Press.

Bullard, R.D. (2001) 'Environmental justice in the 21st century: Race still matters', *Phylon*, 49 (3/4): 151–71.

Bullard, R.D. & Johnson, G.S. (2000) 'Environmentalism and public policy: Environmental justice: Grassroots activism and its impact on public policy decision making', *Journal of Social Issues*, *56*(3), 555–78.

Bullard, R. D. and Wright, B. H. (1990) The quest for environmental equity: Mobilizing the African–American community for social change. *Society & Natural Resources*, 3(4), 301–311.

Bullard, R., Warren, R. and Johnson, G. (2005) *The Quest for Environmental Justice: Human Rights and the Politics of Pollution*, San Francisco: Sierra Club Books.

Burac, M. (2005) 'The struggle for sustainable tourism in Martinique', in S. Baver and B. Lynch (eds) *Beyond Sun and Sand: Caribbean Environmentalism*, New Jersey: Rutgers University Press.

Byrne, J. and Wolch, J. (2009) 'Nature, race, and parks: Past research and future directions for geographic research', *Progress in Human Geography*, 33: 743–65.

Byrne, J., Wolch, J. and Zhang, J. (2009) 'Planning for environmental justice in an urban national park', *Journal of Environmental Planning and Management*, 52: 365–92.

Carlisle, S. (2010) 'Access and marginalization in a beach enclave resort', in S. Cole and N. Morgan (eds) *Tourism and Inequality: Problems and Prospects*, Oxford: CAB International.

Chester, G. and Drimwal, S. (2012) *The Potential Economic Benefits of Protecting and Presenting Cape York*, Cairns: EcoSustainability Pty Ltd.

Colchester, M. (2004) 'Conservation policy and indigenous peoples', *Environmental Science & Policy*, 7: 145–53.

Cole, S. and Morgan, N. (eds) (2010) *Tourism and Inequality: Problems and Prospects*, Oxford: CAB International.

Cutter, S.L. (1995) 'Race, class and environmental justice', *Progress in Human Geography*, 19: 111.

Di Chiro, G. (1992) 'Defining environmental justice: Women's voices and grassroots politics', *Socialist Review*, 22: 92–130.

Disko, S. (2010) 'World heritage sites in indigenous peoples territories: Ways of ensuring respect for indigenous cultures, values and human rights', in O. Dieter, Z. Walther and A. Marie-Theres (eds) *World Heritage and Cultural Diversity*, Cottbus: German Commission for UNESCO.

Draper, D. (1997) 'Touristic development and water sustainability in Banff and Canmore, Alberta, Canada', *Journal of Sustainable Tourism*, 5(3), 183–212.

Faber, D. (1998) *The Struggle for Ecological Democracy: Environmental Justice Movements in the United States*, New York: The Guilford Press.

Fennell, D. (2003). Ecotourism (2nd ed) London: Routledge.

Fennell, D. and Dowling, R. (2003) *Ecotourism Policy and Planning*, Wallingford: Cabi Publishing.

Ferguson, L. (2011) 'Promoting gender equality and empowering women? Tourism and the third Millennium Development Goal', *Current Issues in Tourism* 14: 235–49.

Floyd, M. and Johnson, C. (2002) 'Coming to terms with environmental justice in outdoor recreation: A conceptual discussion with research implications', *Leisure Sciences*, 24: 59–77.

Geisler, C. and Lesoalo, E. (2000) 'Rethinking land reform in South Africa: An alternative approach to environmental justice', *Sociological Research*, 5(2).

Gössling, S., Peeters, P., Hall, C.M., Ceron, J.-P., Dubois, G., Lehmann, L.V. and Scott, D. (2010) 'Tourism and water use: supply, demand, and security – an international review', *Tourism Management*, 33: 1–15.

Grandoit, J. (2005) 'Tourism as a development tool in the Caribbean and the environmental by-products: The stresses on small island resources and viable remedies', *Journal of Development and Social Transformation*, 2: 89–97.

Hales, R., Rynne, J., Howlett, C., Devine, J. and Houser, V. (2013) 'Indigenous free prior informed consent: A case for self determination in world heritage nomination processes', *International Journal of Heritage Studies*, 19: 1–18.

Heil, M. and Selden, T. (2001) 'International trade intensity and carbon emissions: A cross–country econometric analysis', *The Journal of Environment & Development*, 10: 35–49.

Higgins-Desbiolles, F., Whyte, K. and Tedmanson, D. (2013) 'Tourism and environmental justice' in D. Dustin and K. Schwab (eds) *Just Leisure: Things That We Believe In*, Illinois: Sagamore Publishing.

Holden, A. (2000) *Environment and Tourism*, London: Routledge.

Holmes, J. (2011) 'Contesting the future of Cape York Peninsula', *Australian Geographer*, 42: 53–68.

Jamal, T. and Camargo, B. (2014) 'Sustainable tourism, justice and an ethic of care: Toward the just destination', *Journal of Sustainable Tourism*, 22(1): 11–30.

Jeffreys, S. (1999). Globalizing sexual exploitation: Sex tourism and the traffic in women. *Leisure Studies*, 18(3), 179–196.

Jenner, P. and Smith, C. (1992) *The Tourism Industry and the Environment*, London: Economist intelligence unit.

Krueger, L. (2009) 'Protected areas and human displacement: Improving the interface between policy and practice', *Conservation and Society*, 7: 21.

Lee, S. and Jamal, T. (2008) 'Environmental justice and environmental equity in tourism: missing links to sustainability', *Journal of Ecotourism*, 7: 44–67.

McCool, S. (2012) 'Distributing the benefits of nature's bounty: A social justice perspective'. Paper presented at International Symposium on Managing Benefit Sharing in Changing Social Ecological Systems, Windhoek, Namibia, June 2012.

McCool, S.F. and Moisey, R.N. (eds) (2001) *Tourism, Recreation and Sustainability: Linking Culture and the Environment*, New York: CABI Publishing.

Meletis, Z. and Campbell, L. (2009) 'Benevolent and benign? Using environmental justice to investigate waste-related impacts of ecotourism in destination communities', *Antipode*, 41: 741–80.

Meyer, D. (2010). Pro-poor tourism: can tourism contribute to poverty reduction in less economically developed countries?. In S. Cole and N. Morgan (eds), *Tourism and inequality: Problems and prospects*, 164–182. Wallingsford: CABI.

Mohai, P. and Bryant, B. (1992) 'Environmental injustice: Weighing race and class as factors in the distribution of environmental hazards', *University of Colorado Law Review*, 63: 921.

Mohai, P., Pellow, D. and Roberts, J. (2009) 'Environmental justice', *Annual Review of Environment and Resources*, 34: 405–30.

Nepal, S. K. (2000) Tourism in protected areas: the Nepalese Himalaya, *Annals of Tourism Research*, 27(3), 661–681.

Newton, D.E. (1996) *Environmental Justice: a reference handbook*. Santa Barbara, CA: ABC-CLIO.

Nicholson-Lord, D. (1993) 'Mass tourism is blamed for paradise lost in Goa', *The Independent*, 27: 10–11.

Nyong, A., Adesina, F. and Osman, E. (2007) 'The value of indigenous knowledge in climate change mitigation and adaptation strategies in the African Sahel', *Mitigation and Adaptation Strategies for Global Change*, 12: 787–97.

OECD-UNEP (2011) *Climate Change and Tourism Policy in OECD Countries*, Organisation for Economic Co-operation and Development (OECD), Geneva: United Nations Environment Programme.

Pezzullo, P. (2007) *Toxic Tourism: Rhetorics of Pollution, Travel, and Environmental Justice*, Tuscaloosa: The University of Alabama Press.

Pizzini, M.V. (2006) 'Historical connections and future trends in the coastal zone, the environment movement of Puerto Rico', in S. Baver and B. Lynch (eds) *Beyond Sun and Sand: Caribbean Environmentalism*, New Jersey: Rutgers University Press.

Porter, R. and Tarrant, M. (2001) 'A case study of environmental justice and federal tourism sites in southern Appalachia: A GIS application', *Journal of Travel Research*, 40: 27–40.

Posner, E. and Sunstein, C. (2007) 'Climate change justice', *Georgia Law Journal*, 96: 1565.

Rawls, J. (2001) *Justice as Fairness: A Restatement*, Cambridge: Harvard University Press.

Richter, L.K. (1995) 'Exploring the political role of gender in tourism research', in W. Theobald (ed.) *Global Tourism: The Next Decade*, Oxford: Butterworth-Heinemann.

Salem, N. (1995) 'Water rights', *Tourism in Focus*, 17: 4–5.

Scheyvens, R. (2012) 'Pro-poor tourism: Is there value beyond the rhetoric?', *Critical Debates in Tourism*, 57: 124.

Schilcher, D. (2007) Growth versus equity: The continuum of pro-poor tourism and neoliberal governance. *Current Issues in Tourism*, 10(2-3), 166–193.

Schlosberg, D. (2013) 'Theorizing environmental justice: The expanding sphere of a discourse', *Environmental Politics*, 22: 37–55.

Schroeder, R. (2008) 'Environmental justice and the market: The politics of sharing wildlife revenues in Tanzania', *Society and Natural Resources*, 21: 583–96.

Scott, D. and Becken, S. (2010) 'Adapting to climate change and climate policy: Progress, problems and potentials', *Journal of Sustainable Tourism*, 18: 283–95.

Scott, D., Peeters, P. and Gössling, S. (2010) 'Can tourism deliver its "aspirational" greenhouse gas emission reduction targets?', *Journal of Sustainable Tourism*, 18: 393–408.

Stonich, S.C. (1998) 'Political ecology of tourism', *Annals of Tourism Research*, 25: 25–54.

Tarrant, M. and Cordell, H. (1999) 'Environmental justice and the spatial distribution of outdoor recreation sites: An application of geographic information systems', *Journal of Leisure Research*, 31: 18–34.

Taylor, D. (2011) 'The evolution of environmental justice activism, research, and scholarship: Environmental practice', *Environmental Politics*, 13: 280–301

Thomas, D. and Twyman, C. (2005) 'Equity and justice in climate change adaptation amongst natural-resource-dependent societies', *Global Environmental Change*, 15: 115–24.

Torres, R. and Momsen, J. (2005) 'Gringolandia: The construction of a new tourist space in Mexico', *Annals of the Association of American Geographers*, 95: 314–35.

Tsosie, R. (2007) 'Indigenous people and environmental justice: The impact of climate change', *University of Colorado Law Review*, 78: 1625.

—— (2009) 'Climate change, sustainability and globalization: Charting the future of indigenous environmental self-determination', *Environmental and Energy Law and Policy*, 4: 188.

Ukayli, M. and Husain, T. (1988) 'Comparative evaluation of surface water availability, wastewater reuse and desalination in Saudi Arabia', *Water International*, 13: 218–25.

United Nations University (2008) 'Indigenous peoples and climate change', paper presented at Internatial Expert Group Meeting on Indigenous Peoples and Climate Change, Darwin, April 2008.

Weaver, D. (1998) *Ecotourism in the Less Developed World*, New York: CAB International.

Whyte, K. (2010) 'An environmental justice framework for indigenous tourism', *Journal of Environmental Philosophy* 7: 75–92.

Williams, L. (2012) 'Sex Tourism', in *Wiley-Blackwell Encyclopedia of Globalization*, New Jersey: Wiley. DOI: 10.1002/9780470670590.wbeog516.

Wilson, A. (1997) *Ukrainian Nationalism in the 1990s: A Minority Faith*, Cambridge: Cambridge University Press.

World Commission on Environment (1987) *Report of the World Commission on Environment and Development: Our Common Future*, Oxford: Oxford University Press.

Zebich-Knos, M. (2008) 'Ecotourism, park systems, and environmental justice in Latin America', in D.V. Carruthers (ed.) *Environmental Justice in Latin America: Problems, Promise, and Practice*, London: MIT Press.

Zhang, Y., Tarrant, M. and Green, G. (2008) 'The importance of differentiating urban and rural phenomena in examining the unequal distribution of locally desirable land', *Journal of Environmental Management*, 88: 1314–19.

12

Consumptive and non-consumptive tourism practices

The case of wildlife tourism

Brent Lovelock

Consumption '...a vast range of human practices and mental and feeling states (shopping, buying, acquiring, desiring, daydreaming, fantasizing) all of which involve complex relations and attachments to an infinite variety of objects and experiences' (Dunn 2008: 1).

Consumptive wildlife tourism 'A form of leisure travel undertaken for the purpose of hunting or shooting game animals, or fishing for sports fish, either in natural areas or in areas created for these purposes' (Lovelock 2008: 4).

Non-consumptive wildlife tourism 'A human recreational engagement with wildlife wherein the focal organism is not purposefully removed or permanently affected by the engagement' (Duffus & Dearden 1990: 215).

Introduction

The practice of consumption has become a defining element of many postmodern tourism-generating societies (Bocock 1993). Within such societies, tourism, as a significant form of leisure, plays an important role in shaping and defining consumption, and has been suggested to be the 'paradigm case' for all modern consumption (Campbell 1995). Unfortunately, the nature of tourism consumption is problematic – to the extent that it is seen as a barrier to achieving sustainable tourism outcomes (Sharpley 2006). Given the central roles of consumption and of touristic consumption, and the potential problems associated with touristic consumption, it is pertinent to address issues of consumption (and non-consumption) in this chapter.

The focus of this chapter is on how we consume nature through tourism, and in particular, how tourism consumes wildlife. Whether or not to allow consumptive use of wildlife for tourism is one of the most controversial topics of contemporary wildlife management and conservation (Meguro & Inoue 2011). Wildlife tourism has become a flashpoint for the debate about the nature of touristic consumption, and about what is consumptive and what is non-consumptive – a discussion that has increasingly been framed as a debate over what is 'right' and what is 'wrong'.

The chapter has three main goals. First, to explain what consumption means from a number of perspectives, and in particular in relation to wildlife tourism. Consumptive wildlife tourism is situated within broader debates about consumption. Then the focus is on how tourism consumes wildlife, and the meanings and relative impacts of consumptive and non-consumptive uses of wildlife. The discussion then examines the case of ecotourism, which is considered within this consumptive/non-consumptive framework. Since ecotourism is often held as a 'role model' for the tourism industry, it is important to develop some clarity around how and what ecotourism consumes. Note that the common terminology of 'consumptive' and 'non-consumptive' is used throughout the chapter while it is acknowledged that this dichotomy is open to challenge.

Consumption as a market-based activity

Consumption is a broad concept and defies simple definition, but consists of 'activities potentially leading to and actually following from the acquisition of a good or service by those engaging in such activities' (Belk 2007: 731). Such a definition of consumption, however, implies that it is something that occurs only within 'the market'. Commentators such as Cook believe that we find all our leisure, including tourism, within consumer society: 'We don't live near or beside consumer society, but within it' (Cook 2006: 313). The counterargument is that not all leisure (and we can use the same argument for tourism) can be equated with consumption (Stebbins 2009). For example, if we consider nature-based and wildlife tourism, much of this has some elements of commercialisation, but there are also many non-commercial aspects. It is thus possible to identify a category of 'non-consumptive leisure' which includes activities that cost nothing or have a negligible cost (Stebbins 2009: 118). Stebbins' proposition is that consumption and leisure occupy 'in significant measure' separate worlds and that 'leisure and consumption are not an identity' (2009: 126).

> Whereas economists view the act of purchasing a good or service as lying at the heart of consumption, a leisure-studies based understanding of the consumptive process places the accent elsewhere…[and] minimises the significance of the demarcating act of buying or renting something.
>
> *(Stebbins 2009: 132)*

Certainly not all tourism activities fall within this scope of commercialised leisure either, and particularly much nature-based tourism and wildlife tourism is non-commercial. Thus to define all these activities as consumption, within the sense that the consumer (and the commodity) is subsumed within a capitalist system of 'domination and manipulation' (Dunn 2008: 116) is too restrictive.

Consumption as the creation of meaning

Considering the broad possibilities of tourism (and wildlife tourism), the above market-based conceptualisation of consumption is too narrow for our discussion here. Rather, a broader interpretation may be more appropriate whereby consumption (at least within postmodern late-capitalist societies) 'has assumed a dominant and significantly more complex role than simple utilitarian need satisfaction' (Sharpley 2006: 18). Thus consumption may be considered to include:

...a vast range of human practices and mental and feeling states (shopping, buying, acquiring, desiring, daydreaming, fantasizing) all of which involve complex relations and attachments to an infinite variety of objects and experiences.

(Dunn 2008: 1)

In this sense, consumption is increasingly associated with the creation of meaning where 'the object of consumption is not so much tangible products as coded cultural meanings' (Dunn 2008: 4). Such a broader interpretation of consumption is useful when considering the debate over wildlife uses, as it allows us to consider in a more holistic manner, the implications of consumption within this context. For example, the so-called consumptive wildlife tourism activities, of hunting, fishing and killing of wildlife, have often been considered 'beyond the pale' of acceptable tourism activities, because of a range of ethical and ecological concerns. By participating in, allowing, or condoning, such activities, what meanings are being created by our consumptive practices, as tourists, as tour operators, and as an industry? We might also ask what the relationships are between the 'meanings' that are created by such consumptive practice and the more tangible, physical consequences of the consumption.

Consumption as a user of resources

Perhaps the most understandable and significant conceptualisation of consumption involves its function as a user (reducer, extractor or destroyer) of resources. Within the tourism and wildlife literature, this is the most common approach to consumption. On the most basic level, the distinction between consumptive and non-consumptive uses differentiates between touristic uses and extractive, primary-industry based uses of natural resources. Tourism in this sense is considered non-consumptive. Wildlife-related examples of this interpretation of consumptiveness include turtle tourism (non-consumptive) versus turtles as a source of meat and turtle shells (consumptive) (Hart *et al.* 2013) and shark tourism (non-consumptive) versus sharks as a source of shark fin meat (consumptive) (Gallagher & Hammerschlag 2011).

But this chapter is mainly concerned with how tourism itself is dissected into consumptive and non-consumptive activities, and as noted earlier, wildlife tourism has been a target of this partition. To date, wildlife tourism has been simplistically divided into two categories, consumptive and non-consumptive. Such a classification is innately attractive, and probably largely derives from early work on wildlife tourism, and most notably that of Duffus and Dearden (1990), who addressed the need to better understand wildlife-oriented recreation at a time of substantial growth in the scale and scope of the activity. Their focus was on 'Non-consumptive wildlife-oriented recreation', which they defined as 'a human recreational engagement with wildlife wherein the focal organism is not purposefully removed or permanently affected by the engagement' (1990: 215). This definition built upon earlier understandings of non-consumptive use, and upon the basic precepts 'that use provides an experience rather than a product, and that one person's activities do not detract from the experiences available for another person in the same area' (Duffus & Dearden 1990: 215). Some have traced the origins of the consumptive/non-consumptive dichotomy back to early resource management, particularly of water, where consumptive use is that which makes water unavailable for further uses (Tremblay 2001), or more generally where consumptive use is a use of a resource that reduces the supply (Mimi 2011 in Fennell 2012).

The emphasis on *removal of or permanent effect on* wildlife (Duffus & Dearden 1990) has been influential in subsequent analyses of consumptive wildlife tourism, and is apparent in a number of works (e.g. Reynolds & Braithwaite 2001; Newsome *et al.* 2005; Novelli *et al.* 2006;

Lovelock 2008; Tisdell 2010; Dobson 2012; Fennell 2012). Buckley, for example, defines consumptive nature-based tourism as hunting or fishing, and non-consumptive as including 'all activities based on watching animals or plants or enjoying scenery' (2009: 399). Adherence to this simplistic dichotomy persists despite the original proponents' acknowledgement of the 'myth of the non-consumptive user' (Wilkes 1979) and of the problems of such a dichotomous classification, with its implication that 'one class of activities has an impact on the resource and the other does not' (Pomerantz *et al.* 1988: 58). Indeed, they go on to warn that *any* close contact between humans and nature can cause changes to the focal species, to other species and to the habitat, and suggest that non-consumptive uses (their definition) that have a 'high goal orientation, such as specialised wildlife viewing, differ little from consumptive use' (Duffus & Dearden 1990: 215). They propose a continuum of human–wildlife interaction, but, as noted above, notwithstanding this continuum, the basic dichotomy has persisted as a mode of analysis within the field. It has been frequently, uncritically and inconsistently applied (Tremblay 2001), not only within academic literature, but also in wildlife and parks management (e.g. SANParks 2011). This is despite observations that, from a management perspective, it may be meaningless to make such a distinction between consumptive and non-consumptive use, as *all* visitors create impacts (McKercher 1996).

Tremblay believes that the term 'non-consumptive' has been used in association with wildlife viewing 'to support the desirability of the activity without much questioning' (2001: 81). He notes an 'erroneous connection' between non-consumptive wildlife tourism and 'low impacts or noble motives' (2001: 82).

> One primary difficulty with the term 'consumptive' lies with this connotation with 'consumption'. It often reduces to an arbitrary perception that this broad category of activities is close to typical consumption, whereas others are not.
>
> *(Tremblay 2001: 82)*

Thus consumptive activities may be wrongly associated with commercialised activities, as opposed to non-consumptive activities having an inherently greater experiental component. Tremblay rejects this, pointing to research that suggest that both consumptive and non-consumptive wildlife tourism can involve valuable 'experiential intensities' (Tremblay 2001: 82). Others agree that consumptive activities often provide more intense and embodied encounters with wildlife, when compared with wildlife viewing (e.g. Franklin 2008; Reis 2009).

A growing number of commentators (e.g. McKercher 1996; Tremblay 2001; Lemelin 2006; Lovelock 2008; Fennell & Nowaczek 2010) have argued to reconsider or to abandon the dichotomy, not only because it is misleading about the real and relative impacts of various wildlife tourism activities, but because it impacts upon our potential to develop a range of consumptive and less-consumptive wildlife opportunities that may be complementary from both production and consumption perspectives (Tremblay 2001: 85). Such an approach may ultimately lead to more sustainable outcomes, both in terms of the environment and the economy. Novelli *et al.'s* (2006) research in Southern Africa tends to support this view. They acknowledge that while consumptive and non-consumptive wildlife tourism may be mutually exclusive at the local scale, there are opportunities at district and national levels for the development of *both*, and that the two are commonly practised side-by-side. It has also been suggested that consumptive uses such as hunting may be beneficial in countries where other forms of tourism are not viable (e.g. for political reasons) or in remote and peripheral regions (Lindsey *et al.* 2006). The important point to note, however, is that for consumptive uses to contribute to sustainable outcomes, appropriate governance structures and the involvement of local communities are required (Deere 2012). This equally applies to non-consumptive uses.

Is the killing of animals sustainable?

While it is not the purpose of this chapter to address the overall sustainability of consumptive versus non-consumptive wildlife tourism activities, suffice to say that a range of positions are demonstrated in the literature. Two major works on wildlife tourism take strong positions against consumptive wildlife tourism, Shackley in her (1996) book describes it as 'destructive tourism', while Newsome *et al.* (2005) go so far as to purposely exclude consumptive uses from their analysis, in what is otherwise a valuable and comprehensive coverage of wildlife tourism. Part of this rejection of consumptive wildlife tourism arises from arguments developed in the context of endangered species (e.g. that consumptive uses detract from the gene pool of target populations, through removing the largest individuals, and impacting the natural evolutionary process of the target species (Stebbins calls this 'the survival of the smallest' (2009: 156); see also Deere 2012). But such arguments don't necessarily apply to a wider range of wildlife (Tremblay 2001).

Furthermore, the categorisation of wildlife tourism activities as consumptive or non-consumptive in order to help understand and manage their impacts is simplistic and misleading (Tremblay 2001). A number of reviews of the effects of non-consumptive wildlife tourism clearly identify a range of significant impacts, including direct injury or death, disruption of activities or increase in stress levels, and loss of or modification to habitat (e.g. Boyle & Samson 1985; Green & Higginbottom 2000; Blanc *et al.* 2006; Thurstan *et al.* 2012). One study that considers the impacts of non-consumptive tourism activities within marine reserves paradoxically identifies 'high-risk non-consumptive activities' – which include wildlife observation (Thurstan *et al.* 2012: 1099).

Overall, it is apparent that there is a range of serious impacts associated with non-consumptive uses. This has largely been attributed to the commercialised aspect of these activities. Wildlife viewing often involves participants with a lower willingness-to-pay (cf. consumptive uses) and accordingly, profit is mainly addressed through economies of scale. This results in visitation being concentrated in time and space, resulting in crowding, intrusion into the habitat and the need for extensive infrastructure (Baker 1997).

Case Study

Is ecotourism consumptive?

Consumptiveness is central to the ecotourism debate (Fennell & Nowaczek 2010). Ecotourism is often touted as being non-consumptive and contrasted in a favourable light to 'consumptive use', being described as 'low impact, non-consumptive and locally oriented' (Fennell 1999: 43). Ecotourism is also seen as a form of *alternative consumption*, whereby consumption becomes a moral act, an act of caring (Bryant & Goodman 2004). In the case of ecotourism, the act of caring is focused on both conservation outcomes and community benefits.

There is, however, a strain of literature that is critical of ecotourism. Sharpley, for instance, claims that 'ecotourist' 'is a label that is becoming increasingly meaningless' (2006: 19). Importantly, some critics take particular issue over ecotourism's labelling as non-consumptive.

Meletis and Campbell (2007) point out the irony of labelling ecotourism, which is an elite (and *conspicuous*) form of consumption as non-consumptive. They argue that such labelling perpetuates a 'Western-influenced, pro-preservation and anti-extraction conception of ecotourism and masks the heterogenous nature of peoples, places and activities that comprise ecotourism' (Akama 2008; Meletis & Campbell 2007: 853).

Critics also point to the other ways that ecotourism can be consumptive, and note that:

> ...by focusing on the direct removal of the species in defining consumptive use, the figurative consumption (including visual consumption) associated with ecotourism and impacts thereof are overlooked.
>
> (Meletis & Campbell 2007: 854)

Such figurative consumption would encompass the visual or tourist gaze (Urry 2002), and is relevant to the discussion here in that the primacy or hegemony of visual consumption may lead to inappropriate industry behaviours in order to satisfy the gaze. The 'ecotourist gaze' (Meletis & Campbell 2007) for example, may lead to ecotour guides and attraction staff developing harmful practices where wildlife is habituated and effectively put on display to perform for watching ecotourists. This can lead to direct impacts on the wildlife and habitat – even if no consumptive use (killing/removal) is occurring (Meletis & Campbell 2007). The role of 'ocular consumption' in wildlife tourism is also stressed by Lemelin (2006). While the gaze itself 'may be virtually harmless, this form of leisure is still dependent on the transformation of landscapes and tourism infrastructures (transportation, accommodation, services etc) which may or may not be sustainable' (Lemelin 2006: 518).

The indirect 'consumptions' of ecotourism have also been noted, for example, the broader off-site environmental impacts from tourists' energy and water consumption. Restricting the focus of consumption to the direct killing or removal of species masks this associated and potentially more important component of so-called non-consumptive activities (Meletis & Campbell 2007). While ecotourism is touted as an alternative form of consumption, a thorough analysis of such alternative consumptions 'may only reaffirm the primacy of both consumption and capitalism' so that even supposedly non-consumptive activities can ultimately be seen as products of neo-liberal policies (Meletis & Campbell 2007: 861). In this sense, ecotourism is a form of consumption first and foremost (Ryan *et al.* 2000) where the ecotourist gaze is the product that is purchased and consumed (Lemelin 2006).

Where do consumptive uses such as hunting and fishing 'fit in'?

Some believe that consumptive uses can be considered as ecotourism and suggest that in some contexts 'consumptive ecotourism' may reflect the original goals of ecotourism more closely than wildlife viewing (Lovelock 2008). For example, Novelli *et al.* (2006) in their study of consumptive activities in Namibia and Botswana, present evidence that consumptive activities are more beneficial than non–consumptive activities such as photographic tourism, and that consumptive tourism has 'a positive and additive economic role to play in the development of tourism sectors in southern Africa...and has the potential to contribute to the ever-sought after sustainable tourism development' (2006: 76, 77).

Increasingly, touristic hunting has been portrayed as a conservation tool (Lovelock 2008) with the recognition of 'conservation hunting'. While seemingly counterintuitive, hunting is argued to add value to wildlife and to provide an incentive for communities to protect it (Foote & Wenzel 2008; Dowsley 2009). Indeed, countries with bans on consumptive uses have seen a decline in their wildlife, whereas hunting has supported the successful reintroduction of formerly endangered species (Tisdell 2010; Deere 2012).

Consumptive uses also contribute to conservation and sustainability goals through the intense and embodied encounters with wildlife that are involved. Participants in consumptive activities develop a strong knowledge of and attachment to the species, habitats and ecosystems in which they engage in their activity, and can become stronger and more effective advocates for nature than those who simply watch wildlife (Franklin 2008). But despite the recognition of the conservation and community benefits of consumptive wildlife tourism, and its repackaging (e.g. as conservation hunting), it appears that this offers little protection from ethics-based arguments against such activities.

Moral arguments for (and against) hunting and fishing

Consumptive activities such as hunting and fishing are highly controversial on ethical grounds and the moral integrity of the consumptive act itself is questioned (Oian 2013). In the mainly touristic contexts in which angling and hunting do not have obvious roles in terms of subsistence, 'their legitimacy depends on cultural, moral and political views and definitions, and is therefore potentially fragile and ready to be challenged' (Oian 2013: 183).

It is also beyond the scope of this chapter to consider the ethical case for or against consumptive uses, but suffice it to say that the killing of animals is mainly opposed on animal rights and animal welfare grounds. Arguments are made on the basis of causing harm to sentient beings, and to recognise the intrinsic (rather than utilitarian) value of animals (for a fuller coverage of the debate around the ethics of consumptive wildlife tourism, see Singer 2001; Regan 2004; Fennell 2012; Lovelock & Lovelock 2013).

What is clear about *non*-consumptive wildlife activities, though, is that because of the actual and potential harms identified for these activities, we cannot simply assume that they 'reflect and convey morally superior values' (Tremblay 2001: 83). However, introducing the *intent* to cause harm into our moral framework, does challenge this position. Dobson (2012), while acknowledging arguments against the consumptive/non-consumptive dichotomy, makes a moral distinction between the two; it is the *intended* outcome of an action that should be the criterion used to decide if a particular form of wildlife tourism is acceptable or not. Employing the 'Doctrine of Double Effect', an ethical framework that distinguishes between an intended outcome of an action and what is merely foreseen as a side effect, allows us to 'unpack the subtle ethical differences' between consumptive and non-consumptive activities (2012: 96). The *intent* of the consumptive wildlife tourist (i.e. a hunter or fisher) to cause harm sets their actions apart ethically from non-consumptive wildlife viewing activities. Based upon moral obligations and related factors, Burns *et al.* (2011) propose a useful set of principles that would allow the interrogation of *any* wildlife tourism activity, consumptive or non-consumptive.

Conclusion

The act of consumption may be conceptualised in a number of ways: as a market-based activity, as a creator of meanings, and a user (or destroyer) of resources. We propose that consumption can also be positioned as a moral act, creating harm and/or benefits. Touristic consumption is situated within and across all of these fields, and, depending on the nature of the consumption, our attention may be drawn to any one of or combination of these conceptualisations. Thus, an object of tourism consumption (e.g. wildlife) may be consumed in a variety of ways by different tourists. This complicates the attainment of sustainable consumption activities (e.g. sustainable wildlife viewing) in that some goals 'will be subordinated to other desired outcomes' (Sharpley 2006: 19). Arguably, for an ambiguous activity such as consumptive wildlife tourism, *consumption as a moral act* has been and will continue to be central in determining its ongoing sustainability.

It is also apparent that there are problems with the consumptive/non-consumptive labelling of tourism activities in terms of: identifying the real impacts of tourism activities; the meanings that are created through such consumption; and the lost opportunities for an integrated approach to tourism development. It would be much better to conceptualise wildlife tourism (and nature-based tourism as a whole, for that matter) on a continuum of consumptiveness. We should start to use the terms consumptive and *less-consumptive* (rather than consumptive and non-consumptive).

A key question that arises from our discussion concerns the character of the commodity that is being consumed within wildlife tourism, and whether or not what is being consumed varies substantially from consumptive to non-consumptive wildlife tourism. Arguably, the distraction in this debate has been the act of killing, and a view that the end goal of the consumptive activities of hunting and fishing is to kill. That is akin to saying that the end goal of non-consumptive wildlife viewing activities is simply to capture a photograph. The kill is but one aspect of a more holistic experience that largely mimics aspects of conventional non-consumptive wildlife viewing. While the act of killing (or capturing, sometimes temporarily) may be important (as might be the fish, flesh, hide, venison, tusks or antlers), to conceptualise hunting or fishing as the consumption of death is astray. Such a conceptualisation is implicated in the difficulty with seeing that consumptive and non-consumptive wildlife activities, experientially, have much more in common than some would like to concede, and prevents us from considering them in a more integrated way – or as Novelli *et al*. (2006: 77) put it, as 'two sides of the same coin'. The ethical argument against killing (i.e. consumption as an *immoral* act) has blinded us to more favourable interpretations and analyses of consumptive wildlife tourism. Rather than rejecting one side of an obviously flawed dichotomy, perhaps our focus should be on how all forms of wildlife tourism and tourism in general can be practised in a less-consumptive but more meaningful manner.

Key reading

Fennell, D.A. (2012) *Tourism and Animal Ethics*, London: Routledge.
Lovelock, B.A. (ed.) (2008) *Tourism and the Consumption of Wildlife: Hunting, shooting and sportfishing*. London: Routledge.
Lemelin, R.H. (2006) 'The gawk, the glance, and the gaze: ocular consumption and polar bear tourism in Churchill, Manitoba, Canada', *Current Issues in Tourism*, 9: 516–534.
Meletis, Z.A. and Campbell, L.M. (2007) 'Call it consumption! Reconceptualizing ccotourism as consumption and consumptive', *Geography Compass*, 1: 850–70.
Tremblay, P. (2001) 'Wildlife tourism consumption: consumptive or non-consumptive?', *International Journal of Tourism Research*, 3: 81–86.

References

Akama, J.S. (2008) 'Controversies surrounding the ban on wildlife hunting in Kenya: An historical perspective', in B.A. Lovelock (ed.) (2008) *Tourism and the Consumption of Wildlife: Hunting, Shooting and Sportfishing*, London: Routledge.

Baker, J.E. (1997) 'Trophy hunting as a sustainable use of wildlife resources in southern and eastern Africa', *Journal of Sustainable Tourism*, 5: 306–21.

Belk, R. (2007) 'Consumption, mass consumption, and consumer culture', in G. Ritzer (ed.) *The Blackwell Encyclopedia of the Social Sciences*, Cambridge, USA: Blackwell.

Blanc, R., Guillemain, M., Mouronval, J., Desmonts, D. and Fritz, H. (2006) 'Effects of non-consumptive leisure disturbance to wildlife', *Rev. Ecol. (Terre Vie)*, 61: 117–33.

Bocock, S. (1993) *Consumption*, London: Routledge.

Boyle, S.A. and Samson, F.B. (1985) 'Effects of nonconsumptive recreation on wildlife: A review', *Wildlife Society Bulletin*, 13(2): 110–16.

Bryant, R.L. and Goodman, M.K. (2004) 'Consuming narratives: The political ecology of "alternative" consumption', *Transactions of the Institute of British Geographers*, 29(3): 344–66.

Buckley, R.C. (2009) *Ecotourism: Principles and Practices*, Wallingford: CABI.

Burns, G.L., MacBeth, J. and Moore, S. (2011) 'Should dingoes die? Principles for engaging ecocentric ethics in wildlife tourism management', *Journal of Ecotourism*, 10(3): 179–96.

Campbell, C. (1995) 'The sociology of consumption', in D. Miller (ed.) *Acknowledging Consumption: A Review of New Studies*, London: Routledge.

Cook, D.T. (2006) 'Leisure and consumption', in C. Rojek, S.M. Shaw and A.J. Veal (eds) *A Handbook of Leisure Studies*, New York: Palgrave Macmillan.

Deere, N.J. (2012) 'Exploitation or conservation? Can the hunting tourism industry in Africa be sustainable?', *Environment*, 53(4): 21–33.

Dobson, J. (2012) 'Ethical issues in trophy hunting', in O. Moufakkir and P.M. Burns (eds) *Controversies in Tourism*, Wallingford: CABI.

Dowsley, M. (2009) 'Inuit organized polar bear sport hunting in Nunavut Territory, Canada', *Journal of Ecotourism*, 8(2): 161–75.

Duffus, D.A. and Dearden, P. (1990) 'Non-consumptive wildlife-oriented recreation: A conceptual framework', *Biological Conservation*, 53: 213–31.

Dunn, R.G. (2008) *Identifying Consumption: Subject and Objects in Consumer Society*, Philadelphia: Temple University Press.

Fennell, D.A. (1999) *Ecotourism: An Introduction*, London: Routledge.

Fennell, D.A. (2012) *Tourism and Animal Ethics*, London: Routledge.

Fennell, D. and Nowaczek, A. (2010) 'Moral and empirical dimensions of human–animal interactions in ecotourism: Deepening an otherwise shallow pool of debate', *Journal of Ecotourism*, 9(3): 239–55.

Foote, L. and Wenzel, G. (2008) 'Conservation hunting concepts, Canada's Inuit, and polar bear hunting', in B.A. Lovelock (ed.) *Tourism and the Consumption of Wildlife: Hunting, Shooting and Sport Fishing*, London: Routledge.

Franklin, A. (2008) 'The "animal question" and the "consumption" of wildlife', in B.A. Lovelock (ed.) *Tourism and the Consumption of Wildlife: Hunting, Shooting and Sportfishing*, London: Routledge.

Gallagher, A.J. and Hammerschlag, N. (2011) 'Global shark currency: The distribution, frequency, and economic value of shark ecotourism', *Current Issues in Tourism*, 14: 797–812.

Green, R.J. and Higginbottom, K. (2000) 'The effects of non-consumptive wildlife tourism on free-ranging wildlife: A review', *Pacific Conservation Biology*, 6: 183–97.

Hart, K.A., Gray, T. and Stead, S.M. (2013) 'Consumptive "versus" non-consumptive use of sea turtles? Stakeholder perceptions about sustainable use in three communities near Cahuita National Park, Costa Rica', *Marine Policy*, 42: 236–44.

Lemelin, R.H. (2006) 'The gawk, the glance, and the gaze: Ocular consumption and polar bear tourism in Churchill, Manitoba, Canada', *Current Issues in Tourism*, 9: 516–534.

Lindsey, P.A., Alexander, R., Frank, L.G., Mathieson, A. and Romanach, S.S. (2006) 'Potential of trophy hunting to create incentives for wildlife conservation in Africa where alternative wildlife-based land uses may not be viable', *Animal Conservation*, 9: 283–91.

Lovelock, B.A. (ed.) (2008) *Tourism and the Consumption of Wildlife: Hunting, Shooting and Sportfishing*, London: Routledge.

Lovelock, B.A. and Lovelock, K. (2013) *The Ethics of Tourism: Critical and Applied Perspectives,* London: Routledge.

McKercher, B. (1996) 'Differences between tourism and recreation in parks', *Annals of Tourism Research,* 23(3): 563–75.

Meguro, T. and Inoue, M. (2011) 'Conservation goals betrayed by the uses of wildlife benefits in community-based conservation: The case of Kimana Sanctuary in southern Kenya', *Human Dimensions of Wildlife,* 16(1): 30–44.

Meletis, Z.A. and Campbell, L.M. (2007) 'Call it consumption! Reconceptualizing ecotourism as consumption and consumptive', *Geography Compass,* 1: 850–70.

Newsome, D., Dowling, R. and Moore, S. (2005) *Wildlife Tourism: Ecology, Impacts, and Management,* Clevedon: Channel View.

Novelli, M., Barnes, J.I. and Humavindu, M. (2006) 'The other side of the ecotourism coin: Consumptive tourism in Southern Africa', *Journal of Ecotourism,* 5(1/2): 62–79.

Oian, H. (2013) 'Wilderness tourism and the moralities of commitment: Hunting and landscapes in Norway', *Journal of Rural Studies,* 32: 177–85.

Pomerantz, G.A., Decker, D.J., Goff, G.R. and Purdy, K.G. (1988) 'Assessing the impact of recreation on wildlife: A classification scheme', *Wildlife Society Bulletin,* 16(1): 58–62.

Regan, T. (2004) *The Case for Animal Rights,* Berkeley: University of California Press.

Reis, A.C. (2009) 'More than the kill: Hunters' relationships with landscape and prey', *Current Issues in Tourism,* 12(5/6): 573–87.

Reynolds, P.C. and Braithwaite, D. (2001) 'Towards a conceptual framework for wildlife tourism', *Tourism Management,* 22(1): 31–42.

Ryan, C., Hughes, K. and Chirgwin, S. (2000) 'The gaze, spectacle and ecotourism', *Annals of Tourism Research,* 27: 148–63.

SANParks (2011) *SANParks Biodiversity Monitoring Programme: Resource Use (Consumptive).* Available at: ftp://ftp.sanparks.org/Cape%20Research%20Centre/Biodiversity%20Monitoring%20System/Resource%20Use.MP.Draft2.12%20August%202011.pdf (accessed 24 September 2013).

Shackley, M. (1996) *Wildlife Tourism,* London: International Thomson Business Press.

Sharpley, R. (2006) 'Ecotourism: A consumption perspective', *Journal of Ecotourism,* 5(1,2): 7–22.

Singer, P. (2001) *Animal Liberation,* New York: Harper Collins.

Stebbins, R.A. (2009) *Leisure and Consumption: Common Ground/Separate Worlds,* Basingstoke: Palgrave Macmillan.

Thurstan, R.H., Hawkins, J.P., Neves, L. and Roberts, C.M. (2012) 'Are marine reserves and non-consumptive activities compatible? A global analysis of marine reserve regulations', *Marine Policy,* 36: 1096–1104.

Tisdell, C.A. (2010) *Sharing Nature's Wealth through Wildlife Tourism: Its Economic, Sustainability and Conservation Benefits,* Available at: http://ideas.repec.org/p/ags/uqseee/93404.html (Accessed 20 September 2013).

Tremblay, P. (2001) 'Wildlife tourism consumption: Consumptive or non-consumptive?', *International Journal of Tourism Research,* 3: 81–86.

Urry, J. (2002) *The Tourist Gaze,* Thousand Oaks, US: SAGE Publications.

Wilkes, B. (1979) 'The myth of the non-consumptive user', *Park News,* 15: 16–21.

13

Tourism and cultural change

Melanie Kay Smith

Socio-cultural impacts The impacts of tourism which affect the lifestyles, traditions and culture(s) of local residents or hosts in a tourism destination. This might include the commercialisation of culture (e.g. mass production of arts and crafts; the staging of dance or other performances), demonstration effects (e.g. local people copying tourist behaviour), as well as major changes in social practices and rituals.

Host–guest The complex relationship between local residents living in a destination and the tourists who visit. This relationship has been analysed in depth in anthropological studies of tourism, but recent theories of tourism, including mobility theory, recognise the complexity of this relationship which cannot be reduced to such a simple binary.

Indigenous Local people or communities who are native to a specific place or destination. The term 'indigenous tourism' is often used to describe visits to communities or tribes who live in remote or fragile locations and who have very specific cultural traditions and lifestyles.

Authentic A contentious term which relates to the extent to which cultural practices and rituals have remained faithful to their traditional origins. The concept of 'staged authenticity' refers to forms of culture which are performed and adapted especially for tourists.

Co-creation The notion that tourists and consumers want to help shape their own experiences and engage in more creative activities. This usually involves active and interactive rather than passive activities.

Introduction

Culture in the context of tourism has (to simplify) been variously defined as being about heritage, the arts, or a whole way of life of people (Richards 2001; Smith 2003). This has brought with it a plethora of debates about conservation, interpretation, representation, identity, visitor management, commodification, authenticity and, of course, sustainability.

Most tourists at some point in their travels experience a cultural interaction, whether deliberately or unintentionally, and even if they are not defined as cultural tourists, they will sooner or later become agents of cultural change.

In terms of cultural tourism, the market has fragmented into niche markets such as heritage tourism, arts tourism, festival tourism and indigenous tourism, and many tourists are starting to consume culture in a different way. Europa Nostra estimated that 50 per cent of European tourism is related to heritage, and the ATLAS (2009) research programme showed that over 50 per cent of cultural tourists visit museums and monuments. However, today's cultural tourist is just as likely to be in search of 'popular', 'everyday' 'low' or 'street' culture as they are likely to visit a heritage site or museum (Richards 2011). Palmer and Richards (2010) suggest that culture is now a relational good shared by the many rather than the elite few. Nevertheless, the act of travel is still mainly the practice of a (relative) worldwide elite and the cultural changes which occur are still most likely to affect visited rather than visiting populations. The quest for 'ordinary' and 'everyday' culture in remote and fragile locations can be far more disturbing and destructive for local people than the pursuit of must-see cities or monuments.

Clearly, culture exists independently of tourism. It is a site of contested meaning and a dynamic concept which cannot or should not be subjected to fossilisation. However, in a tourism context, it has been tempting to try to preserve not only historical monuments but also the everyday lives and traditions of people. Egotistically enough, such measures are more often than not for the benefit of tourists and the tourism industry rather than out of genuine concern for the welfare of local people. Given the choice, many of them might prefer investment in clean drinking water, electricity or schooling rather than the conservation of monuments or the continuation of cultural traditions.

It was originally assumed that cultural tourism was a more 'sustainable' form of tourism than many other kinds (e.g. mass beach tourism). Cultural tourists were supposed to be fewer in number, they were well educated, higher spending and on the whole, they were thought to be better behaved! As stated by Smith and Richards (2013: 1). 'The idea that cultural tourists benefit the places they visit not only economically but because they are more culturally sensitive and aware is implicit in the positioning of cultural tourism as "good tourism" against more seemingly frivolous or less lucrative forms of travel.' However, the OECD report on *The Impact of Culture on Tourism* (2009) noted that cultural tourism accounted for almost 360 million international tourism trips in 2007, or 40 per cent of global tourism. Therefore the phenomenon of mass cultural tourism is increasingly becoming a cause for concern, whether it is the budget airline-induced proliferation of long weekend breaks in the historic cities of Europe, or backpackers hill-tribe trekking in Asia. Cities become overcrowded, monuments are eroded and communities' lives change beyond recognition, sometimes for the better but more often for the worse. Destinations which might be seen as paradise for tourists can become hell for locals because of the social and cultural changes that tourism engenders. Examples could include the extreme commercialisation of culture in Hawaii where desperate attempts have been made to reinstate 'authenticity' and evoke cultural pride; the over-visitation of Venice which led to residents moving out of the city centre and more 'serious' cultural tourists staying away; the overcrowding of Barcelona where residents started urging tourists to go home; the full-moon parties in Thailand, which are offensive to local people; or the stag and hen parties who use historic Central and Eastern European cities as a playground, but who have little or no interest in culture or communities.

Sustainability, tourism and cultural change

When it comes to issues of sustainability, the literature about tourism and cultural change tends to focus on socio-cultural impacts of tourism, host–guest relations and indigenous or community-based tourism. Many of the seminal early works have their foundations in anthropology (e.g. Smith 1977, 1989). One of the main strands of anthropological studies of tourism is social and cultural change in addition to semiology and political economy (Selwyn 1996). The anthropology of tourism has gradually shifted from largely negative ethnographic critiques of the impacts of tourism on lives and culture to a more balanced discussion of tourism as a social and cultural phenomenon. This is reflected, for example, in the work of Macleod and Carrier (2010) where the authors provide an assessment of both the positive and negative aspects of tourism on communities, their lives and their cultures. Socio-cultural impacts can include homogenisation or standardisation of culture; demonstration effects (where local people emulate tourist behaviour); commodification of traditions and rituals (e.g. commercial adaptations of arts and crafts); and staged authenticity (where local people perform or produce culture purely for the consumption of tourists). Table 13.1 provides a summary of the main impacts of tourism on culture.

The impacts presented in the table are not binary opposites of course, nor are they as clear cut as they may first appear. More sophisticated models of sustainable tourism need to pay special attention to context, the culture of specific communities and even to individuals. For example, it would be a generalisation to say that younger generations of local communities are enthusiastic about working in tourism, whereas older generations are resistant. Some fathers may be happy for their wife or daughter to make a good living in tourism, perhaps even better than their own, whereas it threatens the masculinity of others and can undermine whole social and familial structures in some communities. Pride in culture and strengthening of identities is generally seen to be a positive impact, but only if it does not support forms of patriotism and nationalism which descend into racism, persecution or exclusion. Standardisation or homogenisation are also seen as fairly dirty words in the context of culture. This can be true if everywhere starts to look the same and a form of 'placelessness' is created. However, it is also well documented that many tourists like to remain in the bubble to a certain extent and play it safe in chain hotels, fast food restaurants like McDonald's with their clean toilets and lack of food poisoning, and Starbucks where a good cappuccino is guaranteed! It cannot be assumed that so-called cultural tourists are any different, especially in historic European cities where the majority arrive by budget airlines and stay in the cheapest hotel in their search engine.

Table 13.1 Tourism and cultural change

'Positive' impacts of tourism on culture	'Negative' impacts of tourism on culture
Spotlight on local communities and their culture	Over-exposure of local communities and their culture
Strengthening of cultural identity	Loss of cultural identity
Preservation of the authenticity of traditions	Staged authenticity and the dilution of cultural traditions
Cross-cultural exchange and mutual education	Cultural conflicts and undesirable demonstration effects
Highlighting of cultural uniqueness and diversity	Standardisation of culture
Whole communities benefiting from tourism	Generational or gender clashes because of tourism

Uniqueness is probably a positive aspiration for many destinations, but only if this does not mean the total eradication of local cultures. Some might argue that some Middle Eastern or Asian model(s) of removing heritage buildings, displacing communities and developing skyscraper cities with unique architecture is a somewhat radical and not altogether desirable form of cultural change. Richards (2013: 299) also notes the irony when destinations seek to develop their uniqueness through cultural tourism, but because of 'serial reproduction' 'many places follow similar strategies in order to achieve their uniqueness, which ends up making those places feel and look the same'.

Cross-cultural exchange

Cross-cultural exchange is lauded as a positive outcome of tourism development, but it should be remembered that the relationship between tourists and locals is still often unequal, unspontaneous and limited in time and space. Demonstration effects are usually seen as negative (e.g. dressing like tourists, drinking alcohol, partying and emulating other aspects of tourists' 'free and easy' lifestyles). However, it is debatable how far local communities should be denied access to the same opportunities as tourists, especially in destinations which are non-seasonal, where tourism becomes a permanent way of life and source of income. As stated earlier, the conservation of certain dimensions of culture is desirable in the context of sustainable tourism, but fossilisation and denial of social and economic opportunities is not. If tourism is deemed to be a harmful influence from the outset because the structure of local community life is very tight and residents already have a self-sufficient livelihood and good quality of life, then development should not be encouraged or permitted. Unfortunately, communities may be enthusiastic about the prospect of tourism development without fully grasping the possible, and even inevitable, implications. Sensitivity is required to explain the potential impact without resorting to paternalistic or patronising rhetoric.

Authenticity

Authenticity is a complex and contentious term, and the concept is constantly being revisited in the context of tourism as it is difficult to determine what and for whom is authentic and whether authenticity is actually even desirable. For example, many cultural tourists who visit indigenous tribal communities are reluctant to stay in primitive accommodation with no electricity or running water, to watch locals hunting or to eat strange or unfamiliar foods. Beer (2013) provides a comprehensive analysis of authenticity in the context of cultural tourism from a philosophical perspective. It is often considered from two sides: objective authenticity (e.g. Wang 1999) and existential authenticity (e.g. Steiner & Reisinger 2006). It is generally agreed that objective authenticity which is genuine and consensual (i.e. everyone agrees on what it is) is rare, as most experiences or perceptions of authenticity are socially constructed and negotiable. Genuinely authentic practices are not diluted, abridged or simplified to make them more accessible, cheaper or more attractive or entertaining for tourists. However, these traditions may have been changed or modified over the centuries and may be further adapted when practices are shifted from one context or generation to another. It is also debatable as to whether the majority of tourists know or even care what is and what is not authentic. The same is true of local communities, especially in contexts where traditions have been discontinued and later revived. Macleod (2013) discusses the concept of 'cultural configuration', which involves the intentional manipulation of culture to present only certain dimensions. Although this can be for contentious political reasons, it can also result in benefits for a destination which wants to project a positive image. He also writes of the discrepancies between what local people want to show and what tourists actually want to see. Nevertheless, conservationists and historians would argue that one of the aims of sustainable development is to ensure that authentic cultural practices continue to exist whether they are consumed or not. This goes back to the notion that culture exists independently of tourism and tourists, a fact which many developers forget.

Case Study

Tourism and cultural change in Mali

Mali is one of the poorest countries in the world; however, it is home to a number of World Heritage sites, cultural and ceremonial events, as well as music, dance and handicraft traditions. European tourists have been visiting since 1931 but tourism grew exponentially in the 1980s to visit what guide books described as a 'living museum'. Over the past few years, the Mali government made tourism development a priority. Ninety per cent of tourists visit primarily to come to Dogon Land, which is a World Heritage Site and the jewel of Malian tourism. For the past 1,000 years local inhabitants (now around 300,000) had hidden themselves from the world by carving their villages out of a cliff that was 200 km long. Baxter (2001) quotes one Mali tourism officer as saying: 'The magic of Dogon country is its inaccessibility, which has protected the authenticity of the culture and the people till now.' However, access to Dogon country is now available to anyone with the desire and the means to get there. Even though Dogon culture could withstand centuries of pressure from Islamic conquerors, Mandingo empire-builders, Fulani slave-seekers and Christian missionaries, tourism has proved to be a much more destructive influence in terms of cultural change. Examples include the Sigui dance of the masks, which is supposed to be performed in great secrecy only once every 60 years, following the cosmology of the star Syrius, from which the Dogon believe they originally came. Although the next authentic Sigui dance is scheduled for 2020, the Dogon people started performing an imitation every day for tourists. Baxter (2001) quotes a Mali tourism officer as saying: 'It's like something you'd see at an airport...tourism demystifies rituals and fetish carvings, eroding all their meaning.' Craddock (2011) also quoted a study which stated that 'the "sacred character" of rituals has become diluted'. Many local people are even selling off authentic cultural artefacts.

In addition to the erosion of culture and authenticity through increasing access to tourists, Mali has experienced even greater crises. Tourists have been vulnerable to kidnap since 2009 and a political coup in 2012 made it a no-go area for tourists. Cultural artefacts have also been damaged. The government tried to rebuild the tourism industry in 2011, however Craddock (2011) stated that 'the country's campaign to reinstate tourism as a pillar of national GDP carries cultural dilemmas. By further commodifying sacred areas like Dogon, Mali runs the risk of killing the goose that lays the golden egg.' Nevertheless, the economic temptation was too much to resist, as the tourism sector was Mali's third-biggest revenue generator. In 2011, almost 200,000 tourists visited the country, each spending at least $100 (£62) a day: barely 10,000 visited in 2012 (Ford & Allen 2013). Many local people have become both desperate and destitute having lost their livelihood from tourism. Such crises clearly render destinations unsustainable, regardless of how they have been developed. This case study also illustrates the tension between economic and cultural sustainability, showing that however negative the impacts of tourism on culture, economic dependency on tourism is a common 'hazard' in developing countries. However, with more limited and sensitive management of cultural tourism, economic benefits could have been derived without being detrimental to cultural continuity. Craddock (2011) quotes a study in which 94 per cent of 32 Malian tourism professionals agreed that 'tourism agencies do not do enough to educate tourists about how to interact with sacred places in the Dogon area'. Perhaps the only positive outcome of this crisis is that Mali now has the opportunity to re-think its future tourism strategy.

Acculturation

Anthropologists tend to study the process of acculturation or permanent cultural change in indigenous societies, although it has proved almost impossible to isolate the impacts of tourism from the influence of wider social, environmental, technological and other changes. As stated by Robinson and Picard (2006: 35) 'while international tourism is implicated in the globalisation thesis it is only part of a much wider process of global cultural change and inter-change'. This makes measuring sustainable tourism extremely difficult, if not impossible. While indicators of sustainable tourism have been developed to monitor changes in the natural environment, measuring cultural change is problematic also because of the multiplicity of subjectivities involved. This means using mainly qualitative research methods or unfeasibly large samples of respondents for quantitative research. Indicators usually include socio-economic and socio-cultural impacts of tourism, including issues relating to standard of living, quality of life and happiness of local residents. Questions might also focus on perceptions of societal and cultural change. It is usually accepted that cultural changes occur primarily to the indigenous society's lives, customs, traditions and values rather than to those of the tourist, especially in the case of remote communities. There is still generally an assumption that host communities are relatively powerless and subordinate in the face of global tourism. Hall and Tucker (2004) showed how colonial thinking and discourse are far from over in contemporary tourism, especially as many Europeans may be nostalgic about imperialism, and may even idealise it. Ever since human beings embarked on the process of exploration and travel, there has been a prevailing assumption that the exploring or travelling societies are superior to those who are being visited. Such theories of culture were even perpetuated by philosophers like Hegel. Explorers, settlers, conquerors, anthropologists, Christian missionaries and tourists alike tended to be surprised by the relatively primitive conditions in which tribal or indigenous communities were living. Strategies of reform often began in an attempt to convert those communities to more modern ways of living, but often using force or cruelty.

However, in recent years, debates about sustainability and the declining wellbeing of capitalist societies has forced social scientists to question whose way of life is really superior and what could be learnt from local and indigenous communities. In his analysis of contemporary health and wellbeing, Weil (2013) suggests that the human body was not designed for the modern post-industrial environment and that lives in the developed world have mainly gone from hard and generally content to easy but often depressed compared to our more 'primitive' ancestors. Very primitive humans hunted and ate what they needed, they struggled to stay alive and died young. However, subsequently many tribal groups have learnt to live more in harmony with nature seeing themselves as belonging to the land rather than the land belonging to them. However, capitalist societies live in permanent settlements that are often far from nature, and the environment and culture are seen as unlimited resources which are there to be exploited for maximum profit. Some researchers have even suggested that the artificial separation of human societies from nature is causing health problems, for example, Nature Deficit Disorder (Louv 2005). There is little correlation between high standard of living and optimum wellbeing or happiness. The Happy Planet Index (New Economics Foundation 2012) shows that even where life is relatively long and supposedly happy, the high carbon footprint of the societies concerned means that the sustainability of the planet is by no means guaranteed.

Community-based tourism

Discussions about the sustainability of cultural tourism have tended to produce community-based tourism models. Some of the issues which have become central to studies of community-based tourism include image creation, representation and the construction of social identities, which all directly or indirectly address the concept of power and are embedded within discourses of political economy. Butler and Hinch (1996: 5) stated that tourism should be planned and managed so that 'indigenous people dictate the nature of the experience and negotiate their involvement in tourism from a position of strength'. In their later publication (Butler & Hinch 2007) they suggest that indigenous peoples had succeeded in some cases in improving self-determination and involvement. Zeppel (2006) gives examples of successful community-based ecotourism projects where communities participated and controlled decision making, as well as receiving training and employment opportunities and developing entrepreneurial skills. On the positive side, tourism can lead to public recognition of and support for traditions and can help to revive cultural practices and renew community pride in them. Cultural tourism is one way in which displaced or politically marginalised indigenous peoples can start to rebuild their communities and to renew their sense of pride in their culture and identity. There is also more recognition of intangible heritage and culture. Overall, there has been a positive shift in the tourism literature from looking mainly at the impacts of tourism on indigenous lifestyles and cultures to documenting and advocating political self-determination and more active participation of indigenous peoples in tourism development. However, Picard (2013) argues that few community-run projects manage to become economically viable because of the imposition of idealistic models of community utopia by international development agents, which ignore the social relationships that govern community life at a local scale.

Conclusions

It should not only be assumed that tourism changes the lives of local communities with little or no impact on the lives of tourists. Much of the recent work on tourism and quality of life (e.g. Uysal, Perdue & Sirgy 2012) shows that the act of travel can greatly improve quality of life and individual trips can sometimes change lives forever, especially if they are specifically focused on health, wellness or self-development (Puczkó & Smith 2012). Many capitalist societies, especially in Europe, are currently living through a period of great turbulence, where the environment, politics, economics and social systems have reached an apparent crisis. It seems that the world is at a turning point where human beings need to acknowledge the consequences of their actions and to take greater responsibility for their lives, fellow human beings and the planet. Social and cultural change is needed and tourism may be one of the vehicles for exchanging sustainable values. However, contrary to earlier theories of tourism and cultural change, tourists may have much to learn from host communities about sustainable living and the protection of natural and cultural resources. There may be some examples of this in the form of indigenous ecotourism, which Zeppel (2006: 1) describes as 'nature-based attractions or tours owned by Indigenous people, and also indigenous interpretation of the natural and cultural environment including wildlife'. Picard (2013) and Selwyn (2013) also give the example of host–guest interaction in the context of hospitality, arguing that the true meaning of the concept as an inherent social value has been lost in the development of an almost purely commercial hospitality industry. Traditional or 'true' hospitality may be more likely to be found amongst indigenous communities. However, hospitality has its limits when the ratio of locals to tourists increases beyond any kind of social carrying capacity (again, difficult to calculate or measure).

Further critiques have been forthcoming regarding past analyses of tourism, cultural change and the relationship with communities. Robinson (2013) questions the usefulness of grand narratives of tourism and binaries like host–guest, especially given the changing nature of contemporary mobilities where the differentiation between local resident and tourist is increasingly complex. As stated earlier, many tourists are starting to engage in forms of tourism which bring them closer to and even make them indistinguishable from local residents. Hannam and Roy (2013) argue that tourism is now an integral rather than a marginal part of everyday social and cultural life, therefore it is becoming harder to distinguish between tourism and other mobilities. This is certainly true of large cosmopolitan cities, but it is perhaps less true of fragile and remote locations. It is the latter which appear to need the greatest attention in terms of managing cultural change. On the other hand, as stated earlier, tourism is not the only factor of change.

'Postmodern' consumers and tourists also want to help shape their own experiences in a process of so-called 'prosumption' or 'co-creation'. They often want to be changed by their experiences and engage in self-development. Creative tourism is one way of providing this (Richards 2013). Depending on how it is defined and executed, creative tourism can arguably provide small-scale, sustainable experiences, although Richards (2013: 302) warns that: 'The use of creativity to develop tourism (also) runs the risk of strengthening the tendency towards colonization of the lifeworld by the forces of commerce'. However, there is potential for positive cross-cultural interactions and education in Richards and Raymonds' (2000: 16) definition that creative tourists 'get closer to local people, through informal participation in interactive workshops and learning experiences that draw on the culture of their holiday destinations' and UNESCO's (2006: 3) definition of creative tourism as 'travel directed toward an engaged and authentic experience, with participative learning in the arts, heritage, or special character of a place, and it provides a connection with those who reside in this place and create this living culture'. Maybe the process of 'co-creation' can therefore be extended to local communities as well as tourists allowing them also to have more positive life experiences and greater opportunities for self-development. At the same time, tourists can learn something about sustainable living and returning to nature by experiencing the lives and practices of many indigenous communities throughout the world.

Key Reading

MacLeod, D.V.L. and Carrier, J.G. (eds) (2010) *Tourism, Power and Culture: Anthropological Insights*, Bristol: Channel View.

Robinson, M. and Picard, D. (2006) *Tourism, Culture and Sustainable Development*, Paris: UNESCO.

Smith, M.K. (2009) *Issues in Cultural Tourism Studies*, London: Routledge.

Smith, M.K. and Richards, G. (eds) (2013) *The Routledge Handbook of Cultural Tourism*, London: Routledge.

Zeppel, H. (2006) *Indigenous Ecotourism: Sustainable Development and Management*, Wallingford: CABI.

References

Baxter, J. (2001) *Mali: What Price Tourism?* BBC News, 16 April. Available at: http: //news.bbc.co.uk/2/hi/africa/1280076.stm (accessed 18 September 2013).

Beer, S. (2013) 'Philosophy and the nature of the authentic', in M.K. Smith and G. Richards, (eds) *The Routledge Handbook of Cultural Tourism*, London: Routledge.

Butler, R. and Hinch, T. (eds) (1996) *Tourism and Indigenous Peoples*, London: International Thomson Business Press.

—— (2007) *Tourism and Indigenous Peoples: Issues and Implications*, Oxford: Butterworth-Heinemann.

Craddock, A. (2011) *Rebuilding Tourism in Mali*, Think Africa Press, 19 August. Available at: http://thinkafricapress.com/mali/rebuilding-tourism-mali (accessed 18 September 2013).

Ford, T. and Allen, B. (2013) 'Tourism in Mali fades away as instability leads to hardship', *The Guardian*, 9 January. Available at: www.theguardian.com/world/2013/jan/09/tourism-mali-fades-away-instability (accessed 18 September 2013).

Hall, C.M. and Tucker, H. (eds) (2004) *Tourism and Postcolonialism*, London: Routledge.

Hannam, K. and Roy, S. (2013) 'Cultural tourism and the mobilities paradigm', in M.K. Smith and G. Richards (eds) *The Routledge Handbook of Cultural Tourism*, London: Routledge.

Louv, R. (2005) *The Last Child in the Woods*, Chapel Hill: Algonquin Books.

Macleod, D.V.L. (2013) 'Tourism, anthropology and cultural configuration', in M.K. Smith and G. Richards (eds) *The Routledge Handbook of Cultural Tourism*, London: Routledge.

MacLeod, D.V.L. and Carrier, J.G. (eds) (2010) *Tourism, Power and Culture: Anthropological Insights*, Bristol: Channel View.

New Economics Foundation (2012) *Happy Planet Index*. Available at: www.happyplanetindex.org/assets/happy-planet-index-report.pdf (accessed 24 February 2013).

OECD (2009) *The Impact of Culture on Tourism*, Paris: OECD

Palmer, R. and Richards, G. (2010) *Eventful Cities: Cultural Management and Urban Revitalisation*, London: Routledge.

Picard, D. (2013) 'Cosmopolitanism and hospitality', in M.K. Smith and G. Richards (eds) *The Routledge Handbook of Cultural Tourism*, London: Routledge.

Puczkó, L. and Smith, M.K. (2012) 'An analysis of TQoL domains from the demand side', in M. Uysal, R.R. Perdue and M.J. Sirgy (eds) *Handbook of Tourism and Quality-of-Life Research: Enhancing the Lives of Tourists and Residents of Host Communities*, Dordrecht: Springer.

Richards, G. (2001) 'The development of cultural tourism in Europe', in G. Richards (ed.) *Cultural Attractions and European Tourism*, Wallingford: CABI.

—— (2011) 'Creativity and tourism: The state of the art', *Annals of Tourism Research*, 38: 1225–53.

—— (2013) 'Tourism development trajectories: From culture to creativity?', in M.K. Smith and G. Richards (eds) *Routledge Handbook of Cultural Tourism*, London: Routledge.

Richards, G. and Raymond, C. (2000) 'Creative tourism', *ATLAS News*, 23: 16–20.

Robinson, M. (2013) 'Talking tourists: The intimacies of inter-cultural dialogue', in M.K. Smith and G. Richards (eds) *Routledge Handbook of Cultural Tourism*, London: Routledge.

Robinson, M. and Picard, D. (2006) *Tourism, Culture and Sustainable Development*, Paris: UNESCO.

Selwyn, T. (ed.) (1996) *The Tourist Image: Myths and Myth-making in Tourism,* Chichester: John Wiley & Sons.

Selwyn, T. (2013) 'Hospitality', in M.K. Smith and G. Richards (eds) *Routledge Handbook of Cultural Tourism,* London: Routledge.

Smith, M.K. (2003) *Issues in Cultural Tourism Studies,* London: Routledge.

Smith, M.K. and Richards, G. (eds) (2013) *Routledge Handbook of Cultural Tourism,* London: Routledge.

Smith, V.L. (ed.) (1977, 1989) *Hosts and Guests: An Anthropology of Tourism,* Philadelphia: University of Pennsylvania Press.

Steiner, C.J. and Reisinger, Y. (2006) 'Understanding existential authenticity', *Annals of Tourism Research,* 33: 299–318.

UNESCO (2006) *Discussion Report of the Planning Meeting for 2008 International Conference on Creative Tourism,* Santa Fe, New Mexico, 25–27 October 2006.

Uysal, M., Perdue, R. and Sirgy, M. J. (eds) (2012) *Handbook of tourism and quality-of-life research: enhancing the lives of tourists and residents of host communities,* Dortrecht: Springer.

Wang, N. (1999) 'Rethinking authenticity in tourism experience', *Annals of Tourism Research,* 26: 349–70.

Weil, A. (2013) *Spontaneous Happiness: Step-by-step to Peak Emotional Wellbeing,* London: Hodder & Stoughton Ltd.

Zeppel, H. (2006) *Indigenous Ecotourism: Sustainable Development and Management,* Wallingford: CABI.

Part 3
Management tools and concepts

14

Environmental indicators and benchmarking for sustainable tourism development

Heather Zeppel

Benchmarking 'Benchmarking is a standard by which something can be measured or judged and allows a company to compare itself against others in its industry sector' (GSTC 2013a).

Indicator 'Indicators are suitable tools to inform, monitor, control and to plan all environmentally relevant activities at different levels' (Hamele & Eckardt 2006: 10).

Environmental indicator 'An environmental indicator is a measure, generally quantitative, that can be used to illustrate and communicate complex environmental phenomena simply, including trends and progress over time – and thus helps provide insight into the state of the environment' (EEA 2012: 27).

Environmental performance indicator 'An environmental performance indicator is a specific measure of environmental performance comparable at the process, site and/or organisation level' (Styles *et al.* 2012: 11).

Sustainability indicators 'Sustainability indicators are information sets which are formally selected for a regular use to measure changes in key assets and issues of tourism destinations and sites' (Vereczi 2007a).

Introduction

This chapter reviews environmental indicators and benchmarking for sustainable tourism. Environmental indicators are objective measures of environmental quality and the impacts of tourism while benchmarking assesses tourism performance on key environmental criteria. Sustainability indicators assess levels of energy and water consumption, waste, pollution and greenhouse gas emissions from tourism. These tools also evaluate the positive contribution of tourism in conserving natural resources, landscapes and biodiversity. Sustainable tourism indicators (STI) have been developed and applied since the early 1990s, in response to national policies on sustainable development, resource efficiency and reducing emissions. Indicators underpin tourism planning and regulations, certification schemes and standards. They aim to minimise negative environmental impacts and maximise the benefits of tourism.

This chapter discusses the role and function of indicators, assesses STI developed by the World Tourism Organization, STI applied in Samoa, Europe and Australia, and the Global Sustainable Tourism Criteria. It also critically reviews research from 1993 to 2013 about the development and use of sustainable tourism indicators in different tourism sectors and areas.

Sustainability indicators

Indicators for sustainable development address social, ecological and economic criteria for managing impacts and assist the transition towards sustainable communities and businesses. Indicators are tools that provide measurable information to guide decision-making on tourism or resource management. They function as 'signals of important trends and changes', and 'also serve as performance measures for progress towards sustainability' (WTO 2004: 463).

Environmental and social indicators measure changes in the state or condition of the natural environment and of society. Indicators also reflect desired conditions for sustainability as set by tourism or management agencies. To be useful, sustainability indicators need to be observable; measurable; respond to changing use conditions; cover appropriate scales (temporal, spatial); include a mix of components (e.g. social, cultural, economic, ecological); address a range of indicator functions/types (i.e. driving force, pressure, state, impact, response); and relate to management objectives for an area (Wight 1998). Data for indicators is expressed as a number (quantity, volume, distance or cost), ratio, percentage figure or other measure (e.g. kWh for energy). The main types of indicators are: descriptive (current situation); performance (targets); efficiency (improvement); and policy effectiveness (EEA 2012). Indicators measure the distance between the present (or past) situation and defined future objectives for a sustainable environment (e.g. reduced energy use, increased wildlife). Key impact or environmental quality indicators are selected in management approaches, with standards specified for designated use zones (Wight 1998). These indicators assess energy, water and waste management, tourism type/intensity, and the environmental condition of natural areas (wildlife, landscapes). Environmental indicators are applied at the national and regional level, for tourism destinations and use sites (e.g. beaches, mountains and protected areas), tourism companies and enterprises (White et al. 2006; WTO 2004). Key issues for indicators include their relevance, feasibility, credibility, clarity and comparability along with operational concerns such as managing, reporting and monitoring of data. Indicators assist tourism decision-making and planning (lower costs/reduce risks), identify impacts and emerging issues, measure environmental performance and evaluate progress or decline in tourism sustainability (WTO 2004). Sustainability indicators can be used as benchmarks to compare environmental performance over time and with other tourism enterprises or destinations. Sustainable tourism indicators have been devised for Spain and England (White et al. 2006), the European Union (European Commission 2012) and the Caribbean (Caribbean Tourism Organization 2000). The next section evaluates use of sustainable tourism indicators.

Applying sustainable tourism indicators

WTO sustainable tourism indicators

The UN World Tourism Organization (WTO) has developed sustainable tourism indicators since the early 1990s (WTO 1993, 1996, 2004, 2005). A report on indicators by an international working group (WTO 1993) was followed by a guide for tourism managers on developing and using indicators (WTO 1996). A guidebook on sustainable development indicators for tourism destinations outlined WTO's baseline criteria for sustainability (WTO 2004). It listed 12 baseline issues for tourism including five areas of resource management (energy, water usage, drinking water, wastewater and solid waste). The 12 indicators included measures of energy and water use or conservation, and volumes of waste or wastewater produced/treated:

Energy management

- Per capita consumption of energy from all sources (overall, and by tourist sector)
- % of businesses participating in energy conservation programs, or applying energy saving policy and techniques
- % of energy consumption from renewable resources (at destinations, establishments)

Water availability and conservation

- Water use: (total volume consumed and litres per tourist per day)
- Water saving (% reduced, recaptured or recycled)

Drinking water quality

- % of tourism establishments with water treated to international potable standards
- Frequency of water-borne diseases: no./% of visitors reporting water-borne illnesses

Wastewater management

- % of sewage from site receiving treatment (to primary, secondary, tertiary levels)
- % of tourism establishments (or accommodation) on treatment system(s)

Solid waste management

- Waste volume produced by the destination (tonnes) (by month)
- Volume of waste recycled (m^3)/Total volume of waste (m^3) (by different types)
- Quantity of waste strewn in public areas (garbage counts) (WTO 2004: 245).

The guidebook provided destination applications of these core indicators in varied tourism environments (e.g. coastal, desert and mountain areas, heritage sites, trails and protected areas) and sectors (e.g. ecotourism, convention centres, theme parks and cruise ships). Additional environmental indicators for key sectors covered air pollution, controlling noise levels, managing visual impacts of tourism facilities and infrastructure, and green purchasing.

Convention centres included indicators for environmental management of the supply chain such as the percentage use of disposable or reusable containers, and green purchasing policies (e.g. bulk purchase, preference to providers of environmentally friendly products) that highlighted organisational and cost savings along with environmental benefits (WTO 2004).

Natural and sensitive ecological sites included 16 indicators for four key areas of ecosystem management (water quality; air, noise pollution; impacts on flora and fauna, and aesthetics). The guide discussed applications of the indicators in tourism planning and management, such as protecting natural and cultural resources, assessing carrying capacity, in public reporting, as standards in certification programs, and in benchmarking enterprises. It noted industry programs such as the Tour Operators Initiative, Green Globe, Earth Check and International Hotels Environmental Initiative use core indicators to benchmark tourism sustainability. The WTO guidebook also included 25 global case studies of indicator development, use and impacts for enterprises, islands, protected areas, winter tourism, sites, regions and nations.

Samoa sustainable tourism indicators

A sustainable tourism indicator framework for Samoa was based on key sustainability issues identified in village surveys, key informant interviews and secondary sources. A methodology based on the TOMM (Tourism Optimisation Management Model) project developed for Kangaroo Island (South Australia), and adaptive management, were employed (Miller & Twining-Ward 2005; Twining-Ward 2001, 2003, 2004, 2007; Twining-Ward & Butler 2002). A project advisory committee identified 270 possible tourism indicators with 57 screened for technical and user-friendly issues. This yielded 20 sustainable tourism indicators used in monitoring Samoan tourism, with 'acceptable ranges' set for each indicator based on secondary baseline results and local knowledge. The final 20 indicators included eight environmental, three economic, five socio-cultural and four sustainable tourism indicators. The environmental indicators included tourism village participation in land conservation and marine protection; tourist participation in nature tourism and marine tourism; hotels using sewage treatment and composting biodegradable waste; water usage per guest night in hotels, and water quality at tourism sites. A related *Indicator Handbook* specified the desired sustainability trend along with data requirements, sources and collection techniques for each indicator (Twining-Ward 2003). Results for the 20 tourism indicators for the year 2000 found 11 indicators were rated as poor (e.g. sewage treatment; environmental assessment; operators adopting sustainable practices; water quality tests); eight indicators were rated acceptable (e.g. composting biodegradable waste hotel water usage; social benefits), with just one rated as good (village protocol). In response, a sustainable tourism action plan addressed priority areas such as building village engagement in conservation, sustainable tourism training for guides and operators, and environmental impact legislation. The *Samoa Tourism Development Plan 2002–2006* included these items but monitoring based on indicators stalled as key project members left and resources were moved to other areas.

European sustainable tourism indicators

Europe has developed and used environmental and sustainable tourism indicators since 2000. This has been driven by European Union (EU) policies on sustainable development and resource efficiency, and the European Charter for Sustainable Tourism in Protected Areas. The European Environment Agency (EEA) has devised 225 indicators covering: climate change (45); environmental scenarios (44); transport (38); energy (29); biodiversity (27); water (15); air pollution (11); tourism (7); fisheries (3); land and soil (2); agriculture (2); and waste (2). EEA tourism indicators have been devised since 2000 to support EU tourism policy and the Community Agenda 21 for European Tourism. A core set of seven tourism indicators, based on international sources (WTO, Eurostat), national tourism data and expert input, focused on the environmental impacts of tourism transport and development. In 2001, the EEA reported on four specific indicators for: tourism intensity, tourism travel by transport modes, household expenditure for tourism and recreation, and tourism eco-labelling. It noted the growing impact of tourism on islands and by ownership of second homes, high water usage by hotels, and limited uptake of eco-labelling schemes by tourism (Pelletreau 2004). The EEA has not updated this tourism indicator data. A 2007 EEA report on tourist arrivals noted lack of progress in implementing EU sustainable tourism policies or tourism industry targets.

A report on *Environmental Initiatives by European Tourism Businesses* (Hamele & Eckardt 2006) included data on indicators for energy, water and waste at European accommodation. Data from 466 accommodation businesses in 15 EU countries was analysed to provide average use and benchmark data on energy and water usage and waste volumes per overnight stay by type of enterprise (camping site, bed & breakfast, and 2, 3, 4 and 5 star hotels). Water usage in swimming pools and waste costs for restaurant meals were also calculated. This benchmark data allowed European hotels to assess and rate their environmental performance. On average, 4 and 5 star hotels had the lowest energy demand/usage per overnight stay. A recent report further outlined environmental best practice, key indicators and benchmarking of environmental performance for the European tourism sector (European Commission 2012). It was based on EMAS, the EU's voluntary eco-management and audit scheme for environmental reporting, with indicators for energy efficiency, material efficiency, water, waste, emissions and biodiversity. This tourism report included indicators and benchmark criteria for environmental standards and certification, green procurement, and energy, water and waste management. It included sustainability guidelines and specific targets on resource efficiency for destinations, tour operators, accommodation, kitchens and campsites.

An EU eco-innovation project produced a sustainable tourism toolkit for environmental management with seven training modules. Sustainability indicators and benchmarking for tourism businesses and destinations were covered in module four (Move It 2012). The 45 tourism indicators were compiled according to EMAS Regulation No. 1221/2009 guiding the EU's voluntary environmental reporting scheme, and international standards (i.e. Global Sustainable Tourism Criteria). For tourism businesses, 30 core indicators covered seven key areas of environmental performance in tourism: energy and material efficiency, water, waste, biodiversity, mobility and emissions. Another 15 indicators covered indirect environmental aspects such as supplies, guests, employees (i.e. environmental training) and public relations (i.e. environmental publications). The module included benchmark data on energy, water and waste usage for European hotels, and software to evaluate performance. Other related core indicators for tourism destinations were economic, environment and public health criteria. The 12 environmental indicators for EU destinations covered environmental certification, resource conservation, reducing negative impacts, and biodiversity conservation. The case study provides a summary of 12 environmental tourism indicators used in Queensland, Australia.

Case Study

Environmental tourism indicators for Queensland, Australia

In 2009, EC3 Global developed a set of environmental indicators for the Queensland tourism industry based on best practice case studies, industry consultation, and tourism data. This addressed a key objective of the Queensland Tourism Strategy to 'develop a practical and effective suite of social and environmental indicators to measure and manage the impacts of tourism on the environment and communities'. The indicators supported five key goals for sustainable tourism in Queensland: reducing average consumption of non-renewable resources, responding to environmental challenges, policies for sustainable tourism growth, increased visitor awareness of natural attractions, and sustainable use of protected areas. The 12 environmental tourism indicators and measures were divided into core and comprehensive indicators:

Core indicators:

1. Carbon footprint of the Queensland tourism industry
2. Energy use
3. Water use
4. Waste sent to landfill
5. Response to climate change by tourism operators
6. Regional sustainability policies

Comprehensive indicators:

7. Average energy use, water use and waste sent to landfill per visitor night
8. Adaptation activities (now Core Indicator 5)
9. Visitor education and awareness of conservation
10. Carbon offsetting
11. Compliance of tourism operators with regulations for protected areas
12. A positive policy environment for tourism

Measures were suggested for each indicator, and reporting items as trend data, or against national best practice per visitor night. Recommended measures for core indicators were:

1. estimated greenhouse gas emissions per visitor via tourism satellite accounts;
2. take-up of renewable energy sources by tourism operators, and industry best-practice energy consumption;
3 and 4: industry measures to reduce water/waste, and industry best practice for water consumption/waste sent to landfill;
5. % of surveyed operators participating in adaptation and mitigation, and number of certified Queensland tourism operators; and
6. number of regional tourism organisations with a sustainability policy.

The measures for comprehensive indicators were:

7. average energy/water use/waste by certified operators;
9. % of visitors involved in conservation;
10. % of visitors using carbon offsetting;
11. number of fines issued to tourism operators; and
12. number of extended permits for tourism operators, and number of local governments encouraging better environmental practices.

A 2010 benchmark survey of tourism operators assessed their energy, water and waste activities and sustainability policies, by sectors, and for each region of the state.

Sources: Colmar Brunton (2010); EC3 Global (2009); Tourism Queensland (n.d.) www.tq.com.au

Global sustainable tourism criteria

In 2012, the Global Sustainable Tourism Council released their Global Sustainable Tourism Criteria (GSTC) with indicators for (1) hotels and tour operators, and (2) destinations. These sustainable tourism criteria were developed over a three-year period with input from over 30 tourism organisations, businesses and tourism experts. GSTC is the first global framework establishing a benchmark for sustainable travel by companies, agencies and tourists, with 11 established certification programs for sustainable tourism also recognised as GSTC standards (GSTC 2013b). The GSTC are part of the tourism industry's response to the United Nations' Millennium Development Goals for environmental sustainability and poverty alleviation. The GSTC indicators include 37 criteria based around four main themes of: sustainability management; maximising social and economic benefits; cultural protection; and reducing environment impacts (GSTC 2013a). The GSTC Criteria for Hotels and Tour Operators analysed more than 4,500 criteria from over 60 certification schemes, other voluntary criteria, and 1,500 comments. The GSTC Criteria for Destinations were based on WTO destination level indicators, GSTC Criteria for Hotels and Tour Operators, and other sustainability principles, guidelines, and certification criteria. It was piloted in six early-adopter destinations in 2012. Five global tourism companies have committed to using and promoting the GSTC (Amadeus, Melia, Royal Caribbean Cruises, Sabre Holdings and TUI Travel) (WTO 2012).

In the GSTC Criteria for Hotels and Tour Operators, the environmental criteria included: conserving resources (purchasing policies, consumable goods, energy and water consumption); reducing pollution (emissions, transport, waste water, waste, harmful substances, and other pollution); and conserving biodiversity, ecosystems and landscapes (wildlife, captive wildlife, alien species, conservation, and wildlife/ecosystem interactions). Sustainable management also included 'use locally appropriate sustainable practices and materials' in buildings or facilities. In the GSTC Criteria for Destinations, environmental criteria included: 'Demonstrate sustainable destination management' (climate change adaptation, sustainability standards, and promotion of sustainability claims), and 12 criteria for 'Maximize benefits to the environment and minimize negative impacts' (i.e. environmental risks, protect sensitive environments and wildlife, greenhouse gas emissions, energy conservation, water management, security and quality, wastewater, solid waste reduction, light and noise pollution, and low impact transport). These criteria suggest measuring emissions and energy consumption and monitoring other resource usage. The GSTC criteria suggest what should be done to progress each aspect of sustainability while the indicators recommend ways of complying with the criteria. The GSTC does not prescribe how to implement or measure sustainability or when a goal has been met. It specifies minimum requirements for tourism businesses and destinations to protect resources and promote responsible travel practices; it does not specify or quantify sustainability targets for tourism. The next section reviews research looking at sustainable tourism indicators from 1993 to 2013.

Research on sustainable tourism indicators

Research evaluates environmental goals and targets for sustainable tourism indicators (STI). This includes the selection of appropriate tourism indicators and developing frameworks for STI (Blackstock *et al.* 2006; Ceron & Dubois 2003; Clarke 1997; Dubois 2005; European Commission 2001; EUROSTAT 2006; Fernandez & Rivero 2009; Hughes 2002; Hughey *et al.* 2004; James 2003, 2004; Ko 2005; Manning 1999; McCool *et al.* 2001; Miller 2001; Payne 1993; Sirakaya *et al.* 2001; Wight 1998; WTO 1993, 2004). Key issues include the selection of sustainability indicators, measurement criteria, implementation and monitoring. STI were selected by experts in the Delphi method (Miller 2001), or consultation with stakeholders. WTO's (2004) sustainability indicators were used to evaluate tourism in Cuba (Perez *et al.* 2013), Quebec (Tanguay *et al.* 2013), and South Africa (Mearns 2012).

Applied studies utilise STI to assess the impacts and benefits of tourism in protected areas, for rural and coastal tourism, community tourism, and in nature-based tourism. One key area is indicators to manage visitor impacts in national parks (Buckley 1999; Moore *et al.* 2003; Tonge *et al.* 2005) with case studies of the Cairgorms in Scotland (Blackstock *et al.* 2008; Crabtree & Bayfield 1998), Cape Range in Australia (Moore & Polley 2007), and the protected Karaj River in Iran (Jalilian *et al.* 2012). These focus on indicators of biophysical impacts (waste, water) and management frameworks to minimise visitor impacts in parks, including environmental levies/permit fees, and environmentally certified park businesses.

Other studies assess bio-indicators for a coral reef (Hughes 2002; Li 2004), fragility (Petrosillo *et al.* 2006), the ecological footprint (Hunter & Shaw 2007), and carrying capacity (Castellani & Sala 2012), as effective tools to measure tourism impacts. These highlight issues with assessing tourism impacts and management constraints for sustainability.

Regional case studies evaluate STI for tourism planning in rural areas (Blancas *et al.* 2011; Cardin & Alvarez-Lopez 2011; Park & Yoon 2011); cultural destinations (Lozano-Oyola *et al.* 2012); coastal regions (Blancas *et al.* 2010); and island tourism (Lim & Cooper 2009; Twining-Ward & Butler 2002), focusing on selecting, implementing and monitoring of STI. Earth Check indicators for resource efficiency and operations were included in a sustainable tourism plan for North Stradbroke Island in Australia (Sustainable Tourism Services 2002). A study of STI by New Zealand local authorities found regional councils preferred ecological indicators while tourism agencies prioritised economic and social indicators (Dymond 1997). Other studies evaluate STI for managing community tourism (Choi & Sirakaya 2006; Goodstein 2007), and ecotourism ventures (Mearns 2011, 2012); and tourist perspectives of sustainability (Cottrell & Duim 2003; Cottrell *et al.* 2004). A key area is developing STI for tourism destinations (Sirakaya *et al.* 2001) with case studies assessing tourism areas in the Mediterranean (Farsari & Prastacos 2001a), and Crete (Farsari & Prastacos 2001b); in Switzerland (Johnsen *et al.* 2008), Quebec (Rajaonson & Tanguay 2012; Tanguay *et al.* 2013) and Cuba (Perez *et al.* 2013). An eco-resort in Australia was assessed with 18 indicators including environmental condition, resource use and benefits (Schianetz & Kavanagh 2008). These studies utilise descriptive, composite or systemic indicator systems to assess sustainability in destinations, integrating expert data and/or input from stakeholders.

Business case studies investigate 10 oil use indicators for tourist transport (Becken 2008), 20 STI for small tourism enterprises (Roberts & Tribe 2008), and 35 energy-saving and carbon reduction indicators for natural attractions in Taiwan (Horng *et al.* 2012). Key studies assess energy benchmarking issues for eco-resorts and other accommodation (Warnken *et al.* 2005), hotels (Chan 2012), and at European airlines where fuel efficiency indicators are not comparable (Chan & Mak 2005). Other global studies evaluate a sustainable tourism benchmarking tool (Cernat & Gourdon 2007, 2010), and a sustainable performance index to assess tourism policy (Castellani & Sala 2010), and environmental sustainability (Bojanic 2011). There is a growing focus on benchmarking destinations (Kozak 2002), through industry adoption of eco-labels or certification (Kozak & Nield 2004; Vereczi 2007b), sustainability accounting (Buckley 2012), and by environmental performance criteria (Styles *et al.* 2012). However, these eco-schemes are voluntary with minimal adoption by the mainstream tourism industry.

Conclusions

This chapter reviewed the development and application of environmental tourism indicators. These sustainability indicators cover energy, water, waste, emissions, and tourism intensity. WTO's (2004) sustainability indicators are used to evaluate the impact of tourism in several areas, while the Global Sustainable Tourism Criteria provide minimum standards without targets. The European Union has set accommodation benchmark data for energy, water and waste. Case studies highlight issues with using indicators to assess tourism impacts and progress.

This review found there is a tendency to select indicators that are observable and easy to measure while other social or community issues may be overlooked. The lack of local data, staff or resources limits the adoption and long-term monitoring of sustainability indicators. Targets, thresholds and standards also need to be established for environmental indicators, based on legal guidelines, policy targets, physical limits, benchmarking and expert input. EU countries and selected tourism agencies mainly focus on indicators with cost-saving measures such as the kilowatts of energy saved, litres of water conserved or amount of waste recycled.

Allied indicators assess the adoption of eco-labelling, conservation of biodiversity and ecosystem management for sustainable tourism. Apart from the European Union, varied frameworks for indicators limit the benchmarking of environmental performance by tourism. Tourism operators, residents and management agencies also have different sustainability priorities: tourism agencies address economic and social benefits but not ecological impacts. Future challenges include linking core indicators across local, regional and national tourism. This will reinforce key environmental indicators as measures of sustainable tourism progress.

Key Reading

EC3 Global (2009) *Environmental Indicators for Tourism in Queensland: Feasibility Assessment, Final Report*, prepared for Tourism Queensland. Available at:
www.tq.com.au/tqcorp_06/fms/tq_corporate/industrydevelopment/Tourism%20 Queensland%20Environmental%20Indicators%20-%20Final%20Report%20May%20 2009%20EC3%20Global.PDF (accessed 11 March 2013).

European Commission (2012) *Reference Document on Best Environmental Management Practice in The Tourism Sector*, Seville: European Commission.

Global Sustainable Tourism Council (2013) *Indicators*. Available at: www.gstcouncil.org/ resource-center/progress-indicators.html.

Miller, G. and Twining-Ward, L. (2005) *Monitoring for a Sustainable Tourism Transition: The Challenge of Developing and Using Indicators*, Wallingford: CABI.

World Tourism Organization (2004) *Indicators of Sustainable Development for Tourism Destinations: A Guidebook*, Madrid: WTO.

References

Becken, S. (2008) 'Developing indicators for managing tourism in the face of peak oil', *Tourism Management*, 29: 695–705.

Blackstock, K.L., McCrum, G., Scott, A. and White, V. (2006) *A Framework for Developing Indicators of Sustainable Tourism*, Aberdeen: Macaulay Institute.

Blackstock, K.L., White, V., McCrum, G., Scott, A. and Hunter, C. (2008) 'Measuring responsibility: An appraisal of a Scottish National Park's sustainable tourism indicators', *Journal of Sustainable Tourism*, 16: 276–97.

Blancas, F. J., Caballero, R., Gonzalez, M., Lozano-Oyola, M. and Perez, F. (2010) 'Global programming synthetic indicators: An application for sustainable tourism in Andalusian coastal counties', *Ecological Economics*, 69: 2158–72.

Blancas, F.J., Lozano-Oyola, M., Gonzalez, M., Guerrero, F.M. and Caballero, R. (2011) 'How to use sustainability indicators for tourism planning: The case of rural tourism in Andalusia (Spain)', *Science of the Total Environment*, 412–13: 28–45.

Bojanic, D. (2011) 'Using a tourism importance-performance typology to investigate environmental sustainability on a global level', *Journal of Sustainable Tourism*, 19: 898–1003.

Buckley, R. (1999) 'Tools and indicators for managing tourism in parks', *Annals of Tourism Research*, 26: 207–10.

—— (2012) 'Sustainable tourism: Research and reality', *Annals of Tourism Research*, 39: 528–46.

Cardin, M. and Alvarez-Lopez, C.J. (2011) 'Sustainability criteria and indicators for rural tourism', *Spanish Journal of Rural Development*, 2: 81–96.

Caribbean Tourism Organization (2000) *Sustainable Tourism Standards and Indicators for the Caribbean*, Barbados: Caribbean Tourism Organization.

Castellani, V. and Sala, S. (2010) 'Sustainable performance index for tourism policy development', *Tourism Management*, 31: 871–80.

—— (2012) 'Carrying capacity of tourism system: Assessment of environmental and management constraints towards sustainability', in M. Kasimoglu (ed.) *Visions for Global Tourism Industry: Creating and Sustaining Competitive Strategies*, Rijcka, Croatia: Intech Europe.

Cernat, L. and Gourdon, J. (2007) *Is the Concept of Sustainable Tourism Sustainable? Developing the Sustainable Tourism Benchmarking Tool*, UNCTAD, Geneva: United Nations. Available at: http://unctad.org/en/Docs/ditctncd20065_en.pdf (accessed 11 March 2013).

—— (2012) 'Paths to success: Benchmarking cross-country sustainable tourism', *Tourism Management*, 33: 1044–56.

Ceron, J.P. and Dubois, G. (2003) 'Tourism and sustainable development indicators: The gap between theoretical demands and practical achievements', *Current Issues in Tourism*, 6: 54–75.

Chan, W. (2012) 'Energy benchmarking in support of low carbon hotels: Development, challenges, and approaches in China', *International Journal of Hospitality Management*, 31: 1130–42.

Chan, W.W. and Mak, B. (2005) 'An analysis of the environmental reporting structures of selected European airlines', *International Journal of Tourism Research*, 7: 249–59.

Choi, H.C. and Sirakaya, E. (2006) 'Sustainability indicators for managing community tourism', *Tourism Management*, 27: 1274–89.

Clarke, J. (1997) 'A framework of approaches to sustainable tourism', *Journal of Sustainable Tourism*, 5: 224–33.

Colmar Brunton (2010) *Tourism Queensland Tourism Operators Environmental Indicators Benchmark 2010*, Tourism Queensland. Available at: www.tq.com.au/fms/tq_corporate/research/destinationsresearch/queensland/FINAL%20REPORT%20Queensland%20Tourism%20Operator%20Environment%20Indicators%20Study%202010.PDF (accessed 11 March 2013).

Cottrell, S.P. and Duim, R. (2003) 'Sustainability of tourism indicators: A tourist perspective assessment in Costa Rica and The Netherlands', *The Environment Paper Series*, 6: 2–9.

Cottrell, S.P., Duim, R., Ankersmid, P. and Kelder, L. (2004) 'Measuring the sustainability of tourism in Manuel Antonio and Texel: A tourist perspective', *Journal of Sustainable Tourism*, 12: 409–31.

Crabtree, B. and Bayfield, N. (1998) 'Developing sustainability indicators for mountain ecosystems: A study of the Cairgorms, Scotland', *Journal of Environmental Management*, 52: 1–14.

Dubois, G. (2005) 'Indicators for an environmental assessment of tourism at a national level', *Current Issues in Tourism*, 8: 140–54.

Dymond, S. (1997) 'Indicators of sustainable tourism in New Zealand: A local government perspective', *Journal of Sustainable Tourism*, 5: 279–93.

EC3 Global (2009) *Environmental Indicators for Tourism in Queensland: Feasibility Assessment, Final Report*, prepared for Tourism Queensland. Available at: www.tq.com.au/tqcorp_06/fms/tq_corporate/industrydevelopment/Tourism%20Queensland%20Environmental%20Indicators%20-%20Final%20Report%20May%202009%20EC3%20Global.PDF (accessed 11 March 2013).

European Commission (2001) *The Use of Indicators in the Measurement of Progress in the Process of Quality Improvement in Tourism,* Brussels: European Commission.
—— (2012) *Reference Document on Best Environmental Management Practice in the Tourism Sector,* Final Draft June 2012, Brussels: European Commission. Available at: http://susproc.jrc.ec.europa.eu/activities/ emas/documents/TOURISM_BP_REF_DOC_2012j.pdf (accessed 11 March 2013).
European Environment Agency (EEA) (2012) *Environmental Indicator Report 2012,* Luxembourg: EU. Available at: www.planbleu.org/portail_doc/environmental_indicator_report2012_EEA.pdf (accessed 11 March 2013).
EUROSTAT (2006) *Methodological Work on Measuring the Sustainable Development of Tourism. Part 2: Manual on Sustainable Development Indicators for Tourism,* Luxembourg: EU.
Farsari, Y. and Prastacos, P. (2001a) 'Sustainable tourism indicators for Mediterranean established destinations', *Tourism Today,* 11: 103–21.
—— (2001b) 'Sustainable tourism indicators: Pilot estimation for the municipality of Hersonissos, Crete', International Scientific Conference 'Tourism on Islands and Specific Destinations', University of the Aegean, Chios, 14–16 December 2000. Available at: http://faculty.wwu.edu/~zaferan/Ithaca%20 Curriculum/tourism%20economy/Sustainablity%20Malia.pdf (accessed 11 March 2013).
Fernandez, J.I.P. and Rivero, M.S. (2009) 'Measuring tourism sustainability: Proposal for a composite index', *Tourism Economics,* 15: 277–96.
Goodstein, C. (2007) 'SmartVoyager: Protecting the Galapagos Islands' in R. Black and A. Crabtree (eds) *Quality Assurance and Certification in Ecotourism,* Wallingford, UK: CABI.
GSTC (2013a) *Indicators.* Available at: www.gstcouncil.org/resource-center/progress-indicators.html (accessed 11 March 2013).
—— (2013b) *The Global Sustainable Tourism Criteria.* Available at: www.gstcouncil.org/sustainable-tourism-gstc-criteria.html (accessed 11 March 2013).
Hamele, H. and Eckardt, S. (2006). *Environmental Initiatives by European Tourism Businesses: Instruments, Indicators and Practical Examples,* Saarbrucken: European Commission. Available at: http://sutour.ier. uni-stuttgart.de/englisch/downloads/sutour_lores_en.pdf (accessed 11 March 2013).
Horng, J.S., Hu, M.L., Teng, C.C. and Lin, L. (2012) 'Energy saving and carbon reduction management indicators for natural attractions: A case study of Taiwan', *Journal of Sustainable Tourism,* 20: 1125–49.
Hughes, G. (2002) 'Environmental indicators', *Annals of Tourism Research,* 29: 457–77.
Hughey, K.F.D., Ward, J.C., Crawford, K.A., McConnell, L., Phillips, J.G. and Washbourne, R. (2004) 'A classification framework and management approach for the sustainable use of natural assets used for tourism', *International Journal of Tourism Research,* 6: 349–63.
Hunter, C. and Shaw, J. (2007) 'The ecological footprint as a key indicator of sustainable tourism', *Tourism Management,* 28: 46–57.
Jalilian, M.A., Danehkar, A. and Fami, H.S.A. (2012) 'Determination of indicators and standards for tourism impacts in protected Karaj River, Iran', *Tourism Management,* 33: 61–63.
James, D. (2003) 'Local sustainable tourism indicators', in J.J. Lennon (ed.) *Tourism Statistics: International Perspectives and Current Issues,* Andover, UK: Cengage Learning.
—— (2004) 'Local sustainable tourism indicator', *Estudios Turisticos,* 161–62: 219–30.
Johnsen, J., Bieger, T. and Scherer, R. (2008) 'Indicator-based strategies for sustainable tourism development', *Mountain Research and Development,* 28: 116–21.
Ko, T.G. (2005) 'Development of a tourism sustainability assessment procedure: A conceptual approach', *Tourism Management,* 26: 431–45.
Kozak, M. (2002) 'Destination benchmarking', *Annals of Tourism Research,* 29: 497–519.
Kozak, M. and Nield, K. (2004) 'The role of quality and eco-labelling systems in destination benchmarking', *Journal of Sustainable Tourism,* 12: 138–48.
Li, W. (2004) 'Environmental management indicators for ecotourism in China's nature reserves: A case study in Tianmushan Nature Reserve', *Tourism Management,* 25: 559–64.
Lim, C.C. and Cooper, C. (2009) 'Beyond sustainability: Optimising island tourism development', *International Journal of Tourism Research,* 11: 89–103.
Lozano-Oyola, M., Blancas, F.J., Gonzalez, M. and Caballero, R. (2012) 'Sustainable tourism indicators as planning tools in cultural destinations', *Ecological Indicators,* 18: 659–75.
Manning, T. (1999) 'Indicators of tourism sustainability', *Tourism Management,* 20: 179–81.
McCool, S.F., Moisey, R.N. and Nickerson, N.P. (2001) 'What should tourism sustain? The disconnect with industry perceptions of useful indicators', *Journal of Travel Research,* 40: 124–31.

Mearns, K.F. (2011) 'Using sustainable tourism indicators to measure the sustainability of a community-based ecotourism venture: Malealea Lodge and Pony Trek Centre, Lesotho', *Tourism Review International*, 15: 135–47.

—— (2012) 'Lessons from the application of sustainability indicators to community-based ecotourism ventures in Southern Africa', *African Journal of Business Management*, 6: 7851–60.

Miller, G. (2001) 'The development of indicators for sustainable tourism: Results of a Delphi survey of tourism researchers', *Tourism Management*, 22: 351–62.

Miller, G. and Twining-Ward, L. (2005) *Monitoring for a Sustainable Tourism Transition: The Challenge of Developing and Using Indicators*, Wallingford, UK: CABI.

Moore, S.A. and Polley, A. (2007) 'Defining indicators and standards for tourism impacts in protected areas: Cape Range National Park, Australia', *Environmental Management*, 39: 291–300.

Moore, S.A., Smith, A.J. and Newsome, D.N. (2003) 'Environmental performance reporting for natural area tourism: Contributions by visitor impact management frameworks and their indicators', *Journal of Sustainable Tourism*, 11: 348–75.

Move It (2012) *Module IV Indicators & Benchmarking: Sustainability Indicators for Tourism Businesses and Destinations, EMAS easy tools and concepts for SME's in the tourism sector*, Stockholm Environment Institute. Available at: www.move-it.eu/wp-content/uploads/2012/09/Move_IT_module_4_ENG.pdf (accessed 11 March 2013).

Park, D.B. and Yoon, Y.S. (2011) 'Developing sustainable rural tourism evaluation indicators', *International Journal of Tourism Research*, 13: 401–15.

Payne, R.J. (1993) 'Sustainable tourism: Suggested indicators and monitoring techniques' in J. Nelson, R. Butler and G. Wall (eds) *Tourism and Sustainable Development: Monitoring, Planning, Managing*, Waterloo, Ontario: Department of Geography, University of Waterloo.

Pelletreau, A. (2004) 'European Environment Agency indicators: Tourism and the environment in the European Union', in *Indicators of Sustainable Development for Tourism Destinations: A Guidebook*, Madrid: WTO.

Perez, V., Guerrero, F., Gonzalez, M., Perez, F. and Caballero, R. (2013) 'Composite indicator for the assessment of Cuban nature-based tourism destinations', *Ecological Indicators*, 29: 316–24.

Petrosillo, I., Zurlini, G., Grato, E. and Zaccarelli, N. (2006) 'Indicating fragility of socio-ecological tourism-based systems', *Ecological Indicators*, 6: 104–13.

Rajaonson, J. and Tanguay, G.A. (2012) 'Strategy for selecting sustainable tourism indicators for the Gaspesie and Iles de la Madeleine regions', *Teoros*, 1: 77–84.

Roberts, S. and Tribe, J. (2008) 'Sustainability indicators for small tourism enterprises – an exploratory perspective', *Journal of Sustainable Tourism*, 16: 575–94.

Schianetz, K. and Kavanagh, L. (2008) 'Sustainability indicators for tourism destinations: A complex adaptive systems approach using systemic indicator systems', *Journal of Sustainable Tourism*, 16: 601–28.

Sirakaya, E., Jamal, T.B., and Choi, H.S. (2001) 'Developing indicators for destination sustainability', in D. B. Weaver (ed.) *The Encyclopedia of Ecotourism*, Wallingford, UK: CABI.

Styles, D., Schoenberger, D. and Galvez, J.L. (2012) *Environmental Performance and Benchmarking in the Tourism Sector: Technologies, Best Practices and Indicators*, Smart Destination Forum, Barcelona, April 2012, European Commission. Available at: http://susproc.jrc.ec.europa.eu/activities/emas/documents/EMAS-Tourism-SRD-Smart_Dest_Forum.pdf (accessed 11 March 2013).

Sustainable Tourism Services (2002) *Sustainable Tourism Vision – North Stradbroke Island*, on behalf of: Redlands Tourism, Tourism Queensland, Redland Shire Council, Brisbane: STS. Available at: www.more2redlands.com.au/SiteCollectionDocuments/_Moreto/Moreto%20Documents/Business%20documents/NSI_Visioning_Report_2.pdf (accessed 11 March 2013).

Tanguay, G.A., Rajaonson, J. and Thereen, M.C. (2013) 'Sustainable tourism indicators: Selection criteria for policy implementation and scientific recognition', *Journal of Sustainable Tourism*, 21: 862–79.

Tonge, J., Moore, S., Hockings, M. and Bridle, K. (2005) *Developing Indicators for the Sustainable Management of Visitor Use of Protected Areas in Australia*, Qld: Sustainable Tourism CRC.

Tourism Queensland (n.d.) 'Tourism Environmental Indicators Fact Sheet'. Available at: www.tq.com.au/fms/tq_corporate/industrydevelopment/Tourism%20Environmental%20Indicators%20Fact%20Sheet.PDF (accessed 11 March 2013).

Twining-Ward, L. (2001) 'Monitoring sustainable tourism in Samoa', *UNEP Industry and Environment*, 24: 3–4.

—— (2003) *Indicator Handbook: A Guide to the Development and Use of Samoa's Sustainable Tourism Indicators*, Apia, Samoa: South Pacific Regional Environment Programme.

—— (2004) 'Samoa sustainable tourism indicator project (SSTIP)', in *Indicators of Sustainable Development for Tourism Destinations: A Guidebook:* Madrid: WTO.

—— (2007) 'Adapting the indicator approach – practical applications in the South Pacific', in R. Black and A. Crabtree (eds) *Quality Assurance and Certification in Ecotourism,* Wallingford, UK: CABI.

Twining-Ward, L. and Butler, R. (2002) 'Implementing sustainable tourism development on a small island: Development and use of sustainable tourism development indicators in Samoa', *Journal of Sustainable Tourism,* 10: 363–87.

Vereczi, G. (2007a) 'Statistical and sustainability indicators concerning tourism', Second Expert Group Meeting World Heritage Periodic Reporting UNESCO Headquarters 22–23 January 2007. Available at: http://whc.unesco.org/uploads/events/documents/event-368-15.ppt (accessed 11 March 2013).

—— (2007b) 'Sustainability indicators for ecotourism destinations and operations', in R. Black and A. Crabtree (eds) *Quality Assurance and Certification in Ecotourism,* Wallingford, UK: CABI.

Warnken, J., Bradley, M. and Guilding, C. (2005) 'Eco-resorts vs. mainstream accommodation providers: An investigation of the viability of benchmarking environmental performance', *Tourism Management,* 26: 367–79.

White, V., McCrum, G., Blackstock, K.L. and Scott, A. (2006) *Indicators of Sustainability & Sustainable Tourism: Some Example Sets,* Aberdeen: The Macaulay Institute. Available at: www.macaulay.ac.uk/ruralsustainability/ExampleSetsofIndicators.pdf (accessed 11 March 2013).

Wight, P. (1998) 'Tools for sustainability analysis in planning and managing tourism and recreation in the destination', in C.M. Hall, and A.A. Lew (eds) *Sustainable Tourism: A Geographical Perspective,* Harlow, Essex: Longman.

World Tourism Organization (WTO) (1993) *Indicators for the Sustainable Management of Tourism,* International Working Group on Indicators of Sustainable Tourism, Madrid: WTO. Available at: www.iisd.org/pdf/2011/indicators_for_sustainable_tourism.pdf (accessed 11 March 2013).

—— (1996) *What Tourism Managers Need to Know: A Practical Guide to the Development and Use of Indicators of Sustainable Tourism,* Madrid: WTO.

—— (2004) *Indicators of Sustainable Development for Tourism Destinations: A Guidebook,* Madrid: WTO. Available at: www.iittm.org/doc/Indicators-of-Sustainable-Development-for-Tourism-Destinations-A-Guide-Book-by-UNWTO.pdf (accessed 11 March 2013).

—— (2005) *Indicators of Sustainable Tourism for Yangshuo China,* Madrid: WTO. Available at: http://sdt.unwto.org/sites/all/files/docpdf/china_0.pdf (accessed 11 March 2013).

—— (2012) *Leading Travel Companies Commit to Sustainable Tourism Through the Global Sustainable Tourism Criteria,* Press release, 16 January 2012, Madrid: WTO. Available at: http://sdt.unwto.org/sites/all/files/pdf/standards_support_press_release_16jan12_0.pdf (accessed 11 March 2013).

15

Certification and labeling

Sonya Graci and Rachel Dodds

Certification A voluntary procedure that assesses, audits and gives written assurance that a facility product, process or service meets specific standards.

Ecolabeling is an award that is given to a business or activity that has significantly better performance compared to the other businesses in its sector. Only the best performers that show exemplary performance, according to the established criteria, receive the ecolabel.

Environmental and social criteria Criteria for certification that is based on environmental and social values and ethics.

Global Sustainable Tourism Criteria is an effort to come to a common understanding of sustainable tourism and will be the minimum that any tourism business should aspire to reach.

Introduction

Certification and ecolabeling have been used in many industries and its application to tourism began in the mid-1990s. There are several certification and labeling schemes related to tourism, and specifically sustainable tourism, which will be discussed in this chapter. The terms certification and labeling are often used interchangeably but mean different things. Certification is awarded to businesses or activities that comply with a set of standards and generally requires more than what legal regulations do. Standards can be divided into *product* standards, reflecting the appropriate characteristics a product is expected to have, or *process* standards, reflecting the appropriate characteristics from products to final distribution (Dodds & Joppe 2009a). Labeling, which occurs through giving an ecolabel, is an award that is given to a business or activity that has significantly better performance compared to the other businesses in its sector. Only the best performers that show exemplary performance, according to the established criteria, receive the ecolabel. As the industry changes and more businesses adopt good practices, the requirements for receiving the ecolabel are raised, so that only the better environmental performance is rewarded (Bien 2007).

Certification for sustainable tourism

Certification for sustainable tourism is based on the premise of measuring and monitoring a tourism company or destination's sustainable management. Certification is a way of ensuring that an activity or a product meets certain standards (Bien 2007). In most industries, standards or certification programs have been developed by the private sector to deal with external pressure. Certification is defined as a "voluntary procedure that assesses, audits and gives written assurance that a facility product, process or service meets specific standards. It awards a marketable logo to those that meet or exceed baseline standards" (Honey & Rome 2001: 8). Sustainable tourism certification consists of programs that measure a range of environmental, socio-cultural and economic equity issues both internally (within business, service or product) and externally (on the surrounding community and physical environment) (Honey & Rome 2001). Within the tourism industry, different organizations have developed certification programs measuring different aspects of tourism, from quality for the entire tourism industry, to sustainability for all sectors and ecotourism (Bien 2007). Currently, there are over 100 certification programs worldwide. These vary in terms of methods, quality, criteria contents and scope.

In the tourism industry, certification is widely discussed; however, there are numerous certification and ecolabeling programs at the regional, national and international level. These programs vary in process and performance standards and provide a confusing state for industry, government and consumers. Certification programs have been developed for accommodations, golf courses, beaches, protected areas, boat tours, ecolodges and naturalist tour guides. Recently the Global Sustainable Tourism Criteria have been developed as a minimum baseline for all certification programs to adhere to; however, these do not include all certification programs – only those that relate to the hospitality and tourism industry, therefore may not be all encompassing.

The earliest case of certification was with the chemical industry and their Responsible Care Program that began as the result of the chemical industry needing to increase their corporate social responsibility after a major chemical spill in 1984. After the Rio Earth Summit, in 1992, the impetus for further environmental certification began. The ISO 14001 generic standard for environmental management systems was released in 1996 and became popular as a universal environmental certification system (Bien 2007). Environmental certification of tourism services began in Europe in 1987 with the Blue Flag Campaign for beaches. In the decade between the Earth Summit in 1992 and the International Year of Ecotourism in 2002, more than 60 environmental tourism certification programs were developed. Most were based in Europe, few took socio-cultural factors into account and all were voluntary.

There are many different types of certification systems, as well as related awards and ecolabels, and there is much confusion about how they differ. The purpose of certification has been to achieve voluntary standards of performance that meet or exceed baseline standards or legislation. The process starts with a body that sets credible certification standards (through standards that are industry relevant, measurable and obtainable). The applicant or business then is evaluated according to the indicators, and if successful, receives recognition, usually through the form of a logo, to inform the consumer that they have met minimum criteria (Dodds & Joppe 2009a). To be considered reliable, certification programs should have a third-party audit and effective assessment as well as clearly defined accreditation criteria. The certifier must be without conflict of interest and the indicators should be recognized by an accreditation body.

Elements of a credible certification system include the following key attributes. Although these attributes are for general certification programs and not necessarily ones for sustainable tourism, it is applicable as a baseline for credible systems. These include the following:

- Adequate, appropriate standards developed/accepted by all affected interests – interpretation of standards;
- Trained, qualified assessors;
- Professional/ethical operations at all levels with no biases or conflicts of interest;
- Qualified, financially stable certifying body – if there are multiple certifiers, an accreditation mechanism is needed;
- Even-handed certification and accreditation;
- Transparency;
- Defined procedures;
- Appeals mechanism;
- Recognition by relevant agencies and/or customers–compliance with accepted criteria (e.g. ISO/IEC Guides) facilitates recognition; and
- Acceptance in the marketplace or by regulators – marketing and promotion (Toth 2002: 96).

There are many tourism certification schemes that relate to sustainability. Green Globe, Travelife and Blue Flag are the best known from an international industry certification program. There are also a number of NGO or country initiatives such as the Costa Rican "Certification for Sustainable Tourism," Canada's Green Leaf Eco-Rating Program for Hotels, and the Australian Ecotourism program to name a few. The International Organization of Standardization (ISO) also does certification although not solely for the tourism industry. ISO developed international standards that ensure products and services are safe, reliable and of good quality. These include ISO 9001 for quality management, ISO 14001 for environmental management, ISO 20121 for event management, ISO 26000 for social responsibility and ISO 50001 for energy management. Even though ISO is not specific to tourism, many tourism organizations have adopted this certification. Despite the several programs developed for sustainable tourism on both a regional and industry level and pertaining to destinations, hotels and ecotourism, these programs may not include all elements of a successful program as discussed by Toth (2002). This has resulted in many issues for consumers as they are unsure of credibility, and the value of the certification is therefore reduced with too many on the market.

Benefits of sustainable tourism certification

There are, however, several benefits to certification. Certification helps businesses to improve themselves. Going through a certification process is educational. Many certified businesses have stated that one of the greatest benefits of the certification was to teach them the elements of sustainability in their operations and focus their attention on the changes they need to make in their business. A better operating business tends to be more efficient and attracts more clients (Bien 2007; Dodds & Joppe 2009a, 2009b). Certification also tends to reduce operating costs. This has been found in almost every type of business certification. In tourism, it has been shown to dramatically reduce the costs of water, electricity and fossil fuels without reducing the quality of service (Bien 2007). Certification can also provide a marketing advantage to certified businesses, as consumers learn to recognize credible certification brands (Bien 2007; Font 2002a; Font et al. 2003). It is thought to give companies a competitive advantage and increased linkages into the distribution chain and to consumers through marketing, all of which is assumed to give businesses competitive advantage through the clearly identified logo (Dodds & Joppe 2005). The ecolabel associated with certification provides tourists with environmentally and socially responsible choices as it helps consumers to know which businesses are truly socially and environmentally responsible and to make choices on this basis. As certification programs become better known, this may produce tangible benefits in a business's reputation and popularity. Certification also increases public awareness of responsible business practices as it provides the ability to distinguish sustainable practices from green washing. It can showcase best practice, assist with training of management procedures and achieve compliance beyond legislative compliance. It raises industry standards in health, safety, environment and social stability and lowers the regulatory costs of environmental protection. In addition, by requiring economic benefits for communities, certification can help reduce poverty, especially in rural areas (Bien 2007; Dodds & Joppe 2009b).

Issues with sustainable tourism certification

Determinants of success of schemes have been linked to marketing which, to date, has been largely unsatisfactory, due to the large number of programs and within these programs the small number of certified businesses and therefore reduced appeal to large operators to use them in their product choice. According to UNWTO (2005: 18): "Tourism certification systems and ecolabels among other voluntary initiatives have been officially adopted or supported by national or local governments in a number of countries. The effectiveness of such systems, or the level to which they are clearly recognized and respected by consumers have not been reported." Also the sheer number of schemes and labels makes it difficult for tour operators to incorporate as they would have to educate the consumer about the standards behind each one and the differences among them. The sheer number of certification and ecolabeling programs makes it confusing to consumers and waters down the value of the certification. Too many certification programs lead to mistrust amongst consumers and a lack of value about what it all means. According to the UNWTO (2005) "the proliferation of voluntary initiatives and ecolabels, and the lack of stringent procedures and standards of many of them, create confusion and affect credibility among consumers" (cited in Dodds & Joppe 2005: 20).

Not only is there a lack of awareness among consumers regarding certification programs, tour operators and travel providers have also confirmed that there is a low consumer demand for the certified product and a general tiredness with labels of all kinds. Government involvement, funding and awareness are limited and usually focused on their own country. Most certification is voluntary but there is little consensus that certification is actually viable. In all cases of certification, there is very little uptake in regards to the whole industry with a small percentage of businesses being certified (Dodds & Joppe 2005, Newton *et al.*, 2004, Dodds & Joppe 2009a, 2009b). This is currently being tackled by the Travelife program that is being supported by most major tour operators in Europe and is currently being expanded globally.

In addition, programs are often focused only on environmental values and do not include social indicators. This has been addressed by ISO 26000 – the certification for social responsibility. The new Global Sustainable Tourism Criteria also addresses this; however, this is not a certification program. The debate over the years has been focused on whether process or performance indicators should be used in certification and which provides the best baseline for tourism businesses. Certification based on process, focuses on implementing a system, not so much meeting performance indicators such as a percentage reduction by a certain time.

Sonya Graci and Rachel Dodds

Process-based systems

The most commonly used process-based systems are ISO 14001 for environmental management systems. They certify businesses that have established and documented systems for assuring the improvement of quality or environmental performance. They do not, however, determine any specific performance results other than the company's own and those required by law. They must show continuous improvement but only compared to their own prior performance. Thus, for example, two hotels may both be certified with ISO 14001, while one might implement excellent state-of-the-art water and energy conservation systems and the other might have overuse of water and energy, as long as each could demonstrate improvement from year to year of its own performance. This is the fundamental problem with process-based systems: as long as the business complies with the law and has mechanisms in place to ensure that its management system continuously improves relative to itself, it can be certified. It receives a certification of its effort, not its actual performance. ISO certifies the business or activity, not what it produces, which in the case for tourism, is lodging in a hotel room, a meal, a tour or transportation (Bien 2007).

Performance-based systems

Performance-based systems certify whether or not a business or activity complies with a set of objectives and criteria. For example, how many litres of water per guest per night does a hotel consume? This allows a direct comparison between two businesses to show which one has better environmental performance. Performance-based certification is best suited to small and medium-sized businesses, which compromise some 80–90% of tourism businesses worldwide. They tend to be cheaper to implement than ISO 14001 or other types of environmental management systems such as ISO 26000 that includes social indicators and ISO 20121 that is for the greening of events. Performance-based programs such as the Costa Rican Certification for Sustainable Tourism and Green Globe have more tangible criteria that permit comparisons among certified businesses and measure achievement and results (Bien 2007; Font 2003; Font 2002b). Below is a discussion of international performance-based systems. There are multiple programs but only Green Globe, Travelife and Blue Flag will be featured as these are international programs.

Green Globe

Green Globe is an international standard applicable to tourism businesses, activities and destinations worldwide. Its programs include benchmarking followed by certification. Measurability and implementation of this scheme, however, has been questioned due to a multi-checkmark scheme that can be confusing to the traveler. Green Globe certification consists of three program levels: affiliate, benchmarking and certification. Logos are awarded to each level, but they are slightly different (e.g. A is awarded for joining but level C has a checkmark which shows a different compliance level).

Blue Flag

The Blue Flag is a voluntary ecolabel awarded to beaches and marinas in 46 countries across Europe, South Africa, Morocco, Tunisia, New Zealand, Brazil, Canada and the Caribbean. There are currently 3,850 beaches certified. The Blue Flag program works towards sustainable development of beaches and marinas through strict criteria dealing with water quality, environmental education and information, environmental management, and safety and other services (Blue Flag 2013).

Travelife

Travelife is a certification system designed by the travel industry for hotels and accommodations, travel agents and tour operators (Travelife 2013). Focusing on 99 sustainability criteria, the program awards bronze, silver or gold status. Currently most major tour operators in the UK and Europe are moving towards having their hotel suppliers be certified.

Global Sustainable Tourism Criteria

This is an effort to come to a common understanding of sustainable tourism and will be the minimum that any tourism business should aspire to reach. The criteria are organized around four main themes: effective sustainability planning; maximizing social and economic benefits for the local community; enhancing cultural heritage; and reducing negative impacts to the environment. Although the criteria are initially intended for use by the accommodation and tour operation sectors, they have applicability to the entire tourism industry (GSTC 2013; Harms 2013).

Beginning in 2007, a coalition of 27 organizations formed the Partnership for Global Sustainable Tourism Criteria. Since then, the coalition has consulted with close to 100,000 tourism stakeholders, analyzed more than 4,500 criteria from more than 60 existing certification and other voluntary sets of criteria and received comments from over 1,500 individuals. The Sustainable Tourism Criteria have been developed in accordance with the ISEAL Code of Best Practice and as such will undergo consultation and input every two years until feedback is no longer provided or unique (GSTC 2013). ISEAL Alliance is the global membership association for sustainable practices.

The criteria are part of the response of the tourism community to the global challenges of the United Nations Millennium Development Goals. Poverty alleviation and environmental sustainability including climate change are the main issues that are addressed through the criteria. These are expected to serve as basic guidelines for businesses of all sizes to become more sustainable and help business choose sustainable tourism programs that fulfill these global criteria. It also is intended to serve as guidance for travel agencies and consumers in choosing suppliers and sustainable tourism programs. The criteria indicate what should be done, not how to do it or whether the goal has been achieved (GSTC 2013; Harms 2013).

The criteria are the baseline standard for certification, government and other voluntary programs, as well as for education and training bodies such as universities. These criteria are not a global certification but a benchmark and guide for certification programs to meet and adhere to. A global certification system that is based on these criteria may be beneficial to the industry to reduce confusion and increase value and marketing.

The future of sustainable tourism certification

If certification is to continue to move forward, sustainability criteria need to be assessed to include quality assurance as well as health and safety standards as this is crucial to selling a better product. Although eco-certification claims to address environmental and sometimes social criteria, basic health and safety factors are not always considered and some certified ecolodges in Central America have been found to lack elementary hygiene and safety. Although ISO 9001 addresses quality assurance, it is not linked to other schemes and has only been adopted by some individual hotels rather than entire chains or others in the tourism sector. The main selection criteria for customers to choose their travel packages remain price, safety and quality. Environmental and social criteria will only be considered when these primary criteria are satisfied.

Certification incentives could help build industry buy-in. Tax write-offs, preferential access to areas (e.g. beach property or remote parks) and preferential marketing to supporting schemes would be beneficial; however, the majority of businesses use certification as a means of cost savings, improving management practices and to comply with requirements for corporate reporting (Dodds & Joppe 2009b). The main weakness of certification is the overall lack of reporting and monitoring (Font 2002a; Dodds & Joppe 2005, 2009b). Certification has been seen to positively affect resource management but does not necessarily deal with labor or social issues and therefore most companies who promote their certification also provide additional forms of public corporate reporting.

Certification does not appear to have a significant effect on spreading sustainable tourism practices overall nor on allowing SMEs to gain better access to international markets (Dodds & Joppe 2009a, 2009b; Fairweather, Maslin & Simmons 2005). The focus on educational and training campaigns for the industry, as well as education of the consumer, could have higher initial impacts than attempting to move certification forward to become more mainstream.

Overall there is a need to agree on international standards that can be addressed step by step and seen as appropriate by local and international operators. This has been the purpose of the Global Sustainable Tourism Criteria by establishing minimum baseline criteria. However, there is also a need to link quality with environmental and social criteria in guidelines, reporting and accreditation efforts by consolidating criteria and charters. In addition they should be made to be sector specific as the differences in business realities among the various supply chain agents is considerable. Standards also need to be flexible enough to fulfill regional needs.

An international certification system, if developed, should include the following elements:

- Flexibility in letting the organization decide to certify a product, facility or entire operation
- Process and performance-based indicators requiring an environmental management system and providing benchmarks for compliance
- Third-party auditing for credibility
- A clear ecolabeling system which enables consumers to distinguish level of sustainability
- A partnership model with governments and other certification programs to have a consistent system in place
- Ongoing continuous improvement
- Transparency in the process
- Marketing and promotion with a universally recognized logo

Both industry and government must assume their respective responsibilities. Industry will need to adopt and implement sustainable supply and government will need to develop, implement and enforce policies that regulate minimum standards for sustainability. Certification programs are to promote voluntary initiatives to be above and beyond regulation and governments must play a role to promote and award early adopters, rather than focusing on baseline compliance.

Recommendations

If certification is to continue and be successful, a number of criteria are needed. First, there is a need for one global body to monitor and promote industry-wide criteria. Second, there should be more business-to-business marketing rather than business-to-consumer, as consumer awareness and interest are extremely low (this is currently being attempted by Travelife, however, with good uptake to date). Third, demand needs to be created among consumers through increased industry responsibility reporting and educational campaigns. Fourth, if certification is to be successful, there is a need to achieve critical mass. Currently, few companies worldwide have achieved certification and therefore there are few certified products to choose from. In the Americas as well as Europe, there have been efforts to amalgamate certification schemes; however, the complexity of programs and politics in different countries has not permitted much success. Fifth, quality must be linked with environmental and social management so that certified products can guarantee that a level of quality has been achieved and the "experience" of the product is still elevated (Dodds & Joppe 2005; Dodds & Joppe, 2009b).

The following needs to occur in order for certification to become more successful and implemented on a wider scale:

- Agreement on international standards that can be addressed step by step and seen as appropriate by local and international operators. This is the role of the Global Sustainable Tourism Criteria; however, it is yet to be seen how this translates into implementation.
- Link quality with environmental and social criteria in guidelines, reporting and accreditation efforts.
- Pressure associations to integrate and implement certification.
- Consolidate guidelines and charters to be wide reaching and industry specific (tour operators, hotels, etc.).
- Develop methods to identify free riders and ensure that green washing does not occur in certification programs.
- Adopt certification or use certified products through supply chain partners.
- Governments to reward businesses that implement certification through tax breaks, incentives, marketing, preferential treatment.
- Pressure industry associations to report on how they are achieving more sustainable tourism (e.g. industry associations are asking their members to sign up to guidelines and charters but few are enforcing this as a criteria for membership and even fewer are pushing certification schemes or ecolabeling).
- Facilitate arenas to share best practices between sectors (hotels, tour operators, airlines and cruise lines) so that they can learn from one another.
- Legislate or provide incentives to businesses who adopt internationally recognized certification schemes or standards within their country.

(Dodds & Joppe 2005, 2009b)

With all actors focusing on supporting certification and having an agreed upon international standard, it may be a viable tool. All stakeholders, however, (government, industry, trade associations, suppliers, businesses and community) need to undertake certification of their products and promote it to the consumer for global change. Continuous improvement is also necessary to continue to evolve the standards and increase the level of sustainability in the tourism industry.

Key Reading

Bien, A. (2007) *A Simple User's Guide to Certification for Sustainable Tourism and Ecotourism*, IDB Publications.

Dodds, R. and Joppe, M. (2009) 'Have certification programs allowed SME's in LDC's access to market?', *Tourism & Territories Journal*, 1: 237–61.

Global Sustainable Tourism Council *Global Sustainable Tourism Criteria*. Available at: www. gstcouncil.org/sustainable-tourism-gstc-criteria.html

Honey, M. and Rome, A. (2001) *Protecting Paradise: Certification Programs for Sustainable Tourism and Ecotourism*, Washington DC: Institute for Policy Studies.

References

Bien, A. (2007) *A Simple User's Guide to Certification for Sustainable Tourism and Ecotourism*, IDB Publications.

Blue Flag (2013) *Homepage*. Available at: www.blueflag.org (accessed 20 May 2013).

Dodds, R. and Joppe, M. (2005) *CSR in the Tourism Industry: The Status of and Potential for Certification, Codes of Conduct and Guidelines*, Washington: IFC/World Bank.

—— (2009a) 'The demand for, and participation in corporate social responsibility and sustainable tourism – implications for the Caribbean', *ARA Journal of Travel Research*, 2: 1–24.

—— (2009b) 'Have certification programs allowed SME's in LDC's access to market?', *Tourism & Territories Journal*, 1: 237–61.

Fairweather, J., Maslin, C. and Simmons, D.G. (2005) 'Environmental values and response to ecolabels among international visitors to New Zealand', *Journal of Sustainable Tourism*, 13: 82–98.

Font, X. (2002a) *Critical Review of Certification and Accreditation in Sustainable Tourism Governance*, Leeds Metropolitan University, UK.

—— (2002b) 'Environmental certification in tourism and hospitality: Progress, process and prospects', *Tourism Management* 23: 197–205.

—— (2003) *Labelling & Certification: Benefits & Challenges for Sustainable Tourism Management & Marketing*, Leeds Metropolitan University, UK. Available at: http://ecoclub.com/news/050/expert.html#1 (accessed 1 July 2005).

Font, X., Sanabria, R. and Skinner, E. (2003) 'Sustainable tourism and ecotourism certification: Raising standards and benefits', *Journal of Ecotourism*, 2: 213–18.

Global Sustainable Tourism Council (GSTC) (2013) *Global Sustainable Tourism Criteria*. Available at: www.gstcouncil.org/sustainable-tourism-gstc-criteria.html (accessed 1 April 2013).

Harms, E. (2013) 'The Global Sustainable Tourism Council' in K. Bricker, R. Black and S. Cottrell (eds.) *Sustainable Tourism & the Millennium Development Goals*, Burlington: Jones & Bartlett Learning.

Honey, M. and Rome, A. (2001) *Protecting Paradise: Certification Programs for Sustainable Tourism and Ecotourism*, Washington DC: Institute for Policy Studies.

Newton, T., Quiros, N., Crimmins, A., Blodgett, A., Kapur, K., Lin, H.C., Luo, T., Rossbach, K. and Dunnevin, D. (2004) *Assessing the Certification for Sustainable Tourism (CST) Program in Costa Rica*, Costa Rica: NEAP. The School for Field Studies (SFS).

Toth, R. (2002) 'Exploring the concepts underlying certification', in M. Honey (ed.) *Ecotourism & Certification: Setting Standards in Practice*, Washington: Island Press.

Travelife (2013) *Homepage*. Available at: www.travelife.org/ (accessed 30 May 2013).

16

Life cycle assessment

Viachaslau Filimonau

Product life cycle is all the stages a product goes through during its lifespan, from its manufacture, through its use and maintenance, to its end-of-life disposal. The life cycle of some typical tourism-related products is estimated (in years): passenger car (12–15), road infrastructure (60–70), hotel building (50–100), hotel furniture (6–10), hotel room textiles (4–5).

'Direct' environmental impact (footprint, effect) is the impact arising from the operational (i.e. product use) stage of a product life cycle. The carbon footprint generated as a result of fuel combustion in a car engine when driving is an example of 'direct' environmental impact.

'Indirect' ('hidden', 'grey' or 'embodied') environmental impacts (footprints, effects) are the impacts generated during the non-operational phases of a product life cycle. For example, the processes of vehicle manufacture, its delivery to the final user, its maintenance and disposal, all contribute to 'indirect' environmental impacts. The 'indirect' environmental impacts also relate to the capital goods and infrastructure and supply chain industries.

Capital goods and infrastructure are the goods (e.g. machinery, electric equipment, electronic devices) used in the production of commodities and employed to support the operation of these commodities. Tourism-related examples include roads which serve tourism transport, automotive fuel production processes, factories that manufacture aircraft, personal computers used at a hotel reception. To produce and maintain the capital goods and infrastructure, environmental resources (e.g. energy) are required. Hence, they have the 'indirect' environmental footprint (e.g. carbon footprint) embodied in them.

Tourism supply chain (side) is the system of resources required to produce a tourism product or deliver a tourist service. It ranges from the supply of raw materials through the production and delivery of end products to the customer. Food procurement, contracted vehicle fleet and outsourced laundry services are examples of supply chain in hotels. Supply chain consumes energy and resources which results in the 'indirect' environmental releases.

Introduction

Tourism generates significant environmental impact; the necessity to reduce this impact has been repeatedly emphasized. Reliable environmental assessment methods are required to produce accurate estimates. To this end, a number of impact appraisal tools have been applied in tourism, such as an ecological footprint analysis, environmental impact assessment, input–output analysis and carrying capacity (Filimonau et al. 2011b). Despite the recent developments in the area, existing tools have a number of shortcomings. As a result, the potential of these methods to account for the full diversity of environmental impact from the tourism industry is limited (Lundie et al. 2007). The necessity to refine existing and to develop new, more advanced, techniques for environmental assessment in tourism has been recognized (Schianetz et al. 2007).

The challenge of assessing the full diversity of the environmental impact from tourism

Tourism environmental impacts are multi-dimensional and range from carbon footprint generation and water consumption to water eutrophication, acidification and ozone layer depletion (Gössling 2002; see also Chapter 3). The primary focus of environmental assessment in tourism has been on the contribution of the industry to the global carbon (Gössling et al. 2005) and water footprint (Gössling et al. 2012) as these are deemed to be the major environmental impact categories attributed to tourism operations. There is evidence to suggest that other environmental effects from tourism are also significant and should not, therefore, be excluded from analysis. The study by Koroneos et al. (2005) demonstrates, for instance, that tourism makes a large contribution to global acidification due to kerosene combustion in aircraft engines. Further studies emphasize the harmful effect of acidification on human health and marine ecosystems (Gössling 1999) and establish the inter-linkages between the issues of global acidification and climate change (Caldeira & Wickett 2003). Given the diversity of tourism impacts, it is crucial that environmental assessment tools in tourism can appraise *all or the majority* of its impacts. The ability to compare the relative damaging effects of different environmental impacts from tourism operations would also be a valuable feature. This could enable policy makers and tourism managers to prioritize the areas where the primary impact mitigation is necessary. Existing methods struggle to address this task.

Another shortcoming of the current techniques for assessing the environmental impact of tourism is the limited capability to account for the full scale of a *single, specific* impact. The focus of existing appraisals is on the 'direct' or operational environmental effects which represent only a fraction of the total environmental impact from tourism products. There are additional, 'indirect' environmental impacts attributed to the non-operational stages of a tourism product life cycle. These stem, for example, from industrial processes required to extract raw materials, manufacture tourism products and deliver them to the consumer. Maintenance and end-of-life disposal also make a contribution to the 'indirect' environmental effects (see Figure 16.1). The 'indirect' environmental footprint is, for example, embodied in the capital goods and infrastructure used to support the industrial processes at different stages of a product life cycle. The 'indirect' environmental impacts are further magnified by the breadth and diversity of the tourism supply chain (Frischknecht et al. 2007). The combination of the 'direct' and 'indirect' environmental impact of a tourism product is known as the 'life cycle environmental effect' (Patterson & McDonald 2004).

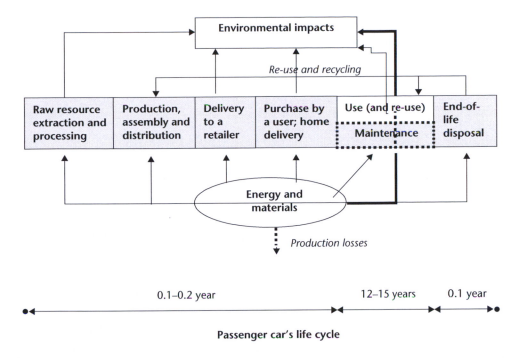

Figure 16.1 'Direct' (white colour box, thick arrows) and 'indirect' (grey colour boxes, thin arrows) environmental impacts arising during a product life cycle.

Evidence from the non-tourism literature suggests that the 'indirect' environmental effects from tourism products can be significant and their exclusion from impact appraisals may result in underestimates of the total environmental footprints. König *et al.* (2007) studied the life cycle impacts of a hotel in Portugal and found that the amount of energy required to construct a hotel building equates to 20 per cent of the total energy consumption within the building's operational life cycle of 80 years. Barrett and Scott (2003) posit that the 'indirect' environmental footprint associated with vehicle manufacture and maintenance may account for about 30 per cent of the total environmental impact attributed to public transport in the United Kingdom. The study on the environmental footprint of sport events by Collins *et al.* (2009) found that the 'indirect' contribution from the supply-side industries can be equal to 45–64 per cent of the total. These examples suggest that the scope of current impact assessments in tourism must be extended to account for the 'indirect' environmental footprint.

Life-cycle assessment as a holistic method for environmental appraisal

Life cycle assessment (LCA) is an established tool for evaluating the environmental performance of individual products or services throughout their life cycle (Patterson & McDonald 2004). The concept of LCA was proposed in the 1990s and, since then, it has been cited as the most appropriate, well-established and developed method for holistic environmental assessment (Junnila 2004). LCA identifies and quantifies the energy and material consumed during a product's life cycle, evaluates the associated environmental releases and further appraises the corresponding impacts on the environment (Koroneos *et al.* 2005).

LCA has a broad international acceptance in the scientific community as a means to improve environmental performance of products or services and to set targets for environmental impact prevention and reduction (Ortiz *et al.* 2009). It has been identified as a strong scientifically grounded support tool for environmental decision making in different sectors of the global economy (Koroneos *et al.* 2005). LCA has been successfully applied in many disciplines to appraise the environmental impact of a number of products and services ranging from wine to biofuels.

The LCA method has a number of advantages. The key strength from the standpoint of tourism environmental assessment is that it can appraise the magnitude of both 'direct' and 'indirect', life cycle-related, environmental impacts (Berners-Lee *et al.* 2011). These are estimated by specialized research groups for a broad range of products and services and summarized in the form of extensive life cycle inventories, such as the Ecoinvent database (Frischknecht & Rebitzer 2005). These databases enable inclusion or exclusion of the 'indirect' environmental impacts associated with, for example, infrastructure and capital goods (Frischknecht *et al.* 2007). To simplify the use of life cycle inventories and enable detailed impact analysis, a number of dedicated LCA software packages have been developed, such as SimaPro (see www.pre-sustainability.com/simapro-lca-software), GaBi (see www.gabi-software.com) and Umberto (see www.umberto.de).

The LCA method can help to estimate the 'indirect' environmental footprint from the supply chain industries. It can capture up to 50 per cent of the total 'indirect' environmental impacts related to the first-, second- and third-orders of suppliers (Berners-Lee *et al.* 2011). This is a significant development compared to the conventional tools for environmental assessment in tourism which either do not address the 'indirect' environmental impacts, or are limited to the appraisal of first-order suppliers (Lundie *et al.* 2007). The LCA method is more accurate as it can appraise a fuller magnitude of the 'indirect' environmental impacts associated with the supply chain and capital goods and infrastructure of tourism products.

Another advantage of LCA is its ability to appraise the environmental effects from a broad range of impact categories, such as climate change, resource depletion, human toxicity, ozone layer depletion, eutrophication, acidification, aquatic eco-toxicity, ionizing radiation and photochemical smog formation (Frischknecht *et al.* 2007), thus covering the diversity of tourism-related environmental impacts. Furthermore, LCA enables a comparative analysis of environmental effects by normalizing them to a certain reference value with further weighting of their relative importance. It establishes the key damaging impacts that can further be targeted by mitigation measures.

Importantly, the international standards for environmental appraisal recognize the value of LCA analysis. The greenhouse gas conversion factors for corporate reporting developed by the UK's Department for Environment, Food and Rural Affairs (Defra) integrate the 'indirect' carbon impacts from the capital goods and infrastructure into its inventory (Defra 2013). The Greenhouse Gas Protocol, an international accounting tool for corporate carbon footprint, highlights the importance of life cycle considerations and emphasizes the necessity to appraise the 'indirect' carbon footprint embodied in the supply-side industries (GHG Protocol 2011).

The methodological framework for LCA assessment

The LCA methodology has been internationally appraised and reflected in the ISO 14040 series of standards (ISO 2006). LCA consists of four distinctive stages (see Figure 16.2):

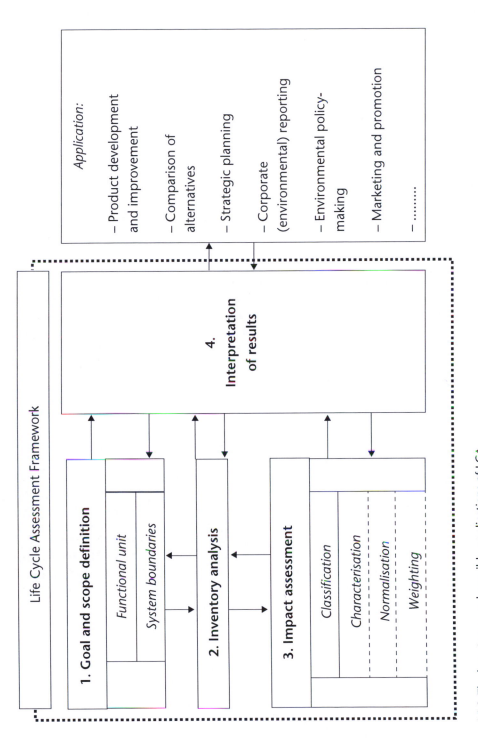

Figure 16.2 The key stages and possible applications of LCA.
Source: adapted from ISO 14040 (2006)

1   *Goal and scope definition* (explains the study purpose, defines a functional unit for analysis and sets up system boundaries);
2   *Life cycle inventory* (collects and systemizes data);
3   *Impact assessment* (evaluates the magnitude of environmental impacts);
4   *Interpretation* of results (draws conclusions and provides recommendations for environmental improvements).

All data in LCA are related to a basis for comparison, the functional unit which is defined as the quantified performance of a product or service. In terms of tourist accommodation, for example, '1 guest night stay in a hotel' with associated environmental impacts can represent a suitable functional unit for analysis. For leisure transport, '1 km driven by a passenger car' can be used as a functional unit.

Precise definition of system boundaries (i.e. processes included and excluded from appraisal) is a distinctive feature of the LCA method which enables subsequent scenario analysis. For instance, for holiday packages, a system boundary can be drawn upon the 'door-to-door' concept that suggests that LCA will appraise all environmental impacts generated in the result of a tourist's absence from home. Although the setup of system boundaries for LCA may involve a subjective element, this issue is typical for all environmental assessment techniques.

The general framework of impact assessment employed by LCA (stage 3 in Figure 16.2) consists of classification, characterization, normalization and weighting. The ISO 14040 series of standards prescribe that the classification and characterization steps that convert the impact assessment outcome into an easy-to-understand quantitative indicator for specific impact categories (e.g. kg of CO_2 produced) are mandatory elements of assessment, while normalization and weighting lead to a unique indicator across all impact categories, showing the relative significance of each specific impact is discretionary.

Types of LCA

Two major categories of LCA can be distinguished: process-based LCA and input–output LCA (Lenzen 2000). The input–output LCA represents a derivative of the large-scale economic input–output assessment generally applied at 'macro' levels, such as national industries and economic sectors. The process-based LCA is a conventional form of environmental life cycle analysis carried out on a 'micro' level of specific products and services.

There is no agreement in the literature about which category of LCA is more accurate. There is evidence that the input–output LCA generates higher estimates of environmental impacts (Junnila 2006). The lower estimates of environmental footprints made by the process-based LCA may be due to the so-called truncation errors (Lenzen 2000). The process-based LCA fails to account for *all* environmental contributions on the higher (i.e. above the 3rd layer of suppliers) orders of a product system as these can be of infinite order. Hence, there will be a bias as there are always additional or yet unknown processes that will be overlooked. The omission of some upstream processes is the primary reason for truncation errors; hence, their occurrence is inevitable when the process-based LCA method is applied (Berners-Lee *et al.* 2011). Nonetheless, the input–output LCA is also limited as it fails to account for the environmental impacts associated with the use phase of a product life cycle. To address the shortcomings of the two methodologies, a 'merged' LCA (i.e. a combination of the process-based LCA and the economic input–output LCA) has been proposed and is currently under development.

Simplified LCA

The primary goal of LCA is to evaluate the *overall* impact of a product under review. The assessment is truly holistic since it handles a range of different environmental impact categories. Such complex assessments are not always necessary as they often result in laborious data collection. The simplified LCA methods can be employed when, for instance, a single environmental impact, such as climate change, needs to be appraised. These simplified LCA tools have been developed with the aim to provide quick, but cost–effective analysis (Menzies *et al.* 2007). The simplified LCA methods represent a feasible solution when, for example, the available resources and quality of the obtained data are insufficient for a rigorous LCA.

The simplified LCA methods are based on the 'screening' and 'streamlining' approach, using a reduced inventory of the system under review and identifying only the most critical processes or 'hot spots'. These are subject to further and fuller analysis and some processes with minor contributions are eliminated or estimated. This method allows a researcher to draw reliable conclusions, with acceptable uncertainties, but concurrently results in significant savings of research budgets and time (Menzies *et al.* 2007).

Life cycle energy analysis (LCEA) represents an example of a simplified LCA method (Filimonau *et al.* 2011b). LCEA is based on the original four-step LCA methodology but it focuses on energy and consequent carbon footprint as the only measure of environmental impact. Similar to the traditional LCA, LCEA makes the life cycle inventory where energy flows within the system under review are identified and appraised. The impact of these energy flows is assessed by converting the energy use data into a carbon footprint. LCEA does not replace conventional LCA; instead, it has been designed to present a more detailed analysis of energy for those products and services whose primary environmental impacts are known to relate to energy consumption (Menzies *et al.* 2007).

LCA in tourism

There is limited evidence of the application of LCA in tourism. Furthermore, the focus of existing LCA studies on national tourism industries and specific tourist accommodation establishments (see Table 16.1) is limited as it does not address the totality of holiday travel, accounting for a whole range of tourism products, such as transport, accommodation and activities. More research on LCA in tourism has been conducted in Italy (De Camillis *et al.* 2010), but its outcome is not in the public domain. Some research has emphasized the need to apply the life cycle perspective in tourism but did not directly use the LCA method (see, for example, World Wide Fund for Nature – UK 2002). The limited number of studies on the LCA utility in tourism underlines the necessity for more in-depth research into this area.

Limitations of LCA

There are a few possible explanations to the limited application of LCA in tourism. Poorly understood evaluation potential and limited knowledge on the advantages of the LCA method for comprehensive impact appraisal among tourism policy makers, managers and academics is deemed to be the key reason. Data intensity of analysis and costs of impact inventory databases may provide another partial explanation.

The tourism industry is complex as it operates a number of products and services, often with extensive supply-side industries. Supply chains of hotels can, for example, be of infinite order and some suppliers can even be difficult to identify. This suggests that the data required for

Table 16.1 LCA application in tourism

Study	Object of LCA analysis	Geographical scope
Process-based LCA		
Castellani & Sala (2012)	1-week holiday travel and hotel stay	Italy
El Hanandeh (2013)	Religious travel	Saudi Arabia
Filimonau *et al.* (2011a)	Budget hotels	UK
Kuo *et al.* (2005)	Meal boxes in tourism catering	Taiwan
König *et al.* (2007)	Holiday resort	Portugal
Rosselló-Batle *et al.* (2010)	Budget hotels	Spain
Sára *et al.* (2004)	Budget hotels	Italy
De Camillis *et al.* (2008)		
Input-output LCA		
Berners-Lee *et al.* (2011)	Large tourism business	UK
Patterson & McDonald (2004)	National tourism industry	New Zealand
Rosenblum *et al.* (2000)	Hotel industry	USA

LCA of some tourism products can be laborious to collect. The situation is further complicated if the supply chain industries are based overseas, particularly in developing countries, as the life cycle inventories of environmental impacts employed by LCA have developed states as their primary focus. Despite ongoing research to develop life cycle databases for developing markets, LCA of tourism products originating from outside Europe and North America may have restricted accuracy.

The cost of LCA databases and software packages may serve as another limitation. Due to the significant time and effort invested in collecting and systemizing the life cycle data on environmental impacts, prices range from €1,800 to €21,000, depending on the type and duration of the user licence and software functionality. While large companies can potentially afford the costs, small and medium-sized enterprises may struggle to pay such high subscription fees.

Some categories of life cycle data inventories, such as carbon impacts from short-haul air travel in Europe, lack precision due to the inconsistencies attributed to the definition of flying distances in Europe and North America. Most accurate estimates can, therefore, be obtained only when the LCA figures are combined with the numbers extracted from the Europe-focused environmental impact inventories, such as Defra.

Lastly, the LCA method is best applied for the assessment of environmental impact. The potential of LCA to holistically appraise the socio-economic effects is less well established (Schianetz *et al.* 2007). While research is being conducted to rectify this gap, this may represent a significant shortcoming given the large number of adverse non-environmental effects attributed to tourism.

Case Study

LCA of the Accor Hotel Group

In 2011 the Accor Hotel Group commissioned PwC to holistically analyze the Group's environmental footprints using the LCA method. To this end, PwC combined data on resource consumption from Accor hotels operating in 90 countries. The impacts were assessed in the five impact categories (energy use, climate change, water consumption, water eutrophication and waste generation) as arisen from the chosen 11 functional areas (Accor Sustainable Development Department 2011).

Table 16.2 indicates the results of the LCA analysis for the 'climate change' impact category. The life cycle of an average Accor hotel building is assumed to equate to 100 years and the carbon footprint is estimated in 'tonnes of CO_2-equivalents'. The analysis includes the 'direct' or operational carbon impacts generated as a result of on-site energy consumption and a range of the 'indirect' carbon effects. These are attributed to the life cycle of hotel buildings (i.e. the carbon footprint embodied in the building's construction, regular refurbishments and disposal) as well as to the contributions made by supply-side operations, such as hotel room furniture and office equipment procurement, food and beverages purchases, outsourced laundry services and employee transportation.

Table 16.2 LCA of the Accor Hotel Group operations, 'climate change' impact category

Item	'000 Tonnes of CO_2 equivalent	%
Energy consumption on-site	2 420	66.1%
Hotel air-conditioning	73.9	2.0%
Waste management	75.8	2.1%
Outsourced laundries	48.0	1.3%
Food and beverage services	495.0	13.5%
Construction and renovation	165.0	4.5%
Room furniture	75.1	2.1%
Housekeeping products	0.7	0.0%
Office equipment and supplies	11.9	0.3%
Employee travel	303.0	8.3%
Total	3 660.0	100%

Source: Derived from Accor Sustainable Development Department (2011)

The study demonstrates that the 'direct' or operational carbon impacts from the Accor Hotel Group account for 70 per cent of its total contribution to the global carbon footprint. The share of the 'indirect' carbon impacts is also significant. Importantly, these would have been excluded had the analysis been conducted using conventional methods for carbon footprint appraisal in tourism.

Procurement of food and beverages and employee travel make the largest contribution to 'indirect' carbon impacts from the Accor Hotel Group's operations with shares of 13.5 per cent and 8.3 per cent, respectively. The carbon footprint embodied in the hotel buildings and room/office equipment is smaller, yet is still significant (circa 7 per cent) (Accor Sustainable Development

Department 2011). The outcome of this study demonstrates the value of LCA as a more holistic method of environmental appraisal of tourism products and services. It suggests that environmental footprint reduction strategies should focus not only on hotel operations, but also on hotel suppliers. The study also shows that 'indirect', non-operational carbon impacts can be particularly high for tourism products and services with shorter life cycles, such as transport, catering and activities.

Conclusions

Despite the ongoing financial recession, tourist demand is growing and this is reflected in the accelerated impact of tourism on the environment. While the importance of reducing the environmental footprints from tourism is broadly recognized, the implementation of effective mitigation measures has been hampered. This is partly because accurate estimates of the magnitude of environmental impacts from tourism products are difficult to produce as the current environmental appraisal techniques are limited in number and quality of analysis. The diversity and complexity of tourism impacts impose the key challenge. Existing methods need to be refined, or new tools need to be developed, to ensure they comply with the requirements of holistic tourism environmental assessment. The new, improved technique(s) should be capable of making comprehensive appraisals of tourism environmental impacts, accounting for their diversity (i.e. range of impacts) and full magnitude (i.e. 'direct' and 'indirect' effects).

LCA is an established method of environmental assessment which has been broadly applied in a number of domains but has only recently been introduced to tourism. It offers a number of new insights into the appraisal of tourism impacts due to its proven capability to holistically account for a broad range of environmental effects, most notably those arising from the non-use phases of a tourism product life cycle related to capital goods and infrastructure and supply-side industries. The evidence of LCA application in tourism to date has been limited; this notwithstanding, a small number of available studies have indicated that existing figures on the environmental footprint from tourism products may have been underestimated. They exclude contributions made by the non-operational stages of a product life cycle and supply chain industries. The LCA method has the potential to enhance the quality of environmental appraisals in tourism by making them more accurate and rigorous. It also highlights the new areas for environmental impact mitigation (e.g. hotel suppliers, vehicle manufacturing processes) that would have remained undisclosed should conventional appraisal techniques have been applied to the environmental analysis of tourism products.

While there is a clear need for a broader use of LCA in tourism environmental assessment, there are a number of challenges which may hamper its adoption. Given the high cost of LCA databases and software packages, small and medium-sized tourism enterprises, which constitute the majority of the tourism business market, may struggle to allocate resources to LCA-based environmental appraisals. The issue with data access and quality of available data may represent another barrier. To address these challenges, it is recommended that academics take the lead and produce a number of representative LCA case studies targeting the key tourism products in the primary tourist markets. It is argued that this could: (1) improve our understanding of the complexity and magnitude of tourism impacts; (2) demonstrate the value and further test the applicability of the LCA method in the tourism domain; (3) contribute to the generalization of the LCA results; and (4) enable comparative analysis of LCA with traditional methods for environmental assessment in tourism. This enhanced knowledge could influence managerial decisions, provide scientific underpinning to policy measures and raise consumer awareness of the environmental impact of tourism.

Key Reading

Filimonau, V., Dickinson, J., Robbins, D. and Huijbregts, M.A.J. (2011) 'Reviewing the carbon footprint analysis of hotels: Life cycle energy analysis (LCEA) as a holistic method for carbon impact appraisal of tourist accommodation', *Journal of Cleaner Production*, 19: 1917–30.

Filimonau, V., Dickinson, J. E., Robbins, D. and Reddy, M.V. (2011) 'A critical review of methods for tourism climate change appraisal: Life cycle assessment as a new approach', *Journal of Sustainable Tourism*, 19: 301–24.

Frischknecht, R., Althaus, H.J., Bauer, C., Doka, G., Heck, T., Jungbluth, N., Kellenberger, D. and Nemecek, T. (2007) 'The environmental relevance of capital goods in life cycle assessments of products and services', *International Journal of Life Cycle Assessment*, 12: 7–17.

Patterson, M.G. and McDonald, G. (2004) *How Clean and Green is New Zealand Tourism? Lifecycle and Future Environmental Impacts*, Lincoln, New Zealand: Manaaki Whenua Press.

Schianetz, K., Kavanagh, L. and Lockington, D. (2007) 'Concepts and tools for comprehensive sustainability assessments for tourism destinations: A comparative review', *Journal of Sustainable Tourism*, 15(4): 369–89.

References

Accor Sustainable Development Department (2011) *The Accor Group's Environmental Footprint: First Multi-Criteria Life-Cycle Analysis for an International Hospitality Group*, Accor Sustainable Development Department, December 2011. Available at: www.accor.com/fileadmin/user_upload/Contenus_Accor/Developpement_Durable/img/earth_guest_research/2011_12_08_accor_empreinte_environnementale_dp_bd_en.pdf (accessed 14 June 2014).

Barrett, J. and Scott, A. (2003) 'The application of the ecological footprint: A case of passenger transport in Merseyside', *Local Environment*, 8: 167–83.

Berners-Lee, M., Howard, D.C., Moss, J., Kaivanto, K. and Scott, W.A. (2011) 'Greenhouse gas footprinting for small businesses – the use of input–output data', *Science of the Total Environment*, 409: 883–91.

Caldeira, K. and Wickett, M.E. (2003) 'Anthropogenic carbon and ocean pH', *Nature*, 425: 365.

Castellani, V. and Sala, S. (2012) 'Ecological footprint and life cycle assessment in the sustainability assessment of tourism activities', *Ecological Indicators*, 16: 135–47.

Collins, A., Jones, C. and Munday, M. (2009) 'Assessing the environmental impacts of mega sporting events: Two options?' *Tourism Management*, 30: 828–37.

De Camillis, C., Petti, L. and Raggi, A. (2008) 'LCA: A key-tool for sustainable tourism?' Paper presented at the Eighth International Conference on EcoBalance, Tokyo, Japan, 10–12 December 2008.

De Camillis, C., Raggi, A. and Petti, L. (2010) 'Tourism LCA: State-of-the-art and perspectives', *International Journal of Life Cycle Assessment*, 15: 148–55.

Defra (2013) '*2012 Guidelines to Defra/DECC's GHG Conversion Factors For Company Reporting*, Defra. Available at: www.defra.gov.uk/publications/files/pb13773-ghg-conversion-factors-2012.pdf (accessed 2 April 2013).

El Hanandeh, A. (2013) 'Quantifying the carbon footprint of religious tourism: The case of Hajj', *Journal of Cleaner Production*, 52: 53–60.

Filimonau, V., Dickinson, J., Robbins, D. and Huijbregts, M.A.J. (2011) 'Reviewing the carbon footprint analysis of hotels: Life cycle energy analysis (LCEA) as a holistic method for carbon impact appraisal of tourist accommodation', *Journal of Cleaner Production*, 19: 1917–30.

Filimonau, V., Dickinson, J.E., Robbins, D. and Reddy, M.V. (2011) 'A critical review of methods for tourism climate change appraisal: Life cycle assessment as a new approach', *Journal of Sustainable Tourism*, 19: 301–24.

Frischknecht, R. and Rebitzer, G. (2005) 'The Ecoinvent database system: A comprehensive web-based LCA database', *Journal of Cleaner Production*, 13: 1337–43.

Frischknecht, R., Althaus, H.J., Bauer, C., Doka, G., Heck, T., Jungbluth, N., Kellenberger, D. and Nemecek, T. (2007) 'The environmental relevance of capital goods in life cycle assessments of products and services', *International Journal of Life Cycle Assessment*, 12: 7–17.

Gössling, S. (1999) 'Ecotourism: A means to safeguard biodiversity and ecosystem functions?' *Ecological Economics*, 29: 303–20.

—— (2002) 'Human-environmental relations with tourism', *Annals of Tourism Research*, 29: 539–56.

Gössling, S., Peeters, P., Ceron, J.P., Dubois, G., Patterson, T. and Richardson, R.B. (2005) 'The eco-efficiency of tourism', *Ecological Economics*, 54: 417–34.

Gössling, S., Peeters, P., Hall, C.M., Ceron, J.P., Dubois G., Lehmann, L.V. and Scott, D. (2012) 'Tourism and water use: Supply, demand, and security. An international review', *Tourism Management*, 33: 1–15.

GHG Protocol (2011) *The Greenhouse Gas Protocol Initiative. The Foundation for Sound and Sustainable Climate Strategies*, The Greenhouse Gas Protocol. Available at: www.ghgprotocol.org/ (accessed 2 April 2013).

ISO (2006) *ISO 14040:2006, Environmental Management – Life Cycle Assessment – Principles and Framework*, ISO, Geneva, Switzerland, 2006.

Junnila, S. (2004) 'The environmental significance of facilities in service sector companies', *Facilities*, 22: 190–98.

—— (2006) 'Empirical comparison of process and economic input-output life cycle assessment in service industries', *Environmental Science & Technology*, 40: 7070–76.

König, H., Schmidberger, E. and de Cristofaro, L. (2007) 'Life cycle assessment of a tourism resort with renewable materials and traditional techniques'. Paper presented at the Portugal SB07, Sustainable Construction, Materials and Practice – Challenge of the Industry for the New Millennium Conference, Lisbon, Portugal, 12–14 September.

Koroneos, C., Dompros, A., Roumbas, G. and Moussiopoulos, N. (2005) 'Advantages of the use of hydrogen fuel as compared to kerosene', *Resources Conservation and Recycling*, 44: 99–113.

Kuo, N.W., Hsiao, T.Y. and Lan, C.F. (2005) 'Tourism management and industrial ecology: A case study of food service in Taiwan', *Tourism Management*, 26: 503–8.

Lenzen, M. (2000) 'Errors in conventional and input-output-based life-cycle inventories', *Journal of Industrial Ecology*, 4: 127–48.

Lundie, S., Dwyer, L. and Forsyth, P. (2007) 'Environmental-economic measures of tourism yield', *Journal of Sustainable Tourism*, 15: 503–19.

Menzies, G.F., Turan, S. and Banfill, P.F. (2007) 'Life-cycle assessment and embodied energy: A review', *Proceedings of the Institution of Civil Engineers Construction Materials*, 160: 135–43.

Ortiz, O., Castells, F. and Sonnemann, G. (2009) 'Sustainability in the construction industry: A review of recent developments based on LCA', *Construction and Building Materials*, 23: 28–39.

Patterson, M.G. and McDonald, G. (2004) *'How Clean and Green is New Zealand Tourism? Lifecycle and Future Environmental Impacts'*, Lincoln, New Zealand: Manaaki Whenua Press.

Rosenblum, J., Horvath, A. and Hendrickson, C. (2000) 'Environmental implications of service industries', *Environmental Science & Technology*, 34: 4669–76.

Rosselló-Batle, B., Moiá, A., Cladera, A. and Martínez, V. (2010) 'Energy use, CO_2 emissions and waste throughout the life cycle of a sample of hotels in the Balearic Islands', *Energy and Buildings*, 42: 547–58.

Sára, B., Raggi, A., Petti, L. and Scimìa, E. (2004) 'Implementation of LCA to services: Case studies in the hospitality industry'. Paper presented at the Sixth International Conference on EcoBalance, Tsukuba, Japan, 25–27 October.

Schianetz, K., Kavanagh, L. and Lockington, D. (2007) 'Concepts and tools for comprehensive sustainability assessments for tourism destinations: A comparative review', *Journal of Sustainable Tourism*, 15: 369–89.

World Wide Fund for Nature – UK (2002) *Holiday Footprinting: A Practical Tool for Responsible Tourism*, Godalming: WWF-UK.

17

Carbon management

Stefan Gössling

Carbon accounting The *measurement and reporting* of emissions of CO_2 and other greenhouse gases, including direct/indirect emissions. Depending on system boundaries, this can also include the supply chain.

Carbon audit The *measurement* of emissions of CO_2 and other greenhouse gases in a business or destination. This can include direct and indirect emissions from the core business, as well as those included in the supply chain.

Carbon footprint The amount of carbon dioxide and other greenhouse gases emitted as a result of a given activity. Can include a tourist trip, a business, destination, or country.

CO_2-equivalent Comparison of various greenhouse gases in terms of their contribution to global warming. Includes long-lived greenhouse gases such as methane (CH_4), nitrous oxides (NOx), hydrofluorocarbons (HFCs), perfluorocarbons (PFCs) and sulphur hexafluoride (SF_6), all of which are comparable on the basis of their Global Warming Potential, which is expressed as CO_2-equivalent.

Mitigation An intervention to lower greenhouse gas concentrations in the atmosphere, either through reducing sources or enhancing sinks.

introduction

Tourism is dependent on movement and, for most tourist trips, energy-intense transport modes are used, specifically aircraft and cars, which together account for 75 per cent of all energy use in tourism (UNWTO-UNEP-WMO 2008). Tourists also stay in hotels or other accommodation; they may participate in various activities, or eat in restaurants. All of these aspects of a holiday or business trip require energy, and as most of this energy is fossil fuel-based, the sector contributes to considerable emissions of greenhouse gases (GHGs). On a global scale, some 5 per cent of all CO_2 emissions are a result of tourism activities (UNWTO-UNEP-WMO 2008) and the sector's overall contribution to global warming is even greater because of short-lived, non-CO_2 emissions released by aircraft at flight altitude in the upper troposphere and lower stratosphere. Taking these effects into consideration, tourism may be responsible for 5.2–12.5 per cent of global warming in 2005 (the range attributed to uncertainties; Scott *et al.* 2010).

Stefan Gössling

The development of global tourism is likely to lead to considerably higher emissions in the future. The United Nations World Tourism Organization (UNWTO 2012; UNWTO UNEP 2011) anticipates that the number of international tourist arrivals will increase by 3.3 per cent per year on average between 2010 and 2030 (i.e. an average increase of 43 million arrivals per year) reaching an estimated 1.8 billion arrivals by 2030. Similar figures have been presented by aircraft manufacturers Boeing (2012) and Airbus (2012), which expect passenger growth rates in the order of 4.9 per cent per year over the next 20 years. Such growth in international tourist arrivals, in all likelihood matched by growth in domestic travel volumes, will represent a major increase in energy use. Compounding this, average distances travelled appear to increase, as do per tourist trip numbers, and the use of more energy-intense transport (Gössling 2010; Scott et al. 2012). The conflict arising out of these developments is shown in Table 17.1, which outlines emission estimates and business-as-usual projections (UNWTO-UNEP-WMO 2008; WEF 2009) in comparison to mitigation targets as postulated by World Tourism and Travel Council (WTTC 2009) and as calculated on the basis of IPCC estimates (2007).

Table 17.1 shows that tourism's contribution to emissions is considerable, and will continue to grow. In a business-as-usual scenario to 2035, which considers changes in travel frequency, length of stay, travel distance and technological efficiency gains, UNWTO-UNEP-WMO (2008) projects that CO_2 emissions from tourism will grow by 135 per cent by 2035 compared to 2005 (totalling 3.059 Gt CO_2). A similar estimate has been presented by the World Economic Forum (2009), with tourism emissions growing to 3.164 Gt CO_2 by 2035. Notably, most of this growth will be associated with air travel. In comparison, sustainable 'aspirational' targets to 2035 as formulated by the World Tourism and Travel Council (2009) suggest maximum emissions from the sector in the order of 0.652 Gt CO_2 (i.e. about one-fifth of trend scenarios). Likewise, a 5 per cent allocation of emissions from tourism to sustainable emission targets as implied in a 2°C maximum global warming scenario demands an emission reduction to 0.940 Gt CO_2 by 2035. Clearly, none of these mitigation scenarios is realistic, even under optimistic assumptions of technological innovation (cf. Gössling et al. 2013; Scott et al. 2010). Carbon management thus becomes increasingly important (i.e. an effort that strategically introduces technical, managerial, marketing, policy and behavioural changes to reduce emission in tourism).

Table 17.1 Tourism sector emissions and mitigation targets

| Year | Emission estimates and BAU projections (CO_2) | | Mitigation targets | |
	UNWTO-UNEP-WMO (2008)	WEF (2009)	WTTC (2009) *	5% allocation of overall GHG emissions to tourism **
2005	1.304 Gt	1.476 Gt	-	
2020	2.181 Gt	2.319 Gt	0.978 Gt	1.254 Gt
2035	3.059 Gt	3.164 Gt	0.652 Gt	0.940 Gt

*** Pathway that limits global average temperature increase to below 2°C; assuming CO_2 continues to representing approximately 57% of the median estimate of 44 Gt CO_2-e total GHG emissions in 2020 and 2035 and the tourism sector continues to represent approximately 5% of global CO_2 emissions over the same time frame.

Source: Gössling et al. 2013

Strategy

Carbon management seeks to implement strategic actions to reduce emissions of CO_2 and other greenhouse gases. Carbon management is relevant for all stakeholders in tourism, including airlines, railways, cruises, buses, car rental and other transport providers, accommodation and activity providers, destination marketing organizations, as well as (online) travel agents and tour operators. From a strategic point of view, carbon management seeks to reduce emissions by considering where changes are significant, and where these can be implemented without disrupting economic structures or entailing financial losses.

To identify options to reduce emissions, it is important to consider the most relevant sub-sectors, holiday types and travellers. As outlined, transport is particularly relevant for mitigation, and specifically aviation (40%) and car travel (32%) make the most significant contributions to climate change. From a 'per trip' perspective, in particular the number of long haul flights and cruise trips needs to be reduced, as these holiday forms are the most energy intense. For instance, a single return trip Europe–Australia at emissions in the order of 4.5 t CO_2 is equivalent to global average per capita emissions per year (for further information see Chapter 39, Low-carbon and post carbon travel). Finally, from a 'per capita' contribution viewpoint, focus would have to be on frequent long-haul travellers (i.e. in particular, business travellers participating in regular intercontinental first class flights (see Table 17.2). There is overlap between these categories of travellers/trips.

Furthermore, it is important to consider a number of important ratios: aviation accounts for only 17 per cent of all tourist trips (domestic and international), but 40 per cent of emissions, while the car accounts for 49 per cent of tourist trips (domestic and international), and 32 per cent of emissions (UNWTO-UNEP-WMO 2008). A calculation for the EU shows, for instance, that the 6 per cent of the most energy intense tourist trips cause 47 per cent of CO_2-equivalent emissions (Peeters *et al.* 2004). To replace an average flight by an average car trip would consequently reduce emissions of CO_2 by 78 per cent, and replacing a long haul flight (10,000 km) by a long drive (1,000 km) reduces emissions by more than 90 per cent (UNWTO-UNEP-WMO 2008). Out of these observations, a number of general rules for carbon management can be derived. To reduce emissions in a significant way, it is necessary to:

- Reduce long-distance travel, and to increase the share of tourism focusing on closer destinations;
- To increase length-of-stay in order to counter the trend of shorter and more frequent trips, essentially with the goal to 'bind vacation days', and hence to reduce transport demand;
- To achieve changes in the transport modes used (i.e. to move from the use of aircraft and car to bus and rail where feasible, and to avoid cruises altogether);
- To foster mechanisms that make travellers choose energy efficient transport modes, and avoid those that increase emissions, such as first class flights or private aircraft;
- To encourage low-carbon spending (i.e. the consumption of goods and services that entail low emissions) 'binding income' at low emission cost.

Table 17.2 Energy intensities in tourism

Aviation, cars	Responsible for 72% of CO_2 emissions from tourism
Individual holidays	Long-haul flights
	Cruises (169 kg CO_2 per day on board)
Individual travellers	Business traveller, frequent flyer: > 25 t CO_2 per year

Source: Eijgelaar *et al.* 2010; Gössling 2010; Gössling & Cohen 2014

Furthermore, carbon management seeks to reduce energy use and to increase energy efficiencies, to encourage the use of renewable energy and sustainable biofuels, with a view to the economics involved. For example, there is evidence that accommodation providers can reduce energy use by 10–15 per cent by training their employees as to how these can save energy. To facilitate carbon management, benchmark indicators can be used to facilitate carbon management such as energy use or emissions per tourist or per market, in comparison to revenue or turnover (e.g. the ratio of emissions in kg CO_2 to € turnover). These can be derived from audits or carbon footprint assessments (i.e. by combining emission data with economic data).

Carbon footprint

The concept refers to emissions of carbon dioxide (CO_2) associated with the production or consumption of a good or service, and is sometimes also referred to as a carbon audit, or carbon accounting. The term originates from the concept of ecological footprints developed by Mathias Wackernagel and William Rees (1998), who express environmental consumption as area use to assess and visualize sustainability. Depending on scope, carbon footprints can be assessed for individual services or activities, travellers, trips, tourism businesses, cities, destinations, or countries. Carbon footprints measure the amount of CO_2 involved in the consumption of a given good or service, and usually include other long-lived greenhouse gases such as methane (CH_4), nitrous oxides (NOx), hydrofluorocarbons (HFCs), perfluorocarbons (PFCs) and sulphur hexafluoride (SF_6), all of which are comparable on the basis of Global Warming Potentials, and expressed as CO_2 equivalents. Of importance in the context of tourism is that various short-lived greenhouse gases from aviation make a considerable contribution to global warming, but are difficult to compare to long-lived greenhouse gases, and thus often excluded in carbon audits. While carbon footprints are useful to understand the carbon intensity of consumption, and to compare performances based on benchmarks, difficulties arise out of the choice of system boundaries and the inclusion of direct as well as indirect, short- and long-lived emissions. A focus on CO_2 emissions from transport and accommodation as a simplified approach may often be sufficient to gain insights regarding a tourism system's carbon intensity (Gössling 2013).

Carbon management by sub-sector

The following section considers the role of various stakeholders in reducing emissions, and their specific opportunities to engage in carbon management. Table 17.3 provides an overview. Note that the table is not exhaustive and only provides examples of possible actions.

As outlined in the stakeholder and carbon management matrix, there exist a wide range of options for engaging in carbon management. Examples presented in the table include opportunities for destination marketing organizations to encourage low-carbon travel to the destination (e.g. as promoted by the network Alpine Pearls, (www.alpine-pearls.com)). Policies for online distribution platforms could include the definition of standards for carbon labels, so that offers become comparable in terms of their carbon footprint. Tour operators might switch from offering holidays in fixed packages towards marketing these on a per day basis. In this business model, the first days of a holiday will become disproportionally more expensive, as these involve the expensive transport to/from the destination. Staying longer becomes

Table 17.3 Stakeholder and carbon management dimension matrix

Type of mitigation/ Stakeholder	Technical	Managerial	Marketing	Policy	Behavioural	Research & Development
Destination marketing organizations					Stimulate low-carbon travel to destination	
Internet-based distribution platforms				Define standards for carbon labels		
Tour operators			Market holidays based on 'per day' offers			
Airlines		Cooperate with and become financially engaged with railways				Specific research to support change
Car manufacturers	Focus on e-mobility, small car designs					
Train operators		Purchase 'green' power				
Coach operators			Offer low-carbon travel			
Accommodation providers				Introduce mandatory energy audits and standards		
Activity provider					Encourage low-carbon activity choices	

proportionally cheaper, as each additional day in the destination entails a comparably low extra cost. Airlines are currently competing with railways on distances of up to 1,000 km. If airlines became financially involved in railways, their interest in cooperation would increase, and more flights would be replaced by rail journies. Car manufacturers could focus on the development of e-mobility, and engines adjusted to lower speeds. Train operators could run trains on electricity sourced from renewable energies – notably from newly developed energy sources, to avoid purchasing their share of renewable energy in the existing power mix at a premium, while other customers would receive a higher share of power from coal or nuclear sources. Coach operators might focus on offering low-carbon travel to a younger clientele, to create a lasting interest in this mode of transport. Finally, activity providers could encourage their customers to focus on low-carbon choices. All stakeholders can make use of research and development to support restructuring processes.

Destinations

The following section focuses on destinations. Destinations are key units in climate change mitigation efforts, because they can mobilize and coordinate different stakeholders to strategically engage in carbon management. Measures can range from the restructuring of markets to decisions to become car-free, restrictions on individual motorized transport, focus on organic food use, and negotiations with power suppliers to provide energy from renewable energies. Where stakeholders cooperate to achieve change towards greater sustainability, they have considerable influence on value chains, suppliers and governance (Gössling et al. 2012). Fundamentally new destination branding concepts have also often had the effect of attracting new tourist groups. For instance, the Alpine Pearls destinations with their focus on bicycles, e-mobility and public transport have become attractive for tourists, not least because average speeds decline, and noise and air pollution are reduced (Dickinson & Lumsdon 2010). When cities become attractive for walks and bicycle tours, this can also open up for innovation, including new tourism products such as guided tours by bicycle or inline skates, now offered in many European destinations. Bicycle cities can fundamentally transform urban living, and make cities far more liveable, as exemplified by Copenhagen, the self-declared 'city of cyclists'. While there is a wide range of technical, political, behavioural and research-related opportunities to facilitate change, the focus in this section is on systemic change (i.e. low-carbon destination management).

There are many examples of destinations working proactively with carbon management. These include large ski resorts such as Aspen Snowmass, USA (Gössling 2010); regions such as South West England (Whittlesea & Owen 2012); and networks covering several countries such as the Alpine Pearls (Gössling 2010). For any destination or business, strategic mitigation has to begin with an inventory of energy consumption and associated emissions, followed by an identification of suitable strategies to reduce emissions, and the monitoring of progress towards a specific low-carbon future goal. Greenhouse gas inventories can be simple or more complex (Gössling 2013), and destinations can work on the basis of a range of indicators, such as per tourist emission intensities or eco-efficiencies. 'Per tourist emission intensity' focuses on transport emissions per tourist for different markets (Gössling et al. 2008, 2013; for an alternative approach see Becken's (2008) 'oil indicators'). The second indicator involves the calculation of eco-efficiencies to combine a CO_2 indicator with an economic value, expressed as kg $CO_2/€$ turnover. This indicator allows for more strategic considerations regarding economically feasible options to reduce emissions (Gössling et al. 2005).

Per tourist emissions are easiest calculated on the basis of transport distances, as the journey to/from the destination is likely to account for 60–90 per cent of the overall emissions caused by a vacation. As shown in Table 17.4, emissions can be calculated for the main markets by multiplying average travel distances with the number of arrivals from a given market, thus creating benchmarks for comparison between destinations. Table 17.4 shows, for instance, that Samoa can attract an international tourist at almost one-third of the 'carbon cost' of an arrival in the Seychelles. Further analysis can break up these results by focusing on emissions associated with main markets, which are an indicator of economic dependency. In such an approach, Cuba with a share of 26 per cent of arrivals from Canada is less vulnerable at 556 kg CO_2/tourist than Madagascar, with a 52 per cent share of arrivals from France at almost four times the carbon cost (2.159 kg CO_2/arrival).

To reduce a destination's carbon intensity, arrival to emission ratios can be calculated, based on a comparison of the percentage of arrivals from one market with the emissions caused by this market (see Table 17.5). For instance, tourists from the USA account for 67 per cent of arrivals in Anguilla, but cause only 55 per cent of overall emissions. The resultant ratio is 0.82 (55 divided by 67). The lower the ratio, the better the market for the destination in terms of energy intensities, with ratios < 1 indicating that the market is causing lower emissions per tourist than the average tourist (and vice versa). Arrivals from source markets with a ratio < 1 should thus be increased in comparison with the overall composition of the market in order to decrease emissions, while arrivals from markets with a ratio >1 should decline. In the case of Anguilla, the replacement of a tourist with a ratio of >1 in favour of one tourist from the USA (ratio 0.8) would thus, from a GHG emissions point of view, be beneficial. However, as arrivals from the USA in this case already dominate overall arrivals, it needs to be evaluated whether the destination becomes more vulnerable by increasing its dependence on this market.

Another approach focusing on holiday types was recently presented by de Bruijn et al. (2010) on the basis of 'emissions per day' for the Netherlands, showing that holidays of the Dutch by cycle and train, as well as non-organized holidays, have a relatively small carbon footprint,

Table 17.4 Energy characteristics of tourism in case study islands, 2005

Country	Average weighted emissions per tourist, air travel (return flight; kg CO_2)[1]	Internat. tourist arrivals (2005)	Total emissions, air travel (1000 ton CO_2)	Emissions per tourist, main market (return flight; kg CO_2) Percentage: share of total arrivals[1]
Anguilla	750	62,084	47	672 (USA; 67%)
Bonaire	1,302	62,550	81	803 (USA; 41%)
Comoros	1,734	17,603	31	1,929 (France; 54%)
Cuba	1,344	2,319,334	3,117	556 (Canada; 26%)
Jamaica	635	1,478,663	939	635 (USA: 72%)
Madagascar	1,829	277,422	507	2,159 (France; 52%)
Saint Lucia	1,076	317,939	342	811 (USA; 35%)
Samoa	658	101,807	67	824 (New Zealand; 36%)
Seychelles	1,873	128,654	241	1,935 (France; 21%)
Sri Lanka	1,327	549,309	729	606 (India; 21%)

(1) Calculation of emissions is based on the main national markets only, using a main airport to main airport approach (in the USA: New York; Canada: Toronto; Australia: Brisbane).

Source: Gössling et al. (2008)

Table 17.5 Market structure and emissions ratio*

	Anguilla	Bonaire	Comoros	Cuba	Jamaica	Madagascar	Saint Lucia	Samoa	Seychelles	Sri Lanka
1st market	USA	USA	France	Canada	USA	France	USA	New Z.	France	India
Emissions ratio[1]	0.8	0.5	1.4	0.4	0.8	1.2	0.9	0.7	1.2	0.3
2nd market	UK	Netherl.	Reunion	UK	–	Reunion	UK	A. Samoa	Italy	UK
Emissions ratio[1]	2.5	1.6	0.3	1.8		0.1	2.0	0.1	1.0	1.4
3rd market	–	–	–	Spain	–	Italy	Barbados	Austral.	Germany	Germany
Emissions ratio[1]				1.9		1.0	0.1	1.1	1.2	1.4
4th market	–	–	–	Italy	–	–	Canada	–	UK	USA
Emissions ratio[1]				2.1			1.0		1.2	2.0
5th market	–	–	–	France	–	–	–	–	–	Australia
Emissions ratio[1]				2.0						1.2
6th market	–	–	–	Germany	–	–	–	–	–	France
Emissions ratio[1]				2.6						1.4

*Includes only markets with shares of at least 5% of total tourist arrivals.

(1) The arrivals/emission ratio is a measure of the share of tourists from one market compared to these tourists' share in overall emissions.

Source: Gössling et al. 2008

whereas holidays by plane, those spent in hotels, and organized holidays have a relatively high environmental impact. The average footprint of Dutch holidays is 49 kg CO_2 per day, and allows for a relative comparison of carbon intensity to other holiday types:

- cruises (+265 per cent);
- intercontinental (long-haul) holidays (+200 per cent);
- holidays by airplane (+102 per cent);
- holidays in hotels/motels (+78 per cent);
- organized holidays (+35 per cent);
- outbound holidays (+27 per cent).

Vacation types with low environmental impacts per day are:

- domestic cycling holidays (−76 per cent);
- outbound holidays by train (−55 per cent);
- all camping holidays with a tent (−50 per cent);
- domestic holidays (−47 per cent);
- all non-organized holidays (−39 per cent);
- all nearby outbound holidays, e.g. in Belgium (−31 per cent).

These results provide insights for destinations with regard to the development of low-carbon tourism products, but they do not consider the economic implications of such systemic changes. More comprehensive approaches would thus seek to combine the focus on emissions with economic indicators, such as eco-efficiencies (Gössling *et al.* 2005). On an incoming tourism basis (by nationality), the usefulness of an eco-efficiency approach is illustrated in Figure 17.1 for Amsterdam, where tourist nationalities were found to have substantially varying eco-efficiencies. Results allow identification of the tourist nationality with the highest spending patterns in relation to emissions and, vice versa, high emitters in relation to spending. The eco-efficiency approach can also be applied to various tourist types (e.g. day visitors, nationals, overseas tourists), tourism sub-sectors (hotels, restaurants, retail), on a product value-chain basis (see also Hille *et al.* 2007). It thus opens up new opportunities to work strategically with emission reductions, because energy use is not generally proportional to the profitability of tourism products, opening up opportunities for optimization, including the potential to increase the profitability of the sector (Gössling *et al.* 2005; see also Perch-Nielsen *et al.* 2010).

In the context of systemic change, it should also be mentioned that tourism systems appear seldom optimized with regard to spending and length of stay. In many destinations, there appears to be a number of travellers who have not spent their full holiday budgets, or who may have wished to stay longer. Rather than focusing on mass markets and volume growth, destinations may thus explore options to maximize income from the existing system.

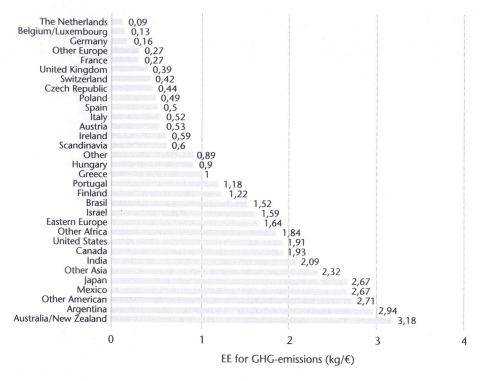

Figure 17.1 Eco-efficiency by source market for Amsterdam 2002

Source: Gössling et al. (2005)

Case Study

Economic policy instruments in France and the UK

In November 2008, the UK Parliament enacted the *Climate Change Act 2008*, which sets a binding target to reduce UK emissions by 80 per cent by 2050, compared with the base year 1990, with an interim target of at least 20 per cent lower CO_2-eq emissions by 2020. The Act focuses on trading schemes for the purpose of limiting GHG emissions or the encouragement of activities that reduce such emissions or remove GHG from the atmosphere. Tourism is not mentioned in the Act, but it is understood that all sectors should be part of emission reductions. As of 1 November 2010, the UK introduced a new air passenger duty (APD) for aviation, which replaced its earlier, two-tiered APD (HMRC 2013). The new APD distinguishes four geographical bands, representing one-way distances from London to the capital city of the destination country/territory, and based on two rates, one for the lowest class, the other for other classes of travel (see Table 17.6). Although no studies exist as yet regarding the impact of the new APD, it can be assumed that low-cost airlines as well as long-haul travel will be affected by cost increases, particularly if these coincide with increasing oil prices. This is because low-cost airlines may no longer be able to sell tickets based on an understanding that such journeys are bargains and entailing virtually no cost (the APD will add €27 to these ticket costs), and long-haul journeys may become too expensive (the APD will add €193 to ticket costs).

Table 17.6 UK air passenger duties

Destination Bands and distance from London (miles)	Reduced rate from: (for travel in the lowest class of travel available of the aircraft)		Standard rate from: (for travel in any other class of travel)		Higher rate from: (for travel in aircraft of 20 tonnes or more equipped to carry fewer than 19 passengers)	
	1 April 2012	1 April 2013	1 April 2012	1 April 2013	1 April 2012	1 April 2013
Band A (0–2,000)	£13	£13	£26	£26	N/A	£52
Band B (2,001–4,000)	£65	£67	£130	£134	N/A	£268
Band C (4,001–6,000)	£81	£83	£162	£166	N/A	£332
Band D (over 6,000)	£92	£94	£184	£188	N/A	£376

However, if a class of travel provides for seating in excess of 1.016 metres (40 inches) then the standard or higher (rather than the reduced) rate of APD applies.

Another example is the bonus–malus system introduced by France in December 2007, which rewards purchases of low-emission cars and punishes purchases of high-emission cars. In 2011, this 'feebate' (fee–rebate) system had four bonus and four malus classes, which, in 2012, were expanded to contain 10 malus and 5 bonus classes (see Table 17.7). Purchases of highly efficient cars are rewarded with up to €7,000, while purchases of cars with emissions above 200 g CO_2 per km are fined €6,000.

Table 17.7 Emission and 'feebate' (fee-rebate) classes in the French bonus-malus system for cars for 2013

Emissions of CO_2 per km (g)	Bonus/malus (€)	Paid by
0–20	7,000	Bonus paid by government
21–50	5,000	
51–60	4,500	
61–90	550	
91–105	200	
136–40	100	Malus paid by car owner
141–45	300	
146–50	400	
151–55	1,000	
156–75	1,500	
176–80	2,000	
181–85	2,600	
186–90	3,000	
191–200	5,000	
> 200 g	6,000	

Source: Government of France (2012)

Conclusion

The chapter has shown that a wide range of carbon management options exist to reduce emissions from tourism, including technological, managerial, marketing, policy and behavioural changes. All of these will have to be utilized to accomplish absolute emission reductions in tourism, as the system is in a rapid expansion process, and mitigation objectives as postulated by various organizations for the sector cannot be achieved without a concerted effort at de-carbonization. Yet, achieving emission reductions does not have to be costly, and can even entail considerable savings, if managed properly. At the same time, a focus on carbon management will help business to prepare for a future in which energy consumption and emissions will be more costly, and where energy-intense operations increase vulnerabilities.

Key Reading

Gössling, S. (2010) *Carbon Management in Tourism: Mitigating the Impacts on Climate Change*, London: Routledge.

Scott, D., Hall, C.M. and Gössling, S. (2012) *Tourism and Climate Change: Impacts, Mitigation and Adaptation*, London: Routledge.

References

Airbus (2012) *Global Market Forecast 2012–2031*. Available at: www.airbus.com/company/market/forecast/ (accessed 23 November 2012).

Becken, S. (2008) 'Developing indicators for managing tourism in the face of peak oil', *Tourism Management*, 29: 695–705.

Boeing (2012) *Current Market Outlook 2012–2031*. Available at: www.boeing.com/commercial/cmo (accessed 23 October 2012).

de Bruijn, K., Dirven, R., Eijgelaar, E. and Peeters, P. (2010) *Travelling Large in 2008: The Carbon Footprint of Dutch Holidaymakers in 2008 and the Development Since 2002,* Breda, the Netherlands: NHTV Breda University of Applied Sciences. NRIT Research and NBTC–NIPO Research.

Dickinson, J. and Lumsdon, L. (2010) *Slow Travel and Tourism*, London: Earthscan.

Eijgelaar, E., Thaper, C. and Peeters, P. (2010) 'Antarctic cruise tourism: The paradoxes of ambassadorship, "last chance tourism" and greenhouse gas emissions', *Journal of Sustainable Tourism*, 18: 337–354.

Gössling, S. (2010) *Carbon Management in Tourism: Mitigating the Impacts on Climate Change,* London: Routledge.

—— (2013) 'National emissions from tourism: An overlooked policy challenge?' *Energy Policy*, 59: 433–42.

Gössling, S. and Cohen, S. (2014) 'Why sustainable transport policies will fail: European Union climate policy in the light of transport taboos', *Journal of Transport Geography*, 39: 197–207.

Gössling, S., Peeters, P.M., Ceron, J.-P., Dubois, G., Patterson, T. and Richardson, R.B. (2005) 'The eco-efficiency of tourism', *Ecological Economics*, 54: 417–34.

Gössling, S., Peeters, P. and Scott, D. (2008) 'Consequences of climate policy for international tourist arrivals in developing countries', *Third World Quarterly*, 29: 873–901.

Gössling, S., Hall, C.M, Ekström, F., Brudvik Engeset, A. and Aall, C. (2012) Transition management: A tool for implementing sustainable tourism scenarios?', *Journal of Sustainable Tourism,* 20: 899–916.

Gössling, S., Scott, D. and Hall, C.M. (2013) 'Challenges of tourism in a low-carbon economy', *Wiley Interdisciplinary Reviews Climate Change*, 4(6): 525–38.

Government of France (2012) *Bonus-Malus*. Paris: Ministère de L'Écologie, du Développement durable, des Transports et du Logement. Available at: www.developpementdurable.gouv.fr/Le-bonus-ecologique-c-est-facile.html (accessed 17 May 2013).

Hille, J., Aall, C. and Grimstad Klepp, I. (2007) *Miljøbelastninger Fra Norsk Fritidsforbruk—En Kartlegging* (Environmental impacts of Norwegian leisure consumption – an overview). Available at: www.vestforsk.no/index.html/rap port/miljobelastninger-fra-norsk-fritidsforbruk-en-kartlegging (accessed 20 September 2012).

HM Revenue and Customs (HMRC) (2013) *Air Passenger Duty – Introduction*. Available at: http://customs.hmrc.gov.uk/channelsPortalWebApp/channelsPortalWebApp.portal?_nfpb=true&_pageLabel=pageExcise_InfoGuides&id=HMCE_CL_001170&propertyType=document (accessed 17 May 2013).

Intergovernmental Panel on Climate Change (IPCC) (2007) *Fourth Assessment Report: Climate Change 2007, WGI. 2007*, Cambridge University Press, Cambridge.

Peeters, P.M., van Egmond, T. and Visser, N. (2004) *European Tourism, Transport and Environment,* Breda, the Netherlands: NHTV Breda University of Applied Sciences, Centre for Sustainable Tourism and Transport.

Perch-Nielsen, S., Sesartic, A. and Stucki, M. (2010) 'The greenhouse gas intensity of the tourism sector: The case of Switzerland', *Environmental Science & Policy*, 13: 131–40.

Scott, D., Peeters, P. and Gössling, S. (2010) 'Can tourism deliver its aspirational greenhouse gas emission reduction targets?' *Journal of Sustainable Tourism*, 18: 393–408.

Scott, D., Hall, C.M. and Gössling, S. (2012) *Tourism and Climate Change: Impacts, Mitigation and Adaptation*, London: Routledge.

United Nations World Tourism Organization (UNWTO) (2012) *UNWTO Tourism Highlights 2012 Edition*, Madrid: UNWTO.

United Nations World Tourism Organization (UNWTO) and United Nations Environment Programme (UNEP) (2011) 'Tourism: Investing in the green economy', in UNEP, *Towards a Green Economy*, Geneva: UNEP.

United Nations World Tourism Organization (UNWTO), United Nations Environment Programme (UNEP) and World Meteorological Organization (WMO) (2008) *Climate Change and Tourism: Responding to Global Challenges*, Madrid: UNWTO.

Wackernagel, M. and Rees, W. (1998) *Our ecological footprint: reducing human impact on the earth*. Gabriola Island: New Society Publishers.

WEF (World Economic Forum) (2009) *Towards a Low Carbon Travel & Tourism Sector*, Davos: World Economic Forum.

Whittlesea, E.R. and Owen, A. (2012) 'Towards a low carbon future—the development and application of REAP Tourism, a destination footprint and scenario tool', *Journal of Sustainable Tourism*, 20: 845–65.

WTTC (World Travel and Tourism Council) (2009) *Leading the Challenge*, London: World Travel and Tourism Council. Available at: www.wttc.org/site_media/uploads/downloads/leading_the_challenge_on_clima.pdf (accessed 17 May 2013).

18

Sustainable tourism legislation and regulation

John M. Jenkins and Mucha Mkono

Legislation is created by a legislature (e.g. a parliament, which has the authority to enact legislation, and which is the arm of government empowered to do so). Legislation is law to which regulations refer or from which regulations arise.

Institutions are an established law, regulative principle, convention, custom, usage, practice, organisation or other element in the political or social life of a society or an organised community.

Complexity systems are inherently complex, have non-linear relationships and display far-from-equilibrium characteristics.

Introduction

This chapter examines research on legislation and regulation with specific reference to sustainable tourism. It is presented in the context of an increasingly globalised socio–political and economic landscape. The terms legislation and regulation are used in their broadest senses. References to these terms range from their application to laws promulgated by governments and international jurisdictions to national public policies to self-regulation, certification and accreditation. The latter are often used by industry groups seeking to promote social and corporate regulation and behavioural change in businesses, tourists and government authorities (Forsyth 1997; Perez–Salom 2000; Levi-Faur & Levi-Faur 2011).

This chapter is structured thematically. It begins by defining legislation and regulation and then briefly analyses legislative instruments and tools. The implications of globalisation for sustainable tourism regulation are discussed, and the significance of global governance institutions to such arrangements is described. This section is followed by a brief reflection on the role of indicators in the regulation and legislation of sustainable tourism. A case study of Barbados provides an empirical scenario seeking to link theory and practice. Finally, citing the complexity of the system, complexity science is briefly discussed as a viable and potentially alternative framework for future research in the field.

Regulatory and legislative tools and instruments

Each nation state has a system of government, and indeed, a broader political system (e.g. see Haywood 2007). Systems of government range widely; for example, from a national (and single) government possessing almost complete territorial jurisdiction, to a federal system characterised by a government empowered by a constitution, with lower-level territorial governments also empowered either by the same constitution or by legislation. Each level of government would usually have constitutionally or otherwise assigned powers so as to not overlap significantly with one another. However, inevitably these powers do overlap and often lead to tensions between governments at different levels and complexity in engagement for citizens, industry, interest groups and other stakeholders (Haywood 2007). Furthermore, in systems such as the Westminster system, a national or state/territorial Parliament will incorporate a separation of powers, such as those in the United Kingdom, the United States and Australia. Each nation has various courts of law and other institutional arrangements which, although unable to create legislation, do interpret and make judgments about legislation and regulations.

Legislation is, therefore, created by a legislature, which has the authority to enact it and which is the arm of government empowered to do so. Legislation is law to which regulations refer or from which regulations arise. Legislation and regulations establish the framework for responsibility and accountability, and for promulgating, monitoring and enforcing rules and laws (Forsyth 1997; Perez-Salom 2000; Mau 2008) within and around what are broadly described as institutional arrangements.

Institutions have been defined as 'an established law, custom, usage, practice, organisation, or other element in the political or social life of a people; a regulative principle or convention subservient to the needs of an organised community or the general needs of civilization' (Scrutton 1982: 225). As Hall and Jenkins (1995: 21) put it:

> We might think of institutions as a set of rules which may be explicit and formalised (e.g. constitutions, statutes and regulations) or implicit and informal (e.g. organisational culture, rules governing personal networks and family relationships). Thus institutions are an entity devised to order interrelationships between individuals or groups of individuals by influencing their behaviour.

The legislation and regulations of nation states and their territories are, therefore, critical elements of the institutional arrangements briefly described above. They provide the broad parameters through which any sustainability and sustainable tourism principles and practices are developed, interpreted, implemented and reviewed. Various legislative and regulatory tools are at the disposal of government and regulatory bodies seeking to achieve sustainability goals. Government regulatory instruments, supported by legislation, can be introduced to prohibit or require certain courses of action on the part of tourists, businesses and other stakeholders. For instance, policies for energy efficiency, reducing greenhouse gas emissions and limiting consumption of natural resources are now widespread in the UK, Europe, North America, Australia and New Zealand.

Various types of regulations limit emissions and the discharge of pollutants by businesses (Bramwell & Alletorp 2001; Becken & Patterson 2006). The forces or tensions in the emergence of policies in these arenas have reflected what Forsyth (1997) noted regarding the debate on regulation; that is, that these debates frequently tend towards finding acceptable middle ground between the extremes of laissez-faire allocation of resources according to market forces, and the drastic command-and-control mechanisms through state legislation. Nevertheless, it has been widely argued that government intervention, through legislation and regulation, is needed to promote behavioural change in travel, tourism and leisure (e.g. Sinclair & Jayawardena 2003; McKercher, Prideaux, Cheung & Law 2010).

Regulatory instruments can be adopted outside government intervention. To show their commitment to sustainable development, tourism companies have increasingly adopted a variety of voluntary initiatives as a form of self-policing or self-regulation (Ayuso 2006, 2007). Environmental auditing as a means of monitoring environmental impacts and performance has been one example that has developed in the resorts and accommodation sectors (Ding & Pigram 1995), though with varying degrees of success.

Bramwell and Alletorp (2001) argue that the response to environmental concerns about tourism has largely relied on individual and corporate responsibility through industry self-regulation. Self-regulating action networks are formed to 'bring solutions to specific issues and problems' (Erkuş-Öztürk & Eraydın 2010: 115). Bramwell and Alletorp (2001) further suggest that self-regulation is a pragmatic choice for business if it is understood that such measures will be of benefit (e.g. by improving its image and increasing short-term profits). The most common self-regulation instruments in the tourism and hospitality industries include codes of conduct, best environmental practices, accreditation, certification, eco-labels, environmental performance indicators, and environmental management systems (Ayuso 2006, 2007). The 1993 International Hotels Environment Initiative, driven through corporate leadership, is a notable example of self-regulation in the hospitality sector, focusing on environmental management and recycling waste (Forsyth 1997; Scanlon 2007).

In recent years, the carbon market is central to the success of sustainable tourism initiatives at an international level, as tourism increasingly depends on air transport, which contributes the largest proportion of the growth of greenhouse gas emissions in the transport industry (Gössling et al. 2007). The carbon market is a composite of regulatory and voluntary mechanisms. The former operated under the Kyoto Protocol, an international agreement which sets binding targets for emission reductions by signatory countries, and which is premised on carbon trading through the Clean Development Mechanism (CDM) and Joint Implementation (JI) schemes (Steffen et al. 1998; Reilly et al. 1999; O'Neill & Oppenheimer 2002; Victor 2004; Santilli et al. 2005; Gössling et al. 2007). Under these regulations, companies which have exceeded their carbon allowances have the option to purchase Certified Emissions Reductions (CERs), or Emission Reduction Units (ERU), from carbon offset suppliers (Gössling et al. 2007). However, the effectiveness of carbon markets as regulatory tools for reducing carbon emissions has been questioned (Gössling et al. 2007). Most recently, Gossling (2013), citing reports from the OECD and UNEP, noted that climate policy with respect to tourism will achieve little if left to global institutions or airlines, and that tourism policies in many countries actually promote long-haul travel, increase emissions and stand in stark contrast to the policy goals countries have signed up to. In December 2012, the Protocol was amended (Doha Amendment to the Kyoto Protocol); a number of countries (e.g. Canada and Russia) are no longer signatories.

Nonetheless, voluntary carbon offsetting schemes have been growing steadily in number and scope, fuelled by various factors, including personal and corporate goals to reduce the impact on the environment, by undertaking environmental management initiatives (Bramwell & Alletorp 2001; Gössling et al. 2007). However, voluntary compensation schemes have been criticised for 'creating and fostering the idea that there are simple solutions to unsustainable lifestyles' (Gössling et al. 2007: 230). In the case of airlines, it has been argued that the schemes could enable them (the airlines) to claim that they are already doing everything they can, a scenario which would not lead to more innovation towards better carbon emission management (Gössling et al. 2007).

Governments and tourism industry operators have been seeking to create circumstances in which market forces, including non-government organisations or industry associations, perform regulatory functions. Accreditation and certification schemes or systems seeking to promote sustainability of natural and cultural resources are popular self-regulatory tools in the tourism industry (Rivera 2002; Font *et al.* 2003). Certification is a voluntary procedure, which purports to assess, monitor and document assurance that a business, product, process, service, or management system meets specific requirements (Honey & Rome 2001; Mycoo 2006). Research on accreditation and certification has grown considerably in the past two decades, in parallel with the growth in market interests (Harris & Jago 2001; Lynes & Dredge 2006).

From a critical perspective, it is legitimate to question the motives of business in adopting environmental management practices, voluntary and otherwise, and Best and Thapa (2013) draw upon many studies to support their concerns with respect to the accommodation sector. However, they highlight barriers and constraints to adoption linked to factors such as location, knowledge, cost of implementation and access to appropriate technologies. Subsequently, they look to not only motives (and facilitators), but also to these barriers and constraints. Whether such practices are adopted because they are good for the environment, or because they serve as a marketing tool in response to market pressures (Forsyth 1997), is only one consideration in a complex interplay of factors affecting decisions. That said, some scholars argue that voluntary instruments for sustainability may only be adopted to pre-empt possible regulation, or to legitimise unsustainable business practices (Baker & Miner 1993; Brophy *et al.* 1995; Forsyth 1997). It is important to state also that legislation and regulatory instruments are themselves subject to various limitations. For example, where legislation sets minimum standards which companies must meet, will businesses have any incentive to exceed those standards? Regulatory approaches, however, typically place responsibility for monitoring sustainability compliance on a government inspectorate which is often poorly resourced for the mandate (Bramwell & Alletorp 2001; Pigram & Jenkins 2006).

Regulation and legislation are part of governance, which encapsulates the broader deployment of power in managing the tourism system (Dinica 2009; Beaumont & Dredge 2010, Bramwell 2011; Zahra 2011). Governance involves all the processes for the regulation and mobilisation of social action, and for producing social order (Bramwell & Lane 2011). Increasingly, governance transcends national boundaries, making 'global governance' a more apt approach for understanding regulatory and legislative processes in the contemporary tourism environment. This paradigmatic transition is reflected in the growing research on the role of international institutions and, in some cases, taking a global perspective on the issue of tourism sustainability (and elements of this broad concept), as opposed to localised case studies (Perez-Salom 2000; Holden 2003; Dinica 2009).

Global governance and sustainable tourism policy

In practice, since the 1980s, the international community has been taking steps to regulate tourism for sustainable outcomes. International institutions such as the World Tourism Organization (now UNWTO) have been very involved in that regard, but with mixed success. The first reference to UNWTO's environmental concerns can be found in the Manila Declaration on World Tourism and the Acapulco Documents addressing the Right to Holidays (both adopted in 1980) (Perez-Salom 2000). The UNWTO's environmental concerns were consolidated by the 1989 World Tourism Conference's Hague Declaration on Tourism (Perez-Salom 2000; Roe & Urquhart 2001), and the Mediterranean Action Plan, established through a transnational collection of experts – referred to as an epistemic community, promoting international pollution controls by influencing governmental learning, objectives and international relations (Haas 1989).

With these in mind, it is evident that individual countries must look beyond domestic policy in designing their sustainable tourism agendas, and incorporate – or at least acknowledge – internationally prescribed/negotiated value systems, even when they advocate divergent points of view. International governance, therefore, possesses persuasive authority over governments, as the latter are aware that nations which do not conform to the spirit of international governance, at the very least, risk being ostracised. Notably, the climate change debate has escalated into mainstream discourse on tourism regulation; the industry's links with pollution, particularly through air travel, has created a vast amount of literature (Belle & Bramwell 2005; Amelung *et al.* 2007; Buzinde *et al.* 2010; Hares *et al.* 2010; Buckley 2011; Cohen *et al.* 2011; Scott 2011; Zeppel & Beaumont 2012). However, policy decisions for climate change and tourism depend on 'value-driven decisions made in the context of uncertainty and complex socioeconomic, cultural, and political relationships' among domestic and international actors (Belle & Bramwell 2005: 32). It is perhaps reasonable to suggest, therefore, that, if governance is complex, global governance is even more so. Table 18.1 shows examples of international institutions that are involved in global governance for sustainable tourism.

While international governance literature focusing on the regulation of impact on the physical environment is abundant (though not always successful and effective), other areas of international concern have somewhat been neglected. Tourism's links with security risks such as terrorism and the spread of infectious diseases, for example, are yet to gain mainstream attention among scholars, although there are a small number of studies (e.g. Sönmez *et al.* 1999; Bhattarai *et al.* 2005; Hall 2011a). One way of explaining this could be to observe that these issues, being politically and religiously charged, might be viewed as 'sensitive' discourse and, as such, become risky terrain for researchers.

Table 18.1 Examples of international institutions in global governance for sustainable tourism

International institution/Instrument	Regulatory roles/contribution
World Tourism Organisation (UNWTO) www2.unwto.org/	International forum for tourism policy and issues. UN agency which promotes sustainable and responsible tourism.
United Nations Environment Programme www.unep.org/	Main areas of focus include voluntary regulatory initiatives, such as environmental codes of conduct; best practice.
Commission on Sustainable Development www.icsu.org/what-we-do/projects-activities/un-csd	Works to ensure transparency and visibility of sustainable development issues within the United Nations.
Global Code of Ethics for Tourism www.unwto.org/ethics/index.php	Reference point for international sustainable tourism. Article 3 of the Code refers specifically to sustainable tourism development. The Code includes a mechanism for enforcement of its provisions.
The Council of Europe http://hub.coe.int/	The Council has adopted several recommendations for regulating sustainable tourism in sensitive areas, including protected areas and coastal areas.

The role of indicators and evaluation

The development and implementation of indicators has become an important element of sustainable tourism regulation and there is no shortage of frameworks or lists of them (e.g. Dymond 1997; Farsari & Prastacos 2001; Miller 2001; Twining-Ward & Butler 2002; Miller & Twining-Ward 2005; White *et al.*, 2006). However, although the application of indicators in outdoor recreation management settings in western countries has a lengthy history spanning at least four decades (Pigram & Jenkins 2006), the development and application of sustainability indicators for tourism is a relatively new area of research in that field (Farsari & Prastacos 2001). Advocacy for their implementation in the tourism industry is growing (Twining-Ward & Butler 2002); in fact some have suggested that without indicators the term 'sustainability' is meaningless (Twining-Ward & Butler 2002).

An indicator is something that helps you to comprehend where you are, which way you are going and how far you are from where you want to be (Miller 2001). Sustainable tourism indicators provide an early warning system that indicates or highlights areas of concern, enabling relevant decision makers to implement necessary policy changes and corrective measures (White *et al.* 2006). The main function of indicators, therefore, is communication of information relating to the issues they address (White *et al.* 2006).

One attempt by an international body to develop indicators of sustainable tourism has been undertaken by the World Tourism Organization via its Environment Task Force (Twining-Ward & Butler 2002). The UNWTO's goal in that undertaking was to produce sustainable tourism indicators that would guide managerial decision making in the tourism industry (Twining-Ward & Butler 2002). Its indicators for sustainable tourism are listed in Table 18.2.

At local, regional, national and international levels there are already a large number of organisations involved in the development of indicators for sustainable development, such as the European Environment Agency (EEA), the United Nations Environment Programme (UNEP), the United Nations Development Programme (UNDP), The World Bank, the World Watch Institute, the International Institute of Sustainable Development (IISD), the New Economics Foundation (NEF), the United Nations Commission for Sustainable Development (UNCSD) and, as already indicated, the World Tourism Organization (UNWTO).

Table 18.2 World Tourism Organization's indicators for sustainable tourism

Indicator	Description example
Site protection	Category of site protection according to International Union for Conservation of Nature (IUCN)
Stress	Tourist numbers visiting a site (per annum/peak month)
Use intensity	Intensity of use in peak periods (persons per hectare)
Social impact	Ratio of tourists to locals (peak period and over time)
Development control	Existence of environmental review procedure or formal site controls
Waste management	Percentage of sewage from site receiving treatment
Planning process	Existence of organised regional plan for tourism
Critical ecosystems	Number of rare/endangered species
Consumer satisfaction	Level of satisfaction by visitors
Local satisfaction	Level of satisfaction by locals
Tourism contribution to local economy	Proportion of total economic activity generated by tourism

Source: adapted from Twining-Ward & Butler (2002)

Indicators perform various functions. They can be used to: evaluate and compare past and current situations to enable assessment of progress towards sustainability; make predictions about what might occur in the future based on an evaluation of the impact of resource use and resource utilisation changes on sustainability; and shape future directions by contributing to the development of policies which encourage progress towards sustainability by altering the behaviour of business, tourists or other groups (White *et al.* 2006). Different types of indicators are relevant for different audiences and stages in sustainability policy cycles (Miller 2001; White *et al.* 2006), so the selection of indicators needs to clearly reflect which facet of sustainability is being measured (Miller 2001; White *et al.* 2006).

Good indicators have been described as possessing characteristics such as relevant, acceptable, collaboratively developed, credible, easy to monitor, robust to manipulation, stable, timely, responsible, understandable, policy relevant, measurable, representative, flexible, proactive, flexible, and suited to suit local needs (Dymond 1997; Farsari and Prastacos 2001; Miller 2001; Miller and Twining-Ward 2005; White *et al.* 2006). Miller (2001) asserts that the principal criterion for selecting good indicators is that they measure the phenomena intended to be measured, although he concedes that some phenomena are inherently difficult to measure. Second in importance, he opines, is that indicators are policy relevant. General public interest and participation is also important for the successful implementation of indicators (Twining-Ward & Butler 2002; White *et al.* 2006). In other words, to be effective, the development and implementation of indicators should be consultative, including the contribution of all relevant stakeholders (White *et al.* 2006), and should reflect the space- and time-specific context of the locality under study (Twining-Ward & Butler 2002).

However 'good' they are, indicators only provide an indication of change and will only ever be partial (White *et al.* 2006). Further, as White *et al.* (2006) point out, indicators themselves require constant review and updating over time, suggesting that implementing indicators is a dynamic process. Many countries are lagging behind in the development and implementation of indicators, and this scenario is reflected in the dearth of well-contextualised case study research. Where indicators are not deployed, the likely result is a haphazard approach to management of a destination or a geographical environment generally, and physical, socio-cultural and economic environments specifically.

Case Study

Sustainable tourism regulation and self-regulation initiatives in Barbados

Tourism accounts for more than 10 per cent of the Gross Domestic Product (GDP) of the island economy of Barbados (Mycoo 2006). After a long history of environmental neglect, the promotion of mass tourism in and around this fragile ecosystem has created a need for strong policy intervention and stricter enforcement of protective legislation (Belle & Bramwell 2005). Mycoo (2006) argues that unregulated interaction of market incentives and the relatively weak mitigating forces of modern island tourism tend, over time, to institutionalise a growth process which is not sustainable in the long term. Such a market-driven ethic, she argues, maximises short-term commercial benefit at the expense of long-term environmental integrity – a legacy which persists in an environment of weak sustainability legislation. As a result, for example, about 30 per cent of the Caribbean's coral reef is now threatened by the discharge of untreated domestic and hotel waste (Mycoo 2006).

Mycoo (2006) identifies two key regulatory initiatives that have been undertaken in recent years to reverse sustainability policy failure in Barbados and, especially, training/capacity building, and green certification. With reference to the former, the Caribbean Environment Programme (www.cep.unep.org/about-us) sponsored by the United Nations Environment Programme (UNEP) has three key sub-programmes:

- Assessment and Management of Environment Pollution (AMEP);
- Specially Protected Areas and Wildlife (SPAW);
- Communication, Education, Training and Awareness (CETA).

The tourism industry in Barbados has also adopted self-regulation initiatives, primarily by seeking Green Globe 21 certification (Mycoo 2006; Charara *et al.* 2011). The certification criteria are based on Agenda 21 and ISO 14001 and cover minimum requirements for waste reduction, reuse and recycling, energy efficiency, conservation and management, an environmentally sensitive purchasing policy, social and cultural development, hazardous waste disposal, company transportation and its impact on the environment, land use planning and management, and environmental/historic site protection (Mycoo 2006). However, as Mycoo (2006) notes, certification is contentious, as it is seen by some as strengthening big business, thus threatening the viability of smaller, locally owned enterprises.

The Physical Development Plan of 1970 and the National Development Plan of 1979 helped to discourage overdevelopment in coastal areas. Additionally, coastal setback distances have been implemented as a regulatory measure, as per the Coastal Zone Management Unit, prescribing the distance to a certain feature within which all or certain types of development are prohibited (Mycoo 2006). Setback distances, therefore, create buffer zones between the ocean and coastal infrastructure, minimising beach erosion and other negative environmental impacts. Table 18.3 lists examples of Barbados's regulatory policies for sustainable tourism development. However, several questions arise from this Barbadian case. For example:

- How does the government measure the effectiveness of its regulatory instruments?
- Whose interests are represented or compromised within legislative and regulatory frameworks?
- How are conflicting views with respect to sustainable tourism regulation managed and/or reconciled?

Table 18.3 Sustainable tourism regulatory measures in Barbados

Sustainable tourism regulatory measures	Details
Coastal setback policy	Town and Country Planning Development Order 1972. Since 2006, a 30-metre setback distance from high tide mark is compulsory for all new coastal development.
Public access policy	Since 1995, all enclosures of beachfront properties need a grant of permission from the Chief Town Planner.
Density and overcrowding policy	Permitted density of 150 beds per 0.5 hectares on the south coast and 110 beds per 0.5 hectares on the west coast.
Building height restriction policy	Since 1999, maximum hotel height is 19 metres.
Water demand management policy	From 1997, the Town and Country Planning Department has required all buildings, other than houses, to instal a rainwater storage tank for secondary usage. Hotels must have on-site water-recycling facilities for golf courses and landscaped areas.
Water pollution mitigation and market incentives	No outfall should be built that causes the discharge of wastewater directly into coastal waters without at least primary level treatment. Other reforms to manage water pollution include the implementation of the Marine Pollution Act (1968) and the formation of an Environmental Standards Review and Assessment Committee (ESRAC). Under the Tourism Development Act 2002, a tax credit of 20% of capital cost of wastewater improvement is allowed.
Energy reduction policy/ market incentives	Fiscal incentives for energy conservation, such as rebates and subsidies on solar heating. Concessions enable manufacturers to import materials duty free, and provide consumers with full or partial tax deductions for the cost of the heaters.

Source: Adapted from Mycoo (2006)

Future directions: complexity science as an alternative lens

In this chapter we briefly discussed selected research on sustainable tourism regulation and legislation. The literature suggests that successful regulation and legislation occurs in an intricate web of relationships among various tourism stakeholders at local, regional, national, international and global levels. Regulatory processes should, therefore, be suited to this complex environment, and indicators of sustainability should take into consideration the web of complex interrelationships and interdependencies of resources and stakeholders in the tourism system (Sirakaya *et al.* 2001).

In tourism, regulation and legislation serve to mitigate environmental, economic, cultural and social impacts by imposing limits on various elements of the system such as prices, the extent and nature of resource utilisation, the nature of employment, growth and development plans, and demand (Forsyth 1997; Perez-Salom 2000; Goodwin & Roe 2001; Wall & Xie 2005; Mycoo 2006). However, regulation and legislation are complicated by various sustainability problem attributes, including the latter's pervasive uncertainty, the interconnectivity of sustainability problems, and the mismatch between government, regulatory space and ecological boundaries (Hall 2011b).

Not surprisingly, the complexity of the tourism system is a recurrent theme in sustainability research. This reality poses the question as to the appropriateness of frameworks and approaches adopted in the existing research. Of course, each approach has its own merits and problems. For instance, case studies, as we have shown in the Barbadian example, produce detailed, context-specific accounts of phenomena, but may not capture external factors which have a bearing on the dynamics of the tourism system. Nor, as our case study questions imply, can the effectiveness of frameworks be readily identified. Here we suggest that an alternative approach, capable of capturing the interconnectedness of various actors in the tourism system is required. Specifically, we recommend future research give consideration to a 'complexity science' approach.

A complexity science worldview posits that systems are inherently complex, have non-linear relationships and display far-from-equilibrium characteristics (McDonald 2009). Complex systems are, by nature, dynamic, unpredictable and continually fluctuating. 'Internal and external influences impact on all components which are hierarchical in nature, consisting of subsystems, and are influenced by underlying behaviours that result in unpredictable outcomes' (McDonald 2009: 456). What this means is that any change to one of the tourism system's components, in scope or force, is likely to impact the rest of the system. As McDonald highlights, it is undesirable that tourism research continues to take a reductionist approach which does not recognise the inherent complexity of the tourism system.

Key Reading

Bramwell, B. and Alletorp, L. (2001) 'Attitudes in the Danish tourism industry to the roles of business and government in sustainable tourism', *International Journal of Tourism Research*, 3: 91–103.

Forsyth, T. (1997) 'Environmental responsibility and business regulation: The case of sustainable tourism', *Geographical Journal*, 163: 270–80.

McDonald, J.R. (2009) 'Complexity science: An alternative world view for understanding sustainable tourism development', *Journal of Sustainable Tourism*, 17: 455–71.

Mycoo, M. (2006) 'Sustainable tourism using regulations, market mechanisms and green certification: A case study of Barbados', *Journal of Sustainable Tourism*, 14: 489–511.

White, V., McCrum, G., Blackstock, K. and Scott, A. (2006) *Indicators and Sustainable Tourism: Literature Review*, Aberdeen: The Macaulay Institute.

References

Amelung, B., Nicholls, S. and Viner, D. (2007) 'Implications of global climate change for tourism flows and seasonality', *Journal of Travel Research*, 45: 285–96.

Ayuso, S. (2006) 'Adoption of voluntary environmental tools for sustainable tourism: Analysing the experience of Spanish hotels', *Corporate Social Responsibility and Environmental Management,* 13: 207–20.

—— (2007) 'Comparing voluntary policy instruments for sustainable tourism: The experience of the Spanish hotel sector', *Journal of Sustainable Tourism*, 15: 144–59.

Baker, J. and Miner, K. 1993. 'Corporate environmentalism: Cooperation or co-optation?', *Journal of Environment and Health*, 56: 25–27.

Beaumont, N. and Dredge, D. (2010) 'Local tourism governance: A comparison of three network approaches', *Journal of Sustainable Tourism*, 18: 7–28.

Becken, S. and Patterson, M. (2006) 'Measuring national carbon dioxide emissions from tourism as a key step towards achieving sustainable tourism', *Journal of Sustainable Tourism*, 14: 323–38.

Belle, N. and Bramwell, B. (2005) 'Climate change and small island tourism: Policy maker and industry perspectives in Barbados', *Journal of Travel Research*, 44: 32–41.

Best, M.N. and Thapa, B. (2013). 'Motives, facilitators and constraints of environmental management in the Caribbean accommodations sector', *Journal of Cleaner Production*, 52: 165–75.

Bhattarai, K., Conway, D. and Shrestha, N. (2005) 'Tourism, terrorism and turmoil in Nepal', *Annals of Tourism Research*, 32: 669–88.

Bramwell, B. (2011) 'Governance, the state and sustainable tourism: A political economy approach', *Journal of Sustainable Tourism*, 19: 459–77.

Bramwell, B. and Alletorp, L. (2001) 'Attitudes in the Danish tourism industry to the roles of business and government in sustainable tourism', *International Journal of Tourism Research*, 3: 91–103.

Bramwell, B. and Lane, B. (2011) 'Critical research on the governance of tourism and sustainability', *Journal of Sustainable Tourism*, 19: 411–21.

Brophy, M., Netherwood, A. and Starkey, R. (1995) 'The voluntary approach: An effective means of achieving sustainable development?', *Eco-Management and Auditing*, 2: 127–32.

Buckley, R. (2011) '20 answers: Reconciling air travel and climate change', *Annals of Tourism Research*, 38: 1178–81.

Buzinde, C.N., Manuel-Navarrete, D., Kerstetter, D. and Redclift, M. (2010) 'Representations and adaptation to climate change', *Annals of Tourism Research*, 37: 581–603.

Charara, N., Cashman, A., Bonnell, R. and Gehr, R. (2011) 'Water use efficiency in the hotel sector of Barbados', *Journal of Sustainable Tourism*, 19: 231–45.

Cohen, S.A., Higham, J.E.S. and Cavaliere, C.T. (2011) 'Binge flying: Behavioural addiction and climate change', *Annals of Tourism Research*, 38: 1070–89.

Ding, P. and Pigram, J.J. (1995) 'Environmental audits: An emerging concept in sustainable tourism development', *Journal of Tourism Studies*, 6: 2–10.

Dinica, V. (2009) 'Governance for sustainable tourism: A comparison of international and Dutch visions', *Journal of Sustainable Tourism*, 17: 583–603.

Dymond, S.J. (1997) 'Indicators of sustainable tourism in New Zealand: A local government perspective', *Journal of Sustainable Tourism*, 5: 279–93.

Erkuş-Öztürk, H. and Eraydın, A. (2010) 'Environmental governance for sustainable tourism development: Collaborative networks and organisation building in the Antalya tourism region', *Tourism Management*, 31: 113–24.

Farsari, Y. and Prastacos, P. (2001) 'Sustainable tourism indicators for Mediterranean established destinations', *Tourism Today*, 1: 103–21.

Font, X., Sanabria, R. and Skinner, E. (2003) 'Sustainable tourism and ecotourism certification: Raising standards and benefits', *Journal of Ecotourism*, 2: 213–18.

Forsyth, T. (1997) 'Environmental responsibility and business regulation: The case of sustainable tourism', *Geographical Journal*, 163: 270–80.

Goodwin, H. and Roe, D. (2001) 'Tourism, livelihoods and protected areas: Opportunities for fair-trade tourism in and around National Parks', *International Journal of Tourism Research*, 3: 377–91.

Gössling, S. (2013) 'National emissions from tourism: An overlooked policy challenge?', *Energy Policy*. DOI: http://dx.doi.org/10.1016/j.enpol.2013.03.058

Gössling, S., Broderick, J., Upham, P., Ceron, J.-P., Dubois, G., Peeters, P. and Strasdas, W. (2007) 'Voluntary carbon offsetting schemes for aviation: Efficiency, credibility and sustainable tourism', *Journal of Sustainable Tourism*, 15: 223–48.

Haas, P.M. (1989) 'Do regimes matter? Epistemic communities and Mediterranean pollution control', *International Organization*, 43: 377–403.

Hall, C.M. (2011a) 'Biosecurity, tourism and mobility: Institutional arrangements for managing biological invasions', *Journal of Policy Research in Tourism, Leisure and Events*, 3(3): 256–80.

—— (2011b) 'Policy learning and policy failure in sustainable tourism governance: From first- and second-order to third-order change?', *Journal of Sustainable Tourism*, 19: 649–71.

Hall, C.M. and Jenkins, J.M. (1995) *Tourism and Public Policy*. London: Routledge.

Hares, A., Dickinson, J. and Wilkes, K. (2010) 'Climate change and the air travel decisions of UK tourists', *Journal of Transport Geography*, 18: 466–73.

Harris, R. and Jago, L. (2001) 'Professional accreditation in the Australian tourism industry: An uncertain future', *Tourism Management*, 22: 383–90.

Haywood, A. (2007) *Politics*, (3rd edition), Palgrave, MacMillan: Basingstoke, England.

Holden, A. (2003) 'In need of new environmental ethics for tourism?', *Annals of Tourism Research*, 30: 94–108.

Honey, M. and Rome, A. (2001). *Protecting paradise: Certification programs for sustainable tourism and ecotourism*, Washington DC: Institute for Policy Studies.

Levi-Faur, D. and Levi-Faur, D. (2011) 'Regulation and regulatory governance', in Levi-Faur, D. and Levi-Faur, D. (eds) *Handbook on the Politics of Regulation*, Cheltenham: Edward Elgar.

Lynes, J.K. and Dredge, D. (2006) 'Going green: Motivations for environmental commitment in the airline industry. A case study of Scandinavian Airlines', *Journal of Sustainable Tourism*, 14: 116–38.

Mau, R. (2008) 'Managing for conservation and recreation: The Ningaloo Whale Shark experience', *Journal of Ecotourism*, 7: 208–20.

McDonald, J.R. (2009) 'Complexity science: An alternative world view for understanding sustainable tourism development', *Journal of Sustainable Tourism*, 17: 455–71.

McKercher, B., Prideaux, B., Cheung, C. and Law, R. (2010) 'Achieving voluntary reductions in the carbon footprint of tourism and climate change', *Journal of Sustainable Tourism*, 18: 297–317.

Miller, G. (2001) 'The development of indicators for sustainable tourism: Results of a Delphi survey of tourism researchers', *Tourism Management*, 22: 351–62.

Miller, G. and Twining-Ward, L. (2005) *Monitoring for a Sustainable Tourism Transition: The Challenge of Developing and Using Indicators*, Cambridge: CABI.

Mycoo, M. (2006) 'Sustainable tourism using regulations, market mechanisms and green certification: A case study of Barbados', *Journal of Sustainable Tourism*, 14: 489–511.

O'Neill, B.C. and Oppenheimer, M. (2002) 'Climate change: Dangerous climate impacts and the Kyoto Protocol', *Science*, 296: 1971–72.

Perez-Salom, J.-R. (2000). 'Sustainable tourism: Emerging global and regional regulation', *Georgia International Environmental Law Review*, 13: 801–36.

Pigram, J.J. and Jenkins, J.M. (2006) *Outdoor Recreation Management*, London: Routledge.

Reilly, J., Prinn, R., Harnisch, J., Fitzmaurice, J., Jacoby, H., Kicklighter, D., Melillo, J., Stone, P., Sokolov, A. and Wang, C. (1999) 'Multi-gas assessment of the Kyoto Protocol', *Nature*, 401: 549–55.

Rivera, J. (2002) 'Assessing a voluntary environmental initiative in the developing world: The Costa Rican Certification for Sustainable Tourism', *Policy Sciences*, 35: 333–60.

Roe, D. and Urquhart, P. 2001. *Pro-poor Tourism: Harnessing the World's Largest Industry for the World's Poor*, IIED: London.

Santilli, M., Moutinho, P., Schwartzman, S., Nepstad, D., Curran, L. and Nobre, C. (2005) 'Tropical deforestation and the Kyoto Protocol', *Climatic Change*, 71: 267–76.

Scanlon, N.L. (2007) 'An analysis and assessment of environmental operating practices in hotel and resort properties', *International Journal of Hospitality Management*, 26: 711–23.

Scott, D. (2011) 'Why sustainable tourism must address climate change', *Journal of Sustainable Tourism*, 19: 17–34.

Scrutton, R. (1982) *A Dictionary of Political Thought*, London: Pan Books.

Sinclair, D. and Jayawardena, C. (2003) 'The development of sustainable tourism in the Guinas', *International Journal of Contemporary Hospitality Management*, 15: 402–7.

Sirakaya, E., Jamal, T. and Choi, H.-S. (2001) 'Developing indicators for destination sustainability', *The Encyclopedia of Ecotourism*, 411–32.

Sönmez, S.F., Apostolopoulos, Y. and Tarlow, P. (1999) 'Tourism in crisis: Managing the effects of terrorism', *Journal of Travel Research*, 38: 13–18.

Steffen, W., Noble, I., Canadell, J., Apps, M., Schulze, E.-D. and Jarvis, P.G. (1998) 'The terrestrial carbon cycle: Implications for the Kyoto Protocol', *Science*, 280: 1393–94.

Twining-Ward, L. and Butler, R. (2002) 'Implementing STD on a small island: Development and use of sustainable tourism development indicators in Samoa', *Journal of Sustainable Tourism*, 10: 363–87.

Victor, D.G. (2004) *The Collapse of the Kyoto Protocol and the Struggle to Slow Global Warming*, Princeton: Princeton University Press.

Wall, G. and Xie, P.F. (2005) 'Authenticating ethnic tourism: Li dancers' perspectives', *Asia Pacific Journal of Tourism Research*, 10: 1–21.

White, V., Mccrum, G., Blackstock, K. and Scott, A. (2006) *Indicators and Sustainable Tourism: Literature Review*, Aberdeen: The Macaulay Institute.

Zahra, A.L. (2011) 'Rethinking regional tourism governance: The principle of subsidiarity', *Journal of Sustainable Tourism*, 19: 535–52.

Zeppel, H. and Beaumont, N. (2012) 'Climate change and tourism futures: Responses by Australian tourism agencies', *Tourism and Hospitality Research*, 12: 73–88.

19

Promoting voluntary behaviour change for sustainable tourism

The potential role of social marketing

Dao Truong and C. Michael Hall

Social marketing is the use of marketing principles and methods to encourage and enable individual and organisational behaviour change for the public good.

Introduction

There is increasingly widespread recognition that most environmental problems are caused by human behaviours and thus can be mitigated by changing such behaviours (Oskamp 2000; Takahashi 2009). Major changes in individual and public behaviours and values are therefore regarded as integral to long-term sustainable tourism (Hall 2013; Higham, Cohen, Peeters & Gössling 2013; Oskamp 2000; Peeters 2013; Takahashi 2009). For example, with respect to tourism and climate change, tourists are the part of the tourism system that by their capacity to change their behaviours rapidly are the most easily adaptable to impacts of climate change (Gössling *et al.* 2012; Scott *et al.* 2012). Therefore, there is increasing research into how to best achieve behaviour change and what variables (e.g. attitudes, beliefs, social contexts) are the most important determinants of such change (McKenzie-Mohr 2000; Oskamp 2000).

However, although attitudes and beliefs can be changed through information, educational, or economic measures, they do not necessarily lead to desirable behaviour change (Hall 2014). This is because individual behaviour choices are not only determined by personal preferences but also by the social-technical contexts, institutions, and environments in which individuals are embedded (Gössling, Hall *et al.* 2009; Hall 2013; Kotler & Lee 2008, 2009). Education does not necessarily provide meaningful incentives in exchange for behaviour change (Kaczynski 2008). As a result, increased attention has thus been given to the marketing field and to social marketing in particular, which is rooted in and utilises the tools of generic marketing to promote voluntary behaviour change, and may have an important role to play in the behavioural change process with respect to tourism and sustainability (Andreasen 2002; Hall 2014; Kotler & Lee 2008; Truong & Hall 2013). Although social marketing has demonstrated its effectiveness in various fields, it has captured surprisingly limited attention from the tourism industry and researchers (Bright 2000; Dinan & Sargeant 2000; Lane 2009; Truong & Hall 2013). Therefore, it is the purpose of this chapter to examine how and to what extent social marketing has been studied in the tourism field. It first briefly chronicles the development of social marketing and discusses its conceptual underpinnings. It then reviews social marketing research in the tourism literature with respect to topics, perspectives, and methods. Finally, limitations to the chapter are discussed and implications for further research indicated.

Social marketing: A brief history

The origin of social marketing is usually traced back to Wiebe (1951) who posed the question *Can brotherhood be sold like soap?* Wiebe (1951) suggested that a social change programme would be more likely to succeed if it were more similar to that of commercial marketing. Social marketing was then not recognised as a formal concept. However, marketing was adopted by international development agencies in an effort to distribute contraceptives (Andreasen 2006) and provide health education in developing countries (MacFadyen *et al.* 1999). The success of these efforts helped broaden the marketing concept to its application to social and environmental concerns (Andreasen 2006).

The 1970s was marked by the formalisation of the term *social marketing* and its early development. Kotler and Zaltman (1971: 5) defined social marketing as "the design, implementation and control of programmes calculated to influence the acceptability of social ideas and involving considerations of product planning, pricing, communication, distribution and marketing research". However, the idea of using marketing to solve social issues was opposed by some scholars. Luck (1974) was concerned that the economic exchange concept would be threatened by an intangible product or value. A person, he argued, receiving a free service was not a customer because s/he exchanged nothing with the service provider. Some feared the power of marketing in disseminating social ideas could have substantial ethical ramifications (MacFadyen *et al.* 1999). Others were even afraid the social marketing concept would threaten the reputation of marketing as it might be used to promote non–mainstream causes, or that the proposed behaviour change might not be in society's interest (Fox & Kotler 1980). Although opposition to social marketing was expressed, its popularity grew nevertheless. The result was that the social marketing concept continued to be applied, particularly in developing countries. It was also redefined to embrace the marketing of ideas (Kotler & Roberto 1989) and a greater consideration of ethical issues (Laczniack, Lusch & Murphy 1979).

By the 1980s, scholars were no longer concerned about the possibility of applying marketing to social issues. Instead, they paid more attention to how it should be applied (MacFadyen *et al.* 1999). Fox and Kotler (1980) depicted the move of social marketing from a social advertising approach to social communications and promotion. While social advertising mainly articulates information to influence attitudes and behaviours, social communications and promotion utilise personal selling and editorial support. Social marketing replaces these approaches by adding at least four elements: marketing research, product development, incentives, and facilitation. Bloom (1980) examined the ways social marketing programmes were evaluated, indicating that poor design and implementation affected many studies, leading to calls for more studies to lay a more rigorous theoretical foundation for the field (Bloom and Novelli 1981).

Research in the 1990s (e.g. Hastings & Haywood 1991) contributed to social marketing's increasing popularity in the field of public health in particular (Ling *et al.* 1992). Andreasen (1994: 110) provided an influential definition of social marketing as "the application of commercial marketing technologies to the analysis, planning, execution and evaluation of programmes designed to influence the voluntary behaviour of target audiences in order to improve their personal welfare and that of society of which they are a part". Although this, in turn, has led to substantial discussion as to the extent to which social marketing should be understood as a field in its own right, which also influences commercial marketing theory and practice (Lefebvre 1996; MacFadyen *et al.* 1999).

Since 2000, social marketing has continued to be applied in various sectors. It is not only seen as an effective way of improving public health, but is also perceived as holding important potential for fostering public safety, family planning, human rights, environmental protection, and community development (Foxall *et al.* 2006; Truong & Hall 2013). The approach has also become extremely significant within neoliberal policy orientations in which individual freedom of choice is given priority over regulatory approaches via the creation of new social norms over time – what is sometimes referred to as "nudging" (Dolan *et al.* 2010; Thaler & Sunstein 2008). Nevertheless, it would certainly be wrong to characterise all social marketing as operating within a neoliberal governance regime (Hall 2014). As discussed below, there is a strong tradition of critical social marketing which recognises the importance of institutional regime change in seeking to encourage more sustainable forms of consumption and production (Farrell & Gordon 2012). The theoretical underpinnings of social marketing are discussed next.

Social marketing: Conceptual underpinnings

The conceptual foundations of social marketing have been a topic of debate since the term was first coined (Dann 2010; Hall 2014). MacFadyen *et al.* (1999) suggested that the social marketing concept consisted of four elements: audience orientation, exchanges, a long-term planning process, and the general public as the target audience. Andreasen (2002) added two more elements, namely voluntary behaviour change and competition, to constitute a set of six elements. These elements are presented below.

Voluntary behaviour change

Social marketing utilises the tools of generic marketing to solve social problems where the final goal is behaviour change (Andreasen 1994; Donovan 2011; Kotler & Lee 2008). It is unique in that it expands from the mainstream marketing domain to solve social causes (Andreasen 2002; Stead, Gordon, Angus & McDermott 2007). However, the behaviour change must be voluntary, rather than compulsory or coercionary (Donovan 2011; Stead *et al.* 2007). Social marketing influences people to accept a target behaviour or stop a harmful behaviour for individual and collective benefits of their own volition. Hence, without the objective or outcome of behaviour change in the target audience, programmes are not considered social marketing (Tabanico & Schultz 2007). The outcome of behaviour change is also used to evaluate the success of social marketing programmes (Andreasen 1994; Tabanico & Schultz 2007). If only a more positive attitude is seen in the target audience after intervention, a social marketing programme is not successful (Redmond & Griffith 2006). That said, voluntary behaviour change is regarded as the "bottom line" of social marketing programmes.

An exchange

Promoting behaviour change requires an exchange between social marketers and the target audience. Exchange is thus the second basic element of social marketing (Peatie & Peatie 2003; Smith 2000). It is defined as a situation where two or more parties interact with one another to gain benefit from something of value (Kotler & Zaltman 1971). Bagozzi (1975) classified exchange into restricted exchange, generalised exchange, and complex exchange. Restricted exchange refers to the relationships between two parties. Generalised exchange involves reciprocal relationships between at least three parties where each party gives to another but receives from someone other than to whom s/he gives. Complex exchange consists of the mutual relationships between three or more parties where each party is directly engaged in at least one relationship. Skidmore (1975) indicated that individuals will engage in an exchange if the resulting awards are valued, if the exchange is likely to produce valued rewards, and if the perceived benefits outweigh the perceived costs. Thus, to encourage voluntary behaviour change, social marketers need to exchange something the target audience are interested in or want (Hastings & Saren 2003). They may even need to attach more value to the proposed behaviour so that it can be maintained by the target audience (Andreasen 2006). To this end, social marketers need to identify both internal and external barriers to the sustainable maintenance of the proposed behaviour (Tabanico & Schultz 2007).

The notion of exchange in social marketing is, however, not without problems. Since the benefits promoted by social marketers are often intangible, unforeseeable, and long-term, it is difficult to convince the target audience (Kotler & Lee 2008, 2009). It may also be difficult for social marketers to communicate the benefits of the proposed behaviour in case the target audience do not have adequate knowledge and skills to provide constructive responses. Thus, in order to promote voluntary exchange, a long-term planning process is required.

Long-term planning process

The development of a social marketing programme is long-term, continual, and consists of a number of steps (Kotler & Lee 2008). The social marketing planning process is carried out in a similar fashion to that of commercial marketing. Although there are slightly different versions of the process (see Hall 2014: 78) it is generally recognised that it starts with the description of the programme background, purpose, and focus. The internal and external environment is then analysed. This results in the segmentation of the target audience, determination of objectives and goals, and identification of competition and barriers. Next, a strategic marketing mix is developed (see Table 19.1) and a monitoring and evaluation plan is outlined. Finally, budgets and funding sources are sought and an implementation plan completed (Kotler & Lee 2008).

However, it is more difficult to conduct social marketing as opposed to commercial marketing because it involves encouraging long-term behavioural change as opposed to product purchase within a more complex and, sometimes, contested environment (Kotler & Zaltman 1971). First, it is more difficult to define behaviour and its benefits. Second, it is harder to generate demands for that behaviour. Third, it is harder to reach the target audience (MacFadyen et al. 1999). Whilst commercial marketing seeks to meet shareholders' objectives, social marketing aims to bring about collective welfare for society overall. This long-term vision is an important advantage of social marketing (Andreasen 1994). Yet, it makes social marketing more challenging because the benefits of the proposed behaviour are not direct and foreseeable in the short term. One way to overcome this difficulty is to conduct effective audience research and segmentation.

Table 19.1 The social marketing mix

Elements	Description
Product	This element refers to the idea, behaviour, or service to be promoted to the target audience (Smith 2000). The social product consists of the core or actual product that is the benefits of behaviour change, and the supplementary product comprising of tangible objects and services to facilitate behaviour change (Kotler & Zaltman 1971; Wood 2008).
Price	The price element represents the barriers that the target audience must overcome to accept and maintain the proposed social product (Kotler & Zaltman 1971; Smith & Strand 2008). It may include the actual time they spend, the effort they make, the physical discomfort they experience, the opportunity cost they incur, and/or the status loss they may suffer.
Place	Refers to where the target audience perform the proposed behaviour (Bloom & Novelli 1981; Kotler & Lee 2008). To encourage this performance, social marketers may make the places closer, more accessible, and more appealing to the target audience (Kotler & Lee 2008).
Promotion	This element refers to the ways the social product is communicated to the target audience. It includes advertising, public relations, audience orientation, education, counselling, community organisation, and interpersonal support (Kotler & Zaltman 1971; Smith 2000). It also includes interactive media and electronic channels (Wood 2008).
Politics/Policy	Apart from the above four main Ps, a social marketing mix may include politics and/or policy, especially when the support of policy-makers, political parties, interest groups, and/or community activists is required to ensure successful behaviour change (Andreasen 2002; Hall 2014; Smith 2000).

Audience research and segmentation

The fourth element of social marketing is audience research and segmentation. This is because social marketing is audience-focused where the target audience are the active participants of the change process (Gordon 2011; Smith 2000). For social marketers, audience research provides insights into the audience's needs, wants, attitudes, perceptions, and behaviours (Donovan & Henley 2010) as well as factors influencing their choices (Griffin 2006). For marketing organisations, it allows them to optimise the resources of their own and their partners (Maibach 2003). Generally, audience research in social marketing requires more in-depth analyses and approaches than commercial marketing because of the complex environments within which it is situated (Donovan & Henley 2010).

After audience research, a process of segmentation is undertaken (Smith & Strand 2008). It is defined as the division of audience into homogeneous segments within which similar strategies are adopted (Kotler & Lee 2009). The number of segments does vary. A social marketing programme may consist of only one or several segments. These segments are common in terms of age, income, geographic locations, needs, wants, motivations, values, or behaviours (Kotler & Lee 2008, 2009). One or more of these variables may be chosen or combined to ensure that people of the same segments have similar behaviours and those of different segments demonstrate different behaviours. The segmentation should also ensure segment sizes are reasonably large so that a marketing mix can be developed effectively.

Not only individuals, but also wider publics

As well as individuals as the target audience (downstream level), social marketing can be adopted to change the behaviour of a wider range of publics. This means to ensure the success of any social marketing programme, the behaviour of other people relevant to the target audience also needs to change (Andreasen 1994; Gordon 2011; Kotler & Lee 2009). These people may include interest groups, the media, stakeholders, organisations, and policy-makers (Donovan & Henley 2010; Gordon 2011). Referred to as the "upstream" level, these people and organisations to some extent control the social and institutional context in which individual behaviour choices are made (Gordon 2011; Kotler & Lee 2008). Targeting the upstream level also helps social marketers avoid being criticised for blaming their own target audience, whose behaviours are not always under their control. It potentially makes downstream efforts less manipulative and overcomes structural barriers to change. That said, social marketing could be more comprehensive by targeting both downstream and upstream levels, a factor that may be especially important in responding to climate change or waste management for example (Hall 2014).

Maibach (2003), in contrast, argues that social marketing is not about influencing law- and policy-makers who enforce regulations to achieve behaviour change. Andreasen (1994), while acknowledging the efficacy of coercion, claims that it is not part of social marketing. However, Donovan (2011: 11) contends that social marketing should include legal and policy strategies because it exists in "a sea of regulations". Laws and policies are part of the working environment for social marketers and are part of the context in which target behaviours are motivated (Donovan 2011). Smith and Strand (2008) even ascribe the failure of social marketing programmes to the exclusion of regulatory measures, implying that policies and regulations should be a component of social marketing. Yet, targeting the "upstream" level often requires in-depth research to inform policies and regulations, where lobbying and media advocacy plays an important role (Gordon 2011), as well as becoming more sensitive to the political implications of social marketing strategies (Hall 2014).

Competition

The sixth element fundamental to social marketing is competition (Smith 2000). Competition always exists because the ultimate goal of social marketing is voluntary behaviour change. It may be an undesirable/less-desirable behaviour that the target audience tend to continue or an alternative to the proposed behaviour (Dann & Dann 2009). At the upstream level, competition may occur between policies proposed by social marketers and other policies with their advocates (Maibach 2003). Andreasen (1994) classified social competition into four levels: desire competition, generic competition, service form competition, and enterprise competition. Despite acknowledging this useful approach, Peatie and Peatie (2003) argued that competition was still examined from a commercial perspective. Expanding on the idea of desire competition, they considered social marketing "a battle of ideas". In this "battle", competitive ideas emerge in four ways: counter-marketing (because social marketers advocate behaviour opposite to commercial marketers), social discouragement (this may consist of social values and peer pressure), apathy (which prevents change or behaviour adoption), and individuals' involuntary disinclination to change their behaviour (Peatie & Peatie 2003). Hence, social marketers need to understand not only the perceived benefits and costs related to the proposed behaviour, but also the perceived benefits and costs related to the competing behaviour (Maibach 2003; Smith & Strand 2008). They also need to move beyond individual audience to influence other relevant stakeholders because competition occurs at both downstream and upstream levels as noted. The next section will proceed to review social marketing research in the tourism literature.

Social marketing research in tourism

Although social marketing has been applied in a number of different areas where behavioural modification and change has been sought, it has received relatively scant research attention in tourism and related literature. However, since 2000 a small but growing number of scholars have sought to explore the potential of social marketing for enhancing societal welfare, including with respect to sustainable tourism development (George & Frey 2010; Shang *et al.* 2010; Truong & Hall 2013). These studies have targeted both individual (e.g. tourists) and organisational change (e.g. tourism businesses). A summary of tourism research on social marketing by topics, perspectives, and methods is given in Table 19.2.

The term *social marketing* was first mentioned in a tourism context by Cowell (1979), although the first substantive examination of the concept was Bright (2000), who argued that the potential to improve the well-being of individuals and society has not been fully embraced by traditional profit-driven marketing. Marketing techniques, which can be used by governmental and non-governmental organisations, may have some potential to enhance social benefits, leading to increased attention to social marketing. Given the multi-faceted benefits of recreation and tourism activities, Bright (2000) argued that the use of social marketing to communicate these to the wider public would help to improve the quality of life for individuals and society. Bright (2000) also stated that social marketing is consistent with the social or public welfare philosophy that drives the work of public recreation professionals, implying that tourism naturally fits in well with the social marketing concept given that it is considered one form of recreation.

Table 19.2 Tourism studies on social marketing by topics, perspectives, and methods

	Description	Examples
Topics	General social marketing discourse	Bright (2000); Kaczynski (2008); Truong & Hall (2013)
	Attract and manage (potential) pro-environmental tourists	Beeton (2001); Beeton & Benfield (2002); Beeton & Pinge (2003); Dinan & Sargeant (2000); Kim et al. (2006); Mair & Laing (2013)
	Gender equity (in tourism advertising)	Chhabra et al. (2011); Sirakaya & Sonmez (2000)
	Sustainable/responsible tourism operation and management	George & Frey (2010); McKenzie-Mohr et al. (2012); Shang et al. (2010)
Perspectives	Downstream (e.g. tourists, tourism businesses and organisations)	Beeton (2001); Beeton & Benfield (2002); Beeton & Pinge (2003); Dinan & Sargeant (2000); Peeters et al. (2009)
	Upstream (e.g. tourism businesses, destination marketing organisations)	Chhabra et al. (2011); George & Frey (2010); Shang et al. (2010); Sirakaya & Sonmez (2000)
Methods	Qualitative	Beeton (2001); Beeton & Benfield (2002); Beeton & Pinge (2003); Bright (2000); Kaczynski (2008); Truong & Hall (2013)
	Quantitative	Chhabra et al. (2011); George & Frey (2010); Kim et al. (2006); Shang et al. (2010)

Social marketing may focus on the identification and attraction of markets that best match the characteristics of a tourism product. Dinan and Sargeant (2000) argued that tourism development might produce severe economic and environmental impacts on local communities if it attracted the "wrong" type of tourist whose demonstrated behaviours were incongruent with local contexts. It was thus crucial that sustainable practices be adopted and the nature of the destination respected. Dinan and Sargeant (2000) proposed two strategies. The first concentrated on the segment of sustainable tourists who were attracted primarily by the natural beauty and historical values of the destinations, while the second focused on the least sustainable tourists where a social marketing mix was used to encourage them to adopt a visitors' code of conduct. Likewise, Peeters et al. (2009) suggest the use of social marketing to influence tourists' behaviour in choosing destinations, travel modes, and consumption patterns, where research and segmentation is conducted to understand tourists' needs, wants, and motivations.

Kotler and Levy (1971: 76) defined demarketing as "that aspect of marketing that deals with discouraging customers in general or a certain class of customers in particular on either a temporary or permanent basis". In tourism Beeton (2001) introduced the concept of demarketing to move Australians away from involvement in gambling and towards spending money on domestic holidays. This process consists of two steps: first, demarketing is adopted to discourage gambling behaviour; second, remarketing is utilised to encourage holiday taking behaviour. This shift may benefit local communities since the gambling expenditure will accrue to local tourism organisations through domestic holidays (Beeton & Pinge 2003). More significantly with respect to environmental dimensions of sustainability Benfield (2001) and Beeton & Benfield (2002) argued that demarketing could also be used as a form of demand control for environmentally sensitive areas. Such an approach was also suggested by Wearing et al. (2007) for developing a greater focus on more targeted audience and ecological messages in national park marketing, which reflected earlier work by Hall and McArthur (1998) with respect to natural and cultural heritage management.

The potential contribution of social marketing to the development of environmentally friendly consumption behaviours is an increasingly significant theme in the tourism literature (Gössling, Hultman et al. 2009; Peeters et al. 2009). Kim et al. (2006) examined the psychological constructs of visitors attending the International Festival of Environmental Film and Video held in Brazil and proposed social marketing as means of improving participants' environmental awareness. They indicated that the highly pro-environmental group of visitors was more likely to attend the festival given its thematic relevance to their existing psychological constructs. Kim et al. (2006) suggested that by adopting social marketing approaches, the balance between the host community's long-term environmental interests, sociocultural constructs, and customers' expectations could be maintained. However, the behavioural impacts of the psychological constructs were not examined. In addition, other factors influencing the target visitors' choice of behaviour (e.g. peer influence) were ignored. Similarly, drawing on the Transtheoretical Model and social marketing to examine the pro-environmental intentions and behaviours of attendees at an Australian event, Mair and Laing (2013) find that the event attracted individuals who were already committed to sustainable behaviour. However, they suggest that events can be an important context for promoting pro-environmental behaviour change. Although such elements of social marketing as behaviour change, exchanges, and upstream targeting were utilised, the competition element was missed (Mair & Laing 2013).

Tourism research on social marketing also targets behaviour change in tourism operators. Shang et al. (2010) note that a number of hotels have adopted social marketing to encourage customers to reuse towels and linen while also reducing operating costs and improving their image (see also McKenzie-Mohr et al. 2012). Shang et al. (2010) reveal that customers' reuse intentions are much influenced by the presence of a reuse request card printed with hotel logos. They also indicate that benefits to towel and linen reuse programmes could be maximised if the savings are donated to charity, meaning that hotel guests' behavioural change could be enhanced if the hotels were more conscious of social concerns, rather than their own interest. George and Frey (2010) examine social marketing to encourage tour business owners in Cape Town to adopt positive attitudes and behaviours towards responsible tourism practices. They indicate that, although local tourism firms do not hold negative attitudes towards responsible tourism practices, their performance is not satisfactory. Barriers facing these firms in implementing change are also identified. Social marketing strategies are thus needed to enable change to support the future sustainable development of tourism (George & Frey 2010).

Social marketing has also been applied to tourism advertising. Sirakaya and Sonmez (2000) revealed that women are often depicted in a traditional way as submissive, subordinate, and dependent on men, and noted the potential implications of social marketing to change the behaviour of tourism marketing organisations towards promoting gender equity. Similarly, Chhabra *et al.* (2011) indicated that tourism advertising organisations could adopt social marketing to dispel gendered images in their advertising with the generation of two main benefits. First, tourism organisations can better attract women as a lucrative target segment. Second, they can improve their members and customers' awareness about the ethics of marketing (Chhabra *et al.* 2011).

In exploring the idea of adopting social marketing in the domain of public leisure services by distinguishing it from cognate concepts (e.g. societal marketing – a concern with the social effects of commercial marketing), Kaczynski (2008) argued that social marketing is a more superior and credible mechanism for leisure services delivery. While differences between societal and social marketing are well noted in the marketing literature (Andreasen 1994; MacFadyen *et al.* 1999), they may still need to be considered by tourism scholars.

Truong and Hall (2013) examined the social marketing characteristics of tourism projects in Vietnam using Andreasen's (2002) six benchmark criteria (as discussed above). The authors found 21 projects that matched all the criteria, suggesting that some tourism projects might have already been developed using the social marketing concept, although they did not label themselves in social marketing terms. Truong and Hall (2013) suggested that social marketing might be a contributing approach to natural resource conservation and poverty alleviation in tourist destinations. It could be applied to encourage behaviour change in both destination residents and authorities. Truong and Hall (2013) also noted that more empirical studies are needed to demonstrate the effectiveness of social marketing in tourism.

In 2013, the *Journal of Sustainable Tourism* (JOST) devoted a special issue to behaviour change mechanisms and sustainable tourism (Volume 21, Issue 7). This was the result of the 2012 Psychological and Behavioural Approaches to Understanding and Governing Sustainable Tourism Mobility Workshop held in Freiburg (Germany), where some attention was drawn to social marketing (Hall 2013; Higham *et al.* 2013; Peeters 2013). Yet, none of the published papers in JOST provided any empirical findings that proved the effectiveness of social marketing in tourism (although see Eijgelaar & de Kinderen (2014) and Le-Klähn *et al.* (2014) in Cohen *et al.* (2014) that also included papers from the workshop). There may be several major reasons for this. First, social marketing is still a new topic in tourism studies. Second, actual evidence of tourism projects that were implemented using the social marketing concept is lacking. Most previous research was conceptual in nature, which sought to explore the theoretical aspects of social marketing. Although some studies were methodologically informed, they were not actual applications of social marketing in tourism. Instead, they aimed to develop and test variables/hypotheses in the context of social marketing applications (e.g. George & Frey 2010;

Shang *et al.* 2010). Third, there is a possible lack of understanding of social marketing as well as generic marketing and business overall (Lane 2009).

The absence of many empirical tourism studies on social marketing should not be cause to underestimate the utility of social marketing or to claim the irrelevance between the two fields. Rather, it demonstrates that tourism researchers and practitioners have thus far paid comparatively limited attention to social marketing although they may be aware of the concept. Indeed, the lack of interplay between the fields is evidenced by Truong and Hall (2013) arguably being the first empirical tourism paper in the social marketing literature. This situation, therefore, offers important opportunities for further research.

Further research

As discussed above, social marketing remains a new area for tourism researchers. A majority of tourism studies on social marketing are conceptual or otherwise tested variables/hypotheses and provided implications for social marketing. Evidence demonstrating the relationship between social marketing and tourism is sparse and tends to be attraction based (Hall 2014). Therefore, empirical studies are needed to examine the effectiveness and relative value of social marketing and add to the evidence base of social marketing itself. This is particularly significant in two ways. First, it will draw greater attention of tourism researchers and practitioners to social marketing as a potential means of promoting sustainable tourism. Second, it will generate greater awareness of social marketing scholars and practitioners to the field of tourism.

Yet, the lack of empirical studies that demonstrate the effectiveness of social marketing in tourism does raise the question as to some tourism projects using social marketing principles but not labelling themselves as such. As indicated earlier, Truong and Hall (2013) found 21 tourism projects implemented in Vietnam that matched the six benchmark criteria proposed by Andreasen (2002), although they did not consider themselves social marketing interventions. This finding has two important implications. First, it suggests that tourism practitioners (e.g. project consultants/managers) might have used several or all elements of the social marketing concept to guide project design, implementation, and evaluation but did not refer it to the field. Second, it helps to reinforce the earlier argument that social marketing remains under-researched in tourism studies. Nevertheless, as Truong and Hall (2013) noted, the labelling and evaluation of social marketing interventions largely depends on the applicable criteria. Therefore, tourism researchers may also contribute to devising appropriate sets of key criteria for labelling and evaluating social marketing interventions within a tourism–specific context. That said, both theoretical and practical contributions to the social marketing debate on the part of tourism researchers are needed and should be encouraged.

Previous research suggests that effective social marketing campaigns tend to use theories and models to guide their interventions (Thackeray & Neiger 2000). These are rooted in different disciplines such as social psychology (e.g. Transtheoretical Model), sociology (e.g. Social Learning Theory), and economics (e.g. Supply Chain Theory) (Luca & Suggs 2013; Hall 2014), but their application in social marketing interventions is often uneven and poor (Luca & Suggs 2013; Hall 2014). Similarly, while some tourism studies on social marketing (e.g. Mair & Laing 2013) reported using theory, most others were not theoretically informed. Therefore, future research must examine the utility of theories and models in developing behavioural interventions with respect to sustainability. Answers may be sought to the questions as to if the presence of an underlying theory or model necessarily results in effective interventions, if effective interventions necessarily constitute proof of a theory's value, and if the effectiveness of a theory or model can be easily tested. It may then be possible to add theory and model use as a criterion to Andreasen's (2002) six social marketing benchmarks.

Social marketing research in the tourism field has focused on motivating behaviour change at both the downstream (e.g. tourists) and upstream (e.g. corporate) levels. Yet, the critical dimension of social marketing has rarely been examined. Critical social marketing "is concerned with the application of marketing knowledge, concepts, and techniques to enhance social as well as economic ends. It is also concerned with analysis of the social consequence of marketing policies, decisions and activities" (Lazer & Kelley 1973: ix; see also Gordon 2011). A critical approach to social marketing may hold substantial potential for improving marketing theory and practice, informing downstream and upstream social marketing, and adding to the evidence base of social marketing itself (Gordon 2011). Within the tourism context, a critical social marketing approach may be useful given that the business and policy strategies of most tourism organisations primarily focus on increased tourist numbers and industry growth that may further increase the environmental impacts of tourism. Critical social marketing may also help contribute to improving gender equity in tourism development (Chhabra et al. 2011). Critical social marketing may also be combined with upstream social marketing, for instance, to raise public awareness about the effects of airlines' marketing policies (e.g. frequent flyer programmes) on tourists' increasing mobility and consumption (Hibbert et al. 2013). Appropriate policy changes may thus be advocated.

Further research is also possible to investigate social marketing as a contributor to poverty alleviation via tourism given its recognised role in sustainable tourism development (Zapata et al. 2011). If poverty is ascribed to ineffective policies and structural arrangements (Blank 2003), then upstream social marketing may be important. In case poverty is due to the attitudes and behaviours of poor people (Amsden 2012; Moore 2012), downstream social marketing may be significant in promoting positive behaviour change in these people (Kotler & Lee 2009). This is particularly important in the tourism context given that some tourist destinations are home to poor ethnic minorities who depend on natural resources for subsistence, resulting in rapid environmental degradation (UNEP 2011). Poor people's subsistence lifestyles also contribute to widening income gaps in society, cultivating social inequality, and threatening economic viability (Kirchgeorg & Winn 2006). Criticising poor people's lifestyles is neither to deny the hardships that they suffer nor to provide a sole explanation for the poverty situation in any destination. Rather, it emphasises that poverty has detrimental effects on economic, social, and environmental sustainability and affects resilience. To this end, alternative livelihoods are needed and tourism businesses can help to improve poor people's living conditions, thereby contributing to sustainable tourism overall (UNEP 2011). Upstream social marketing may, therefore, help to change the self-interested practices of tourism businesses towards socially responsible business practices.

Conclusion

Sustainability is one of the most important issues facing the world today and will remain so in the future. Environmental sustainability is arguably the focal point of sustainable development, although equal importance is also attached to economic and social sustainability. Changes in individual and public behaviours are essential for sustainability. These behaviour changes are even more significant when it is recognised that most environmental problems facing the world today are primarily the consequences of human behaviour (McKenzie-Mohr 2000; Oskamp 2000; Takahashi 2009).

Tourism is central to the debate over global sustainability due to both the contributions it can make to sustainable development and the challenges it may present. First, this is due to the dynamics and growth of the sector and its economic importance to national economies and local destinations. Second, tourism often involves the participation and interactions between tourists, the industry, the environment, and local communities. To achieve a sustainable tourism future, behaviour changes in all stakeholders are required, and social marketing may hold important potential given its demonstrated effectiveness in differing sectors. However, there is a lack of studies exploring the potential contribution of social marketing to sustainable tourism with a large majority of research being conceptual in nature. This chapter supports Lane's (2009: 26) observation that social marketing remains a relative "blank" for sustainable tourism researchers. It emphasises that this "blank" has since not been substantially "filled" by tourism researchers. Therefore, the value of social marketing for sustainable tourism remains unclear, the main barrier, which is also the most important limitation, being the absence of empirical findings needed to demonstrate the efficacy of social marketing in tourism. Nevertheless, this chapter contributes to shaping debate about future research on social marketing and potentially engaging tourism scholars in broadening the research agenda, particularly beyond technological (and other) approaches and into social marketing as a promising contributor to sustainable tourism.

Key reading

Beeton, S. and Benfield, R. (2002) 'Demand control: The case for demarketing as a visitor and environmental management tool', *Journal of Sustainable Tourism*, 10: 497–513.

Beeton, S. and Pinge, I. (2003) 'Casting the holiday dice: Demarketing gambling to encourage local tourism', *Current Issues in Tourism*, 6: 309–22.

Hall, C.M. (2014) *Tourism and Social Marketing*, Abingdon: Routledge

McKenzie-Mohr, D., Schultz, P.W., Lee, N.R. and Kotler, P. (2012) *Social Marketing to Protect the Environment: What Works*, Thousand Oaks, CA: Sage.

Truong, V.D. and Hall, C.M. (2013) 'Social marketing and tourism: What's the evidence?', *Social Marketing Quarterly*, 19: 110–35.

References

Amsden, A.H. (2012) 'Grass roots war on poverty', *World Economic Review, 1*: 114–31.

Andreasen, A.R. (1994) 'Social marketing: Its definition and domain', *Journal of Public Policy and Marketing, 3*: 108–14.

—— (2002) 'Marketing social marketing in the social change marketplace', *Journal of Public Policy and Marketing, 21*: 3–13.

—— (2006) *Social Marketing in the 21st Century*, Thousand Oaks, CA: Sage.

Bagozzi, R.P. (1975) 'Marketing as exchange', *Journal of Marketing, 39*: 32–39.

Beeton, S. (2001) 'Cyclops and Sirens – Demarketing as a proactive response to negative consequences of one-eyed competitive marketing', in *Travel and Tourism Research Association 32nd Annual Conference Proceedings*, Idaho: Travel and Tourism Research Association.

Beeton, S. and Benfield, R. (2002) 'Demand control: The case for demarketing as a visitor and environmental management tool', *Journal of Sustainable Tourism, 10*: 497–513.

Beeton, S. and Pinge, I. (2003) 'Casting the holiday dice: Demarketing gambling to encourage local tourism', *Current Issues in Tourism, 6*: 309–22.

Benfield, R. (2001) '"Good things come to those who wait": sustainable tourism and timed entry at Sissinghurst Castle Garden, Kent', *Tourism Geographies*, 3: 207–17.

Blank, R.M. (2003) 'Selecting among anti-poverty policies: Can an economist be both critical and caring?', *Review of Social Economy, 61*: 447–69.

Bloom, P.N. (1980) 'Evaluating social marketing programs: Problems and prospects', in R.P. Bagozzi, K.L. Bernhardt, P.S. Busch, D.W. Cravens, J.F. Hair and C.A. Scott (eds) *Marketing in the 80's*, Chicago, IL: American Marketing Association.

Bloom, P.N. and Novelli, W.D. (1981) 'Problems and challenges in social marketing', *Journal of Marketing, 45*: 79–88.

Bright, A.D. (2000) 'The role of social marketing in leisure and recreation management', *Journal of Leisure Research, 32*: 12–17.

Chhabra, D., Andereck, K., Yamanoi, K. and Plunkett, D. (2011) 'Gender equity and social marketing: An analysis of tourism advertisements', *Journal of Travel and Tourism Marketing, 28*: 111–28.

Cohen, S.A., Higham, J.E.S., Gossling, S. and Peeters, P. (eds) (2014) *Understanding and Governing Sustainable Tourism Mobility: Psychological and Behavioural Approaches*', Abingdon: Routledge.

Cowell, D. (1979) 'Marketing in local authority sport, leisure and recreation centres', *Local Government Studies, 5*(4): 31–43.

Dann, S. (2010) 'Redefining social marketing with contemporary commercial marketing definitions', *Journal of Business Research, 63*: 147–53.

Dann, S. and Dann, S. (2009) *Insight and Overview of Social Marketing*. Available at: www.premiers.qld.gov. au (accessed 1 September 2011).

Dinan, C. and Sargeant, A. (2000) 'Social marketing and sustainable tourism: Is there a match?', *International Journal of Tourism Research, 2*: 2–14.

Dolan, P., Hallsworth, M., Halpern, D., King, D. and Vlaev, I. (2010) *MINDSPACE: Influencing Behaviour through Public Policy*, London: Cabinet Office and Institute for Government.

Donovan, R. (2011) 'Social marketing's mythunderstandings', *Journal of Social Marketing, 1*: 8–16.

Donovan, R. and Henley, N. (2010) *Principles and Practice of Social Marketing: An International Perspective*, Cambridge: Cambridge University Press.

Eijgelaar, E. and de Kinderen, D. (2014) 'Carbon offsetting: Motives for participation and impacts on travel behaviour', in S.A. Cohen, J.E.S. Higham, S. Gossling and P. Peeters (eds) *Understanding and Governing Sustainable Tourism Mobility: Psychological and Behavioural Approaches*, Abingdon: Routledge.

Farrell, T. and Gordon, R. (2012) 'Critical social marketing: Investigating alcohol marketing in the developing world', *Journal of Social Marketing, 2*: 138–56.

Fox, K.F.A. and Kotler, P. (1980) 'The marketing of social causes: The first ten years', *Journal of Marketing, 44*: 24–33.

Foxall, G.R., Castro, J., James, V., Yani-de-Soriano, M. and Sigurdsson, V. (2006) 'Consumer behavior analysis and social marketing: The case of environmental conservation', *Behavior and Social Issues, 15*: 101–24.

George, R. and Frey, N. (2010) 'Creating change in responsible tourism management through social marketing', *South African Journal of Business Management, 41*: 11–23.

Gordon, R. (2011) 'Critical social marketing: Definition, application and domain', *Journal of Social Marketing, 1*: 82–99.

Gössling, S., Hall, C.M. and Weaver, D. (eds) (2009) *Sustainable Tourism Futures: Perspectives on Systems, Restructuring and Innovation*, London: Routledge.

Gössling, S., Hultman, J., Haglund, L, Källgren, H. and Revahl, M. (2009) 'Voluntary carbon offsetting by Swedish air travellers: Towards the co-creation of environmental value?', *Current Issues in Tourism, 12*: 1–19.

Gössling, S., Scott, D., Hall, C.M., Ceron, J-P. and Dubois, G. (2012) 'Consumer behaviour and demand response of tourists to climate change', *Annals of Tourism Research, 39*: 36–58.

Griffin, D. (2006) 'Social issue exchange: An exploration of determinants and outcomes', Doctoral Dissertation, Griffith University, Australia. Available at: www4.gu.edu.au (accessed 1 June 2011).

Hall, C.M. (2013) 'Framing behavioural approaches to understanding and governing sustainable tourism consumption: Beyond neoliberalism, "nudging" and "green growth"?', *Journal of Sustainable Tourism, 21*: 1091–1109.

—— (2014) *Tourism and Social Marketing*, Abingdon: Routledge.

Hall, C.M. and McArthur, S. (1998) *Integrated Heritage Management*, Norwich: The Stationery Office.

Hastings, G. and Haywood, A.J. (1991) 'Social marketing and communication in health promotion', *Health Promotion International, 6*: 135–45.

Hastings, G. and Saren, M. (2003) 'The critical contribution of social marketing: Theory and practice', *Marketing Theory, 3*: 305–22.

Hibbert, J., Dickinson, J.E., Gössling, S. and Curtin, S. (2013) 'Identity and tourism mobility: An exploration of the attitude-behaviour gap', *Journal of Sustainable Tourism, 21*: 999–1016.

Higham, J., Cohen, S.A., Peeters, P. and Gössling, S. (2013) 'Psychological and behavioural approaches to understanding and governing sustainable mobility', *Journal of Sustainable Tourism, 21*: 949–67.

International Union for Conservation of Nature (IUCN) (1980) *World Conservation Strategy*, Morges: IUCN.

Kaczynski, A.T. (2008) 'A more tenable marketing for leisure services and studies', *Leisure Sciences, 30*: 253–72.

Kim, H., Borges, M.C. and Chon, J. (2006) 'Impacts of environmental values on tourism motivation: The case of FICA, Brazil', *Tourism Management, 27*: 957–67.

Kirchgeorg, M. and Winn, M.I. (2006) 'Sustainability marketing for the poorest of the poor', *Business Strategy and the Environment, 15*: 171–84.

Kotler, P. and Lee, N.R. (2008) *Social Marketing: Influencing Behaviors for Good*, Thousand Oaks, CA: Sage.

—— (2009) *Up and Out of Poverty: The Social Marketing Solutions*, Upper Saddle, NJ: Prentice Hall.

Kotler, P. and Levy, S.J. (1971) 'Demarketing, yes, demarketing', *Harvard Business Review, 49*(6), 74–80.

Kotler, P. and Roberto, E.L. (1989) *Social Marketing – Strategies for Changing Public Behavior*, New York: The Free Press.

Kotler, P. and Zaltman, G. (1971) 'Social marketing: An approach to planned social change', *Journal of Marketing, 35*: 3–12.

Laczniak, G.R., Lusch, R.F. and Murphy, P.E. (1979) 'Social marketing: Its ethical dimensions', *Journal of Marketing, 43*: 29–36.

Lane, B. (2009) 'Thirty years of sustainable tourism: Drivers, progress, problems – and the future', in S. Gössling, C.M. Hall and D. Weaver (eds) *Sustainable Tourism Futures: Perspectives on Systems, Restructuring and Innovation*, London: Routledge.

Lazer, W. and Kelley, E.J. (1973) *Social Marketing: Perspectives and Viewpoints*, Homewood, IL: Richard D. Irwin.

Le-Klähn, D., Hall, C.M. and Gerike, R. (2014) 'Promoting public transport in tourism', in S.A. Cohen, J.E.S. Higham, S. Gossling and P. Peeters (eds) *Understanding and Governing Sustainable Tourism Mobility: Psychological and Behavioural Approaches*, Abingdon: Routledge.

Lefebvre, R.C. (1996) '25 years of social marketing: Looking back to the future', *Social Marketing Quarterly, 3*: 51–58.

Ling, J.C., Franklin, B.A.K., Lindsteadt, J.F. and Gearon, S.A.N. (1992) 'Social marketing: Its place in public health', *Annual Review of Public Health, 13*: 341–62.

Luca, N.R. and Suggs, L.S. (2013) 'Theory and model use in social marketing health interventions', *Journal of Health Communication, 18*: 20–40.

Luck, D.J. (1974) 'Social marketing: Confusion compounded', *Journal of Marketing, 38*: 70–72.

MacFadyen, L., Stead, M. and Hastings, G. (1999) 'A synopsis of social marketing', *Health Promotion International, 9*: 59–63.

Maibach, E.W. (2003) 'Explicating social marketing: What is it, and what is not it?', *Social Marketing Quarterly, 8*: 7–13.

Mair, J. and Laing, J.H. (2013) 'Encouraging pro-environmental behaviour: The role of sustainability-focused events', *Journal of Sustainable Tourism*, DOI: 10.1080/09669582.2012.756494.

McKenzie-Mohr, D. (2000) 'Promoting sustainable behaviour: An introduction to community-based social marketing', *Journal of Social Issues, 56*: 543–54.

McKenzie-Mohr, D., Schultz, P.W., Lee, N.R. and Kotler, P. (2012) *Social Marketing to Protect the Environment: What Works*, Thousand Oaks, CA: Sage.

Moore, S. (2012) 'Instead of being disgusted by poverty, we are disgusted by poor people themselves', *The Guardian*, 16 February: 10.

Oskamp, S. (2000) 'Psychological contributions to achieving an ecologically sustainable future for humanity', *Journal of Social Issues, 56*: 373–90.

Peatie, S. and Peatie, K. (2003) 'Ready to fly solo? Reducing social marketing's dependence on commercial marketing theory', *Marketing Theory, 3*: 365–85.

Peeters, P.M. (2013) 'Developing a long-term global tourism transport model using a behavioural approach: Implications for sustainable tourism policy making', *Journal of Sustainable Tourism, 21*: 1049–69.

Peeters, P., Gössling, S. and Lane, B. (2009) 'Moving towards low-carbon tourism: New opportunities for destinations and tour operators', in S. Gössling, C.M. Hall and D.B. Weaver (eds) *Sustainable Tourism Futures: Perspectives on Systems, Restructuring and Innovations,* London: Routledge.

Redmond, E.C. and Griffith, C.J. (2006) 'A pilot study to evaluate the effectiveness of a social marketing-based consumer food safety initiatives using observation', *British Food Journal, 108*: 753–70.

Scott, D., Gössling, S. and Hall, C.M. (2012) *Tourism and Climate Change,* Abingdon: Routledge.

Shang, J., Basil, D.Z. and Wymer, W. (2010) 'Using social marketing to enhance hotel reuse programs', *Journal of Business Research, 63*: 166–72.

Sirakaya, E. and Sonmez, S. (2000) 'Gender images in state tourism brochures: An overlooked area in socially responsible tourism marketing', *Journal of Travel Research, 38*: 353–62.

Skidmore, W. (1975) *Theoretical Thinking in Sociology,* Cambridge: Cambridge University Press.

Smith, W.A. (2000) 'Social marketing: An evolving definition', *American Journal of Health Behaviour, 24*: 11–17.

Smith, W.A. and Strand, J. (2008) *Social Marketing: A Resource Guide for Social Change Professionals,* Washington DC: Academy for Educational Development.

Stead, M., Gordon, R., Angus, K. and McDermott, L. (2007) 'A systematic review of social marketing effectiveness', *Health Education, 107*: 126–91.

Tabanico, J.J. and Schultz, P.W. (2007) 'Community-based social marketing', *BioCycle,* August: 41–47.

Takahashi, B. (2009) 'Social marketing for the environment: An assessment of theory and practice', *Applied Environment Education & Communication, 8*: 135–45.

Thackeray, R. and Neiger, B.L. (2000) 'Establishing a relationship between behavior change theory and social marketing: Implications for health education', *Journal of Health Education, 31*: 331–35.

Thaler, R.H. and Sunstein, C.R. (2008) *Nudge: Improving Decisions about Health, Wealth and Happiness,* London: Yale University Press.

Truong, V.D. and Hall, C.M. (2013) 'Social marketing and tourism: What's the evidence?', *Social Marketing Quarterly, 19*: 110–35.

United Nations Environment Programme (UNEP) (2011) *Towards a Green Economy: Pathways to Sustainable Development and Poverty Eradication.* Available at: www.unep.org/greeneconomy (accessed 1 April 2013).

Wearing, S., Archer, D., and Beeton, S. (2007) *The Sustainable Marketing of Tourism in Protected Areas,* Gold Coast, Australia: Sustainable Tourism Cooperative Research Centre.

Wiebe, G.D. (1951) 'Merchandising commodities and citizenship on television', *Public Opinion Quarterly, 15*: 679–91.

Wood, M. (2008) 'Applying commercial marketing theory to social marketing: A tale of 4Ps (and a B)', *Social Marketing Quarterly, 14*: 76–85.

Zapata, M.J., Hall, C.M., Lindo, P. and Vanderschaeghen, M. (2011) 'Can community-based tourism contribute to development and poverty alleviation?' *Current Issues in Tourism, 14*: 725–49.

20

Managing visitors to the natural environment

David Newsome and Susan Moore

Management strategies include the designation of protected areas and development of management plans. Practical aspects of management include both managing and influencing visitors and the sites that they visit. Managing the tourism industry involves both voluntary and regulatory strategies.

Planning is defined as setting goals and then developing the actions needed to achieve the nominated goals.

Sustainability is achieved via a combination of approaches that include various means of controlling the size, type and spatial extent of activities in combination with educational programmes. These approaches are used in conjunction with green design and the application of technologies to reduce the ecological footprint of tourism.

Voluntary management approaches include the application of codes of conduct and guidelines, certification and the employment of environmental management systems.

Introduction

Nature–based tourism and public interest in the natural environment continues to rise. Up to 20 per cent of all tourism (990 million international tourist arrivals in 2011) focuses on natural and protected areas and wildlife in the natural environment (Buckley 2009; UNWTO 2012). A critical issue in relation to such tourism activity is how people interact with and affect the environment in terms of development pressures, visitor access and activities. Newsome *et al.* (2013) have documented a range of impacts, many of which can be negative, arising from tourism and recreation in natural areas. Sources of negative impact include access via roads and trails, trampling beyond trail networks, camping, operation of built facilities such as resorts, use of coastal environments and the edges of rivers and lakes, visits to caves and mountain environments and wildlife tourism.

The need to understand a wide range of impacts is comprehensively explored in Kuss *et al.* (1990), Liddle (1997), Hammitt and Cole (1998), Buckley (2004), Newsome *et al.* (2005) and Newsome *et al.* (2013). Potential impact scenarios that occur in tandem with the rapid and complex growth of natural area tourism make adequate protection and management of nature-based tourism destinations vitally important. Any negative impacts that may degrade ecological conditions (the tourism resource) and visitor satisfaction (the tourism experience) therefore need to be anticipated and minimised via tourism planning and the employment of various management strategies.

The aim of this chapter, therefore, is to outline the vital role of planning and the ways that natural areas and their visitors can be managed. Such approaches include an overview of the role of tourism planning frameworks and a brief consideration of the suite of management strategies and actions that are available to tourism planners and managers.

Managing the environmental context: the vital role of planning

Planning is essential for effective and cost-efficient management of negative environmental impacts and enhancing the visitor experience. A variety of planning frameworks are available to underpin the management of natural area tourism. In the tourism context, planning is defined as setting goals and then developing the actions needed to achieve them. Such goals include the nature of visitor experience and the extent that the tourism resource can or cannot be modified.

The most important recreation/tourism planning frameworks are the Recreation Opportunity Spectrum (ROS), Limits of Acceptable Change (LAC), the Visitor Impact Management framework (VIM) and the Tourism Optimisation Management Model (TOMM). A detailed explanation of these frameworks in provided by McCool *et al.* (2007) and Newsome *et al.* (2013).

The main objective of all these frameworks is to provide tourism opportunities for visitors and to protect the natural environment at the same time. The nominated frameworks have some important common features including: their ability to integrate well with general management and tourism management planning; requiring management actions and monitoring to be undertaken; and their applicability to different settings in both terrestrial and marine situations. LAC, VIM and TOMM provide data on the impact of visitor use which need management action and require information on measurable indicators and standards which can be assessed against management objectives.

ROS can be broadly applied, from places only accessible on foot where there are no facilities through to highly developed destinations, such as resorts and lodges. It uses physical, social and managerial characteristics to describe and compare opportunity classes determined by access, remoteness, naturalness and size, contact with other visitors and acceptability of visitor impacts. Managerial characteristics include making decisions about the level of facility development and the amount of on-site regulation such as site development and signage to be applied in a tourism situation. Any one of these characteristics can be manipulated to provide a chosen recreation opportunity, ranging from primitive to a highly modified destination/management footprint (Clark & Stankey 1979).

The LAC planning framework is a process for deciding what environmental and social conditions are acceptable and helps identify management actions to achieve the nominated and desired conditions. LAC differs from ROS in the setting of measurable standards for managing recreation and tourism in natural areas (see case study). In contrast, ROS is a process for recognising and designating different recreation/tourism opportunity classes. Because acceptability is a societal value judgement, stakeholder involvement is essential. Stakeholders, such as managers, tourism operators and tourists can provide judgements regarding the acceptability of various impacts and in some cases can provide monitoring information to assist management (Clark & Stankey 1997).

Case Study

Managing the impacts of coral reef tourism at Koh Chang National Marine Park, Thailand

Coral reef ecosystems are highly valued tourism destinations. Scuba diving and snorkelling are common recreational activities on most of the world's coral reef systems. There are around 17 million divers worldwide. However, snorkelling activity exceeds scuba diving as many more people can participate because there are few requirements for training or special equipment. The impact of snorkelling on coral reefs includes local damage to susceptible corals, disturbance of sediments, abrasion and the direct breakage of corals (e.g. Plathong *et al.* 2000; Harriott 2002; Leujak & Ormond 2008; Hannak *et al.* 2011).

Such impacts can be mitigated by education, employing a code of practice, briefing and the direct supervision of snorkellers and the provision of resting buoys and flotation platforms on which snorkellers can rest (Harriott 2002). Sometimes, however, management actions are reactive rather than proactive, but the application of a planning framework can provide the setting for stronger management into the future.

Roman *et al.* (2007) described the application of the LAC planning framework in an effort to address environmental impacts of snorkelling at Koh Chang National Marine Park, Thailand. The LAC process enabled the identification of resource (i.e. biophysical) and social indicators and standards for managing the snorkelling activity of some 30,000 people per year. The resource conditions identified by Roman *et al.* (2007) included coral mortality, diversity and vulnerability to trampling. Assessment of social conditions via a questionnaire included visitor perceptions of coral mortality and diversity and the number of other people snorkelling at the site.

Reef-transect surveys focused on coral mortality, identified as an important indicator for unacceptable change, with the results used to formulate a standard of 35–50 per cent coral mortality. A range of levels of tourist access were suggested by Roman *et al.* (2007), with the most vulnerable, highly valued sites having limited access. In terms of mitigating biophysical impacts and reducing crowding, a generic standard of 30–35 snorkellers was proposed, with the proviso for downward adjustment for low tourist visitation zones and upward adjustment for more intensively visited areas.

The (VIM) planning framework provides a focus on visitor impacts and involves a review of existing data and management objectives – again through the selection of indicators and standards that identify unacceptable impacts. Like LAC, if selected standards are exceeded, then the causes need to be determined and the appropriate management actions employed to mitigate the problem.

The TOMM planning framework was developed specifically for tourism planning in natural areas and has great functionality as a regional planning directive encompassing political, socio-cultural and economic contexts while retaining a central focus on tourism. Because such planning can encompass land and waters owned and/or managed by a diverse group of people, a large number of stakeholders are potentially involved. According to McArthur (2000), the framework comprises context description (policies, plans, community values, product characteristics, growth patterns, market trends and opportunities, positioning and branding), a monitoring programme (selection of indicators and standards to identify optimal conditions) and implementation (development of suitable management strategies).

Planning is critical for sustainability as it allows impacts to be recognised and managed. All the frameworks described satisfy the conditions of objective setting, data collection, collation and analysis with the development of alternatives and recognition of the implementation of suitable management as a crucial final stage. They focus on determining how much change is acceptable rather than trying to determine how much use is too much. Furthermore, they all provide for adaptive management by establishing management objectives and related actions, and require a monitoring programme that provides scope for feedback and subsequent changes.

McCool et al. (2007) observe that planning is essential for dealing with the complexity and uncertainty that often characterises tourism in highly valued, sensitive, environments. Moreover, planning is important given the combined impact of increasing visitor pressure, global climate change and the influence of other activities emanating from the landscape in which tourism exists. Despite this, as yet, visitor planning frameworks have not been widely adopted in the management planning process for natural area tourism (see chapter 30). The absence of planning, therefore, hinders the development of a strong management philosophy in managing tourism activity and associated sustainable tourism resource management (Newsome et al. 2013).

Managing tourists in the natural environment

A fundamental management strategy is the creation of a protected area (to protect the natural environment) followed by development of a management plan specifying human use. Management plans may or may not have provision for tourism management depending on the purpose of the reserve and the resources available to manage it. The International Union for Conservation of Nature (IUCN) identifies seven categories of protected area including strict nature reserve, national park and habitat/species management areas (IUCN 2013). A detailed account of the creation, design and governance of reserved areas is beyond the scope of this chapter but suffice to say these are important mechanisms and the first stage in managing a natural area (Newsome et al. 2013).

The governance of a protected area, the administrative and policy structures within which management takes place, is an important influence on management effectiveness. For protected areas where tourism is an integral component, the traditional form of governance has been a government ownership model with funding from societal taxes (Eagles 2008, 2009). More recently, there has been a shift to governance arrangements based on partnerships between commercial tourism providers and government agencies, and arrangements with indigenous and other local people in increasingly central and important roles.

Within specific protected areas zoning is a management strategy that falls under the umbrella of tourism planning frameworks such as ROS and LAC (e.g. see case study). The rationale behind zoning is multi-faceted, including protection of the natural environment from the environmental impacts of recreation and tourism through the allocation of no use and restricted areas. Zoning also provides choice for visitors as well as separating incompatible visitor uses in space and time. For example, zoning can spatially separate hikers from motor vehicles and mountain bikers from horse riders. Temporal zoning can be used to protect wildlife, such as seabirds, during breeding. Where breeding is also a wildlife tourism attraction, zoning can separate visitors from wildlife according to calculated safe approach distances demarcated by barriers, hides or viewing platforms.

Beyond the strategies of reservation and zoning, the practicalities of management involve site and visitor management actions. Site management helps to control the impact of visitors through actions at sites where use is occurring, while visitor management focuses on managing the visitors themselves through actions such as regulating visitor numbers and group size, interpretation and other forms of communication, and law enforcement and policing. Both site and visitor management actions, such as re-designing a picnic site, building a boardwalk to manage the impact of hiking in sensitive environments, or restricting the number of visitors to a sensitive coral cay, can be specified in protected area management plans.

Site management includes the design and management of tourism infrastructure and facilities such as roads, walk trails, resorts, eco-lodges, campsites, day-use areas, and water-related facilities such as jetties and pontoons. Such site management relies on locating and directing visitor activity to the more resilient parts of the landscape where possible, as well as designing and managing sites and facilities to minimise visitor impact. For example, the majority of visitors can be directed to day-use areas that have been designed for durability via site hardening, the provision of facilities such as toilets and where educational material about codes of visitor behaviour are located. Beyond such an area formed (hardened) walk trails can be located and enhanced with directional signage and interpretive panels. Sites providing access to scenic areas and vistas that receive significant visitation can be hardened through the construction of viewing platforms and visitor impacts thus managed.

In terms of managing visitors themselves (i.e. visitor management) educational approaches are frequently employed to inform visitors of specific activities such as 'where to go' and 'what to do' in conjunction with advice on prohibited activity and behaviours. Visitor management also involves the regulation of specific uses and numbers visiting a site, as well as limitations on group size and length of stay at a particular location. Management actions such as limiting access and restrictions on visitor numbers in natural areas, although controversial, may have to be considered further as a management strategy (Eagles & McCool 2002). Many popular, accessible protected areas, wildlife hotspots and World Heritage sites are experiencing increased visitor pressure and the negative impacts of congestion and crowding. Using advance reservations, queuing and the charging of fees to regulate and reduce visitor numbers could be applied in conjunction with other actions like de-marketing and pre-trip educational information about peak activity periods and restrictions.

Managing the nature tourism industry

The tourism industry as it relates specifically to protected and natural areas comprises the location and operation of permanent built facilities such as eco-lodges, temporary accommodation such as tented campsites, tour companies that provide transport and guiding services, and independent tour guides. The environmental impacts associated with the construction and operation of built facilities and the activities of tourism are detailed in Buckley (2004) and Newsome et al. (2013). The previous sections have described site-based management of visitor impacts and experiences and managing visitors themselves (which may occur on- or off-site). Managing the tourism industry, rather than visitors themselves, is the subject of this section.

Such management involves two major approaches: regulatory and voluntary strategies. For many protected areas, regulatory approaches are administered by government agencies via the issuing of licences and leases. Voluntary approaches include industry codes of conduct, engagement by a tourism enterprise in a certification programme and/or employment of an environmental management system to assist in reducing their impact on the environment and ensure high-quality visitor experiences.

Leases are a regulatory management strategy in widespread use. They are issued to tourism businesses occupying permanent premises, normally for long periods of time. Leases generally provide exclusive occupancy rights for a company or individual who has invested significant amounts of money in tourism infrastructure. Examples of such infrastructure include eco-lodges, hotels, tea rooms, souvenir shops and jetties located within protected areas. Licences are a legally binding arrangement, ensuring access to a protected area or areas for a licensee; in turn, there are specific requirements on licensees regarding their behaviour in such areas. For example, a licence for an operator offering dolphin-watching tours can specify that they must undertake a monitoring programme and provide suitable, accurate information to enhance visitor satisfaction and ensure conservation objectives are met.

Voluntary management approaches include the application of codes of conduct and guidelines, certification and the employment of environmental management systems. Furthermore, the United Nations World Tourism Organization (UNWTO) has developed a code of ethics, part of which explicitly pertains to safeguarding the natural environment (UNWTO 2012).

Codes of conduct and guidelines are designed to influence the attitudes and behaviour of tourists and the tourism industry. Such codes are frequently developed and promoted by industry associations and government agencies responsible for tourism activity taking place in protected areas. For example, codes of conduct relating to the viewing of marine turtles laying their eggs have been developed by wildlife management agencies around the world. Such codes usually include limiting the number of tourists in each tour, and prohibition of the use of flashlights, avoidance of excessive noise and sudden movements, positioning of tourists behind the turtle and staying low, and allowing the turtle to return to the ocean without interruption (see e.g. Waayers *et al.* 2006). Guidelines developed by the Whale and Dolphin Conservation Society have been designed to foster minimal impact and responsible whale watching (see e.g. Carlson 2008). These guidelines include: minimising boat speed and avoiding sudden changes in boat direction; specified approach distances; utilisation of minimal disturbance approach directions and angles of approach; reduced noise levels; avoidance of pursuit, encirclement or separation of whales; and allowing whales to control the duration and nature of the experience.

Eco-certification is another voluntary mechanism that has promoted good environmental practice. Haaland and Aas (2010) posit that certification involves assessing a facility, product, services or management system using known and specified standards. Such standards are developed and set by tourism industry organisations such as Ecotourism Australia (EA) where the aim is to improve quality and sustainability by practising minimal impact tourism operations, reducing non-renewable resource consumption, fostering the use of renewable resources and alternative energy, and promoting recycling practices (EA 2012). Certified tourism operators can then promote their 'quality' products to potential tourists with the aim of attracting 'green travellers' as well as showcasing sustainable practices and educating other tourists about minimal impact environmental practices (Buckley 2002). Ultimately tourists will be in a better position to choose better quality products, which are sanctioned by professional organisations. Tourism operators who obtain certification are generally in a better position to gain government/land manager issued leases and licences within competitive environments, particularly where there are only a restricted number of such permits available.

The final voluntary strategy is environmental management systems (EMS), such as the International Standard ISO 14001, the aim being to improve environmental performance (Ayuso 2007). EMS was originally designed to improve the environmental practices of traditional industries such as manufacturing and mining. Such an approach is also applicable to other industries such as tourism where reducing resource consumption and waste production can have significant environmental (and often economic) benefits. In fostering responsible tourism operations and working towards sustainable tourism Marr Consulting Services (2008) developed an environmental best practice toolkit for the Canadian tourism industry, with a focus on resource consumption and services. The toolkit addresses important indicators of good environmental practice such as waste management, water use, reducing the carbon footprint, and carbon neutrality. One area of attention is in reducing the carbon impact of travel and the energy requirements of buildings via carbon offsets, such as tree planting, and energy-efficient building design, for example by the use of solar energy.

Managing nature tourism for sustainability

Managing for sustainability involves a combination of approaches that collectively give rise to a solid management framework. For example, in many cases of wildlife tourism there will be the application of controls on the size of tourist groups (via tour operator licences), regulation of the scale and frequency of interaction (zoning), separation of tourists from the wildlife (site management) and education and interpretation as may be specified in a tour operator licence. Such combined approaches, when applied in conjunction with greening programmes, set the scene for comprehensive management that fosters sustainability.

A range of design and management features can be employed to lesson the footprint of built facilities and also foster sustainable tourism (Andereck 2009). These include: architecture compatible with the local environment; landscaping with native plants; energy-efficient systems/energy conservation; renewable energy systems; recycling; items made of recycled materials; water use reduction programmes; composting toilet systems and grey water systems. Such approaches are likely to be supported by clients, especially those tourists who have a positive orientation towards nature (Andereck 2009). Client views can clearly reinforce 'green design' efforts made by ecotourism facility providers. 'Green facilities' and sustainable environmental management practices can go a long way in fostering appropriate attitudes towards natural areas and management directed towards sustainable tourism (Lee & Moscardo 2005).

For all this to take place requires an awareness of the applied science of nature-based tourism, a desire to manage the environment for sustainability, and resources such as adequate funding and staffing (see e.g. Fennel 2008; Buckley 2009; Newsome et al. 2013). Resources and funding especially influence management capacity and management effectiveness. It has already been noted that tourism planning frameworks have not been extensively applied. Furthermore, it has become apparent that many protected areas in which tourism takes place are inadequately managed and fail to reach an acceptable level of management effectiveness (Leverington et al. 2010). Hockings et al. (2006) developed six major indicators of an effective management cycle that are applicable in the tourism context. Planning is one of these and central to effective tourism management. A fundamental intent of the protected area management effectiveness (PAME) assessments is supporting adaptive management through monitoring and then using the resultant feedback to inform and improve management.

Furthermore, protected area management effectiveness indicators developed by Leverington et al. (2010) are directly applicable in the tourism context. These indicators include the adequacy of staff training, the extent and severity of threats, management of impact, adequacy of infrastructure and facilities, and visitor satisfaction. Such approaches and indicator development reinforce the fact that mechanisms exist to assess the effectiveness of tourism management and the means to foster sustainable approaches to tourism in the natural environment.

Conclusion

The management of tourism in the natural environment, especially valued ecosystems, comprises designating the resource as a protected area and subsequent zoning, the planning of activities and the application of various site management actions such as planned, designed and maintained hiking trails, viewpoints and wildlife interaction areas. Visitors to natural areas are also managed according to direct regulation or communication and education. It is also becoming more important to understand visitor motivations and their levels of satisfaction, particularly with the type and extent of management they experience as part of their visit.

The tourism industry, as well as natural area destinations, is managed to maintain environmental quality and positive and appropriate tourist experiences. This is achieved through regulatory approaches (e.g. licences and leases) and according to voluntary strategies (e.g. certification and environmental management systems). Management will only be effective where there is adequate resourcing and staffing levels to undertake and maintain management actions. Many protected areas around the world, which are also important tourism destinations, are poorly funded and staffed, leading to a degradation of management capacity and poor management effectiveness.

Key Reading

Ayuso, S. (2007) 'Comparing voluntary policy instruments for sustainable tourism: The experience of the Spanish hotel sector', *Journal of Sustainable Tourism*, 15: 144–59.

McCool, S.F., Clark, R.N. and Stankey, G.H. (2007) *An Assessment of Frameworks Useful for Public Land Recreation Planning*, General Technical Report, PNW-GTR-705, Portland, Oregon: United States Department of Agriculture (Forest Service), Pacific Northwest Research Station.

Newsome, D., Dowling, R. and Moore, S.A. (2005) *Wildlife Tourism*, Clevedon: Channel View Publications.

Newsome, D., Moore, S. and Dowling, R. (2013) *Natural Area Tourism: Ecology, Impacts and Management*, 2nd edn, Clevedon: Channel View Publications.

References

Andereck, K.L. (2009) 'Tourists' perceptions of environmentally responsible innovations at tourism businesses', *Journal of Sustainable Tourism*, 17: 489–99.

Ayuso, S. (2007) 'Comparing voluntary policy instruments for sustainable tourism: The experience of the Spanish hotel sector', *Journal of Sustainable Tourism*, 15: 144–59.

Buckley, R. (2002) 'Tourism ecolabels', *Annals of Tourism Research*, 29: 183–208.

—— (2004) *The Environmental Impacts of Tourism*, CABI Publishing, UK.

—— (2009) *Ecotourism: Principles and Practices*, Wallingford, UK: CABI.

Carlson, C. (2008) *A Review of Whale Watch Guidelines and Regulations Around the World*, Whale and Dolphin Conservation Society, USA.

Clark, R.N. and Stankey, G.H. (1979) *The Recreation Opportunity Spectrum: A Framework for Planning, Management, and Research* (General Technical Report PNW-98), Portland, Oregon: Department of Agriculture, Forest Service, Pacific Northwest Forest and Range Experiment Station.

—— (1997) 'Historical development of limits of acceptable change: Conceptual clarifications and possible extensions', in S.F. McCool and D.N. Cole (eds) *Proceedings from a Workshop on Limits of Acceptable Change and Related Planning Processes: Progress and Future Directions, University of Montana's Lubrecht Experimental Forest, Missoula, Montana, May 20–22, 1997* (Gen. Tech. Rep. INT-GTR-371), Ogden, Utah: US Department of Agriculture Forest Service, Rocky Mountain Research Station.

Eagles, P.F.J. (2008) 'Governance models for parks, recreation, and tourism', in K.S. Hanna, D.A. Clark and D.S. Slocombe (eds) *Transforming Parks and Protected Areas: Policy and Governance in a Changing World*, New York: Routledge.

—— (2009) 'Governance of recreation and tourism partnerships in parks and protected areas', *Journal of Sustainable Tourism*, 17: 231–48.

Eagles, P.F.J. and McCool, S.F. (2002) *Tourism in National Parks and Protected Areas: Planning and Management*, Wallingford: CABI Publishing.

Ecotourism Australia (EA) (2012) *Homepage*. Available at: www.ecotourism.org.au/index.asp. (accessed 21 February 2012).

Fennell, D. (2008) *Ecotourism*, 3rd edn, London: Routledge.

Haaland, H. and Aas, O. (2010) 'Eco-tourism certification – does it make a difference? A comparison of systems from Australia, Costa Rica and Sweden', *Scandinavian Journal of Hospitality and Tourism*, 10: 375–85.

Hammitt, W.E. and Cole, D.N. (1998) *Wildland Recreation: Ecology and Management*, New York: Wiley.

Hannak, J.S., Kompatscher, S., Stachowitsch, M. and Herler, J. (2011) 'Snorkelling and trampling in shallow-water fringing reefs: Risk assessment and proposed management strategy', *Journal of Environmental Management*, 92: 2723–33.

Harriott, V.J. (2002) *Marine Tourism Impacts and their Management on the Great Barrier Reef*, Technical Report No 46, Townsville, Australia: CRC Reef Research Centre.

Hockings, M., Stolton, S., Dudley, N., Leverington, F. and Courrau, J. (2006) *Evaluating Effectiveness: A Framework for Assessing the Management of Protected Areas*, Gland, Switzerland: International Union for Conservation of Nature and Natural Resources.

Kuss, F.R., Graefe, A.R. and Vaske, J.J. (1990) *Visitor Impact Management: A Review of Research*, Vol.1, Washington DC, USA: National Parks and Conservation Association.

Lee, W.H. and Moscardo, G. (2005) 'Understanding the impact of ecotourism resort experiences on tourists' environmental attitudes and behavioural intentions', *Journal of Sustainable Tourism*, 13: 546–65.

Leujak, W. and Ormond, R. (2008) 'Quantifying acceptable levels of visitor use on Red Sea reef flats', *Aquatic Conservation*, 18: 930–44.

Leverington, F., Costa, K.L., Pavese, H. and Hockings, M. (2010) 'A global analysis of protected area management effectiveness', *Environmental Management*, 46: 685–98.

Liddle, M. (1997) *Recreation Ecology: The Ecological Impact of Outdoor Recreation and Ecotourism*, London: Chapman and Hall.

Marr Consulting Services (2008) *Green Your Business: Toolkit for Tourism Operators*, Tourism Industry Association of Canada, Canadian Tourism Commission and Parks Canada. Available at: www.marrcc.com/toolkit.html. (accessed 1 March 2012).

McArthur, S. (2000) 'Visitor management in action: An analysis of the development and implementation of visitor management models at Jenolan Caves and Kangaroo Island', PhD thesis, University of Canberra.

McCool, S.F., Clark, R.N. and Stankey, G.H. (2007) *An Assessment of Frameworks Useful for Public Land Recreation Planning*, General Technical Report, PNW-GTR-705, Portland, Oregon: United States Department of Agriculture (Forest Service), Pacific Northwest Research Station.

Newsome, D., Dowling, R. and Moore, S.A. (2005) *Wildlife Tourism*, Clevedon, UK: Channel View Publications.

Newsome, D., Moore, S. and Dowling, R. (2013) *Natural Area Tourism: Ecology, Impacts and Management*, 2nd edn, Clevedon, UK: Channel View Publications.

Plathong, S., Inglis, G.J. and Huber, M.E. (2000) 'Effects of self-guided snorkeling trails in a tropical marine park', *Conservation Biology*, 14: 1821–30.

Roman, G.S.J., Dearden, P. and Rollins, R. (2007) 'Application of zoning and "limits of acceptable change" to manage snorkelling tourism', *Environmental Management*, 39: 819–30.

UNWTO (2012) *World Tourism Barometer, May 2012*, Madrid: United Nations World Tourism Organization.

Waayers, D., Newsome, D. and Lee, D. (2006) 'Observations of non-compliance behaviour by tourists to a voluntary code of conduct: A pilot study of turtle tourism in the Exmouth region, Western Australia', *Journal of Ecotourism*, 5: 211–22.

21

Tourism and corporate social responsibility

Tim Coles, Emily Fenclova and Claire Dinan

Corporate social responsibility (CSR) is an approach to business administration where, in addition to the more traditional issues of profitability and other shareholder concerns, closer voluntary consideration of ethical, social and environmental issues as well as the organisation's varied stakeholders is taken in operations and value creation.

Narrow business case is the specific and direct relationship between CSR and corporate financial performance, usually revealed through secondary data analysis, using such indices as revenue, profits, profitability and share price.

Wider business case is the broader arguments setting out the ways in which CSR can contribute to competitive advantage of a business including, but not restricted to: positive effects on image; increased revenue; reputational risk reduction; attracting or retaining more highly qualified and motivated staff; and cost reduction (e.g. from enhanced environmental management).

Introduction

What is the purpose of a tourism business? This is not a trick question and there is a perfectly legitimate, albeit axiomatic, answer. Nevertheless, this simple question forces us to stop and contemplate an issue that so many business people, regulators, policy-makers, academics and students take for granted. Beyond the obvious answer that a business's purpose is to make money, it is a question that many struggle to answer.

Debates about the role of business in general have been protracted and heavily contested for over half a century. Milton Friedman (1970: 126), the American economist, was in absolutely no doubt. For him, 'there is one and only one social responsibility of business – to use its resources and engage in activities designed to increase its profits'. His views have been interpreted as a throwback to the movement that gathered traction in the 1950s and 1960s, towards recognising and acting on the wider social, environmental and even cultural responsibilities of business. Tracing its genealogy back to the employee welfare and community schemes of nineteenth-century philanthropists, several luminaries had argued that business does not operate in isolation, entirely separate from society and the environment that exists around it. Instead, business have a duty of stewardship to those who work for them, who live in the communities where they operate, to respect the environments from which they derive value, and not just to act on behalf of their investors, shareholders and customers.

Friedman's views and others like them sparked a counter-critique which might these days seem quite curious. At a time when sustainable development is the predominant organisational and societal paradigm, Lee (2008) has noted that making the case for corporate social responsibility (CSR) is no longer the key issue. Expectations have changed. In many advanced industrial economies, it is almost unacceptable for business, companies and corporations *not* to act in such a manner. As such, the principal concern is how business should act to optimise a range of benefits, and hence justify the decisions and approaches they take. Set against this background, this chapter examines how CSR has been researched in travel and tourism. CSR is notoriously difficult to define. After a short, but important, discussion of the concept, the chapter examines the academic body of knowledge on CSR in the tourism sector and its main features. The distinctive epistemological and methodological implications arising from recent research are then discussed, while the final section summarises the main findings and examines the prospects for the future.

The alphabet soup of responsible business: CSR, CSER, CR, CP...

Definitional discussions can be dry and dull, but exchanges about this particular concept are especially important in establishing how it is understood as well as how knowledge about it has been, and should be, produced, as we will discuss later. First of all, it is important to note that CSR is a 'fuzzy' concept that has consumed considerable time and energy as academics have grappled with the task of defining it definitively and precisely. This has been a frustrating task because, as several now orthodox (although not faultless and uncontested) definitions make clear, the multi-dimensionality of the concept and its aspirations make it elusive and problematic to capture its essence in a single statement. For instance, the World Business Council for Sustainable Development (WBCSD 1999: 3) views CSR as 'the continuing commitment by business to behave ethically and contribute to economic development while improving the quality of life, of the workforce, and their families, as well as the local community and society at large' while, to the European Commission, CSR is a 'concept whereby companies integrate social and environmental concerns in their business operations and in their interactions with their stakeholders on a voluntary basis' (CEC 2006: 5).

One of the main issues is that responsibility is a socially constructed and culturally negotiated term (Van de Mosselaar *et al.* 2012); this has led to debate about terminology and relative emphases. For instance, although by far the most conspicuous term referring to the need for greater, more widespread responsibility in business administration, corporate *social* responsibility (CSR) is argued to unduly privilege the social at the expense of other dimensions, like the importance of business in environmental stewardship in an age when the latter is paramount in the public discourse on sustainable development. Not surprisingly, the term 'corporate social and environmental responsibility' (CSER) has emerged as a compromise. Even this, though, has its limitations in so far as the economic role of a business is invisible from the moniker and, without any economic activity, there is no business and no need to be responsible! Furthermore, it places emphasis more on externalities, as opposed to promoting responsibility across the full array of internal business functions and operations. According to Porter and Kramer (2006),

CSR is most effective where it is embedded throughout the entire value chain rather than being perceived as some sort of additional 'bolt on' activity that is conducted after the fact by business looking to mitigate their impacts. 'Corporate responsibility' (CR) is a relatively anodyne term that can be criticised for its somewhat vague connotations, while CSR has been frequently confused with the much more limited idea of 'corporate philanthropy' (CP). While charitable activities may be significant expressions of a business's apparent ethos of responsibility, they should not be the only manifestations. Indeed, an enduring issue in CSR research has been the long-term fascination with philanthropy and charitable activities (see Fenclova & Coles 2011).

Beyond these, several other terms have made it into the 'responsibility lexicon', including: 'social responsibility' (SR), 'corporate citizenship', 'company sustainability management' and 'corporate sustainability and responsibility'. Corporate citizenship conceptualises business through its relationship with the state and other (for instance, supra-national) regulatory bodies. Rights are bestowed on enterprises to conduct their business throughout a territory but there is an expectation that they will discharge their obligations properly to the state and citizens, for instance by paying taxes, acting in the best interests of local communities, not polluting the environment and so on. The final two terms appear to have merit by connecting sustainable development and responsible business administration in an overt and literal sense. Corporate sustainability management may nevertheless be criticised for appearing to be a pragmatic solutions-based term that is conceptually awkward: for instance, why should the responsible business require a specific division dealing with sustainability when CSR should be about the principles of sustainable development being central to, and woven through, all business activities? *Prima facie*, corporate sustainability and responsibility implies – somewhat erroneously – two distinct, connected but ultimately different sets of ideas. Tautologically, it is impossible to conduct irresponsible sustainability.

Clearly, it is impossible here to explore these issues in far greater depth. However, there are three important implications for tourism studies of CSR in this discussion. First, CSR is best conceptualised at the level of the individual business as a means of delivering higher aspirations for, and collective action necessary to achieve, sustainable development (Plume 2009). While sustainable development may be best regarded as a macro-level or 'macro-social' concern (Lee 2008), CSR is essentially a micro-level phenomenon at the level of the firm. CSR is concerned with how the 'triple bottom line' is affected by the operations of an organisation, the extent to which the business is conscious of these impacts, and how it acts voluntarily to ensure its outcomes are optimised. As an approach to business administration, CSR requires organisations to question the extent to which their *internal* practices and stakeholders adhere to, and deliver on, the principles of sustainable development. Thus, CSR is not just 'sustainable development for business' in that it deals with more than just the traditional, macro-level concerns of social, environmental and economic issues. As Dahlsrud (2008) points out, of 38 interpretations of CSR, most contained more than mere rehearsals of the sustainable development-influenced 'triple bottom line'. The five most common components of CSR included in most, although not all, statements were stakeholder engagement by business; the voluntary nature of the commitment to (greater) responsibility; and consideration of the full range of social, economic *and* environmental dimensions and implications of business decisions. The latter point is significant because it emphasises once more that CSR should not be about selectivity; rather, responsible firms should aspire to whole business approaches and be responsible across the piece. Finally, given the wide range of labels, monikers and descriptors used to characterise responsible business administration, in researching this form of activity within travel, tourism and hospitality organisations there is a need to set the search parameters carefully. As the concept is multi-faceted, research that claims to contribute to the body of knowledge on CSR in the tourism sector is conceptually inappropriate if it focuses exclusively on just one domain of responsibility.

CSR research on travel, tourism and hospitality organisations

Research on CSR in the tourism sector falls into two broad categories. The first (and smaller) group of studies is consistent with the view of CSR as a complex, integrative multi-dimensional concept; a second (but much larger group) contains CSR-related studies (i.e. studies that focus on only one aspect of CSR). In the latter, CSR is viewed in a more liberal, flexible and often selective manner where there is only partial coverage of the five key components of the concept. Often such studies are on topics that pertain to, and will be of interest to, tourism academics and practitioners of CSR. Ultimately though, their primary focus is elsewhere (e.g. business ethics, pro-poor tourism, supply chain management, codes of conduct, 'green' or 'social' marketing, eco-labelling and certification schemes).

Most conspicuous among the first group have been a series of studies on the nature of CSR activity; in other words, how far has the concept penetrated the tourism sector and to what extent is CSR proactively practiced, promoted and managed within tourism business and organisations? For example, in an important early contribution Miller (2001) interviewed 35 senior representatives of major operators in the UK tourism industry and found that responsibility was not as widespread as might have been expected for reasons of industry structure and fear of negative PR. Notwithstanding, the market offered the potential to trigger more responsible behaviour from the industry. Sheldon and Park (2011) demonstrated a high level of awareness in their sample of 274 American business. The majority had engaged in some form of CSR activity and nearly a quarter had a designated lead for CSR. Environmental, rather than socio-cultural, actions had been favoured while the main barriers to further implementation were a lack of resources and understanding of the next steps. Reporting activities among the top 150 hotel companies were examined by de Grosbois (2012). Nearly three-quarters were able to demonstrate a commitment to CSR in one aspect or another, but only just over one-third were able to provide details of goals, fewer still reported on how they performed, and just under one-third presented no information about their CSR activities whatsoever. Holcomb et al. (2007) closely examined responsibility reporting among ten top hotel chains. It was notable that 80 per cent had some form of socially responsible reporting, usually relating to charitable activities. There were, however, conspicuous gaps in reporting on the environment, CSR vision and values. Most recently, in a novel twist, Font et al. (2012: 1544) have identified what they term a 'disclosure-performance gap'. They benchmarked the CSR policies and practices of ten international hotel groups and found that 'corporate systems are not necessarily reflective of actual operations'. Larger hotels groups had more comprehensive policies accompanied by larger gaps in implementation. Conversely, while smaller hotel groups tended to concentrate on environmental management, there was greater congruence between what they claimed and delivered.

Collectively, this and other work like it raises two questions. The first is how best to judge the level of activity within the sector? An immediate answer may depend, metaphorically, on whether the glass is half empty or half full. There is clear evidence of activity taking place in the sector and some may even contend that this progress is more widespread than current empirical research has reported or indeed is able to capture. An alternative view may be that it is concerning that such a widespread idea in business administration and education would appear not to have permeated among an even-wider proportion of tourism enterprises. From a more scholarly perspective, the second question is – as worthy and as informative as each of these studies is in its own right – how best to judge the current level of understanding of CSR in the tourism sector? First of all, it is useful to put the overall size of the corpus into perspective. In their analysis of trends in CSR research across business and management studies, Aguinis and Glavas (2012) examined 690 journal articles, books and book chapters. In their review of tourism studies of CSR, Coles *et al.* (2013) identified fewer than 50 contributions that have been published since 2000 in which CSR has been considered in the more conceptually appropriate sense.

In fact, there has been a clear but modest increase in interest since the middle of the last decade. One possible reason for this may have been a Think Tank held by Business Education for Sustainable Tourism (BEST) in 2006 which brought the subject to greater prominence among the tourism academy. At this meeting, 19 papers were presented; Dwyer and Sheldon (2007: 94) subsequently published an agenda for future research. Their list of over 50 potential topics was 'intended to be indicative of the challenges for research rather than a definitive set of research topics'. Be that as it may, many of the topics had been the subject of attention already in other sectors which, in turn, inferred that research on tourism CSR was some way behind that of other sectors of economic activity even at that time. Moreover, it is not entirely clear whether the knowledge gap has closed in the interim. Although their agenda highlighted many fruitful ideas to pursue, the rate of increase in tourism studies of CSR would not appear to have matched the burgeoning literature in other sectors. One potential criticism that could be levelled at their comprehensive exposition is that it presents what appears to be a daunting task with little sense of where the academy should first focus its efforts.

Of course, tourism research on CSR is a subset of a larger body of knowledge on CSR in management and business studies. One way to evaluate progress in understanding tourism CSR is to compare current studies with the work conducted on other sectors of economic activity. Several meta-analyses of CSR research have been published that identify broad themes that characterise the literature beyond tourism. For instance, Lindgreen and Swaen (2010) identified five strands of research on CSR which provide an initial framework for such a benchmarking exercise, namely: studies of CSR implementation; the business case for CSR; measurement of CSR; stakeholder engagement; and CSR communications. Implementation refers to putting responsibility into practice while research on measurement examines the many technologies (i.e. indexes and reporting schemes) that are used to monitor and report on responsibility. Research on the business case focuses on the pragmatic issue of whether it makes sense for commercial organisations to act in a more responsible manner. The penultimate theme concerns identifying the stakeholders connected to particular organisations, the nature of their respective stakes, and how their social relations are mediated with the business. Finally, there has been considerable analysis of how and why organisations communicate, not least because this can play a major role in the success of CSR programmes or initiatives.

Examined against this broad framework, Coles *et al.* (2013) argue that tourism studies of CSR have made notable advances ostensibly in the areas of implementation, the (narrow) business case, and stakeholder engagement, especially at the destination level. In contrast, measurement and communications have been largely overlooked. As noted above, tourism research on implementation has focused primarily on awareness and understanding of the term within the sector as well as the type of practices and activities that are being conducted 'in the name of CSR'. There has been notable work, especially through a suite of studies, on the narrow rationale for (more widespread) adoption of CSR through analyses of corporate financial performance (Lee & Heo 2009; Lee & Park 2009, 2010). Perhaps not surprisingly given the emphasis on stakeholders in research on sustainable tourism during the last decade, several studies have concentrated on how they interpret and respond to the claims and practices of responsibility by organisations. Indeed, the interaction between Intrawest and the local community to develop Whistler–Blackcomb in an appropriate manner has been a notable instance of a long-standing research interest on stakeholders in tourism CSR (see e.g. Williams *et al.* 2007). As the next step, the academy was encouraged to focus on the wider business case and measurement as two mutually reinforcing themes. In a sector traditionally dominated by short business horizons, the benefits of acting in a more responsible manner have to be much clearer, while claims that the sector is acting more responsibly ring hollow if there is insufficient corroboration (Coles *et al.* 2013).

Knowledge production on CSR in the tourism sector

The juxtaposition of tourism research on CSR with the mainstream body of knowledge is instructive in several further ways. The relationship between the two literatures may be characterised as reticent. There has been little reference to tourism studies of CSR in the mainstream corpus, while the latter has only selectively drawn upon the former. Arguably, given the size and scope of the respective literatures, the tourism academy has more to gain from greater engagement with the mainstream. Yet, very few studies of tourism CSR engage with theoretical and analytical frameworks developed from research on other sectors. To date, the most routine form of engagement has been to draw on key concepts and approaches to delimiting CSR set out by 'thought leaders' like Friedman, Carroll and Porter.

In contrast, there has been far less attention paid to more recent innovations in theory. For example, Ketola (2006) has pointed out that, although CSR is a multi-faceted concept, in practice within organisations each dimension is not afforded equal importance. Instead, she noted nine permutations or 'profiles' that typified CSR behaviour. Coles *et al.* (2011) found that this framework had important explanatory potential in focus group research on key stakeholders' expectations of the responsibility of low-fares airlines (LFAs) in three UK regions during the recession. Most starkly, the group from Northern Ireland took an anthropogenic view, whereas those in the Highlands and Islands of Scotland had a more techno-centric perspective. In earlier work, they found that a series of frameworks on the implementation of CSR were helpful in framing the progress made by LFAs (Coles *et al.* 2009). For example, Mirvis and Googins' (2006) four-stage diagnostic model offered a way to benchmark CSR implementation. Although difficult to apply, on the balance of the evidence, CSR activity among LFAs was best described at that time as 'elementary' or (for certain dimensions) 'engaged' (i.e. at the two lower levels of development). Furthermore, Kramer and Kania's (2006) distinction between 'offensive' and 'defensive' strategies suggested that LFAs viewed CSR more defensively as an opportunity to protect brand and reputation. This is a recurring theme. Among Dutch tour operators, Van de Mosselaer *et al.* (2012: 87) argue that there has been a shift from CSR as a more defensive mode of thinking, to a more positive, proactive position resulting from the 'institutionalisation of moral responsibility'. Central to this reorientation has been the advocacy of trade associations 'in promoting CSR in the industry itself'.

This work and a range of studies on the Hilton and Scandic hotel chains (Bohdanowicz & Zientara 2008, 2009) are notable for a further epistemological reason, namely: they highlight the benefits from primary data collection on CSR within tourism business and through access to a wide range of internal stakeholders. As CSR is characterised by an internal–external duality, this methodological observation may seem odd; however, the majority of tourism research on CSR has been conducted from outside the firm 'looking in' as it were. Instead, it has relied heavily, in some cases even exclusively on secondary data sources with the case study as a principal methodological approach. Alongside CSR reporting produced by organisations themselves, particularly rich veins have been data they have submitted as part of corporate disclosures and processed by business data services (Lee & Heo 2009; Lee & Park 2009, 2010). Press releases, web pages, newspapers and other documents already in the public domain have been widely adopted (see Holcomb *et al.* 2007; Coles *et al.* 2009, 2011; Cowper-Smith & de Grosbois 2010; de Grosbois 2012).

There has been some discussion about the implications of the predominant methodological approaches and data sources. On the one hand, Bohdanowicz and Zientara (2012: 114) contend that secondary sources are reliable because in the information age claims about responsibility can be easily verified and hence there are unjustifiable corporate risks for companies in providing false or inaccurate information. On the other hand, several studies have concluded that secondary sources only partially represent the full extent of CSR strategies, practices or initiatives going on within particular business or across the sector (Holcomb *et al.* 2007; Font and Zientara 2012). Attempts to compare CSR practices among major airlines were frustrated by variability in the quality and quantity of the content they had put in the public domain (Cowper-Smith & de Grosbois 2010). In turn, this points more widely to the fact that variations in the availability of, and access to, data sources almost inevitably means that each study uses different evidence, measures and/or surrogates of CSR. Allied to the uniqueness inherent in the case-study approach, this makes inter-business, cross-sectoral and geographical comparisons awkward to the point of being somewhat meaningless because they are so general. Bohdanowicz and Zientarac's (2012) impressive survey of environmental initiatives among top international hotel chains makes this point all too clearly. Theirs is an extremely comprehensive portrayal of an array of measures hotels have introduced as testament to their commitment to environmental responsibility. Their account reinforces the view in the mainstream literature that the precise nature of CSR activity in an organisation is socially constructed around its individual corporate priorities. Clearly, tourism research on CSR would benefit from greater empirical observation within the firm and the mixing of methods and data sources allows for a more complete view of CSR pertaining to an organisation to be formed (Coles *et al.* 2009). However, making clear, direct and meaningful comparisons on a 'like-for-like' basis among business or across different types of travel, tourism and hospitality business has been – and currently remains – extremely difficult.

Conclusion

In essence, CSR is an approach to business administration where, in addition to the more traditional issues of profitability and other shareholder concerns, closer voluntary consideration of ethical, social and environmental issues as well as the organisation's varied stakeholders is taken in operations and value creation. Clearly, there are close conceptual connections with the principles of sustainable development, but CSR should be understood as more than merely 'sustainable development for business'. It is an approach that requires business to consider its purpose more carefully, almost in the sense of making a case for a licence to operate. No longer is it possible – or indeed welcome – for a business to exist solely for financial gain without consideration of its wider responsibilities to a range of human (i.e. societies, communities) and non-human actors (i.e. the environment, culture) across the range of its internal and external activities, operations and practices. In an age of sustainable development, its right to operate is accompanied by a series of obligations. These are especially important considerations for those sectors, like tourism, where business routinely operate across borders, between cultures, and where there are potentially strong tensions between producers and residents (i.e. hosts and guests).

A more sympathetic reading would be that research on the tourism sector suggests that this is understood, if it has not always been easy for scholars to verify empirically. Rather, the true extent of CSR activity in the tourism sector – and hence its contribution to sustainable development – is difficult to discern, arguably even under-represented. Responsibility is, in fact, a more widespread ethos and practice if a more flexible definition and selective instances, not whole business approaches, are considered. Of course, the empirical evidence can be read quite differently and this position can be readily contested. However, irrespective of which way the discourse is read, the fact is that tourism studies of CSR are still largely focused on the extent to which CSR is practised and hence how far the case for more responsible approaches to business administration has been successfully made. At a time when the tourism sector is under fire for its contributions to carbon emissions and global environmental change (see Chapter 3), this places tourism scholarship of CSR some way behind that dealing with other high-impact sectors like mining, logging and tobacco. As Lee (2008) has argued, the nature of enquiry has shifted elsewhere and the predominant focus is now on how to make CSR function most effectively and in the best interests of as wide a range of stakeholders as possible. In other words, elsewhere the debate has shifted from legitimation and justification of CSR towards careful examination of the extent to which CSR may result in the most beneficial behaviour change and contributions to sustainable development. The pillars of more sustainable development should not be erected on shaky foundations, however. Further research is necessary on establishing the wider business case as well as measuring more precisely the extent of activity. It is only through the latter in particular, that an adequate evidence base will be assembled and a clear, less contentious, view of the state of CSR activity in the tourism sector will emerge.

Key Reading

Coles, T.E., Fenclova, E. and Dinan, C.R. (2013) 'Tourism and corporate social responsibility: A critical review and research agenda', *Tourism Management Perspectives*, 6: 122–41.

de Grosbois, D. (2012) 'Corporate social responsibility reporting by the global hotel industry: Commitment, initiatives and performance', *International Journal of Hospitality Management* 31: 896–905.

Font, X., Walmsley, A., Cogotti, S., McCombes, L. and Häusler, N. (2012) 'Corporate social responsibility: The disclosure-performance gap', *Tourism Management*, 33: 1544–53.

Miller, G. (2001) 'Corporate responsibility in the UK tourism industry', *Tourism Management*, 22: 589–98.

Sheldon, P. and Park, S-Y. (2011) 'An exploratory study of corporate social responsibility in the US travel industry', *Journal of Travel Research*, 50: 392–407.

References

Aguinis, H. and Glavas, A. (2012) 'What we know and don't know about corporate social responsibility: A review and research agenda', *Journal of Management*, 38: 932–68.

Bohdanowicz, P. and Zientara, P. (2008) 'Corporate social responsibility in hospitality: Issues and implication. A case study of Scandic', *Scandinavian Journal of Hospitality and Tourism*, 8: 271–93.

—— (2009) 'Hotel companies' contribution to improving the quality of life of local communities and the well-being of their employees', *Tourism and Hospitality Research*, 9: 147–58.

—— (2012) 'CSR-inspired environmental initiatives in top hotel chains', in D. Leslie (ed.) *Tourism Enterprises and the Sustainability Agenda Across Europe*, Farnham: Ashgate.

Coles, T.E., Dinan, C.R. and Fenclova, E. (2009) *Corporate Social Responsibility Among Low-Fares Airlines: Current Practices and Future Trends*, Exeter: University of Exeter. Available at: www.exeter.ac.uk/slt/newspublications/publications/ (accessed 7 June 2010).

Coles, T.E., Fenclova, E. and Dinan, C. (2011) 'Responsibilities, recession and the tourism sector: Perspectives on CSR among low-fares airlines during the economic downturn in the UK', *Current Issues in Tourism*, 14: 519–36.

—— (2013) 'Tourism and corporate social responsibility: A critical review and research agenda', *Tourism Management Perspectives*, 6: 122–41.

Commission of the European Communities (CEC) (2006) *Implementing the Partnership for Growth and Jobs: Making Europe a Pole of Excellence on Corporate Social Responsibility*. Available at: http://eur-lex.europa.eu/LexUriServ.do?uri=COM:2006:0136:FIN:EN:PDF (accessed 25 November 2008).

Cowper-Smith, A. and de Grosbois, D. (2010) 'The adoption of corporate social responsibility practices in the airline industry', *Journal of Sustainable Tourism*, 19: 59–77.

Dahlsrud, A. (2008) 'How corporate social responsibility is defined: An analysis of 37 definitions', *Corporate Social Responsibility and Environmental Management*, 15: 1–13.

de Grosbois, D. (2012) 'Corporate social responsibility reporting by the global hotel industry: Commitment, initiatives and performance', *International Journal of Hospitality Management*, 31: 896–905.

Dwyer, L. and Sheldon, P.J. (2007) 'Corporate social responsibility for sustainable tourism', *Tourism Review International*, 11: 91–95.

Fenclova, E. and Coles, T.E. (2011) 'Charitable partnerships among travel and tourism businesses: Perspectives from low-fares airlines', *International Journal of Tourism Research*, 13: 337–54.

Font, X., Walmsley, A., Cogotti, S., McCombes, L. and Häusler, N. (2012) 'Corporate social responsibility: The disclosure–performance gap', *Tourism Management*, 33: 1544–53.

Friedman, M. (1970) 'The social responsibility of business is to increase its profits', *The New York Times Magazine*: 32–33 and 122–26.

Holcomb, J.L., Upchurch, R.S. and Okumus, F. (2007) 'Corporate social responsibility: What are the top hotel companies reporting?' *International Journal of Contemporary Hospitality Management*, 19: 461–75.

Ketola, T. (2006) 'From CR-psychopaths to responsible corporations: Waking up the inner sleeping beauty of companies', *Corporate Social Responsibility and Environmental Management*, 13: 98–107.

Kramer, M. and Kania, J. (2006) 'Changing the game: Leading corporations switch from defence to offence in solving global problems', *Stanford Social Innovation Review*, Spring: 20–27.

Lee, M-D.P. (2008) 'A review of the theories of corporate social responsibility: Its evolutionary path and the road ahead', *International Journal of Management Reviews*, 10: 53–73.

Lee, S. and Heo, C.Y. (2009) 'Corporate social responsibility and customer satisfaction among US publicly traded hotels and restaurants', *International Journal of Hospitality Management*, 28: 635–37.

Lee, S. and Park, S.-Y. (2009) 'Do socially responsible activities help hotels and casinos achieve their financial goals?', *International Journal of Hospitality Management*, 28: 105–12.

—— (2010) 'Financial impacts of socially responsible activities on airline companies', *Journal of Hospitality & Tourism Research*, 34: 185–203.

Lindgreen, A. and Swaen, V. (2010) 'Corporate social responsibility', *International Journal of Management Studies*, 12: 1–7.

Miller, G. (2001) 'Corporate responsibility in the UK tourism industry', *Tourism Management*, 22: 589–98.

Mirvis, P. and Googins, B. (2006) 'Stages of corporate citizenship', *California Management Review*, 48: 104–26.

Plume, K. (2009) 'CSR – Einführendes zu einem Trend', in S. Krause (ed.) *Dokunmentation des Symposiums Corporate Social Responsibility im Tourismus*, Hamburg: GATE e.V.

Porter, M.E. and Kramer, M.R. (2006) 'Strategy & society: The link between competitive advantage and corporate social responsibility', *Harvard Business Review*, December: 1–14.

Sheldon, P. and Park, S-Y. (2011) 'An exploratory study of corporate social responsibility in the US travel industry', *Journal of Travel Research*, 50: 392–407.

Van de Mosselaer, F., van der Duim, R. and van Wijk, J. (2012) 'Corporate social responsibility in the tour operating industry: The case of Dutch outbound tour operators', in D. Leslie (ed.) *Tourism Enterprises and the Sustainability Agenda Across Europe*, Farnham: Ashgate.

WBCSD (1999) Corporate Social Responsibility, Genf: World Business Council for Sustainable Development.

Williams, P., Gill, A. and Ponsford, I. (2007) 'Corporate social responsibility at tourism destinations: Toward a social licence to operate', *Tourism Review International*, 11: 133–44.

22

Wildlife tourism

"Call it consumption!"

James Higham and Debbie Hopkins

Wildlife tourism Watching and interacting with animals, incorporating free-ranging and captive wildlife, fauna and flora (Newsome & Rodger 2012).

Global governance "The sum of the many ways individuals and institutions, public and private, manage their common affairs" (Carlsson *et al.* 1995: 2). Addressed in this chapter through three meta-discourses: green governmentality, ecological modernization and civic environmentalism.

Global environmental change Human-induced environmental change on a global scale, or a significant fraction of the total/global environmental phenomenon (Gössling & Hall 2006) including endangered species.

Whale watching Commercial tourist ventures including opportunities for people to observe, swim with, touch, or feed cetaceans in the wild from shore, sea or air (Higham, Bejder & Williams, 2014).

Non-consumptive wildlife tourism Commercial tourist interactions with wildlife which do not result in the immediate/permanent removal of individual animals from a population; contrasts consumptive/lethal human interactions (e.g. hunting, fishing).

Introduction

Human interactions with wildlife represent a significant and growing part of the global tourism economy (Newsome & Rodger 2012). While these interactions range across the wild–captive continuum, this chapter addresses human interactions with free-ranging wild animals. Phenomenal growth in demand for wildlife tourism (Curtin 2010) has been predicated upon the widespread assumption that viewing non–human animals in the wild is non-consumptive, and thus more desirable than consumptive activities such as hunting. The growth in demand for wildlife experiences, now considered to be a $46 billion (£30 billion) global industry has been well documented in the literature (Newsome & Rodger 2012). Whale watching, which is used to illustrate various discussions throughout this chapter, highlights this remarkable growth. In a relatively short timeframe, whale watching has developed into a US$2.1 billion *per annum* global industry (O'Connor *et al.* 2010), with considerable capacity for further growth (Cisneros-Montemayor *et al.* 2010). Industrial wildlife tourism on this scale has been described as a form of periodic transformation in the global capitalist economy (Neves 2010).

This global transformation calls for a critical analysis of wildlife tourism. The field is now well served by research that measures the ecological impact of tourism, using the methods and techniques of the natural sciences (Williams *et al.* 2002; Bejder *et al.* 2006; Cui, Xu & Wall 2012). This research has informed debates surrounding planning and management at sites where wildlife–tourist interactions take place (see Higham, Bejder & Lusseau 2009). However, this chapter seeks to broaden this focus to question the global context within which local wildlife tourism experiences are produced and consumed. It situates wildlife tourism in the context of global environmental change and biodiversity governance (Gössling & Hall 2006; Hall 2007). Importantly, the macro scale of analysis brings global threats to biodiversity, including habitat destruction, pollution and resource degradation (among others), into the wildlife tourism conversation. Within this context, a critique of the concept of "non-consumptive" wildlife tourism is central to this chapter. Specifically, it addresses the fallacy of "non-consumptive" human interactions with wildlife, when viewed through the lenses of global environmental change (Gössling & Hall 2006) and global capitalist transformation (Neves 2010).

Human interactions with wildlife: global discourses

"Non-consumptive" wildlife viewing has grown from humble origins (Higham, Bejder & Williams 2014). Once the domain of modest numbers of dedicated enthusiasts, or "specialists" (Duffus & Dearden 1990), it has moved rapidly into the mainstream of commercial tourism (Knight 2009). With this has come a proliferation and diversification of opportunities to encounter (Newsome & Rodger 2012), and platforms from which to view wildlife (Higham, Lusseau & Hendry 2008). Furthermore, it has been associated with increasing spatio-temporal pressures to accommodate tourists in proximity to wild animals (Lusseau & Higham 2004). Successful commercial wildlife viewing concentrates groups of tourists in locations where interactions with wild animals are predictable and constant (Whittaker 1997). This is typically in critical wildlife habitats (Higham & Lusseau 2004), where important feeding, resting, socialising and reproduction behaviours occur. This course of tourism development is associated with widespread sustainablity concerns (Higham *et al.* 2014). Local wildlife tourism practices are, of course, set within the context of global governance, which is a context that may lead to the foundational concept of "non-consumptive" wildlife tourism being drawn into question.

Global scale: discourses/governance and biodiversity

Given the industrial scale that wildlife tourism has assumed (Neves 2010; Newsome & Rodger 2012), a starting point for our critique is the global wildlife tourism system. The global scale of analysis may be situated within discourses of global environmental change and the biodiversity crisis (Hall 2007). Global biodiversity describes the degree of diversity of life forms on earth and the accompanying genetic diversity, which is implicated in human health in various ways. The emergence of anatomically modern humans has been associated with the Holocene extinction phase, with catastrophic and ongoing biodiversity loss arising principally from wholesale habitat modification and ecological destruction (Gössling & Hall 2006). Global biodiversity loss arises from a wide range of physical, social, economic and political issues (Gössling & Hall 2006). The global response to the biodiversity crisis has been led by the United Nations Convention on Biodiversity (UNCBD), which was established at the Earth Summit (Rio de Janeiro) in 1992. Ten years later, at the World Summit on Sustainable Development (Johannesburg, 2002), the 2010 Biodiversity Target was established with the aim of stabilizing biodiversity loss by that year.

By 2006 biodiversity action plans (species recovery plans in the USA) had been established in four countries (Great Britain, New Zealand, Tanzania and the United States). However, the failure to arrest the global decline in biodiversity resulted in 2010 being declared the UN International Year of Biodiversity; in recognition of the continuing biodiversity crisis, the UN has declared 2011–20 the United Nations Decade of Biodiversity (UNEP 2013). The UNDBD addresses six thematic programmes (agricultural; dry and sub-humid lands,; forests; inland waters; island, marine and coastal; and mountain biodiversity). It also identifies nineteen "cross-cutting issues" that are considered important to all thematic areas (UNEP 2013), one of which is titled "tourism and biodiversity." The rhetoric associated with tourism is illuminating. Tourism continues to be recognized as "…the world's largest single industry" (UNEP 2013: np), and Ahmed Djoghlaf (Executive Secretary, Convention on Biological Diversity) observes that: "The powerful forces that shape the essence of tourism, including the human urge to see and experience the natural world, must continue to be harnessed to support the achievement of the goals of the Convention" (UNEP 2013: np). This position assumes the compatibility of economic growth through tourism, and the goals of the UN biodiversity convention.

The thematic programmes addressing global biodiversity are integrated with manifold cross-cutting issues (e.g. climate change, economics and trade, food production systems, transport and communication, education and public awareness), and have implicated many sectors including energy, agriculture and forestry (UNEP 2013). It is remarkable, however, that hitherto direct address to tourism has been so limited (Gössling & Hall 2006). Holden (2009) states that this will change as tourism becomes increasingly constrained by environmental policy. Tourism is an energy-intensive and natural resource-dependent industry (Becken 2008; see Chapter 3) that both contributes to and is harmed by the effects of global environmental change including biodiversity loss. This "resource paradox" gives urgency to discussions surrounding the tourism–environment relationship (Williams & Ponsford 2009). Yet there is complexity in defining the boundaries of tourism, which in turn, creates difficulty in allocating responsibility or singling out one sector, heavily integrated with "cross-cutting issues," as environmentally benign (Perch-Nielsen et al. 2010). In this chapter we engage three "meta-discourses": green governmentality, ecological modernization and civic environmentalism, to explore the fields of tourism, environmental governance and biodiversity. In doing so, we also critique global governance frameworks specifically as they relate to national and regional/local scales of wildlife tourism.

Governance: The global–local nexus

There are widely diverging definitions of governance (Biermann & Pattberg 2012). While the Commission on Global Governance defines governance as "the sum of the many ways individuals and institutions, public and private, manage their common affairs" (Carlsson et al. 1995: 2), other definitions include "the combined efforts of international and transnational regimes" (Young 1999: 11) and "the sum of the world's formal and informal rule systems" (Rosenau 2002: 4). Similarities in these definitions of global environmental governance include the involvement of a wide range of actors and groups of actors charged with the management of global commons resources. Consequently, global environmental governance is often called upon to address discourses of environmental sustainability and is deeply embedded in the sustainable development rhetoric (e.g. 65th meeting (2010) of the General Assembly, the United Nations). The physical and social complexity of global environmental resource governance has received academic attention (Pahl-Wostl 2009; Underdal 2010), identifying that globally relevant environmental issues are often characterized by vast temporal and spatial scales, along with scientific uncertainty (Meadowcroft 2007; Rauschmayer *et al.* 2009).

Global environmental resource governance processes are used to "formalize" human–environment relationships. However, preventing the overuse, depletion and eventual exhaustion of natural resources (including flora and fauna) is no simple task. The development of modern society on a trajectory of unsustainable growth, parallels the relentless mass consumption of natural resources, which, in turn, has triggered a range of chronic environmental issues including biodiversity loss (Carter 2007; Pelletier 2010). Current global governance regimes are often depicted as technocentric, with a political and scientific focus, and neglecting the societal dimensions of these issues. Consequently, socio-cultural aspects have been added to some definitions of global resource governance (Adger *et al.* 2009), thereby engaging governance systems not only with the environment but also with society. Nevertheless, the human–environment relationship has been compounded by governance failures (Bäckstrand *et al.* 2010), and the increasingly complex landscape for resource governance and management to address the global environmental crisis.

Historically, the economic and developmental successes and intentions of the tourism industry have generated greater attention than concerns over the unsustainable natural resource consumption of the tourism sector (Romeril 1989; Cater 1995). Tourism is dependent on finite resources, and operates in delicate ecosystems including small islands and alpine regions (Cohen 1978). The implications of global environmental change for tourism, as manifest through climate change, habitat loss and resource depletion, are serious and now widely documented (Gössling & Hall 2006). Yet the contribution of the tourism industry to global environmental change and biodiversity loss is yet to receive serious attention. The UNCBD and national biodiversity action plans (where they exist) represent important global governance regimes. International non-government organizations (e.g. Greenpeace, WWF, International Fund for Animal Welfare (IFAW)) and inter-governmental commissions (e.g. International Whaling Commission (IWC); Commission for the Conservation of Antarctic Marine Living Resources (CCAMLR)) also contribute to the global governance of wildlife tourism, bearing influence over regional/local policies and practices.

In order to examine and critique environmental governance systems across spatial scales, three "meta-discourses" in environmental governance (Bäckstrand & Lövbrand 2007): green governmentality, ecological modernization and civic environmentalism, are used as conceptual lenses and provide a way to frame the changes and developments in environmental resource governance over time. The main biodiversity narratives translate from the wider environmental discourses, including the many dualisms which help to perpetuate the global environmental crisis: local v global, North v South, public v private, decentralized v centralized, economy v environment (Bäckstrand & Lövbrand 2007). Moreover, the systems in place to govern environmental resources (e.g. institutions, bureaucracies etc.) are limited by conflicts, power, knowledge asymmetry and irrationality of actors (Paavola 2007; Pelletier 2010; Bäckstrand *et al.* 2010).

Green governmentality

Green governmentality has emerged from the Foucauldian concepts of "biopower" and "governmentality" (Darier 1999), combined with a "green twist" (Bäckstrand & Lövbrand 2007: 54), whereby governance transitions to include tenants of the human–environment relationship. Nevertheless, green governmentality is depicted as a top-down discourse, technocentric and expert-oriented. As a result, alternative (non–elite) understandings of environmental resource issues are marginalized with elite perspectives favoured and consequently power asymmetries can be perpetuated through the green governmentality framework (Boehmer-Christiansen 2003). Furthermore, Rutherford (2007) argues that green governmentality is intertwined with narratives of the "fragile earth" warranting regulation, management and governing. Indeed, she goes on to argue that even some non-governmental organizations are functioning within this framework, with regulatory, policymaking and environmental monitoring roles.

The green governmentality discourse is characterized by global scale power, mega-science and the prioritization of big business (Bäckstrand & Lövbrand 2007). The discourse is seen to be promoting the role of science in monitoring and recording the environment, thus suggesting manageability and control, or human stewardship of the natural environment (Rutherford 1999; Bäckstrand & Lövbrand 2007). This, Rutherford (2007) finds, has merged with growing connections between corporations and environmental funding; as evidenced by the Disney Wildlife Conservation Fund. Moreover, the dominance of green governmentality and scientific measurement of environmental resource issues presumes that scientific mapping can guide the human–environment relationship back to a point of sustainability (Crutzen 2002). This meta-discourse has dominated early environmental governance systems, and continues through to the present day's "framework-protocol" approach, and this includes the UN Convention on Biodiversity.

Ecological modernization

While green governmentality focuses on the capacity of centralized governance systems to "manage" the environment and measure environmental issues, the ecological modernization discourse is grounded in capitalist ideology, the promotion of private-level decision making (as opposed to state intervention) and capital accumulation. This is explained by Bäckstrand and Lövbrand (2007: 129) as: "the compatibility between economic growth and environmental protection." Thus ecological modernization identifies a synergy between a liberal market order and the goals of sustainable development. Proponents of green governmentality argue that capitalism has the capacity to be environmentally friendly resulting from the employment of "green regulations" (Hajer 1995). However, this discourse has been critiqued for proposing that institutions of modernity can resolve environmental problems, indeed Bäckstrand (2004: 710) finds a dichotomy between modernity as the "overarching cause of environmental destruction" and modernity as a solution for environmental ills. In terms of application, it has been argued that ecological modernization, as with many governance systems, works to neglect the inherently social elements of environmental degradation, resource depletion and biodiversity loss. This, in turn, reduces the importance of individuals and continues to focus on elite participation in policymaking endeavors.

Critiques of ecological modernization focus on what Christoff (1996) would describe as a "weak" form of ecological modernization. This form of ecological modernization is criticized for perpetuating centralized, top-down environmental governance, and the dominance of scientific elitism in environmental governance. "Weak" ecological modernization is also the "predominant discourse in global policy rhetoric and practice" (Bäckstrand & Lövbrand 2007: 129). This contrasts with a "strong" form of ecological modernization which, among other differences, calls for the participation and inclusion of civil society in environmental governance processes. Thus Christoff (1996) highlights the spectrum of ecological modernization thought, with the "strong" version providing a more nuanced application.

Overall, the ecological modernization meta-discourse differs from that of green governmentality by challenging state-centric, science-based negotiations. It promotes a decentralized liberal market order, through which business opportunities are sought through "green technologies." Thus the main difference between these meta-discourses is the reliance on government or business endeavor. Consequently, they are fairly compatible in terms of application – indeed it has been argued that global environmental governance relies on both green governmentality and ecological modernization concurrently (Bäckstrand & Lövbrand 2007). This is evident through the United Nations favored the "framework-protocol" method, which has been exercised through a range of environmental discourses during the past three decades.

Civic environmentalism

While green governmentality and ecological modernization are congruent in many of their main features, the meta-discourse of civic environmentalism has emerged as a counter-critique of the neoliberal framing of environmental governance. In essence, civic environmentalism argues that the two former narratives fail to prioritize the environment (Byrne *et al.* 2004). Dominant neoliberalism framing of environmental governance commodifies the environment, fails to challenge the rampant consumerism of the global North, and calls for *management* of nature. Much like ecological modernization, civic environmentalism has both "radical" and "reform"-oriented narratives. On the one hand, the "radical resistance" stance of civic environmentalism is highly critical of current environmental governance regimes. It emphasizes asymmetric power relations as a root cause of environmental degradation. Consequently, radical civic environmentalists advocate fundamental changes to current consumption-driven lifestyles and call for prioritization of the environment over the economy (Bäckstrand & Lövbrand 2007).

The reform-oriented account of civic environmentalism focuses on methodological differences and promotes multi-stakeholder participation to gain specialized, non-scientific expertise into environmental resource governance. It is argued that public confidence in multilateral institutions will increase as a result of enhanced accountability and transparency in the governance process. An additional benefit from this approach is the range of alternative voices which can gain prominence in the governance processes (Rauschmayer *et al.* 2009). Consequently, the civic environmentalism meta-discourse challenges the many dualisms confronting and adding complexity to global environmental politics by calling for "cross-sectorial cooperation between market, state and civil society actors" (Bäckstrand & Lövbrand 2007: 124).

The key distinctions between the three meta-discourses of green governmentality, ecological modernization and civic environmentalism are primarily analytical for there is significant interaction and overlap between them (Bäckstrand & Lövbrand 2007). Progress in understanding these discourses highlights wider-ranging perspectives, leading to spectrums of thought. For example, Fogel (2004) identifies an increasingly reflexive version of green governmentality, where local actors are introduced to the global policy arena in response to the local scale complexities which are often overlooked by global governance systems. This more moderate version of green governmentality draws parallels with the reform-oriented version of civic environmentalism, perhaps responding to the critiques provided from this discourse to develop UN-induced "good governance" (Van der Heijden 2008). Finally, reflexive green governmentality, strong ecological modernization and the reformist civic environmentalism discourse all situate global environmental crises within the context of the meta-sustainable development narratives. This was evidenced by Tschakert and Olsson (2005) who identified the synergies between the Conventions on Climate Change, Biodiversity, and Desertification.

Global human (tourist) interactions with wildlife

It is futile to consider wildlife tourism in isolation from the current global environmental crisis. It is here that the tenants of green governmentality and ecological modernization should be interrogated. The viability of wild animal populations must be understood within the context of a rapidly degrading global environment, wherein wild animals (individuals, populations and species) are subject to the overwhelming pressures of all forms of human exploitation, both direct and indirect (Gössling & Hall 2006), consumptive and "non-consumptive." Wildlife tourism must be situated within the broader global processes exerting influence upon species and genetic biodiversity. Within the context of global whale watching these influences, according to Williams (2014), include fisheries by-catch, vessel strikes, noise, toxic poisoning, the ingestion of plastics and other non-biodegradable materials, and other forms of chronic environmental pollution. Broader degradation of the coastal and marine environment arises from other inexorable pressures of human development: agricultural pesticides, tidal energy generation, seabed mining, and coastal/marine oil exploration and recovery, all of which are extending into more remote and extreme global environments (Hammond 2006; Williams 2014).

It is evident, then, that wildlife tourism can not be seen as a benign, "non-consumptive" activity, treated in isolation from the global environmental crisis. Wildlife viewing is now part of mainstream commercial tourism (Knight 2009). With this course of development has come a proliferation and diversification of opportunities to encounter wildlife (Higham, Lusseau & Hendry 2008), and growing pressures on wildlife populations that are already subject to the stresses of large-scale environmental change. It makes little sense, for example, to consider tourist viewing of puffins (*Fratercula arctica*) in the North Sea islands in isolation from the puffin wreck (population decimation) resulting from climatic change as manifest in prolonged extreme weather during the northern spring of 2013 (BBC 2013). The uncritical treatment of wildlife tourism under the circumstances does a disservice to the pursuit of sustainability.

Wild animals are also human-averse (Knight 2009) and respond to a human presence as they do any form of predation (Bejder *et al.* 2009). To ignore this tension is to remain entrenched in the neoliberal framing of green governmentality and ecological modernization. The global politics of whale watching have been driven by the economic development agenda (Higham *et al.* 2014). Whale watching has been morally elevated above whale hunting practices, without careful consideration of the potential impacts of this form of wildlife tourism (Neves 2010). To counter the case for continued whale hunting, whale watching has been portrayed as a form of nature conservation. The recent history of whale watching is one in which complex issues have been simply and uncritically stated based on intuitive appeal and politico-economic agendas (Neves 2010; Higham, Bejder & Williams 2014).

Little scholarly attention has been paid to the consequences of global environmental change for wildlife tourism (Gössling & Hall 2006). Hall (2007) highlights the importance of scale in assessing the sustainability of wildlife tourism, while Becken and Schellhorn (2007) call for an "open-system" approach to this subject. They argue that local/regional studies are incomplete, in the absence of attention paid to the global system. It is under the open-system approach, they claim, that consideration of global issues "clearly challenge the widely accepted link between (wildlife) tourism and nature conservation" (Becken & Schellhorn 2007: 99). There is little doubt, for example, that changes in sea surface temperature due to global climate change will alter the distribution and abundance of cetaceans, with implications for the presence and frequency of occurrence of species that are of interest to tourists (Lambert, et al. 2010). While whale watch operators will be subject most immediately to such changes, it is climate change mitigation that poses a considerable challenge to the entire industry, not to mention the tourism sector more broadly (Gössling & Hall 2006; Gössling & Upham 2009; Scott, Hall & Gössling 2012). These issues deeply challenge the mainstream neoliberal rhetoric of green governmentality and ecological modernization in ways that cannot be ignored.

Human–wildlife interactions: "Call it consumption!"

The language of "non-consumptive" wildlife tourism is long-standing. It dates to the "Whales Alive" conference (Boston, MA) in 1983 where the IWC made the case for new forms of "non-consumptive" whale utility (O'Connor et al. 2010). The notion of "non-consumptive" whale watching, in contrast to the immediate and lethal outcomes of hunting, is intuitively appealing (Duffus & Dearden 1990). The two practices: one that is lethal and the other that protects target animals appear to have little or nothing in common (Knight 2009). In fact, the broad treatment of human interactions with wild animals highlights the indistinct boundaries between apparently distinct forms of human utility. The "Big Five" of African wildlife tourism refers to the African elephant (*Loxodonta Africana*), lion (*Panthera leo*), rhinoceros (*Diceros bicornis*), buffalo (*Syncerus caffer*) and leopard (*Panthera pardus)*, which derives from their earlier status as hunting trophies. Wildlife tourism is, in this case, simply a variation of the hunting safari. The consumptive/non-consumptive binary invites critique because there are, in fact, inherent contradictions in such unitary terminology (Tremblay 2001).

When subject to critique, it emerges that the consumptive/non-consumptive dichotomy is deceptive and misleading (Lemelin 2006). It is, in fact, the case that hunting is lethal at the level of individual animals but may simultaneously be sustainable at the population level if carefully managed (Tremblay 2001). Furthermore, wildlife viewing may be described as a form of "ocular consumption" (Lemelin 2006). While the act of viewing may be relatively harmless, the development of industrial-scale commercial viewing comes with various elements of environmental transformation (Lemelin 2006). Such elements of transformation for so-called "non-consumptive" wildlife tourism may include increased volume and speed-of-surface marine transportation, with implications for cetacean vessel strikes (Lammers, Pack, Lyman & Espiritu 2013), which may negatively impact local animal populations and the capacity of wildlife tourism systems (Higham & Lusseau 2007, 2008).

Building on this line of debate, Knight (2009) states that the practices of hunting and viewing wild animals actually have much in common. In order to locate and observe wild animals, tourist operators use the techniques of the hunter. Both systematically identify and pursue target animals. Both trigger alarm and anti-predatory responses in these wild animals due to human approach (Tremblay 2001; Knight 2009). Tourist satisfaction is determined by close, unobstructed and sustained interaction (Orams 2000) and perhaps feeding and touch (Muloin 1998) all of which may cause non-lethal but cumulative stress (Orams, 2004). Ultimately, "in both contexts nature is produced first and foremost according to capitalist principles, which problematizes the pervasive assumption that whale-watching correlates primarily and directly with conservation" (Neves 2010: 719).

Applying evolutionary theory to the non-lethal impacts of whale watching Bejder *et al.* (2009) consider how wild animals respond to non-lethal forms of human disturbance. They propose that wild animals use highly evolved anti-predator responses which do not distinguish between lethal and non-lethal stimuli (Christiansen & Lusseau, 2014). Rather, animals take exactly the same ecological considerations into account whenever human disturbance or any other risk of predation is encountered (Lima & Dill 1990; Frid & Dill 2002; Beale & Monaghan 2004). These contributions add further weight to the argument that whale watching, while non-lethal in the immediate spatial-temporal context of the wildlife encounter, may have biologically significant consequences for cetaceans (Bejder *et al.* 2006). This draws the assumptions of "non-consumptive" wildlife tourism into deep question. In the words of Meletis and Campbell (2007: 850), "call it consumption!"

Case Study

Humans and whales – the global/local nexus

Viewing cetaceans – the "giants of the deep"– in the open ocean triggers emotions of awe and intrigue (Higham *et al.* 2014). Few wild animal species have such deeply engaging and emotional appeal (Hammond 2006). The experiential value of cetaceans has resulted in expressions of widespread abhorrence towards whale hunting, and the phenomenal growth of whale watching (O'Connor *et al.* 2010; Cisneros-Montemayor *et al.* 2010). Whale hunting practices have historically been the subject of conflicting views in terms of utility, sustainability, economic development, cultural identity, nationhood and sovereignty (Allen 2014). Despite the near extinction of many species of whales (Hammond 2006) "scientific," commercial and traditional whaling continues in some parts of the world, while whales have become "standard bearers" of marine conservation (Corkeron 2006), even in parts of those societies where whale hunting persists.

Global governance relating to whale stocks is the charge of the International Whaling Commission (IWC) which, in 1982, adopted the moratorium on commercial whaling (Higham *et al.* 2014). Following intense campaigning by the IFAW in the early 1990s, the Southern Ocean Whale Sanctuary (50 million km^2 of ocean south of latitude 40°S) was established by the IWC in 1994 to ban commercial whaling in the oceans surrounding Antarctica. Although Japanese "scientific" whaling in the Southern Ocean has continued under protest, that was legally stopped in April 2014 following a case that was heard by the International Court of Justice. Commercial whaling continues in northern Norwegian and Icelandic waters (Rasmussen 2014; Andersson, Gothall & Wende 2014).

Despite protection measures in some parts of the world, considerable uncertainty surrounds cetacean populations at the species level (Hammond 2006). Furthermore, Williams (2014) documents various global (marine vessel strikes, noise, toxic poisoning and other forms of chronic environmental pollution) and regional (fisheries depletion and by-catch, tidal energy generation, seabed mining and marine oil drilling) practices that impact the viability of cetacean populations. In the case of the 2010 Deepwater Horizon/BP oil spill (Gulf of Mexico), where 101 dead marine mammals were recovered, it was estimated that only 2 per cent of cetacean deaths were actually recorded (Williams *et al.* 2011). It is futile to consider tourism (inclusive of wildlife tourism) in isolation from these driving forces of global environmental change (Gössling & Hall 2006).

In 1993, the IWC recognized whale watching as a legitimate commercial activity that allowed for the sustainable use of cetaceans in the wild (Orams 2000). Firmly rooted in the global ecological modernization discourse, this legitimacy articulates a compatibility between economic growth and environmental protection that has been the subject of increasing tension (Wheeller 1994; Neves 2009). However, since 1995, the IWC Scientific Committee has confronted a variety of scientific issues concerning whale watching. Indeed, in 1998, a sub-committee of the IWC was established to specifically consider the possible effects of commercial whale watching on cetaceans, and to provide expert advice on visitor management practices (O'Connor *et al.* 2010). In 2006, the IWC conceded that "there is compelling evidence that the fitness of individual odontocetes repeatedly exposed to whale-watching vessel traffic can be compromised and that this can lead to population-level effects" (IWC 2006). This consensus has been reached in light of recent studies indicating that repeated disturbance can lead to displacement from preferred habitat and reduced fitness at the population level (Bejder *et al.* 2006).

Meaningful responses to these studies have been blunted by the prevailing ecological modernization discourse. Indeed Neves (2009: 721) argues that "the efforts of some of the world's most prominent E-NGOs to save whales from being hunted to extinction have produced and propagated whale-watching as a quintessentially and uniformly benign activity." This political position has countered efforts to recognize that whale watching may have cumulative effects even though the intention is that interactions are non-lethal (Bejder *et al.* 2006; Christiansen & Lusseau 2014). It has also prevented acceptance that whale watching must be strictly managed within sustainable limits (Neves 2010). Such a move towards civic environmentalism would mark a significant break from the rhetoric of sustainable "non-consumptive" whale watching, and serve as a move towards recognizing and managing whale watching as a form of consumption (Higham *et al.* 2014).

Conclusion

Dominant neoliberal approaches to environmental governance continue to commodify the environment in the interests of consumption and economic development (Harvey 2011). The global wildlife tourism phenomenon represents a significant transformation in the global capitalist economy (Wheeller 1991; Hall 1994; Neves 2010), which requires us to question the founding assumptions of "non-consumptive" wildlife tourism. This chapter contemplates wild animals as global common pool resources (Moore & Rodger 2010), which are subject to a range of global and local environmental threats confronting the morbidity and mortality of individual wild animals, populations and species (Higham & Lusseau 2007). It defines global governance and then reviews the green governmentality discourse, which is characterized by the prioritization of big business (Bäckstrand & Lövbrand 2007). It then considers ecological modernization, which identifies a synergy between a liberal market order and the goals of sustainable development, arguing that capitalism has the capacity to be environmentally friendly (Hajer 1995). This chapter sees value in civic environmentalism as a counter-discourse to the dominant neoliberal framings of environmental governance, which fail to challenge rampant consumerism or give adequate priority to the environment (Byrne *et al.* 2004). In particular, the value of reform-oriented civic environmentalism lies in promoting multi-stakeholder participation to gain specialized and non-scientific expertise to influence environmental resource governance.

Within the context of global governance and global environmental change (Gössling & Hall 2006) we consider the long-standing notion of wildlife viewing as "non-consumptive" to be untenable. We endorse Knight's (2009) view that hunting and viewing wildlife are fundamentally similar, despite the obvious contrast in immediate outcomes for target animals. We also endorse Lemelin's (2006) notion of "ocular consumption." The case of whale watching is illuminating. Neves (2010) observes that the assumptions underpinning "non-consumptive" utility of cetaceans have been deliberately perpetuated through the mechanisms of global governance, including inter-governmental commissions, the public communication strategies of international environmental NGOs, and the global marketing practices of commercial tourism operators. She contests "…the reductionism that is entailed in taking for granted that the relation between (whale-watching), economic development/growth, and conservation is essentially and universally benign" (Neves 2010: 721). Such assumptions "…undermine the possibility of distinguishing between different types of whale-watching and the degree to which they effectively live up to conservationist goals" (Neves 2010: 721). The assumptions that underpin "non-consumptive" whale watching effectively cloak wildlife tourism in a "green mantle" (Wheeller 1994), (falsely) setting it apart from other rapacious means by which humanity consumes nature. It seems unlikely that a global–local sustainability paradigm will be achieved until some form of civic environmentalism prevails.

Key Reading

Bejder, L., Samuels, A., Whitehead, H., Gales, N., Mann, J., Connor, R.C., Heithaus, M.R., Watson-Capps, J., Flaherty, C. and Krutzen, M. (2006) 'Decline in relative abundance of bottlenose dolphins exposed to long-term disturbance', *Conservation Biology*, 20: 1791–98.

Gössling, S. and Hall, C.M. (eds) (2006) *Tourism and Global Environmental Change. Ecological, Social, Economic and Political Interrelationships*, London: Routledge.

Higham, J.E.S., Bejder, L. and Williams, R. (eds) (2014) *Whale-watching, Sustainable Tourism and Ecological Management*, Cambridge: Cambridge University Press.

Lemelin, R.H. (2006) 'The gawk, the glance, and the gaze: Ocular consumption and polar bear tourism in Churchill, Manitoba, Canada', *Current Issues in Tourism*, 9: 516–34.

Neves, K. (2010) 'Cashing in on cetourism: A critical ecological engagement with dominant E-NGO discourses on whaling, cetacean conservation, and whale-watching', *Antipode*, 42: 719–41.

References

Adger, W.N., Lorenzone, I. and O'Brien, K.L. (eds) (2009) *Adapting to Climate Change: Thresholds, Values, Governance*, Cambridge: Cambridge University Press.

Allen, S. (2014) 'From exploitation to adoration: The historical and contemporary contexts of human-cetacean interactions', in J.E.S. Higham, L. Bejder and R. Williams (eds) *Whale-watching, Sustainable Tourism and Ecological Management*, Cambridge: Cambridge University Press.

Andersson, T.D., Gothall, S.E. and Wende, B.D. (2014) 'Iceland and the resumption of whaling: An empirical study of the attitudes of international tourists and whale watch tour operators', in J.E.S. Higham, L. Bejder and R. Williams (eds) *Whale-watching, Sustainable Tourism and Ecological Management*, Cambridge: Cambridge University Press.

Bäckstrand, K. (2004) 'Scientisation vs. civic expertise in environmental governance: Eco-feminist, eco-modern and post-modern responses', *Environmental Politics*, 13(4), 695-714.

Bäckstrand, K. and Lövbrand, E. (2007) 'Climate governance beyond 2012: Competing discourses of green governmentality, ecological modernisation and civic environmentalism', *The Social Construction of Climate Change: Power, Knowledge, Norms, Discourses*, Aldershot: Ashgate.

Bäckstrand, K., Khan, J. and Kronsell, A. (2010) *Environmental Politics and Deliberative Democracy: Examining the Promise of New Modes of Governance*, Cheltenham: Edward Elgar.

BBC (2013) *Thousands of Puffins May Be Dead in North Sea Storms*. Available at: www.bbc.co.uk/news/uk-scotland-north-east-orkney-shetland-21941240 (accessed 6 May 2013).

Beale, C.M. and Monaghan, P. (2004) 'Human disturbance: People as predation-free predators?', *Journal of Applied Ecology*, 41: 335–43.

Becken, S. (2008) 'Developing indicators for managing tourism in the face of peak oil', *Tourism Management*, 29: 695–705.

Becken, S. and Schellhorn, M. (2007) 'Ecotourism, energy use and the global climate: Widening the local perspective', in J.E.S. Higham (ed.) *Critical Issues in Ecotourism: Understanding a Complex Tourism Phenomenon*, Oxford: Elsevier.

Bejder, L., Samuels, A., Whitehead, H., Gales, N., Mann, J., Connor, R.C., Heithaus, M.R., Watson-Capps, J., Flaherty, C. and Krutzen, M. (2006) 'Decline in relative abundance of bottlenose dolphins exposed to long-term disturbance', *Conservation Biology*, 20: 1791–98.

Bejder, L., Samuels, A., Whitehead, H., Finn, H. and Allen, S. (2009) 'Impact assessment research: Use and misuse of habituation, sensitisation and tolerance in describing wildlife responses to anthropogenic stimuli', *Marine Ecology Progress Series*, 395: 177–85.

Biermann, F. and Pattberg, P. (2012) 'Global environmental governance revisited', in F. Biermann and P. Pattberg (eds) *Global Environmental Governance Reconsidered*, MIT Press: Cambridge MA.

Boehmer-Christiansen, S. (2003) 'Science, equity, and the war against carbon', *Science, Technology & Human Values*, 28: 69.

Byrne, J., Glover, L., Inniss, V., Kulkarni, J., Mun, Y., Toly, N. and Wang, Y. (2004) 'Reclaiming the atmospheric commons: Beyond Kyoto', *Climate Change: Perspectives Five Years After Kyoto*, Plymouth: Science Publishers.

Carlsson, I., Ramphal, S., Alatas, A. and Dhalgren, H. (1995) *Our Global Neighbourhood: The Report of the Commission on Global Governance*, Oxford: Oxford University Press.

Carter, N. (2007) *The Politics of the Environment: Ideas, Activism, Policy*, Cambridge: Cambridge University Press.

Cater, E. (1995) 'Environmental contradictions in sustainable tourism', *The Geographical Journal*, 161.

Christiansen, F. and Lusseau, D. (2014) 'Understanding the ecological effects of whale-watching on Cetaceans', in J.E.S. Higham, L. Bejder and R. Williams (eds) *Whale-watching, Sustainable Tourism and Ecological Management*, Cambridge: Cambridge University Press.

Christoff, P. (1996) 'Ecological modernisation, ecological modernities', *Environmental Politics*, 5: 476–500.

Cisneros-Montemayor, A.M., Sumaila, U.R., Kaschner, K. and Pauly, D. (2010) 'The global potential for whale-watching', *Marine Policy*, 34: 1273–78.

Cohen, E. (1978) 'The impact of tourism on the physical environment', *Annals of Tourism Research*, 5: 215–37.

Corkeron, P.J. (2006) 'How shall we watch whales?', in D.M. Lavigne (ed.) *Gaining Ground: In Pursuit of Ecological Sustainability*, Guelph, ON: International Fund for Animal Welfare.

Crutzen, P. (2002) 'Geology of mankind', *Nature*, 415: 23.

Cui, Q., Xu, H. and Wall, G. (2012) 'A cultural perspective on wildlife tourism in China', *Tourism Recreation Research*, 37: 27–36.

Curtin, S. (2010) 'Managing the wildlife tourism experience: The importance of the tour leaders', *International Journal of Tourism Research*, 12: 219–36.

Darier, E. (1999) *Discourses of the Environment*, Wiley-Blackwell.

Duffus, D.A. and Dearden, P. (1990) 'Non-consumptive wildlife-oriented recreation: A conceptual framework', *Biological Conservation*, 53: 213–31.

Fogel, C. (2004) 'The local, the global and the Kyoto Protocol', *Earthly Politics: Local and Global in Environmental Governance*: 103–25.

Frid, A. and Dill, L. (2002) 'Human-caused disturbance stimuli as a form of predation risk', *Conservation Ecology* 6: 11–26.

Gössling, S. and Hall, C.M. (eds) (2006) *Tourism and Global Environmental Change: Ecological, Social, Economic and Political Interrelationships*, London: Routledge.

Gössling, S. and Upham, P. (eds) (2009) *Climate Change and Aviation: Issues, Challenges and Solutions*, London: Earthscan.

Hajer, M. (1995) *The Politics of Environmental Discourse: Ecological Modernization and the Policy Process*, New York: Oxford University Press.

Hall, C.M. (1994) 'Ecotourism in Australia, New Zealand and the South Pacific: Appropriate tourism or a new form of ecological imperialism?' in Cater, E. and Lowman, G.L. (eds) *Ecotourism: A Sustainable Option?* Chichester: John Wiley and Sons.

—— (2007) 'Scaling ecotourism: The role of scale in understanding the impacts of ecotourism', in J.E.S. Higham (ed.) *Critical Issues in Ecotourism: Understanding a Complex Tourism Phenomenon,* Oxford: Elsevier.

Hammond, P. (2006) 'Whale science – and how (not) to use it', *Significance,* June 2006: 54–58.

Harvey, D. (2011) *The Enigma of Capital and the Crises of Capitalism,* London: Profile Books.

Higham, J.E.S. and Lusseau, D. (2004) 'Ecological impacts and management of tourist engagements with cetaceans', in R. Buckley (ed.) *Environmental Impacts of Ecotourism,* Wallingford: CAB International.

—— (2007) 'Urgent need for empirical research into whaling and whale-watching', *Conservation Biology,* 21: 554–58.

—— (2008) 'Slaughtering the goose that lays the golden egg: Are whaling and whale-watching mutually exclusive?', *Current Issues in Tourism,* 11: 63–74.

Higham, J.E.S., Lusseau, D. and Hendry, W. (2008) 'The viewing platforms from which animals are observed in the wild: A discussion of emerging research directions', *Journal of Ecotourism,* 7: 132–41.

Higham, J.E.S., Bejder, L. and Lusseau, D. (2009) 'An integrated and adaptive management model to address the long-term sustainability of tourist interactions with cetaceans', *Environmental Conservation,* 35: 294–302.

Higham, J.E.S., Bejder, L. and Williams, R. (eds) (2014) *Whale-watching, Sustainable Tourism and Ecological Management,* Cambridge: Cambridge University Press.

Holden, A. (2009) 'The environment-tourism nexus: Influence of market ethics', *Annals of Tourism Research,* 36: 373–89.

IWC (2006) "International whaling commission's 58th annual meeting in St. Kitts and Nevis 2006", Retrieved from http://iwcoffice.org/_documents/commission/IWC58docs/iwc58docs.htm

Knight, J. (2009) 'Making wildlife viewable: Habituation and attraction', *Society and Animals,* 17: 167–84.

Lambert, E., Hunter, C., Pierce, G.J. and MacLeod, D. (2010) 'Sustainable whale-watching tourism and climate change: Towards a framework of resilience, Special Issue; Tourism: Adapting to climate change and climate policy', *Journal of Sustainable Tourism,* 18: 409–27.

Lammers, M.O., Pack, A.A., Lyman, E.G. and Espiritu, L. (2013) 'Trends in collisions between vessels and North Pacific humpback whales (*Megaptera novaeangliae*) in Hawaiian waters (1975–2011)', *Journal of Cetacean Resource Management,* 13(1): 73–80.

Lemelin, R.H. (2006) 'The gawk, the glance, and the gaze: Ocular consumption and polar bear tourism in Churchill, Manitoba, Canada', *Current Issues in Tourism,* 9: 516–34.

Lima, S.L. and Dill, L.M. (1990) 'Behavioral decisions made under the risk of predation: A review and prospectus', *Canadian Journal of Zoology,* 68: 619–40.

Lusseau, D. and Higham, J.E.S. (2004) 'Managing the impacts of dolphin-based tourism through the definition of critical habitats: The case of bottlenose dolphins (*Tursiops* spp.) in Doubtful Sound, New Zealand', *Tourism Management,* 25(5): 657–67.

Meadowcroft, J. (2007) 'Who is in charge here? Governance for sustainable development in a complex world', *Journal of Environmental Policy & Planning,* 9: 299–314.

Meletis, Z.A. and Campbell, L.M. (2007) 'Call it consumption! Re-Conceptualizing ecotourism as consumption and consumptive', *Geography Compass,* 1: 850–70.

Moore, S.A. and Rodger, K. (2010) 'Wildlife tourism as a common pool resource issue: Enabling conditions for sustainability governance', *Journal of Sustainable Tourism,* 18: 831–44.

Muloin, S. (1998) 'Wildlife tourism: The psychological benefits of whale-watching', *Pacific Tourism Review,* 2: 199–213.

Neves, K. (2010) 'Cashing in on Cetourism: A critical ecological engagement with dominant E-NGO discourses on whaling, cetacean conservation, and whale-watching', *Antipode* 42: 719–41

Newsome, D. and Rodger, K. (2012) 'Wildlife tourism', in A. Holden and D. Fennell (eds) *A Handbook of Tourism and the Environment,* London: Routledge.

O'Connor, S., Campbell, R., Cortez, H. and Knowles, T. (2010) *Whale-watching Worldwide: Tourism Numbers, Expenditures and Expanding Economic Benefits,* special report for the International Fund for Animal Welfare prepared by Economists at Large, Yarmouth, MA: International Fund for Animal Welfare.

Orams, M.B. (2000) 'Tourists getting close to whales, is it what whale-watching is all about?', *Tourism Management,* 21: 561–69.

—— (2004) 'Why dolphins may get ulcers: Considering the impacts of cetacean based tourism in New Zealand', *Tourism in Marine Environments*, 1: 17–28.

Paavola, J. (2007) 'Institutions and environmental governance: A reconceptualization', *Ecological Economics*, 63: 93–103.

Pahl-Wostl, C. (2009) 'A conceptual framework for analysing adaptive capacity and multi-level learning processes in resource governance regimes', *Global Environmental Change*, 19: 354–65.

Pelletier, N. (2010) 'Of laws and limits: An ecological economic perspective on redressing the failure of contemporary global environmental governance', *Global Environmental Change*, 20: 220–28.

Perch-Nielsen, S., Sesartic, A. and Stucki, M. (2010) 'The greenhouse gas intensity of the tourism sector: The case of Switzerland', *Environmental Science & Policy*, 13: 131–40.

Rasmussen, M. (2014) 'The whaling versus whale-watching debate: The resumption of Icelandic whaling'. In J.E.S. Higham, L. Bejder and R. Williams (eds) *Whale-watching, Sustainable Tourism and Ecological Management*, Cambridge: Cambridge University Press.

Rauschmayer, F., Van Den Hov, S. and Koetz, T. (2009) 'Participation in EU biodiversity governance: How far beyond rhetoric?', *Environment and Planning C: Government and Policy*, 27: 42–58.

Romeril, M. (1989) 'Tourism and the environment: Accord or discord?', *Tourism Management*, 10: 204–8.

Rosenau, J.N. (2002) 'Globalization and governance: Sustainability between fragmentation and integration,' paper presented at the Conference of Governance and Sustainability: New Challenges for the State, Business and Civil Society, Berlin, September 2002.

Rutherford, P. (1999) 'The entry of life into history', *Discourses of the Environment*: 37–62.

Rutherford, S. (2007) 'Green governmentality: insights and opportunities in the study of nature's rule', *Progress in Human Geography*, 31(3), 291–307.

Scott, D., Hall, C.M. and Gössling, S. (2012) *Tourism and Climate Change: Impacts, Adaptation and Mitigation*, London: Routledge.

Tremblay, P. (2001) 'Wildlife tourism consumption: Consumptive or non-consumptive?', *International Journal of Tourism Research*, 3: 81–86.

Tschakert, P. and Olsson, L. (2005) 'Post-2012 climate action in the broad framework of sustainable development policies: The role of the EU', *Climate Policy*, 5: 329–48.

Underdal, A. (2010) 'Complexity and challenges of long-term environmental governance', *Global Environmental Change*, 20: 386–93.

United Nations Environment Programme (2013) *Convention on Biodiversity*. Available at: www.cbd.int/programmes (accessed 6 May 2013).

Van der Heijden, H. (2008) 'Green governmentality, ecological modernisation or civic environmentalism? Dealing with global environmental problems', *Environmental Politics*, 17: 835–39.

Wheeller, B. (1991) 'Tourism's troubled times: Responsible tourism is not the answer', *Tourism Management*, 12: 91–96.

—— (1994) 'Ecotourism: A ruse by any other name', in C. Cooper and A. Lockwood (eds) *Progress in Tourism, Recreation and Hospitality Management*, Vol. 7. London: Belhaven Press.

Whittaker, D. (1997) 'Capacity norms on bear viewing platforms', *Human Dimensions of Wildlife*, 2: 37–49.

Williams, P.W. and Ponsford, I.F. (2009) 'Confronting tourism's environmental paradox: Transitioning for sustainable tourism', *Futures*, 41: 396–404.

Williams, R. (2014) 'Threats facing cetacean populations: The global context'. In J.E.S. Higham, L. Bejder and R. Williams (eds) *Whale-watching, Sustainable Tourism and Ecological Management*, Cambridge: Cambridge University Press.

Williams, R., Trites, A.W. and Bain, D.E. (2002) 'Behavioural responses of killer whales (*Orcinus orca*) to whale-watching boats: Opportunistic observations and experimental approaches', *Journal of Zoology*, 256: 255–70.

Williams, R., Gero, S., Bejder, L., Calambokidis, J., Kraus S.D., Lusseau, D., Read, A.J. and Robbins, J. (2011) 'Underestimating the damage: Interpreting cetacean carcass recoveries in the context of the Deepwater Horizon/BP incident', *Conservation Letters*, 4: 228–33.

Young, O.R. (1999) *Governance in World Affairs*, Ithaca: Cornell University Press.

23

Stories of people and places
Interpretation, tourism and sustainability

Gianna Moscardo

Interpretation 'An educational activity which aims to reveal meanings and relationships through the use of original objects, by first hand experience, and by illustrative media, rather than simply to communicate factual information' (Tilden 1977: 33).

Tourist experience A tourist experience comprises a distinctive set of events and/or activities, occurring in a particular location and within a specific time period, outside of the everyday realm, that provide meaning and significance to the tourist's identity and social interactions (Moscardo 2009).

Commodification Refers to the 'extent to which a heritage place has been modified through adoption of a commercial focus for tourism purposes' (Hughes & Carlsen 2010: 17).

Social marketing The use of 'marketing principles and techniques to influence a target audience to voluntarily accept, reject or abandon a behaviour for the benefit of individuals, groups, or society as a whole' (Kotler, Roberto & Lee 2002: 5).

Introduction

In 1992, Irish commentator Fintan O'Toole challenged the growing use of interpretation at Irish tourist attractions quoting Susan Sontag's words, 'interpretation is the revenge of the intellect upon the world. To interpret is to impoverish, to deplete the world – in order to set up a shadow world of "meanings"'(1992: 12). O'Toole argued that the provision of tourist interpretation had become excessive, interfering with the ability of visitors to have their own experiences and to create their own meanings and that it turned nature and culture into commercial products. Fifteen years later, he raised similar concerns about the development of interpretation at the Cliffs of Moher, this time claiming that 'you can be entertained, mildly educated, fed, relieved and gently parted from some money [but] you cannot be moved' (O'Toole 2007: 16). These concerns are consistent with those listed by Bramwell and Lane (2005) in their brief critical review of interpretation. While, O'Toole (1992, 2007) recognises the importance of managing visitor impact and safety, he questions if interpretation is the best way to achieve these goals. More than 20 years later this challenge remains largely unanswered but, arguably, it has become a more important question as tourism is increasingly under pressure to demonstrate its contribution to sustainability. This chapter will define interpretation, focusing on why and how it is used in different tourism contexts, arguing that it has four main functions: creating visitor experiences, assisting in visitor management, supporting tourism development; and (potentially) contributing to sustainability more broadly. The chapter will take each of these four functions and, using a selective review of key papers published in the last 10 years, highlight key trends and major issues.

Interpretation: definitions and functions

A simple way to define interpretation is to list some of the common places where it happens (e.g. museums, zoos, historic houses, guided trails and conservation areas) and the common tools that interpreters use (e.g. guided talks, signs, exhibitions, films and brochures). These places and tools share a common theme – the provision of information about the place being visited. The most commonly accepted definition of interpretation is that provided by Tilden (see key concepts above) which emphasises three elements: education, meaning and experience. Similarly, Moscardo (2001) reported that the most common words used in interpretation definitions were: education, explanation, discovery, awareness, enjoyment and inspiration. So there is consensus that interpretation is a type of educational or persuasive communication activity. Despite this consensus, there is also divergence about the primary function or purpose of interpretation (Ablett & Dyer 2009). An examination of both academic literature and tourism practice suggests four main functions. The first, and most common, is that of interpretation as visitor management (see Brown, Ham & Hughes 2010). The second related function is interpretation as visitor experience (Marschall 2012). The third is that of interpretation for tourism development (Firth 2011). Finally, there is a growing interest in the idea of interpretation in tourism contexts as a tool for encouraging more sustainable lifestyles (Lai *et al.* 2009). In this last function, tourist interpretation begins to merge with the concept of social marketing. The following sections explore each of these four approaches to interpretation identifying major themes, key issues and emerging trends.

Interpretation as visitor management

The most commonly reported function for interpretation, especially in environmental conservation areas, is that of assisting in the management of visitors (Ablett & Dyer 2009). Interpretation can assist site managers by:

- providing information about, and motivation for, visitors to adopt minimal impact behaviours;
- spreading visitors throughout a site to relieve congestion; and
- offering substitute experiences that reduce impacts in fragile areas (Kim, Airey & Szivas 2011).

A large proportion of the available research into interpretation has focused on assessing its effectiveness in this visitor management role. One stream in this research examines whether or not interpretation in general is an effective management tool (Littlefair & Buckley 2008). Overall, this research concludes that while there are some cases where interpretation has been effective, this is not a consistent conclusion, thus supporting arguments that interpretation has to be well designed and effectively delivered to achieve management objectives (Stamation *et al.* 2007) and that interpretation often varies significantly in terms of quality, intensity and content (Mayes & Richins 2009).

A second stream of interpretation evaluation research explores these variations conducting research that analyses the effectiveness of particular interpretive strategies (Powell & Ham 2008). Reviews of this style of research also report mixed evidence in terms of interpretation outcomes (Littlefair & Buckley 2008). Of particular importance in this work are the consistent calls for improvements to the research methods used. Issues identified include:

- poor research design with limited use of valid experimental techniques;
- an over-reliance on behavioural intentions and/or self-reported behaviours with few measures of actual behaviour change;
- concentration on relatively simple quantitative measures of knowledge gain and attitude change;
- a focus on immediate post-visit measures with very few longer-term assessments of impacts; and
- the use of a limited range of explanatory concepts reflecting a lack of understanding of the range of variables involved in behaviour change (Ballantyne & Packer 2011; Hughes 2013; Kim, Airey & Szivas 2011; Lee & Moscardo 2005; Miller *et al.* 2010; Munro *et al.* 2008; Powell & Ham 2008; Weiler & Smith 2009).

One consistent suggestion for improving research methods in interpretation effectiveness has been to explore more qualitative techniques that allow for a wider range of variables to be recognised and analysed (Anderson 2012). A second suggestion has been to adopt the use of new computer and mobile technologies (Yalowitz & Bronnenkant 2009).

Interpretation as visitor experience

The rise of new mobile and social media has also become a major trend in the design and delivery of interpretation. Bohlin and Brandt (2013), for example, critically examine the use of digital guides as an interpretive method, especially at historic sites. They argue that such guides should be able to provide tourists with a wider range of alternative perspectives, although few currently do that. Kang and Gretzel analysed the effectiveness of podcasts in museums (2012a) and national parks (2012b) and again concluded that these new communication tools could be used effectively to interpret places, but that there are issues with user familiarity and comfort with technology use. Finally, Lombardo and Damiano (2012) describe the development and potential of mobile phone applications that can be used as a personal guide to a tourist place. As with the other new technologies, mobile apps offer tourists the ability to have greater control over their experience, to customise or personalise their experience, and to access different perspectives or stories about places. These three themes are consistent with what has been called the 'experiential turn' in tourism (Lindberg, Hansen & Eide 2013).

This 'experiential turn' is not limited to tourism, having also been used in the broader literature on consumer behaviour (Darmer & Sundbo 2008), in marketing (Schmitt 1999) and in numerous other areas including education (Boud 2012). In the areas of consumption and marketing it can be traced back to Pine and Gilmore's (1999) book on the experience economy which proposed that consumers are seeking experiences which are more than products and advocating a dramaturgical approach to understanding the consumption experience. Although it could be argued that tourists have always purchased or consumed experiences, the experiential turn in tourism refers to a more explicit desire by tourists to engage in personalised, immersive, often themed activities that can be clearly labelled and presented as an experience beyond that of simply visiting a place and/or relaxing and escaping their everyday world (Berridge 2012; Gretzel, Fesenmaier & O'Leary 2006; Moscardo 2009). Table 23.1 summarises the elements that have been proposed as important for creating tourist experiences.

Interpretation can be linked to this experiential turn in three main ways. First, interpretation offers a way to support this creation of a tourist experience. The addition of more intensive and extensive information about the history, culture, nature and/or uniqueness of a place contributes to the sense of an experience beyond merely visiting. Again it can be argued that this process is not a new one for tourism, with MacCannell (1976) describing the creation of tourist attractions through a process of site sacralisation, which included the introduction of interpretation as a key step.

The difference in the last decade has been the explicit use of interpretation in a wider range of contexts than have been traditionally seen as in need of specific interpretation. An example of this can be found in food tourism, also known as culinary and gastronomic tourism; all labels that refer to tourism products focused on the production and consumption of food including food-themed events and festivals, regional food-themed touring routes, specialist restaurants, cooking classes and visits to places of food production such as wineries, chocolate factories, distilleries and orchards (Ignatov & Smith 2006). All of these food tourism experiences include some degree of interpretation, but this is especially apparent in the development of interpretation in places of food production where tourists are provided with opportunities to learn about the history, production and cultural significance of the relevant food, as well as the opportunity to develop their tasting and connoisseurship skills (Jacobsen 2008). As more places adopt this type of approach, there is evidence that tourists are increasingly coming to expect interpretation and it makes an important contribution to the satisfaction they experience (Moscardo 2010; Moscardo & Ballantyne 2008).

The second link between interpretation and experience is the convergence in the characteristics that are seen as important for creating effective consumer/tourist experiences and the features of effective interpretation. Factors reported as contributing to satisfaction in both areas include the need to offer tourists the chance to engage with, and participate in, the activities on offer, the provision of multiple and different perspectives on a topic, the consistent use of strong themes, the provision of variety on a number of dimensions and the use of stories (Moscardo 2009, 2010).

Table 23.1 Key characteristics of consumer experiences

Experience characteristic
Immersion in a multisensory, themed setting
A focus on authenticity in a range of dimensions including the social interactions with others
Opportunities for customisation and personalisation of the activities engaged in leading to what is called experience co-creation
Opportunities to learn and enhance personal and cultural capital through engagement with offered interpretation
Activities built around stories/narratives

Sources: Berry & Carbone 2007; Hollenbeck, Peters & Zinkham 2008; Jacobsen 2008; Mascarenhas, Kesavan & Bernacchi 2006; McGoun *et al.* 2003; Moscardo 2010; Pine & Gilmore 1999; Poulsen & Kale 2004.

This convergence supports the third link between interpretation and experience: the explicit adoption of key experiential features in interpretation programmes and activities (Broomall 2013; Chronis 2012; Czajkowski 2011; Leighton 2006). Of particular importance has been the adoption of dramaturgical approaches and the increasing attention paid to stories. Pine and Gilmore (1999) highlighted the idea of consumption as theatre, applying a dramaturgical approach in which the service or sales setting is the stage. This can include props, the staff playing various supporting roles and an experience designed to encourage the consumers to play an active role in creating their own story (Harris, Harris & Baron 2003; Stuart & Tax 2004). When applied to the tourist interpretive experience there are several levels or styles of drama that can be described. At the most basic level, interpretive guides, both live and through various electronic forms, can act as narrators telling the visitor audience stories about the place. At the next level, the interpretive staff can provide what has been called 'first person' or 'live' interpretation – where they play the part of actual or fictional characters acting out various scenes (Williams 2013). In these performances the tourists can be either a passive audience or can be invited to be part of the performance in various ways. At another level, parts of the physical site become a stage, which can be enhanced by the provision of props, such as costumes for tourists to wear. Tourists are encouraged to perform key roles in a story, which can be recorded and then shared with others. At the most intense level, tourists are involved in the development of a theatrical performance from beginning to presentation using the interpretation provided to help develop ideas, stories, scripts and actions in what Hughes, Jackson and Kidd (2007) refer to as 'participatory drama'. The key element in all types of performance is the use of stories to improve interpretation effectiveness (Kidd 2011).

Interpretation as tourism development

This renewed emphasis on interpretation storytelling is central to the third function of interpretation as tourism development (Mitsche *et al.* 2013). According to Urry and Larsen (2011: 54) organisations and groups 'seeking to revitalise decaying places and commercialise cultural institutions such as theatres and museums, increasingly turn [them] into "experience-scapes"'. This process is an extension of the use of interpretation to create or enhance tourist experiences. In this function, interpretation is used as the justification for tourism development, especially in cultural or heritage development. Interpretation is seen as a tool to support a commercial tourist experience that provides the necessary financial, political and social support required for heritage conservation and/or preservation in a process called commodification (Hughes & Carlsen 2010). While the idea of using tourist interpretation to sustain cultural heritage may be well-intentioned, commodification is a complex and challenging process (Bramwell & Lane 2005). On the one hand, the interpretation of places, history and culture to transform them into tangible economic assets may be the only viable option for their conservation (Porto, Leanza & Cascone 2012) and the telling of stories to both tourists and residents can support positive perceptions of the destination (Firth 2011; Marschall 2012). On the other hand, commodification can lead to conflict over which stories to tell, changes to the heritage to make it more commercially acceptable and damage to the perceived authenticity of the site (Bramwell & Lane 2005). The issue of whose story gets told in interpretation is a longstanding one (Moscardo 2001) and is bound up in the power struggle between different actors associated with the heritage being interpreted (Wong 2013). Even where there may be consensus about what should be told to tourists, there is still the issue of adapting the story to suit their perceived expectations and sensitivities. Difficult and challenging stories such as those related to slavery are often left out of the interpretation (Best & Phulgence 2013; Wong 2013).

There has also been considerable opposition to the use of tourism to redevelop heritage sites (Ross 2006) with some concerns that the heritage interpretation aspect can be used as a cover to justify more extensive commercial development (Leite 2013). In this case the interpretation itself can become a good story used to rationalise what might otherwise be seen as selfish commercial interests. Finally, there is also little evidence that heritage interpretation as tourism development is especially effective at generating the necessary financial benefits or promised local opportunities (Chirikure *et al.* 2010).

Interpretation for sustainability

These concerns about the negative impact of tourism brings us to the fourth and final function of interpretation: the promotion of sustainability beyond the destination and/or holiday experience. This is an extension of interpretation as tourist management on site and is a response to those who would argue that tourism needs to do more than just minimise its negative impact and maximise its positive impact. There are increasing calls for tourism itself to be a strategy for encouraging more sustainable lifestyles beyond the destinations visited and beyond the holiday or travel experience (Jamrozy 2007; Lai *et al.* 2009). In this function tourist interpretation becomes a part of a larger social marketing approach to encourage more responsible and sustainable action. Social marketing seeks to take the principles of marketing and apply them to changing behaviour towards some ideal of social good. Pomering, Noble and Johnson (2011) and Truong and Hall (2013) offer more detailed analyses of how social marketing could be applied to tourism to encourage greater sustainability (see also Chapter 19).

Interpretation could play an important role in social marketing applications in tourism by focusing on encouraging the values, knowledge and attitudes necessary to support sustainable lifestyles. This is, however, likely to be a very difficult task – the available evidence suggests that many tourists, even those who are generally environmentally responsible at home, do not see a need to engage in sustainability actions while travelling (Barr & Prillwitz 2012; Miao & Wei 2013). Maier and Laing (2013) provide evidence that even when tourists do engage in interpretation activities about sustainable lifestyles, they are likely to be already committed to sustainability action and seeking positive feedback for the actions they already take rather than extending their commitment to sustainability, casting further doubt on the likely changes that tourist interpretation can achieve.

Case Study

Interpretation and dark tourism

'Dark tourism' was defined by Foley and Lennon (1996: 198) as 'the phenomenon which encompasses the presentation and consumption (by visitors) of real and commodified death and disaster sites'. It has become a topic of considerable research interest in recent times. Interpretation plays an important role in the tourist experiences at these dark tourism sites (Cohen 2011). Two contrasting examples of dark tourism can be found at the Arizona Memorial in Hawai'i which interprets the 1941 Japanese attack on Pearl Harbour that brought the USA into the Pacific arena of World War Two. The tourist experience provided at this site is very controlled and structured and starts at the Visitors Centre, where tourists are required to attend an audio-visual presentation of the story of the USS Arizona, a battleship that was sunk during the attack, resulting in the deaths of 1,102 sailors and marines. After this, tourists can view a range of interpretive displays which focus heavily on first-person stories. They are then taken by boat to a shrine built over the submerged wreck of the ship which serves as a memorial to those killed during the attack. This provides an example of a site where interpretation plays a major role in the creation and management of the tourist experience. The history of the site's development and its interpretation is also an example of the conflict that interpretation can generate, with considerable debate about control of the site, the nature and content of the interpretation, the aims of both the interpretation and allowing tourists onsite, and the way the tourist experience should be organised (Bergman 2013).

The Arizona Memorial focuses on the start of the war between Japan and the USA. The Nagasaki Atomic Bomb Museum and Peace Park, one of several such sites in Japan, focuses on the end of the war, in particular the USA nuclear bombing of Hiroshima and Nagasaki in 1945. Like the Arizona Memorial, this dark tourism site combines both a shrine and memorial to those who died, with a specific interpretive building. Like the Arizona Memorial, the focus of the interpretation is on stories, especially first-hand accounts of the event and its aftermath. Like the Arizona Memorial, the site also has a long history of conflict over how it should be developed and what should be interpreted (Williams 2012). Despite these similarities, the style of interpretation used in Nagasaki is very different to that of the Arizona Memorial, with tourists having much greater freedom and independence to organise their own experience with a stronger focus on the wider implications of the event for issues of global peace and security.

The difference in the interpretive approaches used at these two dark tourism sites reflects a number of factors, not least of which is the difference in culture between Japan and the United States. Wong (2013) argues that many interpretive situations are cross-cultural, with differences between the cultures of the tourists and of the places being visited and between those doing the interpretation and the tourists. Research into dark tourism has mostly used more qualitative approaches; these have highlighted the importance of recognising tourist characteristics, such as personal life history, culture and motivation, in understanding their responses (Biran, Poria & Oren 2011; Dunkley, Morgan & Westwood 2011).

Interpretation futures

It is common in futures studies to consider three main types of futures: predictive or probable futures which examine what is likely to happen, explorative or possible futures which seek to understand what might happen, and normative or preferable futures, which seek to determine the future that is desired and how it might be achieved (Bishop, Hines & Collins 2007). A predictive or probable future for interpretation would include a continued central role in the creation of tourist experiences, a greater focus on stories as a key interpretive technique, and an increased reliance on mobile technologies and social media as interpretive tools. An explorative or possible future for interpretation would see it becoming more widespread across a range of different settings and making a greater use of drama to give tourists a stronger role in their interpretive experience.

Finally, we can consider normative or preferable futures and it is clear that this interpretation future would include a shift from an exclusive focus on tourists' onsite behaviours and experiences to seeking to encourage more sustainable action beyond the site and travel experiences. This aspirational future will not, however, be easy to achieve as the practice of interpretation can be challenging, the available research into interpretation has been limited in its methodological approaches and the resulting evidence provides only partial support for the effectiveness of interpretation in changing tourist knowledge, attitudes and/or actions. Returning to O'Toole's (1992) critique of interpretation, we can conclude that it is not easy to provide enough interpretation to manage the impact of tourism and to provide tourists with the information they might need to make their own interpretations about the site. New technologies do offer some hope in this regard as they could allow for greater personalisation of the interpretive experience and the presentation of a range of different perspectives. The challenge for tourism academics is to support these changes with more sophisticated approaches to interpretation research.

Key Reading

Ballantyne, R., Packer, J. and Falk, J. (2011) 'Visitors' learning for environmental sustainability: Testing short- and long-term impacts of wildlife tourism experiences using structural equation modelling', *Tourism Management*, 32: 1243–52.

Cohen, E.H. (2011) 'Educational dark tourism at *In Populo Sites*', *Annals of Tourism Research*, 38(1): 193–209.

Moscardo, G. (2009) 'Understanding tourist experience through mindfulness', in M. Kozak and A. Decrop (eds) *Handbook of Tourist Behaviour: Theory and Practice*, New York: Routledge.

Moscardo, G. and Ballantyne, R. (2008) 'Interpretation and tourist attractions', in A. Fyall, A. Leask and S. Wanhill (eds) *Managing Tourist Attractions,* 2nd edn, London: Elsevier.

Truong, V.D. and Hall, C.M. (2013) 'Social marketing and tourism: What is the evidence?', *Social Marketing Quarterly*, 19(2): 110–35.

References

Ablett, P.G. and Dyer, P.K. (2009) 'Heritage and hermeneutics: Towards a broader interpretation of interpretation', *Current Issues in Tourism*, 12(3): 209–33.

Anderson, D. (2012) 'A reflective hermeneutic approach to research methods investigating visitor learning', in D. Ash, J. Rahm, and L.M. Melber (eds) *Putting Theory into Practice: Tools for Research in Informal Settings*. Rotterdam: Sense Publishers.

Ballantyne, R. and Packer, J. (2011) 'Using tourism free-choice learning experiences to promote environmentally sustainable behaviour: The role of post-visit "action resources"', *Environmental Education Research*, 17(2): 201–15.

Barr, S. and Prillwitz, J. (2012) '"Green travellers" Exploring the spatial context of sustainable mobility styles', *Applied Geography*, 32, 798–908.

Bergman, T. (2013) *Exhibiting Patriotism: Creating and Contesting Interpretations of American Historic Sites*, Walnut Creek: Left Coast Press.

Berridge, G. (2012) 'Designing event experiences', in S.J. Page and J. Connell (eds) *The Routledge Handbook of Events*, London: Routledge.

Berry, L.L. and Carbone, L.P. (2007) 'Build loyalty through experience management', *Quality Progress*, 40(9): 26–32.

Best, M.N. and Phulgence, W.F. (2013) 'Interpretation of contested heritage at an attraction in St. Lucia', *Journal of Heritage Tourism*, 8(1): 21–35.

Biran, A., Poria, Y. and Oren, G. (2011) 'Sought experiences at (dark) heritage sites', *Annals of Tourism Research*, 38(3): 820–41.

Bishop, P., Hines, A. and Collins, T. (2007) 'The current state of scenario development: An overview of techniques', *Foresight*, 9(1): 5–25.

Bohlin, M. and Brandt, D. (2013) 'Creating tourist experiences by interpreting places using digital guides', *Journal of Heritage Tourism*. Available at: http://dx.doi.org/10.1080/1743873x.2013.799173

Boud, D. (2012) 'Problematising practice-based education', In J. Higgs, R. Barnett, S. Billet, M, Hutchings and F. Trede (eds) *Practice-based Education: Perspectives and Strategies,* Rotterdam: Sense Publishers.

Bramwell, B. and Lane, B. (2005) 'Interpretation and sustainable tourism: The potential and pitfalls', *Revista Interamericana de Ambiente y Turismo*, 1(1): 20–27.

Broomall, J.J. (2013). 'The interpretation is a-changin': Memory, museums, and public history in Central Virginia', *Journal of the Civil War Era*, 3(1): 114–24.

Brown, T.J., Ham, S.H., and Hughes, M. (2010) 'Picking up litter: An application of theory-based communication to influence tourist behaviour in protected areas', *Journal of Sustainable Tourism*, 18(7): 879–900.

Chirikure, S., Manyanga, M., Ndoro, W. and Pwiti, G. (2010) 'Unfulfilled promises? Heritage management and community participation at some of Africa's cultural heritage sites', *International Journal of Heritage Studies*, 16(1–2): 30–44.

Chronis, A. (2012) 'Tourists as story-builders: Narrative construction at a heritage museum', *Journal of Travel & Tourism Marketing*, 29(5): 444–59.

Cohen, E.H. (2011) 'Educational dark tourism at an *In populo site*', *Annals of Tourism Research*, 38(1): 193–209.

Czajkowski, J.W. (2011) 'Making space for interactive learning in the galleries of the Detroit Institute of Arts', *Journal of Museum Education*, 36(2): 171–78.

Darmer, P. and Sundbo, J. (2008) 'Introduction to experience creation', in J. Sundbo and P. Darmer (eds) *Creating Experiences in the Experience Economy*, Cheltenham: Edward Elgar.

Dunkley, R., Morgan, N. and Westwood, S. (2011) 'Visiting the trenches: Exploring meanings and motivations in battlefield tourism', *Tourism Management*, 32: 860–68.

Firth, T.M. (2011) 'Tourism as a means to industrial heritage conservation: Achilles heel or saving grace?' *Journal of Heritage Tourism*, 6(1): 45–62.

Foley, M. and Lennon, J.J. (1996) 'JFK and dark tourism: A fascination with assassination', *International Journal of Heritage Studies*, 2(4), 198–211.

Gretzel, U., Fesenmaier, D.R. and O'Leary, J.T. (2006) 'The transformation of consumer behaviour', in D. Buhalis and C. Costa (eds) *Tourism Business Frontiers: Consumer, Products and Industry,* Oxford: Elsevier.

Harris, R., Harris, K. and Baron, S. (2003) 'Theatrical service experiences: Dramatic script development with employees', *International Journal of Service Industry Management,* 14(2): 184–99.

Hollenbeck, C.R., Peters, C. and Zinkham, G.M. (2008) 'Retail spectacles and brand meaning: New insights from a brand museum case study', *Journal of Retailing*, 64(3): 334–53.

Hughes, C., Jackson, A. and Kidd, J. (2007) 'The role of theater in museums and historic sites: Visitors, audiences, and learners', in N.L. Bresler (ed.) *International Handbook of Research in Arts Education*, Rotterdam: Springer.

Hughes, K. (2013) 'Measuring the impact of viewing wildlife: Do positive intentions equate to long-term changes in conservation behaviour?', *Journal of Sustainable Tourism*, 21(1): 42–59.

Hughes, M. and Carlsen, J. (2010) 'The business of cultural heritage tourism: Critical success factors', *Journal of Heritage Tourism*, 5(1): 17–32.

Ignatov, E. and Smith S. (2006) 'Segmenting Canadian culinary tourists', *Current Issues in Tourism*, 9(3): 235–55.

Jacobsen, J.K. (2008) 'The food and eating experience', in J. Sundbo and P. Darmer (eds) *Creating Experiences in the Experience Economy*, Cheltenham: Edward Elgar.

Jamrozy, U. (2007) 'Marketing of tourism: A paradigm shift toward sustainability', *International Journal of Culture, Tourism and Hospitality Research*, 1(2): 117–30.

Kang, M. and Gretzel, U. (2012a) 'Perceptions of museum podcast tours', *Tourism Management Perspectives*, 4: 155–63.

—— (2012b) 'Effects of podcast tours on tourist experiences in a national park', *Tourism Management*, 33: 440–55.

Kidd, J. (2011) 'Performing the knowing archive: Heritage performance and authenticity', *International Journal of Heritage Studies*, 17(1): 22–35.

Kim, A.K., Airey, D. and Szivas, E. (2011) 'The multiple assessment of interpretation effectiveness: Promoting visitors' environmental attitudes and behavior', *Journal of Travel Research*, 50(3): 321–34.

Kotler, P., Roberto, N. and Lee, N. (2002) *Social Marketing: Improving the Quality of Life,* 2nd edn, Thousand Oaks: Sage Publications.

Lai, P.H., Sorice, M.G., Nepal, S.K. and Cheng, C.K. (2009) 'Integrating social marketing into sustainable resource management at Padre Island National Seashore: An attitude-based segmentation approach', *Environmental Management*, 43(6): 985–98.

Lee, W. and Moscardo, G. (2005) 'Understanding the impact of ecotourism resort experiences on tourists' environmental attitudes and behavioural intentions', *Journal of Sustainable Tourism*, 13(6): 546–65.

Leighton, D. (2006) '"Step back in time and live the legend": Experiential marketing and the heritage sector', *International Journal of Nonprofit and Voluntary Sector Marketing*, 12(2): 117–25.

Leite, R.P. (2013) 'Consuming heritage: Counter-uses of the city and gentrification', *Vibrant: Virtual Brazilian Anthropology*, 10(1): 165–89.

Lindberg, F., Hansen, A.H., and Eide, D. (2014) 'A multi-relational approach for understanding consumer experiences within tourism', *Journal of Hospitality Marketing & Management*, 23(5): 487–512.

Littlefair, C. and Buckley, R. (2008) 'Interpretation reduces ecological impacts of visitors to world heritage site', *AMBIO: A Journal of the Human Environment*, 37(5): 338–41.

Lombardo, V. and Damiano, R. (2012) 'Storytelling on mobile devices for cultural heritage', *New Review of Hypermedia and Multimedia*, 18(1–2): 11–15.

MacCannell, D. (1976) *The Tourist: A New Theory of the Leisure Class*, Berkeley: University of California Press.

Mascarenhas, O.A., Kesavan, R. and Bernacchi, M. (2006) 'Lasting customer loyalty', *Journal of Consumer Marketing*, 23(7): 397–405.

Mair, J. and Laing, J.H. (2013) 'Encouraging pro-environmental behaviour: The role of sustainability focused events', *Journal of Sustainable Tourism*. Available at: http://dx.doi.org/10.1080/09669582.2013.7564954

Marschall, S. (2012) 'Sustainable heritage tourism: The Inanda Heritage Route and the 2010 FIFA World Cup', *Journal of Sustainable Tourism*, 20(5): 721–36.

Mayes, G. and Richins, H. (2009) 'Dolphin watch tourism: Two differing examples of sustainable practices and pro-environmental outcomes', *Tourism in Marine Environments*, 5(2/3): 201–14.

McGoun, E.G., Dunkak, W.H., Bettner, M.S. and Allen, D.E. (2003) 'Walt's street and Wall Street: Theming, theatre and experience in finance', *Critical Perspectives on Accounting*, 14: 647–61.

Miao, L. and Wei, W. (2013) 'Consumers' pro-environmental behaviour and the underlying motivations: A comparison between household and hotel settings', *International Journal of Hospitality Management*, 32: 102–12.

Miller, G., Rathouse, K., Scarles, C., Holmes, K. and Tribe, J. (2010) 'Public understanding of sustainable tourism', *Annals of Tourism Research*, 37(3): 627–45.

Mitsche, N., Vogt, F., Knox, D., Cooper, I., Lombard, P. and Ciaffi, D. (2013) 'Intangibles: Enhancing access to cities' cultural heritage through interpretation', *International Journal of Culture, Tourism and Hospitality Research*, 7(1): 68–77.

Moscardo, G. (2001) 'Cultural and heritage tourism: The great debates', in B. Faulkner, G. Moscardo and E. Laws (eds) *Tourism into the Twenty First Century: Reflections on Experience,* London: Cassells Academic.

—— (2009) 'Understanding tourist experience through mindfulness', in M. Kozak and A. Decrop (eds) *Handbook of Tourist Behaviour: Theory and Practice*, New York: Routledge.

—— (2010) 'The shaping of tourist experience: The importance of stories and themes', in M. Morgan, P. Lugosi and J.R.B. Ritchie (eds) *The Tourism and Leisure Experience: Consumer and Managerial Perspectives*, Bristol: Channel View.

Moscardo, G. and Ballantyne, R. (2008) 'Interpretation and tourist attraction', in A. Fyall, A. Leask and S. Wanhill (eds) *Managing Tourist Attractions*, 2nd edn, London: Elsevier.

Munro, J.K., Morrison-Saunders, A. and Hughes, M. (2008) 'Environmental interpretation evaluation in natural areas', *Journal of Ecotourism*, 7(1): 1–14.

O'Toole, F. (1992) 'The emperor's map makes us tourists in our own land', *The Irish Times*. Available at: www.irishtimes.com/newspaper/archive/1992/1007/Pg012.html#Ar01201

—— (2007) 'Taming the Cliffs of Moher', *The Irish Times*. Available at: www.irishtimes.com/newspaper/archive/2007/0206/Pg016.html#Ar01602

Pine, B.J. and Gilmore, J.H. (1999) *The Experience Economy*, Boston: Harvard Business School Press.

Pomering, A., Noble, G. and Johnson, L.W. (2011) 'Conceptualising a contemporary marketing mix for sustainable tourism', *Journal of Sustainable Tourism*, 19(8): 953–69.

Porto, S.M.C., Leanza, P.M. and Cascone, G. (2012) 'Developing interpretation plans to promote traditional rural buildings as built heritage attractions', *International Journal of Tourism Research,* 14: 421–36.

Poulsson, S.H.G. and Kale, S.H. (2004) 'The experience economy and commercial experiences', *The Marketing Review*, 4(3): 267–77.

Powell, R.B. and Ham, S.H. (2008) 'Can ecotourism interpretation really lead to pro-conservation knowledge, attitudes and behaviour? Evidence from the Galapagos Islands', *Journal of Sustainable Tourism*, 16(4): 467–89.

Ross, G. (2006) 'Heritage lost or fortune found: issues and dilemmas concerning tourist development within local communities', *Etropic: Electronic Journal of Studies in the Tropics*, 5. Available at www.jcu.edu.au/etropic

Schmitt, B. (1999) 'Experiential marketing', *Journal of Marketing Management*, 15(1–3): 53–67.

Stamation, K.A., Croft, D.B., Shaugnessy, P.D., Waples, K.A. and Briggs, S.V. (2007) 'Education and conservation value of whale watching', *Tourism in Marine Environments*, 4(1): 41–56.

Stuart, F.I. and Tax, S. (2004) 'Toward an integrative approach to designing service experiences: Lessons learned from the theatre', *Journal of Operations Management*, 22: 609–27.

Tilden, F. (1977) *Interpreting Our Heritage*, Chapel Hill: The University of North Carolina Press.

Truong, V.D. and Hall, C.M. (2013) 'Social marketing and tourism: What is the evidence?', *Social Marketing Quarterly*, 19(2): 110–35.

Urry, J. and Larsen, J. (2011) *The Tourist Gaze 3.0,* London: Sage.

Weiler, B. and Smith, L. (2009) 'Does more interpretation lead to greater outcomes? An assessment of the impacts of multiple layers of interpretation in a zoo context', *Journal of Sustainable Tourism*, 17(1), 91–105.

Williams, P. (2012) 'The memorial museum identity complex: Victimhood, culpability, and responsibility', in B.M. Carbonell (ed.) *Museum Studies: An Anthology of Contexts*, 2nd edn, Maldon: Blackwell Publishing.

—— (2013) 'Performing interpretation', *Scandinavian Journal of Hospitality and Tourism*. Available at: http://dx.doi.org/10.1080/15022250.2013.796228

Wong, C.U.I. (2013) 'The sanitization of colonial history: Authenticity, heritage interpretation and the case of Macau's tour guides', *Journal of Sustainable Tourism*. Available at: http://dx.doi.org/10.1080/09669582.2013.790390

Yalowitz, S.S. and Bronnenkant, K. (2009) 'Timing and tracking; Unlocking visitor behavior', *Visitor Studies*, 12(1): 47–64.

24

Tourism in the future(s)

Forecasting and scenarios

Daniel Scott and Stefan Gössling

Forecasting To predict or estimate a future event or trend in a phenomenon of interest. For the tourism sector, forecasts generally focus on indicators of tourism demand, including, for example: tourist arrivals (international and domestic), same-day visitors (day trips), overnight stays, accommodation occupancy rates, transportation mode occupancy rate (seats sold), and visitor spending.

Scenario Scenarios utilize broad perspectives to explore multiple interactions among major known drivers of change and to identify the strategic implications of so-called 'game changers' that could result in high-impact, non-linear changes to a tourism business, destination or even the global tourism sector.

Introduction

The future belongs to those who prepare for it today.

Malcolm X (1925–1965)

The need for insight into the future to guide better decision making in the present permeates many aspects of our personal life and professional work. At a personal level, homeowners want to know what mortgage interest rates will be for the next several months or years. Farmers want to know commodity prices six months ahead to decide what crop to plant and then know the weather several days ahead to decide when to plant that crop or use irrigation. Tour operators want to know what demand for travel to a city or country will be in the next month, season or year. Investors want insight into a myriad of factors influencing individual stock or commodity prices, from interest and currency exchange rates to energy prices to regulatory changes to consumer demand for specific products and services. Governments need foresight on equally diverse and complex factors vital to their national interests, including economic growth, employment, education, social benefits (e.g. healthcare, retirement pensions), crime and migration/relocation patterns.

Daniel Scott and Stefan Gössling

In this era of rapid technological, economic, social and political change, where globalization has increased the connectivity and complexities of economic and governance systems, the need for foresight has arguably never been greater. The tumultuous events of the first decade of the twenty-first century, including the 2001 terrorist attacks on the United States, the emergence of smartphone technology and social media, the 2008 financial crisis and lingering economic recession, the Arab Spring movement, and the Asian and Japanese tsunamis, have further reinforced the importance of understanding and preparing for an uncertain and interconnected future. One indicator of the renewed interest in future preparedness comes from a longitudinal survey on the use of a range of management tools by large businesses worldwide that has been conducted since the early 1990s. The survey revealed an abrupt increase in the use of contingency and scenario-planning techniques following the 11 September 2001 terrorist attacks on the United States (nearly doubling to over 70 per cent of responding companies) (Rigby & Bilodeau 2007). The much-increased use of these techniques has been sustained through the end of the decade (Rigby & Bilodeau 2011).

The tourism sector has been no exception to the challenges of persistent social, technological, economic, environmental and political (STEEP) changes and major disruptive events of this century. Consider how tourism has been revolutionized on a global scale by information and communication technologies, the emergence of low-cost airlines, threats of aircraft-focused terrorism, economic growth and political changes that have led to the emergence of major new regional markets like Brazil, Russia, India, China and South Africa (BRICS) and, in contrast, the financial crisis and prolonged impact on mature Organisation for Economic Co-operation and Development (OECD) markets. Planning for a 'business as usual' (BAU) future in turbulent times is a dangerous strategy for any tourism organization, from the small and medium-sized enterprises that are so vital to the sector to super-national tourism organizations like the United Nations World Tourism Organization (UNWTO) (Gössling & Scott 2012).

This chapter provides an overview of the tools and techniques available to the tourism sector to explore the implications of well-established trends and to navigate the uncertainty of other future trends and events. The chapter is organized into two main sections that focus on the different approaches used to understand two distinct domains of knowledge about the future. The forecasts section focuses on techniques to assess well-established trends or influencing factors to provide day-to-day and bounded annual operational intelligence (e.g. how cyclical economic conditions and currency exchange rates might influence seasonal visitation or how demographic changes (population growth, ageing) and energy prices over the next 10 years will influence the evolution of specific tourism markets). The scenario section then examines techniques for exploring the greater complexities and uncertainties of the more distant future, which is beyond the normal planning horizons of business and governments. Scenarios utilize broader perspectives to explore multiple interactions among major known drivers of change and to identify the strategic implications of so-called game changers, black swans, or x-factors, that could result in high-impact, non-linear changes to a tourism business, destination or even the global tourism sector. The strengths, limitations and value of applying forecasting and scenarios techniques in the tourism sector are discussed.

Forecasts

The aim of forecasting is to predict or estimate a future event or trend in a phenomenon of interest. For the tourism sector, forecasts generally focus on indicators of tourism demand, including, for example: tourist arrivals (international and domestic), same-day visitors (day trips), overnight stays, accommodation occupancy rates, transportation mode occupancy rate (seats sold) and visitor spending. Accurate forecasts of how many tourists will be visiting an area, where they will stay, what they will do and spend while they are there, and how key markets are changing over time are essential to efficient tourism operations and promotion. Other indicators of sustainability (see UNWTO 2004) may be considered in forecasts as influences on tourism performance, but are rarely provided as forecast outcomes. In this respect, forecasting approaches in the tourism sector offer a narrow perspective on the future of tourism sustainability. Nonetheless, forecasting offers highly important information for tourism operations planning and destination marketing, both of which are important for improving sustainable tourism.

The history of tourism forecasting research and practice began in the 1960s, with most of the early applications in Europe and North America (Goh & Law 2002). For example, when the British Tourist Authority was created in 1969, it was already forecasting that inbound tourism would increase from less than 6 million visitors in 1969 to 10 million by 1975 (9.5 million visitors were recorded) (VisitBritain 2009). Tourism forecasting has evolved considerably over the last 40 years, particularly as the development and gradual accumulation of more robust tourism data over longer timeframes has facilitated the application of a broader range of analytical forecasting techniques.

Today, tourism forecasts are abundant, with most national tourism organizations or designated government departments providing extensive analysis on domestic, inbound and outbound tourism trends, as well as monthly, quarterly/seasonal and annual forecasts at the national and sub-national scale. These trend analyses and near-term forecasts are intended to support tourism businesses and government agencies in operational decision making and improve competitiveness.

Multi-year forecasts are also available in several countries as part of tourism policy development and strategic planning initiatives (e.g. New Zealand to 2019 [Government of New Zealand 2013], Britain to 2020 [VisitBritain 2012]), often with a special focus on expected change in key international travel markets or market segments and with confidence intervals to quantify uncertainty associated with longer-term projections. The UNWTO provides 20-year forecasts of international tourist arrivals (see Table 24.1) to provide insight into the future development of the tourism economy, to promote the salience of tourism in the global economy, and for policy development. The most recent long-range forecast suggests that international arrivals will increase from 940 million in 2010 to between 1.4 and 2.0 billion in 2030, with the share of international arrivals to emerging economies surpassing those of advanced economies for the first time sometime between 2015 and 2020 (UNWTO 2011). This continued growth trend, which would see the number of international tourists double over the next 20 years, and the evolving geographic distribution of tourism demand has major implications for the sustainability of tourism, illustrating the value of long-range forecasts for sustainable tourism research and policy agenda-setting.

No single technique is the best suited to all tourism forecasting needs. With the diverse forecasting situations, resources and capacities that exist in the global mosaic of tourism businesses and government agencies, the United Nations World Tourism Organization and the European Travel Commission (ETC) (2008) has provided a summary guide detailing the types of forecasting techniques widely used in tourism, including the type of forecasting application and time horizon each are most appropriate for, the data and resource (financial and expertise) requirements, and their respective accuracy (see Table 24.2). Although both qualitative and quantitative forecasting techniques are used in tourism, numerically precise (but not to be equated with 'accurate') predictions from quantitative forecasting are by far more common in professional practice.

Table 24.1 Long-term forecasts of global and regional international tourist arrivals

	2010 Baseline (millions)	2020 (millions)	2030 (millions)		
			Slow economic recovery[1]	Central estimate	Transport costs continue to fall[1]
Global	940	1360	1400	1809	2000
Africa	47	85	98	134	140
Americas	150	199	196	248	280
Asia-Pacific	207	355	420	535	600
Europe	479	620	574	744	820
Middle East	56	101	112	149	160

Data Source: UNWTO (2011) *Tourism Towards 2030: Global Overview*

[1] Extrapolated from regional distribution UNWTO (2011) central estimate.

Table 24.2 Comparison of major tourism forecast approaches

Characteristics	Quantitative		Qualitative
	Extrapolation techniques	Causal techniques	Expert Panel/ Delphi
Type of data used	Time series	Varied data sources	Expert knowledge
Data input needs	High (multi-year)	High	Low
Expertise needed	Low/medium	Medium/high	Medium/high
Development cost	Low	High	Low/medium
Ease of implementation	Easy	Moderate/difficult	Easy/Moderate
Appropriate time horizon	Short (1 year or less)	Short to long (1–10 years)	Short to long (1–10 years)
Best suited application	Short-term forecasts in relatively stable markets (minimal disruptions and complexity)	Understanding influences on observed trends and forecasts in evolving markets	Understanding observed trends and forecasts where complex situations exist (e.g. following a major disruptive event)
Accuracy	High in appropriate applications	Medium	Medium (though rarely evaluated)

Adapted from: UNWTO and ETC (2008).

Quantitative forecasting techniques can be classified into two main types: extrapolative and causal. Extrapolative techniques, as the name implies, rely on extrapolating observed historical trends, often referred to as a 'time series', into the future. For example, if international tourism arrivals in a country have increased between 3 and 5 per cent annually for the last 10 years, a simple extrapolation–based forecast would be that arrivals in the next year would increase at the average of the last 10 years. Extrapolative forecast techniques only consider change to the tourism indicator of interest and do not consider how changes in other external factors (tourism or non-tourism) could influence that specific performance indicator. Therefore, extrapolative techniques are most accurate for short-term forecasts in fairly stable tourism markets that have not been influenced by highly disruptive events during the particular time series (low complexity) (see Table 24.2). While no minimum length of time series is needed for extrapolation-based forecasts, those that are longer are likely to improve forecast accuracy. Similarly, statistical techniques that give more weight to recent observations (i.e. the last three of 10 years) or account for the influence of exceptional years (e.g. when a special event like the Olympics took place in the destination or there was a natural disaster) are often used improve the accuracy of extrapolative approaches.

Where simplifying assumptions form the basis of forecasts or where disruptions occur, projections may deviate considerably from actual developments. As an example, the Ministry of Water, Energy, Construction, Lands and Environment (MWECLE 1993) and the Commission for Tourism (1998) in Zanzibar, Tanzania, expected tourist arrivals in the Zanzibar islands to increase from 86,495 in 1997 to 550,000 in 2015. After a period of political turmoil and the economic recession in 2008, arrivals totaled 168,223 in 2012, with little hope of continued growth (Zanzibar Association of Tourism Investors 2013).

The relative accuracy of tourism forecast techniques have been evaluated in four major comparative studies (Witt & Witt 1995; Li *et al.* 2005; Song & Li 2008; Athanasopoulos *et al.* 2011). The most recent and comprehensive of these compared the relative performance of extrapolation (time series) and causal models (with explanatory variables) using the same tourism data, and found that extrapolative (time series) approaches provided more accurate monthly, seasonal and one-year forecasts than causal models (Athanasopoulos *et al.* 2011).

Because extrapolation-based forecast techniques are univariate, they provide no explanatory power for how tourism markets may change beyond short timeframes when there is less continuity in the influences on tourism. For example, in the late 1990s, after a period of sustained growth, arrivals from several major European markets began to decline substantially in several Caribbean destinations. Figure 24.1 shows this trend for arrivals from Germany and France to the Bahamas, while at the same time the markets in Sweden and the Netherlands remained relatively stabile and the UK market increased. Where more complex market change is occurring, simple extrapolative techniques can provide misleading forecasts over a three–five year period and, importantly, provide no insight into the differential trends in key markets. To understand why most, but not all, of these inbound markets were declining require causal and/ or expert-based techniques.

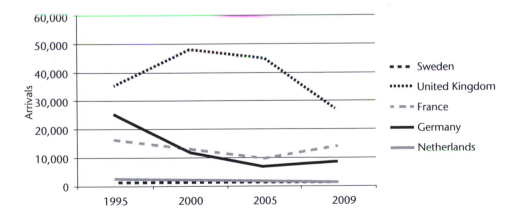

Figure 24.1 Differential trends in European market arrivals to Bahamas

Causal forecast methods examine relationships between the tourism performance indicator of interest (dependent variable) and other influencing factors (independent variables) that can be specific to the tourism sector (e.g. number of air travel route connections, transportation costs) or external to the tourism sector (e.g. general economic indicators like gross domestic product [GDP] or currency exchange rates). Table 24.3 outlines many of the factors commonly included in causal forecast models as well as a sample of other potentially important influencing factors that are not typically considered. Causal models come in many forms, ranging from simple regression analysis of key influencing variables to complex structural models that seek to quantify interdependencies of multiple dependent and independent variables. Data requirements increase with the complexity of the causal model and can limit their application in data-poor destinations where reliable tourism performance monitoring over many years is not available.

Table 24.3 Important factors influencing the tourism sector

	Factors commonly considered in causal forecast models	Major drivers considered in scenarios
Social	Population size; population growth; age distribution; historical social/ cultural ties (diaspora); threats to personal safety/crime rate.	Role of social media for consumer referrals and targeted social action; mismanagement of population ageing; widespread youth unemployment and family dynamics; discovery of extraterrestrial life.
Technology	Transport mode; efficiency gains in fuel use.	Role of information and communication technology in travel bookings; cyber attack; robotics in service sector.
Economic	Economic growth (GDP); currency exchange rates; personal income trends (GINI); travel price; economic links/ free trade agreements.	Sudden financial crisis/systemic financial failure of governments; international economic sanctions; new free trade agreements; prolonged spike in world oil price; growing income disparity.
Environment	Travel distance/time; climate (at source market and destination).	Legacy of natural disasters (earthquake, tsunami, hurricane/ typhoon); disease outbreaks (SARS, avian flu)/pandemic; new regulatory regimes (carbon tax); food shortage versus large-scale biofuel production; abrupt climate change and impact on natural assets (coastal areas, heritage sites, snow cover).
Political	Travel taxation; fees; charges; subsidies.	Changes in travel taxation; arrival/departure taxes; levies to finance conservation; accommodation taxes; fuel subsidies; changes in border regulations (China's preferred country status, entry into the EU, break-up of EU); political unrest (Arab Spring); regional instability; WMD terrorist attack.

Critical advantages of causal models are that they can provide insight into changing tourism markets and provide forecasts of how markets with less continuity may continue to evolve in response to changes in major external or internal drivers listed in Table 24.3. Because causal models seek to understand the influence of key factors on tourism performance, they can also be used as a policy analysis tool to provide insight into the implications of planned policy interventions such as the imposition of new taxes on tourists (e.g. destination marketing tax at hotels or airport departure tax) or new investments in marketing. These forecast techniques can also provide powerful support for the positions of lobby groups. For example, there have been a number of forecasts of the potential impact of the substantial increases in the United Kingdom's (UK) Air Passenger Duty (APD) or the cancellation of this excise tax on departing passengers. Departure taxes on air travelers have been strongly opposed by the aviation and tourism industries (e.g. International Air Transport Association 2013; Forsyth *et al.*, 2014), and the APD has been heavily criticized from within the UK for reducing the competitiveness of national air carriers, adversely impacting the national economy by reducing international tourism to the UK and restricting business travel necessary for overseas business development. A consortium of British airlines commissioned a study that forecast that the removal of the APD would result in an increase in GDP (0.45% in the first year) and employment (60,000 jobs by 2020) (PricewaterhouseCoopers 2013). Similar conclusions were reached by a World Travel and Tourism Council (WTTC) forecast model which concluded that canceling the APD would create over 90,000 jobs in the UK and add GBP 4.2 billion in annual economic activity (Oxford Economics, 2011).

Similar forecast modeling techniques have also been used to explore other dimensions of tourism sustainability. For example, although the UK government has made it clear that its APD is a revenue-generating excise tax on travelers to compensate for air travel exemptions to value added taxes, the increase in APD costs was partially rationalized as being supportive of the nation's strengthening greenhouse gas (GHG) emission reduction targets. The government projected that this rise in APD will save around 1.1 million tonnes of carbon dioxide in 2010–2011 (House of Commons Environmental Audit Committee 2007). A causal model developed by Mayor and Tol (2007) came to a very different conclusion, forecasting that a doubling of the APD cost would potentially have the perverse effect of marginally increasing CO_2 emissions because, despite the higher fee on non–European Union (EU) flights, it would slightly reduce the relative price difference between near and far holidays, making more distant holiday destinations comparably cheaper.

Other studies that have used similar causal modeling of travel cost sensitivity have examined the impact of the introduction of small carbon taxes, like those proposed for the entry of aviation into the EU Emission Trading System. They also forecast very limited impact on demand for air travel, even for long-haul destinations (Tol 2007; Gössling *et al.* 2008; Pentelow & Scott 2010, 2011; Cohen *et al.* 2011, see further discussion in Chapters 3 and 33).

Causal econometric models have also been used to explore the distant future consequences of projected climate change, in conjunction with a range of other macro-scale factors (e.g. population growth, per capita income and other variables common to causal forecast models) on aggregate international tourism demand and the potential geographical redistribution of tourist arrivals (Hamilton *et al.* 2005; Berrittella *et al.* 2006; Bigano *et al.* 2006). Broadly, global tourism demand is forecast to be largely unaffected by climatic changes. The models forecast changes in geographic distribution of demand, where tourists from temperate nations that currently dominate international travel adapt their travel patterns to take advantage of new climatic opportunities closer to home. Demand for international travel to subtropical, tropical and some Middle Eastern countries is projected to decline, with fewer arrivals from temperate nations and increased out-bound travel from these nations.

These global-scale models with multi-decadal forecasts of tourism demand are necessarily simplified and have important limitations that have been discussed by the authors (Hamilton *et al.* 2005; Berrittella *et al.* 2006) and others (Gössling & Hall 2006; Eugenio-Martin & Campos-Soria 2010; Weaver 2011). Similar concerns about tourism data quality, model spatial and temporal resolution, understanding of demand-influencing variables (and the absence of some variables thought to be important for tourist decision making), and reliance on projections from other models with known limitations, apply to all long-range forecast models in tourism.

Increasingly, contingency analysis is being applied to better reflect the uncertainty in longer-range causal model forecasts. Instead of a single forecast of the future, contingency analysis examines how changes in key assumptions or influencing factors could alter outcomes and provide a range of future forecasts. For example, unlike the UNWTO's initial long-term forecast, which provided a single forecast for global international tourist arrivals in 2020 (UNWTO 2001), the more recent 2030 forecasts shown in Table 24.1 considered some varied assumptions of economic growth and transport costs (UNWTO 2011). In this way, contingency analysis begins to take on some of the characteristics of scenario-based planning, which is discussed in the next section.

Qualitative forecasting methods such as expert panels and the Delphi technique are used much less in the tourism sector. However, these expert-based judgment techniques are valuable in highly uncertain circumstances (e.g. post-tsunami, terrorist attack, epidemic) where time-series approaches are rendered ineffective and empirical causal models are inadequate to capture the scope of unprecedented events and the nuanced impact on tourist decision making. Expert panels bring together diverse expertise to interactively discuss how events may impact tourism demand and interact with other major drivers of tourism. Often experience from analogous events in another destination or country can provide vital insight into panel-based forecasts. The Delphi technique is similar in that it seeks input from diverse experts, but it is usually done without bringing experts together by using multiple rounds of surveys and expert feedback to achieve a consensus forecast.

Both expert panels and Delphi techniques are highly flexible. These approaches can be used to provide valuable input into the development and interpretation of quantitative forecast approaches. The New Zealand Ministry of Business Innovation and Employment adopted an innovative combined-method approach when it set out to prepare its newest multi-year tourism forecasts (for 2013–2019). Quantitative modeling utilizing short-term (income, price and exchange rate effects) and longer-term structural drivers (demographic and market shifts) were combined with industry knowledge from a technical committee consisting of the Ministry, Air New Zealand, the Tourism Industry Association, Auckland International Airport, the New Zealand Institute of Economic Research and Tourism New Zealand. This combined forecast approach was used to quantify key uncertainties and allow the expert-panel to include 'what-if' questions in model outputs (Government of New Zealand 2013).

Scenarios

Pierre Wack (1985), who was credited as one of the pioneers of scenario planning at Royal Dutch/Shell in the 1960 and 1970s, reminds us that:

> Forecasts are not always wrong; more often than not, they can be reasonably accurate. And that is what makes them so dangerous. They are usually constructed on the assumption

that tomorrow's world will be much like today's. They often work because the world does not always change. But sooner or later forecasts will fail when they are needed most: in anticipating major shifts in the business environment that make whole strategies obsolete.

Institutional planning in business, government and non-governmental organizations generally does not handle uncertainty well. Traditional trend-analysis-based forecasting encourages organizations to place a high value on a single view of the future, often represented as an 'official organizational future'. This BAU outlook is not static, but is predicated on an extrapolation of the most probable observed trends and the inherent assumption that these trends will not deviate substantially over the next several years or even decades in the case of long-range forecasts. Wilkinson and Kupers (2013) observe that this BAU view of the future reflects the human tendency to comprehend familiar patterns and often results in an optimism bias that leaves the organization vulnerable to being blindsided by unexpected, disruptive events.

In contrast to forecasts, scenario-based planning does not extrapolate current trends. Its explicit purpose is to constructively challenge the assumptions inherent in the mental maps of organizations and key decision makers to uncover strategic blind spots. Scenario planning forces thinking outside of the proverbial 'box' by introducing elements of uncertainty that confront the BAU biases of organizations.

Scenario planning is a technique used to manage high levels of complexity and uncertainty inherent in preparing for a fundamentally unknowable future. Scenarios are not forecasts or predictions; they are alternate representations of plausible futures. Scenario planning is sometimes confused with contingency analysis, such as in the UNWTO and ETC (2008) *Handbook on Tourism Forecasting* which calls for developing estimated probabilities of scenario occurrence. Scenario development is not about identifying the most likely (right) future, but about developing highly distinct, plausible futures that require in-depth interpretation and often very different strategic responses.

Many attribute the origins of systematic scenario planning to military organizations in the twentieth century, though less formalized, intuitive approaches undoubtedly occurred long before. Scenario planning was subsequently adopted as a business management tool in the 1960s and 1970s to better understand the consequences of unusual or extreme situations, such as Royal Dutch/Shell's pioneering application of scenarios that considered dramatically increased world oil prices prior to the 1973 oil crisis.

Scenario planning has enjoyed something of a revival among academics and practitioners in the last decade (Varum & Melo 2010). Scenario analysis has become an integral part of planning for uncertain futures across a wide range of economic sectors and major global issues, including: energy (e.g. International Energy Agency 2011, 2012), demography (e.g. UN 2012), economic development (e.g. International Monetary Fund 2012), climate change (e.g. Intergovernmental Panel on Climate Change 2013), technology (e.g. Rockefeller Foundation 2010), biodiversity and ecosystem change (e.g. Hassan *et al.* 2005; Leadley *et al.* 2010), transportation and mobility (e.g. Schäfer & Victor 2000), agriculture and food production (e.g. Godfray *et al.* 2010), and water security (e.g. Cosgrove & Cosgrove 2012). As Gössling and Scott (2012) point out, the implications of these major scenario exercises have rarely been interpreted for tourism, and thus far represent a missed opportunity for the tourism community to benefit from the tremendous expertise of other academic disciplines and professions concerned with planning for an uncertain future.

Scenario planning is a highly flexible technique, characterized by numerous approaches, each with strengths and limitations, supporters and detractors (Keough & Shanahan 2008; Moriarty

2012). Nonetheless, scenario planning generally proceeds through a number of common stages (Schoemaker 1991; Varum & Melo 2010).

- *Problem definition/project scoping:* What is the strategic topic or focal question that the organization wants to examine? Why has it prioritized this analysis and how does it relate to the future strategy of the organization? What is the current BAU (official) future perceived by the organization? What is the time horizon the scenarios are to examine? Who are the stakeholders to be involved? For example, Vorster *et al.* (2013: 1) recently developed a scenario-building process for South Africa, but with high applicability to all long-haul destinations, with the core problem statement that: 'unconstrained growth in aviation emissions will not be compatible with 2050 climate stabilisation goals, and that the stringency and timing of public policy interventions could have far-reaching impacts – either on the market for future growth of long-haul travel or the natural ecosystem on which tourism depends'.
- *Establish current-future drivers of change:* Determine the wide range of change drivers that will be considered in the scenario analysis. Reflect on the salience of past drivers and whether these factors will remain fundamental uncertainties in the future. For scenarios to be effective, they cannot be devoid of links to current management situations and concerns over changes in contemporary key trends. Table 24.3 provided illustrative examples of major drivers of STEEP change that could be included in tourism scenario planning. It is clear that scenario planning can incorporate a much broader perspective of sustainability than is typical in forecasting approaches. Engaging highly diverse participants is fundamental to success at this stage (Berkhout & Hertin 2002). The perspectives of people from different regions, generations, social groups and professional experience that matter most to the organization must be brought together. A range of techniques can be used to develop a list of change drivers, including interviews or a workshop to collect the views of key informants in the organization and sector. Bringing participants together in interactive settings is generally recommended to allow more creative and insightful perspectives about the future to emerge through debate.
- *Ranking of drivers*: Although many drivers of change will be of interest to stakeholders engaged in the scenario-planning process, a critical task is to identify the most salient factors that could lead to distinctly different futures, which will comprise the foundation of the scenarios. A wide range of techniques can be used at this stage, including a workshop that allows participants to debate the importance of drivers and their associated critical uncertainties or the Delphi technique which allows participants to remotely and anonymously provide feedback on the thoughts of others. Dwyer *et al.* (2008) provide four tourism sector-specific criteria that can be helpful to guide the ranking of drivers: (1) the elements of the tourism sector that will be affected; (2) the degree of certainty associated with the driver of change; (3) the timescale within which change will manifest; and (4) the magnitude and irreversibility of change.
- *Initial scenario-building*: Scenario-building is a sub-process within broader scenario-planning exercises. A logical framework is created to bring combinations of the most salient drivers together into an initial, manageable, set of scenarios. Initial scenarios should be robust in that they are grounded in the recent experience of the organization and its broader economic sector (and geographic region if applicable), internally consistent, and plausible. This is the stage to critically examine the working scenarios for obvious contradictions and to determine whether the scenario is believable to the diverse stakeholders involved in the process. The purpose of an initial set of scenarios is to scope out a diverse range of futures

that could happen, some that the stakeholders involved may want to happen and others they do not want to happen (sometimes represented as 'extreme worlds' portending totally utopian and dystopian futures), to ensure the mental maps of the participants and organization will be challenged.

- *Reduce working scenarios to a final set of scenarios*: The final set of scenarios is generally recommended to be four or less, so the scenarios focus on the most relevant drivers and interpreting the implications is a manageable task for key decision makers. One recommended approach is for participants to prioritize the two most critical uncertainties and use these as a basis of what is sometime referred to as a '2x2 scenario matrix', resulting in four equally plausible, often evocatively named, scenarios. For example, a scenarios analysis that examined the potential impacts of the evolving global climate change policy regime on long-haul tourism to South Africa to 2050 generated two undesirable scenarios called the 'grim reaper' and 'fallen angel', a desirable future called 'green lantern', and a fourth scenario 'Florence Nightingale' was deemed implausible and removed from the analysis (Voster *et al.* 2013). Similarly, the UK's Forum for the Future (2009) developed scenarios to 2023, including 'boom and burst', 'divided disquiet', 'price and privilege' and 'carbon clampdown', to understand the implications of climate change, population growth and shortages of oil and other resources for outbound tourism and specific market segments. The selected final scenarios need to be clearly differentiated futures, not mere variations of a central BAU future. They should strive for persuasive storylines that can be effectively communicated among diverse stakeholders. Inviting external review of the detailed storylines of the final scenarios to 'fact check' their credibility with experts in key fields can be helpful to ensure their plausibility. For the final scenarios to be useful for action–oriented decisions, they must challenge the organization's BAU future and its associated assumptions, as well as be highly relevant to the most important strategic issues facing the organization (as determined in stages 1 and 3). A criticism of some scenario exercises is that they devolve into futurist musings with little relevance to current situations, providing limited value for decision making. The identification of indicators that can provide signals about the direction of key uncertainties provides additional value as an early warning system.
- *Interpret implications of scenarios for decision making*: Identifying the major implications of the scenarios on the organization and then including the risks and opportunities associated with different strategic choices is fundamental to translating scenario development into action. This is best done by re-engaging key decision makers in the organization from stage 1, as well as other external stakeholders who could provide valuable perspectives from outside the organization, to consider the challenges presented by the final scenarios. What would be the impact of each scenario on decision making for a range of tourism actors (i.e. from tourism ministers, to airline and hotel CEOs, to destination marketers, to tourism insurance providers and investors)? What would each need to do differently, as individuals or collectively, in order to succeed in the alternate futures outlined? This sector-wide collaborative response was the vision of the UK's 'Tourism 2023: Scenarios for Sustainable Tourism' initiative.
- *Revisit and review scenarios*: Scenario planning has often been criticized as a one-time exercise that is rarely an ongoing component of long-range strategic planning. Proponents contend that what is required to provide optimal value from scenario planning is a periodical commitment to review scenarios to incorporate new information, as well as monitoring predefined indicators which would provide early insight into key uncertainties.

As Varum *et al.* (2011) and Moriarty (2012) point out, there have been a number of methodological-oriented critiques of scenario planning as it has continued to mature towards a more praxis-based technique. Other critics of scenario planning argue that, fundamentally, there is only anecdotal evidence to support the value of scenarios for actionable decision making; there is, too rarely, critical reflection on scenario planning outcomes or the credibility of the proposed scenarios themselves.

Proponents counter that the value of scenario planning is not in the predictive power of the constructed futures, but in their much broader value to the organization(s) involved (Rohrbeck & Schwarz 2013). Scenarios do not claim to be predictions of 'the' future and should not be confused with crystal balls. Instead, the value of scenario planning comes from the process of collective learning, improved organizational/inter-organization communication, capacity building, and strategic alignment within an organization/sector, as well as greater insight into how strategic decisions are being made. Well-designed scenarios make key assumptions about the 'official' BAU future explicit, reveal risks associated with uncertainties in those core assumptions, provide strategic foresight by identifying risks and opportunities not recognized through traditional forecasts and planning processes and identifying early warning indicators that provide an enhanced capacity to recognize and respond to change, and create a formal context through which to test unconventional policies and business lines.

Conclusion

As the global tourism system is affected by, and must to respond to, an increasing number of interconnected challenges, including ongoing uncertainty related to the financial and sovereign debt crisis, the new geography and market preferences of major tourist flows from emerging economies, the new realities of mobility in a world of fluctuating energy prices and the shift toward a low-carbon economy, threats of terrorism and political upheaval, demographic change with near- and long-term implications for travel patterns of youth and seniors, and the consequences of climate and environmental change for destination attributes and attractiveness, the need for foresight and techniques that can contribute to future preparedness will only increase. Forecasting techniques are widely utilized in the tourism sector and can provide essential insight into well-established near-term trends, but are not capable of coping with the uncertainty of longer-term trends, let alone some of the important uncertainties that will have an immense influence on the future of sustainable tourism. Existing forecasting tools also have limited application for broader dimensions of sustainability that are likely to be more important to the tourism sector in the decades ahead. While scenario planning has had a more limited application in tourism to date, it could become increasingly valuable for navigating these future challenges.

The next generation of tourism scholars and professionals reading this chapter will need to develop innovative ways to explore these sustainability challenges. Collectively, we need to ask some salient questions. What has the tourism sector learned from the major disruptive events of the first decade of the twenty-first century (effective recovery strategies, limits to coping range)? Which of the major risks to regional or global tourism listed in Table 24.3 has the tourism sector evaluated? How vulnerable are the UNWTO projections of tourism growth to 2030 to these unfolding trends or disruptive events? What strategies have been developed to cope with these risk factors should they unfold? In other words, what future(s) is tourism ready for? The answer to these questions is disconcerting considering the increasingly important contribution many perceive tourism will make to the future global economy.

References

Athanasopoulos, G., Hyndman, R., Song, H. and Wu, D. (2011) 'The tourism forecasting competition', *International Journal of Forecasting*, 27(3): 822–44.

Berkhout, F. and Hertin, J. (2002) *Foresight Futures Scenarios: Developing and Applying a Participative Strategic Planning Tool*. University of Sussex.

Berrittella, M., Bigano, A., Roson, R. and Tol, R. (2006) *General Equilibrium Analysis of Climate Change Impacts on Tourism*, Working Paper No. 17. Ecological and Environmental Economics (EEE) Programme.

Bigano, A., Hamilton, J., Maddison, D. and Tol, R. (2006) 'Predicting tourism flows under climate change: An editorial comment on Gössling and Hall (2006)', *Climatic Change*, 79: 175–180.

Cohen, S., Higham, J. and Cavaliere, C. (2011) 'Binge flying: Behavioural addiction and climate change', *Annals of Tourism Research*, 38: 1070–89.

Commission for Tourism (1998) *Tourist Arrivals on Zanzibar 1997*. Zanzibar: Tanzania.

Cosgrove, C.E. and Cosgrove, W.J. (2012) *The Dynamics of Global Water Futures Driving Forces 2011–2050*. Paris: United Nations Educational, Scientific and Cultural Organization. Available at: http://unesdoc.unesco.org/images/0021/002153/215377e.pdf. Accessed 27 May 2012.

Dwyer, L., Edwards, D., Mistilis, N., Roman, C., Scott, N. and Cooper, C. (2008). *Megatrends Underpinning Tourism to 2020: Analysis of Key Drivers for Change*. Gold Coast: CRC Sustainable Tourism.

Eugenio-Martin, J.L. and Campos-Soria, J.A. (2010) 'Climate in the region of origin and destination choice in outbound tourism demand', *Tourism Management*, 31: 744–53.

Forsyth, P., Dwyer, L., Spurr, R. and Pham, T. (2014) 'The impacts of Australia's departure tax: Tourism versus the economy?' *Tourism Management*, 40: 126–36.

Forum for the Future (2009) *Tourism 2023: Four Scenarios, a Vision and a Strategy for UK Outbound Travel and Tourism*. Available at: www.forumforthefuture.org/sites/default/files/images/Forum/Projects/Tourism2023/Tourism_2023_full_report_web_version.pdf. Accessed 27 May 2012.

Godfray, H.C.J., Beddington, J.R., Crute, I.R., Haddad, L., Lawrence, D., Muir, J.F., Pretty, J., Robinson, S., Thomas, S.M. and Toulmin, C. (2010) 'Food security: The challenge of feeding 9 billion people', *Science*, 327: 812–18.

Goh, C. and Law, R. (2002) 'Modeling and forecasting tourism demand for arrivals with stochastic nonstationary seasonality and intervention', *Tourism Management*, 23: 499–510.

Gössling, S. and Hall, C.M. (2006) 'Uncertainties in predicting tourist travel flows based on models', *Climatic Change*, 79: 163–73.

Gössling, S. and Scott, D. (2012) 'Scenario planning for sustainable tourism: an introduction', *Journal of Sustainable Tourism*, 20(6): 773–78.

Gössling, S. Peeters, P. and Scott, D. (2008) 'Consequences of climate policy for international tourist arrivals in developing countries', *Third World Quarterly*, 29: 873–901.

Government of New Zealand (2013) *New Zealand's Tourism Sector Outlook: Forecasts for 2013–2019*. Ministry of Business Innovation and Employment. Available at: www.med.govt.nz/sectors-industries/tourism/tourism-research-data/forecasts/2013-19-forecasts. Accessed 15 November 2013.

Hamilton, J., Maddison, D. and Tol, R. (2005) 'Climate change and international tourism: A simulation study', *Global Environmental Change*, 15: 253–66.

Hassan, I., Scholes, R. and Neville, A. (eds) (2005) *Millennium Ecosystem Assessment. Ecosystems and Human Well-Being: Current State and Trends: Findings of the Condition and Trends Working Group*. Washington DC: Island Press.

House of Commons Environmental Audit Committee (2007) *Pre-Budget 2006 and the Stern Review* (Fourth Report of Session 2006–7). London: HMSO.

Intergovernmental Panel on Climate Change (IPCC) (2013) 'Summary for Policymakers', in *Climate Change 2013: The Physical Science Basis. Contribution of Working Group I to the Fifth Assessment Report of the Intergovernmental Panel on Climate Change*. Available at: www.ipcc.ch/report/ar5/wg1/#.Upyi_aUrTHg. Accessed 10 November 2013.

International Air Transport Association (IATA) (2013) *Impact assessments of proposed or implemented changes in taxation policy affecting the airline industry and its users*. Available at: www.iata.org/publications/economics/public-policy/Pages/taxation.aspx. Accessed 29 October 2013.

International Energy Agency (2011) *World Energy Outlook 2011*. Paris: International Energy Agency. Available at: www.iea.org/publications/freepublications/publication/WEO2011_WEB.pdf. Accessed 12 November 2013.

—— (2012) *World Energy Outlook 2012*. Paris: International Energy Agency. Available at: www.iea.org/newsroomandevents/speeches/weo_launch.pdf. Accessed 12 November 2013.

International Monetary Fund (2012) *World Economic Outlook April 2012: Growth Resuming, Dangers Remain*. Washington, DC: IMF.

Keough, S. and Shanahan, K. (2008) 'Scenario planning: Toward a more complete model for practice advances', *Developing Human Resources,* 10(2): 166–78.

Leadley, P., Pereira, H.M., Alkemade, R., Fernandez-Manjarrés, J.F., Proença, V., Scharlemann, J.P.W. and Walpole, M.J., (2010) *Biodiversity Scenarios: Projections of 21st century change in biodiversity and associated ecosystem services*. Convention on Biological Diversity, Montreal, Canada. Available at: www.diversitas-international.org/activities/research/biodiscovery/cbdts50en.pdf. Accessed 27 May 2012.

Li, G., Song, H. and Witt, S.F. (2005) 'Recent developments in econometric modelling and forecasting', *Journal of Travel Research,* 44: 82–99.

Mayor, K. and Tol, R.S.J. (2007) 'The impact of the UK aviation tax on carbon dioxide emissions and visitor numbers', *Transport Policy*, 14: 507–13.

Ministry of Water, Energy, Construction, Lands and Environment (MWECLE) (1993) *Tourism Zoning Plan: Main Report*. Zanzibar: Tanzania.

Moriarty, J.P. (2012) 'Theorising scenario analysis to improve future perspective planning in tourism', *Journal of Sustainable Tourism,* 20(6).

Oxford Economics (2011) *An Alternative APD Regime*. Available at: www.oxfordeconomics.com/Media/Default/economic-impact/public-policy-assesment/an-alternative-apd-regime.pdf. Accessed 12 November 2013.

Pentelow, L. and Scott, D. (2010) 'The implications of climate change mitigation policy and oil price volatility for tourism arrivals to the Caribbean', *Journal of Tourism Hospitality and Planning Development,* 7(3), 301–15.

—— (2011) 'Aviation's inclusion in international climate policy regimes: Implications for the Caribbean tourism industry', *Journal of Air Transport Management*, 17: 199–205.

PricewaterhouseCoopers (2013) *The Economic Impact of Air Passenger Duty: A Study by PwC*. London, UK: PricewaterhouseCoopers LLP. Available at: http://corporate.easyjet.com/~/media/Files/E/Easyjet-Plc-V2/pdf/content/APD-study-full.pdf. Accessed 20 November 2013.

Rigby, D. and Bilodeau, B. (2007) 'A growing focus on preparedness', *Harvard Business Review*. Available at: http://hbr.org/2007/07/a-growing-focus-on-preparedness/ar/1. Accessed 12 November 2013.

—— (2011) *Management Tools & Trends 2011*. 11 May 2011 Bain Brief. Available at: www.bain.com/publications/articles/Management-tools-trends-2011.aspx. Accessed 12 November 2013.

Rockefeller Foundation (2010) *Scenarios for the Future of Technology and International Development*. New York: The Rockefeller Foundation.

Rohrbeck, R. and Schwarz, J. (2013) 'The value contribution of strategic foresight: Insights from an empirical study of large European companies', *Technological Forecasting and Social Change,* 80(8): 1593–1606.

Schäfer, A. and Victor, D.G. (2000) 'The future mobility of the world population', *Transportation Research A*, 34: 171–205.

Schoemaker, P.L.H. (1991) 'When and how to use scenario planning: A heuristic approach with illustration', *Journal of Forecasting*, 10: 549–64.

Song, H. and Li, G. (2008) 'Tourism demand modelling and forecasting – A review of recent literature', *Tourism Management*, 29: 203–20.

Tol, R.S.J. (2007) 'The impact of a carbon tax on international tourism', *Transportation Research Part D*, 12: 129–42.

UN (2012) *United Nations Population Division Home Page*, various pages. Available at: www.un.org/esa/population. Accessed 25 May 2012.

United Nations World Tourism Organization (UNWTO) (2001) *Tourism 2020 Vision*. Madrid: World Tourism Organization.

—— (2004) *Indicators of Sustainable Development for Tourism Destinations: A Guidebook*. Madrid: UNWTO.

—— (2011) *Tourism Towards 2030: Global Overview*. Madrid: UNWTO.

United Nations World Tourism Organization and the European Travel Commission (2008) *Handbook on Tourism Forecasting Methodologies*. Madrid: United Nations World Tourism Organization and Brussels:

European Travel Commission. Available at: http://pub.unwto.org/WebRoot/Store/Shops/ Infoshop/48EA/1B51/FFDF/0971/B7DC/C0A8/0164/D9AF/081003_handbook_tourism_ forecasting_excerpt.pdf. Accessed 12 November 2013.

Varum, C. and Melo, C. (2010) 'Directions in scenario planning literature – A review of the past decades', *Futures*, 42(4): 355–69.

Varum, C.A., Melo, C., Alvarenga, A. and de Carvalho, P.S. (2011) 'Scenarios and possible futures for hospitality and tourism', *Foresight*, 13: 19–35.

VisitBritain (2009) *Foresight* – Issue 64. Available at: www.visitbritain.org/Images/Foresight%20Issue%20 64_tcm29–14796.pdf. Accessed 4 December 2013.

—— (2012) *Foresight* – Issue 100. Available at: www.visitbritain.org/Images/Foresight%20-%20issue%20 100_tcm29–30520.pdf. Accessed 4 December 2013.

Vorster, S., Ungerer, M. and Volschenk, J. (2013) '2050 Scenarios for long-haul tourism in the evolving global climate change regime', *Sustainability*, 5(1): 1–51.

Wack, P. (1985) 'Scenarios: Uncharted waters ahead', *Harvard Business Review*, September. Available at: http://hbr.org/1985/09/scenarios-uncharted-waters-ahead/ar/1. Accessed 4 December 2013.

Weaver, D. (2011) 'Can sustainable tourism survive climate change?', *Journal of Sustainable Tourism*, 19: 5–15.

Wilkinson, A. and Kupers R. (2013) 'Living in the Futures', *Harvard Business Review*, May 2013. Available at: http://hbr.org/2013/05/living-in-the-futures/ar/1. Accessed 29 October 2013.

Witt, S.F. and Witt, C.A. (1995) 'Forecasting tourism demand: A review of empirical research', *International Journal of Forecasting*, 11: 447–75.

Zanzibar Association of Tourism Investors (2013) *New Tourism Arrival Figures for Zanzibar – 2012.* Available at: http://198.136.54.91/~wwwzati/new-tourism-arrival-figures-for-zanzibar-2012/. Accessed 4 December 2013.

25

Local-scale environmental impacts and management of tourism

Ralf Buckley

Impact Effect of human activity, in this case tourism, on either the natural or human social environment; commonly used with negative connotations, but positive impacts are also possible, though infrequent.

Environmental impact assessment Formal technical process, commonly prescribed under legislation, for identifying and predicting the probable impacts of potential human developments in advance, as one input to planning and development approval processes.

Recreation ecology Subfield of ecology which focuses on measurement and mechanisms of impacts produced by outdoor recreation, including commercial outdoor tourism; also includes ecological study of the consequences of tourist behaviour and of impact management measures.

Introduction

Tourism generates a wide variety of environmental impacts associated with the various forms of transport, accommodation, and recreational activities, at all scales from global to very local (Buckley 2004, 2009a, 2011a, 2012). This chapter focuses on the local-scale impacts of tourism, principally those associated with accommodation and activities, and in particular, on those with greatest environmental significance. In general, these involve impacts or threats to species or ecosystems of high conservation value. Construction of a new hotel or resort in a rural or wilderness area with relatively undisturbed vegetation and wildlife, for example, is much more significant environmentally than construction of a similarly sized hotel in an urban area. Likewise, construction of transport infrastructure corridors is of greater environmental significance if those corridors cut or otherwise disturb areas of high conservation value.

Local large-scale impacts

Management of local-scale impacts generally involves only a few, identifiable stakeholders, land tenures and government agencies. This contrasts with large-scale impacts such as those associated with climate change (Gössling 2011), global water consumption (Gössling *et al.* 2011), and the production and transport of material goods including food. These are all manifested essentially as marginal modifications to non-tourism aspects of human society and economy. Managing these impacts thus necessarily involves the manipulation of highly complex interlinked systems. Even where basic physical mechanisms are straightforward, the social and political aspects commonly prove intractable.

To reduce the contribution of air travel to climate change, for example, requires either reducing total air traffic, improving the fuel use efficiency of air traffic, or both. Improving efficiency has limited prospects alone, and any politically practicable mechanism for reducing aggregate traffic is likely to involve changing the cost of air travel. There are several confounding factors, however, which make such measures difficult to implement in practice. First, any deliberate policy intervention, such as a carbon tax, can be swamped by unrelated market mechanisms such as oil prices, or social factors such as population growth and redistribution of wealth. Second, cost-related measures commonly cross over from tourism into other sectors, sometimes with unintended social equity effects. For example, increasing water rates to reduce high consumption by tourists would also affect local residents. Third, if one type of discretionary expenditure, such as air travel, becomes more expensive, then people divert their resources into different types of expenditure, with different types of impact (Buckley 2011b). Assessing and managing the global-scale impacts of the entire tourism sector thus involves macrosocial measures at an intergovernmental scale. These are beyond the scope of this chapter, but are considered elsewhere in this volume.

Impact assessment approaches

Broadly, most countries use three main mechanisms to assess and manage local-scale impacts. The first is through environmental protection legislation (e.g. for the control of air, water and noise pollution, and the protection of listed endangered species). Commonly this applies across all land tenures and at all scales, but in practice it is much more effective for more intense and localised impacts where the source and hence the persons responsible are readily identifiable. The second is through development control legislation, including requirements for environmental impact assessment (Warnken & Buckley 1998). These requirements, and their implementation in practice, differ greatly between countries and jurisdictions, and also between different types of development. In most cases, they contain scoping steps or mechanisms which are intended to focus attention on impacts of greatest environmental significance, whether related to pollution or biodiversity conservation (Buckley 2008). Application of development control and EIA legislation across different land tenures differs between jurisdictions. In some cases, different systems apply for public and private lands respectively.

The third main mechanism is through the management agencies of public lands, whether allocated for protection, primary industries production, recreation, or multiple uses. These agencies typically establish regulations and management plans, subject to the overarching mandate and establishing legislation of the relevant agencies, in order to control different types of human activity including tourism. Often these three different approaches overlap, or apply simultaneously. Thus, for example, management measures inside a national park may focus largely on controlling the behaviour and impact of individual visitors, but may also specify regulations relating to any proposals for private development or other commercial operations, which apply in addition to cross-tenure pollution control and EIA requirements.

Impact types and mechanisms

Nominally at least, one of the main aims of all the approaches outlined above is to identify areas of high conservation value and risk, and minimise human activities and impacts in those areas. The remainder of this chapter, therefore, reviews relevant literature on the identification, mechanisms, measurement, and management of these local-scale negative impacts of tourism and recreation activities on the natural environment, particularly in areas of high conservation value. It draws on previous reviews by Buckley (2004, 2009a, 2011a, 2012).

Under some circumstances tourism can also make positive contributions to the conservation of threatened species and the operation of protected areas (Buckley 2010a); and in some cases at least, these contributions may be highly significant (Buckley et al. 2012; Morrison et al. 2012; Steven et al. 2013). Indeed, at local scale it is argued that at some sites and for some tourism enterprises, the net contribution to conservation is positive even after allowing for negative impacts (Buckley 2009b, 2010b; Buckley & Pabla 2012). These cases, however, constitute only a very small proportion of the global tourism industry, which overall, is far from sustainable (Buckley 2011a, 2012). Even for these cases, and even considering only the local scale, positive contributions can only outweigh negative impacts if the latter are understood, monitored, managed and minimised. It is these aspects which are addressed here.

Impacts of tourism differ between transport, accommodation, and activity components; between wilderness, rural, and urban levels of land development; and between different climates, terrain types, and ecosystems (Buckley 2011a, 2012). Environmental management for fixed-site tourism development is largely integrated into local government planning, including project-style EIA, infrastructure standards, and building regulations (Buckley 2008). Such developments may produce a range of environmental impacts (Buckley 2004, 2011a) including: vegetation clearance and loss of wildlife habitat (Roux-Fouillet et al. 2011); air and water pollution; noise, light, and visual disturbance to native fauna (Halfwerk et al. 2011; Kociolek et al. 2011; Thiel et al. 2008); road-kill and barriers to wildlife movements (Lian et al. 2011); and introduction of feral animals, pathogens, and weeds.

A similar range of impacts are produced by smaller-scale tourism activities, including those permitted inside protected areas. These are particularly significant in areas of high conservation value. Most relevant research has focused on direct, immediate, localised, and easily identified impacts, such as vegetation trampling and wildlife disturbance. There is much less research on indirect, delayed, or diffuse impacts which may not be detectable without careful controlled experimentation; on the effects of timing or patterns in repeated disturbances (Buckley 2013). Impacts depend on ecosystem, activity, season, and tourist numbers and behaviour (Buckley 2004, 2011a; Monz et al. 2013; Remacha et al. 2011). There are case studies where even a single disturbance has caused a major and ecologically significant impact on the global populations of individual threatened species, particularly birds (Buckley 2004, 2011a; Kerbiriou et al. 2009). Different species are differentially sensitive to disturbance (Buckley 2004; Steven et al. 2011).

Some of the more widespread and ecologically significant impacts include: loss of habitat and fragmentation (Jorge 2008); introduction of invasive species and pathogens (Muehlenbein et al. 2010; Pickering & Mount 2010; Whinam et al. 2005); increases in parasitism; trampling damage to vegetation and soil (Monz et al. 2013); disruptions to plant pollination (Kolb 2008) and dispersal (Moran et al. 2009); and disturbances to animal behaviour, energetics, communications and physiology (Beale & Monaghan 2004; Huang et al. 2011; MacArthur et al. 1982; Maréchal *et al.* 2011; Nimon *et al.* 1995; Rode *et al.* 2006; Steven *et al.* 2011; Velando & Munilla 2011; Wang *et al.* 2011).

Landowners and managers in areas subject to tourism impacts can deploy a well-tested toolkit of management measures (Buckley 1998, 2009a). Regulatory measures include: permits, zoning, seasonal closures, group size limits, activity restrictions, and restrictions or requirements for particular equipment or behaviours. Economic measures include a range of fees, often coupled with permit systems, but commonly limited by equity considerations and administrative costs. Interpretive measures have similar goals to regulatory measures and are intended to operate through voluntary compliance by informed visitors. They are much less effective, except under limited circumstances (Boon *et al.* 2008; Littlefair & Buckley 2008). Physical measures involve construction of infrastructure to localise and control impacts using facilities such as tracks, lookouts, campsites, and toilets. These are locally effective, but can create secondary impacts and change visitor perceptions and behaviour. Such infrastructure is commonly constructed by the landowner or land management agency itself: public in the case of parks and public forests, private for freehold land. Cases of privately owned infrastructure tourism in public protected areas are uncommon, and most reflect historical legacies of various types (Buckley 2010c).

Case Study

Impacts of Arctic and Antarctic tourism

Opportunities for tourists to visit polar regions have increased greatly in recent decades. Waters once plied only by the pioneering tours of the *Lindblad Explorer* are now traversed every summer by smaller ~100-berth expedition cruise vessels, and cruise ships with several thousand berths. These vessels visit Polar regions via sub-Arctic or sub-Antarctic coasts and islands. These ecosystems are of very high conservation value as breeding and feeding sites for migratory birds, marine mammals, and penguins in the southern hemisphere. The potential for environmental impact from tourism is thus particularly high. Land-based air access, which has long been available to Arctic destinations such as Longyearbyen in Svalbard and Pond Inlet on Canada's Baffin Island, is now becoming available on blue ice airstrips in the Antarctic, as well as formerly closed Russian sections of the Arctic. Particularly in the Antarctic, these flights provide tourist access to areas of polar ice well inland from the ice edge, including sites used as breeding colonies by otherwise undisturbed bird species. In addition, tourists may be taken to the rare ice-free valleys, where plant growth is extremely slow and any impacts very long-lasting.

Management and monitoring of these impacts is particularly difficult in the Antarctic, where under the *Antarctic Treaty* there are no local laws or compliance authority. There have been attempts at self-regulation via the International Association of Antarctic Tour Operators (IAATO), but membership is voluntary and compliance is not enforced. In addition, even if IAATO Codes of Practice were enforceable and followed, they may not be strict enough to manage impacts effectively. As one example, one of the most critical impacts of tourism is disturbance to nesting seabirds on sub-Antarctic islands. The IAATO code provides that tourists should not approach closer than five metres. This code is routinely breached by individual tourists; but in addition, nesting birds such as skuas, albatrosses, and penguins show behavioural, physiological, and hormonal signs of stress even when approached slowly and quietly, by a single individual, to distances further than five metres (Buckley 2010d; Giese 1996; Giese & Riddle 1999; Nimon *et al.* 1995).

In Polar and sub-Polar environments, birds must nest in the open, on the ground or sometimes on cliff ledges. Nests are under constant surveillance and attack by predatory gulls and skuas, some of which attack their own as well as other bird species. If nesting adults leave their eggs or chicks unattended for even a moment, they lose their entire year's reproductive output. When tourists approach nests, therefore, the adult birds stay in place as long as they dare. This, however, does not mean that they are unstressed. They become agitated, clack their beaks repeatedly, salivate copiously, and show other behavioural signs of distress. More sophisticated experiments using dummy eggs fitted with transmitters and monitoring devices show that birds become distressed well before any behavioural symptoms are visible; and also that different species, and different individuals, are differentially sensitive to disturbance. Similar considerations apply for cliff-nesting birds in the Arctic, such as guillemots and razorbills; and also for marine mammals such as seals, sealions, and walrus, which breed on land, and also use rocky haul-out areas to conserve energy when not feeding. Especially for species previously decimated by sealing and in some cases also by disease, pollution, and overfishing of prey fish species, repeated disturbances by tourists can lead to increased pup mortality.

In the earlier days of Polar tourism when access was only by expedition cruise vessels, tourists arrived infrequently and in small numbers. They were self-selected for an interest in polar environments; received detailed on-board briefings about minimal-impact practices and codes of behaviour; were taken ashore in small groups with staggered arrivals; and were always accompanied by trained guides who generally ensured that minimal-impact practices were followed. More recently, however, large-scale cruise ships have started to arrive at the same sites, sometimes several each day in peak seabird breeding season; these tourists are unfamiliar with minimal-impact practices, unaware and perhaps uncaring of environmental concerns, untrained and unguided. The cruise ships aim to land as many visitors as possible in a short period of time, and they are essentially unsupervised. Their impact is thus potentially far more severe than for the small vessels. The only real control is that the cruise ships have only a few inflatable boats, and this limits the total number of tourists on shore at any one time.

In addition to wildlife disturbance onshore, large cruise ships bring water pollution and significant risks. Although, in theory, the MARPOL Convention and the *Antarctic Treaty* require ships to retain waste on board, in practice there is no surveillance, and vessels can discharge human sewage, food residues, and a wide variety of other rubbish such as containers and packaging materials. Since all of these are generated on a *per capita* basis, large cruise ships potentially create far more impact than smaller expedition vessels or commercial cargo ships. In addition, whilst most expedition cruise vessels are at least ice strengthened and able to survive minor collisions, large cruise ships are not, and run the risk of spilling fuel oil if they run aground or hit an iceberg.

Most of the impacts outlined above relate to ship-borne tourism. In addition, however, there have been a number of proposals to construct relatively large tourist hotels in the Antarctic, with air access. Once again, impacts are related to the total number of people, so tourist hotels would generate proportionately more impacts than existing scientific bases. In the Arctic there are already numerous human settlements, but most of them small, and tourist accommodation is currently limited. This could also change in future.

Conclusions

Research on local-scale environmental impacts of tourism has examined only a few types of impact for a very small proportion of the plants, animals, and ecosystems affected (Buckley 2004, 2009a, 2011a, 2013; Monz *et al.* 2013). As commercial pressures to increase private tourism development and high-impact types of recreation in protected areas continue to increase, reliable scientific research on the impacts of tourism and recreation, and the effectiveness of management measures, becomes increasingly critical.

Key Reading

Buckley, R.C. (ed.) (2004) *Environmental Impacts of Ecotourism*, Wallingford: CAB International.

Buckley, R.C. (2011) 'Tourism and environment', *Annual Review of Environment and Resources*, 36: 397–416.

Buckley, R.C. (2012) 'Sustainable tourism: Research and reality', *Annals of Tourism Research*, 39: 528–46.

Liddle, M.J. (1997) *Recreation Ecology: The Ecological Impact of Outdoor Recreation*, Dordrecht: Kluwer Academic Publishers.

Monz, C.A., Pickering, C.M. and Hadwen, W.D. (2013) 'Recent advances in recreation ecology and the implications of different relationships between recreation use and ecological impacts', *Frontiers in Ecology and the Environment*, DOI: 10.1890/120358.

References

Beale, C.M. and Monaghan, P. (2004) 'Human disturbance: People as predation-free predators?', *Journal of Applied Ecology*, 41: 335–43.

Boon, P.I., Fluker, M. and Wilson, N. (2008) 'Ten-year study of the effectiveness of an educative programme in ensuring the ecological sustainability of recreational activities in the Brisbane Ranges National Park, south-eastern Australia', *Journal of Sustainable Tourism*, 16: 681–97.

Buckley, R.C. (1998) 'Tools and indicators for managing tourism in parks', *Annals of Tourism Research*, 26: 207–10.

Buckley, R.C. (ed.) (2004) *Environmental Impacts of Ecotourism*, Wallingford: CAB International.

Buckley, R.C. (2008) 'Thresholds and standards for tourism environmental impact assessment', in M. Schmidt, J. Glasson, L. Emmelin and H. Helbron (eds) *Standards and Thresholds for Impact Assessment*, Heidelberg: Springer.

—— (2009a) *Ecotourism: Principles and Practices*, Wallingford: CAB International.

—— (2009b) 'Parks and tourism', *PLoS Biology*, 7: e1000143.

—— (2010a) *Conservation Tourism*, Wallingford: CAB International.

—— (2010b) 'Safaris can help conservation', *Nature*, 467: 1047.

—— (2010c) 'Private tourism in public parks', in Y-C. Hsu (ed.) *Issues Confronting the Management of the World's National Parks*, National Dong Hua University, Taipei. Proceedings of the Conference held on 2–3 August 2010, Taiwan.

—— (2010d) 'Arctic and sub-Antarctic', in *Conservation Tourism*, Wallingford: CAB International.

—— (2011a) 'Tourism and environment', *Annual Review of Environment and Resources*, 36: 397–416.

—— (2011b) '20 Answers: Reconciling air travel and climate change', *Annals of Tourism Research*, 38: 1178–81.

—— (2012) 'Sustainable tourism: Research and reality', *Annals of Tourism Research*, 39: 528–46.

—— (2013) 'Frontiers in recreation ecology', *Frontiers in Ecology and the Environment*, 8: 399–400.

Buckley, R.C. and Pabla, H.S. (2012) 'Tourism ban won't help Indian tigers', *Nature*, 489: 33.

Buckley, R.C., Guy Castley, J., Pegas, F., Mossaz, A.C. and Steven, R. (2012) 'A population accounting approach to assess tourism contributions to conservation of IUCN-redlisted mammals', *PLoS ONE*, 7: e44134.

Giese, M. (1996) 'Effects of human activity on Adelie penguin *Pygoscelis adeliae* breeding success', *Biological Conservation*, 75: 157–64.

Giese, M. and Riddle, M. (1999) 'Disturbance of emperor penguin chicks by helicopters', *Polar Biology*, 22: 366–71.

Gössling, S. (2011) *Carbon Management in Tourism*, Abingdon: Routledge.

Gössling, S., Peeters, P., Hall, C.M., Ceron, J.-P., Dubois, G., Lehman, L.V. and Scott, D. (2011) 'Tourism and water use: Supply, demand and security: And international review', *Tourism Management*, 33, 16–28.

Halfwerk, W., Holleman, L.J.M., Lessells, C.M. and Slabbekoorn, H. (2011) 'Negative impact of traffic noise on avian reproductive success', *Journal of Applied Ecology*, 48: 210–19.

Huang, B., Lubarsky, K., Teng, T. and Blumstein, D.T. (2011) 'Take only pictures, leave only…fear? The effects of photography on the West Indian anole', *Current Zoology*, 57: 77–82.

Jorge, M.L.S.P. (2008) 'Effects of forest fragmentation on two sister genera of Amazonian rodents', *Biological Conservation*, 141: 617–23.

Kerbiriou, C., Le, Viol, I., Robert, A., Porcher, E., Gourmelon, F. and Julliard, R. (2009) 'Tourism in protected areas can threaten wild populations: From individual response to population viability of the chough *Pyrrhocorax pyrrhocorax*', *Journal of Applied Ecology*, 46: 657–65.

Kociolek, A.V., Clevenger, A.P., St. Clair, C.C. and Proppe, D.S. (2011) 'Effects of road networks on bird populations', *Conservation Biology*, 25: 241–49.

Kolb, A. (2008) 'Habitat fragmentation reduces plant fitness by disturbing pollination and modifying response to herbivory', *Biological Conservation*, 141: 2540–49.

Lian, X., Zhang, T., Cao, Y., Su, J. and Thirgood, S. (2011) 'Road proximity and traffic flow perceived as potential predation risks: Evidence from the Tibetan antelope in the Kekexili National Nature Reserve, China', *Wildlife Research*, 38: 141–46.

Littlefair, C. and Buckley, R.C. (2008) 'Interpretation reduces ecological impacts of visitors to World Heritage Areas', *Ambio*, 37: 338–41.

MacArthur, R.A., Giest, V. and Johnston, R.H. (1982) 'Cardiac and behavioural responses of mountain sheep to human disturbance', *Journal of Wildlife Management*, 46: 351–58.

Maréchal, L., Semple, S., Majolo, B., Qarro, M., Heistermann, M. and MacLarnon, A. (2011) 'Impacts of tourism on anxiety and physiological stress levels in wild male Barbary macaques', *Biological Conservation*, 144: 2188–93.

Monz, C.A., Pickering, C.M. and Hadwen, W.D. (2013) 'Recent advances in recreation ecology and the implications of different relationships between recreation use and ecological impacts', *Frontiers in Ecology and the Environment*, DOI: 10.1890/120358.

Moran, C., Catterall, C.P. and Kanowski, J. (2009) 'Reduced dispersal of native plant species as a consequence of the reduced abundance of frugivore species in fragmented rainforest', *Biological Conservation*, 142: 541–52.

Morrison, C., Simpkins, C., Castley, J.G. and Buckley, R.C. (2012) 'Tourism and the conservation of critically endangered frogs', *PLoS ONE*, 7: e43757.

Muehlenbein, M.P., Martinez, L.A., Lemke, A.A., Ambu, L., Nathan, S., Alsisto, S. and Sakong, R. (2010) 'Unhealthy travelers present challenges to sustainable primate ecotourism', *Travel Medicine and Infectious Diseases*, 8: 169–75.

Nimon, A.J., Schroter, R.C. and Stonehouse, B. (1995) 'Heart rate of disturbed penguins', *Nature*, 374: 415.

Pickering, C.M. and Mount, A. (2010) 'Do tourists disperse weed seed? A global review of unintentional human-mediated terrestrial seed dispersal on clothing, vehicles and horses', *Journal of Sustainable Tourism*, 18: 239–56.

Remacha, C., Pérez-Tris, J. and Delgado, J.A. (2011) 'Reducing visitors' group size increases the number of birds during educational activities: Implications for management of nature-based recreation', *Journal of Environmental Management*, 92: 1564–68.

Rode, K.D., Farley, S.D. and Robbins, C.T. (2006) 'Behavioural responses of brown bears mediate nutritional effects of experimentally introduced tourism', *Biological Conservation*, 133: 70–80.

Roux-Fouillet, P., Wipf, S. and Rixen, C. (2011) 'Long-term impacts of ski piste management on alpine vegetation and soils', *Journal of Applied Ecology*, 48: 906–15.

Steven, R., Pickering, C.M. and Guy Castley, J. (2011) 'A review of the impacts of nature based recreation on birds', *Journal of Environmental Management*, 92: 2287–94.

Steven, R., Castley, J.G. and Buckley, R.C. (2013) 'Tourism revenue as a conservation tool for threatened birds in protected areas', *PlosOne*, 8: e62598.

Thiel, D., Jenni-Eiermann, S., Braunisch, V., Palme, R. and Jenni, L. (2008) 'Ski tourism affects habitat use and evokes a physiological stress response in capercaillie *Tetrao urogallus*: A new methodological approach', *Journal of Applied Ecology*, 45: 845–53.

Velando, A. and Munilla, I. (2011) 'Disturbance to a foraging seabird by sea–based tourism: Implications for reserve management in marine protected areas', *Biological Conservation*, 144: 1167–74.

Wang, Z., Li, Z., Beauchamp, G. and Jiang, Z. (2011) 'Flock size and human disturbance affect vigilance of endangered red–crowned cranes', *Biological Conservation*, 144: 101–5.

Warnken, J. and Buckley, R.C. (1998) 'Scientific quality of tourism EIA', *Journal of Applied Ecology*, 35: 1–8.

Whinam, J., Chilcott, N. and Bergstrom, D.M. (2005) 'Subantarctic hitchhikers: Expeditioners as vectors for the introduction of alien organisms', *Biological Conservation*, 2: 207–19.

Part 4

Sectoral approaches to tourism and sustainability

26

Foodservice in tourism and sustainability

Brian Garrod

Foodservice provider An organisation that prepares and sells food and drinks directly to tourists in the destination or transit zones.

Food tourism Tourism activities that are motivated primarily by the pursuit of pleasurable and memorable food and drink experiences.

Food miles The distance that a specific item of food, or the sum of its component ingredients, travels before it reaches the consumer.

Carbon footprint The amount of carbon dioxide and other greenhouse gas emissions directly emitted into the atmosphere by a specific entity.

Food management The process of controlling the purchasing, preparation and presentation of food.

Introduction

Food is, by definition, a significant part of the tourism experience: tourists have to eat some time, somewhere in the destinations in which they are staying and while they are in transit to and from those destinations. Food has also long been an important secondary motivation for people to visit a destination: the opportunity to sample the distinctive, even 'exotic' foods of the destination is something that can be attractive to tourists (Nield *et al.* 2000). Food also increasingly represents a primary motivator or attraction for people to visit a destination, in the form of food (or gastronomic or 'gastro') tourism (Povey 2012). In this chapter, as in much of the literature, the term 'food' is taken to include 'drinks' of all kinds.

While self-catering remains a popular option (Leslie 2007), many tourists will be staying in serviced accommodation and many, whether they choose to stay in self-catered or serviced accommodation, will also 'eat out' during the course of their stay. This is where the 'foodservice sector' enters the equation. The foodservice sector can be defined as the sum of those organisations that prepare and sell food directly to consumers. In tourism destinations it is most probable that some of these consumers will be tourists, others day visitors and others still local residents. Gössling *et al.* (2011) estimate that tourists consume at least 200 million meals a day (about the same number as a country the size of the UK), a substantial proportion of which will be prepared and served to them by foodservice providers.

It is important also to recognise that the foodservice sector comprises not only more formal outlets, such as restaurants, cafés, diners, fast-food chains and so forth, but also informal food outlets such as street-food stalls and food-hawkers (Gössling *et al.* 2011). As well as the understandable overlap with the hospitality and accommodation sectors, foodservice is also a vital component of the transport sector, including food served while in transit on trains, ferries, cruise ships and aeroplanes, as well as at the respective terminals. Foodservice is also part of the attractions sector, not only in the form of cafes and coffee shops located in attractions, but also in terms of the wide range of food-related visitor attractions that exist. Examples include vineyards, brewery and whisky-distillery tours (Hall *et al.* 2012; McBoyle & McBoyle 2008). Food products are also sometimes sold as souvenirs (Sims 2009). As such, foodservice constitutes an important part of the tourism experience, across almost all of its many forms and provider sectors.

Given the importance of food in tourism, it is perhaps surprising that it has not been the subject of significant attention by academics. Chan *et al.* (2010: 990), for example, remark that 'despite the central role of dining in the holiday experience, the interface between food and tourism has received scant research attention', adding that 'research on tourist food consumption is in its infancy, and is still establishing the basic tenets'. Policy makers have also tended to under-emphasise the role of food in tourism, although there have been some significant exceptions, one of these being the Countryside Agency's 'Eat the View' strategy, which sought to encourage tourism businesses in England to connect better with their local economy by using and selling locally produced food products (Garrod *et al.* 2006). Two areas where published research is considered to be particularly sparse are among small businesses (Tzchentke *et al.* 2008) and in the self-catering sector (Leslie 2007).

While there has been little discussion of the role of food in tourism, there has been some emphasis on the role of food as a primary motivator for tourism: the phenomenon referred to above as 'food tourism'. Research undertaken in this area includes studies of food festivals (e.g. Chang & Yuan 2011), food tourism initiatives (e.g. Everett 2009) and food as a component of destination brand image (e.g. Hjalager & Corigliano 2000; Lin *et al.* 2011). As such, the emphasis tends to be on the tourism that is generated through an interest in food, rather than the role of foodservice in the pursuit of sustainable tourism and destinations.

Tourism foodservice and sustainability

Of the limited amount of research linking foodservice and tourism, very little has focused specifically on issues of sustainability. Henderson's (2009) review of food tourism, for example, identifies literature on food as a tourist attraction, as a determinant of tourist satisfaction, as a generator of feelings of involvement and place attachment, in creating and maintaining destination image and reputation, and as a niche tourism product. In none of these categories is sustainability raised as an issue and nor is it discussed as a category in its own right. Henderson goes on to outline current challenges for tourism food providers, including hygiene, international differences in food culture, competition and quality issues (including provenance and authenticity). Significantly, however, sustainability is not discussed as an issue.

This is not to suggest that there has been a total absence of studies attempting to link tourism foodservice and sustainability; rather that any such studies have been published lack prominence in the literature. A useful study by Sims (2009), for example, argues that food plays an important role in sustainable tourism because it can appeal to visitors' demands for 'authenticity'. This, she argues, is connected to the localness of food, which has implications for 'economic, cultural and environmental sustainability' because 'locally sourced products can result in benefits for both hosts and guests' (Sims 2009: 321). Four main arguments are then put forward with regard to the benefits of local food: first, that it is likely to result in a stronger local multiplier effect; second, that it can lead to a reduced carbon footprint; third, that it can produce a source of competitive advantage for a destination; and fourth, that the production of 'alternative' foods can be a useful means of addressing falling farm incomes. This is said to imply that using local food in tourism can help to promote 'all-round sustainability' or 'integrated rural tourism' (Sims 2009: 323). A weakness of the study, however, is that there is a tendency here to conflate 'authentic' with 'local', and 'local' with 'sustainable', neither of which is necessarily the case.

Reynolds (1993) also argues that food plays an important role in determining the cultural dimension of sustainability, although his analysis focuses on the harm that tourism can do to authentic food cultures. His study of the impact of tourism in Bali, Indonesia, notes a significant reduction in indigenous ethnic dishes found on restaurant menus in tourist areas over time. He adds that food is 'therefore…perhaps one of the last areas of authenticity that is affordable on a regular basis by the tourists' (Reynolds 1993: 49).

Another important connection between food and tourism noted by Sims (2009) is that food is a vital part of the embodied tourism experience: the tourist not only sees food but also smells, tastes, touches and even sometimes even hears it. Chan *et al.* (2010) also note that the consumption of food utilises all five senses. This implies that the tourism experience needs to be conceptualised in more than simply visual terms. Everett (2009: 337) also discusses food as an embodied experience, arguing that food enables the tourist literally to internalise the tourism destination. As such, food is an important 'communicator of meaning' in the tourism experience (Everett 2009: 340). Without explicitly saying so, the paper expects the reader to deduce that, without the important mediating role of food, tourism sustainability would be more difficult to achieve.

Finally, a study by Telfer and Wall (1996) notes that the relationship between food and tourism often implies competition for land use with agriculture. This may have implications for the sustainability of the destination area as agriculture becomes progressively crowded out or transformed to meet the needs of tourists. Where local food production cannot meet the needs of tourists, high leakage rates may result as the tourism industry fills the gap with food imports. As such, the study does note the link between tourism food and sustainability. As with most of the foregoing studies, however, the focus is on the use of local or imported food products.

It is, therefore, possible to deduce two outstanding features of the food and tourism literature to date. The first is that issues of sustainability are often only implied, for example by the couching of arguments in terms of destination branding or tourist satisfaction. The second is that there has been a tendency to assume that local food is more sustainable food. This links the debate to that of the concept of 'food miles', to which the chapter now turns.

Food miles

The consumption and production of food has a wide range of sustainability considerations attached to it, including the use of chemical fertilisers and pesticides on farms, soil erosion, animal welfare considerations, the human health implications of mass food-production systems, economic multiplier effects, effects on farm-worker health, and many more. The concept of food miles tends, however, to focus on the transport of food. The argument is that any given foodstuff will travel physically 'from farm to fork' and the distance travelled can serve as a measure of its sustainability. Transporting food has an impact on the environment, such as expending fossil fuels and exhaust emissions, which tend to correlate strongly with distance travelled. 'Local' is therefore held to be more 'sustainable'.

It can be argued, however, that the food miles concept, appealing as it may seem, can be very deceptive. First, calculating the number of food miles embodied in a meal can be very difficult, particularly when it uses a variety of foods with ingredients sourced from different suppliers in different parts of the world. A further complicating factor in the case of tourism foodservice is that it is the consumers who are moving to the food, rather than the food moving to the consumer. Doubtless this is why so few studies using food miles have been published in the tourism context.

Other important shortcomings have been identified with regard to the concept of food miles. In particular, the assumption that the food mile fully captures the sustainability implications of consuming the food product requires closer inspection. A particular problem is that the transportation of food, environmentally unfriendly as it can be, only tends to make up a small proportion of the overall environmental impact of consuming a food product. Indeed, Weber and Matthews (2008) argue that only 11% of life-cycle greenhouse gas (GHG) emissions associated with the consumption of food in the USA is due to its transport, with only 4% being generated by the actual delivery of the food from the producer to the consumer. Their study finds that dietary change – such as eating less red and more white meat, or eating more vegetables – would be more effective than attempting to reduce the number of food miles involved by buying only locally produced food.

Saunders et al. (2006) reach a similar conclusion in their study of New Zealand food products. Indeed, their study demonstrates that applying a whole life-cycle approach may lead to very different results than are suggested by the calculation of food miles. Thus, for example, while some New Zealand food products clearly involve many food miles when they are imported half way across the world to the UK, they can still have a lower environmental impact than equivalent, but locally sourced, products. A great deal depends on how the food is transported and stored. In the case of New Zealand apples, for example, the majority of the transport can be by bulk carrier by sea, which tends to have much lower environmental impact per unit of product than transport in smaller quantities by road. Seasonality also comes into play in the calculation, as British apples would require storage if they are to be available out of season, which is when the New Zealand apples would be ready for the UK market.

Another shortcoming of food miles, as noted by authors such as Pretty et al. (2005), is that the external costs of transport are omitted from the calculation. External costs are the social (non-market) costs of a production or consumption activity, which are not generally taken into account in the decision-making calculus of buyers and sellers. An example is the traffic congestion on roads caused, in part, by food delivery vehicles. These costs can be significant with Pretty et al. (2005) estimating that the external costs of food transported by road in the UK to be upwards of £3.5 billion per year. Food transportation by different modes of transport, in different contexts, will clearly have different external costs associated with it. The important point, however, is that these costs are not routinely accounted for when calculating food miles.

The weaknesses of the food miles concept are increasingly being recognised. Some authors have responded by recommending that the concept be replaced by that of 'fair miles'. The idea of a 'fair mile' is to widen the remit of a food mile to capture broader ethical, economic and social aspects of food transport (e.g. Chi et al. 2009; Watkiss 2005). Saunders and Barber (2008: 88), meanwhile, argue that 'Food miles, whist [sic.] still having traction with the popular media and maybe consumers, have lost credibility with the supermarkets and government agencies which have turned their attention to carbon footprinting. The emphasis now must be on measuring the carbon footprint of products'.

Carbon footprinting in tourism

Few studies have applied carbon footprinting in the context of tourism; fewer still have attempted to measure the contribution of tourism foodservice, or the food consumed by tourists, to the overall tourism carbon footprint. The fundamental premise of the carbon footprint is to measure the amount of carbon dioxide and other GHG emissions directly emitted into the atmosphere by a product, person, country, event or organisation. The intention is to take into account all relevant sources of GHG emissions within pre-determined spatial and temporal boundaries. Often a whole life-cycle approach is adopted, attempting to measure the GHG emissions of the target phenomenon 'from cradle to grave'.

Given the significant complexity of the tourism product, this task is clearly a formidable one. Many studies have encountered difficulties with data, especially the earlier ones that attempted to apply the more general concept of the ecological footprint (EF). One such study, for example, was undertaken by WWF-UK (2002). The study set out to calculate the EF for two representative holidays: one based on accommodation in family apartments in Majorca and the other at a four-star hotel in Cyprus. The EFs of the holidays as a whole were found to be equivalent to 5% of the UK average annual EF in the case of Majorca and 14% in the case of Cyprus, implying that 'going on holiday is an expensive proposition in terms of individual environmental sustainability' (WWF-UK 2002: vi). The food component of the EF, meanwhile, accounted for 9% of overall footprint in Majorca and 6% in Cyprus: not an insubstantial proportion. On closer inspection of the methodology, however, it appears that the data-collection demands involved in determining the EF of the food eaten by guests were prohibitive, so the researchers opted to restrict the analysis simply to food miles.

Similar data problems were encountered in another study by Gössling *et al.* (2002) which attempted to calculate the EF of tourism in the Seychelles. The study included 'food and fibre consumption' as one of the categories. However, due to lack of access to data, it was assumed that the tourists' food consumption was essentially the same as it would be were they still at home. Hunter and Shaw (2007) make a similar assumption in calculating the EF of two ecotourism holidays: one from the USA to Costa Rica and the other from the UK to Brazil, extending this simplification to all aspects of the tourists' in-destination stay and focusing their efforts simply on the travel component.

The studies referred to above demonstrate the formidable difficulties involved in calculating the full EF of food as a component of the tourism product. Perhaps the most telling of all, however, is the study by Kuo *et al.* (2005) which attempts to illustrate the 'industrial ecology' approach to managing tourism foodservice for sustainability. Their work focuses on undertaking a detailed life-cycle analysis inventory of meal boxes popular with tourists while they are in transit within Taiwan. This process is in many ways similar to an EF study. The main shortcoming of Kuo *et al.*'s (2005) analysis, however, is that due to data difficulties they focus only on the sustainability of the actual box, completely ignoring the food contained within it.

Sustainable food management practices in tourism

The difficulties in determining even the basic conditions for sustainability of foodservice in tourism leave the sector in great difficulty with regard to determining effective food management practices. In short, what practices should the foodservice provider adopt in order to ensure that they are doing their part, to the maximum effect, in achieving sustainable tourism?

There is no shortage of options or, indeed, advice on which options to take. Hu *et al.* (2010), for example, note 11 recommendations of the Green Restaurant Association, which range from the very general, such as adopting energy-efficiency measures and reducing the use of water, to the very specific, such as using only chlorine-free paper products and non-toxic cleaning products (see Table 26.1). Also included among the recommendations is purchasing policy, which endorses the purchase of organic, local and vegetarian foodstuffs in preference to the conventional, imported and meat based. Other studies also emphasise purchasing policy. Post and Mikkola (2012), for example, examine stakeholder attitudes to the sustainability of foodservice businesses in Nordic countries and find that the issues stressed by participants focus on cooking from scratch, using organic ingredients (whereby 'organic' is considered to be a proxy for 'sustainable'), seasonal foods, foods and ingredients of identified origin (to assess quality, compliance with standards), and local foods in preference to imports. Rimmington *et al.*'s (2006) expert panel study of contract caterers servicing the UK public sector also emphasises purchasing policy, with experts subscribing to the use of domestic food products in preference to imports, provided that quality is maintained and sufficient quantities are available, as well as products with assured provenance and animal welfare assurances. Notably, a number of other recommendations are developed, including providing menu information to enable consumers to make choice-based sustainability considerations, ensuring food is processed using facilities that are resource efficient (in terms of energy, waste, water) and that transport systems from production/processing to the point of consumption are fuel-efficient.

The consensus derived from the available research would seem, therefore, to be that purchasing policies have a major role to play in the sustainability strategies of tourism foodservice providers. This makes a great deal of sense from a systems perspective: if the major inputs into the foodservice system (i.e. foodstuffs and food ingredients) are as sustainable as possible, then there is the greatest opportunity to ensure that the whole system is also sustainable to the greatest possible extent. If, however, the system is being fed with unsustainable inputs, then the task of making the system as a whole sustainable will be substantially more difficult. Food management should, therefore, focus on purchasing decisions.

Table 26.1 Elements of an environmental management system for restaurants

---

1. Energy efficiency and conservation (e.g. lighting, refrigeration, cooking appliances).
2. Water efficiency and conservation (e.g. toilets, sinks, laundry, sprinklers).
3. Recycling and composting, including use of recycled products such as napkins, paper towels, office paper, etc.
4. Purchase of sustainable food products, including organic, locally grown and plant-based foods.
5. Pollution prevention, achieved through reduction, reuse and improving operational practices.
6. Purchase of recycled products, tree-free, biodegradable and organic products.
7. Use of chlorine-free paper products.
8. Use of non-toxic cleaning and chemical products (e.g. dish detergent, disinfectants, toilet bowl cleaner).
9. Use of renewable power, through purchase from a green supplier.
10. Green building and construction, to reduce or eliminate negative impacts on the environment, occupants and the local community.
11. Employee education by training employees about green practices.

Source: Hu *et al.* (2010)

Gössling *et al.* (2011), however, challenge this proposition. Their argument first divides the foodservice production process into three stages – purchasing, preparation and presentation – which they describe as 'the 3Ps of food management' (Gössling *et al.* 2011: 536). Examining first the evidence on purchasing, Gössling *et al.* review the evidence from outside of the tourism literature on the carbon footprint (or GHG–intensity) of a range of different foodstuffs. Their analysis focuses particularly on locally produced foods, organic foods and foods that are in season. The study's findings are salutary in that little consistent evidence can be found to prefer any of these product characteristics. The following case study presents this crucial finding in more depth.

Case Study

The difficulties in making food purchasing choices are best illustrated by means of an example. Imagine that you are the manager of a tourism foodservice provider based in Sweden and that you have decided to put a dish on your menu that uses fresh tomatoes. Tomatoes are currently not in season in the Sweden. You could therefore buy them from Spain, where they are grown in unheated greenhouses, or you could buy them from a local producer in the Sweden, where they are grown in heated greenhouses.

The best available data suggest that the GHG intensity in growing the former is 0.456kg CO_2-eq/kg (i.e. their production 0.456kg of carbon dioxide is released for every kilogramme of tomatoes grown). The equivalent figure for the locally produced tomatoes is 7.2 kg CO_2-eq/kg.

Simple comparison would suggest that the most sustainable purchase is from Spain, where the tomatoes do not need to be grown inefficiently in heated greenhouses. But this clearly is not taking into account the need to transport the tomatoes across Europe; surely including the transport implications will swing the balance the other way?

The answer is, probably not. Each kilogramme of tomatoes would involve 0.047 additional kg CO_2-eq by train, 0.98 kg CO_2-eq by truck and 1.77 kg CO_2-eq by air. The latter has a considerable additional impact but it is still a better prospect to buy tomatoes grown in-season in Spain in unheated greenhouses than tomatoes grown out-of-season in Sweden in heated greenhouses.

In other words, the mantra that one should only 'buy local' does not always make sense. Clearly, in this case, it is better to buy the tomatoes from Spain and transport them all the way to Sweden, even by air freight, simply because they are in season in Spain and do not need to be grown in heated greenhouses as the locally produced ones do.

Now let us assume that you are thinking of buying your tomatoes from Denmark instead: should you buy organic tomatoes or conventionally produced ones? The data suggests that the former have a higher GHG-intensity than the latter: the conventionally produced tomatoes implying 19.1 kg CO_2-eq/kg and the organic ones 27.3 kg CO_2-eq/kg. This is not surprising given that the methods of organic production tend to be more carbon intensive. Of course, this is to not to suggest that organic food is less sustainable than its conventionally produced equivalent: merely that the data on GHG-intensity do not reveal the whole story. There are undeniably other major sustainability benefits associated with organic production, including the avoidance of chemicals, fertilisers and irrigation, as well as enhanced animal welfare standards and employee health. Clearly one has to make a decision: do I wish to capture the wider benefits of organic production, even if the GHG-intensity of production is greater?

Source: Gössling *et al.* (2011); Gössling & Garrod (2011)

Gössling *et al.* (2011) therefore recommend that providers focus not only on purchasing decisions but also on the preparation and presentation stages further down the foodservice supply system. With regard to preparation, a number of recommendations are put forward.

First, foodservice providers can do a great deal to improve the sustainability of their operations by adapting their menus so that they require fewer of the foodstuffs that are likely to have negative sustainability implications. This gives the foodservice provider more scope to apply sustainable purchasing policies than simply by seeking to make more sustainable purchasing decisions for the existing menu. This recommendation also extends to the way in which food has to be cooked: for example, removing dishes from the menu that have to be cooked using aluminium foil will enable a foodservice provider to avoid purchasing significant amounts of this product, which is considered to have poor sustainability credentials. Some foodservice providers are already adopting such 'choice-editing' policies (e.g. Scandinavian Service Partners Sweden has already edited out dishes that require fish species identified by the WWF as being threatened) (Gössling *et al.* 2011).

A second plan of action is to investigate how dishes that are to be on the menu are to be prepared. Thus, for example, meat is generally more GHG-intensive than vegetables (Gössling *et al.* 2011), so one potentially more sustainable option is to reduce the meat content of dishes such as salads: it may be even more useful to re-envision meat as a side component to a dish rather than as a core component. Meanwhile, the available evidence suggests that fresh ingredients are generally preferable to semi-processed and preserved products, provided that as little as possible is wasted through trimming or the product not being used before its shelf life has expired. Cooking methods are also important and there are a number of useful techniques that foodservice providers can adopt to reduce their energy usage, for example by auditing energy use per unit turnover to identify dishes using particularly energy-intensive cooking routines.

Third, waste can be avoided by more carefully planning operations. Ideally, the kitchen should only prepare meals to order but this is not always possible. A good compromise, however, might be to collect data on the kinds and amounts of food consumed by different types of guest. In this way, if the front-of-house staff take a booking for a sports team or a stag night, they can anticipate different dishes being needed, in different quantities, than would be the case if, say, a group of pensioners were booking a table (Gössling *et al.* 2011). Another means of avoiding kitchen waste is to purchase good quality, fresh products, that will have a longer shelf life. This will help to ensure that they are used up before they have to be thrown away.

Gössling *et al.* (2011) then go on to suggest some ways in which managing the presentation of food can enhance the sustainability of foodservice operations. Presentation in this context refers to the ways in which foodservice providers serve meals to their customers. This can have significant implications for the way in which the food is prepared, as well as the choice of food components and ingredients. The study makes a number of suggestions about how sustainable food management might be achieved through presentation.

The first is to enable customers to make more sustainable meal choices by printing the relevant information on the establishment's menus. This is a form of 'social marketing' that has not yet been widely adopted in the foodservice sector, although Gössling *et al.* (2011) do mention a Swedish fast-food restaurant that is printing carbon footprint information on its menus. Indeed, social marketing has not been popular in the wider tourism sector. As Peeters *et al.* (2009) remark, this is probably because the tourism sector has traditionally been more concerned with increasing volume and, in doing so, slowly adapting the pattern of demand, rather than attempting to influence consumer choices directly.

A second strategy is to adapt buffets: guests often take more food than they can really eat when dining buffet-style, leaving substantial amounts of uneaten food on their plate. This becomes waste. Buffet diners also tend to choose more meats, which tend to be relatively GHG-intensive, and generally environmentally harmful foods such as prawns. In this respect, Gössling *et al.* (2011) discuss the interesting experiments that have been undertaken at the Maritim pro Arte hotel in Berlin, which have included offering an alternative 'organic' breakfast buffet, with only 52 components compared with around 100 in their conventional breakfast buffet. The hotel also uses smaller plates to try to discourage guests from overloading them. Moreover, some progress in reducing the GHG-intensity of the buffet as a whole has been achieved by displaying the most GHG-intensive foods, such as meat dishes, at the edges of the buffet table. This leaves the least GHG-intensive dishes in the centre of the table, where guests tend to focus their attention. All foods are served in small portions to avoid food being left on the buffet table at end of service. The hotel could also experiment with putting out smaller quantities of each dish on the buffet table and replenishing each one more frequently as guests serve themselves. This mirrors the practice that some airlines have now adopted with regard to serving beverages.

Conclusion

Given the importance of food in the co-production of the tourism experience, in determining tourist satisfaction (or causing dissatisfaction) and in shaping destination images, it is perhaps surprising that so little research has been published on the sustainability of foodservice provision in the tourism context. Research on sustainable tourism has tended either to overlook the role of food or to treat the issue only superficially. Meanwhile, the small amount of research that has been undertaken specifically on the sustainability implications of tourism foodservice operations has tended to rely on relatively simple methodologies, such as the calculation of food miles.

Such findings are probably not so surprising when one considers the enormity of the challenge faced by researchers wishing to understand the sustainability implications of tourism foodservice. Most researchers have baulked at the vast amount of data that would be required to make a satisfactory assessment of the carbon footprints of the food consumed by tourists. Others have investigated the data available from studies of GHG-intensities of food undertaken outside of the tourism context but have found the data inconsistent and therefore inconclusive (as illustrated in the case study in this chapter).

What, then, is the way forward for the tourism foodservice sector so that it can to play its full part in the pursuit sustainable tourism? The solution proposed by Gössling *et al.* (2011) is to look beyond purchasing choices to consider possible strategies that can be applied further down the foodservice chain, specifically at the preparation and presentation stages. These actions are, however, clearly inter-related. As such, it is simply not feasible to implement one in isolation from the others: rather, each foodservice provider needs to identify and adopt a judicious blend of actions to maximise its overall effectiveness in assisting with the drive to more sustainable tourism.

Brian Garrod

Key Reading

Gössling, S., Garrod, B., Aall, C., Hille, J. and Peeters, P. (2011) 'Food management in tourism: Reducing tourism's carbon "foodprint"', *Tourism Management*, 32: 534–43.

Hall, C.M. and Gössling, S. (eds) (2013) *Sustainable Culinary Systems: Local Foods, Innovation, and Tourism & Hospitality*, Abingdon: Routledge.

Henderson, J. (2009) 'Food tourism reviewed', *British Food Journal*, 111: 317–26.

Sims, R. (2009) 'Food, place and authenticity: Local food and the sustainable tourism experience', *Journal of Sustainable Tourism*, 17: 321–36.

References

Chan, R.C.Y., Kivela, J. and Mak, A.H.N. (2010) 'Food preferences of Chinese tourists', *Annals of Tourism Research*, 37: 989–1011.

Chang, W. and Yuan, J.J. (2011) 'A taste of tourism: Visitors' motivations to attend a food festival', *Event Management*, 15: 13–23.

Chi, K.R., MacGregor, J. and King, R. (2009) *Fair Miles: Recharting The Food Miles Map*, London: International Institute for Environment and Development.

Everett, S. (2009) 'Beyond the visual gaze? The pursuit of an embodied experience through food tourism', *Tourist Studies*, 8: 337–58.

Garrod, B., Wornell, R. and Youell, R. (2006) 'Re-conceptualising rural resources as countryside capital: The case of rural tourism', *Journal of Rural Studies*, 22: 117–28.

Gössling, S. and Garrod, B. (2011) 'Tourism, climate change and carbon management: Three case studies', in B. Garrod and A. Fyall (eds) *Contemporary Cases in Tourism: Volume 1*, Oxford: Goodfellow.

Gössling, S., Borgström Hansson, C., Hörstmeier, O. and Saggel, S. (2002) 'Ecological footprint analysis as a tool to assess tourism sustainability', *Ecological Economics*, 43: 199–211.

Gössling, S., Garrod, B., Aall, C., Hille, J. and Peeters, P. (2011) 'Food management in tourism: Reducing tourism's carbon "foodprint"', *Tourism Management*, 32: 534–43.

Hall, C.M., Sharples, L., Cambourne, B. and Macionis, N. (eds) (2012) *Wine Tourism Around the World*, London: Routledge.

Henderson, J. (2009) 'Food tourism reviewed', *British Food Journal*, 111: 317–26.

Hjalager, A-M. and Corigliano, M.A. (2000) 'Food for tourists: Determinants of an image', *International Journal of Tourism Research*, 2: 281–93.

Hu, H-H., Parsa, H.G. and Self, J. (2010) 'The dynamics of green restaurant patronage', *Cornell Hospitality Quarterly*, 51: 344–62.

Hunter, C. and Shaw, J. (2007) 'The ecological footprint as a key indicator of sustainable tourism', *Tourism Management*, 28: 46–57.

Kuo, N-W., Hsiao, T-Y. and Lan, C-F. (2005) 'Tourism management and industrial ecology: A case study of food service in Taiwan', *Tourism Management*, 26: 503–8.

Leslie, D. (2007) 'The missing component in the "greening" of tourism: The environmental performance of the self-catering accommodation sector', *Hospitality Management*, 26: 310–22.

Lin, Y.C., Pearson, T.E. and Cai, L.A. (2011) 'Food as a form of destination identity: A tourism destination brand perspective', *Tourism and Hospitality Research*, 11: 30–48.

McBoyle, G. and McBoyle, E. (2008). 'Distillery marketing and the visitor experience: A case study of Scottish malt whisky distilleries', *International Journal of Tourism Research*, 10: 71–80.

Nield, K., Kozak, M. and LeGrys, G. (2000) 'The role of food service in tourist satisfaction', *Hospitality Management*, 19: 375–84.

Peeters, P., Gössling, S. and Lane, B. (2009) 'Moving towards low-carbon tourism: New opportunities for destinations and tour operators', in S. Gössling, C.M. Hall and D. Weaver (eds) *Sustainable Tourism Futures*, London: Routledge.

Post, A. and Mikkola, M. (2012) 'Nordic stakeholders in catering for sustainability: Chasm between ideology and practice?', *British Food Journal*, 114: 743–61.

Povey, G. (2012) 'Gastronomy and food tourism', in P. Robinson (ed.) *Tourism: The Key Concepts*, London: Routledge.

Pretty, J.N., Ball, A.S., Lang, T. and Morison, J.I. (2005) 'Farm costs and food miles: An assessment of the full cost of the UK weekly food basket', *Food Policy*, 30: 1–19.

Reynolds, P.C. (1993) 'Food and tourism: Towards an understanding of sustainable culture', *Journal of Sustainable Tourism,* 1: 48–54.

Rimmington, M., Carlton Smith, J. and Hawkins, R. (2006) 'Corporate social responsibility and sustainable food production', *British Food Journal*, 108: 824–37.

Saunders, C. and Barber, A. (2008) 'Carbon footprints, life cycle analysis, food miles: Global trade trends and market issues', *Political Science*, 60: 73–88.

Saunders, C., Barber, A. and Taylor, G. (2006) *Food Miles – Comparative Energy/Emissions Performance of New Zealand's Agriculture Industry*, Lincoln University: Agribusiness and Economics Research Unit.

Sims, R. (2009) 'Food, place and authenticity: Local food and the sustainable tourism experience', *Journal of Sustainable Tourism*, 17: 321–36.

Telfer, D. and Wall, G. (1996) 'Linkages between tourism and food production', *Annals of Tourism Research*, 23: 635–53.

Tzchentke, N.A., Kirk, D. and Lynch, P.A. (2008) 'Going green: Decisional factors in small hospitality operations', *International Journal of Hospitality Management*, 17: 126–33.

Watkiss, P. (2005) *The Validity of Food Miles as an Indicator of Sustainable Development*, UK: Department for Environment, Food and Rural Affairs.

Weber, C.L. and Matthews, S. (2008) 'Food-miles and the relative climate impacts of food choices in the United States', *Environmental Science & Technology*, 42: 3508–13.

WWF-UK (2002) *Holiday Footprinting: A Practical Tool for Responsible Tourism*, WWF-UK.

27

Environmental management and online environmental performance assessment tools in the hotel industry

Theory and practice

Paulina Bohdanowicz-Godfrey and Piotr Zientara

Corporate social responsibility (CSR) "A concept whereby companies integrate social and environmental concerns in their business operations and in their interaction with their stakeholders on a voluntary basis" (European Commission 2001: 6).

Environmental management "The processes and practices introduced by an organization for reducing, eliminating, and ideally, preventing negative environmental impacts arising from its undertakings" (Cooper 1998: 112).

Triple bottom line A business reporting framework which includes not only financial, but also social and environmental risks, obligations and opportunities.

Introduction

It is fair to say that, with growing numbers of people realizing the long-term consequences of man–made environmental degradation, there has recently been a shift in attitudes towards nature (Duncan 2013). As tensions intensify between the necessity of protecting the environment and the need to ensure economic growth, the idea of sustainability has come to be seen as crucial to balancing these priorities. In the corporate context, sustainability involves managing the triple bottom line, which includes not only financial, but also social and environmental risks, obligations and opportunities (Hotel Analyst 2012). This evokes the notion of corporate social responsibility (Blowfield & Murray 2011; Porter & Kramer 2011; Hillenbrand *et al.* 2013), which is "a concept whereby companies integrate social and environmental concerns in their business operations and in their interaction with their stakeholders on a voluntary basis" (European Commission 2001: 6) (see also Chapter 21).

Hence, there exists an overlap between the CSR environmental dimension and environmental management, which refers to "the processes and practices introduced by an organization for reducing, eliminating, and ideally, preventing negative environmental impacts arising from its undertakings" (Cooper 1998: 112). It is true that sometimes, in the words of Bohdanowicz and Zientara (2012: 96), "CSR programmes and environmental initiatives are not linked in terms of philosophy and purpose", but the fact remains that, as analysis of corporate manifestos and mission statements suggests, the borderlines between corporate social responsibility and environmental management practice are increasingly blurred. Besides, irrespective of whether companies resolve to go green for ideological or pragmatic motives, the common denominator in these activities is protection of the environment.

All this is of pertinence to the hotel industry, which, as an integral part of hospitality, is one of the main pillars of tourism (Sloan *et al.* 2009; Hawkins & Bohdanowicz 2011). As is widely acknowledged, an unspoiled environment determines, to a large degree, the attractiveness of a tourist destination (Huybers & Bennet 2002). Hotels, however, produce a considerable environmental impact because they consume significant quantities of resources and generate large volumes of waste (Kasim 2009). Indeed, it is estimated, for example, that annual water consumption in the entire sector (worldwide) is in the order of hundreds of millions of cubic metres (Gössling 2002). Likewise, over the last decade, electricity consumption in many hotels has increased by up to 30% (Hawkins & Bohdanowicz 2011). Since there is a strong link between resource consumption and operating costs, such inefficiencies – which *de facto* constitute areas calling for improvement – are likely to affect profitability (Stipanuk 2001).

Although many state-of-the art sustainable and resource-efficient solutions have been traditionally implemented in independent hotels, one has to note that it is the hotel chains that can make a far-reaching difference to the way the sector operates once environmental commitments are implemented across the portfolios (Bohdanowicz & Zientara 2008, 2012). Whilst sustainability and/or CSR philosophy tend to be embedded into the corporate strategies, increasing numbers of companies introduce resource efficiency initiatives as well as more comprehensive sustainability programmes – such as "Omtanke" (Scandic) or "Planet 21 Strategy" (Accor). These programmes encompass a large selection of aspects from resource efficiency, employee engagement to the greening of the supply chain. An emerging trend is to offer design packages compliant with the US Green Building Council (USGBC) Leadership in Energy and Environmental Design (LEED) Green Building Rating System to encourage the construction of more responsible hotels. The new Courtyard by Marriott and Element by Starwood are examples of brands utilizing such an approach to offer their guests a combination of luxury and advanced resource efficiency. Other hotel companies opt to support existing hotels with tools that will assist individual properties in achieving LEED certification (InterContinental Hotel Group). A common theme to all these efforts follows the golden rule that "one cannot manage what one does not measure", which, in turn, emphasizes the importance of tools for measuring and reporting environmental performance.

It is within this context that the present chapter explores the practice of monitoring and reporting environmental performance in the hotel industry. In particular, it aims to provide guidelines on how to develop and operate electronic environmental performance assessment systems. The chapter starts by discussing the problems of environmental management in hotels. We then move on to describe the functioning and characteristics of performance assessment systems. Subsequently, we examine practical aspects related to the development of such tools, as well as the advantages of environmental performance measuring and reporting. Finally, we provide an overview of some of the online environmental/sustainability reporting tools currently employed in the industry. The chapter concludes by summarizing the argument.

Paulina Bohdanowicz-Godfrey and Piotr Zientara

Environmental management in the hotel industry

Sustainability has far-reaching implications for the hotel industry which, in turn, emphasizes the significance of environmental management (Sloan *et al.* 2009). Whilst greening their operations, lodging establishments all over the world have to tackle similar problems (although differences in building location, size, design and services offered account for variations in the intensity with which particular issues manifest themselves). Hawkins and Bohdanowicz (2011) have grouped these into three main categories: (a) "the throw-away culture" (which deals with waste disposal, segregation and recycling), (b) "the carbon challenge" (which bears on energy consumption and, by implication, on carbon dioxide emissions), and (c) "the wet stuff" (which has to do with water efficiency and waste-water treatment). In addition, hotels committed to sustainability should raise green awareness amongst their employees and guests, keep up green supply chains, offer (whenever feasible) locally sourced and/or organic food and, last but not least, collaborate with industry organizations, such as the International Tourism Partnership (ITP) or the Green Hotel Association (GHA) (Hsie, 2012).

The box below presents a step-by-step approach on how to implement an environmental programme in any type of organization.

12 steps to the implementation of an environmental programme

- Acknowledgement of environmental responsibility at the executive level.
- Current status review – an environmental audit to establish current situation and a benchmarking baseline for relevant metrics.
- Policy and commitment – written documents publicized internally and externally.
- Objectives and targets – formulation of SMART (specific, measurable, attainable, realistic and timely) goals. Initially, it may be more appropriate to set optimization objectives relative to one's own performance rather than to external standards.
- Development of a programme and procedures aligned with existing brand standards, contracts and SOP (Standard Operating Procedures). These may need to be modified to serve the overall purpose.
- Raising communication and awareness, involving staff members at all levels. The introduction of any environmental programme ought to be preceded by an intensive information campaign carried out among employees, who should understand why their company implements it. Otherwise, less-committed individuals or those who do not really believe in environmentalism will, after some time, probably start to refrain from applying the rules in their daily operations.
- Development of an action plan – the collaborative effort of individuals at all levels to define improvement activities (initially at a low or no cost), which should be undemanding, but still produce noticeable outcomes. In this way, employees will become acquainted with the concept in a gradual and stress-free way, which is likely to encourage them to take on more tasks later on.
- Implementation of the action plan – all required tools, such as financial resources, technical assistance or managerial support, must be provided to ensure success. Environmental champions and internal competitions may be employed to encourage participation.

- Documentation of the procedures implemented – as support materials for future replication and model expansion.
- Monitoring and feedback – continuous throughout the programme to allow for corrective action when necessary.
- Management review of objectives – on a regular basis to ensure the constant improvement of a facility's environmental performance.
- Sharing successes internally and externally.

There are various organizations that assist tourism managers in implementation of comprehensive environmental programmes and the development of effective environmental management systems by creating standardized frameworks and detailed guidelines. These include the International Tourism Partnership (ITP), GHA, American Hotel & Lodging Association, Considerate Hoteliers (WTO 2004; Conservation International & the Prince of Wales International Business Leaders Forum (CI and IBLF) 2005; ITP 2008). Furthermore, there exist other environmental initiatives and standards, which, albeit not specifically addressed to hospitality businesses, can easily be adopted by the sector, such as ISO 14001 and ISO 50001, the Eco-Management and Audit Scheme, or the Coalition for Environmentally Responsible Economics Roadmap for Sustainable Development. The Carbon Disclosure Project Reporting, UN Global Compact or the Global Reporting Initiative (GRI) (GRI 2002) can be used for the purposes of unification of sustainability-related reporting across the sector. Also of help are the guidelines available within the various eco-labels and certification programmes, such as the LEED, Travelife, Green Globe or Green Key, the UK Green Tourism Business Scheme, or the recently launched TripAdvisor greenleaders (Font & Buckley 2010; Sampaio et al. 2012; Rushmore 2013).

The keys to a long-lasting positive change in operational practices are (1) to engage all the employees in the initiative; and (2) to reliably monitor any performance changes resulting from the implementation of an environmental programme. The former aspect has been widely debated (Chan & Hawkins 2010; Bohdanowicz et al. 2011), whilst the latter follows the rule "one cannot manage what one does not measure" which will be further discussed below.

The role and characteristics of environmental performance assessment systems

Successful monitoring of a property performance requires the creation of a set of procedures and a system that makes regular reporting of performance possible and data collation, storage and feedback creation easy. In its simplest form this can be an Excel file submission via email to a central point of contact or a destination file located on a shared drive, where regular meter readings of main utilities are recorded and supplemented by hotel operational information. With the widespread availability of IT technology, most of the multi-property companies, however, tend to opt for more sophisticated web-based tools, such as US DoE EnergyStar, UNWTO Hotel Energy Solutions e-toolkit, Green Hotels Global created by the Carbon Accounting Company as well as the proprietary systems developed by hotel companies: Scandic Sustainability Indicator Reporting (ScandicSIR), Accor's OPEN tool, Hilton Worldwide's LightStay, InterContinental Hotel Group's GREENengage and Wyndham Worldwide's Green Toolbox.

All these systems aim to help hotel management assess the environmental performance of a particular facility (or a selected group of properties) by offering a wide variety of tabular and/ or graphical presentations. These tools can also be used to provide back-up information for legislative compliance and CSR reporting. They combine measurement (of environmentally sensitive "inputs") with industry-specific "output" indicators and even benchmarking (Stipanuk 2001, 2003; Scott *et al.* 2004). Typical key performance indicators applied in hospitality include utilities use, carbon footprint and waste generation per available or occupied room, per property unit area, guest-night or units of other services offered or sometimes even revenue. This allows managers to learn how a hotel performs against industry norms, competitors with similar characteristics (or other establishments within the portfolio) or against itself over time as well as where improvements may be needed (Hawkins & Bohdanowicz 2011). It is widely recognized that reliable performance assessment systems are central to effective environmental management practice.

Of course, relevant quantitative and qualitative data are a necessity (Bohdanowicz 2007). Information on the following aspects of the hotel operation must be collected from individual facilities (usually on a monthly basis as a minimum): consumption of all energy forms, water and chemicals, waste generation including diversion from landfill, turnover, property operational characteristics such as number of customers, rooms and other service units sold, outdoor and indoor temperature and humidity conditions. It is also essential to find out what eco-friendly measures have already been implemented on site and to get to know employee attitudes towards environmental practice (Bohdanowicz *et al.* 2011). In recent years, the systems have evolved to gather data of a socio-economic character (Kozak 2004). These include information on seasonally adjusted demand, incidence of leakages, compliance with health and safety regulations, gender equality as well as investment outlays in the local economy, poverty alleviation and conservation of cultural heritage.

Many guidelines have been published (within the GRI, Global Compact, CDP, ITP/ WTTC Hotel Carbon Measurement Initiative v.1) on how to collect the information and on how to delineate acceptable system boundaries (GRI 2002; WTO 2004). Nevertheless, the need for good and reliable metrics still remains unmet. Equally importantly, although research has been undertaken into the problems of performance indicators in the hotel industry (Bohdanowicz & Martinac 2007), the accuracy of the published figures have been contested, principally due to the existence of large discrepancies in the reported data (De Burgos-Jiménez *et al.* 2002; Warnken *et al.* 2005). Researchers highlight the differences both in the methodology used to collect data and in the facility characteristics (e.g. weather conditions and climate zone, number of amenities, type of customers served, occupancy, building size and design) used as a point of reference (Leslie 2001; Scott *et al.* 2004; Matson & Piette 2005).

The overall reliability of benchmarking tools has also been questioned (Stipanuk 2003). Some authors argue that for global benchmarks to be reliable, too many hotel sub-categories would be required or extensive databases would need to be created (Warnken *et al.* 2005). Hence, at the moment, there is no universally applicable benchmark tool for the hotel industry and most of the international hotel corporations have developed internal benchmarking schemes to assist individual properties.

It should also be noted that environmental performance assessment systems for hotels are developed by specialized companies or academic institutions. Only some of these become available as free tools and, as a result, there is limited information publicly available (the EnergyStar Portfolio Manager is among the exceptions in that it provides a document explaining the methodology). That makes it hard to draw on someone else's experience and to "transplant" similar systems to other organizations. It is, therefore, extremely important to provide hoteliers and other tourism managers with clear and well-proven guidelines on how to successfully introduce performance-assessment systems in their facilities.

Practical aspects of the development of performance assessment systems

The development of environmental performance systems is challenging. Accordingly, it is worth discussing the key aspects, procedures and main development stages of such an initiative. The procedure outlined here can be adapted to a system developed for any single- or multiple-unit tourism enterprise (Bohdanowicz 2008). Table 27.1 presents possible time spans of particular stages in the tool development, assuming that the environmental policy and strategy are already in place.

When defining the scope and methodology of environmental/sustainability reporting the following aspects should be considered:

- indicators and outputs required from the point of view of CSR, engineering, finance and legal teams, as well as various business levels;
- CSR corporate reports, engineering improvement opportunities, legislation (i.e. UK Energy Efficiency CRC scheme);
- physical boundaries of the system under reporting;
- on-property performance only (equivalent to Scope 1 and 2 of GHG Protocol), or transport and supplies to and from (Scope 3);
- characteristics of the property and need of capturing significant changes;
- property size, year of construction, services offered, structure and mechanical systems installed, implemented innovations and initiatives;
- renovations, extensions, service changes and external influences;
- availability and granularity of the input information and frequency of collection (centralized and/or manual inputs) weighted against the reporting burden;
- monthly utilities based on main meters or sub-meters, occupancy, services offered such as food-covers, meeting hours, etc.;
- weather data;
- availability of centralized inputs from suppliers or other in-house reports;
- standardization of definitions and methodologies of data collection to ensure compliance and reliability;
- instructions on how to read meters, which tariffs and services to include;
- transparency of the methodology and internal processes;
- the above-mentioned instructions;
- documentation on conversion and correction factors, external data sources and mathematical models used;
- alignment of requirements with recognized certification programmes and legislative reporting;
- GRI, UN Global Compact, CDP, UK EE CRC, ITP/WTTC HCMI, etc.;
- LEED, BREEAM, Green Globes, Nordic Swan, TripAdvisor greenleaders, etc.;
- potential of providing selected information externally;
- legislative compliance;
- carbon footprint calculators for the sales teams; and
- "live" business performance displays in-house and online.

Table 27.1 Timeline for the implementation of an environmental reporting and resource management tool

Stage	Time (months)	Actions
1 – Development of the reporting tool	6–8	Definition of the scope and form of the environmental management programme and reporting tool
		Consultation with company representatives and external consultants
		External validation of the methodology
		Development of the programme, tool and supporting materials
		Software testing
		Provision of necessary infrastructure in all units (i.e. computers, handheld devices)
2 – Introduction of the programme and reporting tool	1–2	Introduction of the environmental programme and reporting system to the business by the top management
		Nomination of environmental champions in all business units
		Installation of the reporting system in all units
3 – Training	2–4	1. Online modules or classroom type workshops detailing the system (data sources, data acquisition methodology, reporting procedure, output reports, possible limitations of the tool)
		2. Regular Question & Answer virtual sessions led by the support team or tool developer
		Separate training modules may be required for different business roles to accommodate the interest and needs
4 – Creation of the reporting culture	3–6	Careful monitoring of the data quality and reporting status of individual properties
		Regular reminders of the need to report on time
		Continuous support and encouragement for employees to raise awareness and develop a routine of regular and correct reporting (special consideration given to individuals new to the tool)
		Management support for the initiative
5 – Data collection	Up to 12	Constant collection of the data in the system, centralized sources can be used Environmental programme and training can be initiated
6 – Initiation of resource saving program	When 12 months of data available	Setting environmental (resource reduction) goals (with the past 12 months as a base year) as discussed in the box on 12 steps to implementation
		The tool used to monitor progress and performance of individual units
7 – Data validation	At least annually	Validation (preferably external) of the accuracy of data reported

The key points of consideration in the development of a computerized tool itself include:

- user-friendly, flexible, modern and visually attractive interface aligned with the company branding;
- availability of standardized as well as easy-to-customize reports providing instantaneous feedback to the various levels of business users;
- added business benefits in terms of benchmarking, identifying improvement opportunities and providing relevant suggestions;
- user-customized landing page;
- networking capability for users;
- capability of automated/direct data transfer from other systems and bulk data uploads;
- multiple levels of internal and third-party data validation (automated and manual);
- accessibility via multiple device types;
- strategy to ensure all sales and acquisitions are captured;
- data and access security;
- flexibility of further development, adaptations, expansion and addressing ad hoc requests;
- effective and efficient infrastructure to cope with large amounts of data; and
- technical support for users.

The ever-increasing popularity and potential impact of social networking calls for similar features in the environmental reporting tools to allow users to communicate with their peers, exchange ideas and collectively address challenges. Practical experience indicates that making environmental/sustainability reporting mandatory within the management contract or brand standard requirements facilitates penetration of the solution across the business and helps encourage the creation of a proper reporting culture.

Once the system is operational, it is imperative that it constantly receives strong corporate support. Continuity of the system's utilization may be achieved by frequent references being made to it by senior management, while hotel managers and environmental champions should be encouraged to report and discuss the hotel environmental status with all staff members on a regular basis. It can also be used to evaluate the commitment level of area and hotel managers and serve as a support tool in recognition programmes.

A well designed and implemented performance-assessment system may certainly bring considerable benefits at an individual as well as corporate level. These benefits can be referred to as both business and non-business, and include improved bottom line due to reduced operational costs, the potential for an increased market-share and preservation of limited natural resources. More attractive CSR images may further enhance customer and employee loyalty.

Online sustainability reporting tools in practice

The advances in IT technology have led to the propagation of online sustainability reporting tools. Table 27.2 presents a selection of some of the most prominent systems currently available within and for the hospitality sector. From a practical point of view, it is worth mentioning that all these tools require the input of basic building information and monthly reporting of utility and operational information for each property.

As Table 27.2 indicates, there are a wide variety of online tools in use within the industry. This is a good sign as it means more businesses are taking their environmental performance and its monitoring more seriously. Whether they are doing so for altruistic or purely pragmatic reasons is the subject of another debate. The most important thing is that the sector has taken

Table 27.2 Key features of online sustainability reporting tools

	ScandicSIR (Sustainability Indicator Reporting)	LightStay	GREENengage	Green Hotels Global (as adopted by Marriott International)	EnergyStar	Hotel Energy Solutions e-toolkit
Business owner	Scandic	Hilton Worldwide	InterContinental Hotel Group	The Carbon Accounting Company	US Department of Energy	UN World Tourism Organization
Launch date	1996 (version 1)	2008	2009	2011–12	2000	2011
Reduction targets, KPIs	2007–25: Fossil CO_2: 100%	2008–14: Energy: 20%, CO_2: 20%, Waste: 20%, Water: 10%	2010–12: Energy: 6–10% (managed and owned); 2013–17: CO_2: 12%, Water (in water stressed areas): 12%	2009–20: Energy: 20%; Water: 20%	Set by individual users	Set by individual users
Achievements	1996–2012: Energy: 24%, CO_2: 60%, Water: 21%, Waste: 45%	2008–12: Energy: 12.2%, CO_2: 12.8%, Waste: 24.0%, Water: 10.2%, Savings: USD$ 253	2010–12: Energy: 11.7%; 2011–12: CO_2: 19%	2007–12: Energy: 16.5%; GHG: 13.3%; Water: 11.6%	N/A	N/A
Sustainability reporting	Mandatory for all	Mandatory for all via Brand Standard	Mandatory for owned and managed, voluntary for franchised	Mandatory via Brand Standard	Voluntary, no fee	Voluntary, no fee
Portfolio coverage	No information available	100% in Jan 2013	50% in Jan 2013	58% in Jan 2013	North America	EU
Reporting of environmental practices in place	Technology and culture	Technology and culture	No info available	Technology and culture	Energy and water technology only	Energy technology only

	ScandicSIR (Sustainability Indicator Reporting)	LightStay	GREENengage	Green Hotels Global (as adopted by Marriott International)	EnergyStar	Hotel Energy Solutions e-toolkit
Data validation	Internal and external via Nordic Swan where relevant	Internal and external via KEMA Inc. and DEKRA Certification Inc.	Assurance process on hotel achievements, GRI process	Internal and on-site spot audits by GreenHotelsGlobal	Internal based on E-Tracker tool	No information available
Report spectrum	Medium	High	High	Medium	High	Low
Benchmarking	Energy, CO_2, water, waste and active chemicals against other hotels, country average, Nordic Swan criteria where available	Energy, CO_2, water, waste, environmental practices score against brand and neighbours	Energy and water against similar hotels	No information available	Energy against data in Commercial Buildings Energy Consumption Survey database	Energy against the data in the database
Improvement suggestions	No information available	Sustainability Improvement Planner and Project Database	Action Plan and IHG Green Solutions	No information available	Within EnergyStar framework only	Energy efficiency and renewable energy projects with ROI
Carbon footprint calculation	Internal indicators and country KPIs publicly available on Sustainability Live Report Calculator	Internal indicators and external Meeting Calculator and Report for customers via Connect+	Internal indicators and Carbon Calculator for customers	Internal indicators (incl. weather corrected)	Internal indicators	Internal absolute volume
ITP/WTTC HCMI v.1	No information available	Incorporated	Incorporated	Incorporated	N/A	N/A
Social networking	Forum and network of coordinators	Neighbour function and forum	Blog and forum	No information available	N/A	N/A

Table 27.2 Key features of online sustainability reporting tools cont'd

	ScandicSIR (Sustainability Indicator Reporting)	LightStay	GREENengage	Green Hotels Global (as adopted by Marriott International)	EnergyStar	Hotel Energy Solutions e-toolkit
Internal certification	No	No	4 levels: Partner, Achiever, Innovator, Leader	No	Rating	N/A
Used for external reporting	Sustainability Live Report website: www.scandic-campaign.com/livereport	CR reporting, support for UK CRC reporting	CR reporting, for corporate customers, support for CDP, UK CRC; some results displayed online	No details on Marriott arrangement; GreenHotelsGlobal provides standardized metrics free of charge to meeting/event planners and corporate travel professionals	As needed by individual users	As needed by individual users
External certification	Nordic Swan	ISO 14001	Approved for LEED pre-certification	Aligned with APEX/ASTM Standards for Green Meetings and Events	EnergyStar	N/A

Sources: Company websites (CSR sections) and press releases as accessed 5–6 October 2013, www.scandic.com, www.hiltonworldwide.com, www.ihgplc.com, www.greenhotelsglobal.com, www.marriott.com, www.energystar.gov, hes.e-benchmarking.org

steps to measure its environmental performance which, in turn, is likely to lead to more pro-active management of resources in the near future.

Conclusion

There is no doubt that performance-assessment systems, which show how a hotel performs against industry norms or in comparison with its peers with similar characteristics (or other establishments within the portfolio) or with itself over time, are of high value to hotel managers and engineers alike. Individual businesses may either opt to acquire one of the many commercially available tools and adapt it to their specific *modus operandi* or develop their own tool. Each of these options offers certain benefits but invariably requires support from the company management as well as active (and pro-active participation) of employees.

It is, however, worth noting that these tools are not devoid of limitations. Hence special attention needs to paid to certain aspects. These include the quality of input data coming from individual properties, the reliability and accuracy of international benchmarks or lack of thereof, as well as the uniformity of reporting methodologies. As things stood in 2013, neither of these challenges has been satisfactorily addressed (though efforts are being made to that end).

Such undertakings as the ITP/WTTC Hotel Carbon Measurement Initiative merit particular recognition since they promote much-needed collective action. The above initiative, while bringing together over 20 hotel companies, helped to reach consensus on the common methodology for measuring carbon emissions. Similar schemes are needed for other utilities and environmental outputs.

In order to successfully address the challenge of international and uniform benchmarking, development of the "Lego-like" construction of benchmarks should be considered. This concept holds that hotel establishments are disaggregated into service modules, such as guestrooms, catering outlets, conference/business centres, etc., each having individual efficiencies/performance indicators. These indicators would then be combined and weighted (depending on the services offered and their share in the overall area or revenue generated) to produce the overall evaluation of a facility. The actual performance of a given property could then be compared to an individual benchmark. This idea deserves consideration since, with the advances in IT technology and growing interest in pro-active management of environmental resources, development of such solutions becomes increasingly feasible.

Despite the yet unsolved challenges, it would be hard to deny the benefits the environmental performance-assessment systems bring – both to hotel companies and the environment. In fact, elimination (or reduction) of inefficiencies (which translates into savings and lower operating costs) coupled with reduced environmental impacts and a more ecologically aware workforce justify non-negligible investment outlays. We hope, therefore, that the present chapter will help practitioners to put into place and operate such systems, irrespective of whether they will do so for purely economic reasons or out of a deep conviction that companies should behave responsibly vis-à-vis the environment and their stakeholders.

Key Reading

Bohdanowicz, P. (2008) 'Theory and practice of environmental management in hotel chains', in S. Gössling, C. M. Hall and D. Weaver (eds) *Sustainable Tourism Futures: Perspectives on Systems, Restructuring and Innovations*, London: Routledge.

Bohdanowicz, P., Zientara, P. and Novotna, E. (2011) 'International hotel chains and environmental protection: Analysis of Hilton's *we care!* programme (Europe, 2006–8)', *Journal of Sustainable Tourism*, 19(7): 797–816.

ScandicSIR Sustainability Live Report. Available at: www.scandic-campaign.com/livereport

References

Blowfield, M. and Murray, A. (2011) *Corporate Responsibility*, Oxford: Oxford University Press.

Bohdanowicz, P. (2007) 'A case study of Hilton environmental reporting as a tool of corporate social responsibility', *Tourism Review International*, 11(2): 115–31.

—— (2008) 'Theory and practice of environmental management in hotel chains', in S. Gössling, C.M. Hall and D. Weaver (eds) *Sustainable Tourism Futures: Perspectives on Systems, Restructuring and Innovations*, London: Routledge.

Bohdanowicz, P. and Martinac, I. (2007) 'Determinants and benchmarking of resource consumption in hotels – Case study of Hilton International and Scandic in Europe', *Energy and Buildings*, 39: 82–95.

Bohdanowicz, P. and Zientara, P. (2008) 'Corporate social responsibility in hospitality: Issues and implications. A case study of Scandic', *Scandinavian Journal of Hospitality and Tourism*, 8(4): 271–93.

—— (2012) 'CSR-inspired environmental initiatives in top hotel chains', in D. Leslie (ed.) *Tourism Enterprises and the Sustainability Agenda across Europe*, Farnham: Ashgate.

Bohdanowicz, P., Zientara, P. and Novotna, E. (2011) 'International hotel chains and environmental protection: Analysis of Hilton's *we care!* programme (Europe, 2006–8)', *Journal of Sustainable Tourism*, 19(7): 797–816.

Chan, E.S.W. and Hawkins, R. (2010) 'Attitude towards EMS in an international hotel: An exploratory case study', *International Journal of Hospitality Management*, 29(4): 641–51.

Conservation International and the Prince of Wales International Business Leaders Forum (CI and IBLF) (2005) *Sustainable Hotel Siting, Design and Construction*, London: CI & IBLF, Nuffield Press.

Cooper, I. (1998) 'Emerging issues in environmental management', in K. Alexander (ed.) *Facility Management: Theory and Practice*, London: Spon Press.

De Burgos-Jiménez, J., Cano-Guillén, C.J. and Céspedes-Lorente, J.J. (2002) 'Planning and control of environmental performance in hotels', *Journal of Sustainable Tourism*, 10(3): 207–21.

Duncan, E. (2013) 'All creatures great and small', *Economist*, 408(8853), 14 September: 3–16.

European Commission (2001) *Promoting a European Framework for Corporate Social Responsibility*, COM(2001) 366 Final, Brussels.

Font, X. and Buckley, R.C. (2010) *Tourism Ecolabelling: Certification and Promotion of Sustainable Management*, Wallingford: CABI.

Gössling, S. (2002) 'Global environmental consequences of tourism', *Global Environmental Change*, 12: 283–302.

Global Reporting Initiative (GRI) (2002) *Sustainability Reporting Guidelines*, Boston: GRI.

Hawkins, R. and Bohdanowicz, P. (2011) *Responsible Hospitality: Theory and Practice*, Woodeaton, Oxford: Goodfellow Publishers.

Hillenbrand, C., Money, K. and Ghobadian, A. (2013) 'Unpacking the mechanism by which corporate responsibility impacts stakeholder relationships', *British Journal of Management*, 24(1): 127–46.

Hotel Analyst (2012) *The 'Value' of Sustainability for the Hotel Sector*, London: ZeroTwoZero Communications.

Hsie, Y-C. (2012) 'Hotel companies' environmental policies and practices: A content analysis of their web pages', *International Journal of Contemporary Hospitality Management*, 24(1): 97–121.

Huybers, T. and Bennet, J. (2002) *Environmental Management and the Competitiveness of Nature-based Tourism Destinations*, Cheltenham: Edward Elgar Publishing.

International Tourism Partnership (2008) *Environmental Management for Hotels*, London: ITP.

Kasim, A. (2009) 'Managerial attitudes towards environmental management among small and medium hotels in Kuala Lumpur', *Journal of Sustainable Tourism*, 17: 709–25.

Kozak, M. (2004) *Destination Benchmarking: Concepts, Practices and Operations*, Wallingford: CABI Publishing.

Leslie, D. (2001) 'Serviced accommodation, environmental performance and benchmarks', in S. Pyo (ed.), *Benchmarks in Hospitality and Tourism*, Binghampton: Haworth Press.

Matson, N.E. and Piette, M.A. (2005) *High Performance Commercial Building Systems – Review of California and National Benchmarking Methods, Working Draft*, Berkeley: Ernest Orlando Lawrence Berkeley National Laboratory.

Porter, M. and Kramer, M.R. (2011) 'Creating shared value', *Harvard Business Review, January–February*, 62–77.

Rushmore, J. (2013) *TripAdvisor greenleaders program presentation*, The Travel Foundation Annual Meeting, The Crystal, London UK, 17 September 2013.

Sampaio, A.R., Thomas, R. and Font, X. (2012) 'Small business management and environmental engagement', *Journal of Sustainable Tourism*, 20(2): 179–93.

Scott, J.A., Beckenham, T. and Watt, M. (2004) *Travel and Tourism Industry Benchmarking Methodologies*, London: Green Globe 21, Earth Check Pty Ltd.

Sloan, P., Legrand, W. and Chen, J.S. (2009) *Sustainability in the Hospitality Industry, Principles of Sustainable Operations*, Oxford: Elsevier.

Stipanuk, D.M. (2001) 'Energy management in 2001 and beyond: Operational options that reduce use and cost', *The Cornell Hotel and Restaurant Administration Quarterly*, 42(3): 57–71.

—— (2003) *Hotel Energy and Water Consumption Benchmarks, Final Report*, Washington DC: American Hotel & Lodging Association.

Warnken, J., Bradley, M. and Guilding, C. (2005) 'Eco-resorts vs. mainstream accommodation providers. An investigation of the viability of benchmarking environmental performance', *Tourism Management*, 26: 367–79.

WTO (2004) *Indicators of Sustainable Development for Tourism Destinations – a Guidebook*, Madrid: World Tourism Organization.

28

Built attractions and sustainability

John Swarbrooke

> **Visitor attractions** Man-made buildings, structures and sites that are designed specifically to attract visitors and which are purpose-built to meet the needs of these visitors.
>
> **Heritage** The things we want to keep.

Introduction

In the debates that have been taking place across the world in recent years about the impact of tourism, relatively little attention has been focused on the visitor attractions sector. Instead, the carbon footprint of air travel, the use of resources by hotels, and the effects of mass market tour operation on destinations have been the dominant themes in both the academic literature and even the news media.

The lack of focus on the attractions sector in the discussions about sustainable tourism may be because most attractions are not thought to have the highly visible and measurable impact associated with the carbon emissions of airliners or the 'food miles' of the ingredients used in hotel restaurants (see Chapters 2 and 26). However, it may reflect the fact that the visitor attractions sector has, in recent years, seen far fewer high-profile attraction projects than was the case in the 1980s and particularly the 1990s. In this era we saw the creation of mixed-use waterfront developments in the seaboard cities of the USA and Europe as well as the opening of Disneyland Paris and the Guggenheim Museum in Bilbao. This was also the period in which industrial heritage and open-air museums flourished. These were arguably step-change developments in the attractions sector; since then, most new developments have largely been imitations of these types of attractions. Nevertheless, attractions do have an impact, both positive and negative and, occasionally, a new attraction can attract public attention in terms of these. For instance, when Ski Dubai opened in 2005, many questioned the environmental impact which operating such a facility in a desert environment would have. This chapter uses a broad definition of sustainable tourism that embraces environmental sensitivity, social equity and economic viability.

The definition of built attractions

As the focus of this chapter is on built attractions let us begin by defining how the term will be used. The phrase will be used to encompass two types of attractions, namely:

- Man-made buildings, structures and sites that were designed for a purpose other than attracting visitors but which now attract significant numbers of visitors. This category might include for example places of worship, royal palaces and disused industrial sites.
- Man-made buildings, structures and sites that are designed specifically to attract visitors and which are purpose-built to meet the needs of these visitors (e.g. this would cover theme parks and art galleries).

This broad definition means that the term could be applied to everything from a heritage centre to a zoo, a steam railway to an archaeological site, a shopping mall to a theatre, a marina to an amusement park.

However, the situation is even more complex than this in two main ways. First, these tangible built attractions are also the venue for intangible events that have their own impact. Second, there is some blurring of the boundaries between built attractions and other sectors of tourism. For example, hotels such as the Burj el Arab in Dubai have become built attractions in their own right due to their architecture and reputation. People visit them as architectural icons – even if they never sleep in the hotel – in the same way that they might visit a cathedral.

The impacts of built attractions

In common with the rest of the tourism sector it is possible to divide the impact of built attractions into environmental, economic and social although there are clearly inter-relationships between the three. As with the case of tourism as a whole, the impacts can be both positive and negative and are affected by a range of factors including how the attraction is owned and managed, its location, visitor numbers and its role within the local community.

In general, built attractions are perceived to have less negative impacts than other elements of tourism (e.g. air travel). However, in measuring the impact of a visit to an attraction we have to include all the impacts, including the carbon footprint of the journey there, as well as the impacts associated with the purchase of food and drink and souvenirs. In a complex system such as tourism it is very difficult to isolate the environmental impact of built attractions (see Chapter 16).

We are starting to see research on the resource impacts of visits to built attractions, such as the work of Farreny et al. (2012), who calculated the energy and water usage figures per visit for 28 museums in the province of Catalunya in Spain. We have also seen in recent years that the creation of new built attractions can bring real environmental benefits in the form of recycling derelict buildings into attractions. In waterfront areas from New York to Barcelona we have seen the creation of new aquarium attractions, IMAX cinemas, contemporary art museums and leisure shopping complexes in former dockside warehouses and factories. These, in turn, have been used as the flagship developments for ambitious, but not always successful, urban regeneration schemes.

The economic benefits of built attractions are rarely quantified but they can be substantial in terms of both jobs and revenue. However, their impact goes beyond this – in many destinations the existence of a particular attraction is what brings tourists to the destination; the attraction can fairly claim to be responsible for a share of overall revenue in all businesses within the destination. This is as true of the Louvre in Paris as it is of Disney in Orlando or the casinos of Macau. If attractions are able to open and attract visitors all year around they can help reduce the seasonality which often undermines destination sustainability. However, as attractions are generally very costly to develop and often involve public sector investment, there are potential opportunity costs.

The social impact of attractions is perhaps the most difficult to identify, but it should be seen in terms of the impact not only on the local community but also on the visitors themselves. We know from the wider tourism literature how important tourism is for local communities, but visiting attractions can change the lives of the visitors too, causing them to change their attitudes about everything from war to wildlife conservation. Built attractions have a particularly significant impact on the lives of young people as many of them feature in educational visits organised by schools and colleges.

Sustainability challenges and built attractions

Given the diversity and complexity of the built attraction sector, trying to identify key sustainability issues is a challenging task. The first challenge appears to be that attraction operators do not seem to be devoting much attention to the issue of sustainability.

The author conducted an informal search of the websites of 20 leading built attractions around the world in April 2013. Of these, 11 made no mention of any sustainability-related issues including the Louvre in France, Ski Dubai, the Guinness Storehouse in Ireland, the Georgia Aquarium in the USA, Stonehenge in the UK, Marina Bay Sands Casino in Singapore, Universal Studios, Notre Dame de Paris, the Guggenheim Museums, Terra Mitica in Spain and the Ngong Ping Cultural Village in Hong Kong. Of the others, four – Sovereign Hill in Australia, Colonial Williamsburg in the USA, the British Museum, and the Swiss Transport Museum – talked about their education work with schools. However, this was simply about promoting their services to attract visitors. San Diego Zoo talked about its conservation work but that also relates to how it attracts visitors and develops brand loyalty. The Taj Mahal in India had a short code of conduct for visitors and pointed out that cars could not be driven close to the structure. The Eden Project in the UK had a significant amount of content on sustainability as this is a key theme at the attraction that was developed to find a new use for a derelict industrial site. The Empire State Building in New York had a major section about what it described as its 'sustainability retrofit', showing how refurbishment work was reducing the negative impact of the building on energy use. Finally, only one organisation appeared to be engaging with a sustainability agenda in an holistic manner and that was, not surprisingly, Walt Disney through its Disney Citizenship programme. This covers all Disney companies, however, not just the theme parks and resorts.

These results show that sustainability and sustainable development is not yet a major consideration for most attraction operators. This is in stark contrast to other sectors such as tour operation, air transport and hotels which have all increasingly felt the need to be seen to be addressing sustainability in recent years.

For many attractions there appears to be a growing problem of the sustainability of the attractions themselves. In the 1980s and 1990s we saw the development of many new built attractions, particularly in Europe, often using public funding. With the current economic recession and the growth in competition from destinations around the world a number of formerly successful attractions appear to be struggling to survive or are operating less successfully than they were. Those funded from the public sector tend not to have the funding to undertake the constant updating that is needed to ensure continued success. Many European attractions have also relied heavily on European Union funding, so may not be economically viable in the long term. If attractions fail, the impact can be devastating, particularly in destinations which are heavily reliant upon one or two attractions. There can then be a domino effect on other local attractions and then on local businesses which depend on visitor expenditure (see Miman *et al.* 2010).

In some more affluent parts of the world we appear to be in an era when certain types of built attractions have become a sort of status symbol, on a scale perhaps not seen before. There is possibly a mind-set that says if we can afford it and the technology exists, we build it, perhaps with little regard for the broader concept of sustainability. It could certainly be suggested that we have seen examples of this phenomenon in recent years in the oil-rich Gulf States with its plethora of tall buildings, sites reclaimed from the sea, shopping malls, and even a ski slope in the desert!

A major area of controversy in the built attraction sector relates to wildlife attractions such as zoos. The growing interest in animal rights – although by no means a universal trend – has led to questions being raised about animals being kept confined and displayed for the entertainment of visitors. Yet, at the same time, there is no doubt that the work of many zoos has helped to conserve threatened species. Frost (2011) examines some of the issues surrounding the ethical dimension of wildlife attractions (see Chapter 30).

One of the few ideas that no one seems to disagree with in sustainable tourism is the need to engage consumers in sustainability and get them actively involved (Gössling *et al.* 2012). Many also talk about 'educating' consumers that seems to be synonymous with trying to persuade them to behave in certain ways (see Chapter 19). We have seen this very strongly in both tour operations and the hotel sector. However, this is a problematic approach when we are far from certain yet of what behaviour is most conducive to sustainability given our limited knowledge of cause and effect in relation to actions we ask customers to take in tourism. What seems like a good idea today may turn out to be a problem tomorrow. However, in terms of wildlife attractions at least, it seems from the work of Smith *et al.* (2012) that zoo visitors do not object to being given messages encouraging behaviour change, which is good news for the marketers of such attractions.

A very different issue in terms of the market is the matter of equity and social inclusion and widening access to built attraction experiences. In the field of cultural attractions such as museums and art galleries there have been some excellent examples of outreach work designed to bring in visitors from all social classes and ethnic communities. Sometimes, in heritage attractions, the choice of stories to be told – or perhaps more commonly the stories that will not be told – excludes people from particular ethnic communities or subcultures within the society.

Pricing is an important issue in relation to social inclusion. In the UK, for example, the government abolished entrance charges to the major national museums to encourage more people to visit them. However, this has provoked some controversy from those who believe it represents an unnecessary subsidy to affluent citizens and foreign tourists. Meanwhile private attractions and those owned by 'not for profit' social enterprises complain that it represents unfair competition and is a threat to their survival.

Moving from the demand to the supply side another challenge in this sector is around the subject of labour, the employees in built attractions. First, there is the question of seasonality, particularly in theme and amusement parks; IAAPA, the trade body for such parks, estimated in 2010 that while parks employed some 600,000 people, 83 per cent of the jobs were seasonal. Many jobs are also casual, with no guaranteed fixed hours per week. While this kind of employment undoubtedly suits some people, it is not conducive to the development of sustainable communities. Someone in such a job cannot easily obtain a mortgage, or develop enough financial security to start a family. This situation is exacerbated by the fact that, in countries such as the UK, many staff in built attractions are on official government minimum wage.

These last two points perhaps lead us on to look at the role of attractions within communities and their contribution to the sustainable development of these communities. Many purpose-built attractions appear to have little direct involvement with their host communities and often they seem to have no published commitments to recruit staff locally or buy the products and services that they need from local suppliers wherever possible. They rarely even talk about supporting local charities and good causes. This is in contrast to what we are increasingly seeing from hotel companies, for example. Indeed, they generally do not seem to recognise the risks that can occur to their reputation due to the actions of their supply chain partners. In 2006, for example, Hong Kong Disneyland faced on-site protests from people complaining about alleged 'sweatshop' conditions at factories that produced merchandise for sale in the outlets at the park. Yet exporting sustainability values to an organisation's supply chain has become a major theme in sustainable tourism in recent years (see Chapter 15).

Heritage attractions are often almost as controversial as wildlife attractions due to the contested nature of heritage in many countries. Communities may choose to present their heritage in ways that either rewrite history or, at the very least, ignore certain periods or marginalise the contribution made by minority communities or even use such communities as 'scapegoats' for negative events. We continue to see museums struggling to deal with issues such as slavery and ethnic violence.

If sustainability is about equity and human dignity as much as about environmental concerns then the whole area of 'dark tourism' raises some interesting ethical dilemmas. Stone, on the website of the Institute for Dark Tourism Research, defined it as 'travel to sites of death, disaster or the seemingly macabre'. This broad definition clearly encompasses a range of sites that have highly emotional personal connections for certain individuals and communities. It is not difficult to see, therefore, the controversy that can surround the presentation of certain sites, particularly in terms of what Sharpley (2012) describes as 'genocide tourism'.

Another aspect of heritage attractions that raises concerns is the way in which attractions can be developed based around the lives of minority communities. This is a trend which is particularly significant in Asia at the moment. In 2005, the Baan Tang Liang village attraction opened in Thailand purporting to give tourists an opportunity to learn about the culture of an indigenous tribe. However, many believe it was merely an excuse to create a voyeuristic photo opportunity for tourists curious to see the unique 'longneck women' of this region. Yang (2011a, 2011b) published a study of the 'Yunnan Ethnic Village', an attraction that presents the architecture and customs of the Yunnan people. However, as the papers noted, some staff complained that they were paid low salaries by the Han entrepreneurs who own the attraction.

The concept of carrying capacity has been with us for many years but for some attractions the issue is not one of physical capacity (see Chapter 20). What is more important is the capacity after which the fabric of the attraction begins to be adversely affected as well as the capacity after which the quality of the visitor experience begins to deteriorate. Clearly this is a very subjective judgement and one where norms may well vary between nationalities and cultures.

In the tour operation sector, a growing element of corporate social responsibility is the notion that tourists should be encouraged to spend their money in destination in ways that spread the benefits of this spending as widely as possible within the local community. This is also a challenge for attraction managers given that most merchandise sold on site may well be made in another country. There are real opportunities for attractions to benefit their host communities by developing partnerships with local handicraft producers and food producers that will enhance the visitor experience as well as bringing more money into the local economy. It is now time for us to look at the question of research in the area of sustainability in the built attraction sector.

Research issues and built attractions

In writing this chapter the author has become painfully aware of the lack of attention that has been paid to built attractions by tourism academics and researchers. There have been no major new texts written during the last five years and very few influential journal papers in the past decade. Literature on the management of attractions is sparse. As Leask (2010: 163) noted, 'this area of study lacks the mature research to underpin the comparison of best practice or to provide a national or international benchmark of visitor attraction quality'.

However, the problem is more fundamental than a lack of literature on the management of attractions; it is the lack of literature on any aspect of built attractions. A review of volumes 33 to 38 of *Tourism Management* covering 2012 and the first part of 2013 shows that of some 175 papers, only six had any real focus on built attractions. Interestingly, there were more papers about natural attractions and event attractions but these were still very few in number. If this field of study is seen as an arid zone then the area of sustainability and built attractions is a veritable desert!

In Volume 20 and the first three issues of volume 21 of the *Journal of Sustainable Tourism*, covering 2012 and the first part of 2013, there were some 81 papers, of which only seven could be said to have any significant focus on built attractions. One point that came out of this modest review of the recent literature in sustainable tourism is that there appears to be much more interest from researchers in sustainability in relation to natural attractions than for built attractions. Therefore, in terms of the future, there is great scope for empirical research on the relationship between sustainability and built attractions.

First, we need more work on the measurement of the impact of attractions in terms of the environment, social and economic impacts. We need to know more about the carbon footprint of attraction visitors and how it varies between different types of attraction. At the same time, we need to study the economic multiplier effects of different types of built attraction as well as exploring the social impact of attractions, such as the effects which new casinos have on gambling behaviour in the host community. These are just three examples of the types of research that are needed to help guide public policy on attraction development.

There also appears to be a great need for further research about consumer behaviour in the sector. It is important for us to discover the extent to which destination image and choice is based on the existence of specific attractions. We also need to investigate perceptions of different types of built attractions and seek to identify types that may be in decline in terms of popularity. Both areas of research should help us to be able to predict where destinations may face a challenge to sustain their markets in the future. In parallel with this research we need to establish if consumers are aware of, or interested in, sustainability issues at built attractions. It would be particularly interesting to explore national and cultural differences in relation to these attitudes.

There is also a paucity of convincing detailed single-attraction case studies concerning the role which attractions play within host communities and their links to sectors such as hotels and transport.

On a corporate level we need studies of the corporate social responsibility policies of attraction operators together with studies of why such policies are not being developed. This research could also address the issue of sustainability and the supply chains of attractions. At the same time it would be useful to have more empirical research on employment in the built attraction sector in terms of casual employment, seasonality, wage rates and turnover.

Finally, it would be interesting to see more studies of the impact of visitor numbers on built attractions. Is it possible to recognise a scale of visitation at which point significant physical deterioration begins to occur. Furthermore, we need to better understand the 'sense of place' at attractions and how this is influenced by visitor numbers.

Case Study

Geevor Tin Mining Museum, Cornwall, UK

Geevor Tin Mining Museum is located in Pendeen in the remote far west of Cornwall in the UK, within the Cornwall and West Devon Mining Landscape World Heritage Site that was designated in 2006. Although an industrial site it is in an area of great natural beauty looking out over the Atlantic Ocean. Until the mine closed in 1990 it produced some 50,000 tons of Black Tin and employed several hundred people. Its closure was a major blow to the local community which was heavily dependent on the mine.

The local community was determined that the site should continue to play a positive role in the community. Following local community lobbying the local authority, Cornwall County Council, acquired the site in 1992 and in 1993 it opened as a museum. In 2000 a 'not for profit' social enterprise, Pendeen Community Heritage, was established to manage the site and the museum.

Major funding of some £3.8 million was attracted from the European Union and national and local government to improve the site and develop new facilities for visitors.

The museum now attracts some 40,000 visitors a year and contributes to sustainability and sustainable development in a number of ways including the following:

- It is conserving a site which is of great significance to the history and lives of the local community as well as being of such global significance as to merit designation as part of a World Heritage Site by UNESCO.
- The existence of the museum has provided impetus for works to reduce contamination of the land caused by the mining activities.
- Part of the development of the site has involved the creation of a nature train covering the 27 hectare site, thus helping visitors to discover the rich flora and fauna found on the site.
- One of the published aims of Pendeen Community Heritage (PCH) is the creation of sustainable employment. The site currently provides paid employment for 22 full-time and part-time staff. All of the jobs are held by local people.
- Geevor provides opportunities for people to work on-site as volunteers organising events, acting as guides, working with the education team or collecting the memories of ex-miners in an oral history project. This is an excellent way for young people to develop skills that increase their employability as well as providing a way in which retired people can add value to their leisure time.
- The museum is run by the community through PCH, which has some 500 members and an elected Board of trustees who are local people.

- Geevor has an outreach programme designed to raise awareness of the history of the mine through which staff deliver presentations off-site at schools and clubs and societies. Between 2010 and 2013 more than 60 presentations had been made to nearly 3,000 people.
- The museum puts a lot of resources into welcoming educational visits from school and college students who use the site as a laboratory to learn about history, wildlife and engineering. Geevor has won awards for its work in this field and between 2010 and 2012 some 6,000 young people visited as part of an educational programme.
- The café is managed as a franchise by a local family and has become renowned for the quality of its 'pasties', the 'pasty' being a food traditionally eaten in Cornwall by miners. It also has a display of paintings from local artists that are available for sale, with the proceeds going to local and community groups.
- The shop sells a range of local products, from jewellery to works of art, thus supporting local SME's.
- Geevor opens all year around which not only means jobs are permanent rather than seasonal but also helps to attract tourists in the off-peak season to the benefit of the local economy.

This brief list illustrates some of the ways in which Geevor and PCH works towards achieving a sustainable environment and local community. However, it faces challenges such as a lack of capital for further investment and reliance on the volatile tourist market as it is in a sparsely populated area with less than 50,000 people within half an hour travel time.

Conclusion

Built attractions play a vital role in tourism as they are the stimuli for trips and are often the most important factor in destination choice. They are, therefore, crucial factors in the broader field of sustainable tourism in that their existence influences everything from the location of new hotels to the creation of new roads and airline routes.

Yet as we have seen, this sector has received far less attention from researchers than most other sectors of tourism in terms of sustainability. If we are to develop more sustainable forms of tourism, we need to address this paucity of research.

Governments also need to be encouraged to develop a more strategic approach towards built attractions, including both new attraction developments and long-established historic sites and buildings. They need to see the potential problems, as well as the benefits, of new attractions such as casinos, shopping malls and marinas as well as recognising the economic benefits that heritage attractions bring to a destination.

As we look to the future of the built attraction sector we need to recognise the changing geography of tourism and acknowledge that many of the innovations in the sector, as well as some of its greatest sustainability challenges, will be found in Asia rather than in Europe or North America.

We must also recognise that shopping is set to continue to grow as a leisure activity and that more and more shopping-based attractions will be developed. This is a fascinating dilemma given that the idea of sustainable development is often predicated on a suggestion that we need to curb the rise of rampant consumerism.

At the same time we are living in an era where traditional boundaries are being challenged and blurred; this will also affect built attractions increasingly in the future. For example, until recently, hospitals belonged clearly in the health sector and people avoided visiting them whenever possible. Now, with the rise of health tourism, a growing number of people are making hospitals the focal point of their vacation as they travel to undertake cosmetic surgery, while a growing number of medical tourists are combining life-saving or life-enhancing surgery with a vacation. Destinations are marketing their wellness facilities as built attractions and entrepreneurs are developing hospitals that look more like five-star hotels.

Yet, at the same time, the diverse built attraction sector will continue to encompass millennia-old historic and religious sites which are being asked to meet the needs of growing numbers of visitors without losing their 'sense of place' and their unique identity. It is clear, therefore, that the future sustainability challenges in this sector will be many and complex and they will need to be tackled in a context that is far broader than just attractions or even tourism.

Key Reading

Leask, A. (2010) 'Progress in visitor attraction research: Towards more effective management', *Tourism Management*, 31: 155–66

References

Farreny, R., Oliver-Solà, J., Escuder-Bonilla, S., Roca-Martí, M., Sevigné, E., Gabarrell, X. and Rieradevall, J. (2012) 'The metabolism of cultural services: Energy and water flows in museums', *Energy and Buildings,* 47: 98–106.

Frost, W. (ed.) (2011) *Zoos and Tourism: Conservation, Education, Entertainment?* Bristol: Channel View.

Gössling, S., Scott, D., Hall, C.M., Ceron, J-P. and Dubois, G. (2012) 'Consumer behaviour and demand response of tourists to climate change', *Annals of Tourism Research,* 39: 36–58.

The International Association of Amusement Parks and Attractions (IAAPA). (no date) *Homepage.* Available at: www.iaapa.org (accessed 1 April 2014).

Institute for Dark Tourism Research (no date) *Homepage.* Available at: http://dark-tourism.org.uk/ (accessed 1 April 2014).

Leask, A. (2010) 'Progress in visitor attraction research: Towards more effective management', *Tourism Management,* 31: 155–66

Miman, A., Okumus, F. and Dickson, D. (2010) 'The contribution of theme parks and attractions to the social and economic sustainability of destinations', *Worldwide Hospitality and Tourism Themes,* 2: 338–45.

Sharpley, R. (2012) 'Towards an understanding of "genocide tourism": An analysis of visitors' accounts of their experience of recent genocide sites', in R. Sharpley and P.R. Stone (eds) *Contemporary Tourist Experience: Concepts and Consequences,* Abingdon: Routledge.

Smith, L.D.G., Curtis, J., Mair, J. and Van Dijk, P.A. (2012) 'Requests for zoo visitors to undertake pro-wildlife behaviour: How many is too many?', *Tourism Management,* 33: 1502–10.

Yang, L. (2011a) 'Minorities, tourism and ethnic theme parks: Employees perspectives from Yunnan, China', *Journal of Cultural Geography,* 28: 311–38.

—— (2011b) 'Ethnic tourism and cultural representation', *Annals of Tourism Research,* 38: 561–85.

29

Destination tourism

Critical debates, research gaps and the need for a new research agenda

Bruce Prideaux

Destination A formal or informal spatial unit in which a number of businesses either formally or informally cooperate to attract tourists by offering a range of experiences grouped together to create a unique image. The term resort is often used interchangeably with destination.

Introduction

Destinations are central to the tourism experience and, for this reason, present researchers with a large range of issues to investigate. As the following discussion highlights, issues related to growth, function and spatial relationships have been of particular interest. It is also apparent that many gaps remain in our understanding of the destination phenomenon. This chapter will briefly consider factors that currently influence the direction of destination development, the antecedents of our current understanding of destinations, highlight the current direction of research and suggest destination-related issues that need to be considered in the future.

Before engaging in a discussion on destinations it is essential to take a step back and consider the role of destinations in the broader context of global tourism trends and the international economy. The current structure of the global industry is to a large extent a reflection of the growth in leisure travel in the developed economies. Europe, North America and, more recently, Japan dominated post–World War Two tourism flows until the late twentieth century. The destinations that emerged during that period reflect the origin of the customers they were built to serve. In the twenty-first century the engine room of tourism growth will shift away from the West towards the newly developing economies of Asia, Africa and South America. A recent forecast by the UNWTO (2011) predicts that past patterns of growth in international arrivals will continue with international arrivals predicted to reach 1.8 billion by 2030, up from 1 billion in 2012 and 277 million in 1980 (see Chapter 1). In a parallel trend, urbanisation of the global population continues at a rapid rate. By the end of the twentieth century, 80% of the population of developed countries lived in cities in contrast to 30% in many developing countries. By 2030 the UN (2012) predicts that 61% of the world's population will reside in cities.

From the early 1980s onwards, debate began in earnest about concerns over mass tourism, carrying capacity and sustainability. The terms 'post-modern', 'post-fordist' and the 'new' tourist entered the research vocabulary. In the decades since, international arrivals have more than tripled, neoliberal economic policies have continued to promote economic growth and new terms such as the experience economy and wellness have become topics of interest. Climate change has emerged as a major issue (Gössling *et al.* 2012) and concerns about sustainability are becoming more pressing. These issues pose critical questions about the future structure of global tourism flows. For example, will the manner in which governments and consumers respond to these issues lead to the emergence of post-carbon tourism and post-carbon destinations?

The magnitude of growth in international arrivals and global urbanisation will generate a range of problems that the tourism literature has barely begun to acknowledge. Beyond issues related to growth and urbanisation are changing patterns of demand for tourism products and experiences and, importantly, the problems that will be caused by climate change. When considered in this context it is apparent that the future role of destinations in the global tourism industry needs to be re-evaluated particularly in relation to concerns about mass tourism, carrying capacity and sustainability.

As Povilanskas and Armaitiene (2011) observed, changing consumer demand and preferences have led to increased competition and shortened life cycles. This trend is likely to continue as the 'post-carbon' destinations of the future begin to take form and struggle with the factors outlined above. While the literature exhibits a growing understanding of many of the components of the destination system including marketing and many aspects of consumer behaviour, demand for travel, distribution systems, image, segmentation analysis, accommodation, events and shopping, there remains a vigorous debate over our theoretical understanding of the destination phenomenon. Significant gaps in knowledge remain including our understanding of the policy environment, governance, post-carbon destinations, tourism's role in very large cities and threats. In the near future a range of factors including rapidly growing tourism demand, urbanisation, loss of global biodiversity and climate change may force a reordering of the international economy as the desire for growth is increasingly constrained by the ability of the global environment to meet the demands placed on it. Viewed from this perspective there is an urgent need to advance our understanding of destinations.

Modelling destination development

The most obvious issue relating to destinations is what are they? Academic, travel trade and consumer views differ. Academic discussion may for example commence with questions of definition, insights from model building, scale, economic structures and function. Butler's (1980) Tourism Area Life Cycle provides one start point. Another might be Ritchie and Crouch's (2003) model of destination competitiveness and sustainability that offers a comprehensive review of the interrelationships that exist between elements of the destination system. Other possible start points could be planning, marketing or policy issues. From a consumer perspective, the travel section in any good weekend newspaper is likely to offer numerous suggestions to this question. The list of destination types from the consumers' perspective is extensive and may be activity or place based. There may also be little consistency in how destinations are described and promoted with the terms *destination* and *resort* at times used interchangeably. Paralleling the inconsistency in the travel trade's definition of destination are academic understandings of destinations which as applied in the literature may range in scale and function from a small rural town to the state or province it is located in, to country scale or even groupings of countries. Does this matter? From the perspective of the tourist as a consumer, probably not; from a research or planning perspective, most definitely.

Academic definitions of destination often reflect disciplinary perspectives with geography, economics, history and management providing the bulk of contributions. A definition emanating from a management perspective may focus on destinations as a product, organisation or network (Haugland *et al.* 2010) while a geographic perspective will often include territory and spatial relationships. From an economic perspective Andergassen *et al.* (2013: 86) building on an earlier definition by Candela and Figini (2012) suggest that a destination is 'a territorial system supplying at least one tourism product able to satisfy the complex requirements of the demand for tourism'. This multiplicity of definitions illustrates the complexity of the destination phenomenon.

While the disciplinary-based approach of the past has added to our understanding of destinations the failure to develop a stronger multi-disciplinary perspective has placed limitations on the scope of previous research, often channelling it into specific forms of destination enquiry such as coastal resorts while neglecting other areas such as large cities. This blindness of the literature was succinctly described by Ashworth (2003: 143) in the following way: 'Those studying tourism neglected cities while those studying cities neglected tourism.' There is an obvious need to move beyond disciplinary-based understanding and also beyond disciplinary boundaries to explore opportunities for multii-disciplinary understandings of destinations. This point will be revisited later in the chapter.

Since its publication in 1980 Butler's seminal paper and Tourism Area Life Cycle (TALC) model has underpinned much of the discussion that has followed in relation to destination and resort development. Early attempts to explain the destination phenomenon can be traced back to 1939 when Gilbert examined the growth of English seaside health resorts and inland towns (see Hall & Page 2014). Other contributions to this question that appeared before Butler include Christaller (1963), Plog (1974), Stansfield (1978) and Miossec (1976). The TALC model and its many modified versions continue to be widely used to explain how destinations evolve, decline and rejuvenate. The model has been widely applied to explain aspects of destination and resort development (Agarwal 2002; Tooman 1997). The TALC has also attracted a number of critiques, many of which focus on its descriptive and its deterministic nature (Baidal, Sanchez & Rebollo 2013) and limited usefulness as a planning model.

Another problem with the model is that it is largely concerned with destinations where tourism has been a key driver in their evolution. The majority of studies using the TALC model have taken this approach. However, a significant proportion of tourism now occurs in cities where tourism is often a relatively small part of the overall economy. Thus, while the TALC might have some applicability in explaining how tourism has evolved in the Gold Coast (Russell & Faulkner 1999), one of Australia's leading beach destinations, it has less use in explaining how major international destinations such as London, New York and Beijing have evolved. While useful for understanding growth in leisure tourism is destinations that have a significant tourism economy it has less applicability in destinations where business travel constitutes a significant percentage of arrivals or where tourism is a small part of the urban economy. In response to the many criticisms and suggested modifications, and to bring together a coherent collection of research on the TALC see Butler (2006a, 2006b).

Despite its limitations the TALC continues to attract significant interest and a growing number of attempts have been made to extend the model. For example, in a commentary on the TALC Hall and Page (2009) stated that the model remains a clear indication of the importance that theory has in underpinning research. Recent work by Giannoni and Maupertuis (2007) into the dynamics of infrastructure investment, policy choice and environmental quality has provided additional theoretical rigour to the TALC model while Lozano *et al.* (2008) built a theoretical model that is consistent with the TALC model. However, as Andergassen *et al.* (2013) point out, these models have no micro-economic foundations which they argue is an essential element of understanding destinations (although see several of the chapters in Butler 2006a, 2006b). In a study of Tenerife in the Canary Islands, Oreja *et al.* (2008) sought to integrate technological perspectives with the TALC. Taking a multi-disciplinary historic approach Garay and Canoves (2010) sought to 'revision' the TALC using it in conjunction with regulation theory to create a framework for describing and understanding the history of Catalonia and its role as a regional tourism destination.

In a move away from the TALC approach to resort development and following a management approach Haugland *et al.* (2010) suggested an integrated multi-level framework based on destination capabilities, coordination at the destination level and inter-destination bridge ties. To date, this model has yet to be tested. More recently Baidal, Sanchez and Rebollo (2013) suggested a new approach to evolutionary analysis of coastal resorts intended to complement previous theoretical models including the TALC.

Other models (Young 1983) and suggestions to explain the destination phenomenon have appeared in the literature. Prideaux (2000), for example, suggested a multi-model approach that included historic, planning and economic elements. In the most recent attempt to explain destination development Ma and Hassink (2012: 90) suggested the use of an evolutionary economic geography (EEG) approach which focuses 'on how the spatial economy transforms itself through irreversible dynamic processes from within over time'.

From a micro-economic perspective Andergassen, Candela and Figini (2013) brought together tourism product and territory (resource empowerment and organisational structure) to analyse destinations as meta-economic organisations. Further work in this area is likely to augment existing research to provide a more comprehensive understanding of the destination phenomenon. Povilanskas and Armaitiene (2011) suggested that changing consumer demand has generated increased rivalry between destinations and shorter life cycles resulting in what Conti and Perelli (2006) describe as greater attention being paid to territories and networks of attractions rather than on the monoculture economies that are a characteristic of traditional mass tourism destinations. In a re-examination of the resort-hinterland relationship Povilanskas and Armaitiene (2011: 1157) employed actor-network theory (ANT) to replace previous notions of 'geographical determinism (centre-periphery, foreground-background, near-distant and macro-micro) with spatial relativism and the notion of networking as the underlying principle of space and mobility ordering'. In another recent contribution to the debate on aspects of destination development Agarwal (2012) observed that although a number of papers had considered exogenous factors such as labour and property markets little attention has been given to endogenous factors such as the economic interdependence that operates between destinations and sectors of the destination economy.

Scale continues to occupy the attention of researchers. Globally, city destinations are growing in size, function and complexity forcing a re-evaluation of the significance of geographic, economic and political boundaries. A recent paper by Agarwal (2012) provides a new perspective on scale and the relationship between place and near-far relations citing a shift in human geography from the discourse on scalar and territorial relativisation toward spatiality where the linear distinction between space and place are rejected. Borders thus become less important while greater value is placed on socio-spatial relations. Given the growing connectedness of many destinations, particularly large cities, and changes in political arrangements where borders are becoming less important, the shift to spatial planning opens new avenues for understanding how destinations will evolve in the future. There is also an urgent need to consider the scale of tourism's contribution to the GDP of cities. Compared to the significant role of tourism in the economies of the coastal resorts that have been subject to intense scrutiny by researchers, the contribution of tourism to the economies of many large cities is relatively small.

The foregoing discussion indicates that the intellectual struggle to understand the many issues related to destinations has generated a lively ongoing debate in the literature. It is also apparent that much of this discussion has focused on relatively small destinations where tourism activity has often been the major element of the local economy. Beach resorts in the UK, Spain and the Mediterranean have provided much of the evidence used in the models and theories suggested. In the year that the TALC was published global arrivals were in the order of 277 million. By 2012 arrivals had exceeded one billion and were expected to continue climbing. Unfortunately, the literature shows little evidence that it has recognised the need to move beyond the patterns of growth that the TALC was developed to explain and refocus on large cities such as New York, London, Beijing, São Paulo and Tokyo which now form the epicentre of a significant percentage of domestic and international tourism flows.

The failure of the literature to take a broader view of destinations has contributed to the current failure to develop a more comprehensive understanding of destinations and how they may respond to the almost tidal wave-like surge in growth forecast over the next two decades. For this element of our theoretical understanding of destinations to progress, more attention needs to be given to alternative approaches including models from other disciplines and the use of multiple linked models to explain various aspects of the destination system.

As suggested above, a multi-disciplinary or even a multi-model approach offers new avenues for understanding. For example, Prideaux (2009) demonstrated how the use of a multiple model approach (including the Beach Evolution Model (Smith 1992), the TALC model (Russell & Faulkner 1999), chaos theory (Russell & Faulkner 1999) and the Resort Development Spectrum) to study destination growth on the Gold Coast of Australia was able to provide a more holistic and multi-dimensional view than could be provided by a single model.

Comparative and competitive advantage and the role of competitiveness

In many countries neoliberal views (Dredge 2010) on economic growth prevail, a position that may explain the hesitancy of many economies to accept the need to give serious consideration to climate change. Growth remains a common mantra while lip service is given to concerns about long-term sustainability. Until there is overwhelming evidence that climate change is a serious challenge this attitude is likely to dominate public and private sector thinking. Irrespective of the prevailing worldview, the fundamentals of the market economy will continue to govern destinations in the future. From a destination perspective measures of success will continue to include yield and profitability regardless of the external policy environment that may range from promotion of growth in the neoliberal worldview of the present to a more sustainable economic model in the future. For this reason it is important to consider issues related to comparative and competitive advantage and the role of competitiveness as they apply to destinations.

In a competitive world all destinations strive to out-compete competitors, often with little thought to implications for long-term sustainability. In the most exhaustive examination of the issue of competitiveness and sustainability to date, Ritchie and Crouch (2003) undertook a comprehensive analysis of competitiveness and sustainability. Their model is arguably the most comprehensive analysis of the interlinking elements of the destination system but, as pointed out previously, does not provide a theoretical exploration for growth.

Destinations need to be mindful of the resources that provide them with opportunities to build on areas of comparative advantage, how these may be developed into a competitive advantage and ensuring ongoing competitiveness. However, as Dwyer and Kim (2003: 373) caution 'it (competitiveness) is a complex concept because a whole range of factors account for it'. The importance of competitiveness is that it enables a destination to create value-added products enabling them to maintain or improve their market position relative to competitors (Hassan 2000: 239). As Prideaux *et al.* (2012: 15) note 'competitiveness in its most basic form is the ability of a destination to identify its key selling propositions, identify markets that are likely to purchase these propositions, create a market space where these products are able to be purchased, identify change and future threats, and have the ability to maintain this process over a long period of time in a manner that is both environmentally and economically sustainable'. Ritchie and Crouch (2000: 5) add that unless a destination is sustainable 'competitiveness is illusory'.

While there is a growing literature on the issue of competitiveness, comparative advantage and competitive advantage, a generally accepted definition of competitiveness has yet to emerge and there has been little headway made in building a more comprehensive model than that advanced by Ritchie and Crouch (2003). Issues raised in the literature in relation to destination competitiveness that require further investigation include the role of innovation, networking, governance and government regulatory activates. For example, it can be argued that innovation lies at the core of ongoing competitiveness. As new cohorts of tourists emerge, either because they have entered a new stage in their family life cycle, or are from new generating areas, new or refreshed products and experiences may be required. Equally, tastes change and once fashionable places and experiences are superseded as consumers seek novelty and inclusiveness in adopting the latest fashions and trends.

Innovation, although arguably a key driver of long-term economic sustainability, is only one of many related factors. Ritchie and Crouch (2003) identify five major groupings of factors and 36 sub-factors each of which has a role to play. In reality, in a system of the nature of a destination, it is difficult to single out one factor as being more important than others because each has a critical role irrespective of apparent importance. Crisis management, for example, becomes important only when a shock is experienced by a destination and must be responded to in a manner that facilitates recovery and resumption of growth. If not responded to adequately the destination may suffer over the long term. As Gurtner (2007) argued in the case of the 2002 Bali bombing, without speedy post-disaster marketing the destination could have suffered long-term decline. Image is almost always important particularly when shocks such as a disaster are experienced but image without adequate attention to infrastructure maintenance will fail to maintain let alone enhance competitiveness.

Sustainability

While academics have long recognised the importance of sustainability, particularly in natural areas, the neoliberal endorsement of growth as a key indicator of national success has often resulted in tourism development that is not sympathetic to its surrounding environment. This is despite an emerging consensus that unless areas visited by tourists are sustainable over the long term, visitor numbers will decline as the quality of the experience deteriorates. While there remains considerable debate about the precise meaning of sustainability and how it may be achieved (Navarro Jurado *et al.* 2012) it is clear that it is an important issue. On the issue of sustainability and its manifestation as the triple bottom line approach Hall *et al.* (2013: 114) observe that 'the continuing contribution of a growing tourism industry to resource consumption and environmental change raises a clear question as to whether "balanced" sustainable tourism or "green economy/growth" approaches are actually achievable'. Given the predicted doubling of tourism flows by 2030 this statement has a great deal of relevance to destinations. It might, for example, lead to a re-evaluation of which destination types are sustainable and which are not. Interventions by governments concerned about climate change may also place limits on tourism activity, particularly mobilities. This is an area that warrants further research.

One factor that has been identified but never satisfactorily defined as having a considerable influence on sustainability is carrying capacity. As Navarro Jurado *et al.* (2012: 1338) observe, the difficulty with applying the concept of carrying capacity is that 'prevailing economic ideology (has) denied the existence of limits'. The recent rapid growth in mainland Chinese visitors to Hong Kong illustrates the issue of social carrying capacity and the ability of host populations to absorb large numbers of visitors (Siu *et al.* 2013).

In recent years a number of authors have raised concerns about the impact that climate change (Pang *et al.* 2013) will have on destinations. Low-altitude ski destinations will face a decline in snow depth and length of season (IPCC 2007) and many natural areas will experience a decline in the complexity of their ecosystems as some species become extinct, others migrate out or migrate in. In a marine context Poloczanska *et al.* (2013) reported that the leading-edge marine species is migrating towards the poles at a rate of about 30–72 kms per decade, much faster than terrestrial species that are migrating towards the poles at a rate of about 6 kms per decade. Destinations that rely on adjoining natural areas as their main 'pull' factors are likely to suffer as the quality of the ecosystem declines. Fortunately a number of researchers are now beginning to look at this issue from a destination perspective (Scott *et al.* 2012; Wong *et al.* 2013).

Conclusion

This brief review of the current state of research into the destination phenomenon indicates that many issues need further investigation and that while there is a growing literature on many of the aspects of destinations our understanding of destinations remains limited. As this chapter has highlighted, there is an urgent need to pay more attention to the challenges of the future. This suggests that far greater emphasis is required on destination research that examines the impact of future growth, change in functions and climate change in terms of planning, policy, governance, infrastructure provision and aspects of consumer demand. As the global economy begins to move to a post-carbon model of growth where our understanding of sustainability will have to evolve to deal with new relationships between economic, social and environmental priorities, the manner in which destination tourism is planned, managed, operates and is demanded by the next post-carbon generation of consumers will require a radical redirection of thought and scholarship.

Moreover, the literature needs to shift its focus from the very narrow definition of destination used in the past to refocus on a broader interpretation that includes cities. As Ashworth (2003) noted, cities have received little attention. With the shift of tourism activity into cities and concerns about sustainability, the future agenda for destination research needs to reflect the new centrality of tourism activity.

Bruce Prideaux

References

Agarwal, S. (2002) 'Restructuring seaside tourism: The resort lifecycle', *Annals of Tourism Research*, 29: 25–55.

—— (2012) 'Resort economy and direct economic linkages', *Annals of Tourism Research*, 39: 1470–94.

Andergassen, R., Candela, G. and Figini, P. (2013) 'An economic model for tourism destinations: Product sophistication and price coordination', *Tourism Management,* 37: 86–98.

Ashworth, G.J. (2003) 'Urban tourism: Still an imbalance in attention?' in C. Cooper (ed.) *Classic Reviews in Tourism,* Clevedon: Channel View.

Baidal, J., Sanchez, I. and Rebollo, J. (2013) 'The evolution of mass tourism destinations: New approaches beyond deterministic models in Benidorm (Spain)', *Tourism Management*, 34: 184–95.

Butler, R. (1980) 'The concept of a tourist area cycle of evolution: Implications for management of resources', *The Canadian Geographer*, 24: 5–12.

Butler, R. (ed.) (2006a) *The Tourism Life Cycle, Vol 1: Applications and Modifications*, Clevedon: Channel View Publications.

—— (2006b) *The Tourism Lifecycle, Vol 2: Conceptual and Theoretical Issues*, Clevedon: Channel View Publications.

Candela, G. and Figini, P. (2012) *The Economics of Tourism Destinations*, Berlin: Springer.

Christaller, W. (1963) 'Some considerations of tourism location in Europe: The peripheral regions in underdeveloped countries' recreation areas', *Regional Science Association: Papers XII, Lund Congress*: 95–105.

Conti, G. and Perelli, C. (2006) Traditional Mass Tourism Destinations: the decline of Fordist tourism facing the rise of vocational diversification. Governance and sustainability in new tourism trends. *Planum. The European Journal of Planning Web site* www.planum.net/topics/documents/Conti_Perelli.pdf.

Dredge, D. (2010) 'Place change and tourism development conflict: Evaluating public interest', *Tourism Management*, 31: 104–12.

Dwyer, L. and Kim, C. (2003) 'Destination competitiveness: Determinants and indicators', *Current Issues in Tourism*, 6: 369–414.

Garay, L. and Canoves, G. (2010) 'Life cycles, stages and tourism history the Catalonia (Spain) experience', *Annals of Tourism Research*, 38: 651–71.

Giannoni, S. and Maupertuis, M. A. (2007) Environmental quality and optimal investment in tourism infrastructures: a small island perspective. *Tourism Economics*, 13(4), 499–514.

Gilbert, E. (1939) 'The growth of inland and seaside health resorts in England', *The Scottish Geographical Magazine*, 55: 16–35.

Gössling, S., Scott, D., Hall, C.M., Ceron, J.P. and Dubois, G. (2012) 'Consumer behaviour and demand response of tourists to climate change', *Annals of Tourism Research*, 39: 36–58.

Gurtner, Y. (2007) 'Crisis in Bali; Lessons in tourism recovery', in E. Laws, B. Prideaux and K. Chon (eds) *Crisis Management in Tourism*, Wallingford: CABI.

Hall, C.M. and Page, S. (2009) 'Progress in tourism management; From the geography of tourism to geographies of tourism – a review', *Tourism Management*, 30: 3–16.

—— (2014) *The Geography of Tourism and Recreation*, 4th edn, Abingdon: Routledge.

Hall, C.M., Scott, D. and Gössling, S. (2013) 'The primacy of climate change for sustainable international tourism development', *Sustainable Development*, 21: 112–21.

Hassan, S. (2000) 'Determinants of market competitiveness in an environmentally sustainable tourism industry', *Journal of Travel Research*, 38: 239–45.

Haugland, S., Ness, H., Gronseth, B. and Aarstad, J. (2010) 'Development of tourism destinations: An integrated multilevel perspective', *Annals of Tourism Research*, 38: 268–90.

Intergovernmental Panel on Climate Change (IPCC) (2007) *Summary for Policy Makers,* in S. Solomon, M. Qin, Z. Manning, M. Chen, K. Marquia, M. Averyt, M. Tignor and H. Miller (eds) *Climate Change 2007: The Physical Science Basis. Contribution of Working Group 1 to the Fourth Assessment Report of the Intergovernmental Panel on Climate Change*, Cambridge, UK and New York, USA: Cambridge University Press.

Lozano, J., Gómez, C. and Rey-Maquieira, J. (2008) 'The TALC hypothesis and economic growth theory', *Tourism Economics*, 14: 727–49.

Ma, M. and Hassink, R. (2012) 'An evolutionary perspective on tourism area development', *Annals of Tourism Research,* 41: 89–109.

Miossec, J.M. (1976) 'Elements pour une Theorie de l'Espace Touristique', *Les Chasiers du Tourisme*, C-36, C.H.E.T., Aix-en-Provence.

Navarro Jurado, E., Tejada Tejada, M., Almeida García, F., Cabello González, J., Cortés Macías, R., Delgado Peña, J., Gutiérrez Fernández, G., Luque Gallego, M., Málvarez García, G., Marcenaro Gutiérrez, O., Navas Concha, F., Ruiz de la Rúa, F., Ruiz Sinoga, J. and Solís Becerra, F. (2012) 'Carrying capacity assessment for tourist destinations: Methodology for the creation of synthetic indicators applied in a coastal area', *Tourism Management*, 33: 1337–46.

Navarro Jurado, E., Damian, I.M. and Fernández-Morales, A. (2013) 'Carrying capacity model applied in coastal destinations', *Annals of Tourism Research*, 43: 1–19.

Oreja, J., Parra, E. and Yanes, V. (2008) 'The sustainability of island destinations: Tourism area life cycle and teleological perspectives. The case of Tenerife', *Tourism Management*, 29: 53–65.

Pang, S., McKercher, B. and Prideaux, B. (2013) 'Climate change and tourism: An overview', *Asia Pacific Journal of Tourism Research*, 18: 4–20.

Plog, S. (1974) 'Why destination areas rise and fall in popularity', *Cornell Hotel and Restaurant Administration Quarterly*, 14: 55–58.

Poloczanska, E.S., Brown, C.J., Sydeman, W.J., Kiessling, W., Schoeman, D.S., Moore, P.J., Brander, K., Bruno, J.F., Buckley, L.B., Burrows, M.T., Duarte, C.M., Halpern, B.S., Holding, J., Kappel, C.V., O'Connor, M.I., Pandolfi, J.M., Parmesan, C., Schwing, F., Thompson, S.A. and Richardson, A.J. (2013) 'Global imprint of climate change on marine life', *Nature Climate Change*, 3: 919–25.

Povilanskas, P. and Armaitiene, A. (2011) 'Seaside resort-hinterland nexus: Palanga, Lithuania', *Annals of Tourism Research*, 38: 1156–77.

Prideaux, B. (2000) 'The resort development spectrum', *Tourism Management*, 21: 225–41.

—— (2009) *Resort Destinations: Evolution, Management and Development,* Oxford: Butterworth Heinemann.

Prideaux, B., Sakata, H. and Thompson, M. (2012) 'Tourist exit survey report: February–September 2012. Annual patterns of reef and rainforest tourism in North Queensland from exit surveys conducted at Cairns Domestic Airport', Report to the National Environmental Research Program, Reef and Rainforest Research Centre Limited, Cairns.

Ritchie, J.R. and Crouch, G.I. (2000) 'The competitive destination: A sustainability perspective', *Tourism Management*, 21: 1–7.

—— (2003) *The Competitive Destination: A Sustainable Tourism Perspective,* Wallingford: CABI.

Russell, R. and Faulkner, B. (1999) 'Movers and shakers: Chaos makers in tourism development', *Tourism Management*, 20: 411–23.

Scott, D., Gössling, S. and Hall, C.M. (2012) *Tourism and Climate Change: Impacts, Adaptation and Mitigation,* Abingdon: Routledge.

Siu, G., Lee, L. and Leung, D. (2013) 'Residents' perceptions toward the "Chinese tourists' wave" in Hong Kong: An exploratory study', *Asia Pacific Journal of Tourism Research*, 15: 446–63.

Smith, R.A. (1992) 'Beach resort evolution', *Annals of Tourism Research*, 19: 304–22.

Stansfield, C. (1978) 'Atlantic City and the resort cycle: Background to the legalisation of gambling', *Annals of Tourism Research*, 5: 238–51.

Tooman, L.A. (1997) 'Applications of the life-cycle model in tourism', *Annals of Tourism Research*, 24: 214–34.

United Nations (UN) (2012) *World Urbanization Prospects: The 2011 Revision,* New York: United Nations.

UNWTO (2011) *Tourism Towards 2030 Global Overview,* Madrid: UNWTO.

Wong, E., Jaing, M., Klint, l., DeLacy, T., Harrison, D. and Dominey-Howes, D. (2013) 'Policy environment for the tourism sector's adaptation to climate change in the South Pacific – The case of Samoa', *Asia Pacific Journal of Tourism Research,* 19: 52–71.

Young, B. (1983) 'Touristization of traditional Maltese fishing-farming villages: A general model', *Tourism Management*, 4: 35–41.

30

Natural heritage, parks and protected areas

Warwick Frost and Jennifer Laing

National parks Narrowly the term given to a designated conservation area or site under the authority of the highest appropriate national authority. In a broader or generic sense it is a term applied to a range of protected areas.

World Heritage An area or site of 'outstanding universal value' designated as World Heritage by UNESCO under the Convention concerning the Protection of the World Cultural and Natural Heritage.

Conventionally divided between natural and cultural, heritage refers to what we – either as societies or individuals – wish to protect and preserve for future generations. An intrinsically human centred concept, it involves subjective judgements and choices as to what is worthy of preservation and what is not. The idea of protected areas for natural heritage is widespread across the globe, with nearly all countries perceiving the value in both their use for tourism and recreation and their role in shaping national and regional identities. According to the International Union for the Conservation of Nature (IUCN), nearly 19 million square kilometres are protected under six categories of protected areas. These are shown in Table 30.1, together with the percentage of land protected under each type.

The most well-known protected area type is that of national parks. Indeed, so entrenched is this category in popular consciousness, that it may be considered as the pre-eminent *brand* in nature conservation (Frost & Hall 2009a). Generally, national parks are established and managed by individual national or regional governments, though as is discussed below, there are a wide range of variations across the globe. While no international standard of national park accreditation exists, the development of World Heritage classifications by UNESCO has taken on that role to a certain extent. In addition, zoos are also widespread and increasingly recognised as having a role in nature preservation.

Table 30.1 Area protected under IUCN categories, 2003

Number	Category	Percentage
1	Strict nature reserve or wilderness area	10.9
2	National park	23.5
3	Natural monument	1.5
4	Habitat/species management area	16.1
5	Protected landscape/seascape	5.6
6	Managed resource protected area	23.3
-	No category	19.0

Source: Hall & Frost (2009: 12–13).

Origins of the conservation ideal

Interest in natural heritage and its protection is conventionally dated to the rise of Romanticism in eighteenth and nineteenth century Western Europe (Nash 1967; Runte 1979; see Chapter 2). Edmund Burke and Jean-Jacques Rousseau promoted the idea that it was in wild and natural places that humans could find beauty and spiritual inspiration. Mountains, in particular, could evoke sublime feelings of awe, exultation and mortality. Such a view was further popularised by poets William Wordsworth and Lord George Byron. These writers provided the genesis of the concept – still prevalent today – that travelling through wilderness and other natural areas could be the catalyst for positive personal transformation. The growth of scientific rationalism also fuelled the notion of nature as worthy of study and protection. In the nineteenth century, these ideas flowed across the Atlantic, taken up by James Fenimore Cooper, Henry David Thoreau and John Muir.

Yellowstone, the first national park

In 1810, Wordsworth described England's Lake District as a 'sort of national property, in which every man has a right and interest who has an eye to perceive and a heart to enjoy' (Wordsworth 1810: 92). In the USA, George Catlin proposed in 1832 that the Great Plains be protected as a 'Nation's Park' and in 1864 the US Congress had established Yosemite as a state park (Runte 1979). However, it was in 1873 that the world's first national park was established at Yellowstone.

Yellowstone came with an instructive creation story, one that could be recounted and applied elsewhere. Parts of it were, perhaps, invented, but its fundamental message struck resonant chords. In 1870 a group of Montana businessmen went exploring in the Yellowstone Mountains. After stumbling upon the Upper Geyser Basin, they relaxed around a campfire, speculating how they could exploit their discovery for tourism. Finally, one of them – lawyer Cornelius Hedges spoke up with an idea:

> He did not approve of any of these plans – that there ought to be no private ownership of any portion of that region, but that the whole of it ought to be set apart as a great National Park.
>
> (*Langford 1905: 117–18*)

Table 30.2 Seven principles arising from Yellowstone

1	The formal term of National Park is coined.
2	Yellowstone is reserved for its natural wonders and monumental scenery. The monumentalism enshrined by Yellowstone will continue to dominate ideas of natural area protection.
3	Nature is preserved for tourism.
4	National Park status is conferred by the national government.
5	The National Park is permanently protected.
6	Establishment arises from scientific investigation.
7	There is little consideration of indigenous peoples.

Source: Frost & Hall (2009b: 28).

Convinced by Hedges' altruism, the others started a campaign for preservation. Established in 1872, Yellowstone remained under federal rather than state control, as Montana was then still a Territory. As the original national park, Yellowstone created a template for future developments. Though not set in stone, it laid down seven key principles as to what a national park was and how it should be established (see Table 30.2).

For Americans, the establishment of Yellowstone has become entwined with the *Frontier Thesis* (Turner 1894), reinforcing a view of American exceptionalism arising from its Western frontier. Nash, reflecting on the Centenary of Yellowstone, argued that 'the concept of a national park reflects some of the central values and experiences in American culture' (Nash 1970: 726). National parks were not only invented by the USA, according to Nash, but also arose as a product of that country's unique physical, social and political environments. Such a view is central to American histories of national parks (e.g. Runte 1979) and was the core premise of the recent documentary series *The National Parks: America's Best Idea* (Burns 2009).

Spread and evolution of the national parks concept

Seeing national parks as a uniquely American institution poses a conundrum. How could the concept be transferred to other countries with quite different conditions? If national parks had been created by unique forces within the USA, how could they work in countries with significantly different natural environments, social structures and political regimes? What happened was that as the idea of national parks spread, it mutated and evolved. The American idea of national parks was not so much duplicated, but rather provided the inspiration for a wide range of variations.

Initially, Yellowstone was an isolated instance. However, it was quickly copied in other parts of the West. By World War One, national parks had been established at Yosemite, Sequoia and General Grant (1890), Mount Rainier (1899), Crater Lake (1902), Glacier (1910) and Rocky Mountain (1915). All were in the image of Yellowstone, mountainous and monumental. Similarly, when national parks were created in the settler societies of Canada and New Zealand, they followed this template. Banff (1885), in the Canadian Rockies combined rugged mountains with hot springs. Tongariro (1887) protected three spectacular volcanic peaks. As in the USA, the economic benefits of tourism were of major importance (Boyd & Butler 2009; Star & Lochhead 2002).

In the other Anglophone settler society of Australia, there was in contrast a rapid divergence from the standard US model. Its first national park in 1879 was on the outskirts of Sydney. Simply called The National Park (later Royal would be added), it encompassed a large area of coastal bush. The rationale for its creation was for the recreational use of the city's population and for the acclimatisation of exotic animals. The concept of monumentalism was completely absent, it was simply available land close to an urban area. At the time, the Australian colonies were separate political entities and the others quickly followed New South Wales' lead. At federation in 1901, responsibility for natural area protection (and tourism) remained with the states and by World War One all of them had established their own national parks (Frost & Hall 2009a).

The Australian system continued to evolve in a way manifestly different from the USA. Each of the states maintained their own system and bowing to public enthusiasm were quick to establish a wide range of national parks. The resulting proliferation was often dogged by a lack of funding – still a major problem today. To illustrate the numbers involved, it is worth considering that our home state of Victoria is about the same size as Wyoming in the USA. Yet, while Wyoming – taking in the Rockies – has only two national parks, Victoria has over 50. Indeed, there are only a handful of countries in the world with more national parks than this one Australian state.

Most of the early national parks in Australia were established for local recreation. Community usage was usually more important than tourism or natural values. Nonetheless, the sheer numbers involved meant there was scope for some very different national parks. In contrast to the USA, coastal national parks were popular, including the Royal (1879), Kuring-Gai Chase (1894), Wilson's Promontory (1898) and Mallacoota (1909). Lamington (1915) was the world's first large rainforest national park. Wyperfeld (1909) protected a flat area of semi-arid vegetation and wildlife. Remote, with little local population and containing no monumental features, it was arguably the world's first national park based on protecting an ecosystem (Frost & Hall 2009a).

In Africa, national parks were established to protect wildlife. In 1919, King Albert of Belgium toured the USA and, around a campfire at Yellowstone, discussed the need for African national parks. This resulted in the 1925 creation of the Albert National Park in the Belgian Congo. This was specifically to protect mountain gorillas and was initially not open to the public. In 1926, South Africa opened Kruger National Park. Again, while Yellowstone was invoked in the arguments in favour of its establishment, it took a very different form. Its purpose was to protect game animals. Indeed, early management focused on reducing predators until it was realised that tourists were attracted as much by lions as by elephants and zebra. After the Second World War, colonial administrators created wildlife focused national parks in Kenya, Tanganyika and Uganda. After independence, these remained protected as iconic tourist destinations (Carruthers 1995; Frost & Hall 2009a; MacKenzie 1988).

Early Asian national parks, were similarly created by colonial authorities in India, Malaysia, Sri Lanka and Indonesia to protect stocks for recreational hunting. As in Africa, this resulted in conflict with local villages, though there is also evidence of support from middle class elites (Jepson & Whittaker 2002; Kathirithamby-Wells 2005; MacKenzie 1988). Two anomalies stand out. In Cambodia in 1924, the French established a national park based on the cultural heritage of Angkor Wat. At the same time, Japan – which had escaped colonisation and had quickly industrialised – looked to Yellowstone as a model for nature protection. The result was 12 mountainous national parks before World War Two (Frost & Hall 2009a).

In Europe, the first national park was established in Sweden in 1909. This was followed by Switzerland (1914), Spain (1918), Italy (1922), Iceland (1928), Ireland (1932) Poland (1932), Romania (1935) and Greece (1938). At first glance it seems curious that so many countries created their first national parks in a period that Eric Hobsbawm has described as the *Age of Catastrophe*. In a period of great uncertainty, conflict, economic and social malaise; why would governments indulge in natural area protection? The answer revolves around using national parks as a symbol to reinforce national cultural identities. Sweden and Spain had previously been much more powerful states; national parks were a good device to rebuild pride (Frost & Hall 2009a; Medina 2009). The others all had a history of being dominated by other European powers and national parks were a way of stating that they were nations. Switzerland inaugurated its national park on 1 August, deliberately chosen for being the Swiss national holiday commemorating the 1291 establishment of the Swiss Confederation. Iceland, newly independent – like many of these countries – created its national park to commemorate the 1,000th anniversary of the world's first parliament. In Italy, Mussolini enthusiastically adopted national parks as American and modern, just the image he was seeking for his new regime (Frost & Hall 2009a).

In contrast, national parks came late to established major powers. It was not until 1949 that Britain established national parks. What it created was distant from Yellowstone. These were for the recreation of nearby urban centres and primarily private land, even including towns. Scotland, for all its monumental highland scenery, would not get a national park until 2000. France only established its first national park in 1963 and Germany in 1969 (Frost & Hall 2009a). The Soviet Union established nature reserves, but would not call them national parks. After all, that was an American term. It would not be until the adoption of *Perestroika* that national parks would be declared in 1983 (Weiner 1999).

Evolution and roles of zoos

Zoos predate national parks, the first public zoo being the Jardin des Plantes in Paris, established in 1794. While they may not have the cachet of national parks and other protected areas, zoos are a major way in which people view and experience natural heritage. Primarily this is animals, though zoos also need to be recognised as constructed attractions presenting natural areas. From their beginnings, zoos were *zoological gardens*, essentially urban parks for recreation and amusement, which were themed around animals – indeed arguably zoos were the first theme parks. From the late nineteenth century onwards, zoo designers strove to place a greater emphasis on naturalness, creating an illusion of immersing the visitor within the display and featuring examples of the natural environments of the exhibits. This trend has more recently led to walk-through exhibits, displays based on habitats (e.g. placing all rainforest fauna together) and an emphasis on appropriate vegetation (Frost 2011; Hancocks 2001).

The most recent change for zoos is that some have sought to reposition themselves as conservation agencies working on a far broader scale. This is, in part, due to criticisms of zoos, but also partly a natural extension of their roles in education and conservation. This has led to zoos extending their operations *ex situ*, particularly into the less-developed areas of Africa, Asia and South America. Initially, the focus was on field stations or partnerships with local agencies to achieve species reintroduction, but this has become more complex with zoos now providing scientific aid and raising funds for such projects. Zoos have also become conservation advocates supporting, and even initiating, campaigns to lobby for protection or change behaviour. Examples of this include campaigns to reduce Western consumption of palm oil (thereby protecting rainforest from clearance) and to recycle mobile phones (for the rare metals which are mined near Gorilla habitat). Such developments take zoos further into conservation education and advocacy than national parks.

World Heritage

World Heritage listing is administered by UNESCO and recognises sites as of importance to all humanity. It is, essentially, an accreditation scheme, as administration and the initiating of the listing resides with the relevant national government. As of 2012, there were 962 World Heritage sites. The majority are cultural heritage. There are 745 in this category (78%), 188 natural (20%) and 29 mixed cultural and natural (3%). Australia has the most natural sites (16), followed by China and the USA with 13 each. This emphasis on cultural listings has been in evidence since the scheme formally started in 1972, but even today, seems as strong as ever. For example, of the 51 sites added to the list in 2011 and 2012, only nine were natural and one a mixture of natural and cultural (all data from http://whc.unesco.org/en/list/). Whether World Heritage listing leads to an increase in tourism is a matter of ongoing debate (Leask & Fyall 2012).

Governance

The governance structures of national parks vary across the globe. There is no international governing body setting standards – World Heritage being essentially an accreditation process for existing parks – and individual countries are free to arrange their national parks however they see fit. As demonstrated in the sections above on their evolution, national parks are tied to issues of national sovereignty and identity and developed in response to local conditions and needs. Accordingly, some are administered nationally and some regionally; the levels of funding and infrastructure vary and some charge admission fees, whereas others are free.

Nature rarely recognises borders, especially when they are arbitrarily drawn straight lines. Throughout the world, there are a large number of instances where national parks for different countries abut each other. While national sovereignty remains, such situations have led to international co-operation through *cross-border* national parks. One of the most well known of these is the Waterton-Glacier International Peace Park, established by Canada and the USA in 1932. Others are found in the Americas, Asia, Africa and in the states system of Australia. While emphasising international co-operation and goodwill, such parks may have difficulties with conflicting cultures and objectives and many are still scarred by cleared border zones (Timothy 2000).

Though established by governments, national parks have always had a contentious relationship with the private sector. Starting with Yellowstone, many were created to manage the provision of visitor amenities by the private sector, particularly accommodation and tours. Juggling the balance between a public agency and private interests has often been difficult and criticisms about commercial over-development extend back into the nineteenth century (Frost & Hall 2009a; Runte 1979). A key issue has been as to what level of physical development – hotels, car parks, shopping centres – should be allowed within the boundaries of a national park. This has led to national parks agencies developing theories of creating different levels (or zones) of activity and impact within protected areas; effectively balancing *sacrificial sites* with back-country wilderness (Eagles & McCool 2002).

At times there have been calls to better govern national parks by shifting them from the public to private sector (Charters, Gabriel & Prasser 1996). Recently the debate has shifted towards the concept of building *partnerships* between parks agencies, private businesses, local destination marketing organisations, host communities and other stakeholders (Eagles & McCool 2002; *Journal of Sustainable Tourism* 2009). Such an approach has the advantage of being more inclusive, though it is also open to charges of *window-dressing*, encouraging privatisation while giving the illusion of greater community engagement. Certainly, this is an area that needs greater critical research from a range of perspectives.

Similarly controversial is the issue of indigenous management. Indigenous peoples comprise 5% of the world's population, though 50% of all national parks and protected areas are on their lands, with that rising to as high as 85% in Latin America and Africa (Zeppel 2006). Starting with Yellowstone, which was imagined as vacant land (see e.g. Langford 1905), there has been a tendency to remove and exclude traditional and indigenous peoples. In recent years, some governments have ventured down the path of returning ownership to indigenous groups and developing co-operative management plans (as in the case of Uluru and Kakadu in Australia). However, there are still widespread issues of indigenous practices (such as traditional hunting) and the lack of employment and other economic benefits for indigenous communities (Strickland-Munro & Moore 2013; Zeppel 2006; see also case study below on Monument Valley).

Visitor management

Visitor management covers a wide range of roles and services. A broad division is between access, protection and interpretation. Depending on circumstances, these may be provided by park management, private businesses, volunteers, stakeholder groups or some combination. For contemporary national parks, effectively balancing these roles and satisfying diverse stakeholders is a major strategic task

Access for visitors includes roads, car parks and walking tracks. In some parks, this may extend to viewing platforms and visitor centres. Access is often divided between main sites, which have a higher level of infrastructure and more remote areas where there is a strategic decision to limit access. In recent years there has been greater attention paid to managing barriers to access for disabled groups. Indeed, English national parks now have encouraging access by marginal groups as one of their main objectives.

Protection works two ways. The visitor needs to be protected from dangers – including wild animals, falls, landslips and poisonous or prickly vegetation. In turn, wild areas need to be protected from damage by visitors – including trampling vegetation, interfering with wildlife and the possibility of causing fires. Strategies for protection need to take into account the unfamiliarity of most visitors with natural areas. Many visitors are urban dwellers, who do not regularly engage with nature. That they are often in a *tourist bubble*, unaware of dangers and their potential impact, increase risks within protected areas. This requires both a strategic approach to risk management, not only among park staff, but also with the private businesses and tours licensed to operate within protected areas (Frost 2004). Traditionally, parks managers have tended to think in terms of *hardening* (building and fencing high usage walkways) and proscriptive signage, though these are sometimes limited in their effectiveness. Some modern trends have increased the impact of visitors, requiring greater infrastructure. These include staging events with large numbers of participants within protected areas and the construction of capital intensive viewing platforms (Zhang *et al.* 2009).

Interpretation provides meaning and understanding for visitors. The pioneering work by national park ranger Freeman Tilden (1957) argued that it needed to be effectively based on story-telling to get across important persuasive messages of conservation. He also argued it needed to be provocative, challenging visitors to think differently, a theme continued by Moscardo (1999). However, despite such a strong theoretical base, protected area interpretation may tend for safe options, pitching at a low level and avoiding controversy. Zoos, in particular, have noticeably cut back on interpretation, relying more heavily on less-structured experiential encounters (Frost 2011). For many protected area managers, the persuasive messages have tended to become linked to branding, agency identification and touting for funding.

Case Study

Monument Valley Navajo Tribal Park

From the Grand Canyon to Monument Valley is only a few hours drive by car, but they are worlds apart. The Grand Canyon is a US National Parks Service showpiece, with a range of accommodation (some dating back to the early twentieth century), visitor centres, sealed walking paths and interpretation. In contrast, Monument Valley is administered by the Navajo Nation as *their* national park through the Navajo Nation Parks and Recreation Department (www. navajonationparks.org). Though one of the iconic and most widely recognised images of the American West, Monument Valley has little of the infrastructure and polish of the Grand Canyon.

Monument Valley comprises a number of spectacular sandstone buttes rising sharply from the desert floor (see Figure 30.1). It is located within the 71,000 km^2 Navajo Nation, on the border of Arizona and Utah. It has featured in many Western films and is most associated with the work of director John Ford (*Stagecoach, Fort Apache, The Searchers*). It continues to be used in modern productions, including *Thelma and Louise, The Lone Ranger* and *Dr Who*. Accordingly, apart from its natural spectacle, it attracts film tourists.

Figure 30.1 The iconic view of Monument Valley

Within the park boundary, the Navajo operate a recently opened hotel. This competes with nearby Goulding Lodge, famous for being the base of film production companies. Both hotels hug the rocky mesas, providing visitors with a sense that they are immersed in the heart of the landscape, not merely gazing in, as at the Grand Canyon. The park used to be open to private vehicles, but recently it has been restricted to authorised tour vehicles and walkers. Roads are dirt and walking tracks little more than sandy paths. This lack of hardening contributes to the visitor experience. Most reasonably fit people would have little difficulty in tackling the hikes, a sharp contrast to the arduous trek to the floor of the Grand Canyon (requiring the National Parks Service to dissuade would-be adventurers). At Monument Valley, the walking tracks are lightly travelled, providing full rein for visitors to imagine they are completely isolated. Again, this is a stark contrast to the overcrowding of the vantage points at the Grand Canyon.

Guided tours are conducted by Navajo guides. Loosely structured, their attraction is in their free-wheeling nature and lack of artificial scripting. For many visitors, this is a rare opportunity to interact with a Native American. Such encounters provide a sense of what has been termed *existential authenticity* (Wang 2000). In such a concept, the interaction with wilderness and traditional peoples stimulates a feeling of re-energising or transformation, an idea that they have been somewhere that is real in contrast to the artificiality of modernity.

Key Reading

Butler, R.W. and Boyd, S.W. (eds) (2000) *Tourism and National Parks: Issues and Implications*, Chichester: Wiley.

Eagles, P.J.F. and McCool, S.F. (2002) *Tourism in National Parks and Protected Areas: Planning and Management*, Wallingford: CABI.

Frost, W. (ed.) (2011) *Zoos and Tourism: Conservation, Education, Entertainment?* Bristol: Channel View.

Frost, W. and Hall, C.M. (eds) (2009) *Tourism and National Parks: International Perspectives on Development, Histories and Change*, London: Routledge.

Runte, A. (1979) *National Parks: The American Experience*, Lincoln: University of Nebraska Press.

References

Boyd, S.W. and Butler, R.W. (2009) 'Tourism and the Canadian national park system: Protection, use and balance', in W. Frost and C.M. Hall (eds) *Tourism and National Parks: International Perspectives on Development, Histories and Change*, London: Routledge.

Burns, K. (2009) *The National Parks: America's Best Idea*, DVD, Public Broadcasting Service.

Carruthers, J. (1995) *The Kruger National Park: A Social and Political History*, Pietermaritzburg: University of Natal Press.

Charters, T., Gabriel, M. and Prasser, S. (eds) (1996) *National Parks: Private Sector's Role*, Toowomba: University of Southern Queensland Press.

Eagles, P.J.F. and McCool, S.F. (2002) *Tourism in National Parks and Protected Areas: Planning and Management*, Wallingford: CABI.

Frost, W. (2004) *Travel and Tour Management*, Sydney: Pearson.

Frost, W. (ed.) (2011) *Zoos and Tourism: Conservation, Education, Entertainment?* Bristol: Channel View.

Frost, W. and Hall, C.M. (eds) (2009a) *Tourism and National Parks: International Perspectives on Development, Histories and Change*, London: Routledge.

—— (2009b) 'Reinterpreting the creation myth: Yellowstone National Park', in W. Frost and C.M. Hall (eds) *Tourism and National Parks: International Perspectives on Development, Histories and Change*, London: Routledge.

Hall, C.M. and Frost, W. (2009) 'Introduction: The making of the national park concept', in W. Frost and C.M. Hall (eds) *Tourism and National Parks: International Perspectives on Development, Histories and Change*, London: Routledge.

Hancocks, D. (2001) *A Different Nature: The Paradoxical World of Zoos and Their Uncertain Future*, Berkeley: University of California Press.

Jepson, P. and Whittaker, R.J. (2002) 'Histories of protected areas: Internationalisation of conservation values and their adoption in the Netherlands Indies (Indonesia)', *Environment and History*, 8: 129–72.

Journal of Sustainable Tourism (2009) 'Special issue: Tourism and protected area partnerships', *Journal of Sustainable Tourism*, 17(2).

Kathirithamby-Wells, J. (2005) *Nature and Nation: Forests and Development in Peninsular Malaysia*, Singapore: Singapore University Press.

Langford, N.P. (1905; 1972 reprint) *The Discovery of Yellowstone Park*, Lincoln: University of Nebraska Press.

Leask, A. and Fyall, A. (2012) *Managing World Heritage Sites*, Hoboken: Taylor and Francis.

MacKenzie, J.M. (1988) *The Empire of Nature: Hunting, Conservation and British Imperialism*, Manchester: Manchester University Press.

Medina, J.S. (2009) 'The national park concept in Spain: Patriotism, education, romanticism and tourism', in W. Frost and C.M. Hall (eds) *Tourism and National Parks: International Perspectives on Development, Histories and Change*, London: Routledge.

Moscardo, G. (1999) *Making Visitors Mindful*, Champaign Ill: Sagamore.

Nash, R. (1967) *Wilderness and the American Mind*, New Haven: Yale University Press.

—— (1970) 'The American invention of national parks', *American Quarterly*, 22: 726–35.

Runte, A. (1979) *National Parks: The American Experience*, Lincoln: University of Nebraska Press.

Star, P. and Lochhead, L. (2002) 'Children of the burnt bush: New Zealanders and the indigenous remnant, 1880–1930', in E. Pawson and T. Brooking (eds) *Environmental Histories of New Zealand*, Melbourne: Oxford University Press.

Strickland-Munro, J. and Moore, S. (2013) 'Indigenous involvement and benefits from tourism in protected areas: A study of Purnulu National Park and Warmun Community, Australia', *Journal of Sustainable Tourism*, 21: 26–41.

Tilden, F. (1957; 2007 edn) *Interpreting Our Heritage*, Chapel Hill: University of North Carolina Press.

Timothy, D.J. (2000) 'Tourism and international parks', in R.W. Butler and S.W. Boyd (eds) *Tourism and National Parks: Issues and Implications*, Chichester: Wiley.

Turner, F.J. (1894) 'The significance of the frontier in American history', in R.W. Etulain (ed.) *Does the Frontier Experience Make America Exceptional?* Boston and New York: Bedford/St Martin's, 1999.

Wang, N. (2000) *Tourism and Modernity: A Sociological Analysis*, Oxford: Pergamon.

Weiner, D.R. (1999) *A Little Corner of Freedom: Russian Nature Protection from Stalin to Gorbachev*, Berkeley: University of California Press.

Wordsworth, W. (1810; 1970 reprint) *Wordsworth's Guide to the Lakes*, Oxford: Oxford University Press.

Zeppel, H. (2006) Indigenous Ecotourism: Sustainable Development and Management, Wallingford: CABI.

Zhang, C.Z., Xu, H.G., Su, T. and Ryan, C. (2009) 'Visitors' perceptions of the use of cable cars and lifts in Wulingyuan World Heritage site, China', *Journal of Sustainable Tourism*, 17: 551–66.

31

Changing audience behaviour

A pathway to sustainable event management

James Musgrave and Stephen Henderson

Sustainable event Objectives must be scoped across the three pillars of sustainable development, the stakeholders involved in the event and location.

Social marketing Utilising tools, techniques and concepts derived from commercial marketing in pursuit of social goals.

Consumer behaviour The study of decision-making processes prior to purchasing services.

Persuasion Techniques that enable a change in attitude or behaviour.

Introduction

To date, the majority of discussion around sustainability has talked at a policy level or a practical level. At its worst, the policy level might be seen as a flag-waving exercise that is trying to differentiate those making policy as 'doing the right thing'. However, working at a practical level can leave those involved considering single issues or just a handful of issues when achieving sustainability requires a much broader, holistic approach. Whilst this is a problem, it might be seen as one of management needing to translate policy into action. In other words, it requires the core, day-to-day management process to organise resources in a way that achieves particular goals.

This chapter explores a more fundamental problem that sits amongst policy, process and people. Though corporations offering products may operate on a sustainable basis in a manner somewhat isolated from the consumer who chooses where and when to consume, event organisers are providing a service at a specific time and place. Therefore, as consumers, the attendees at events may need to make choices about travel, eating, drinking and, possibly, accommodation that are separate to their decision to become part of the audience. In doing this, the audience bring with them their own attitudes and behaviour with regard to sustainability, neither of which may fit with any of sustainability objectives aimed for by the event organiser. Only through the behaviour change of attendees can there be a realisation of a number of key sustainable management practices based around the consumption of natural resources (water, food, fuels) and related waste management. Consequently, in the following discussion we will argue that modifying audience behaviour is the major barrier to be overcome in achieving sustainable events.

Defining the sustainable event

The concept of sustainable development has been proclaimed by some as a watershed moment in society where political and social interests combined in order 'to meet the needs of present generations' without compromising opportunities for future generations (WCED 1987). The economic and political significance of this widely used statement is sometimes undervalued. Fundamentally, it is suggesting a shift in economics whereby market growth is replaced by sustainable development; thus the perpetual insistence of growth and consumption within all strands of society alters. Yet whilst the accomplishment of such 'mega-political' action is scrutinised (Anderson 2002; Pronk 2011) and the definitional debate surrounding 'sustainable development' continues (Ketola 2007; Brown 2003; Dyllick & Hockerts 2002), the term 'sustainable' has evolved and is seen to permeate twenty-first century language. For example, it is commonly used in managerial, technical, administrative, academic and social forums and is now attached to initiatives such as sustainable business, sustainable living, sustainable tourism and now sustainable events (Smith-Christensen 2009).

At its core, the sustainable event is a rather incongruous title; events encourage people to congregate in a particular location for a specific reason and therefore encourage the consumption of resources. Once past this paradox it can be argued that a sustainable event has an opportunity to fulfil important social, cultural and economic roles that, according to Getz (2009), are valued by people. These so-called roles are commonly referred to as the three pillars – a balanced focus on economic, socio-culture and environmental issues (Getz 2009; Laing & Frost 2010; Sherwood 2007). But given the scope of the event industry and its wide-ranging objectives, it is questionable whether a definitive statement on sustainable events can be produced. At this stage it is more reasonable to consider the common factors and terms associated with 'sustainable events' and to consider these from an academic and practitioner perspective.

A sustainable event can be differentiated between environmental sustainability (greening) and the holistic approach to sustainable development (Tinnish & Mangal 2012). The term is further delineated by Laing and Frost (2010) who propose a 'green event' as an event that has a sustainability policy or incorporates sustainable practices into its management and operations. This thinking is further reflected in Graci and Dodds' (2008) approach to planning and executing events. For them, sustainable events can be defined as incorporating the consideration of the environment in order to minimise their negative impact. Indeed, this expectation is, sometimes, boiled down to the principle that all events should adopt measures to reduce, reuse and recycle resources.

Gallagher and Pike (2011) take a pragmatic and resource-based view, suggesting sustainable event management is the key paradigm in which all organisational resources and development decisions are taken. This includes a stakeholder view where relevant authorities and organisations involved in local governance have interest. Capriello and Fraquelli (2008) and Henderson (2011) develop the ideas of scoping the sustainable event objectives in terms of not only the stakeholders but the three pillars of sustainable development. Nonetheless, attempting sustainable event management raises a number of issues of itself. For example, promoting sustainable credentials for every facet of the event might be aspirational but, according to Kearins and Pavlovich (2002), it can impose additional demands under short lead-in times and increased public scrutiny.

Notwithstanding the environmental and social delineation, the economic imperative of event management remains. Carroll (1999) reiterates the need for financial sense and economic responsibility as a priority of any business. Indeed the 'business case' for sustainable events frequently reports on internal cost savings, efficiencies and market attractiveness. Although adhering to principles of sustainable event management will present a notion of due diligence, the measurement of success in sustainable event management practice is not commonplace (Musgrave *et al.* 2012) thus it is difficult to prove these benefits with certainty. Whilst it is accepted that due diligence is a market driven imperative it is also an internal necessity. Getz (2009) proposes that working conditions, meeting minimum health and safety laws and providing opportunities for employees to learn and develop is a factor of sustainable events management, firmly supported by Musgrave (2011) and Musgrave *et al.* (2012). Finally, Mair and Laing (2013) add an additional aspect to their interpretation of sustainable events – the opportunities for sustainable events to educate, inform and encourage sustainable behaviour change among attendees.

These wide-ranging perspectives continue with the proliferation of sustainable event management guidance presented to the events industry – from international standards to consultancy checklists (see Table 31.1). Yet the term *Sustainable Events Management* struggles to be defined in certification standards such as ISO 20121; the APEX/ASTM Environmentally Sustainable Meeting Standards and the Global Reporting Initiative's (GRI) Sector Supplement for Events. APEX/ASTM have a prescriptive approach towards environmental solutions and target eight key areas such as environmental policy; communications; and procurement. Despite these relevant components a benchmark definition is not provided. Within the GRI, sustainability is defined using the aforementioned and often-debated WCED definition. This framework for voluntary sustainability reporting covers key sector-specific issues, including: transport of attendees, recruiting and training of the event workforce, through to planning and managing potential legacies. According to Walker (2012) ISO 20121 includes a balanced approach to the triple bottom line of social ('people'), environmental ('planet') and economic ('profit'); but once again refers to the WCED definition to benchmark its terminology. Whilst ISO 20121 and GRI refer to sustainability as 'sustainable development' arguably it exemplifies the broad nature of the term, adding to the difficulty in transposing understanding and application to management practices within the events industry.

Application of sustainable events management is evident within event associations; however, the ability to define these practices using one term is limited. For example, the International Festival and Event Association (IFEA) refer to the importance of 'community' building both locally and globally. The mission of the International Special Events Society (ISES) is to educate, advance and promote 'principles of professional conduct and ethics', whilst Meeting Professionals International (MPI) is committed to providing members with applied examples of sustainability in practice. The self-proclaimed role of Exhibition and Event Association of Australia (EEAA) is to promote sound health and safety and ethical practice and help member businesses to grow profitably. Eventia provide a definition for the industry using the term 'corporate responsibility' which includes environmental carbon footprint reduction; transportation reduction and ethical and transparent marketing, whilst the Association of Exhibitions and Events (IAEE) concentrate upon honesty and integrity as a brand throughout their documentation. This is not an exhaustive list but highlights the holistic nature of sustainable management and the diverse impact an event business has on its internal and external environment. As the Green Meeting Industry Council purports, the overall direction is an aspirational and long-term commitment to ethical and highly valuable business practice.

Table 31.1 Examples of environmental and sustainable voluntary guidance tools implemented worldwide

Country	Standard
Australia	• Global Eco Labeling
	• Good Environmental Choice
UK	• BS i8901:2009 (Specification for a) Sustainability Management System for Events
	• Green Tourism Business Scheme
	• Industry Green (IG) by Julie's Bicycle: 2007(JB) – Voluntary Measurement Tool
	• Defra Sustainable Events Guide
Sweden	• Good Environmental Choice (Sweden)
	• Swan Eco-label
	• Swedish Standards Institute (SIS), Luger, Live Nation – developing a new environmental manual for festivals
Europe	• European Eco-Management and Auditing Scheme (EMAS)
	• Green Hospitality Programme/Green Hospitality Eco Label or Award (Ireland)
North America	• APEX/ASTM Environmental Sustainable Events standards
	• The Sierra Eco Label
	• The Sustainable Forestry Initiative® Program (SFI)
	• LEED Building Certification
Other	• Global Reporting Initiative: Events Sector Supplement
	• SEXI – The Sustainable Exhibition Industry Project
	• ISO 14001: 2004 Environmental Management System
	• ISO 20121: Sustainable Events
	• ISO 26000: Guidance on Social Reporting

Source: Adapted from Tinnish (2013)

It is clear that sustainable event management pivots between moral and business perspectives and must wrestle with the interactions between internal factors such as people, allocation of financial and physical resources and power structures whilst tackling issues of stakeholder engagement, host community demands and attendee expectations. For this reason Smith–Christensen (2009) proposes a supplement to sustainable event management and moves the argument to integrating responsible and quality components in the management of events. Indeed Conley and Williams (2005) in Getz (2009) argued 'the legitimate concerns of a corporation should include such broader objectives as sustainable growth, equitable employment practices, and long-term social and environmental well-being'. Yet Ching-Fu (2006) proclaims there is discrepancy between event organiser's drive to be environmentally responsible and client demand. But what is evident is that every event organisation, irrespective of size, scale or scope, is inextricably linked to a global marketplace that is increasingly engaged with sustainable initiatives.

Realising the sustainable event

Despite this shift in expectation to engage in sustainable activities Nisbet and Gick (2008) have found that explicit pro-sustainable concern does not correlate with individual action (Kaptein *et al.* 2010; Kollmuss & Agyeman 2002) exemplified by the 'throw away' of many tents by attendees at music festivals (see the case study at the end of the chapter). Whilst this lack of behavioural change is a societal problem that might be addressed via accredited frameworks, as has been noted above, it requires the day-to-day management to translate their ideas in a way that achieves particular goals (Coogan *et al.* 2006; Wen *et al.* 2005). Indeed, to truly take on the ideas behind sustainable events management, it should have set objectives to be achieved that meet a mix of people, planet and profit goals. These ought to recognise the scope of their intended influence, particularly in terms of how they might influence the processes adopted by suppliers and the behaviour of consumers (Henderson 2011). Such a stakeholder approach has been recognised by other writers who see this as essential to achieving sustainability goals. These goals can be achieved by three basic approaches using policy, contracts or persuasion as suit particular stakeholder groups:

Informal policies are, for example, useful in terms of addressing the equitable treatment of staff at the event. Similarly, agreed policies might set aside certain parts of the organisation's profit to be used for good causes. In other words, informal policies are likely to work where the stakeholder who benefits has limited power and/or interest in the corporation.

A corporation might apply *formal contracts* where it wishes to apply its power to meet certain sustainable goals. Typically, this would be a way in which to apply control over suppliers to meet the requirements of the corporation. For example, if the corporation wants the event supplier to use low energy lighting or recyclable food utensils in its supply process.

Applying marketing tools as a means of *persuasion* is the most important challenge for the corporation as it addresses the customer. As a key stakeholder, the customer has many choices in terms of whether and how they get involved with the corporation's event(s).

The simplicity of informal policies and the structured nature of formal contracts are more easily managed than the persuasion of customers. Hence, here, the concentration is on understanding how marketing concepts can help in that persuasion. Thus in developing a successful behaviour change approach within an events context, a number of extended marketing processes is required alongside social marketing thinking and related behavioural theories. These are suggested in Figure 31.1 and furthered in the following sections.

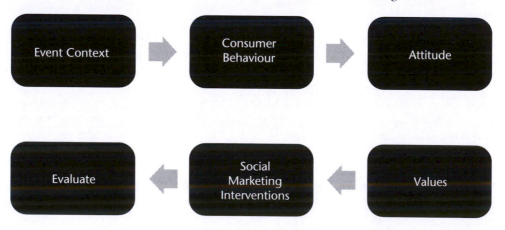

Figure 31.1 A conceptual approach to achieving sustainable event objectives

Context

Recently there has been criticism aimed at marketing interventions developed for the purpose of social behaviour change. More specifically, existing interventions have been simplistic and make little consideration of complex behavioural situations. Unfortunately, the outcome for many is an incomplete understanding of the salient issues; contemporaneously ignoring fundamental variables rather than acknowledging these and the impact these variables have on social marketing strategies. Before these social marketing interventions can be developed, there is a need to recognise the event context where behaviour occurs.

In order to understand this better, a number of writers have begun to address the complexity of the behavioural context. Nicholson and Xaio (2011) developed Skinner's thinking (1953 in Nicholson & Xaio 2011) within the application of the Behavioural Perspective Model (BPM) of Foxall (1996). Foxall *et al.* (2006) also apply this thinking in terms of behavioural change for sustainability. Essentially, the BPM explains how the scope of the behaviour setting is affective in its influence on consumer behaviour (Foxall & Greenley 1998).

Behaviour is influenced by when and where the consumption takes places, as well as past experiences. The attitudes formed from past experiences are furthered by the behavioural setting and either reinforced (as benefits) or punished (as costs) by certain behaviours. These appear as benefits or costs that are seen as utilitarian (functional) or informational (symbolic) in nature and shape the behaviour (primary operant condition) based on the combinations of low and high reinforcement, functional or symbolic consumption.

Certainly, viewing constituent parts of the environment and how they relate to consumer behaviour is a necessity as the context of reality is socially created at both local and broad societal levels. Thus, attempting to separate the consumer from the environment would create artificial interventions and limit successful implementation. An appreciation of where consumption takes place, when and whether or not it is an experience that has been repeated, will influence the behaviour of the individual and indeed the requirements of the social marketing intervention.

Consumer behaviour

When those interested in marketing refer to consumer behaviour, they tend to emphasise purchasing behaviour. A process that involves the recognition of a need, searching information that may help satisfy that need, evaluation of the options, purchase and post-purchase evaluation (Kotler *et al.* 2008). Whilst complex in its detail, these process steps fit neatly with a product such as buying a car or item of clothing. However, one notable absentee step from this process is the consumption itself and, if this was an event, one might wish to persuade attendees to consume in a sustainable manner. So, immediately, the expanded process highlights that achieving sustainable goals requires corporations to influence consumer behaviour (see Figure 31.1) in not only the purchasing choice but the consumption too. Set firmly in the events context, consumption may take place across a few days at a festival and the scope defined within the corporation's objective may extend this to include the travel to and from the event (Henderson 2011).

Whilst these challenges are clearly expansive, consumer behaviour theory tells us that consumers may have low or high involvement in their purchase (Zaichkowsky 1986). In other words, where the choice to attend the event requires little consideration such as going to see a local sports event, the consumer will only be lightly engaged in the purchasing process, particularly, if this is a repeat purchase. If the consumer has a high involvement, perhaps, making decisions about travel and accommodation alongside booking to attend an event, there ought to be a greater opportunity to engage them in the consideration of sustainable event choices, e.g. to travel in a sustainable manner. Therefore, to maximise the chances of truly achieving sustainable objectives, event corporations must look towards marketing interventions designed towards targeted behaviour; the involvement of the actor; whether it is a one time or continuing behaviour; and whether it is performed by individuals or groups (Michie *et al.* 2008).

Attitude

Whatever the levels of engagement during the purchase decision process to attend an event; whether with low or high involvement, positive decisions will involve consumption. During the consumption process, the attendees make further choices that relate to sustainability (e.g. whether to take home their waste and recycle it or to use sustainable water sources provided at the event). Herein lies the principal difficulty for those event corporations wishing to operate in a sustainable manner as the behaviour of consumers requires influencing in a direction that achieves the corporation's goals. Yet, the consumption process could take place over an extended period of time and in a variety of locations with decisions that influence consumption often being taken away from the time and place of consumption. For example, if the event attendee brings along their own food and drink, their decisions on this are made away from the event before they have arrived. Hence, the decision-making process related to attending an event not only has a temporal element but may also occur across different behaviour settings.

Such consumption decisions will depend very much on consumer attitude formed before or at the event depending on the timing of decisions. Theory explains that attitude and consequent behaviour is formed by cognitive (thinking), emotive (feeling) and action (doing). As noted above, different events and different aspects of their consumption suggest that the consumer may engage in different levels of involvement. Hence, the potential for consumers to learn in these situations will also vary and attitudes may form in a rather haphazard manner. What is certain is that they will form attitudes based on the perceived value of certain actions (e.g. the value in taking home litter from the event). Thus the antecedents of value must be recognised, managed and manipulated so that the consumer may be more inclined to make a sustainable choice.

Value

Event corporations that have sustainable goals cannot rest on their laurels assuming that the rise of the ethical consumer will be enough to meet their aim (Kaptein *et al.* 2010; Kollmuss & Agyeman 2002). To do this, there needs to be an understanding of what the consumer perceives as value and worthy of a change in behaviour.

Table 31.2 offers a framework for understanding value (Holbrook 1999) that might be utilised to understand the likely areas of value that consumers are attracted to when adopting sustainable behaviour. Of course, this value may manifest itself at various points in the consumer process that begins with the decision to attend the event and ends on returning home from the event.

The main value typologies apparent in making sustainable choices might be seen as other-oriented rather than self-oriented (i.e. the consumer is making a choice that improves the situation of 'others'). Of course, these 'others' might include relatives or close friends and it is not uncommon for those proposing sustainable choices to suggest that it is 'for the children'.

Table 31.2 Typology of consumer value

		Intrinsic	Extrinsic
Self-orientated	Active	Play	Efficiency
	Reactive	Aesthetics	Excellence or Quality
Other-orientated	Active	Ethics	Status
	Reactive	Spirituality	Esteem

Source: Adapted from Holbrook (1999)

As most of the sustainable choices require action on behalf of the consumer, the active, other-orientated value elements fit better with sustainable choices than the reactive value types. The choices noted above to benefit others are clearly active and intrinsic as the individual sees the chosen action as something virtuous or as is sometimes said, 'doing the right thing'. If, however, 'doing the right thing' might be seen as an action that is taken to impress others, the choice can be seen as active and extrinsic (e.g. the event manager chooses to car share to other events as a means to show a strong commitment to the sustainable agenda).

None of this is meant to suggest that consumers will see value only as one of the categories from the typology suggested by Holbrook. A consumer's perception of value may take on various value types. The aforementioned event manager would recognise the 'status' type value as well as that described as 'ethics'. Furthermore, the wider experience of the event might provide value in a variety of ways depending on the nature of the event. However, what is clear is that value within the sustainable choices is more likely to be active and other-oriented. Indeed, one of the most difficult aspects is that there are self-oriented elements of value that suggest it is more convenient to act in a less sustainable manner. For example, to throw waste on the floor at an event may seem personally efficient in comparison to carrying food containers about our person, or, to travel without car sharing may appear to be convenient but will not help the event achieve their sustainable goals. This suggests that a key role for event management is to introduce circumstances that either encourage sustainable choices based on their basic values as discussed above or consider ways in which to add value for the consumer.

Social marketing

As we can see from above, the discussion has now moved away from informal and formal means to encourage sustainable behaviour into an area where persuasive techniques are more important. To achieve behavioural change alongside event attendance, it is important to turn our attention to social marketing and its persuasive tools. Some touring artists have already recognised these tools as a means to achieve sustainable touring objectives (Henderson 2013).

Peattie and Peattie (2009) refer to social marketing as utilising tools, techniques and concepts derived from commercial marketing in pursuit of social goals. The use of social marketing in relation to the promotion of sustainable consumption is already well established and has been developed to alter health-orientated behaviours through stimulation and facilitation (Haq *et al.* 2008; McKenzie-Mohr 2000).

Andreasen (1994) highlights that such approaches have tended to focus on 'downstream' activity and points to the need for the 'upstream' activity of activists, media, politicians and the like to create an agenda for change. Whilst event managers might add to this by lobbying the 'upstream' stakeholders, their main role is to concentrate on the 'downstream' activities surrounding their events.

In doing so, common marketing principles are applied such as the development of a (social) marketing strategy commonly referred to as an intervention and discussed later in the following section. Clearly, the consumer target for this strategy is already determined by the commercial marketing of the event. That is to say, the event manager puts forward a proposition to a defined target audience that is then targeted by the social marketing strategy to persuade them to behave in a sustainable manner.

Social marketing interventions

Social marketing involves the creation of targeted strategies intended to persuade the target consumer to adopt a different behaviour based on a more valuable proposition. Many writers in this area acknowledge the similarities to typical commercial marketing of products and services: targeted (Ryan & Lauver 2002), driven by communications to the target (Noar *et al.* 2007), innovative communications (Clark *et al.* 2002) and linked to measurable objectives (see also Chapter 19).

Whilst some tools such as the Elaboration Likelihood Model (ELM) are rooted in behavioural thinking, aimed at explaining persuasion and the changing of attitude (Petty & Cacioppo 1984), marketing tends to be driven by the practical elements of the strategy itself. Social marketing strategies focus on the social marketing mix albeit adapted to address behavioural change as opposed to commercial exchange (Kotler & Lee 2008).

The *product* aspect of the strategy is the desired behavioural change and its related benefits as viewed via the value types of Holbrook (1999). From the event perspective, it has been noted that a number of individual buying decisions make up attendance at the event from buying the ticket to choices about travel and subsistence. Each one may need a separate product and its own social marketing mix and, hence, the event manager needs to consider the integration of these strategies to maximise effectiveness (in achieving their objectives) and efficiency (in cost terms).

If we consider the event context as described earlier, *place* in the social marketing mix provides increased complexity in line with typical commercial marketing exchange. When marketing a product or service, the advent of the internet and social media has meant an expanded view of the notion of place as it relates to increased communication methods and sales channels. It acts to emphasise that whilst the behavioural setting of the BPM is the equivalent of the sales channel, the expanded communications that are possible mean that learned history can be extensively influenced too. Similarly, in line with the multi-product decision making noted above, a variety of places may be involved from buying a ticket on the internet to deciding which food to take when in the supermarket.

Naturally, it follows from above that *promotion* is central to not only emphasising the desired behaviour but highlighting the value of the product for the consumer. The BPM model suggests that this value might be indicated via informational reinforcement or by a clear utilitarian benefit. However, the perceived value of a strategy that involves punishment is more debatable. Nevertheless, value needs to be communicated and an integrated marketing communication approach is desirable (Schultz 1992).

Finally, *price* is the cost to the consumer that, as noted above, may or may not involve commercial exchange. Consumers may be viewed as simply balancing the perceived value of the proposed behaviour change against the loss of other perceived benefits and/or a price paid. As the value is often in intangible benefits such as helping others, it's clear that these non-utilitarian aspects add to the sustainable challenge to those pursuing sustainable event objectives. Arguably, this implies that the desired behavioural change requires an underlying cultural shift that sees less benefit in consumption.

Case Study

Festival tents: A case for concern

The wide retail availability and the relative cheapness of tents to accommodate those looking to enjoy themselves at a festival has become a case of concern for festival organisers (Smithers 2011). It has become too easy for festival attendees to enjoy their leisure and depart, leaving the tents in situ for the festival organisers to clear away. Not only does this add cost to the clear-up of the festival site, many of these tents cannot be recycled and are sent to landfill which, typically, incurs a further cost for the organisers. Therefore, whether environmentally aware or not, there are profit-related reasons for the festival promoters to encourage a change in audience behaviour.

One of the reasons cited by festival attendees for leaving their tents is that they 'know' the tents are recycled and used by others. Whilst this does happen at some festivals (Rotary Club 2012; BBC 2012; Wainwright 2012), it is neither universally true nor totally successful as some tents are in too poor a condition to be recycled. This typifies the learned history that a consumer may gather and highlights that their knowledge can not only be inaccurate but also be a convenient truth that leads to an unwanted behaviour based on an inaccurate value proposition.

This type of misunderstanding emphasises why the 'upstream' commentary by activists, environmentalists and others influencing the public agenda is important in establishing an accurate understanding of the impact of different behaviours. With an issue like the disposal of tents the impact is quite clear, yet other environmental problems are fraught with difficulties as the public agenda includes opposing debates (e.g. on climate change).

At the 'downstream' level, the attendee arrives at the festival bringing with them their learned history, there will be an examination of tickets and security checks, though rarely would anyone find their tent inspected. In other words, most festivals offer open behavioural settings and a wide choice of behaviour when deciding on a tent as their favoured accommodation. Recognising this problem, Michael Eavis has suggested that his Glastonbury Festival (A Greener Festival 2013) may require attendees to use pre-erected tents rather than bring their own. In other words, attendance at this particular festival would become a closed setting without choice. Whilst the intervention may have some music fans seeing this action as driven by a profit motive, it would achieve the sustainable objective of eliminating tent waste.

Some (Love Your Tent 2013) have offered informational awareness about the damage caused by leaving a tent for others to clear up, thus suggesting that there is an extrinsic, other-oriented value that might be seen as a reward for taking the tent home. Other rewards can come with spray painting of the festival logo onto the tent (ReTent 2013) that adds value in the form of status for its owner when reused at other festivals.

Another intervention is intended to change the behaviour at the point of purchase rather than at the festival site. The Green Tent Company (2013) encourages the festival attendee to purchase a recyclable tent which does not remove the waste problem but ensures the tents do not go to landfill. Clearly, a different outcome to reusing the tent and requiring the festival management to determine what sustainable behaviour they seek.

Conclusion

This chapter reveals the complex behavioural change that sits in the background of sustainable event management. Whilst acknowledging that there is no agreed definition of a sustainable event, the chapter highlights some important points for those with sustainability goals:

- Various tools are available to guide the event manager but it is essential that objectives are scoped across the three pillars of sustainable development, the stakeholders involved in the event and their location during this involvement.
- Informal policies, formal contracts and persuasive techniques offer a means to achieve sustainability objectives.
- By far the most difficult technique is persuasion where the consumer stakeholder is addressed at various points in an extended consumption process from deciding to attend an event, the journey to the event, activities at the event and the return home.
- The often intangible nature of the value offered during persuasion requires careful consideration as changes in behaviour to meet sustainability objectives tend to offer little utilitarian value.
- To persuade the consumer to behave in a sustainable manner requires social marketing strategies (interventions) which demonstrate the value for the consumer at each of the decision points in this extended consumption process.

Key Reading

Dresner, S. (2006) *The Principles of Sustainability*, London: Earthscan.

Jones, M. (2010) *Sustainable Event Management: A Practical Guide*, London: Earthscan.

Pernecky, T. and Luck, M. (eds) (2012) *Events, Society and Sustainability: Critical and Contemporary Approaches*, London: Routledge.

References

A Greener Festival (2013) *Glastonbury Flags Up Left Behind Tents*. Available at: www.agreenerfestival. com/2013/02/glastonbury-flags-up-dumped-tents-issue/ (accessed 22 March 2013).

Anderson, J.W. (2002) *The International Politics of Sustainable Development*, Sustainable Development, August, Issue Brief 02–15. Available at: <www.rff.org/Publications/Pages/PublicationDetails. aspx?PublicationID=9627> (accessed 2 January 2011).

Andreasen, A.R. (1994) 'Social marketing: Its definition and domain', *Journal of Public Policy and Marketing*, 3: 108–14

BBC (2012) *Wakestock's Abandoned Tents Recycled for Homeless*. Available at: www.bbc.co.uk/news/uk-wales-18995558 (accessed 22 March 2013).

Brown, L. (2003) *Plan B: Rescuing a Plant Under Stress and a Civilisation in Trouble*, London: Earth Policy Institute, W.W Norton and Company.

Carroll, A.B. (1999) 'Corporate social responsibility: Evolution of a definitional construct', *Business & Society*, 38: 268–95.

Capriello, A. and Fraquelli, G. (2008) 'Market-driven management in the event industry: A preliminary conceptual model for community events. Symphonya', *Emerging Issues in Management*, 2: 50–65.

Ching-Fu, C. (2006) 'Applying the analytical hierarchy process (AHP) approach to convention site selection', *Journal of Travel Research*, 45: 167–74.

Clark, M.A., Rakowski, W., Ehrich, B., Rimer, B., Velicer, W., Dube, C., Pearlman, D., Peterson, K. and Goldstein, M. (2002) 'The effect of a stage-matched and tailored intervention on repeat mammography' *American Journal of Preventative Medicine*, 22: 1–7.

Coogan, M.A., Karash, K.H. and Adler, T. (2006) *Changing Travel Behaviour in Environmental Strategies: A New Research Approach,* The New England Transportation Institute Council. Available at: www.newenglandtransportationinstitute.org/changing_travel_behavior.pdf (accessed 17 September 2010).

Dyllick, T. and Hockerts, K. (2002) 'Beyond the business case for corporate sustainability', *Business Strategy and the Environment*, 11: 130–41

Foxall, G.R. (1996) 'The behavioural perspective model: Consensibility and consensuality', *European Journal of Marketing*, 33: 570–96.

Foxall, G.R. and Greenley, G.E. (1998) 'The affective structure of consumer situations', *Environment and Behavior*, 30: 781–98.

Foxall, G.R., Oliveira-Castro, J.M., James, V.K., Yani-de Soriano, M. and Sigurdsson, V. (2006) 'Consumer behaviour analysis and social marketing: The case of environmental conservation', *Behaviour and Social Issues*, 15: 101–24.

Gallagher, A. and Pike, K. (2011) 'Sustainable management for maritime events and festivals', *Journal of Coastal Research*, 61: 158–65.

Getz, D. (2009) 'Policy for sustainable and responsible festivals and events: Institutionalization of a new paradigm', *Journal of Policy Research in Tourism, Leisure and Events*, 1: 61–78.

Graci, S. and Dodds, S. (2008) *Green Festivals and Events Guide, a How to…* ICARUS Foundation. Available at: http://ecoclub.com/library/epapers/15.pdf (accessed 12 January 2012).

Haq, G., Whitelegg, J., Cinderby, S. and Owen, A. (2008) 'The use of personalised social marketing to foster voluntary behavioural change for sustainable travel and lifestyles', *Local Environment*, 13: 549–69.

Henderson, S. (2011) 'The development of competitive advantage through sustainable event management', *Worldwide Hospitality and Tourism Themes*, 3: 245–57.

—— (2013) 'Sustainable touring: Exploring value creation through social marketing', *Arts Marketing: An International Journal*, 3(2): 154–67.

Holbrook, M.B. (1999) 'Introduction to consumer value', in M.B. Holbrook (ed.) *Consumer Value: A Framework for Analysis and Research*, London: Routledge.

Kaptein, M.C., Markopoulos, P., de Ruyter, B. and Aarts, E. (2010) 'Persuasion in ambient intelligence', *Journal of Ambient Intelligence*, 1: 43–56.

Kearins, K. and Pavlovich, K. (2002) 'The role of stakeholders in Sydney's green games', *Corporate Social Responsibility and Environmental Management*, 9: 157–69.

Ketola, T. (2007) 'A holistic corporate responsibility model: Integrating values, discourses and actions', *Journal of Business Ethics*, 80: 419–35.

Kollmuss, A. and Agyeman, J. (2002) 'Mind the gap: Why do people act environmentally and what are the barriers to pro-environmental behaviour?', *Environmental Education Research*, 8: 239–60.

Kotler, P. and Lee, N. (2008) *Social Marketing: Influencing Behaviours for Good*, 3rd edn, Thousand Oaks, California: Sage.

Kotler, P., Armstrong, G., Wong, V. and Saunders, J. (2008) *Principles of Marketing*, 5th European edn, Harlow: Prentice Hall.

Laing, J. and Frost, W. (2010) 'How green was my festival: Exploring challenges and opportunities associated with staging green events', *International Journal of Hospitality Management*, 29: 261–67.

Love Your Tent (2013) *Homepage*. Available at: http://loveyourtent.com/index.php (accessed 22 March 2013).

Mair, J. and Laing, J. (2013) 'Encouraging pro-environmental behaviour: The role of sustainability-focused events', *Journal of Sustainable Tourism*: 1–13.

McKenzie-Mohr, D. (2000) 'Promoting sustainable behaviour: An introduction to community-based social marketing', *Journal of Social Issues*, 56: 543–54.

Michie, S., Johnston, M., Francis, J., Hardeman, W. and Eccles, M. (2008) 'From theory to intervention: Mapping theoretically derived behavioural determinants to behaviour change techniques', *Applied Psychology*, 57: 660–80.

Musgrave, J. (2011) 'Moving towards responsible events management', *Worldwide Hospitality and Tourism Themes*, 3: 258–74.

Musgrave, J., Mulligan, J., Woodward, S., Kenyon, A. and Jones, S. (2012) *The Value of CSR in the Meetings Industry Study Report*. Available at: www.mpiweb.org/Publications (accessed 1 April 2013).

Nicholson, M. and Xiao, S.H. (2011) 'Consumer behaviour analysis and social marketing practice', *The Service Industries Journal*, 31: 2529–42.

Nisbet, E.K.L. and Gick, M.L. (2008) 'Can health psychology help the planet? Applying theory and models of health behaviour to environmental actions', *Canadian Psychology*, 49: 296–303.

Noar, S. M., Benac, C. N., & Harris, M. S. (2007) 'Does tailoring matter? Meta-analytic review of tailored print health behavior change interventions', *Psychological bulletin*, *133*(4), 673-693.

Peattie, K. and Peattie, S. (2009) 'Social marketing: A pathway to consumption reduction?' *Journal of Business Research*, 62: 260–68.

Petty, R.E. and Cacioppo, J.T. (1984) 'Source factors and the elaboration likelihood model of persuasion', *Advances in Consumer Research*, 11: 668–72.

Pronk, J. (2011) 'The quest for sustainability: Some reflections', *Development*, 54: 155–60.

ReTent (2013) *Homepage*. Available at: www.retent.co.uk/ (accessed 22 March 2013).

Rotary Club (2012) *V Festival – Tent Collection*. Available at: www.brewood-rotary.co.uk/tents.htm (accessed 22 March 2013).

Ryan, P. and Lauver, D.R. (2002) 'The efficacy of tailored interventions', *Journal of Nursing Scholarship*, 34: 331–37.

Schultz, D. (1992) 'Integrated marketing communications', *Journal of Promotion Management*, 1: 99–104.

Sherwood, P. (2007) 'A triple bottom line evaluation of the impact of special events: The development of indicators', Doctoral dissertation, Victoria University.

Smith-Christensen, C. (2009) 'Sustainability as a concept within events', in R. Raj and J. Musgrave (eds) *Event Management and Sustainability*, Oxford: CABI.

Smithers, R. (2011) *Thousands of 'Festival' Tents Destined for Landfill*. Available at: www.guardian.co.uk/environment/2011/jul/07/festival-tents-landfill (accessed 22 March 2013).

The Green Tent Company (2013) *Homepage*. Available at: www.thegreententcompany.co.uk/ (accessed 22 March 2013).

Tinnish, S.M. (2013) *Keeping Up with Standards in the New Year*, Meeting Professionals International. Available at: http://chicagompi.org/2013/01/keeping-up-with-standards-in-the-new-year/ (accessed 17 February 2013).

Tinnish, S.M. and Mangal, S.M. (2012) 'Sustainable event marketing in the MICE industry: A theoretical framework', *Journal of Convention & Event Tourism*, 13: 227–49.

World Commission on Environment and Development (WCED) (1987) *Our Common Future, The Bruntland Commission*, Oxford: Oxford University Press.

Wainwright, M. (2012) *Hundreds of Tents Abandoned at Leeds Festival will be Scavenged for Those in Need*. Available at: www.guardian.co.uk/uk/the-northerner/2012/aug/20/leeds-festical-recycling-camping-gear-everything-is-possuble (accessed 22 March 2013).

Walker, A.S. (2012) *Process vs. Performance Standards for Sustainable Meeting and Event Management*, Osgoode CLPE Research Paper No. 17/2012. Available at: http://ssrn.com/abstract=2116342 (accessed 12 January 2013).

Wen, L.M., Orr, N., Bindon, J. and Rissel, C. (2005) 'Promoting active transport in a workplace setting: Evaluation of a pilot study in Australia', *Health Promotion International*, 20: 123–33.

Zaichkowsky, J.L. (1986) 'Conceptualizing involvement', *Journal of Advertising*, 15: 4–14.

32

Small firms and sustainable tourism policy

Exploring moral framing

Rhodri Thomas

Small firms Official definitions vary by country and, in some cases, by sector within the same country. Most official definitions use numerical categories relating to number of employees and/ or turnover. In the United States, for example, to qualify as a small guesthouse or restaurant, the business would have to have a turnover of less than $7m ($30m for a small hotel). The Australian Bureau of Statistics, by contrast, states that trading organisations with up to 19 employees are small; in Europe, a small firm is usually defined as one that employs between 10 and 49 employees. A key characteristic of a small firm for the purposes of this chapter is that it is managed by the owner of the business.

Moral framing A focus on moral or ethical considerations before reaching a decision. In this chapter, it relates to the owner-manager's deliberations.

Corporate social responsibility (CSR) This is generally taken to mean managing a business in a way that improves, rather than damages, society. It encompasses what can seem to be a bewildering array of issues; from those associated with the environment to employment practices. The term is generally used in the context of large firms (corporate) but the 'principles' are also discussed in the small firms literature (see e.g. Garay & Font 2012). Some argue that the idea of CSR is contradictory and its promotion ideological (see e.g. Fleming & Jones 2012).

Introduction

Destination Management Organisations (DMOs) and other public agencies involved in tourism planning are usually either silent on issues of sustainable tourism practices for small firms or advocate actions that represent so-called 'win-win scenarios' (i.e. they serve the private interest of the owner while simultaneously making a positive social contribution). For example, the promotion of measures to reduce energy consumption in the interests of minimising negative externalities is 'sold' to local businesses as a way of cutting costs. Such an approach is superficially appealing but potentially problematic as a foundation stone of policy intervention on two grounds. First, it reflects a conception of small firms and their motivations that is crude and not borne out by the evidence. Owner-managers would probably welcome a reduction in their costs, but to presume significant behaviour change may be precipitated using this approach underestimates the complexity of their decision making (see e.g. Ateljevic & Doorne 2000; Sampaio et al. 2012a). Public sector interventions informed by this kind of conceptualisation have had a minimal impact on the behaviour of small tourism businesses (Dewhurst & Thomas 2003; Thomas et al. 2011; Sampaio et al. 2012b).

The second limitation of promoting what some term the 'doing well by doing good' approach is that it ascribes, in effect, a moral hierarchy whereby 'doing well' (private gain in the form of revenues and profits) is conspicuously subservient to 'doing good' (generating some social benefit); as Kreps and Monin (2011) point out, it is doing well *by* doing good. If 'doing good' ceases to result in 'doing well' then, presumably, small firms would have no reason to persist in activities relating to the former. This chapter is concerned with exploring the advocacy of sustainable practices by considering its moral rather than financial framing.

Small firms and sustainability: Current perspectives

Before considering issues of moral framing, it is appropriate to discuss briefly what is currently understood about small businesses and their sustainable practices in tourism. Most researchers have concentrated their efforts on mapping levels of environmental action and then sought to understand more about the reasons for some running their operations in more or less sustainable ways. To a large extent, the title of a recent article in the *International Journal of Tourism Research* captures the challenge of the latter when it asks 'Why are some engaged and not others? Explaining environmental engagement among small firms in tourism' (Sampaio et al. 2012a). Such research is usually concerned primarily with the environment and promoted in terms of its potential value to the deliberations of public policy-makers. The critical management literature has been almost entirely ignored by tourism scholars (see Fleming & Jones 2012).

Most academic studies suggest that not only is engagement with notions of sustainable tourism limited among small firms but that their knowledge of the environmental and social consequences of their trading, and what they might do to improve any detrimental impacts, is also low (Clarke 2004; Tilley 2000; Sampaio et al. 2012b). Explanations for their inactivity have tended to emphasise the preoccupation of owner-managers with day-to-day operations (McKercher & Robbins 1998), their lack of resources, including knowledge (Vernon et al. 2003; Radwan, Jones & Minoli 2010, 2012) and perceptions that costs might increase as a result of adopting more benign business practices (Dodds & Holmes 2011). There is little evidence of supply chain pressure driving significant environmental reform and consumer demand appears to be having little impact apart from in particular, niche, circumstances (Revell & Blackburn 2007; Kasim & Ismail 2012).

Contemporary theorising and empirical research have resulted in more nuanced readings of the factors influencing small business behaviour in tourism. One important strand of enquiry has been that which has examined lifestyle businesses. Morrison, Carlsen and Weber's (2008) review provides a valuable account of what they term 'lifestyle-oriented small tourism (LOST) firms'. In doing so, they draw attention to various non-economic factors, including the socio-economic context, that shape decisions to form particular kinds of enterprises, and the meanings attached to their business practices by owners. Research on 'commercial home owners' (i.e. those running very small accommodation businesses that are part of their home) by Sweeney and Lynch (2009) develops some of the themes in that context. In essence, this body of work shows that to focus simply on economics is likely to yield limited explanatory insights into the decision-making of small firms in tourism.

Most of the prominent (qualitative) studies of lifestyle businesses draw attention to the distinctive features of the organisations that they have studied and often conclude by promoting a typology as a means of organising their results in a more accessible form (e.g. Tzschentke *et al.* 2008). Typically, these divide small business owners into four or five categories and often incorporate a focus on values as an important dimension of their analysis. Although institutional conditions are alluded to in much of the research cited above, it remains neglected at the expense of a concentration on the role of agency (see Thomas *et al.* 2011; Dorado & Ventresca 2013); a deficiency that is not rectified by this chapter. Developing the work of those who have emphasised the role of values in small business decision-making on environmental matters, Sampaio *et al.* (2012a, 2012b) explain differences in levels of environmental engagement by contrasting not only 'worldviews', which incorporates values, but also self-efficacy (i.e. perceptions of being able to achieve certain goals) and abilities to make sense of and learn from their experience. In this light, they argue that a critical aspect of public policy is to enable those who have a propensity to act to do so by increasing their 'empowerment'. As they note:

> One practical outcome of this research is that environmental programmes aiming to encourage environmental engagement should have 'empowerment' as their ultimate goal. The findings of this research show that empowered (i.e. self-confident and mastery orientated) individuals were much more likely to be engaged in continual environmental improvement. By developing participative policies for empowering individuals rather than simply selling the idea of cost savings, agencies could build the necessary conditions to nurture continual environmental business improvement that appealed to the contrasting community of small businesses in tourism. This implies a fundamental re-thinking among policy-makers of how they approach and seek to influence the behaviour of small firms in tourism. Instead of 'telling' owner-managers what they ought to do, policy-makers might more appropriately develop strategies to empower them to identify the environmental practices best suited to their operation. The development of tailored support could then include a diversity of approaches and measures targeting owner-managers with different patterns of environmental engagement.
>
> (Sampaio et al. 2012a: 247)

It is apparent even from this brief review of the evidence that incentivising small businesses to adopt environmentally and socially benign practices has not been particularly effective. Since the regulation of business behaviour is unpalatable in neoliberal states, commentators have turned to examining the potential value of other means of influencing small businesses in tourism. There is a strong suggestion that engaging in a dialogue that is sensitive to the values of particular businesses, especially where empowerment of the kind described above becomes an outcome, may be more rewarding than simply promoting cost savings as a primary motivator (see also Garay & Font 2012). The remainder of this chapter explores an alternative way of examining the decision-making of small businesses that retains a focus on values with regard to sustainable practices.

Exploring moral framing

Kreps and Monin (2011) propose a categorisation of the moral framing used by actors making decisions imbued with values often associated with sustainability. This is illustrated in Figure

Rhodri Thomas

32.1. Their paper, which is drawn on heavily in this chapter, explores the justifications used for decisions where there is congruence between self-interest (e.g. profit) and wider social concerns (e.g. the environment or local community). Put another way, it is those cases where the outcome would be the same regardless of the justification. A decision to insulate a guest house, for example, may be made primarily to save money or to reduce carbon emissions by being more energy efficient. One concern is that if the motivation is to save money but it is presented as a moral position, it is not likely to be continued if measures to promote sustainability become more expensive.

In Figure 32.1 a distinction is drawn between the public and private, and between the moral and pragmatic framing of organisations' decisions on those things that might be discussed in several ways without affecting the outcome of the decision. In terms of the former, the distinction is whether businesses publicise their decision to engage in a particular activity in ethical terms having also moralised privately (full moralisation) or whether such moralisation only takes place privately. Full moralisation might arise not from anticipated benefits flowing to the business if it is seen to be taking a moral position but because, as a point of principle, the owner feels it is important to declare their position publicly. An equally principled position might lead to owner-managers moralising privately and taking the decision to act in a particular way towards employees or local communities, but then feeling compelled to declare the outcomes of their decisions publicly so as not to be seen to be insensitive to the importance of the issue (again full moralisation).

An absence of moralisation in decision-making (privately or publicly) might arise if owner-managers do not perceive that the issue could be addressed in any terms other than pragmatically. As Kreps and Monin (2011: 105) note: 'because such issues have extremely low moral intensity…they will not be moralized either publicly or privately, simply because it would never occur to anyone to moralize them'. Alternatively, the culture of organisations might lead to a refusal to take decisions on moral grounds.

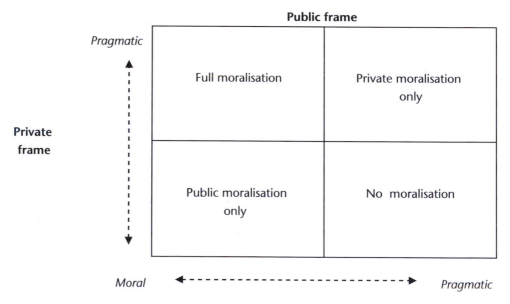

Figure 32.1 Combinations of private and public moralisation

Source: Adapted from Kreps and Monin (2011)

Private moralisation describes those times when an owner-manager moralises privately but is pragmatic (or silent) in public utterances. This may arise from social pressures to conform to certain norms such as being entrepreneurial or to remove the potential for disharmony if public moralising is seen as threatening to group harmony.

In the final category, public moralisation only, the owner-manager may frame an issue as though it were a moral one in public, but privately consider the issue in purely pragmatic terms. In this case, the pressure to conform may arise from being sensitive to the expectations of consumers or others in their business network. For example, small businesses in tourism may feel that they will not be featured or promoted by DMOs unless they adopt the language of sustainability.

Drawing on the work of Butterfield *et al.* (2000), Kreps and Monin (2011) examine the social and psychological factors that might prompt individuals to consider an issue worthy of moralisation (regardless of the outcomes of that moralisation). The first, they note, is based on affect-laden intuition; whether an issue is seen as having a moral dimension will be influenced from an early age. The second they term cognitive 'moral templates' which signal to them that the issue could or should be considered in moral terms. Examples might include a business that systematically excludes certain social groups, which might prompt moral examination of the causes even if nothing changes as a result. The third factor is whether there is a sense that others might be moralising an issue. Clearly, the latter may have a particularly strong influence on public moralisation whereas the former may, less predictably, lead to private or public moralisation. The authors suggest that there are two broad mediating influences: (i) the complexity and reach of the short- and long-term consequences of approaching the decision in a moral way and (ii) when there is a conflict between more than one of the three factors prompting individuals to moralise (e.g. a perception that others are moralising an issue that is not considered to have a moral dimension).

Research on the consequences for small tourism firms of public moralisation would also be valuable. Table 32.1 provides a summary of some potentially positive and negative implications proposed by Kreps and Monin (2011: 114–19). The propositions listed indicate a complex mix of possible outcomes. Positively, from the perspective of the owner-manager, there is the possibility of persuading others of the appropriateness of adopting the moral position, of increasing the popularity of the business by appealing to like-minded consumers and employees, and finally of enabling the owner-manager to avoid guilt at a failure to take action on what is seen as an important social or environmental issue.

By contrast, negative consequences may include perceptions of incompetence (if there is a trade-off between how entrepreneurially oriented and socially oriented businesses are perceived), resentment and accusations of hypocrisy when perceived inconsistencies of management are identified, and the danger for the owner-manager of creating a climate that encourages moralisation within the business by employees beyond what was intended. Examining these propositions from a range of disciplinary perspectives should yield valuable insights into the implications of examining the moral framing of decision-making in small tourism businesses. Although there is some empirical evidence on the consequences of moralisation on larger organisations, little research is available that relates to small firms in tourism. The boxed case study illustrates the issue and suggests the kind of research projects that might be undertaken.

Rhodri Thomas

Table 32.1 Potential consequences of public moralisation

Positive	Persuading others to change behaviour
Increased popularity	
Guilt avoidance	
Negative	Undermining perceptions of competence
Perceptions of hypocrisy	
Intensified moral climate	

Source: Adapted from Kreps and Monin (2011)

Applications to small firms in tourism

The Travel Foundation is a British-based charity created by travel companies to 'enhance the environment, and to improve the well-being of communities in destination countries'. In addition to its advocacy work, it provides toolkits (or advice) for small firms explaining how environmental and social performance might be improved. Its public moralisation epitomises 'doing well by doing good'; there is an emphasis on the cost savings to smaller businesses as well as on the contribution they would make to the welfare of their communities. As the toolkit for tour operators makes clear:

> This step-by-step guide will help you to improve quality, offer more varied, enriched experiences to customers, build greater value into your brand and can also help you reduce costs and operate more efficiently…as well as protecting your most important resource – the destinations that you sell.
>
> *(The Travel Foundation 2013)*

Public agencies that have taken a role in leading tourism policy often make similar observations. A United Nations World Tourism Organization (UNWTO) conference held in Thailand, for example, received 'key messages' from the organisation's Director for the Sustainable Development of Tourism which emphasised the potential of 'green tourism' to reduce costs, satisfy customer demand and to create jobs. Moreover, small and medium-sized enterprises (SMEs) in particular, could expect their competitiveness to be enhanced (UNWTO 2012). Similar perspectives were espoused by several contributors at an Organisation for Economic Co-operation and Development (OECD) sustainable tourism conference (OECD 2012) and by the European Commission Tourism Sustainability Group in passages of its final report dealing with SMEs (European Commission 2007).

There is fragmented evidence in the academic literature of some small firms in tourism who appear to moralise in accordance with the categories listed in Table 32.1. This is illustrated below by taking examples of interview responses quoted in empirical studies of small tourism firms. There are cases where moralisation takes place publicly but is evidently designed to achieve business goals and others which indicate less business instrumentality. Because of the nature of the studies reviewed (i.e. they were all concerned with some aspect of sustainability), there are no illustrations available of owner-managers not identifying an issue as having a moral dimension (even if only for others) when interviewed by researchers.

Full moralisation

...it really got to my conscience, so the next day I phoned the supplier and switched to fair-trade coffee and tea. Now the menus are coming out with fair-trade information, it's in all the rooms so hopefully the message will spread.

(cited in Tzschentke et al. 2008: 129)

(I am) wanting to minimise my impact on the environment and if I can do this and encourage other people to become more aware about the environment and appreciate what we have today and try to improve it for the future

(cited in Poulston & Yiu, 2011: 187)

Private moralisation

I went to Morocco to work. They have nothing in the desert, it's very poor compared to us yet they have so much, their eyes shone and that's because they treasured what they have. Since I got back I've been trying to live with the minimum I need...

(cited in Tzschentke et al. 2008: 129)

My philosophy is that we do what we do which is organics and we do it well. But we don't make a song and dance about it....every business should do what they can to be sensitive to the environment and not try and trade off that and market that to the public.

(cited in Poulston & Yiu 2011: 188)

We're busy on other things. We haven't got the resources to suddenly say 'I know what. I wonder if a new boiler would serve the community'. It's difficult to say (this), but I don't really care.

(restaurant owner-manager cited in Revell & Blackburn 2007: 414)

(separating waste would be) very hard to enforce. On a Saturday night when you've got a restaurant the size we have...we've got 20–25 staff in the building...to stand by the bins and sort of say 'No, not that one. That one there' and at the end of the day you want to grab a plate and shovel the leftovers into a bin.

(restaurant owner-manager cited in Revell & Blackburn 2007: 414)

Public moralisation

Oh we play the game...they'll want to see your environmental policies...your waste management policies...not usually community stuff...whether anyone reads it, I'm not sure. I doubt it, actually.

(business cited in Jenkins 2006: 249)

I want our menu to have a point of difference over other people's menus and by sourcing some organic produce that gives us a difference...I can't really see how it has anything to do with the environment....it is certainly not a reason why I am purchasing organic food. I am not purchasing organic food to save the world.

(cited in Poulston & Yiu 2011: 188)

Perhaps the most interesting cases are those who moralise privately yet do not necessarily communicate their position to consumers, workers or others with whom they come into contact. In this case, they do not have expectations of influencing others or gaining from their moral position. This is quite different from the restaurant and other businesses who moralise publicly, only to make pragmatic business decisions. Not enough is understood at the moment about the role of moralisation in decision-making in small tourism firms and what prompts owner-managers to approach business decisions in this way.

Case Study

Examining moral framing in small tourism firms

Moral framing of decisions in small tourism firms may take several forms from full moralisation to none. Potential examples of these, represented by the comments of various owner-managers, have been found in the published work of academics who have researched small businesses in tourism. This chapter has discussed abstractly some potential triggers for owner-managers choosing to frame a decision pragmatically or morally, even if the outcome would be the same. Little research has been undertaken on this issue to date, however, which constrains the forms of interventions that policy-makers are likely to consider. Greater understanding of why and when small firms in tourism might moralise coupled with an assessment of their consequences might divert attention away from the largely ineffective policy prescriptions advanced currently to more imaginative alternatives.

Potential projects might focus upon these indicative questions:

- What issues are moralised by small firms in tourism?
- When do issues become ones that must be moralised publicly (even if not privately)?
- What are the business models of those that participate in full moralisation?
- Is moralisation a complex process that challenges small business owners?
- Is intervention that engages with cognitive moral templates more likely to yield changes in behaviours than those emerging from affective-laden intuition?

Conclusion

Even though the notion of sustainable tourism has been prominent in academic and certain policy circles for some time, it has attracted scant attention from scholars with an interest in small firms. Important contributions have been made by those who have revealed, *inter alia*, the heterogeneity of operations, the importance of context and the role values can play in determining how owner-managers operate their business. This chapter has promoted a framework for interrogating the connections made between morals (or ethics) and decision-making in small tourism enterprises. It has done so in order to broaden the research agenda that may, in turn, prompt a more fruitful set of policy interventions than those that prevail currently.

Key Reading

Kreps, T.A. and Monin, B. (2011) "Doing well by doing good'? Ambivalent moral framing in organizations', *Research in Organizational Behavior*, 31: 99–123.

Poulston, J. and Yiu, A.Y.K (2011) 'Profits or principles: Why do restaurants serve organic food?', *International Journal of Hospitality Management*, 30: 184–91.

Sampaio, A., Thomas, R. and Font, X. (2012) 'Why are some engaged and not others? Explaining environmental engagement among small firms in tourism', *International Journal of Tourism Research*, 14: 235–49.

Thomas, R., Shaw, G. and Page, S.J. (2011) 'Understanding small firms in tourism: A perspective on research trends and challenges', *Tourism Management*, 32: 963–76.

Tzschentke, N.A., Kirk, D. and Lynch, P. (2008) 'Going green: Decisional factors in small hospitality operations', *International Journal of Hospitality Management*, 27: 126–33.

References

Ateljevic, I. and Doorne, S. (2000) 'Staying within the fence: Lifestyle entrepreneurship in tourism', *Journal of Sustainable Tourism*, 8: 378–92.

Butterfield, K.D., Trevino, L.K. and Weaver, G.R. (2000) 'Moral awareness in business organisations: Influences of issue-related and social context factors', *Human Relations*, 53: 981–1018.

Carlsen, J., Morrison, A. and Weber, P. (2008) Lifestyle oriented small tourism firms, *Tourism Recreation Research*, 33(3), 255–263.

Clarke, J. (2004) 'Trade associations: An appropriate channel for developing sustainable practice in SMEs?', *Journal of Sustainable Tourism*, 12: 194–208.

Dewhurst, H. and Thomas, R. (2003). Encouraging sustainable business practices in a non-regulatory environment: A case study of small tourism firms in a UK national park, *Journal of Sustainable Tourism*, 11(5), 383–403.

Dodds, R. and Holmes, M.R. (2011) 'Sustainability in Canadian B&Bs: Comparing the East versus the West', *International Journal of Tourism Research*, 13: 482–95.

Dorado, S. and Ventresca, M.J. (2013) 'Creative entrepreneurship in complex social problems: Institutional conditions for entrepreneurial engagement', *Journal of Business Venturing*, 28: 69–82.

European Commission (2007) *Action for More Sustainable European Tourism. Report of the Tourism Sustainability Group*. Available at: http://ec.europa.eu/enterprise/sectors/tourism/files/docs/tsg/tsg_final_report_en.pdf (accessed 1 April 2014).

Fleming, P. and Jones, M.T. (2012) *The End of Corporate Social Responsibility: Crisis and Critique*, London: Sage.

Garay, L. and Font, X. (2012) 'Doing good to do well? Corporate social responsibility reasons, practices and impacts in small and medium accommodation enterprises', *International Journal of Hospitality Management*, 31: 329–37.

Jenkins, H. (2006) 'Small business champions for corporate social responsibility', *Journal of Business Ethics*, 67: 241–56.

Kasim, A. and Ismail, A. (2012) 'Environmentally friendly practices among restaurants: Drivers and barriers to change', *Journal of Sustainable Tourism*, 20: 551–70.

Kreps, T.A. and Monin, B. (2011) '"Doing well by doing good"? Ambivalent moral framing in organizations', *Research in Organizational Behavior*, 31: 99–123.

McKercher, B. and Robbins, B. (1998) 'Business development issues affecting nature-based tourism operators in Australia', *Journal of Sustainable Tourism*, 6: 173–88.

Organisation for Economic Co-operation and Development (OECD) (2012) *Green Innovation in Tourism Can Trigger Major Economic, Social and Environmental Benefits*. Available at: www.oecd.org/cfe/greeninnovationintourismcantriggermajoreconomicsocialandenvironmentalbenefits.htm (accessed 5 November 2012).

Poulston, J. and Yiu, A.Y.K. (2011) 'Profits or principles: Why do restaurants serve organics food?', *International Journal of Hospitality Management*, 30: 184–91.

Radwan, H.R.I., Jones, E. and Minoli, D. (2010) 'Managing solid waste in small hotels', *Journal of Sustainable Tourism,* 18: 175–90.

Radwan, H.R.I., Jones, E. and Minoli, D. (2012) 'Solid waste management in small hotels: A comparison of green and non-green small hotels in Wales', *Journal of Sustainable Tourism*, 20: 533–50.

Revell, A. and Blackburn, R. (2007) 'The business case for sustainability? An examination of small firms in the UK's construction and restaurant sectors', *Business Strategy and the Environment*, 16: 404–20.

Sampaio, A., Thomas, R. and Font, X. (2012a) 'Why are some engaged and not others? Explaining environmental engagement among small firms in tourism', *International Journal of Tourism Research*, 14: 235–49.

—— (2012b) 'Small business management and environmental engagement', *Journal of Sustainable Tourism*, 20: 179–93.

Sweeney, M. and Lynch, P.A. (2009). Classifying commercial home hosts based on their relationships to the home, *Tourism and Hospitality Planning & Development*, 6(2), 159–170.

The Travel Foundation (2013) *Greener Tour Operators…A Guide for Small to Medium Sized Businesses.* Available at: www.thetravelfoundation.org.uk/green_business_tools/greener_tour_operators/ (accessed 1 April 2014).

Thomas, R., Shaw, G. and Page, S.J. (2011) 'Understanding small firms in tourism: A perspective on research trends and challenges', *Tourism Management*, 32: 963–76.

Tilley, F. (2000) 'Small firm environmental ethics: How deep do they go?', *Business Ethics: A European Review*, 9: 31–41.

Tzschentke, N.A., Kirk, D. and Lynch, P. (2008) 'Going green: Decisional factors in small hospitality operations', *International Journal of Hospitality Management*, 27: 126–33.

Vernon, J., Essex, S., Pinder, D. and Curry, K. (2003) 'The "greening" of tourism micro-businesses: Outcomes of focus group investigations in South East Cornwall', *Business Strategy and the Environment*, 12: 49–69.

United Nations World Tourism Organization (UNWTO) (2012) *Tourism in the UN Green Economy Report: UNWTO High-level Regional Conference on Green Tourism.* Available at: http://asiapacific. unwto.org/sites/all/files/pdf/2012may_chiangmai_lc_0.pdf (accessed 5 November 2012).

Part 5

Sustainable transport and mobility

33

Sustainable mobility

Erling Holden and Kristin Linnerud

Sustainable development The term was coined in 1987 by the Brundtland Commission as 'development that meets the needs of the present without compromising the ability of future generations to meet their own needs'. Its main characteristics are safeguarding long-term ecological sustainability, satisfying basic human needs, and promoting intragenerational and intergenerational equity.

Sustainable mobility The term was first used in the 1992 EU Green Paper on the Impact of Transport on the Environment. Although no widely accepted definition exists, we suggest that to achieve sustainable mobility, societies must reduce per capita transport energy consumption while simultaneously offering necessary transport services to satisfy basic needs. These services should be based on an affordable and accessible public transport system. Moreover, societies must increase the share of renewable energy used for transport.

Approaches There are three main approaches for achieving sustainable mobility: the efficiency approach, the alteration approach, and the reduction approach. The literature often refers to these approaches as 'improve', 'shift', and 'avoid' strategies.

Policy instruments The goal of achieving sustainable mobility must be accompanied by policy instruments that facilitate its fulfilment; the three main instruments are market-based instruments, information-based instruments, and command-and-control instruments.

Sustainable mobility policies A combination of approaches and policy instruments which potentially can contribute to achieving sustainable mobility.

Introduction

Since launching their 1992 *Green Paper on the Impact of Transport on the Environment*, the European Union has had sustainable mobility as an overriding goal in its transport policy (CEC 1992). Since then, it has continued to pursue this goal in two White Papers (CEC 2001, 2011). In a 1992 Green Paper, the European Union used the term 'sustainable mobility'. Applying the imperative of sustainable development to the transport sector, however, has led to several concepts denoted by terms such as 'sustainable transport', 'sustainable mobility', 'sustainable transportation', 'sustainable transport systems', and 'sustainability issues in transport' (Holden 2007). In the literature on transport and sustainable development, these terms are essentially synonymous. Variants of 'sustainable transport' seem to be the preferred terms in North America, whereas 'sustainable mobility' variants are preferred in Europe (Black 2003). We use 'sustainable mobility' here.

Still, as the European Union emphasizes in its 2011 White Paper, the transport system is not sustainable:

> Looking 40 years ahead, it is clear that transport cannot develop along the same path. If we stick to the business as usual approach, the oil dependence of transport might still be little below 90%, with renewable energy sources only marginally exceeding the 10% target set for 2020. CO_2 emissions from transport would remain one third higher than their 1990 level by 2050. Congestion costs will increase by about 50% by 2050. The accessibility gap between central and peripheral areas will widen. The social costs of accidents and noise would continue to increase.
>
> *(CEC 2011: 4).*

Thus, finding ways to make transport sustainable is high on the political agenda.

This chapter focuses on efforts to achieve sustainable mobility in passenger mobility (including air transport). Nevertheless, these may eventually be relevant for the equally important challenge of achieving sustainable mobility of goods. The chapter has four parts. The first part explains why we presently are facing an unsustainable mobility system. The second shows how the concept of sustainable mobility has changed since its launch in 1992. The third outlines a typology of sustainable mobility. The final part draws attention to a particular challenge regarding sustainable mobility: the already high level of leisure-time mobility and the fast growth of such mobility.

An unsustainable mobility system

For the last 100 years, both population and mobility have grown remarkably. However, whereas population growth shows signs of becoming sustainable, the growth in mobility does not (IEA 2009). While the world's population last century grew by a factor of about four, motorized passenger kilometres and tonne kilometres by all modes each grew on average by a factor of about 100. In particular, mobility has grown extensively during the last four decades. The case study at the end of the chapter shows passenger mobility development in Norway during the twentieth century. A similar pattern exists in the European Union and all other OECD countries (IEA 2009). More than 90 per cent of growth in passenger travel during the last four decades in the European Union (and in other OECD countries) was due to the emergence of two powerful mobility phenomena last century: the private car and later the plane (Black 2003).

The trend of increased travels by road and air is likely to continue for decades (IEA 2012). In a study of future global mobility, Schafer *et al.* (2009) project per-capita mobility in Western Europe to increase from 14,100 passenger kilometres (pkm) yearly in 2005 to 39,100 pkm yearly in 2050. By comparison, they project the average North American's mobility to reach 48,000 km annually by 2050. They reach their conclusions based upon a comprehensive study of travel patterns worldwide, which shows that, on average, a person spends 1.1 hours daily travelling and devotes a predictable fraction of income to travel. These personal travel budgets have been relatively stable across time and countries, and thus Schafer *et al.* (2009) claim that they can be used to predict future travel patterns. Their most important finding is that as we become richer and as technology improves, we will travel faster and further. We would like to add that such will be the case unless scarcity of resources or political decisions prevents us from doing so.

Transport growth has been, according to the OECD, mostly positive: 'It has facilitated and even stimulated just about everything regarded as progress. It has helped expand intellectual horizons and deter starvation. It has allowed efficient production and the ready distribution for widespread consumption. Comfort in travel is now commonplace, as is access to the products of distant places' (OECD 2000: 13). However, the cost – in terms of negative social and environmental impacts – associated with increased motorized mobility by road and air have become increasingly acknowledged. The intensity and scale of these negative impacts have escalated, and are now all too apparent as travel by car and plane has increased. In fact, probably no other activity impacts the environment, both locally and globally, as negatively as transport does. In addition, transport has several negative social impacts:

- Transport is a major consumer of energy and material resources. Almost 30 per cent of worldwide final energy consumption is used for transport. Globally, energy consumption for transport is forecast to grow by 1.5 per cent per year up to 2030. Transport presently uses, and will for decades, mostly non-renewable energy resources (IEA 2010, 2012).
- Producing vehicles and transport infrastructure requires large amounts of materials. Such material use accounts for 20–40 per cent of the consumption of major materials: aggregates, cement, steel, and aluminium. In addition, producing vehicle and transport infrastructure requires large amounts of energy: approximately 20 per cent of the energy consumption during a vehicle's life cycle (OECD 2000; IEA 2009).
- Transport is a major contributor to local, regional, and global pollution of air, soil, and water. Chief among transport's global impacts is its contribution to climate change; transport activity contributes about 20 per cent of anthropogenic CO_2 worldwide and almost 30 per cent of these emissions in OECD countries. Air pollution is the main local and regional impact, with major effects on human and ecosystem health. Transport is a main source of these air pollutants. Air pollution is expected to decline in OECD countries, although not enough to improve air quality to WHO standards. Worldwide, however, air pollution is expected to increase (IEA 2009, 2012).
- Transport infrastructure, mainly roads, consumes about 25–40 per cent of land in OECD urban areas and almost 10 per cent in rural areas. Roads and railways cut natural and agricultural areas into ever-smaller pieces, threatening the existence of wild plants and animals (OECD 2000).
- Yearly, up to 1.2 million people are killed on roads and up to 50 million more are injured. About 30 per cent of the EU's population is exposed to urban traffic noise levels that represent a significant cause of annoyance and ill health. Some 10 per cent of the EU's population is estimated to be seriously annoyed by aircraft noise; however, little change in exposure to high noise levels can be expected during the next decade (Peden *et al.* 2004; OECD 2000).
- Transport infrastructure might disrupt communities. The increasing orientation of urban transport systems toward private vehicles can negatively affect the quality of community life. Urban motorways are sometimes built through established communities, creating physical barriers within them.
- Mobility has not increased for everyone. Lack of access to transport may reduce people's access to basic public and private services, leading to social exclusion, particularly for poor people, disabled people, elderly, women, and the growing number of low-income immigrant groups in developed countries (Root *et al.* 2002; Tillberg 2002; Rudinger 2002; Uteng 2006).

The situation described above characterizes an unsustainable mobility system (Black 2010; Schiller *et al.* 2010; Castillo & Pitfield 2010; Litman & Burwell 2006; Banister 2005; Sperling & Gordon

2009). Without major changes in policies and practices, future transport activity could well continue last century's unsustainable trends. According to the 2011 EU *White Paper on European Transport Policy* (CEC 2011), the principles of sustainable mobility should guide necessary changes in policies and practices: 'a new imperative – sustainable development – offers an opportunity, not to say lever, for adopting the common transport policy' (CEC 2011: 14).

Sustainable mobility: a changing concept

There is, however, as yet no political or scientific agreement on a definition of sustainable mobility. Rather, the concept's focus has, to an increasing extent, reflected socially desirable attributes of local- and project-level problems. A diversity of definitions and interpretations of the concept has been presented; the risk, therefore, is that the concept will become mere rhetoric and of little value in guiding policy makers and scientists. Examples of issues dealt with by these and other studies include: protecting wildlife and natural habitats, reducing noise levels, promoting economic growth, facilitating education and public participation, reducing congestion levels, minimizing accidents and fatalities, ensuring stakeholder satisfaction, enhancing aesthetic dimensions of neighbourhoods, supporting cultural activities, increasing tourism's contribution to GDP, promoting liveable streets and neighbourhoods, and minimizing transport-related crime.

A review shows that the focus of mainstream literature about sustainable mobility indeed has changed during the last two decades (Holden 2007). Sustainable passenger transport problems are being addressed in new ways by researchers representing an increasing number of scientific disciplines applying different methodological approaches (Black & Nijkamp 2002). The concept's definition has changed to include a broader set of passenger transport types like production travel, reproduction travel (e.g. Shiftan *et al.* 2003; Castillo & Pitfield 2010; Amekudzi *et al.* 2009; Banister 2011), and leisure-time travel (e.g. Black & Nijkamp 2002; Mokhtarian 2005; Ory & Mokhtarian 2005; Næss 2006; Banister 2008; Holden & Linnerud 2011). Vilhelmson (1990) distinguishes between three categories of travel: production travel (travel to work and school), reproduction travel (travel to shop and nursery school) and leisure-time travel (travel to recreational activities, on holidays and to visit friends and relatives). This broadening has added to our understanding of the challenges posed by sustainable passenger transport, but has also added to the complexity of how the concept is defined, measured, assessed, and evaluated.

More importantly, the concept's definition has changed to include a broader set of transport's impacts on society. Gudmundsson and Højer (1996) focus on impacts on the environment and social equity. Black (2010) adds impacts on health and security. Lautso & Toivanen (1999) include all these impacts and add quality of life considerations. More recently, several studies have broadened the list of impacts to include economic growth (e.g. Shiftan *et al.* 2003; Castillo & Pitfield 2010; Amekudzi *et al.* 2009).

Thus, sustainable mobility is about to include every aspect of transport which is desirable in society and therefore risks becoming meaningless. To avoid diluting the concept, it may be helpful to clarify the main dimensions of sustainable development by returning to its origin, the Brundtland Report (WCED 1987), and then to adapt these dimensions to sustainable mobility. Based on such clarification and adaptation, we suggest that to achieve sustainable mobility, societies must reduce per capita transport energy consumption while simultaneously offering necessary transport services to satisfy basic needs. These services should be based on an affordable and accessible public transport system. Moreover, societies must increase the share of renewable energy used for transport.

Achieving sustainable mobility: A typology

The main approaches

There are three main approaches for achieving sustainable mobility: the efficiency approach, the alteration approach, and the reduction approach. (In everyday terms, the three approaches can be characterized respectively as 'travel more efficiently', 'travel differently', and 'travel less'.) These three approaches, under different names, represent established knowledge within the sustainable mobility (and sustainable development) literature, for example, the IPAT equation (Commoner 1972; Ehrlich & Holdren 1971); the ASIF equation (Schipper & Lilliu 1999); the ISA model (Dalkmann & Brannigan 2007); the SMART model (Holden 2007); social, technical, and infrastructural emission drivers (Sager *et al.* 2011); and the STPM index (Black 2003).

The efficiency approach for achieving sustainable mobility suggests that environmental problems caused by transport can be reduced and that the lack of accessibility for low-mobility groups can be relieved by developing technology that is more efficient. The concept 'technology' is here used in a broad sense; it includes the use of both 'hard technology' (e.g. developing more efficient vehicle technology and fuels) and 'soft technology' (e.g. developing more efficient transport logistics). Moreover, technology that is more efficient could be implemented in all parts of the transport system: motorized transport, transport infrastructure, and the energy system.

The alteration approach recognizes the urgent need to fundamentally change present transport patterns. Accordingly, the prevailing transport pattern, dominated by the car and the plane, must be changed to one based on collective forms of transport, namely an affordable, well-functioning public transport system. (Although travel by plane is also a collective form of transport, its high energy consumption per passenger kilometre makes it comparable to travel by car). Such a public transport system would lead to increased use of buses, trains, and trams – which are all more energy efficient than cars and planes – and therefore reduce their use. Moreover, an affordable, well-functioning public transport system would increase accessibility for low-mobility groups. In addition, the alteration approach comprises the idea of substituting walking and cycling for motorized travel.

The reduction approach for achieving sustainable mobility does not question the importance of improved efficiency and increased alteration. Indeed, these latter two approaches would, according to the reduction approach, offer some reductions in, for example, energy consumption. However, these reductions are insufficient to meet sustainable mobility's energy goal. Moreover, continuous transport growth negates any reductions in energy consumption achieved by implementing new technology and altering transport patterns. Thus, present transport volume must urgently be decreased – except for those whose basic transport needs are not met – or at least transport growth trends must be changed.

The policy instruments

There are three main policy instruments which facilitate sustainable mobility: market-based instruments, information-based instruments, and command-and-control instruments (Holden 2007; Banister *et al.* 2000). Market-based instruments include taxes and subsidies, which affect our behaviour through their impact on market prices. Ideally, authorities should make all emitters pay a Pigouvian tax (i.e. a tax on emissions equal to its marginal cost to society). An alternative is to use fuel as a proxy for emissions and to levy a differentiated fuel tax. Examples of more indirect ways of addressing the emission problem are to subsidize low-carbon fuels (such as biofuels), to support R&D of low-carbon technologies, and to subsidize public transport. These indirect market-based instruments may, however, have unintended side effects. Subsidizing public transport, for example, may result in some people reducing their use of bicycles (Sandmo 1976).

Information-based instruments involve the assumption that informed consumers will make decisions that are more socially desirable; providing consumers with information that is more detailed concerning the social costs of emissions and concerning the availability of options that are more environmentally friendly will cause them to voluntarily change their behaviour (Stern 1999, 2000). Even if we disregard for the moment the complex relationships between information, attitudes, and behaviour, there are simple examples of possible unintended side effects from using such information-based instruments. If, for example, the information is focused on reducing emissions from one activity (e.g. shifting to more energy-efficient light bulbs), while other mitigating activities are ignored (e.g. reducing the number of flights), then individuals may allocate their mitigation efforts in a way that does not reduce overall emissions.

Control-and-command (CAC) instruments impose standards on products and processes and use physical planning to steer behaviour directly in the desired direction. For instance, authorities could set a minimum vehicular emissions limit or a maximum energy-efficiency level on new cars, they could invest in public transport systems, or they could use land-use planning to reduce travel distances. Again, unintended side effects occur because these policies do not impose equal emissions costs on all emitters. If, for example, a more energy-efficient car will reduce the amount of energy consumed per kilometre, it may also give the driver an incentive to drive further because the fuel cost per kilometre is reduced.

A typology of sustainable mobility policies

A typology for sustainable mobility policies can be constructed using those three approaches and those three policy instruments. Figure 33.1 shows a number of sustainable mobility policies

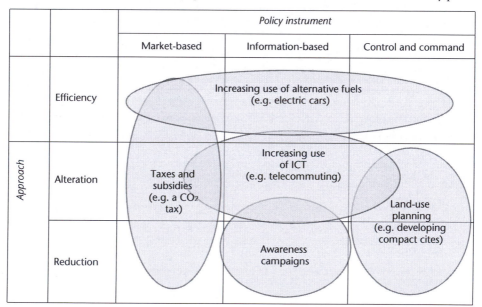

Figure 33.1 A typology for sustainable mobility policies. Each policy (in circles) may be represented by a combination of one or more approaches and one or more policy instruments.

Sources: Holden (2007), Holden and Linnerud (2011). Reprinted by permission of the publishers from 'The Sustainable Mobility Area', in *Achieving Sustainable Mobility* by Erling Holden (Farnham: Ashgate, 2007), p.72. Copyright © 2007.

– a combination of policy approaches and instruments – which can contribute to achieving sustainable mobility.

The policies shown in the figure are chosen due to their prevalence in the literature on sustainable mobility. Moreover, these policies are high on the political agenda in most developed countries.

Troublesome leisure-time travel

Since the 1960s, the growth in leisure-time travel (in particular by car and plane) has increased alarmingly. Although this growth is mostly positive for travellers, it represents a serious challenge for achieving the goal of sustainable mobility.

However, research on leisure-time transport and sustainable development has largely been neglected and is today an underdeveloped field. For example, whereas knowledge of appropriate measures for achieving sustainable *everyday* transport is well established, this is not the case for measures for achieving sustainable *leisure-time* transport (Banister 2005; Black & Nijkamp 2002; Holden 2007). Thus, knowledge is still lacking concerning the complex relation between sustainable mobility, everyday travel, and leisure-time travel.

There are five reasons for increasing the focus on leisure-time travel: First, in the EU and most other developed countries, travel surveys show that leisure-related trips account for one-third of all daily passenger trips (EEA 2008). Due to generally longer average trip lengths, leisure-time travel totals just over half of all daily travel. Moreover, because leisure-time travel – to a larger extent than everyday travel – relies on cars and planes, leisure-time-related energy consumption and CO_2 emissions account for more than 60 per cent of total passenger transport's energy consumption and CO_2 emissions.

Second, as the population ages over the next 20 years, elderly people will spend more time on leisure activities (Banister *et al.* 2000). Much of this may involve long-distance air travel as people have the means, time, and desire to see the world.

Third, as indicated by travel surveys (Holden & Linnerud 2011; Barr *et al.* 2010, Barr, Shaw & Coles 2011), although most of the year people may follow sustainable mobility practices, travelling locally by low-energy modes, they may once (or even twice) yearly travel long distance for leisure, thus negating the positive effects of their sustainable mobility practices. If people cast aside their environmental concerns when travelling for leisure, policy measures like information and awareness campaigns must be rethought.

Fourth, and related to the previous point, a deeper understanding of the factors that influence leisure-time travel is generally lacking. Indeed, leisure has become more than time remaining after work. Instead, it has become a crucial component of our lives (Anable 2002). Thus, the pull and push factors in leisure-time travel decisions tend to be different from those in, say, everyday commuting. Therefore, achieving sustainable mobility requires an understanding of how leisure-time travel differs from other travel.

Fifth, as the understanding deepens, policymaking must change. For example, traditional sustainable mobility policy measures – improved public transport, compact urban form, and green awareness campaigns – are probably less relevant to leisure-time travel. Policy must reflect an understanding of the psychological issues related to leisure-time travel (e.g. leisure-time travel is linked to people's expression of identity). Moreover, leisure-time travel is politically sensitive because it involves notions of freedom, choice, and self-improvement. Sustainable mobility policy measures must reflect all these factors.

Case Study

A study of 'green' attitudes' effect on travel

The study is based on a travel survey of 960 individuals in eight residential areas within the Greater Oslo Region (Holden & Linnerud 2011; Holden & Norland 2005). Variation in energy consumption for everyday and long-distance leisure travel, respectively, was explained in a multiple regression analysis. The explanatory variables included land-use characteristics as well as socioeconomic, sociodemographic, and attitudinal variables.

- *The dependent variables*: Respondents were asked to estimate the distance travelled daily by car, bus, tram, and train in the preceding week. Their estimates were used to measure everyday travel. Moreover, the questionnaire asked respondents to state the number of long-distance leisure trips by plane and car (more than 100 km one way) they had taken during the previous 12 months. All travel distances were converted into yearly energy consumption per individual.
- *The independent variables*: Physical-structural characteristics of the house and the residential area (e.g. type of housing, size, age, access to a private garden, distance from the house to the city centre and nearest sub-centre, housing density, and local land mix); socioeconomic and sociodemographic factors of the household (e.g. sex, age, education, occupation, income, car ownership, and access to a private holiday house); and environmental attitudes (e.g. using a Likert Scale to measure attitude strength, whereby attitudes are measured according to whether a respondent expresses agreement or disagreement with environmental statements).

The analyses (see Figure 33.2) show that respondents who express concern for the environmental consequences of transport have significantly lower household energy consumption related to everyday travel than do other people. However, the concerned individuals travel more by plane for leisure than do others. This contradictory pattern becomes more pronounced (statistically significant), the more specifically the attitudinal variables address environmental issues related to transport. In summary, the overall consumption of energy for transport by people holding positive environmental attitudes is essentially equal to that by people who do not hold such positive environmental attitudes.

To explain the contradictory pattern revealed in Figure 33.2, in-depth interviews of Norwegian households' green attitudes and transport were studied (Holden 2007). The study suggests that there are different mechanisms that influence whether individuals are able to behave in an environmentally friendly way in everyday and leisure travel, respectively. While green individuals strive to act in an environmentally responsible manner in their everyday lives, they seem to have a conflicting need to cast aside their environmental concerns when travelling for leisure. Many respondents indicated that in some situations they have a desire to indulge themselves – to free themselves from the constraints involved in environmentally friendly behaviour. Moreover, they seem to feel that they do their fair share for the environment in their non-leisure time, so they should not have to continue behaving environmentally responsibly during their leisure time. These findings have had a profound influence on sustainable mobility policy based on promoting green attitudes. The finding in the survey and in the in-depth interviews that environmental behaviour depends on the context is supported by findings in a similar UK study by Barr *et al.* (2010).

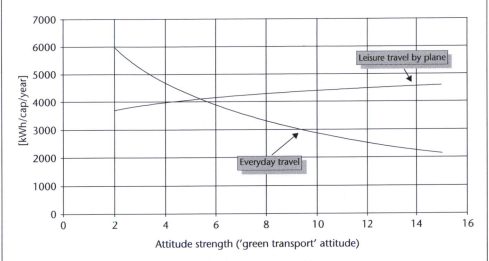

Figure 33.2 Relationship between 'green transport' attitude strength, energy use for everyday travel, and energy use for leisure travel by plane (N = 616)

Source: Holden (2005) 'Attitudes and sustainable household consumption – Household consumption of energy and transport in eight Norwegian residential areas'. The European Network of Housing Research (ENHR) International Housing Conference 2005. Reykjavik, Iceland, 29 June–3 July

Key Reading

Banister, D. (2005) *Unsustainable Transport*, London: Routledge.

Black, W.R. (2010) *Sustainable Transportation: Problems and Solutions*, New York: Guilford Press.

Holden, E. (2007) *Achieving Sustainable Mobility: Everyday and Leisure-Time Travel in the EU*, Aldershot: Ashgate.

Schafer, A., Heywood, J.B., Jacoby, H.D. and Waitz, I.A. (2009) *Transportation in a Climate-Constrained World*, Cambridge, MA: MIT Press.

Schiller, P.L., Bruun, E.C. and Kenworthy, J.R. (2010) *An Introduction to Sustainable Transportation: Policy, Planning, and Implementation*, London: Earthscan.

References

Amekudzi, A.A., Khisty, C.J. and Khayesi, M. (2009) 'Using the sustainability footprint model to assess development impacts of transportation systems', *Transportation Research Part A: Policy and Practice*, 43: 339–48.

Anable, J. (2002) 'Picnics, pets, and pleasant places: The distinguishing characteristics of leisure travel demand', in W.R. Black and P. Nijkamp (eds) *Social Change and Sustainable Transport*, Bloomington: Indiana University Press.

Banister, D. (2005) *Unsustainable Transport*, London: Routledge.

—— (2008) 'The sustainable mobility paradigm', *Transport Policy* 15: 73–80.

—— (2011) 'The trilogy of distance, speed and time', *Journal of Transport Geography*, 19: 950–59.

Banister, D., Stead, D., Steen, P., Åkerman, J., Dreborg, K., Nijkamp, P. and Schleicher-Tappeser, R. (2000) *European Transport Policy and Sustainable Mobility*, London: Spon Press.

Barr, S., Shaw, G., Coles, T.E. and Prillwitz, J. (2010) '"A holiday is a holiday": Practicing sustainability home and away', *Journal of Transport Geography*, 18: 474–81.

Barr, S., Shaw, G. and Coles, T. (2011) 'Times for (Un)sustainability? Challenges and opportunities for developing behaviour change policy. A case-study of consumers at home and away', *Global Environmental Change*, 21: 1234–44.

Black, W.R. (2003) *Transportation: A Geographical Analysis*, London: The Guilford Press.

—— (2010) *Sustainable Transportation: Problems and Solutions*, New York: Guilford Press.

Black, W.R. and Nijkamp, P. (eds) (2002) *Social Change and Sustainable Transport*, Bloomington: Indiana University Press.

Castillo, H. and Pitfield, D.E. (2010) 'ELASTIC – A methodological framework for identifying and selecting sustainable transport indicators', *Transportation Research Part D, Transport and Environment*, 15: 179–88.

Commission of the European Communities (CEC) (1992) *Green Paper on the Impact of Transport on the Environment. A Community Strategy for 'Sustainable Mobility'*, COM (92) 46 Final, Brussels: CEC.

—— (2001) White Paper. *European Transport Policy for 2010: Time to Decide*, COM (2001) 370 Final, Brussels: CEC.

—— (2011) White Paper. *Roadmap to a Single European Transport Area – Towards a Competitive and Resource Efficient Transport System*, COM (2011) 144 Final, Brussels: CEC.

Commoner, B. (1972) 'The environmental cost of economic growth', in R.G. Ridker (ed.) *Population, Resources and the Environment*, Washington DC: Government Printing Office.

Dalkmann, H. and Brannigan, C. (2007) *Transport and Climate Change, A Sourcebook for Policy-Makers in Developing Cities: Module 5e*, Gesellschaft für Technische Zusammenarbeit–GTZ Eschborn.

European Environment Agency (EEA) (2008) *Beyond Transport Policy – Exploring and Managing the External Drivers of Transport Demand*, EEA Technical Report No 12/2008, European Environment Agency.

Ehrlich, P.R. and Holdren, J.P. (1971) 'Impact of population growth', *Science*, 171: 1212–17.

Gudmundsson, H. and Höjer, M. (1996) 'Sustainable development principles and their implications for transport', *Ecological Economics*, 19: 269–82.

Holden, E. (2005) 'Attitudes and sustainable household consumption – Household consumption of energy and transport in eight Norwegian residential areas'. Paper presented at The European Network of Housing Research (ENHR) International Housing Conference 2005. Reykjavik, Iceland, 29 June–3 July.

Holden, E. and Linnerud, K. (2011) 'Troublesome leisure travel: The contradictions of three sustainable transport policies', *Urban Studies*, 48: 3087–3106.

Holden, E. and Norland, I.T. (2005) 'Three challenges for the compact city as a sustainable urban form: Household consumption of energy and transport in eight residential areas in the greater Oslo region', *Urban Studies*, 42: 2145–66.

International Energy Agency (IEA) (2009) *Transport, Energy and CO_2: Moving Toward Sustainability*, Paris: IEA.

—— (2010) *World Energy Outlook 2010*, Paris: IEA.

—— (2012) *Energy Technology Perspectives 2012: Pathways to a Clean Energy System*, Paris: IEA.

Lautso, K. and Toivanen, S. (1999) 'SPARTACUS system for analysing urban sustainability', *Transportation Research Record*, 1670: 35–46.

Litman, T. and Burwell, D. (2006) 'Issues in sustainable transportation', *International Journal of Global Environmental Issues*, 6: 331–47.

Mokhtarian, P.L. (2005) 'Travel as a desired end, not just a means', *Transportation Research Part A: Policy and Practice*, 39: 93–96.

Næss, P. (2006) *Urban Structure Matters*, Abingdon: Routledge.

Organisation for Economic Co-operation and Development (OECD) (2000) *Environmentally Sustainable Transport, Futures, Strategies and Best Practices*, Synthesis Report of the OECD project on Environmentally Sustainable Transport EST: Organisation for Economic Co-operation and Development.

Ory, D.T. and Mokhtarian, P.L. (2005) 'When is getting there half the fun? Modelling the liking for travel', *Transportation Research Part A: Policy and Practice*, 39: 97–123.

Peden, M., Scurfield, R., Sleet, D., Mohan, D., Hyder, A.A., Jarawan, E. and Mathers, C. (eds) (2004) *World Report on Road Traffic Injury Prevention*, Geneva: World Health Organization.

Root, A., Schintler, L. and Button, K. (2002) 'Women and travel: The sustainability implications of changing roles', in W.R. Black and P. Nijkamp (eds) *Social Change and Sustainable Transport*, Bloomington: Indiana University Press.

Rudinger, G. (2002) 'Mobility behaviour of the elderly: Its impacts on the future road traffic system', in W.R. Black and P. Nijkamp (eds) *Social Change and Sustainable Transport*, Indiana, USA: Indiana University Press.

Sager, J., Apte, J.S., Lemoine, D.M. and Kammen, D.M. (2011) 'Reduce growth rate of light-duty vehicle travel to meet 2050 global climate goals', *Environmental Research Letters*, 6: 024018.

Sandmo, A. (1976) 'Direct versus indirect Pigouvian taxation', *European Economic Review*, 7: 337–49.

Schafer, A., Heywood, J.B., Jacoby, H.D. and Waitz, I.A. (2009) *Transportation in a Climate-Constrained World*, Cambridge, MA: MIT Press.

Schiller, P.L., Bruun. E.C. and Kenworthy, J.R. (2010) *An Introduction to Sustainable Transportation: Policy, Planning, and Implementation*, London: Earthscan.

Schipper, L. and Lilliu, C.M. (1999) *Transportation and CO$_2$ Emissions: Flexing the Link. A Path for the World Bank*, Washington: The World Bank.

Shiftan, Y., Kaplan, S. and Hakkert, S. (2003) 'Scenario building as a tool for planning a sustainable transportation system', *Transportation Research Part D: Transport and Environment*, 8: 323–42.

Sperling, D. and Gordon, D. (2009) *Two Billion Cars*, New York: Oxford University Press.

Stern, P.C. (1999) 'Information, incentives, and proenvironmental consumer behavior', *Journal of Consumer Policy*, 22: 461–78.

—— (2000) 'Toward a coherent theory of environmentally significant behavior', *Journal of Social Issues*, 56: 407–24.

Tillberg, K. (2002) 'Residential location and daily mobility patterns: A Swedish case study of households with children', in W.R. Black and P. Nijkamp (eds) *Social Change and Sustainable Transport*, Indiana, USA: Indiana University Press.

Uteng, T.P. (2006) 'Mobility: Discourses from the non-western immigrant groups in Norway', *Mobilities*, 1: 435–62.

Vilhelmson, B. (1990) *Vår Dagliga Rörlighet. Om Resandes Utveckling, Fördelning Och Gränser (Our Daily Mobility. On the Development, Distribution and Limits of Travelling)*, TFB Report 16, Stockholm: The Swedish Transport Board.

World Commission on Environment and Development (WCED) (1987) *Our Common Future*, Oxford: Oxford University Press.

34

The role of aviation in sustainable development of tourism

Paul Peeters and Rob Bongaerts

Sustainable aviation essentially is making use of best available technology, logistics and low-carbon fuels and showing reduced growth or decline of demand toward higher eco-efficiency.

Sustainable tourism cannot develop with an increasing share of air transport.

Sustainability is difficult to assess for most environmental problems caused by aviation except for climate change and to some extent biodiversity.

Introduction

Tourism is much older than air transport. Travel was already a widespread phenomenon during Roman times (Perrottet 2002), when flying was just a myth. Modern tourism started in the nineteenth century due to the invention of rail transport (Prideaux 2001). Air transport emerged in the 1920s, but initially was only for the elite until the introduction of jet aircraft and cheap flight in the 1960s (Prideaux 2001). Tourism often is strongly associated with air transport as if it is the most used transport mode. From statistics this appears not to be the case. Of all 4.8 billion (domestic and international) tourism trips in 2005 just 18% were by air, 43% were by car and the remainder by train, coach or ship (UNWTO-UNEP-WMO 2008). Though the use of air transport is increasing faster than other transport modes, it is envisaged that, even in 2035, the car will still be the most important (UNWTO-UNEP-WMO 2008). Air transport's share in total distance travelled in tourism was 44% and may rise to 68% by 2035 (based on UNWTO-UNEP-WMO 2008). The average distance of tourism trips has increased from about 200 km return in 1900 to almost 1,800 km return in 2005; this is still exponentially rising by about 2.2% per year (Peeters 2013).

Air transport has provided access to many remote places in the world and, to some extent, made the economies of these places fully dependent on long-haul tourism. But the long distances associated with air travel have implications for tourism's impact on the environment, specifically on fossil energy consumption, greenhouse gas emissions, biodiversity at a global level and noise and air quality at the local (airport) level.

According to Zaporozhets *et al.* (2011) the main environmental impacts of aviation are noise nuisance, local air quality (air pollution) and climate change, though there are also issues of land-use, landscape quality and water quality. The three main environmental impacts differ in almost all of their characteristics. Where as noise and air quality typically are localized directly around airports, the impact of climate change is global and independent of the place of emissions. The noise problem was acknowledged in the 1960s after the introduction of the first jets plus the fast growth of air navigation caused serious problems at airports around the world (Zaporozhets *et al.* 2011). Air quality issues are more recent, while the contribution of aviation to climate change was only widely acknowledged with an IPCC special report issued in 1999 (Penner *et al.* 1999). While noise and air quality typically are short-term problems, climate change, though happening now, is mainly of the medium to long term, lasting up to centuries (Lee *et al.* 2010). Noise and air quality directly affect people's health. Greenhouse gases generally have no direct health impact but cause climate change that deteriorates the health of the earth's systems causing a range of socio-economic and ecological issues (IPCC 2007). Finally, the ways of calculating the impact differs (see methods section).

An increasing number of small island states are highly dependent on long-haul international tourism for their exports (Pentelow & Scott 2011). So, in social economic terms, such long-haul travel could be called 'sustainable'. However, the amount of greenhouse gas emissions associated with long-haul travel is actually prohibitive (Scott *et al.* 2010). Based on the triple bottom line, planet, people and profit (the 'triple P' concept) (Elkington 1994), this means that economic development based on long-haul travel (profit and people) is at odds with sustainable environmental development (planet). Still, in the tourism and air transport sectors, the link between air transport and poverty alleviation forms a strong discourse against measures affecting our transport demand (Peeters & Eijgelaar 2013).

Environmental impacts of aviation

Methods

Assessing the environmental sustainability of aviation starts with calculating the environmental impact. The basic method to do so is rather straightforward: simply multiply emission factors by the total transport volume and you get the total emissions (see e.g. Peeters & Williams 2009 for greenhouse gas emissions). However, emissions have a complex relationship with environmental impact. For instance, air quality emissions have to be translated to an impact on the concentration of the pollutant in the local atmosphere; this is a function of diffusion of the pollutant over a wider space, local weather, and complex atmospheric chemistry (Sicard *et al.* 2010). The emissions of CO_2 are more easily related to the concentration of CO_2 in the global atmosphere as it will always fully diffuse. However, aviation also causes a range of other impacts on the climate, including the impact of NO_x, water vapour, sulphate and soot aerosols, contrails and contrail-induced cirrus, which have an immediate, generally short-lived but very powerful impact on climate (Lee *et al.* 2009). Assessing the impact of noise requires complicated model studies in which the noise footprints of all aircraft movements around an airport must be translated to an average noise level, weighted for time of the day and night, on all people living and working within the area. Aviation noise is expressed in decibels (dB), the logarithm of sound pressure (Mahashabde *et al.* 2011). Because the sensitivity of the human ear varies over the frequency range, the noise value is weighted to create a noise indicator that represents perceived noise, not just physical noise. A commonly used weighing method is the A-weighted scale measured in dB(A). An additional problem is that noise around an airport is discontinuous:

it consists of a whole series of single-events (aircraft landing or taking off). By averaging these noise levels over a certain period, the equivalent sound level (ESL) is calculated and constitutes a common cumulative noise metric (Mahashabde *et al.* 2011). The A-weighted day-night-level (DNL), which weighs night-time noise events by adding an additional 10 dB(A), is a commonly used measure in aviation noise assessments. Knowing the noise footprint is just the starting point for assessing the nuisance and health impacts. Important factors are not only the volume of air traffic, but also the density of the population, average wind direction, landscape, the quality of buildings, and the general acceptance of aviation by the population (Kroesen *et al.* 2008). An overview of noise methods is given by Zaporozhets *et al.* (2011), air quality assessments by Mahashabde *et al.* (2011) and greenhouse gas emissions by Peeters and Williams (2009) and Lee (2009).

Noise

Both noise and air quality are local environmental problems that mainly affect the direct surroundings of airports. Aviation noise of less then 40 dB DNL causes almost no annoyance, while a level of 65 dB DNL may, on average, cause annoyance to 30% of the population, though varying up to 75% (Mahashabde *et al.* 2011). In 2010, 24 million people were affected by more than 50 dB DNL (Fleming *et al.* 2007). Large achievements in noise nuisance reductions were made with respect to the start of the jet era in the 1960s. At that time the number of affected people was twenty times larger than it is now (Mahashabde *et al.* 2011). The reduction was caused by regulation, but this is now levelling off or even being reversed. Due to the continued growth of air transport volumes the number of affected people is expected to reach 30 million by 2025 (Fleming *et al.* 2007). Noise levels above 65 dB DNL may cause serious health problems and are estimated to affect some 2 million people in the world (Fleming *et al.* 2007). According to the European Environment Agency (EEA) almost 5 million people in the EU are seriously affected by aircraft noise (about 1% of the whole population) (EEA 2011). For comparison: the number of EU population affected by road noise is 20 times higher. The problem is typically local and many of the main airports are now capacity restricted due to large noise footprints (Zaporozhets *et al.* 2011).

Air quality

Of all aircraft engine emissions about 70% consist of CO_2, 29% of water vapour and only 1% of other emissions, mainly NO_x, carbon monoxide (CO), hydro-carbons (HC) and a range of other air pollutants like particulates and black smoke. The total share of emissions caused by aviation in all local air pollutants is less than 1% (FAA Office of Environment and Energy 2005). Again this share can be very significant around large airports, because airports attract large numbers of car and coach transport at the land-side. According to the FAA Office of Environment and Energy (2005), the emission factors (emissions per seat-kilometre, kg/skm) have reduced over time, but for most pollutants, the growth of air transport demand was larger and caused overall effects to increase.

Climate change

The current contribution of aviation to CO_2 emissions is relatively small at between 2% and 3% (Owen *et al.* 2010). However, the non-carbon impacts on radiative forcing are much larger and total current impact of the aviation industry since 1945 has been estimated to range between

2% and 14% of total man-made radiative forcing (Lee *et al.* 2009). Within the tourism sector, air transport in 2005 had a share of 40% of CO_2 emissions and a share of up to 75% in terms of radiative forcing (UNWTO-UNEP-WMO 2008). However, the main issue is the inability of the aviation sector to improve fuel efficiency faster than demand is growing (Scott *et al.* 2010). One of the main problems of air transport is that it is not just replacing existing surface transport but very much involves a simultaneous mode shift and destination choice shift. Fast transport automatically results in very significant increases in distance per trip caused by the travel time budget that assumes the population average of travel time to a constant (Schäfer 2009; Peeters & Landré 2012). This means that air transport–related emissions are still fast increasing, while at the same time a very strong reduction is required to avoid 'dangerous climate change' (Scott *et al.* 2010). Dangerous climate change has been coined as climate change causing more than a 2°C temperature rise (Schellnhuber *et al.* 2006; Parry *et al.* 1996). Scott *et al.* (2010) show that in a business as usual scenario which includes trends of fuels efficiency improvements based on historic developments the emissions of tourism will surpass the total reducing human emissions by about 2050.

Case Study

Sustainability at Air France-KLM

Being ranked first in the aviation sector of the Dow Jones Sustainability Index, AF-KLM has a reputation for mitigating its environmental impact. In its strategic approach, the company adopted five key issues: combating climate change, minimizing environmental impact, building sustainable relationships with customers, promoting a responsible human resources policy and contributing to local development. The issues mentioned in this chapter: noise, local air quality and climate change are covered by the first two strategic issues. All three issues are, to a large extent, related to aircraft type and fleet age. In the financial year 2011, the average fleet age at AF-KLM was 9.9 years, where the average for all IATA members was 11 years. When we look at the main competitors in their main market, Europe (35% of its revenues are intra-European flights), we see Ryanair and Turkish Airlines having an average fleet age of around four years and 5.6 years respectively. Two other competitors use older aircraft: Lufthansa (11.2 years) and British Airways (13 years).

Noise

Both Air France and KLM have achieved serious noise reduction by adopting a policy called 'Balanced Approach', which comprises a combination of several measures: removing noisy aircraft, increasing flying altitudes, using parallel runways, changing flight paths and introducing Continuous Descent Approach procedures for all its flights. Figure 34.1 shows the achievements for AF-KLM with 2000 as base year. The airline group managed to achieve a decrease in noise levels by 34%, while movements increased by 11%.

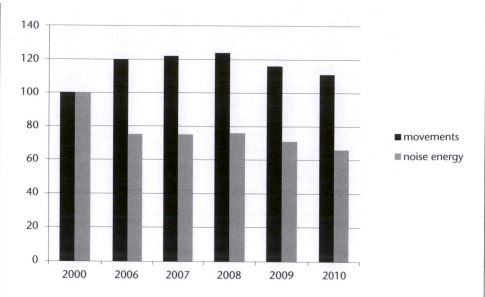

Figure 34.1 Comparing aircraft movements and noise energy (based on Air France and KLM Royal Dutch Airlines 2011: 33)

Local air quality

Local air quality is affected by both aircraft movements and the use of ground transport. The measures taken for noise reduction also affect the air quality in a positive way. At the end of 2010, 45% of Air France's ground equipment was powered by electricity. Air France committed itself to a reduction of commuting transport in the Paris Area, resulting in a 7% decline in car use in 2011 compared to 2005. KLM achieved a 4.8% energy efficiency over 2009 and 2010, mainly achieved by improving operational procedures at Schiphol Airport. This led to better air quality. In 2011, KLM restricted the use of Auxiliary Power Units. Now, the energy necessary for all procedures is delivered by ground support equipment.

Climate change

Every kilogram of fuel burnt causes emissions of 3.2 kg of CO_2, the main greenhouse gas causing climate change. Airlines take numerous measures to reduce emissions, because of the ever-rising cost of fuel. So far, the company has not managed to reduce absolute carbon emissions levels. Between 2001 and 2010 traffic increased by 18%, whereas carbon emissions rose by 4% (Air France and KLM Royal Dutch Airlines 2011: 25). So the company is getting more fuel efficient, but efficiency gains are offset by traffic growth. Carbon neutral growth, an IATA goal for 2050, can only be achieved by using biofuels. AF-KLM is involved in research projects to explore several biofuel options. In June 2011, KLM launched a flight that partly used biofuel.

Other environmental impacts

Air transport causes several other environmental problems like land-use change, water pollution, waste and the discharge of hazardous materials. Most other environmental impacts are relatively small at the global scale. CSR reports of Airports (Schiphol Group 2012), Aircraft manufacturers (EADS 2012) and Airlines (Air France & KLM Royal Dutch Airlines 2012) give more information on these issues. However, be careful when interpreting the information provided in these CSR reports. Though in itself correct, the information is not always put into context. For instance, the total CO_2 emissions caused by operations at Schiphol Airport are reported as 0.1 million metric tonnes (Schiphol Group 2012). This is not very significant compared to the total of 11 million tonnes of CO_2 emissions associated with total Dutch kerosene bunkers sold (CBS 2013). Airbus claims to have reduced the impact on the environment of its production facilities (EADS 2012), but the CSR report fails to mention that operations of an aircraft like the airbus A320 causes 99.9% of the ecological footprint leaving less than 0.1% for manufacturing (Howe *et al.* 2013).

The role of air transport as a vector of diseases has been recognized from as early as 1939 (Whitfield 1939), and is gaining importance with more recent outbreaks like the SARS (severe acute respiratory syndrome) epidemic (Gerencher 2010). Evidence is also mounting that air transport plays a role in the dispersion of alien species including pests (Hulme 2009) which directly threaten biodiversity (EEA 2010).

Sustainable tourism and air transport

Mitigating aviation's emissions

Aviation emissions can be mitigated in four main ways: improving fuel efficiency; advancing operational efficiency; shifting to alternative fuels like biofuels; and implementation of market-based instruments like emission trading, taxes and offsets to temporize demand growth. History shows an improvement of fuel efficiency by 70% between 1960 and 2000 (Peeters & Middel 2007), but the rate of improvement is slowing down (Peeters 2010; Peeters & Middel 2007). Alternative fuels like biofuels have the potential to reduce the carbon footprint for a given amount of air transport (Sgouridis *et al.* 2010). However, they do not reduce emissions to zero as their carbon footprints are assumed to be between 30% and 80% lower on a life-cycle basis (Sgouridis *et al.* 2010). Total capacity to grow biofuels is limited by land-use, food production, nutrients and water constraints (Sims *et al.* 2011). Algae are currently considered a promise for the future (Stephens *et al.* 2010), but a couple of years ago this was also the case for Jatropha nuts, although these promises were not substantiated (Kant & Wu 2011).

Market-based measures refer to taxes and emission trading. Both national taxes on departures and the EU ETS (emission trading system) are not expected to deliver a large impact on demand (Mayor & Tol 2010a). For the ETS this may be due to the rather moderate carbon cost assumption of €23/tCO_2. Due to allowances that are far too generous, the ETS has struggled to generate a reasonable price (Zhang & Wei 2010). It is likely that a trading system capped to a more ambitious reduction of emissions will generate far higher carbon prices (Mandell 2011) and thus have a more significant impact (Scheelhaase *et al.* 2010).

International regulation

One problem within aviation is its international character, making it difficult to regulate emissions. This challenge was taken up by the International Civil Aviation Organization

(ICAO), founded in 1944 at the Chicago convention about international civil aviation (ICAO 2013b). ICAO currently has 192 members, comprising all countries with an aviation industry. The environmental regulations are binding for all member states and were developed by the Committee on Aviation Environmental Protection (CAEP), which was established by the Council in 1983. Before that there were commissions dedicated to noise (Committee on Aircraft Noise, CAN) and engine emissions (Committee on Aircraft Engine Emissions, CAEE (ICAO 2013a). The environmental rules are published in Annex 16 (Environmental Protection) to the *Convention on International Civil Aviation*. Volume I of this Annex gives certification standards for Aircraft Noise (ICAO 2008a) and Volume II for Aircraft Engine Emissions (ICAO 2008b). In October 2010, the 37th Assembly (Resolution A37–19) requested the development of an ICAO CO_2 Emissions Standard (ICAO 2012), which has resulted, so far, in a metric system established on 11 July 2012.

Another approach developed by ICAO is to establish global market-based measures (MBMs) like a global trading system. So far, progress has not been published. There is, however, strong pressure from the EU to deliver, because it has temporarily delayed the inclusion of carbon emissions of non-EU airlines flying to or within EU airspace on the condition that the ICAO delivers structural MBMs by November 2013.

Sustainable tourism scenarios

Several studies have looked at global tourism mitigation scenarios. A recent study (Vorster *et al.* 2012) showed an interesting qualitative analysis of four future scenarios for tourism and aviation. The scenarios are divided over two axes: frozen technology versus carbon-neutral aviation and strict limits versus a lax regime. The carbon-neutral aviation, combined with the strict limits, is the only scenario avoiding dangerous climate change. In this scenario, both tourism and air traffic revenue passenger kilometres (rpk) are increasing unhampered. The scenario is based on the sector's 'carbon neutral' future (ATAG 2005); however, this is unlikely to materialize (Lee *et al.* 2013). Peeters and Dubois (2010) show that tourism demand (i.e. number of trips) can grow as in business as usual, but only under one of two different conditions. Either most car transport shifts to environmentally friendlier electric rail while retaining 2005 levels of global air transport or the car can be used at current shares, but than air transport demand needs to reduce to the level of the 1970s. Several other scenario studies show just an increase of emissions from aviation (Mayor & Tol 2010b; UNWTO-UNEP-WMO 2008). Also Vorster *et al.* (2012) support the idea to decouple tourism and air transport growth and place more emphasis on short-haul markets.

Conclusion

Aviation covers about 17% of all tourism trips, so the role of aviation is significant, even though the car still forms the backbone of tourism. With respect to environmental impact, aviation has a much larger share – up to 75% of the impact of tourism on climate change. Though current share in climate change is moderate, the main problem is the strong growth of greenhouse emissions. Both climate change and biodiversity loss belong to the main global threats to the stability of earth ecosystems (Rockstrom *et al.* 2009). Therefore, 'sustainability' is the best goal for climate change to supply a clear emission reduction path giving a concrete meaning to sustainability. Local impacts: noise and air quality, cannot be defined in such clear terms.

Clearly, tourism is not developing sustainably because of its increasing impact on climate change. The main reason for this is the strong demand for air transport and the concomitant increase of distances travelled per trip. If the tourism sector really seeks to become sustainable it should try to decouple the growth in tourism from the growth in (air) transport travel distances. One way to achieve this is by assessing the eco-efficiency of product portfolios for tour operators and source markets for destinations, and shift both towards a higher eco-efficiency, thus generating more value for fewer emissions (Gössling *et al.* 2005). For the transition to happen, a shift of policies away from demand following air transport investments towards (high and low speed) rail infrastructure and measures impacting transport mode choice away from air transport could be combined with destination policies shifting from long haul to more medium- and short-haul source markets.

Key Reading

Gössling, S. and Upham, P. (2009) *Climate Change and Aviation: Issues, Challenges and Solutions*, London: Earthscan.

Mahashabde, A., Wolfe, P., Ashok, A., Dorbian, C., He, Q, Fan, A., Lukachko, S., Mozdzanowska, A., Wollersheim, C., Barrett, S.R.H., Locke, M. and Waitz, I.A. (2011) 'Assessing the environmental impacts of aircraft noise and emissions', *Progress in Aerospace Sciences*, 47: 15–52.

Upham, P. (2003) *Towards Sustainable Aviation*. London: Earthscan.

Zaporozhets, O., Tokarev, V. and Attenborough, K. (2011) *Aircraft Noise: Assessment, Prediction and Control*, Oxford: Spon Press.

References

Air France and KLM Royal Dutch Airlines (2011) *Together Open & Committed: Corporate Social Responsibility Report 2010–2011*, Paris/Amsterdam: Air France/KLM.

—— (2012) *The Group in 2011: Corporate Social Responsibility Report*, Paris/Amsterdam: Air France/KLM.

Air Transport Action Group (ATAG) (2005) *Aviation & Environment Summit Discussion Paper*, Geneva: Air Transport Action Group.

Centraal Bureau voor de Statistiek (CBS) (2013) *Statline*. The Hague: Centraal Bureau voor de Statistiek. Available at: http://statline.cbs.nl/StatWeb/start.asp?LA=nl&DM=SLNL&lp=Search/Search (accessed 1 May 2013).

Elkington, J. (1994) 'Towards the sustainable corporation: Win-win-win business strategies for sustainable development', *California Management Review*, 36: 90–100.

European Aeronautic Defence and Space Company (EADS) (2012) *Responsibility Made by EADS: EADS 2011 Corporate Responsibility & Sustainability Report*. Leiden: European Aeronautic Defence and Space Company EADS N.V.

European Environment Agency (EEA) (2010) *EU 2010 Biodiversity Baseline*, Copenhagen: European Environment Agency, No. 12.

—— (2011) *Laying the Foundations for Greener Transport. TERM 2011: Transport Indicators Tracking Progress Towards Environmental Targets in Europe*, EEA Report No. 7. Copenhagen: European Environment Agency.

Federal Aviation Administration (FAA) Office of Environment and Energy (2005) *Aviation & Emissions: A Primer*, Washington DC: Federal Aviation Administration, Office of Environment and Energy.

Fleming, G., Malwitz, A., Balasubramanian, S., Roof, C., Grandi, F., Kim, B., Usdrowski, S., Elliff, T., Eyers, C. and Lee, D. (2007) 'Trends in global noise and emissions from commercial aviation for 2000 through 2025', *7th USA/Europe Air Traffic Management R&D Seminar*, Barcelona.

Gerencher, C.L. (2010) *TRB Conference Proceedings: Research on the Transmission of Disease in Airports and on Aircraft: Summary of a Symposium*, Washington DC, 0738–6826.

Gössling, S. and Upham, P. (2009) *Climate Change and Aviation: Issues, Challenges and Solutions,* London: Earthscan.

Gössling, S., Peeters, P., Ceron, J.P., Dubois, G., Patterson, T. and Richardson, R.B. (2005) 'The eco-efficiency of tourism', *Ecological Economics,* 54: 417–34.

Howe, S., Kolios, A.J. and Brennan, F.P. (2013) 'Environmental life cycle assessment of commercial passenger jet airliners', *Transportation Research Part D: Transport and Environment,* 19: 34–41.

Hulme, P.E. (2009) 'Trade, transport and trouble: Managing invasive species pathways in an era of globalization', *Journal of Applied Ecology,* 46: 10–18.

Intergovernmental Panel on Climate Change (IPCC) (2007) *Climate Change 2007: Impacts, Adaptation and Vulnerability. Working Group II Contribution to the Intergovernmental Panel on Climate Change. Fourth Assessment Report,* Geneva: IPCC.

International Civil Aviation Organization (ICAO) (2008a) *Annex 16 to the Convention on International Civil Aviation: Environmental Protection, Volume I, Aircraft Noise,* Montreal, ISBN 978-92-9231-108-7.

—— (2008b) *Annex 16 to the Convention on International Civil Aviation: Environmental Protection, Volume II, Aircraft Engine Emissions,* Montreal: ICAO.

—— (2012) *Aircraft CO_2 Emissions Standard Metric System: ICAO Fact Sheet,* ICAO.

—— (2013a) *Committee on Aviation Environmental Protection (CAEP),* Montreal. Available at: www.icao.int/environmental-protection/pages/CAEP.aspx (accessed 29 April 2013).

—— (2013b) *Homepage,* Montreal. Available at: www.icao.int/ (accessed 29 April 2013).

Kant, P. and Wu, S. (2011) 'The extraordinary collapse of Jatropha as a global biofuel', *Environmental Science & Technology,* 45: 7114–15.

Kroesen, M., Molin, E.J. and van Wee, B. (2008) 'Testing a theory of aircraft noise annoyance: A structural equation analysis', *The Journal of the Acoustical Society of America,* 123: 4250.

Lee, D.S. (2009) 'Aviation and climate change: The science', in S. Gössling and P. Upham (eds) *Climate Change and Aviation: Issues, Challenges and Solutions,* London: Earthscan.

Lee, D.S., Fahey, D.W., Forster, P.M., Newton, P.J., Wit, R.C.N., Lim, L.L., Owen, B. and Sausen, R. (2009) 'Aviation and global climate change in the 21st century', *Atmospheric Environment,* 43: 3520–37.

Lee, D.S., Pitari, G., Grewe, V., Gierens, K., Penner, J.E., Petzold, A., Prather, M.J., Schumann, U., Bais, A., Berntsen, T., Iachetti, D., Lim, L.L. and Sausen, R. (2010) 'Transport impacts on atmosphere and climate: Aviation', *Atmospheric Environment,* 44: 4678–4734.

Lee, D.S., Lim, L.L. and Owen, B. (2013) *Bridging the Aviation CO_2 Emissions Gap: Why Emissions Trading is Needed,* Manchester: Manchester Metropolitan University. Available at: www.cate.mmu.ac.uk/wp-content/uploads/Bridging_the_aviation_emissions_gap_010313.pdf (accessed 4 March 2013).

Mahashabde, A., Wolfe, P., Ashok, A., Dorbian, C., He, Q., Fan, A., Lukachko, S., Mozdzanowska, A., Wollersheim, C., Barrett, S.R.H., Locke, M. and Waitz, I.A. (2011) 'Assessing the environmental impacts of aircraft noise and emissions', *Progress in Aerospace Sciences,* 47: 15–52.

Mandell, S. (2011) 'Carbon emission values in cost benefit analyses', *Transport Policy,* 18: 888–92.

Mayor, K. and Tol, R.S.J. (2010a) 'The impact of European climate change regulations on international tourist markets', *Transportation Research Part D: Transport and Environment,* 15: 26–36.

—— (2010b) 'Scenarios of carbon dioxide emissions from aviation', *Global Environmental Change,* 20: 65–73.

Owen, B., Lee, D.S. and Lim, L. (2010) 'Flying into the future: Aviation emissions scenarios to 2050', *Environmental Science & Technology,* 44: 2255–60.

Parry, M.L., Carter, T.R. and Hulme, M. (1996) 'What is a dangerous climate change?', *Global Environmental Change,* 6: 1–6.

Peeters, P. (2010) 'Tourism transport, technology, and carbon dioxide emissions', in C. Schott (ed.) *Tourism and the Implications of Climate Change: Issues and Actions,* Bingley (UK): Emerald.

—— (2013) 'Developing a long-term global tourism transport model using a behavioural approach: Implications for sustainable tourism policy making', *Journal of Sustainable Tourism,* 21: 1049–69.

Peeters, P.M. and Dubois, G. (2010) 'Tourism travel under climate change mitigation constraints', *Journal of Transport Geography,* 18: 447–57.

Peeters, P. and Eijgelaar, E. (2013) 'Tourism's climate mitigation dilemma: Flying between rich and poor countries', *Tourism Management.* 40: 15–26.

Peeters, P. and Landré, M. (2012) 'The emerging global tourism geography – An environmental sustainability perspective', *Sustainability,* 4: 42–71.

Peeters, P.M. and Middel, J. (2007) 'Historical and future development of air transport fuel efficiency', in R. Sausen, A. Blum, D.S. Lee and C. Brüning (eds) *Proceedings of an International Conference on Transport,*

Atmosphere and Climate (TAC); Oxford, United Kingdom, 26th to 29th June 2006. Oberpfaffenhoven: DLR Institut für Physic der Atmosphäre.

Peeters, P. and Williams, V. (2009) 'Calculating emissions and radiative forcing: Global, national, local, individual', in S. Gössling and P. Upham (eds) *Climate Change and Aviation: Issues, Challenges and Solutions,* London: Earthscan.

Penner, J.E., Lister, D.H., Griggs, D.J. Dokken, D.J. and McFarland, M. (eds) (1999) *Aviation and the Global Atmosphere: A Special Report of IPCC Working Groups I and III,* Cambridge: Cambridge University Press.

Pentelow, L. and Scott, D.J. (2011) 'Aviation's inclusion in international climate policy regimes: Implications for the Caribbean tourism industry', *Journal of Air Transport Management,* 17: 199–205.

Perrottet, T. (2002) *Pagan Holiday: On the Trail of Ancient Roman Tourists,* New York: Random House Trade Paperbacks.

Prideaux, B. (2001) 'Links between transport and tourism – past, present and future', in B. Faulkner, G. Moscardo and E. Laws (eds) *Tourism in the 21st Century: Lessons from Experience,* London: Continuum.

Rockström, J., Steffen, W., Noone, K., Persson, A., Chapin III, F.S., Lambin, E.F., Lenton, T.M., Scheffer, M., Folke, C., Schellnhuber, H.J., Nykvist, B., de Wit, C.A., Hughes, T., van der Leeuw, S., Rodhe, H., Sörlin, S., Snyder, P.K., Costanza, R., Svedin, U., Falkenmark, M., Karlberg, L., Corell, R.W., Fabry, V.J., Hansen, J., Walker, B., Liverman, D., Richardson, K., Crutzen, P. and Foley, J.A.(2009) 'A safe operating space for humanity', *Nature,* 461: 472–75.

Schäfer, A. (2009) *Transportation in a Climate-constrained World,* Cambridge, MA: MIT Press.

Scheelhaase, J., Grimme, W. and Schaefer, M. (2010) 'The inclusion of aviation into the EU emission trading scheme – Impacts on competition between European and non-European network airlines', *Transportation Research Part D: Transport and Environment,* 15: 14–25.

Schellnhuber, H.J., Cramer, W., Nakicenovic, N., Wigley, T. and Yohe, G. (eds) (2006) *Avoiding Dangerous Climate Change,* Cambridge: Cambridge University Press.

Schiphol Group (2012) *Annual Report 2012,* Schiphol Group.

Scott, D., Peeters, P. and Gössling, S. (2010) 'Can tourism deliver its "aspirational" greenhouse gas emission reduction targets?', *Journal of Sustainable Tourism,* 18: 393–408.

Sgouridis, S., Bonnefoy, P.A. and Hansman, R.J. (2010) 'Air transportation in a carbon constrained world: Long-term dynamics of policies and strategies for mitigating the carbon footprint of commercial aviation', *Transportation Research Part A: Policy and Practice,* 45: 1077–91.

Sicard, P., Mangin, A., Hebel, P. and Malléa, P. (2010) 'Detection and estimation trends linked to air quality and mortality on French Riviera over the 1990–2005 period', *Science of the Total Environment,* 408: 1943–50.

Sims, R., Mercado, P., Krewitt, W., Bhuyan, G., Flynn, D., Holttinen, H., Jannuzzi, G., Khennas, S., Liu, Y., O'Malley, M., Nilsson, L.J., Ogden, J., Ogimoto, K., Outhred, H., Ulleberg, O. and van Hulle, F. (2011) 'Integration of renewable energy into present and future energy systems', in O. Edenhofer, R. Pichs-Madruga, Y. Sokona, K. Seyboth, P. Matschoss, S. Kadner, T. Zwickel, P. Eickemeier, G. Hansen, S. Schlömer and C.V. Stechow (eds) *IPCC Special Report on Renewable Energy Sources and Climate Change Mitigation,* Cambridge: Cambridge University Press.

Stephens, E., Ross, I.L., King, Z., Mussgnug, J.H., Kruse, O., Posten, C., Borowitzka, M.A. and Hankamer, B. (2010) 'An economic and technical evaluation of microalgal biofuels', *Nature Biotechnology,* 28: 126–28.

UNWTO-UNEP-WMO (2008) *Climate Change and Tourism: Responding to Global Challenges,* Madrid: UNWTO.

Upham, P. (2003) *Towards Sustainable Aviation,* London: Earthscan.

Vorster, S., Ungerer, M. and Volschenk, J. (2012) '2050 scenarios for long-haul tourism in the evolving global climate change regime', *Sustainability,* 5: 1–51.

Whitfield, F.G.S. (1939) 'Air transport, insects and disease', *Bulletin of Entomological Research,* 30: 365–442.

Zaporozhets, O., Tokarev, V. and Attenborough, K. (2011) *Aircraft Noise: Assessment, Prediction and Control,* Oxford: Spon Press.

Zhang, Y-J. and Wei, Y-M. (2010) 'An overview of current research on EU ETS: Evidence from its operating mechanism and economic effect', *Applied Energy,* 87: 1804–14.

35

The environmental challenges of cruise tourism

Impacts and governance

Machiel Lamers, Eke Eijgelaar and Bas Amelung

Cruise tourism A socio-economic system generated by the interaction between human, organisational and geographical entities, aimed at producing maritime-transportation-enabled leisure experiences (Papathanassis & Beckmann 2011: 166).

Environmental impact Any change of state in the physical environment which is brought about by human interference with the physical environment and has effects which society deems unacceptable in the light of its shared norms (Sloep & van Dam-Mieras 1995: 42).

Marine governance The sharing of policy making competencies in a system of negotiation between nested governmental institutions at several levels (...) on the one hand, and state actors, market parties and civil society organizations of different maritime activities on the other, in order to govern activities at sea and their consequences (Van Tatenhove 2011: 95).

Introduction

Cruise tourism has witnessed tremendous growth over the past decades. From being a predominantly North American market, cruising became more popular in European, Asian and Australian markets and new destinations were added to the portfolio (e.g. Brida & Zapata 2010; Dowling 2006; Weaver & Duval 2008). In 2011, there were around 20 million cruise passengers (CLIA 2013; Peisley 2012). With an annual growth rate of more than 7%, cruising is one of the fastest-growing segments in the global tourism industry (CLIA 2010). The supply of cruise products has also become more diversified. On one side of the spectrum, there are small-scale adventure or luxury cruises to the most remote and vulnerable marine environments (Lamers *et al.* 2012). The opposite side of the spectrum features large-scale cruises on vessels equivalent to floating cities, operating in established cruise destinations, like the Caribbean, the Mediterranean and Northwest Europe (e.g. Brida & Zapata 2010; Wood 2000). In addition to ocean or maritime cruises, river cruising and boating has also gained in popularity in several regions.

430

The economic stakes are high and both cruise companies and coastal destinations advocate increasing flows of cruise vessels and passengers. At the same time, the development of cruise tourism has stirred societal and academic debates about the environmental impact and regulation of cruise mobility (e.g. Dobson & Gill 2006; Johnson 2002; Klein 2007, 2011; Lester & Weeden 2004). Onshore, offshore and global impacts are reported by academics and environmental NGOs. These include air pollution, visitation peaks and infrastructural developments at ports and local attractions, sewage water discharge, dumping of solid waste, biosecurity risks of hull fouling and ballast water discharge, and greenhouse gas emissions (e.g. Farreny et al. 2011; Johnson 2002; Klein 2009; Wood 2002). This literature is fragmented, however, both in terms of their spatial and temporal scope and the environmental impacts addressed.

The literature on cruise tourism regulation is also fragmented. Cruise mobility is considered an under-regulated activity, particularly when viewed from a state agency perspective (e.g. Timothy 2006; Weaver & Duval 2008). However, the regulatory voids in marine governance are increasingly tackled by international organisations and supranational authorities, such as the International Maritime Organization (IMO) and the European Union (EU) (e.g. Van Tatenhove 2011). Cruise tourism clearly is a complex and transnational mobility system governed at multiple levels and by multiple actors, including non-state actors. Changing consumer preferences constitute a regulatory driver towards greener cruise products (Klein 2007; Weaver & Duval 2008). Partly in response to this, cruise companies and industry associations engage in corporate social responsibility (CSR) as well as sustainability partnerships with conservation NGOs (e.g. CLIA 2010; Haase et al. 2009; Klein 2007; Sweeting & Wayne 2006).

Due to the fragmented knowledge about the impact and regulation of cruise tourism, the sector's environmental profile remains unclear and uncontested. To improve this situation, we propose to use a conceptual framework that accounts for the diversity of contexts in which cruise tourism activity takes place. It discerns three interdependent domains (see also Papathanassis & Beckmann 2011), pertaining to on-board, on-the-move and onshore aspects of cruise tourism. The 'hoteling' domain concentrates on on-board hospitality practices, such as catering, laundry, housekeeping, waste handling and entertainment. The 'cruising' domain focuses on routine and emergency operations related to moving the vessels. The 'mooring' domain focuses on embarking and disembarking in hub-harbours and activities at onshore sites and ports. Each of these domains has its own distinct set of activities and impacts, and regulatory arrangements and challenges. As a result, the volume and direction of people and material flows (and thereby impacts) of cruise tourism can be traced in a more complete and natural way. In addition, a comprehensive and integrated analysis can be made of the roles and arrangements of various actors in steering these flows.

For the sake of focus, this chapter is limited to the environmental dimension of maritime cruise tourism and considers only the section of the value chain that relates to the cruise trip itself. We do not claim to meet the integration challenge in the context of this chapter, but we hope that the conceptual approach presented here will inspire further research. In the coming paragraphs we review the literature on the main environmental impact and governance mechanisms of cruise tourism in the three domains of hoteling, cruising and mooring. Afterwards, we illustrate how this plays out in the Antarctic context, discuss some of the main implications for research and policy, and come to a conclusion.

The impacts and regulation of cruise tourism

Hoteling

Cruise ships can be conceptualised as floating hotels or destinations, with facilities for undertaking a range of activities related to lodging, catering and entertaining passengers and crew, similar to land-based tourism resorts (Dowling 2006). Due to the higher numbers of passengers on board cruise ships, the inputs of water, food and materials are typically higher than on other types of sea-faring vessels. So are the volumes of waste streams, such as black water, grey water, bilge water, solid waste, hazardous waste and emissions from on-board waste incineration and electricity generation (Johnson 2002; Klein 2011). A medium-sized cruise ship, carrying around 2,000 passengers and 800 crew members on a one-week voyage, has been estimated to produce approximately 0.75 million litres of black water (i.e. human waste), 3.75 million litres of grey water (i.e. waste water from kitchen sinks, baths, showers, laundry) and eight tonnes of solid waste (Bureau of Transportation Statistics (BTS) 2002).

The environmental performance of a cruise ship's hoteling function depends on the implementation of facilities and technologies on board, such as marine sanitation devices or advanced waste water treatment systems (AWTS), and facilities for separation, compaction, maceration, incineration or storage of solid waste (EPA 2008; Johnson 2002; Klein 2011). For example, AWTS provide a high level of biological treatment, disinfection and removal of solid material of black water and grey water (EPA 2008; Klein 2011). The residues are either stored on board for disposal onshore or controlled discharge in the marine environment (Butt 2007). Application of AWTS technologies has resulted in environmental improvements, but Klein recently argued that discharges still contain very high levels of nutrients, metals and other chemicals, which have a deleterious impact on marine life, fisheries, and eventually marine mammals and human consumers of seafood (Klein 2011).

Whether cruise operators implement and use environmental technologies depends on state regulations in various destinations (Dobson & Gill 2006). The state of Alaska, for example, requires the use of AWTS for cruise ships plying Alaskan waters (Klein 2011; EPA 2008). While having regional benefits, there may be negative spill-over effects attached to such regulations. It has been claimed that these advanced environmental systems are switched off in regions where their use is not required, resulting in the discharge of untreated waste streams (Dobson & Gill 2006). The regulation of waste streams from hoteling has mainly been researched from a state-centred perspective, whereby states stipulate environmental standards in law, impose financial penalties, or deploy voluntary approaches (i.e. Memoranda of Understanding; MOUs) to enhance compliance in their territorial waters (Johnson 2002). Available knowledge in this field has a strong regional bias. The efforts and experiences of North American port-states in regulating waste streams feature frequently in the literature, whereas little is known about port-state regulations and compliance elsewhere in the world.

There are other regulators too, such as the states in which the cruise ships are registered. Cruise companies typically choose to register their ships in states with convenient laws and compliance mechanisms, such as the Bahamas, Panama and Bermuda (e.g. DeSombre 2006; Weaver & Duval 2008). This flag-of-convenience (FOC) system provides a loophole for lower environmental, labour and safety standards, particularly since FOC states often lack the capacity to enforce regulations. This task is increasingly outsourced to corporately run classification societies (CLIA 2010). Further, the IMO is responsible for the development of environmental regulation for cruise ships, and other vessels, in international waters. Through Annexes III, IV and V of the IMO's International Convention for the Prevention of Pollution from Ships (MARPOL) sets the international standards for controlling marine pollution from hazardous waste, sewage and solid waste (Butt 2007; Dobson & Gill 2006), but the IMO depends on port-states and flag-states for enforcement.

There are a number of important non-state actors involved in environmental regulation. The challenge of reducing waste streams has also been taken up by the industry itself by implementing and enforcing regulations and setting industry standards at the transnational level (e.g. Sweeting & Wayne 2006) and at the level of regional seas, such as the Baltic Sea and the Bay of Alaska (CLIA 2010). Non-governmental organisations have been, and continue to be, involved in pushing the envelope of waste stream reduction and recycling in the cruise industry (Klein 2007, 2009). One way of doing that is by providing cruise customers with information about the environmental profile of cruise companies (e.g. in the form of scoring cards that compare the environmental footprint of various cruise ships) (FoE 2012).

Cruising

Cruise ships require a number of essential inputs to become mobile, such as fuel and ballast water. Key outputs, from an environmental viewpoint, are a range of air and water pollutants, and greenhouse gases (GHGs). Cruise ships can be seen as floating power plants and produce a range of emissions. In coastal ports and regions, nitrates, sulphates, particular matter and volatile organic compounds deposited from shipping can be significant, compromising air quality and affecting human health and premature mortality rates. For example, bunker fuels used by cruise ships have a very high sulphur content (Eyring et al. 2010). To improve on this, higher standards of fuel quality have been formulated, which will, of necessity, mean future increases in fuel costs (Peisley 2012). They are therefore opposed by the cruise lines (Klein 2009). Nevertheless, IMO, EU and US-EPA requirements to use low-sulphur fuel are already being implemented in some European and North American emission control areas. Cruising is generally less energy intensive than freight shipping (Buhaug et al. 2009), but it is one of the most energy- and emission-intense forms of tourism transport. An average sea-going cruise produces 1.2 to 1.3 tonnes of CO_2 per passenger, or around 169 kg of CO_2 per passenger per day. Total global CO_2 emissions from sea-going cruise ships have been estimated at 19.17 million tonnes in 2007 – 1.5% of global tourism emissions (Eijgelaar et al. 2010). Including flight emissions caused by the transport of passengers and crew to and from ports of departure, the emissions attributed to cruise trips are double or triple the norm (Walnum 2011).

Over the last decade, cruise companies have achieved considerable reductions in relative fuel use and CO_2 emissions (Carnival 2011; RCC 2012). Rising fuel prices and stricter national and international fuel and emission regulations are the drivers for such efforts. Despite the efficiency gains resulting from technological improvements, however, energy use and emissions from cruise tourism trips remain high and even continue to increase. Relative improvements have been insufficient to realise absolute cuts. This has led Gössling (2011) to believe that a more drastic approach is necessary, consisting of shorter overall distances, lower cruising speeds and alternative ways of propulsion.

Emissions from international shipping are not regulated by the Kyoto Protocol, because of the difficulties in allocating transnational emissions to countries. The Protocol only dictates that Annex I countries should try to limit or reduce GHG emissions from marine bunker fuels by working through the IMO (United Nations Framework Convention on Climate Change (UNFCCC) 1998). After years of slow progress at the IMO, requirements mandating the Energy Efficiency Design Index (EEDI), which is a measure for the CO_2 emission performance, for new ships entered into force in 2013 (MARPOL Annex VI). Although cruise ships are initially excluded from the EEDI, because of the different power demands when compared to cargo ships (European Cruise Council (ECC) 2012), binding limits will likely be introduced for new cruise ships in the coming years. Meanwhile, the IMO's Marine Environment Protection Committee, as well as the EU, are discussing market-based measures to provide incentives for greater fuel efficiency and the reduction of GHG emissions. Cruise companies have been heavily involved in proposing acceptable standards for cruise ships. As part of their corporate responsibility the two largest cruise companies, Carnival Cruise Lines and Royal Caribbean Cruise Lines, have been reporting on their GHG emissions to the Carbon Disclosure Project (CDP) for several years (e.g. CDP 2012a, 2012b). Cruise companies see the trade-offs in climate-related regulations and climatic changes, such as the increasing intensity of tropical cyclones in popular cruise tourism destinations. Regulations result in increasing operational and capital costs, but opportunities also arise to influence policy making by working with regulatory bodies (CDP 2012a, 2012b).

Cruise ships also take in large quantities of ballast water for stabilisation during cruising, and discharge this water at the next port. Ballast water often contains exotic species and bacteria that cause ecological damage to discharge areas and result in economic and public health risks (Copeland 2008). Quantity and quality standards for ballast water discharge have only recently been introduced, primarily in United States' coastal zones. At the global level, the IMO Ballast Water Management Convention has taken over 14 years of negotiation before being adopted in 2004, but has still not entered into force in early 2013 due to insufficient ratification (IMO 2013).

Mooring

A third key domain of cruise tourism concerns the environmental impacts related to mooring activities, such as anchoring, embarking and disembarking in cruise ports, supplying, and the resulting recreational activities onshore. These activities are reported to result in direct environmental impacts, such as local air pollution and damage to coral reefs due to anchoring (Johnson 2002; Lester & Weeden 2004). Further, a considerable proportion of the waste streams produced on cruise ships end up being off-loaded at ports. Depending on how these wastes are processed, their environmental impact may be substantial (Butt 2007), particularly on small islands. For example, the lack of storage facilities and treatment technologies for cruise ship wastes on Caribbean islands has led companies to store their wastes in containers for transport and disposal in their US home ports (Butt 2007). Calling cruise ships also results in a major visitation peak at local destinations that contribute to local waste streams, the use of natural resources and imported products, and the pressure on natural attractions (e.g. national parks, coral reefs) (Klein 2011). In particular, fresh water tends to be scarce on small islands and often needs to be imported from elsewhere to meet the needs of tourists (Johnson 2002). Cruise visitation peaks also result in what Klein (2011) terms 'people pollution', whereby the local population is forced to cope with the environmental and spatial impacts of overcrowding. On top of these short-term effects, increasing numbers of visitors also foster investments in port facilities and infrastructure, for which room needs to be made at the expense of local people, other uses and natural habitat (Johnson 2002; Klein 2011). The immigration wave of external construction and hospitality workers provides an additional strain on the existing natural resources. Strikingly, around 70% of cruise destinations are located in biodiversity hotspots (e.g. the Caribbean or the Mediterranean), which are among the most diverse and vulnerable marine and coastal habitats, and essential for conserving marine species (Sweeting & Wayne 2006).

Environmental impacts from cruise ships calling at ports are regulated and enforced by port-state authorities, whose inspectors will come on board and to which port fees are paid by the cruise operator (Butt 2007). Port-states are responsible for providing facilities and infrastructures that contribute to the mitigation of local environmental impacts. For example, more and more ports are providing cruise ships with the option of connecting to the electricity grid to enable them to shut down their engines and generators and reduce emissions while mooring (i.e. 'cold ironing') (CLIA 2010). However, competition between cruise ports has been reported to result in regulatory laxity (Lester & Weeden 2004). At the same time, the introduction of more stringent regulation in individual ports may cause spill-over effects in areas that lack equivalent rules or proper enforcement (Dobson & Gill 2006; Klein 2007), as was mentioned in the section on hoteling.

By playing divide and rule among ports in cruise destinations, cruise companies can force ports of call to invest valuable public resources in extending or modernising the infrastructure. To secure access to ports of call with extraordinary natural attractions and convenient regulations, cruise companies are increasingly acquiring ownership of cruise terminals from which local communities are excluded (Klein 2011), or even uninhabited islands. Disney Cruise Lines, for example, bought Castaway Cay (Johnson 2002) and Holland America Line acquired Half Moon Cay (Wood 2000). Such practices are criticised for being a private capture of what used to be a public (natural) resource or responsibility, and for making it impossible for local entrepreneurs at other ports of call to offer experiences and services (Klein 2011; Wood 2000). In some cruise tourism regions, such as the Mediterranean and the Baltic Sea, cruise ports are setting up governance networks to collectively set the course for development in their region and prevent large cruise companies from employing the politics of divide and rule. Non-governmental organisations have also developed several strategies to counter or redirect the power of cruise companies. For example, environmental organisations are reporting on measures taken to combat local air pollution (FoE 2012), while large nature conservation organisations have formed partnerships with cruise companies for the protection of marine biodiversity (CLIA 2010).

Case Study

Cruise tourism in Antarctica

Antarctic cruise tourism has grown rapidly from a few thousand visitors in 1990 to over 40,000 passengers in 2008 (Lamers *et al.* 2012). Expedition cruising has been the dominant form of Antarctic tourism since the first organised trip to Antarctica in the 1960s. Expedition cruising involves relatively small ships (200 passengers), landing their passengers at several sites of ecological, historical or scenic interest along their Antarctic itinerary. Since 2000, larger cruise vessels (500 passengers) have also emerged on the Antarctic tourism market.

Until recently, environmental impact assessments focused almost exclusively on 'mooring', for instance disturbance of wildlife during onshore activities. They revealed little evidence of immediate environmental impacts (e.g. Stewart *et al.* 2005). Monitoring programmes are far from comprehensive, however, and in particular the indirect and cumulative impacts of tourism are poorly understood. In fact, no comprehensive or strategic environmental assessment – policy instruments dealing with larger-scale and longer-term issues – has ever been performed for tourism in Antarctica (Lamers *et al.* 2012). Cruise operators have also been reported to illegally dispose of solid waste in the Southern Ocean (Haase *et al.* 2009), but monitoring of waste handling practices in Antarctica is challenging. The impacts of Antarctic cruises on the global climate were recently assessed to be substantial. CO_2 emissions were estimated at 0.53 tonnes per passenger per day for the smaller ships and at 0.29 tonnes for the larger vessels (Farreny *et al.* 2011).

The Antarctic Treaty System (ATS) provides the boundary conditions for all human activities in the Antarctic, including tourism. For example, Antarctic Treaty regulations stipulate how mooring activities should be carried out and how waste should be handled to minimise environmental impact. However, a range of authors have argued for a more comprehensive regulatory mechanism for tourism (e.g. Bastmeijer & Roura 2004; Lamers *et al.* 2012). So far, the Antarctic Treaty parties have relied strongly on self-regulation, entrusting the International Association of Antarctica Tour Operators (IAATO) with the responsibility for enforcing regulations. This self-regulatory arrangement has played a major role in achieving the tour operators' relatively strong record in environmental sensitivity (Haase *et al.* 2009; Splettstoesser 2000). IAATO has put a consistent and practical set of guidelines into place, related to safety requirements, waste treatment, and 'site guidelines' regulating behaviour at sensitive landing sites. Some of IAATO's rules have been adopted by the Antarctic Treaty parties and converted into formal resolutions. The self-regulatory system of cruise tourism in the Antarctic is currently robust and stable, but may be vulnerable to internal and external forces, such as diverging interests of tour operators and Antarctic Treaty parties claiming a stronger role of states in tourism regulation (Haase *et al.* 2009). Recently, the IMO has banned the use of heavy marine fuel in Antarctic waters to avoid major environmental damage in case of an incident with a larger cruise vessel. This measure has, at least temporarily, halted the growth of the larger cruise vessels in Antarctica and, together with the economic recession, resulted in a decrease of visitors to the continent.

Discussion and conclusion

Cruise tourism is a large and rapidly growing segment of tourism. It is a highly international phenomenon, which has largely eluded systematic and comprehensive academic scrutiny. The available evidence on its environmental impact is fragmented and lacks structure. Most knowledge is available on the most localised environmental impacts of cruise tourism, related to air and water pollution and congestion in and around ports-of-call. Some evidence suggests that the regional and global impacts of cruise tourism may be substantial too, but a comprehensive assessment is missing. We have argued that a more integrated analysis of the impact and governance of cruise tourism is needed to obtain a more comprehensive perspective of the environmental sustainability of the sector.

In this chapter we have attempted to provide a structure to the available literature on impacts and regulation, and to suggest a few avenues for further research. We clustered the environmental impact and regulatory efforts in three domains. The hoteling domain, covering all aspects of life on board; the cruising domain, encompassing all facets of propulsion; and the mooring domain, constituted by all activities performed while the ship is by the quay. The nature of the environmental impacts related to each of these domains differs greatly, with the impacts of mooring being much more local than those of shipping, which tend to have global significance.

The scope of this chapter is limited to environmental impacts and governance of these three domains, but could be extended to socio-economic impacts and regulations, or to additional cruise tourism domains (e.g. cruise ship building, air transport). Methodologically, this approach could be enhanced to a full life-cycle assessment of cruise tourism products and enriched with case studies from across the world. Theoretically, this approach could be linked to the emerging social theories on mobilities or networks and flows (e.g. Spaargaren *et al.* 2006; Urry 2007), and theories on multi-actor and multi-level governance (Van Tatenhove 2011). On a practical level, in each of the domains, innovations and policies can lead to improvements in environmental sustainability. Taking a domain perspective allows us to compare and learn from innovations in similar onshore and offshore sectors, such as sustainable cities and hotels, green shipping, decentralised waste management and alternative energy production.

Policymakers grapple with the transboundary nature of the cruise tourism industry and many of its environmental impacts. Stringent regulations in one place may lead to significant spill-over effects in other areas where regulation or enforcement is more lenient. At the same time, there is evidence that fierce competition between ports of call may lead to a race to the bottom with respect to environmental standards. Our analysis of cruise tourism domains suggests that impacts occurring at particular levels of scale have to be matched with governance actions at similar levels. The environmental impacts of cruise tourism occur not only at local levels (e.g. waste handling, visitation peaks), but also at transnational and global levels (e.g. marine discharges, greenhouse gas emissions). Regulation should therefore not only focus on local infrastructure and regulations by port states, but also on intergovernmental governance arrangements and the actions of transnational networks of ports, cruise companies and NGOs. Both research and regulation need to scale up from local to regional and global levels, as these are the same levels at which the cruise tourism industry has been operating for a long time.

Key Reading

Dowling, R.K. (ed.) (2006) *Cruise Ship Tourism*, Wallingford: CABI.

Eyring, V., Isaksen, I.S.A., Berntsen, T., Collins, W.J., Corbett, J.J., Endresen, O., Grainger, R.G., Moldanova, J., Schlager, H. and Stevenson, D.S. (2010) 'Transport impacts on atmosphere and climate: Shipping', *Atmospheric Environment*, 44: 4735–71.

Johnson, D. (2002) 'Environmentally sustainable cruise tourism: A reality check', *Marine Policy*, 26: 261–70.

Klein, R.A. (2011) 'Responsible cruise tourism: Issues of cruise tourism and sustainability', *Journal of Hospitality and Tourism Management*, 18: 107–16.

Papathanassis, A. and Beckmann, I. (2011) 'Assessing the "poverty of cruise theory" hypothesis', *Annals of Tourism Research*, 38: 153–74.

References

Bastmeijer, C. and Roura, R. (2004) 'Regulating Antarctic tourism and the precautionary principle', *The American Journal of International Law*, 98: 763–81.

Brida, J.G. and Zapata, S. (2010) 'Cruise tourism: Economic, socio-cultural and environmental impacts', *International Journal of Leisure and Tourism Marketing*, 1: 205–26.

Buhaug, Ø., Corbett, J.J., Endresen, Ø., Eyring, V., Faber, J., Hanayama, S., Lee, D.S., Lee, D., Lindstad, H., Markowska, A.Z., Mjelde, A., Nelissen, D., Nilsen, J., Pålsson, C., Winebrake, J.J., Wu, W.Q. and Yoshida, K. (eds) (2009) *Second IMO GHG Study 2009*, London: IMO.

Bureau of Transportation Statistics (BTS) (2002) *Maritime Trade and Transportation 2002*, Washington DC: US Department of Transportation BTS.

Butt, N. (2007) 'The impact of cruise ship-generated waste on home ports and ports of call: A study of Southampton', *Marine Policy*, 31: 591–98.

Carbon Disclosure Project (CDP) (2012a) *Investor CDP 2012 Information Request: Carnival Corporation*, CDP.

—— (2012b) *Investor CDP 2012 Information Request: Royal Caribbean Cruises Ltd*, CDP.

Carnival (2011) *Sustainability Report Fiscal Year 2010*, Miami: Carnival Corporation & PLC.

Cruise Lines International Association (CLIA) (2010) *The Overview. 2010 CLIA Cruise Market Overview. Statistical Cruise Industry Data Through 2009*, Fort Lauderdale: CLIA.

—— (2013) *2013 North America Cruise Industry Update*, Fort Lauderdale: CLIA.

Copeland, C. (2008) *Cruise Ship Pollution: Background, Laws and Regulations, and Key Issues*, Washington DC: Congressional Research Service.

DeSombre, E.R. (2006) *Flagging Standards: Globalization and Environmental, Safety, and Labor Regulations at Sea*, Cambridge, MA: MIT Press.

Dobson, S. and Gill, A. (2006) 'Environmental policy challenges for the cruise industry: Case studies from Australia and the USA', in R.K. Dowling (ed.) *Cruise Ship Tourism*, Wallingford: CABI.

Dowling, R.K. (ed.) (2006) *Cruise Ship Tourism*, Wallingford: CABI.

Eijgelaar, E., Thaper, C. and Peeters, P. (2010) 'Antarctic cruise tourism: The paradoxes of ambassadorship, "last chance tourism" and GHG emissions', *Journal of Sustainable Tourism*, 18: 337–54.

Environmental Protection Agency (EPA) (2008) *Cruise Ship Discharge Assessment Report*, Washington DC: US Environmental Protection Agency.

European Cruise Council (ECC) (2012) *2012/2013 Report*, Brussels, Belgium: European Cruise Council.

Eyring, V., Isaksen, I.S.A., Berntsen, T., Collins, W.J., Corbett, J.J., Endresen, O., Grainger, R.G., Moldanova, J., Schlager, H. and Stevenson, D.S. (2010) 'Transport impacts on atmosphere and climate: Shipping', *Atmospheric Environment*, 44: 4735–71.

Farreny, R., Oliver-Solà, J., Lamers, M., Amelung, B., Gabarrell, X., Rieradevall, J., Boada, M. and Benayas, J. (2011) 'Carbon dioxide emissions of Antarctic tourism', *Antarctic Science*, 23: 556–66.

Friends of the Earth (FoE) (2012) *2012 Cruise Ship Environmental Report Card*, Berkeley: FoE.

Gössling, S. (2011) *Carbon Management in Tourism: Mitigating the Impacts on Climate Change*, Abingdon: Routledge.

Haase, D., Lamers, M. and Amelung, B. (2009) 'Heading into uncharted territory? Exploring the institutional robustness of self-regulation in the Antarctic tourism sector', *Journal of Sustainable Tourism*, 17: 411–430.

International Maritime Organization (IMO) (2013) *Ballast Water Management*. Available at: www.imo.org/OurWork/Environment/BallastWaterManagement/Pages/Default.aspx#5 (accessed 4 April 2013).

Johnson, D. (2002) 'Environmentally sustainable cruise tourism: A reality check', *Marine Policy*, 26: 261–70.

Klein, R.A. (2007) 'The politics of environmental activism: A case study of the cruise industry and the environmental movement', *Sociological Research Online*, 12.

—— (2009) *Getting a Grip on Cruise Ship Pollution*, Berkeley, USA: Friends of the Earth.

—— (2011) 'Responsible cruise tourism: Issues of cruise tourism and sustainability', *Journal of Hospitality and Tourism Management*, 18: 107–16.

Lamers, M., Liggett, D. and Amelung, B. (2012) 'Strategic challenges of tourism development and governance in Antarctica: Taking stock and moving forward', *Polar Research*, 31: 1–13.

Lester, J.-A. and Weeden, C. (2004) 'Stakeholders, the natural environment and the future of Caribbean cruise tourism', *International Journal of Tourism Research*, 6: 39–50.

Papathanassis, A. and Beckmann, I. (2011) 'Assessing the "poverty of cruise theory" hypothesis', *Annals of Tourism Research*, 38: 153–74.

Peisley, T. (2012) *Cruises Worldwide – September 2012*, Mintel Oxygen.

Royal Caribbean Cruises Ltd (RCC) (2012) *2011 Stewardship Report*, Miami: Royal Caribbean Cruises Ltd.

Sloep, P.B. and van Dam-Mieras, M.C.E. (1995) 'Science on environmental problems', in P. Glasbergen and A. Blowers (eds) *Environmental Policy in an International Context: Perspectives on Environmental Problems*, London: Arnold.

Spaargaren, G., Mol, A.P.J. and Buttel, F.H. (2006) *Governing Environmental Flows: Global Challenges to Social Theory*, Cambridge, MA: MIT Press.

Splettstoesser, J. (2000) 'IAATO's stewardship of the Antarctic environment: A history of tour operator's concern for a vulnerable part of the world', *International Journal of Tourism Research*, 2: 47–55.

Stewart, E.J., Draper, D. and Johnston, M.E. (2005) 'A review of tourism research in the polar regions', *Arctic*, 58: 383–94.

Sweeting, J.E.N. and Wayne, S.L. (2006) 'A shifting tide: Environmental challenges and cruise industry responses', in R.K. Dowling (ed.) *Cruise Ship Tourism*, Wallingford: CABI.

Timothy, D.J. (2006) 'Cruises, supranationalism and border complexities', in R. Dowling (ed.) *Cruise Ship Tourism*, Wallingford: CABI.

United Nations Framework Convention on Climate Change (UNFCCC) (1998) *Kyoto Protocol to the United Nations Framework Convention on Climate Change*, United Nations.

Urry, J. (2007) *Mobilities*, Cambridge: Polity Press.

Van Tatenhove, J. (2011) 'Integrated marine governance: Questions of Legitimacy', *MAST*, 10: 87–113.

Walnum, H.J. (2011) *Energy Use and CO_2 Emissions from Cruise Ships: A Discussion of Methodological Issues*, Sogndal, Norway: Western Norway Research Institute.

Weaver, A. and Duval, D.T. (2008) 'International and transnational aspects of the global cruise industry', in T. Coles and C.M. Hall (eds) *International Business and Tourism: Global Issues, Contemporary Interactions*, London: Routledge.

Wood, R.E. (2000) 'Caribbean cruise tourism: Globalization at sea', *Annals of Tourism Research*, 27: 345–70.

—— (2002) 'Caribbean of the east? Global interconnections and the southeast Asian cruise industry', *Asian Journal of Social Science*, 30: 420–40.

36

Public transport

Diem-Trinh Le-Klähn

Public transport includes rail, bus, scheduled ferries, taxicabs and other systems that transport members of the public.

Introduction

Besides several economic and social benefits, tourism may have some negative impacts, especially on the environment. Tourists cause 4.4 per cent of global CO_2 and a large part of it (75%) comes from transport (Dubois *et al.* 2011; Peeters & Dubois 2010). To mitigate the emissions from tourism, the emissions from tourism transport must be reduced. Transport, however, is an essential element of the tourism system. It is influential to the tourist experience at the destination (Thompson & Schofield 2007) and determines the attractiveness of the destination (Khadaroo & Seetanah 2008). Maintaining and improving convenience and accessibility for tourists while preserving the environment of the destination is challenging. In other words, sustainable tourism development at a destination should be connected to sustainable mobility (Høyer 2000).

Sustainable transport in tourism has become even more important due to the continuing problems of a growing population, increased traffic congestion and pollution and the impact of climate change. Several attempts have been made to reduce the emissions in tourism transport (Dickinson & Dickinson 2006; Lumsdon & Owen 2004). In 2003, the World Tourism Organization (UNWTO) initiated the Davos Declaration as a statement of its commitment to react promptly to climate change. Shifting to eco-friendly transport modes (e.g. public transport) is one focus of sustainable transport development in tourism.

Public transport (or public transportation, mass transit, public transit) is defined in the *Oxford English Dictionary* as: "forms of transport that are available to the public, charge set fares, and run on fixed routes." According to the International Association of Public Transport (UITP 2013), public transport includes rail, bus, scheduled ferries, taxicabs and other systems that transport members of the public. Public transport has several advantages over other engine-powered modes of transport (e.g. lower cost for passengers, more space for the cities, safer and more energy-efficient (APTA 2013; UITP 2013). It is often viewed as a more sustainable mode of transport than a private car (Le-Klähn & Hall 2014).

Public transport has two major roles in tourism at a destination: as a means of transport which provides accessibility to attractions and as an attraction by itself (Lumsdon & Page 2004). The Nostalgic Istiklal Caddesi tram in Istanbul (Turkey), the Wellington Cable Car (New Zealand) and heritage railways such as the Heritage Express (Australia) are examples of public transport as tourist attractions. As a means of transport, public transport is pivotal for tourists traveling without private vehicles.

Accessibility to a destination is important for tourists (Sorupia 2005) as is the ability to reach attractions at the destination. An efficient public transport system is thus critical to provide accessibility to attractions for tourists, while encouraging more of its use could lead to less use of private vehicles.

This chapter examines the use of public transport in tourism and analyses its potential to replace the car for traveling. Barriers for public transport use and challenges to sustainable tourism transport policies implementation are also discussed.

The use of public transport in tourism

According to the International Association of Public Transport (UITP 2013), public transport at urban, suburban and regional level carried 60 billion passengers in 2008 in the EU-27 region, equivalent to 120 trips per inhabitant per year. The number of people using public transport has seen a steady increase over the last decade (UITP 2013) and this is expected to grow by 1.6–4.4 per cent per year up to 2050 (Dubois et al. 2011).

Public transport is widely used by tourists, especially in urban destinations. However, the choice of public transport varies. The train is quite popular with tourists in Europe, largely due to the extensive rail network as well as public commitment to its use. Tourists traveling in coach tours, which in many cases replaced passenger traffic on existing train routes, form a considerable tourist segment in New Zealand and Australia (Becken 2005).

The tourist users of public transport

Tourist users of public transport include both male and female, and are generally of younger age (Le-Klähn et al. 2014; Farag & Lyons 2012; Quiroga 1990; Thompson & Schofield 2007). A study of public transport use by tourists in Manchester had 73 per cent of the respondents under 35 years old (Thompson & Schofield 2007). Similarly, half of the respondents in a Munich study were in the 18–39 age group (Le-Klähn et al. 2014). This may be because young people are more flexible and more used to public transport systems whereas older tourists often favor traveling in guided tours. As Becken and Gnoth (2004) indicate, 41 per cent of coach tourists in New Zealand were more than 54 years old. However, the situation is different in rural areas. Lumsdon, Downward and Rhoden (2006) found that the majority users of the Wayfarer ticket in the United Kingdom were aged 55–64 and retired. Users of public transport for tourism purposes tend to be well educated and the majority hold a driving license (Farag & Lyons 2012; Le-Klähn et al. 2014; Le-Klähn & Hall 2014).

Barr and Prillwitz (2012) categorized travelers into (1) addicted car users, (2) aspiring green travelers, (3) reluctant public transport users and (4) committed green travelers. Aspiring and committed green travelers are those who have pro-environmental attitudes and would consider and use alternative modes whenever possible. The former group comprises younger middle-aged in higher scale occupational level people whereas the latter includes mostly middle aged people who have managerial or professional occupational background. Reluctant public transport users are often older and retired people who have restricted accessibility to the car (Le-Klähn & Hall 2014).

Visitor satisfaction with public transport services

Tourist users of public transport have different background and characteristics and therefore exhibited diverse perceptions and transport attitudes (Dallen 2007). Their satisfaction with transport is influenced by several factors. Stradling et al. (2007) argued that age and frequency of use are the most influential while factors such as household income, the availability of cars and gender are less significant. A study in Turkey and Mallorca, however, identified cultural background as an important impact (Kozak 2001). For example, British tourists are more satisfied with local transport services during their summer holidays than the Germans. Other influences include word-of-mouth communication, purchase intention and complaints (Kim & Lee 2011). Dimensions of public transport performance measured suggested similarities between overseas visitors and local users (Thompson & Schofield 2007).

Generally, public transport in rural areas (mainly buses) received relatively high satisfaction levels in service dimensions such as comfort, cleanliness, information and driver helpfulness. However, there were also complaints about poor service delivery, unreliability, poor information, bad driving, inferior vehicles, and above all, frequency of services (Guiver et al. 2007).

Public transport is considered as an additional tourism product, which adds to the total tourist experience. However, despite high investment cost and potential value, some public transport systems are still not favored by visitors (Bramwell 1998). Whether or not public transport could replace the car for traveling purposes still remains a topic for debate (Le-Klähn & Hall 2014).

The potential of public transport as an alternative mode for tourists

Barriers for public transport use

Apparently, most tourists are unfamiliar with and may even be intimidated by the public transport systems at their destinations (Lew & McKercher 2006). Nonetheless, barriers for use vary depending on the types of tourists and the destination itself. In rural areas, use of the car is dominant while public transport was little used (Dickinson & Dickinson 2006; Dickinson & Robbins 2007; Dickinson, Robbins & Fletcher 2009; Guiver et al. 2007). Dickinson et al. (2004) suggested that public transport as an alternative to cars is usually more feasible for traveling shorter distances. Reasons against using public transport (particularly buses) include feeling unsafe, a preference for other transport modes (cars, walking or cycling), problems with service provision, unwanted cost, disability and discomfort, and self-image (Stradling et al. 2007). Language could also be another reason: those who speak the local language have more flexibility in their transport choice (Hough & Hassanien 2010).

What makes an effective public transport system for tourists?

Tourists have distinctive needs and travel patterns that are different from the local residents. Public transport operators should adapt their services to their needs. While local residents were concerned with aspects such as quality and safety of the vehicles, visitors to a city emphasized provision of information, service reliability, frequency and punctuality (Kinsella & Caulfield 2011). Unsurprisingly, tourists require more information than the locals (Thompson 2004).

Page (1994, cited in Lew & McKercher 2006) suggested that local public transport systems tend to be used by more adventurous tourists. Tram, train and subway are generally perceived to be easier to use, while buses are seen as more challenging. Therefore, an efficient and reliable public transport system is important, but the system must be easy to use for international visitors as public transport's ease of use has a stronger influence on destination satisfaction than efficiency and safety (Thompson & Schofield 2007).

The design of tourism bus services is another factor attracting visitors. Lumsdon (2006) argued that a bus network which was primarily designed for utility purposes is not likely to be successful. Bus networks therefore have to offer services that suit visitors' needs. Levels of service, types of vehicles, and especially the role of the driving staff are emphasized. One challenge to the delivery of a good bus service is the lack of data regarding the users of tourism buses. The limited knowledge of the market restricted the ability to develop and offer appropriate services and qualities to different customers. Several networks have been designed and operated without a thorough investigation of existing demand patterns. To develop and offer better services, customer information should be included in the tourism transport-planning process. Establishing benchmarks and monitoring programs is essential to determine the levels of demand, user profiles and user motivation on a regular basis.

It is, however, doubtful if improving public transport would encourage more people to use it (Dickinson et al. 2009). Encouraging a modal shift requires a significant commitment from various stakeholders with multi-faceted long-term plans.

How to encourage a modal shift to public transport?

Demand for tourism is expected to be relatively inelastic and will continue to grow steadily in the next few decades (Graham, Papatheodorou & Forsyth 2008). Tourist destinations, therefore, face a dilemma: how to facilitate accessibility for tourists whilst maintaining the destination's attractiveness? How to receive more visitors whilst minimizing negative environmental impacts?

It has been suggested that emission reductions in tourism can only be achieved by a substantial modal shift alongside shortened travel distances and improved low-carbon technologies (Dickinson & Dickinson 2006; Dickinson et al. 2009). Similarly, Guiver et al. (2008) recommended (1) reducing the number of trips and length of trips, (2) switching to alternative transport mode such as walking or cycling, and (3) reducing the number of vehicles used (by car-sharing or using public transport). The disadvantage of the first option is a reduction in the number of tourists, which may affect the tourism industry at the destination. Cycling and walking are environmentally friendly, but have some restrictions (e.g. distance or unsuitable road conditions) and have limitations. The last option, consequently, is the most promising. This view is also shared by other authors, who believe a modal shift to public transport is one significant way to reduce CO_2 emissions (Dubois et al. 2011; Martín-Cejas & Sánchez 2010; Peeters & Dubois 2010). Nonetheless, the implementation of this approach requires commitment both from the tourists and destination management. Policies aimed at encouraging a modal shift often highlight demand management and the involvement of multiple stakeholders.

Demand management

Demand management plays an important role in encouraging a modal shift, in addition to technology and infrastructure improvement (Dubois *et al.* 2011). Gronau and Kagermeier (2007) emphasized the importance of a demand-oriented approach in transport policy. Users' personal characteristics, including attitudes and preferences, should be the focus of transport planning while additional support in the areas of marketing, transparency and quality are also needed. The key requirements for an effective tourism public transport provision include (1) target group identification (nature, family, or sport-oriented), (2) catchment area, (3) situation, (4) quality of the offer and (5) market communication. The authors asserted that demand is of foremost importance and public transport systems should only be established where people are predisposed to use it. Additionally, favorable competition is essential. The quality of public transport (e.g. convenience and accessibility), and intensive and creative market communication are other necessary concerns.

Knowledge of visitor mode choice is vital to manage ridership within destinations and to encourage a modal shift to alternative transport modes. Pettebone *et al.* (2011) suggested that real-time traffic information (intelligent transport systems) could be sent to younger visitors, while for older visitors, enhancing the quality of the travel experience is important to promote public transport use.

Generally tourists have strong preferences for private vehicle use and it is particularly difficult to encourage modal shift in the case of short-haul visitors (Reilly, Williams & Haider 2010). However, Lumsdon, Downward and Rhoden (2006) suggested that a multi-modal ticket may encourage, to some extent, the modal shift by transport users. In the United Kingdom for example, the Wayfarer ticket contributed to a modal shift for tourism trips to the Peak District National Park (Lumsdon *et al.* 2006). This card was a result of a partnership between two major passenger transport executives, transport authorities in Manchester and West Yorkshire and the Country Commission. As a multi-modal, multi-operator ticket, the Wayfarer ticket provides convenience, flexibility and value for money, which makes it more attractive to the visitors. These are especially appealing for older visitors, who have less time restrictions and are more price sensitive.

In terms of marketing strategies, promoting alternatives to the car should be focused on visitor's experience (not on transport modes): relaxed, care-free and enjoyable bus rides, cycling or walking (Dickinson & Robbins 2007). Visitors often appreciate an enjoyable experience with sightseeing onboard using more than one mode of transport (Lumsdon *et al.* 2006).

Other measures include pricing structures, incentives, taxation and emissions quotas. In addition, integrated land use planning, priority for public transport, and policy to influence attitudinal change could also be used (Hall 2004). Installing parking restrictions, car closure and offering alternatives to car are some other possible measurements (Dickinson *et al.* 2004). For a better demand management, visitors' cultural differences and movement patterns should be considered.

Public transport tourist users are diversified in their cultural background and language ability (Sussmann & Rashcovsky 1997). To improve public transport penetration, it is important for transport planners to adapt their policy and marketing plans to various users. Tourists also follow different movement patterns at a destination (Lew & McKercher 2006). Territorial models include no movement, convenience-based movement, concentric exploration and unrestricted movement. Linear path models consist of point-to-point patterns, circular patterns and complex patterns. To successfully target the right customers with the suitable services, transport providers need to understand tourist patterns. Transport management policies and measures should not be based on presumption.

Multiple stakeholders' involvement

Nevertheless, even with a strong knowledge of the market and extensive information, implementation of sustainable strategies may still fail. Determining and implementing sustainable strategies requires involvement of multiple stakeholders (Lumsdon & Owen 2004; Regnerus, Beunen & Jaarsma 2007). Involved parties, especially the area managers are interdependent; cooperation between them is critical for a successful sustainable development (Regnerus *et al.* 2007). The views of both stakeholders and tourists should be considered when planning for sustainable tourism development (Lumsdon & Owen 2004).

Challenges to policy implementation

Providing high quality and excellent transport services is important to encourage transport behavior change. To reduce the use of individual vehicles and encourage a modal shift, the city needs to offer better alternative transport services. However, policies aimed at promoting public transport were often not very successful due to the lack of clear objectives, targets and measures (Eaton & Holding 1996). Regnerus, Beunen and Jaarsma (2007) believed public resistance can be one barrier to the implementation of traffic management. Local politicians need the public support hence any policies that may cause people's unfavor would never be implemented. In areas where a car is a definite necessity, reducing car use is not feasible. Reasons for difficulties in implementing traffic management were believe to be (1) the lack of knowledge about the recreational use of the area, and (2) the interdependence of the actors involved.

Moreover, the ability of tourism attraction managers in influencing tourists' transport mode is questionable (Guiver, Lumsdon & Weston 2008). In fact, managers tended to have doubts about their influence on the number of tourist arrivals, the type of tourists as well as the transport modes they come with. From the management perspective, changing visitors' transport mode arrival is challenging as visitors are believed to determine their mode prior to arrival at the destinations and institutional barriers are significant.

In terms of sustainable transport implementation, urban tourism areas have more advantages as compared to rural areas (Dickinson *et al.* 2004). Attractions in urban areas are in many cases located closer to each other and can normally be reached by public transport. On the other hand, in remote rural areas attractions are potentially more scattered and thus replacement of a car is less likely.

Case Study

City cards for tourists: the case of the CityTourCard in Munich, Germany

Munich is the capital of the Bavaria state and the third largest city in Germany. A commercial, industrial and cultural center, Munich is the second most visited city in Germany (after Berlin) with 5.2 million foreign visitors in 2010 (German National Tourist Board 2011). Munich has a well-developed and extensive traffic and public transport network. The public transport systems in Munich include 442 km of S-Bahn (suburban trains), 95 km of U-Bahn (underground trains), 79 km tram and 454 km of local bus route. The systems are operated by different organizations under the supervision of the Munich Transport and Tariff Association (MVV – Münchner Verkehrs- und Tarifverbund).

In 2011, public transport systems in Munich transported 522 million passengers. Sixty-six per cent of the residents of Munich use the underground, bus and tram several times per week and

---

445

35 per cent of them are daily users of the systems (Sustainable Mobility for Munich 2010). While a large part of users of public transport in Munich is resident, tourists also benefit from the systems. Munich has tremendous appeal to tourists; however, providing excellent public transport services is important to support the growing number of tourists.

City Cards are a type of combination ticket aimed at tourists, which offer unlimited travel on public transport within a chosen time period, free or discounted entrance to several tourist attractions, restaurants, tour packages and some additional benefits. The City Cards are available in many cities especially in Europe with examples including the I amsterdam Card, the ZürichCard, and the Paris City Passport. Introduced in 2007, the Munich CityTourCard (www.citytourcard-muenchen.com) comes in several varieties (see Table 36.1). The Card offers tourists unlimited travel on public transport plus discounts at several attractions.

Table 36.1 Types and prices of the Munich CityTourCard

		Single		Partner	
		CityTourCard	Standard	CityTourCard	Standard
Inner network	One day	9.90€	5.8€	17.9€	10.6€
	Three day	20.9€	14.3€	30.9€	24.6€
Total network	One day	–	11.2€	–	20.4€
	Three day	32.9€	–	53.9€	–

Note: Prices as of April 2013

The CityTourCards are widely distributed at tourist centers, ticket vending machines, MVG/MVV customer centers, and MVG/MVV partners. The integrated ticketing system makes it convenient for passengers to use and transfer between different types (train, subway, tram and bus). However, the CityTourCard seems to have been neglected by visitors in Munich. Table 36.2 shows that although there has been a slight increase in sale from 2007 to 2011, CityTourCard sale only accounts for a minor proportion of the total number of tourist arrivals in Munich.

Table 36.2 Sales of the CityTourCard vs. tourist arrivals in Munich 2007–11

Year	2007	2008	+/-	2009	+/-	2010	+/-	2011	+/-
Tourist arrivals	4,701,717	4,829,683	2.7%	4,983,632	3.2%	5,571,278	11.8%	5,931,052	6.5%
Tickets sold	16,029	24,609	53.5%	41,984	70.6%	59,870	42.6%	70,417	17.6%
% of ticket user	0.3%	0.5%		0.8%		1.1%		1.2%	

Source: Tourism statistics (City of Munich 2011); ticket sale (MVV, personal communication with MVV Marketing director)

One reason for the low sale of the CityTourCard could be related to costs versus benefits. First, compared to the standard tickets, the CityTourCards are more expensive (26–71%) (see Table 36.1). On the other hand, benefits from the cards are small. Most often tourists are entitled to only a discount of €1–3 off or 10–20 per cent discount of the normal prices. Second, the card offers discounts to 62 places, mostly museums, restaurants and beer gardens. However, most important attractions in the city are excluded (e.g. the Residenz, Schloss Nymphenburg, the Pinakothek).

The reason behind the unpopularity of the CityTourCard in Munich is the lack of cooperation between the transport provider and the tourist office. It started with the introduction of the Welcome Card by the company CoCosult following a Berliner success. Thanks to the cooperation between the Tourist Office and participated attractions, more discounts for tourists were offered. By the end of 2006, the Welcome Card, however, was canceled due to a policy decision by the Munich Tourist Office. The CityTourCard was introduced as a replacement by the Munich Transport Company (MVG) without any involvement of the Tourist Office. Tickets are sold in various places although there has been no dedicated marketing strategy to promote its sale.

Conclusion

Public transport is believed to be the most user–friendly transport mode (Sia, Wu & Li 2011). It plays an important role in urban areas and contributes to sustainable development. Public transport (i.e. bus and train) produces a much lower environmental impact compared to other motorized forms of transport (Peeters, Szimba & Duijnisveld 2007). In addition, traveling by public transport provides social engagement and opportunities for interaction (Stradling *et al.* 2007). Despite the benefits that traveling by public transport may bring, giving up their car is arduous for most people. However, given the increasing environmental, social and traffic problems, more people will look for alternatives.

Encouraging a modal shift and promoting public transport use is crucial for all cities. For a successful policy implementation, proactive and effective management is needed, which in turn requires strong knowledge of visitor behavior and attitudes. Tourists are very different in their travel and movement patterns at a destination (McKercher, Wong & Lau 2006). Further examination and understanding of tourists as users of public transport, their demand, expectation and perception of the services are essential.

Key Reading

Dickinson, J.E. and Dickinson, J.A. (2006) 'Local transport and social representations: Challenging the assumptions for sustainable tourism', *Journal of Sustainable Tourism*, 14: 192–208.

Le-Klähn, D-T., Hall, C.M. and Gerike, R. (2014) 'Analysis of visitors' satisfaction with public transport in Munich', *Journal of Public Transportation*, 17(3): in press.

Le-Klähn, D-T. and Hall, C.M. 'Tourist use of public transport at destinations – a review', *Current Issues in Tourism*, accepted.

Lumsdon, L. and Page, S.J. (2004) 'Progress in transport and tourism research: Reformulating the transport-tourism interface and future research agendas', in L. Lumsdon and S.J. Page (eds) *Tourism and Transport*, Oxford: Pergamon.

Thompson, K. and Schofield, P. (2007) 'An investigation of the relationship between public transport performance and destination satisfaction', *Journal of Transport Geography*, 15: 136–44.

References

American Public Transport Association (APTA) (2013) *Facts at a Glance*. Available at: www.publictransportation.org/news/facts/Pages/default.aspx (accessed 25 February 2013).

Barr, S. and Prillwitz, J. (2012) 'Green travellers? Exploring the spatial context of sustainable mobility styles', *Applied Geography*, 32: 798–809.

Becken, S. (2005) 'Towards sustainable tourism transport: An analysis of coach tourism in New Zealand', *Tourism Geographies*, 7: 23–42.

Becken, S. and Gnoth, J. (2004) 'Tourist consumption systems among overseas visitors: Reporting on American, German, and Australian visitors to New Zealand', *Tourism Management*, 25: 375–85.

Bramwell, B. (1998) 'User satisfaction and product development in urban tourism', *Tourism Management*, 19: 35–47.

City of Munich (2011) *Facts and Figures*. Available at: www.muenchen.de/rathaus/home_en/Tourist-Office/Salesguide/Facts-and-Figures (accessed 12 January 2013).

Dallen, J. (2007) 'The challenges of diverse visitor perceptions: Rail policy and sustainable transport at the resort destination', *Journal of Transport Geography*, 15: 104–15.

Dickinson, J.E. and Dickinson, J.A. (2006) 'Local transport and social representations: Challenging the assumptions for sustainable tourism', *Journal of Sustainable Tourism*, 14: 192–208.

Dickinson, J.E. and Robbins, D. (2007) 'Using the car in a fragile rural tourist destination: A social representations perspective', *Journal of Transport Geography*, 15: 116–26.

Dickinson, J.E., Calver, S., Watters, K. and Wilkes, K. (2004) 'Journeys to heritage attractions in the UK: A case study of National Trust property visitors in the south west', *Journal of Transport Geography*, 12: 103–13.

Dickinson, J.E., Robbins, D. and Fletcher, J. (2009) 'Representation of transport: A rural destination analysis', *Annals of Tourism Research*, 36: 103–23.

Dubois, G., Peeters, P., Ceron, J.-P. and Gössling, S. (2011) 'The future tourism mobility of the world population: Emission growth versus climate policy', *Transportation Research Part A: Policy and Practice*, 45: 1031–42.

Eaton, B. and Holding, D. (1996) 'The evaluation of public transport alternatives to the car in British national parks', *Journal of Transport Geography*, 4: 55–65.

Farag, S. and Lyons, G. (2012) 'To use or not to use? An empirical study of pre-trip public transport information for business and leisure trips and comparison with car travel', *Transport Policy*, 20: 82–92.

German National Tourist Board (2011) *Incoming Tourism Germany*, Berlin: German National Tourist Board.

Graham, A., Papatheodorou, A. and Forsyth, P. (eds) (2008) *Aviation and Tourism – Implications for Leisure Travel*, Farnham: Ashgate.

Gronau, W. and Kagermeier, A. (2007) 'Key factors for successful leisure and tourism public transport provision', *Journal of Transport Geography*, 15: 127–35.

Guiver, J., Lumsdon, L., Weston, R. and Ferguson, M. (2007) 'Do buses help meet tourism objectives? The contribution and potential of scheduled buses in rural destination areas', *Transport Policy*, 14: 275–82.

Guiver, J., Lumsdon, L. and Weston, R. (2008) 'Traffic reduction at visitor attractions: The case of Hadrian's Wall', *Journal of Transport Geography*, 16: 142–50.

Hall, D. (2004) 'Transport and tourism: Equity and sustainability issues', in L. Lumsdon and S.J. Page (eds) *Tourism and Transport*, Oxford: Pergamon.

Hough, G. and Hassanien, A. (2010) 'Transport choice behaviour of Chinese and Australian tourists in Scotland', *Research in Transportation Economics*, 26: 54–65.

Høyer, K.G. (2000) 'Sustainable tourism or sustainable mobility? The Norwegian case', *Journal of Sustainable Tourism*, 8: 147–60.

International Association of Public Transport (2013) *What Is Public Transport?* Available at: www.uitp.org/Public-Transport/why-public-transport/index.cfm (accessed 25 February 2013).

Khadaroo, J. and Seetanah, B. (2008) 'The role of transport infrastructure in international tourism development: A gravity model approach', *Tourism Management*, 29: 831–40.

Kim, Y.K. and Lee, H.R. (2011) 'Customer satisfaction using low cost carriers', *Tourism Management*, 32: 235–43.

Kinsella, J. and Caulfield, B. (2011) 'An examination of the quality and ease of use of public transport in Dublin from a newcomer's perspective', *Journal of Public Transportation*, 14: 69–81.

Kozak, M. (2001) 'Comparative assessment of tourist satisfaction with destinations across two nationalities', *Tourism Management*, 22: 391–401.

Le-Klähn, D-T. and Hall, C.M. (2014) 'Tourist use of public transport at destinations – a review', *Current Issues in Tourism*, in press.

Le-Klähn, D-T., Gerike, R. and Hall, C.M. (2014) 'Visitor users vs. non-users of public transport: The case of Munich, Germany', *Journal of Destination Marketing & Management*, DOI: 10.1016/j. jdmm.2013.12.005

Lew, A. and McKercher, B. (2006) 'Modeling tourist movements: A local destination analysis', *Annals of Tourism Research*, 33: 403–23.

Lumsdon, L.M. (2006) 'Factors affecting the design of tourism bus services', *Annals of Tourism Research*, 33: 748–66.

Lumsdon, L. and Owen, E. (2004) 'Tourism transport: The green key initiatives', in L. Lumsdon and S. Page (eds) *Tourism and Transport: Issues and Agenda for the New Millenium*, New York: Elsevier.

Lumsdon, L. and Page, S.J. (2004) 'Progress in transport and tourism research: Reformulating the transport-tourism interface and future research agendas', in L. Lumsdon and S. Page (eds) *Tourism and Transport*, Oxford: Pergamon.

Lumsdon, L., Downward, P. and Rhoden, S. (2006) 'Transport for tourism: Can public transport encourage a modal shift in the day visitor market?', *Journal of Sustainable Tourism*, 14: 139–56.

Martín-Cejas, R.R. and Sánchez, P.P.R. (2010) 'Ecological footprint analysis of road transport related to tourism activity: The case for Lanzarote Island', *Tourism Management*, 31: 98–103.

McKercher, B., Wong, C. and Lau, G. (2006) 'How tourists consume a destination', *Journal of Business Research*, 59: 647–52.

Peeters, P. and Dubois, G. (2010) 'Tourism travel under climate change mitigation constraints', *Journal of Transport Geography*, 18: 447–57.

Peeters, P., Szimba, E. and Duijnisveld, M. (2007) 'Major environmental impacts of European tourist transport', *Journal of Transport Geography*, 15: 83–93.

Pettebone, D., Newman, P., Lawson, S.R., Hunt, L., Monz, C. and Zwiefka, J. (2011) 'Estimating visitors' travel mode choices along the Bear Lake Road in Rocky Mountain National Park', *Journal of Transport Geography*, 19: 1210–21.

Quiroga, I. (1990) 'Characteristics of package tours in Europe', *Annals of Tourism Research*, 17: 185–207.

Regnerus, H.D., Beunen, R. and Jaarsma, C.F. (2007) 'Recreational traffic management: The relations between research and implementation', *Transport Policy*, 14: 258–67.

Reilly, J., Williams, P. and Haider, W. (2010) 'Moving towards more eco-efficient tourist transportation to a resort destination: The case of Whistler, British Columbia', *Research in Transportation Economics*, 26: 66–73.

Sia, R.J.L., Wu, B.H. and Li, J.H. (2011) 'Mass transit as urban tourist transport', *Applied Mechanics and Materials*, 97–98: 1131–34.

Sorupia, E. (2005) 'Rethinking the role of transportation in tourism', *Proceedings of the Eastern Asia Society for Transportation Studies*, 5: 1767–77.

Stradling, S., Carreno, M., Rye, T. and Noble, A. (2007) 'Passenger perceptions and the ideal urban bus journey experience', *Transport Policy*, 14: 283–92.

Sussmann, S. and Rashcovsky, C. (1997) 'A cross-cultural analysis of English and French Canadian's vacation travel patterns', *International Journal of Hospitality Management*, 16: 191–208.

Sustainable Mobility for Munich (2010) *Sustainable Mobility for Munich: Sustainability Report 2010 of Münchner Verkehrsgesellschaft mbH*, Munich: Münchner Verkehrsgesellschaft mbH (MVG).

Thompson, K. (2004) 'Tourists' use of public transportation information: What they need and what they get', paper presented at the Association for European Transport Strasbourg, France, October 2004.

Thompson, K. and Schofield, P. (2007) 'An investigation of the relationship between public transport performance and destination satisfaction', *Journal of Transport Geography*, 15: 136–44.

37

Sustainable space tourism

New destinations, new challenges

David Timothy Duval and C. Michael Hall

Space tourism is the temporary movement of people for non-military and scientific reasons beyond the Earth's atmosphere. The Kármán line, at an altitude of 100 km (62 miles) above sea level, is conventionally used as the start of outer space for regulatory purposes, such as the 1967 UN Outer Space Treaty.

Introduction

Space travel for the purposes of tourism has received a reasonably substantial amount of attention in academic literature. Not withstanding the loss of the *VSS Enterprise*, an experimental space vehicle from Virgin Galactic, in October 2014, and the unknown long-term impact this will have, space tourism nevertheless holds a reasonably high public profile as a result of commercial space tourism ventures such as Virgin Galactic (e.g. *The Guardian* 2014; Ronson 2014) as well as the growth of companies such as Space X (*The Guardian* 2014). Questions often centre around the financial viability of public space travel (Crouch *et al.* 2009; Hempsell 2010; Giacalone 2013; Salt 2013), which will likely mean that market segmentation is unnecessary, at least for the initial period of operation, given that the names of space tourists (such as they are at the time of writing) are easily obtained. Elias (2001) suggested that space tourism needs tickets at US$100,000 each to attract market interest, a figure that appears to be borne out by the pricing of potential space tourism operators, but whether cost functions of orbital or sub-orbital travel can support this remains unclear.

Significant environmental concerns arise from space travel, with the most pressing in the short-term – and which has received the most attention in the astronautical literature – being orbital detritus from launch vehicles and decommissioned or non–functioning purposive orbital vehicles. There is also concern over potential emissions effects on the Earth's atmosphere should growth forecasts come to fruition (Ross *et al.* 2010; Scott *et al.* 2012; see also case study below). Fawkes (2007a, 2007b) estimates that a typical suborbital flight, using technology similar to Bristol Spaceplanes' Ascender, will produce total CO_2 emissions of 6,267 kg per flight and therefore

3,133 kg per passenger. Virgin Galactic has stated that its spaceport will use renewable energy and may even be a net energy producer, which could make it 'carbon negative', and that its suborbital flights will have emissions equivalent to a business–class flight from London to New York (Fawkes 2007a, 2007b). However, such claims need much more detailed analysis and will likely not be verifiable until commercial flights commence (Scott *et al.* 2012).

Not unlike emissions on Earth, or limiting impact through recognised carrying capacities, the focus in space is on mitigation. However, this problem is somewhat compounded by significant advances in technology, with many countries, and indeed private enterprises, actively planning launch vehicles destined for Earth orbit. The result is a new space race involving many actors; in this sense it mirrors the gradual exploitation of sensitive environments on Earth for tourism purposes. As Singer and Musacchio (2011) have argued, there exist significant asymmetric incentives to adopt mitigation strategies, leading to a tragedy of the commons effect.

Space tourism, then, represents an idealised experiment for international and domestic policy implementation (Webber 2013). It reflects an opportunity to determine whether private and public valuation of an environment can co-exist and, at the same time, generate profits as well as measuring externalities from the development of a fragile environment from an early stage. It is further a chance to establish whether there is an agreed–upon level of internalisation of negative externalities. The growth of space tourism in the broader sense also leaves us with some philosophical questions as to whether there is the political will and private sector imperative to mitigate damage to the space environment as well as, a willingness to leave some potential tourism locations untouched (see also Apel 1997). More critically, who will lead the charge to enact global policy and governance in this regard?

This chapter attempts to unravel these and other questions. We start with an exploration of the ethical and philosophical perspectives that can be applied to space explorations. We then tackle the thorny subject of space policy in the context of global governance, concluding that previous efforts have not yet fully adopted what can truly be classed as a 'one-for-all' policy approach. We consider parallels to the current situation regarding emissions mitigation, policy and international air transport and, unfortunately, conclude that the political and economic weight needed does not yet exist. We conclude the chapter with some sobering policy scenarios, and offer a framework that can help position the issue as one of some importance. Whilst the scientific literature has clearly defined various distance bands of space in and around the Earth (e.g. near-Earth orbit, low-Earth orbit), we are here less concerned with these distinctions. Instead, we treat all extra-terrestrial activity for the purposes of tourism as part of a wider definition of 'space tourism'; carried with this are generalisable, but not always applicable, issues of sustainability, resource use, moral and ethical business practices and policy.

Emissions from suborbital flight

A new 'hybrid' rocket engine, which oxidises a solid synthetic hydrocarbon (HC) fuel with N_2O, is the chosen propellant for a number of the suborbital spaceships that will be flying soon (Chandler 2007). Although the stratospheric emissions from a single suborbital rocket are small compared to an orbital rocket, Ross *et al.* (2009, 2010) believe that total suborbital fleet emissions could become comparable to present-day rocket emissions within a decade. Using a global climate model (WACCM3) Ross *et al.* (2010) predict that emissions from 1,000 suborbital launches using this hybrid engine would create a persistent layer of black carbon particulate in the northern stratosphere that could cause potentially significant changes in the global atmospheric circulation and distributions of ozone and temperature. Tropical ozone columns are predicted to decline by as much as 1 per cent, while polar ozone columns increase by up to 6 per cent. Polar surface temperatures rise one degree K regionally and polar summer sea ice fractions shrink between 5 and 15 per cent. After one decade of continuous launches, Ross *et al.* (2010) forecast that globally averaged radiative forcing (RF) from the black carbon would exceed the forcing from the emitted CO_2 by a factor of about 140,000 and would be comparable to the RF estimated from current subsonic aviation. Stratospheric ozone depletion is also significant as it reduces ocean carbon uptake and increases ocean acidification (Lenton *et al.* 2009).

Ethics and philosophy of space exploration/exploitation

In many respects, space is the last remaining imperial and mercantile frontier. Consequently, many of the same philosophical and moral questions that arise from activities that are congruent with imperial and mercantile expansion also apply. A first principle to question is whether there is value to space beyond human interests. At the human interest level, there is obvious considerable scientific and increasing heritage value. The cultural landscapes on space travel are already tourist attractions on Earth and they are obvious sites of tourism exploitation on other planetary bodies and even in Earth orbit (Gorman 2005). Commercial interests (discussed later) are present in the form of tourism development, mining, defence and other activities (Williamson 2003).

In her review of whether space can be considered an environment, Reiman (2009) provides a reasonably comprehensive assessment of the applicability of environmental ethics as they are known for being applied on Earth. The argument against considering space an environment can, according to Reiman, rest on the infinite nature of space (compared to the relatively closed system of Earth), the shift away from precocious environmental problems on Earth, and the fact that the lifeless reality of space lends itself to differential treatment with respect to resource exploitation. Indeed, she questions: 'Do we need to worry about the moral implications of our actions in the vastness of space?' (Reiman 2009: 81).

In support of adopting (or even championing) Earth-based environmental ethics to space (Henry 2009), we return to Reiman's treatment, which suggests that the application of a human perspective, where our interests reign supreme, is neither moral nor logical. The amount of knowledge we possess of space is undoubtedly limited, but growing, so a great many philosophical and environmental ethical tests applied on Earth have not yet had a chance to be tested extra-terrestrially. For example, Williamson (2003: 48) assigns value to space:

> It can be argued that the space environment is valuable because it represents freedom, by providing an almost unlimited expanse for mankind to explore, understand and, if he so wishes, to conquer. So if, for some reason, a part of that expanse – such as a planetary surface – became inaccessible, a part of that freedom would be lost. Placing a value on footprints and historic sites of exploration is difficult, but if it can be done for the Earth, it can be done for the Moon.

From this, Williamson argues for a code of space ethics on the basis that such codes are firmly in place (in some jurisdictions) on Earth for human activities that may result in serious ecological damage. He (2003: 48) argues that a code of space ethics would thus cover 'the impact of our actions in space on each other, on each other's property, on the Earth (which already benefits to some extent from our protection), and on the space environment itself'. Williamson's consideration of an ethical code extends to space tourism, specifically the debris created from low-Earth orbit vehicles and the potential for damage from pollution on planetary bodies (such as the Moon) which lack atmospheric and ecological systems that, unlike Earth, allow for partial or full regeneration. Moreover, should life be discovered on other bodies, which appears increasingly likely, then clearly new ethical concerns emerge. A more precautionary approach (see Chapter 4) would therefore suggest that the adoption of an ethical environmental code in space would be a logical step in the protection of other environments, even though such steps have not been especially successful on Earth.

In shorter time horizons, such as within the next 20 years, an immediate policy issue is the protection of off-Earth heritage sites associated with space exploration. For example, Spennermann (2004: 288) cautions against the exploitation of notable space-centred places, such as the moon landing site from the US Apollo programme as 'literally one wrong step will ruin much of the unique heritage on the Moon'. While the Moon is immediately an obvious location of significant space heritage for tourism, especially given plans for the establishment of space bases on the Moon as well as space tourism flights around the Moon, in the longer term, locations on Mars may similarly require protection given the publicly avowed interest by countries and private enterprise in establishing both a scientific and permanent human presence on the planet. It is worth noting that, as of May 2013, the 1979 Agreement Governing the Activities of States on the Moon and Other Celestial Bodies, better known as the 'Moon Treaty', that sought to create a regulatory regime on planetary bodies similar to that for the sea floor under the UN Law of the Sea had only 17 state parties with a further four states having signed, but not acceded. China, Russia and the USA are not state parties to the agreement. Significantly, this treaty seeks to prevent altering the environment of celestial bodies and requires that states must take measures to prevent accidental contamination and adopt a common heritage of mankind principle.

Indeed, what once belonged to the pages of science fiction is now becoming borderline reality in the commercialisation of space. At one extreme, the potential of terra-forming of other planets for human colonisation and tourism purposes is an obvious example. However, even within existing generations, the development of commercial inter-planetary space travel would clearly require the need for the adoption of strict biosecurity protocols so that Earth organisms, such as bacteria and viruses, were not introduced into a new planetary environment, thereby potentially creating change not only in that body's environment but also in evolutionary processes. Yet the adoption of strict biosecurity protocols would add extra expense to an already expensive mission. In addition, depending on national jurisdictions may not be required under the sponsoring country's laws. In an 'unfettered' commercial space race, it is even possible to imagine 'flags of convenience'.

Space as a contested policy sphere

In this section, we unpack some of the critical parameters against which space tourism policy must evolve. We base our review on common tourism policy issues where sensitive environments are involved. The range of the discussion, then, is framed by wider governmental issues versus questions about how policy is approached and framed and how it applies to individual, corporate and state behaviour (Bensoussan 2010; Griffith & Campbell 2013; Salt 2013). Space is contested along several dimensions. The most obvious is its military significance and, as such, several calls have been made to encourage a peaceful approach to the development of space for commercial purposes (e.g. Som 2010). It is also contested legally: jurisdictions as they are defined for mobility on Earth have not been adopted for space.

A key issue for the governance of space tourism is determining where the atmosphere ends and 'outer space' begins; there is much debate and currently no legal definition (Freeland 2010). The Outer Space Treaty (United Nations 1967) states that there is no national sovereignty over outer space or celestial bodies, that all activities should be used for peaceful purposes, and that states will be liable for any damage caused by their space objects. As of May 2013, 102 countries were parties to the treaty, with another 27 having signed but who have not completed ratification. However, this treaty was developed at a time in which space exploration was almost the exclusive domain of national governments. In the current century, space is becoming increasingly privatised and corporatised; international law has not been able to keep up. Freeland (2010), therefore, argues that space tourism is for the most part 'free' for any state to participate in without prior consent.

Argument 1. Space should be heavily regulated.

There is an argument that space tourism should perhaps be more regulated than terrestrial-based environments because there will be a limited number of active participants in providing space-based tourism experiences given the substantial capital costs involved. This will limit the competitive market. It is reasonable to speculate that the industry will mirror its commercial aviation cousin, where up-front costs and variable operating costs of fuel will be substantial. Indeed, Goehlich (2005) reviewed the economic performance of several launch vehicles and found that variations exist depending on whether they are destined for full or sub-orbit.

Regulatory imperatives include the following:

A. Should nation states be responsible for the environmental damage done by private sector companies offering space tourism? Might this result in extra-terrestrial flags of convenience that more or less mirror the situation with cruise ships?
B. If so, which body shall ultimately take authority for the generation and application of regulations governing space activities? Currently the UN via the United Nations Office for Outer Space Affairs acts as a *de facto* regulatory body. However, this role is increasingly being superseded by national and commercial space activities.

Argument 2. The development of space tourism should not be left exclusively to private sector interests.

Numerous countries have made technological advances that could sustain government-subsidised space-based tourism activities (Dupas & Logsdon 2007):

A. Both Europe and Japan have full capability to produce launch vehicles able to reach the International Space Station.
B. China has already demonstrated their ability to undertake manned space operations, joining the United States and Russia.
C. India has signalled its intent to develop launch vehicles as well and already has an active space programme.

Such development is not restricted to government-funded projects, however. Hertzfeld and Peter (2007) suggest that government support will be necessary to fund space exploration given the high costs involved. Indeed, they further suggest that such support would need multiple government support, but the political feasibility of this remains questionable. For example, the UK's southwest has actively considered Bristol as the site where meaningful development of space exploration and tourism technologies could be developed, but it was recognised that this would take serious commitment from both government and industry (Ashford 2007). Sweden has a high-latitude launch site near Kiruna that already acts as a location for European polar space research and has been mooted as a potential European site for future Virgin Galactic operations (Hobe 2007). Noichim (2008) calls for greater cooperation amongst ASEAN nations in this regard. As is known from wider government policy, if there is an economic or social imperative for government support and operational subsidy it is more likely to find political favour. Beyond the International Space Station and some joint missions there exists little evidence of tangible substantial and systematic government cooperation in space activities. In the immediate term, then, the extent of this cooperation may primarily be almost entirely economic, which it arguably is in the case of many joint missions anyway, with the principles of creating commercial opportunities being offered as the primary reason for inter-governmental support. The environment, however, runs the risk of being left behind in these types of arrangements.

Argument 3. The fragility of space shall require internalisation of the externalities generated from space tourism.

The policy imperative attached to airline emissions in the past decade carries a strong correlation to what is likely possible as space tourism develops. As is widely known, the EU included aviation in its controversial Emissions Trading Scheme (a decision subsequently reviewed), where all airlines operating within and to European zone countries were required to account for specific proportions of the emissions they generated (Scott *et al.* 2012). This generated significant concerns with trade-based partners such as the United States, India and China leading to threats of trade wars. At the time of writing such measures remain unresolved.

The precise details are beyond the scope of our chapter, but the lesson from this is that neither unilateral nor bilateral approaches to the management of airline emissions have yet been shown to be substantially beneficial to the environment. Space-based tourism policy, then, needs to actively be structured where there exists a common (and not differentiated) value attached to space, despite the fact that it remains the medium in which contested business models will eventually develop.

Governance and best practice

It was an agreement reached in Paris in 1919 that set the stage for the regulation of air space above independent nation states. The agreement stipulated that countries carried sovereignty over the airspace above their territory. Not 100 years later, the relevance and significance of this agreement can be called into question given the commercialisation of Earth orbit for tourists is indeed possible, if not highly likely in the near future.

Space is a common pool resource; not entirely unlike lakes, groundwater, forests, and other natural amenities (Weedon & Chow 2012; see also Meek 2012). Resource economists call these 'common property resources' and raise issues with respect to their governance. However, in one sense, space is not a global commons, at least not technically (see Weedon & Chow 2012). There are several reasons for this (see Weedon 2012). First, the private benefits are small, at least relative to the activities of other transport-related commercial activities on Earth. For the foreseeable future, the number of commercial space operations transiting tourists into low-Earth orbit will be small, and the financial viability of these may not be stable. Second, the raw social benefits from tourism will thus stem from private organisations. In other words, if space becomes an environment in which no governmental oversight is held, social benefits will come entirely from, and thus be at the disposal of, private providers of space tourism. Derivatives from taxation, for example, which can be a net positive social contribution, may not be realised.

International cooperation in the management of commercial activities in space will be necessary to ensure environmental stability and avoid destruction of this common property resource (Riess 2005). Ansdell *et al.* (2011b) note that addressing space sustainability requires international engagement, due to the distinct conditions of the space domain that force interdependences between policy actors. A significant issue in the adoption of a pan-governmental approach to managing space tourism policy is that there exist multiple actors, and not everyone has perfect information. In fact, only the US and Russia have space situation analysis, so other actors are not aware of resource impacts or issues, other than what they are told. This imperfect information presents a significant risk to the appropriate development of space tourism. The 2010 United States National Space Policy is explicit in its concern for the environment of space (including recognition of debris and risks of collision) and emphasises the need for international cooperation, but this should be entirely under the auspices of international law. It is precisely this brand of law, however, that has yet to be formally cast and agreed upon internationally. Law is informed by policy, and space policy at the international level is not yet fully developed.

Williamson (2003: 51) proposes that a wider pan-governmental body charged with developing space policy should adopt the following:

- formation and enactment of a policy to maintain and expand the constituency of the body, specifically regarding its international nature;
- formation and enactment of a policy to obtain funding and other support from key space-related organisations;
- formation and enactment of a policy to ensure the promulgation of ideas among the space community and the media; and
- consideration of a 'set of guidelines' or 'code of practice' as a precursor to more formal policies or legislation.

Weedon and Chow (2012) offer some policy responses to the problem of the commons and space. First, they posit a regulatory boundary that separates airspace and low-Earth orbit common pool resources. Second, they argue that space offers unique environmental characteristics. Third, they suggest a need for ensuring that information on development, management and oversight of space tourism activities is properly disseminated among the increasingly diverse range of actors involved in space transport. Weedon and Chow (2012) also argue for a firm regulatory application of international and national laws, which may be somewhat problematic given the already obtuse nature of international legal regulation of terrestrial-based air transport.

One area of debate centres on whether space can have applied to it the tragedy of the commons principle. Milligan (2011) forwards the argument that private sector investment in space requires consideration of private property rights of space. However, this provides a policy challenge that may require changes to existing treaties on the use of space, although there is always the potential for some countries to ignore such treaties. The current situation is that neither privatisation nor the outright rule of domestic law is entirely applicable to space and there is therefore an urgent need to develop new space law that reflects current industrial interests. Nevertheless, potential key state parties, while developing domestic space and space tourism law, do not demonstrate sufficient interest in the urgent development of new legal regimes for space.

Conclusion – Sustainable development: Lessons from terrestrial management

Since the late 1960s, space tourism has always been something 'coming soon' (Salt 2013; Webber 2013). Billings (2006) offers a candid overview for the prospect for space tourism. At the moment, space exploration is confined just to government efforts, but it is becoming increasingly open to entrepreneurs and those with significant net worth, several of which receive significant government support in the development of such ventures. We offer several environmentally informed points as space tourism, or its prospects, continue to unfold as part of a sustainable tourism research agenda for the future:

1   The ticket price paid by space tourists may be exceptionally expensive, at least initially (Goehlich 2005). Would such tourists be willing to pay more to offset the negative environmental externalities of their activities?

2   What will be the relationship between environmental considerations of military activities in space and those devoted specifically to commercial operations? Indeed, there has been some speculation as to the potential difficulties in this regard owing to the International Traffic Arms Regulations (ITAR) statutes. These classify, under US law, launch vehicles in the same manner as so-called 'sensitive munitions', against which there are restrictions on export (Hertzfeld & Peter 2007). This could have significant negative implications for successful private enterprise operations facing substantial costs yet smaller markets (see also Ansdell *et al.* 2011a).

3   What relationship will space tourism have with respect to climate change in general? The wider alignment with climate change and space has been at least recognised formally in policy. For instance, a 2011 European Commission Communication on space strategy and benefits to citizens makes direct links between climate change and space strategy, noting that European space policy 'will help underpin a sustainable use of resources as well as providing better information on climate change. It may thus be used to support policies on climate change adaptation and security and to contribute to crisis prevention and management, with particular emphasis on humanitarian aid, development assistance and civil protection' (European Commission 2011: 4).

Recent work has suggested that, after substantial launches over the course of a decade, there would be a significant increase in RF above existing air travel activities and a potential increase in ground temperature (Ross *et al.* 2010).

Som (2010) argued that a three-pronged approach to space exploration should incorporate public opinion, specific policy and, perhaps most critically, international cooperation. We would argue strongly that considered environmental issues be included. That said, problematic with any assessment and a subsequent push toward 'greening' space tourism is the information vacuum that exists regarding the interaction between human activities and the space environment. It took decades to work out precisely the extent and seriousness of anthromorphic damage caused by humans to the atmosphere. There are several concerns in this regard: first, the relatively low traffic rate of space tourism may render the issue comparatively insignificant by regulatory bodies. Similarly, private sector interests may drive much of the policy agenda relating to regulation, with little guarantee that, in the long term, appropriate efforts will be made to protect the space environment. Orbital junk from launch vehicles poses an immediate threat and does not break down. At the atmosphere level, the common pool resource that is the atmosphere could be at more risk.

Third, the cost of undertaking experimentation and testing the tolerance and limits of the atmosphere may preclude the acquisition of detailed and useful knowledge that could be put to use in policy measures and implementation. Fourth, problematic in any assessment of the damage of tourism activities is defining the scope of the problem. Reporting on a symposium held in 2005 that focused on space law, Hobe and Neumann (2005) highlighted that there lacked a definition of outer space. It would seem, then, that international agreement in this regard is critical.

Finally, space law will require congruence, particularly those in larger trading blocs such as the EU (Rieder *et al.* 2009). We therefore argue that any international efforts targeted at ensuring environmentally conscious developments in space for the purposes of tourism should look to how international agreements over the environmental impact of commercial aviation has unfolded, particularly from a policy perspective.

Key Reading

Freeland, S. (2010) 'Fly me to the moon: How will international law cope with commercial space tourism?' *Melbourne Journal of International Law,* 11: 1–29.

Ross, M., Mills, M. and Toohey, D. (2010) 'Potential climate impact of black carbon emitted by rockets', *Geophysical Research Letters,* 37(24) DOI: 10.1029/2010GL044548

Salt, D.J. (2013) 'Space tourism: Delivering on the dream', *Acta Astronautica,* 92(2): 178–86.

References

Ansdell, M., Ehrenfreund, P. and McKay, C. (2011a) 'Stepping stones toward global space exploration', *Acta Astronautica,* 68: 2098–2113.

Ansdell, M., Delgado, L. and Hendrickson, D. (2011b) *Analyzing the Development Paths of Emerging Spacefaring Nations: Opportunities or Challenges for Space Sustainability?* IAFF 6159: Capstone Research, Secure World Foundation. Available at: http://swfound.org/media/46122/emergingspaceactors_ executive%20summary-august2011.pdf (accessed 2 April 2013).

Apel, W. (1997) 'Space tourism – a promising future?', Space Policy, 13: 279–284.

Ashford, D. (2007) 'New business opportunities in space', *Space Policy,* 23: 241–42.

Bensoussan, D. (2010) 'Space tourism risks: A space insurance perspective', *Acta Astronautica,* 66(11–12): 1633–38.

Billings, L. (2006) 'Exploration for the masses? Or joyrides for the ultra-rich? Prospects for space tourism', *Space Policy,* 22: 162–64.

Chandler, D. (2007) 'Space: Dreams of a new space race', *Nature,* 448: 988–91.

Crouch, I.G., Devinney, M.T., Louviere, J.J. and Islam, T. (2009) 'Modelling consumer choice behaviour in space tourism', *Tourism Management,* 30(3): 441–54.

Dupas, A. and Logsdon, J.M. (2007) 'Creating a productive international partnership in the vision for space exploration', *Space Policy,* 23: 24–28.

Elias, A. (2001) 'Affordable space transportation: Impossible dream or near-term reality?' *Air & Space Europe,* 3(1–2): 121–24.

European Commission (2011) *Communication from the Commission to the Council, The European Parliament, The European Economic and Social Committee and The Committee of the Regions. Towards a Space Strategy for The European Union that Benefits its Citizens,* 52011DC0152. Brussels: European Commission.

Fawkes, S. (2007a) 'Virgin Galactic has been careful to play down any adverse environmental effects caused by SpaceShipTwo tourist flights, but is that enough to satisfy regulators and activists?' *The Space Review.* Available at: www.thespacereview.com/article/813/1 (Accessed 1 April 2010).

—— (2007b) 'Carbon dioxide emissions resulting from space tourism', *Journal of the British Interplanetary Society,* 60: 409–13.

Freeland, S. (2010) Fly me to the moon: How will international law cope with commercial space tourism? *Melbourne Journal of International Law,* 11(1): 1–29.

Giacalone, J.A. (2013) 'The evolving private spaceflight industry: Space tourism and cargo transport', *ASBBS Annual Conference: Las Vegas,* 20(1): 643–50.

Goehlich, R.A. (2005) 'A ticket pricing strategy for an oligopolistic space tourism market', *Space Policy,* 21: 293–306.

Gorman, A. (2005) 'The cultural landscape of interplanetary space', *Journal of Social Archaeology,* 5(1): 85–107.

Griffith, D. and Campbell, M.R. (2013) 'Sub-orbital commercial human space flight and informed consent in the United States', *Acta Astronautica,* 92(2): 263–65.

Hempsell, M. (2010) 'A phased approach to orbital public access', *Acta Austronautica,* 66: 1639–44.

Henry, H. (2009) 'Re-thinking Apollo: Envisioning environmentalism in space', in D. Bell and M. Parker (eds.) *Space Travel & Culture: From Apollo to Space Tourism.* Oxford: Blackwell.

Hertzfeld, H.R. and Peter, N. (2007) 'Developing new launch vehicle technology: The case for multinational private sector cooperation', *Space Policy,* 23: 81–89.

Hobe, S. (2007) 'Legal aspects of space tourism', *Nebraska Law Review,* 86: 439–58.

Hobe, S. and Neumann, J. (2005) 'Global and European challenges for space law at the edge of the 21st century', *Space Policy,* 21: 313–15.

Lenton, A., Codron, F., Bopp, L., Metzl, N., Cadule, P., Tagliabue, A. and Le Sommer, J. (2009). Stratospheric ozone depletion reduces ocean carbon uptake and enhances ocean acidification. *Geophysical Research Letters,* 36(12), DOI: 10.1029/2009GL038227.

Meek, P.A. (2012) 'The CPR approach to space sustainability: Commentaries on Weeden and Chow', *Space Policy,* 28: 173–76.

Milligan, T. (2011) 'Property rights and the duty to extend human life', *Space Policy,* 27: 190–93.

Noichim, C. (2008) 'Promoting ASEAN space cooperation', *Space Policy,* 24: 10–12.

Reiman, S. (2009) 'Is space an environment?', *Space Policy,* 25: 81–87.

Rieder, S., Bruston, J., Mathieu, C. and Schrogl, K-U. (2009) 'Governance of national space activities', *Space Policy,* 25: 133–35.

Riess, C. (2005) 'A new setting for international space cooperation?', *Space Policy,* 21: 49–53.

Ronson, J. (2014) 'Jon Ronson is ready for blast-off. Is Richard Branson?' *The Guardian,* Friday 21 February.

Ross, M., Toohey, D., Peinemann, M. and Ross, P. (2009) 'Limits on the space launch market related to stratospheric ozone depletion', *Astropolitics,* 7(1): 50–82.

Ross, M., Mills, M. and Toohey, D. (2010) 'Potential climate impact of black carbon emitted by rockets', *Geophysical Research Letters,* 37(24) DOI: 10.1029/2010GL044548.

Salt, D. J. (2013) 'Space tourism – Delivering on the dream', *Acta Astronautica,* 92: 178–86.

Scott, D., Gössling, S. and Hall, C.M. (2012) *Tourism and Climate Change,* Abingdon: Routledge.

Singer, M.J. and Musacchio, J.T. (2011) 'An international environmental agreement for space debris mitigation among asymmetric nations', *Acta Astronautica,* 68: 326–37.

Som, S. (2010) 'An international symbol for the sustained exploration of space', *Space Policy,* 26: 140–42.

Spennermann, D.H.R. (2004) 'The ethics of treading on Neil Armstrong's footprints', *Space Policy,* 20: 279–90.

The Guardian (2014) 'Elon Musk unveils Dragon V2 spacecraft for seven astronauts', *The Guardian,* Friday 30 May.

United Nations (1967) *Treaty on Principles Governing the Activities of States in the Exploration and Uses of Outerspace, Including the Moon and other Celestial Bodies.* United Nations Office for Outer Space Affairs. Online. Available at: www.unoosa.org/oosa/SpaceLaw/outerspt.html.

—— (1979) *Agreement Governing the Activities of States on the Moon and Other Celestial Bodies.* United Nations Office for Outer Space Affairs. Online. Available at: www.unoosa.org/oosa/SpaceLaw/outerspt.html.

Webber, D. (2013) 'Space tourism: Its history, future and importance', *Acta Astronautica,* 92(2): 138–43.

Weedon, B. (2012) 'The economics of space sustainability', The Space Review, 4 June

Weedon, B.C. and Chow, T. (2012) 'Taking a common-pool resources approach to space sustainability: A framework and potential policies', *Space Policy,* 28: 166–72.

Williamson, M. (2003) 'Space ethics and protection of the space environment', *Space Policy,* 19: 47–52.

Part 6
Emerging issues and the future

38

Peak Oil and tourism

The end of growth?

Susanne Becken

Peak Oil Point (or period) in time when the maximum rate of petroleum extraction is reached, and after which the rate of production enters terminal decline.

Energy security The term energy security implies that energy supply is reliable, adequate and affordable (Chester 2010).

Conventional oil Mixture of hydrocarbons recoverable (easily and without extra stimulation) at a well from an underground reservoir and liquid at atmospheric pressure and temperature.

Low-carbon tourism Tourism that has minimal emissions of carbon dioxide, thus reducing its impact on the global climate and, at the same time, reducing dependence on fossil fuels.

Hidden hazard Hazards that 'despite serious consequences for the risk bearers and society more generally...pass virtually unnoticed or untended, often continuing to grow in effects until reaching disaster proportions' (Pidgeon, Kasperson & Slovic 2003: 23).

Introduction

It is commonly said that 'oil is the lifeblood of our economy'. The same is true for tourism. Tourism and oil are inextricably interlinked. Tourism is a heavy user of petroleum products, not only for transporting people and goods, but also for many other components of the tourism product, including infrastructure, consumables and hospitality services. Despite growing demand for oil and oil-derived products, there is also increasing concern about a global peak in oil production (UK Energy Research Institute 2009), and what this might mean for tourism and society (Becken 2011). At the very least, increasing scarcity will result in higher oil prices, making tourism more expensive and restraining its growth potential. In more apocalyptic scenarios, rising oil prices will have severe implications for society, development, security and peace (Friedrichs 2010). Attempts to reduce tourism's dependence on fossil fuels align very well with advancing low–carbon economies and carbon management in tourism (Gössling 2010).

In the short term, the main challenge for tourism is the increase in price of oil. As Campbell and Laherrère (1998: 6) summarised: 'The world is not running out of oil – at least not yet. What our society does face, and soon, is the end of the abundant and cheap oil on which all industrial nations depend.' Thus, this chapter provides an insight into what Peak Oil is and how it might affect tourism. A case study from New Zealand is provided to illustrate implications in more detail.

Background on Peak Oil

The real price of oil has oscillated markedly since the oil crises in the 1970s. In 2007, oil prices increased sharply and reached record levels of US$147 per barrel of crude oil in June 2008. Since then, demand has decreased as a result of the Global Financial Crisis. Prices dropped to under $60 per barrel, rising again following the Arab Spring in 2011 to over $100 per barrel.

Multiple factors shape the price of oil and are responsible for its short-term price volatility, but in the long term, prices are mainly driven by world oil supply and demand and by the ultimately available physical resources. Estimates for the so-called 'ultimate reserves' vary depending on the assumptions made, but generally, are believed to range between a total of 2,000 to a maximum of 3,000 or 4,000 billion barrels (e.g. Duncan & Youngquist 1999; Hirsch, Bezdek & Wendling 2005). It is generally believed that we have used around 1,300 billion barrels (Bentley 2002), which – assuming that the ultimate reserve is around 2,600 billion barrels – would represent about half of the global ultimate reserves (Thévard 2012). BP's *Statistical Review of World Energy* (2012) reports 1,622 billion barrels of 'proved reserves' to be exploited. However, Thévard (2012) noted that this figure represents an increase of 20 per cent compared with the previous year, when the *Oil and Gas Journal* only estimated an increase of 3.6 per cent. This discrepancy highlights the notoriously conflicting information on global and national-level oil data, and the lack of transparency and consistency. In addition to 'proved reserves' there are 'probable' and 'possible reserves', some of which – more recently – include estimates of non-conventional oil resources such as tar sands or oil shales. Some of the reserves have been criticised as 'paper barrels', which are artificially created by oil companies or oil-exporting countries for political or commercial reasons (Bell, Dunlop & Glazebrook 2008).

Oil and gas contribute about 35 per cent and 21 per cent to worldwide energy use, respectively. Coal adds a further 25 per cent (International Energy Agency 2006). Hence, in most economies, oil is the dominant energy source, especially as it facilitates most types of transportation (95 per cent of transport relies on petroleum fuels; Intergovernmental Panel on Climate Change 2007). The import of oil constitutes a major cost for most countries, with only 33 countries producing more than they consume. The European Union for example, spends 1.7 per cent of its Gross Domestic Product (GDP) on imported oil; this is forecast to increase to 2.8 per cent for the year 2012 (Thévard 2012). Thus, concerns about energy security are increasing. Such concern is evident in publications such as the report by the German Bundeswehr, Peak Oil (Planungsamt der Bundeswehr 2012) in which the importance of oil for Germany is analysed and security risks are explored systematically. It concludes that Peak Oil is inevitable, and geopolitical shifts in power and dependencies are likely, posing substantial challenges for Germany and the values it currently seeks to embed in its international partnerships.

In 2012, global oil consumption reached a level of 88 million barrels, representing a growth of 2.5 per cent compared with 2011 (BP 2012). Annual global oil production increased by 1.1 million barrels per day (mb/d), an increase of 1.3 per cent compared to 2011, indicating that some of the growth in demand was met by reserves from earlier production. Almost all of the net growth was in Saudi Arabia (+1.2 mb/d), the United Arab Emirates, Kuwait and Iraq; offsetting the loss of supply from Libya of 1.2 mb/d. The US was also able to increase its oil production for a third consecutive year (BP 2012).

When demand increases faster than supply, and when at some point supply will decrease at an unknown rate, the gap between demand and supply will grow further and further. The point of 'peaking of production' will only be known with hindsight. Already in 2007, the global oil demand was larger than production in the same year (86.1 mb/d compared with 85.6 mb/d production; International Energy Agency 2008). Considering that demand continues to grow and global production has only increased marginally, it is possible that the peak is close, has already been reached or indeed has passed. Considering the potential quantities of oil production from unconventional sources (e.g. deep sea, tar sands, extra-heavy oil, tight oil, and synthetic fuels), Thévard (2012) proposes that production will start to decline in 2014 to 2015. This is approximately in line with Aleklett *et al.* (2010) who, in their critique of the International Energy Agency's *World Energy Outlook*, concluded that the forecast production of oil in 2030 is 75.8 million barrels per day and not 101.5 million barrels per day, as suggested by the International Energy Agency (IEA 2008). The IEA has been criticised by many analysts because their forecast is based on the underlying assumption that market mechanisms (and technology development) will prevail and always ensure that supply meets demand (Friedrichs 2011). The IEA is accused of taking an insufficient account of the physical and political realities of oil production.

The rate of decline in global production after Peak Oil (or a plateau) depends on many factors, including the rate of discovery of new fields and the technology available to extract the oil. The world's largest 120 fields make up 50 per cent of production; 70 per cent of global production comes from fields that are at least 30 years old. Recent discoveries have typically been small, with an average size of only 10 billion barrels, well down from an average field size of new discoveries of 527 million barrels in the 1960s and 1970s (Energy Watch Group 2007). One key challenge is the increasing Energy Return on Investment (EROI) ratio. This means that we need to spend increasing amounts of energy to produce oil, with the net energy that is available to society to 'do work' becoming smaller and smaller. In the early days of twentieth century exploration, one barrel of oil was required to find, extract and process 100 barrels; thus the EROI was 100:1. Global EROI for oil in 2005 was 30:1, and that of oil shales, for example, is currently under 5:1 (Thévard 2012).

Tourism's denial of Peak Oil

Peak Oil is an excellent example of a 'hidden hazard' where extreme attenuation of risk results in the risk being unnoticed until it reaches catastrophic dimensions (Pidgeon *et al.* 2003). Kasperson and Kasperson (1991) elaborate that hidden hazards are: (1) globally elusive, (2) ideological, (3) marginal, (4) amplification-driven and (5) value-threatening. The previous section has already provided evidence why Peak Oil is a globally elusive hazard, not only because it is complex, but also because information and knowledge is fragmented, and often purposefully distorted, so that detailed risk assessments are challenging.

Ideologically, and in the context of tourism, the risk of Peak Oil is attenuated because of the systematic elevation of tourism–related benefits, rather than its resource-consuming nature. More specifically, discourses by the UNWTO (e.g. UNWTO 2001), the broader travel industry and society on economic growth, regional development, poverty elimination through tourism, the 'right to travel', hedonic experiences facilitated by travel, and the aspirational goal of education through travel clearly emphasise the 'good' of tourism, leaving little room for questioning underlying risks or impacts. Ideological controversies around oil supplies lead some analysts to avoid the term Peak Oil and refer to energy security instead. Only few have critiqued the moral dimensions of Peak Oil and the system that 'has been so purposefully designed to run on ever increasing supplies of cheap fossil fuel' (Lloyd 2007: 5810). Similarly, very limited research has been undertaken on those societal groups that are most vulnerable to Peak Oil (see also Becken 2011). Despite the wide democratisation of tourism, travel remains a privilege for a minority of the global population. Thus, the concept of tourism, by its very nature, excludes those groups who already live at the margins of their coping capacity.

Peak Oil is also a good example of a hazard that is driven by amplification, which means that the initial risk is increased by amplifying effects. The so-called ripple effect in the social amplification of risk framework (Pidgeon *et al.* 2003) relates to second or third order effects that can exacerbate initial risks. The exponential increase in prices in 2008 illustrated how physical and infrastructural bottlenecks resulted in higher oil prices, which then sparked a speculation frenzy that drove prices to record levels, beyond those that could be explained by physical scarcity. In tourism, there could be societal ripple effects, where suddenly a tipping point is reached that demonises travel and results in the collapse of long-distance tourism. In the meantime, however, tourism is an integral part of human lifestyles and constitutes a core value of many societies around the world. All the different types of tourism statistics are evidence of this. For example, a 2008 study by Scott *et al.* estimated that globally, tourism accounted for 9,147 billion passenger kilometres. Further, recent arrival statistics highlight the continued growth in tourism, especially in the Asia Region. This growth is underpinned by a solid expansion of airline networks, especially those of low-cost carriers. However, it has also been noted that low-cost carriers will suffer most under high oil price scenarios (Yeoman *et al.* 2007).

Clearly, at this point, tourism has not fully grasped the seriousness of Peak Oil and the severe implications of rising oil prices and future shortages. Importantly, this will not only affect how individuals might choose to spend their holidays, and whether low-cost airlines survive, but a reduction in global tourism demand or a redistribution of tourism flows will severely impact tourist destinations. A study undertaken in the United States, for example, found that increased fuel costs led to a drop in demand for hotel rooms (with an elasticity of demand of -1.74), especially in suburban locations and hotels close to highways (Canina, Walsh & Enz 2003). Yeoman *et al.*'s (2007) scenario analysis in Scotland established that 'energy inflation' may result in severe reductions in tourist arrivals. Those destinations that invest heavily into new tourism infrastructure and blindly follow promises of eternal growth will likely suffer severe consequences for their local economies.

Implications

As argued by Becken (2011), the impact of increasing oil prices is complex and includes many dimensions, for example how tourists respond to price signals, how global tourist flows 'contract' to smaller geographic scales, how societal and cultural norms and understanding of mobility (Urry 2008) change, and how quickly politicians respond to the oil challenge. Increases in oil prices not only affect people's willingness and ability to travel but also lead to an increase in prices for many tourism goods and services, including those related to transportation (Becken 2009). In the past, oil price fluctuations have been insufficient to instigate major changes in travel behaviour. A 2006 study, for example, found that historic 'shock' had only a small and short-lived impact on global tourism (UNWTO 2006). This could change once oil prices reach much higher levels and thresholds of price sensitivity are reached.

The New Zealand case study (see below) shows that, while some components of tourism appear to be relatively resilient (at least in the short term) with low-price elasticities, many tourism elements are relatively vulnerable. Overall, tourism appears as an above-average vulnerable sector in the New Zealand economy. The New Zealand government is yet to introduce specific policies to address oil risks, though protective measures relating to tourism marketing, business management and product development, and transport systems could be considered. Ideally, the government would deliberately integrate a range of risk factors, including oil, in the development of their marketing portfolio. Marketing strategies would focus on intra-regional or domestic tourists, and less on long-haul international markets. Considerations of which tourists generate the highest yield would be a critical component of such a strategic approach (Becken & Simmons 2008).

Only few destinations have addressed the risk of Peak Oil. The Sunshine Coast Regional Council is one example, where a region has developed a comprehensive strategy to address both climate change and Peak Oil (Sunshine Coast Council 2010). The strategy includes a risk assessment for selected sectors, including tourism, road transport and the construction sector. It concludes that, thanks to a dominant profile of domestic visitors, the region is less vulnerable to oil prices than other regions in Australia which are more dependent on international visitation. Aside from destination management, tourism businesses are well advised to develop risk management strategies for Peak Oil. Business assistance to reduce oil vulnerability may be most effective in the form of public-private partnerships, such as the Tourism Energy Efficiency Project undertaken jointly by the Energy Efficiency and Conservation Authority and the Tourism Industry Association. Finally, a long-term view of tourism and transport would require investment into alternative low-carbon transport systems.

As discussed in Becken (2009) a range of changes might be conceivable to help tourism adapt to higher oil prices. To date, measures for reducing transport's fossil fuel dependency have largely been focused on developing new technologies (e.g. plug-in hybrid cars) and fuel sources, rather than conceptualising completely new forms of mobility (Urry 2008). The tourism sector provides a wide range of examples that illustrate the use of hybrid or electric cars, biofuel-run buses and other alternatives such as tourist boats running on coconut oil. Also, a number of leading airlines are investing heavily in the development of biofuels for aviation (Becken 2009). However, it has also been demonstrated that the scale of biofuels production will remain insignificant compared with the amount of liquid oil required to meet current and future transportation demands. Patzek (2007) put forward that it is impossible to replace fossil fuels with biofuels due to the low conversion rate of solar energy into usable energy by plants and the lack of space. Thus, low-carbon transport poses a real challenge, if current levels of passenger kilometres are to be maintained or even increased. Substituting fossil fuel intensive modes with low-carbon options provides some reduction potential. The Eurostar, for example, which connects Great Britain with the European continent, resulted in a substantial shift of travel from air to rail with more than 70 per cent of trips between London and Paris now undertaken by train (Johnson & Cottingham 2008). Increased demand for electricity is easier to meet than growing need for fossil fuels (Patzek 2007).

Case Study

New Zealand tourism and oil project

New Zealand is a long-distance destination for most of its markets and, as such, depends heavily on air transportation. Moreover, the tourism product within New Zealand is based on 'touring holidays', which also rely strongly on the availability of affordable transport systems. To understand New Zealand's vulnerability to Peak Oil, a three-year government-funded project in New Zealand investigated the implications of increasing oil prices for international tourism. A number of sub-projects were undertaken to understand consumer behaviour, business responses and macroeconomic impacts.

Research on camper van tourists indicated that higher fuel prices would likely lead to behavioural changes in New Zealand. For example, respondents indicated that they would reduce discretionary consumption on restaurants and attractions; however, they would be unlikely to change their transport behaviour. Indeed, modelling by Becken and Schiff (2011) confirmed that the link between fuel price and transport behaviour over a 10-year period was weak. Variables such as country of origin or length of stay were more important factors than fuel prices and airfares. Coupled with differentiated oil vulnerabilities and levels of price elasticity for different countries (see Schiff & Becken 2011), the importance of market mix for New Zealand's exposure to Peak Oil became evident.

Research on tourism businesses identified the following risk factors for tourism businesses with respect to higher oil prices:

- Exposure: A business that is very energy intensive and particularly dependent on oil is more exposed than energy-efficient businesses that largely rely on electricity.
- Substitution options: Energy source substitution potential depends on both technological options and investment capital.
- Market mix: A diversified market base, including markets with lower price sensitivity reduces vulnerability.
- Diversification: A business that heavily relies on one product is more vulnerable than one with a diverse portfolio.
- Geographic location: Remoteness is not necessarily a risk factor, unless the location is far away from main tourist routes.
- Competition: Higher competition (intra- and inter-industry) means lower profit margins and a potentially higher impact of increasing operating costs (due to higher energy costs).

Using a Computable General Equilibrium model, it became evident that the long-term value of tourism decreases significantly (the real value of tourism exports declined by 4.6 per cent) following a doubling of oil price compared to 2006 levels (Becken & Lennox 2012). An increase in domestic tourism compensated for some of the reduction in international arrivals and export value. The macroeconomic impacts were significantly smaller than the tourism-specific impacts, with a GDP reduction of 1.25 per cent. This indicates that tourism is relatively more vulnerable to oil prices than other sectors. The model also showed that the effect of high oil prices on consumption of New Zealand tourism differs considerably by market. In all cases, the real price of New Zealand tourism as experienced by international tourists rises. However, the real value of consumption may fall substantially (e.g. 29.9 per cent for South Korea) or may even rise slightly (e.g. 0.3 per cent for independent Japanese holiday tourists). In the latter case, the real exchange rate effect is dominating both the negative price and income effects.

Low-carbon transport modes and networks can be efficiently enhanced by 'slow tourism' initiatives, for example cycle tourism (see Chapter 39). In the United Kingdom, Lumsdon (2000) discusses the UK National Cycle Network, which offers connected cycling routes on traffic-free trails, traffic-calming roads and minor roads. Cycle networks also offer substantial benefits for local populations, in addition to tourism development. Clearly, a change in transport systems towards rail, electric vehicles and non-motorised forms of mobility represent a substantial shift in holiday mobility, and potentially the emergence of new societal norms on broader mobility, networks and lifestyles. Long-distance travel would become less frequent and networks might 'shrink' (Becken 2011). Travelling will also require more organisation and less flexibility. Conventional forms of travel will still be available but only for the few and at a higher cost. However, if changes in transport systems are made in time, people will be able to adjust and still be in a position to experience holidays, thus avoiding disastrous disruptions as articulated in the well-known Hirsch report (Hirsch 2005).

Conclusion

This chapter provided a summary of the Peak Oil discussion and its precariousness. Tourism is utterly dependent on cheap (i.e. conventional) oil, and increases in price will impact substantially on its future development. Higher oil prices are believed to lead to reduced incomes in countries of origin and negatively affect travel propensity. Thus, many destinations around the world, especially long-distance destinations and islands, will receive fewer tourist arrivals in the future. Oil prices are also likely to raise production costs and lead to increases in prices for tourism products. Depending on tourists' elasticity of demand, output from tourism will reduce over time. The New Zealand case study provides data for the scenario of a doubling of oil prices.

While research on the cause and effect of oil prices is beginning to emerge, little attention has been paid to understand underlying social values, behaviours and ethics. This chapter argued that several factors contribute to a systematic attenuation of the Peak Oil risk in tourism, making it an excellent example of a hidden hazard. Since travel has elevated to a core value for many, the psychological response is one that tends to deny the risk and emphasises the benefits. Lack of transparency by oil companies and nations, limited discussion in the media and a lack of specific policies are likely to reinforce the inertia around Peak Oil (Wicker & Becken 2013). More psychological research on tourists' and tourism stakeholders' risk perceptions and strategies for dealing with inevitable problems would be important, especially with a view to developing new forms of low-carbon tourism and strengthening tourism's resilience to Peak Oil.

Key Reading

Aleklett, K., Höök, M., Jakobsson, K., Lardelli, M., Snowden, S. and Söderbergh, B. (2010) 'The peak of the oil age – analyzing the world oil production reference scenario in World Energy Outlook 2008, *Energy Policy*, 38: 1398–1414.

Becken, S. (2011) 'A critical review of tourism and oil', *Annals of Tourism Research*, 38: 359–79.

Becken, S. and Lennox, J. (2012) 'Implications of a long-term increase in oil prices for tourism', *Tourism Management*, 33: 133–42.

Friedrichs, J. (2011) 'Peak energy and climate change: The double bind of post-normal science', *Futures*, 43: 469–77.

Lloyd, B. (2007) 'The Commons revisited: The tragedy continues', *Energy Policy*, 35: 5806–18.

Thévard, B. (2012) *Europe Facing Peak Oil*. Study commissioned by the Greens/EFA Group in the European Parliament. Available at: www.greens-efa.eu/fileadmin/dam/Documents/Publications/PIC%20petrolier_EN_lowres.pdf (accessed 20 January 2013).

References

Aleklett, K., Höök, M., Jakobsson, K., Lardelli, M., Snowden, S. and Söderbergh, B. (2010) 'The peak of the oil age – analyzing the world oil production reference scenario in World Energy Outlook 2008', *Energy Policy*, 38: 1398–1414.

Becken, S. (2009) 'Global challenges for tourism and transport: How will climate change and energy affect the future of tourist travel?', in S. Page (ed.) *Transport and Tourism – Global Perspectives*, 3rd edn, Harlow: Pearson Education.

—— (2011) 'A critical review of tourism and oil', *Annals of Tourism Research*, 38: 359–79.

Becken, S. and Lennox, J. (2012) 'Implications of a long term increase in oil prices for tourism', *Tourism Management*, 33: 133–42.

Becken, S. and Schiff, A. (2011) 'Distance models for New Zealand international tourists and the role of transport prices', *Journal of Travel Research*, 50: 303–20.

Becken, S. and Simmons, D. (2008) 'Using the concept of yield to assess sustainability of different tourist types', *Ecological Economics*, 67: 420–29.

Bell, D., Dunlop, I. and Glazebrook, D. (2008) 'Peak oil, risk and opportunity', *Risk Management*, April 2008. Available at: www.greencrossaustralia.org/media/9896031/csa-po-and-risk_mgmnt.pdf (accessed 28 March 2013).

Bentley, R.W. (2002) 'Global oil and gas depletion: An overview. Viewpoint', *Energy Policy*, 30: 189–205.

BP (2012) *Statistical Review of World Energy June 2012*. Available at: www.bp.com/sectionbodycopy.do?categoryId=7500&contentId=7068481 (accessed 28 March 2013).

Campbell, C.J. and Laherrère, J.H. (1998) 'The end of cheap oil', *Scientific American*, March: 60–65.

Canina, L., Walsh, K. and Enz, C. (2003) 'The effects of gasoline-price changes on room demand: A study of branded hotels from 1988 through 2000', *Cornell Hotel and Restaurant Administration Quarterly*, 44 (4): 29–37.

Chester, L. (2010) Conceptualising energy security and making explicit its polysemic nature', *Energy Policy*, 38: 887–95.

Duncan, R.C. and Youngquist, W. (1999) 'Encircling the peak of world oil production', *Natural Resources Research*, 8: 219–32.

Energy Watch Group (2007) *Crude Oil: The Supply Outlook*. EWG Series No 3/2007: Ottobrunn.

Friedrichs, J. (2010) 'Global energy crunch: How different parts of the world would react to a peak oil scenario', *Energy Policy*, 38: 4562–69.

—— (2011) 'Peak energy and climate change: The double bind of post-normal science', *Futures*, 43: 469–77.

Gössling, S. (2010) *Carbon Management in Tourism: Mitigating the Impacts on Climate Change*, London: Routledge.

Hirsch, R.L. (2005) 'The inevitable peaking of world oil production', *Bulletin of the Atlantic Council of the United States*, 16(5): 1–9.

Hirsch, R.L., Bezdek, R. and Wendling, R. (2005) *Peaking of World Oil Production: Impacts, Mitigation and Risk Management*. Prepared for the US Department of Energy. Washington, DC: US Department of Energy.

Intergovernmental Panel on Climate Change (IPCC) (2007) *Climate Change 2007: Mitigation of Climate Change. Working Group II Contribution to the Fourth Assessment. Summary for Policymakers and Technical Summary*. Geneva: IPCC.

International Energy Agency (2006) *World Energy Outlook*. Paris: OECD.

—— (2008) *Oil Market Reports*. Available at: www.oilmarketreport.org/ (accessed 10 October 2008).

Johnson, V. and Cottingham, M. (2008) *Plane Truths: Do the Economic Arguments for Aviation Growth Really Fly?* NEF (New Economics Foundation) Report. London. Available at: www.neweconomics.org (accessed 10 October 2008).

Kasperson, R.E. and Kasperson, J.X. (1991) 'Hidden hazards', in D.G. Mayo and R.D. Hollander (eds) *Acceptable Evidence: Science and Values in Risk Management*, New York: Oxford University Press.

Lloyd, B. (2007) 'The Commons revisited: The tragedy continues', *Energy Policy*, 35: 5806–18.

Lumsdon, L. (2000) 'Transport and tourism: Cycle tourism – a model for sustainable development?', *Journal of Sustainable Tourism,* 8: 361–76.

Patzek, T.W. (2007) 'How can we outlive our way of life?' Paper prepared for the 20th Round Table on Sustainable Development of Biofuels: Is the cure worse than the disease? OECD Headquarters: Paris.

Pidgeon, N., Kasperson, R. and Slovic, P. (2003) *The Social Amplification of Risk*, Cambridge: Cambridge University Press.

Planungsamt der Bundeswehr (2012) *Peak oil* – Sicherheitspolitische Implikationen knapper Ressourcen. Streitkräfte, Fähigkeiten und Technologien im 21. Jahrhundert. Umweltdimensionen von Sicherheit. Available at: www.bundeswehr.de/portal/a/bwde/!ut/p/c4/NYu7DsIwEAT_yBdXG DoiC4kiDU1IGuQkp3DCj-i44IaPxy7YlaaZXRihNLoPrU4oRefhDsNMpymrKS-o3Et29B7fKiMJ Mj7kiQEj9PVYBnOKKJWCUahwZSeJ1ZZYfDU7czGKFhgabVt9aP7RXzPaS9cZc7TX9gZbCO cfRzH_Jg!!/ (accessed 24 March 2013).

Schiff, A. and Becken, S. (2011) 'Demand elasticities for tourism in New Zealand', *Tourism Management*, 32: 564–75.

Scott, D., Amelung, B., Becken, S., Ceron, J.P., Dubois, G., Gössling, S., Peeters, P. and Simpson, M. (2008) *Climate Change and Tourism: Responding to Global Challenges,* Madrid/Paris: United Nations World Tourism Organization (UNWTO) and United Nations Environment Programme (UNEP).

Sunshine Coast Council (2010) *Climate Change and Peak Oil Strategy*. Available at: www.sunshinecoast. qld.gov.au/sitePage.cfm?code=cc-strategy (accessed 24 November 2010.

Thévard, B (2012) *Europe Facing Peak Oil*. Study commissioned by the Greens/EFA Group in the European Parliament. Available at: www.greens-efa.eu/fileadmin/dam/Documents/Publications/ PIC%20petrolier_EN_lowres.pdf (accessed 20 January 2013).

UK Energy Research Institute (2009) *Global Oil Depletion. An Assessment of the Evidence for a Near-term Peak in Global Oil Production*, London.

United Nations World Tourism Organization (UNWTO) (2001) *Tourism 2020 Vision*, Madrid, World Tourism Organization.

—— (2006) *The Impact of Rising Oil Prices on International Tourism,* Special Report Number 26, Madrid: UNWTO.

Urry, J. (2008) 'Climate change, travel and complex futures', *The British Journal of Sociology*, 59: 261–79.

Yeoman, I., Lennon, J.J., Blake, A., Galt, M., Greenwood, C. and McMahon-Beattie, U. (2007) 'Oil depletion: What does this mean for Scottish tourism?', *Tourism Management,* 28: 1354–65.

Wicker, P. and Becken, S. (2013) 'Does concern about energy availability, climate change, and the economic situation influence consumer behaviour?', *Ecological Economics*, 88: 41–48.

39

Low-carbon and post-carbon travel and destinations

Stefan Gössling

Post-carbon travel Travel that makes a negligible contribution to climate change.

CO$_2$-equivalent The contribution of greenhouse gases with long lifetimes (100 years) to global warming, made comparable to CO$_2$.

Slow travel Refers to travel with a 'concern for locality, ecology and quality of life' (Dickinson & Lumsdon 2010), usually involving 'slow' public transport modes, such as trains and buses.

Carbon neutral Implies that an activity does not contribute to climate change, as an amount of greenhouse gas emissions equivalent to those released by the activity is compensated (i.e. saved) against a baseline scenario. This is done in a project, which can focus on either energy efficiency gains, renewable energies replacing fossil fuels, or afforestation.

Carbon offsetting The process of reducing emissions against a business-as-usual baseline in a project, to compensate for greenhouse gas emissions released elsewhere, in the case of tourism usually involving a journey or transport.

Low-carbon tourism Tourism that contributes to emissions lower than the global average for a trip (250 kg CO$_2$).

Introduction

Climate change is increasingly recognized as a major threat to the geophysical, biological and socioeconomic stability of the planet, and there is global consensus that a maximum warming of 2°C as compared to pre-industrial temperatures should not be exceeded. As global warming is a result of the concentration of greenhouse gas emissions in the atmosphere, emissions of, in particular, CO$_2$ as well as other greenhouse gases must be reduced. Tourism accounts for 5 per cent of global emissions of CO$_2$ (UNWTO-UNEP-WMO 2008), and an estimated share of 5.2–12.5 per cent of the overall contribution of anthropogenic emissions of greenhouse gases to global warming (calculation for the year 2005; Scott *et al.* 2010). The sector has consequently some responsibility for contributing to mitigation, specifically in the light of its growth, with an anticipated increase of 135 per cent over 2005 emission levels by 2035, mostly as a result of growth in air travel (UNWTO-UNEP-WMO 2008).

An important aspect of global tourism is that individual travellers and trips make very different contributions to the sector's overall emissions. Currently, a large proportion of the global population does not engage in international tourism at all, with one estimate being that less than 3 per cent of the world's population do fly internationally in a given year (Scott *et al.* 2010). Even among those travelling, individual contributions to emissions are highly unequally distributed. For instance, airline organizations suggest that 2.8 billion passengers are counted annually worldwide (e.g. IATA 2013), but such figures obscure the fact that there are vast differences in aeromobility. Individual travellers have reported that they participate in up to 300 return flights per year (Gössling *et al.* 2009), and a considerable share of long-haul tourism trips fall to a small proportion of the population. For instance, in the European Union (EU 15), 6 per cent of trips caused 47 per cent of emissions (Peeters *et al.* 2004) and in France, 2 per cent of the longest flights account for 43 per cent of aviation emissions (Dubois & Ceron 2009). In the Netherlands, the 4.5 per cent of the most distant trips cause 26.4 per cent of all tourism emissions (de Bruijn *et al.* 2008) (see also Chapter 17). In summary, a small share of both long-haul tourism trips and individual frequent flyers are responsible for a large share of accumulated emissions from tourism.

Because of these interrelationships, low- or post-carbon tourism needs to achieve reductions in individual travel intensities (i.e. the number of trips made by an individual per year); the overall number of long-haul trips, as these are the most relevant aspect pushing global emissions from tourism; as well as reductions in very energy-intense forms of tourism such as cruises. Emissions for various forms of trips have been investigated by UNWTO-UNEP-WMO (2008), Eijgelaar *et al.* (2010) and de Bruijn *et al.* (2010). Figure 39.1 illustrates how emissions from individual trips vary from a few kg of CO_2 (e.g. a bicycle trip in the European Alps) to several tonnes (any long-haul flight, any combination of flight and cruise).

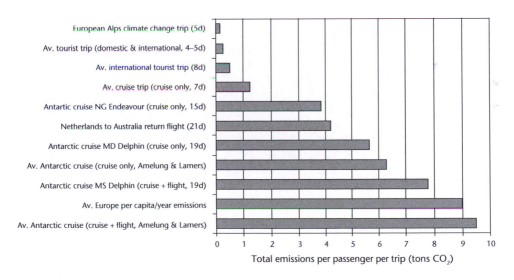

Figure 39.1 Emissions associated with different holiday forms

Source: Eijgelaar *et al.* (2010); Amelung & Lamers (2007)

As travel emissions are also influenced by the specific holiday forms on offer (i.e. tour operators and their marketing strategies) insights can also be derived from a study of the packages on offer. Figure 39.2 shows emissions per customer per day for various German tour operators, as revealed in a carbon accounting process (Gössling 2010). The range in carbon intensities is considerable, from 15 kg CO_2 per day for an operator focusing on hiking holidays to almost half a tonne of CO_2 per day for another operator specializing in long-distance travel.

On the destination level, South–West England has invested considerable resources to identify sustainable emission levels per visitor, in an attempt to define sustainable tourism in the region from a climate change mitigation viewpoint. For this purpose, emissions data for transport, accommodation, food and catering, shopping, attractions, events, services and activities were assessed and fed into a newly developed software tool, REAP Tourism (REAP Tourism 2013). The tool allows quantification on the basis of CO_2. Emissions can be displayed as a total of all tourism, or on a 'per tourist per day' basis. Figure 39.3 shows emissions on a 'per visitor day carbon footprint' basis (i.e. total emissions divided by the number of visitor days). Results indicate that it is meaningful to distinguish 'staying visitors' (tourists) and 'day visitors', as these have different emission profiles and account for unequal shares of overall emissions. South–West Tourism defined global sustainable emissions at 2t CO_2 per capita per year, or 5.5 kg CO_2 per day (Gössling 2010), putting considerable pressure on the destination to reduce per-day per-tourist emissions. As indicated in Figure 39.3, in order for tourism to become sustainable, average carbon footprints would have to decline considerably. For tourists, this means reducing travel distances, while for day visitors, focus should be on the impact of shopping.

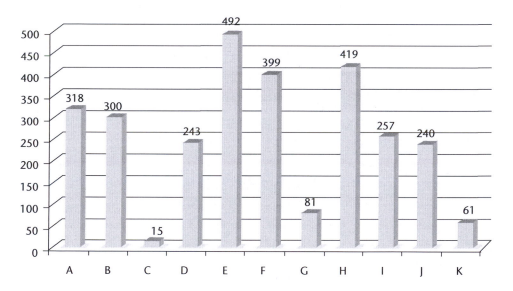

Figure 39.2 Emissions per customer per day, as measured in kg CO_2-equivalent

Source: Gössling (2010)

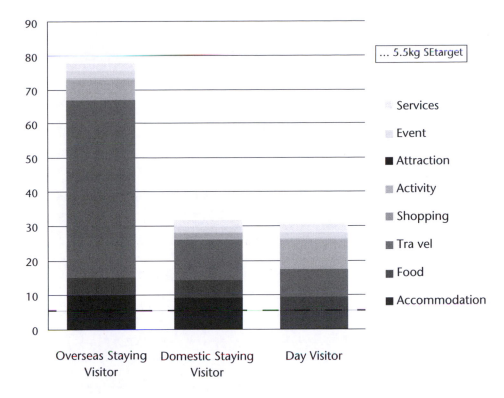

Figure 39.3 South-West England carbon footprint per visitor day (kg CO_2)

Source: REAP Tourism (2013)

Low-carbon tourism

Currently, a tourism trip causes emissions of 250 kg CO_2 on global average (UNWTO-UNEP-WMO 2008). Low-carbon tourism, a term first proposed by Peeters *et al.* (2009), could consequently be described as any tourism with lower than average emissions, a measure that can be applied either globally, nationally or on the destination level (e.g. Gössling *et al.* 2008). Conceptions of low-carbon tourism already exist. For instance, to reduce the carbon intensity of the national tourism system, de Bruijn *et al.* (2010) carried out a detailed analysis for the Netherlands, finding that certain holiday types had a particularly high/low climate impact. For instance, with regard to low-carbon tourism, domestic cycling holidays (−76%), outbound holidays by train (−55%), all camping holidays with a tent (−50%), domestic holidays (−47%), all non-organized holidays (−39%) and all nearby outbound holidays (e.g. in Belgium (−31%)) had far lower than average emissions, suggesting that such holidays should be developed in order to reduce the overall carbon footprint of the national tourism system. De Bruijn *et al.* (2010) also identified holiday types that should be avoided, including cruises (+265%), intercontinental (long-haul) holidays (ca. +200%), holidays by plane (+102%), holidays in hotels/motels (+78%), organized holidays (+35%) and outbound holidays (+27%). Through a strategic focus on holiday forms that entail lower-than-average emissions destinations, as well as tour operators, can lower their carbon intensities and energy dependencies (see also Gössling *et al.* 2008).

Stefan Gössling

Another approach has been suggested for Germany, based on the substitution of transport mode and destination choice (Atmosfair 2012). This approach is based on the observation that there are 'ideal' destinations tourists may favour for various reasons, and that there is some degree of flexibility in destination choices – often, tourists may not be able to visit a specific destination and have to choose an alternative. In this substitution approach, tourists were asked which destination they would favour in case their preferred choice was not available. Results are presented in the following for two examples (Turkey and New Zealand), and the most frequently mentioned substitution choice (Italy and Spain, respectively). Calculations also consider the impact of changes in the transport modes used (train rather than aircraft) as well as the choice of accommodation (pension rather than hotel).

Table 39.1 Substitution of destination and change of transport mode: Turkey

	Original choice: Turkey	New choice: Italy
One way flight distance from Frankfurt:	1,900 km	1,775 km
Length of stay:	14 days	14 days
Travel time (hours):	Aircraft	Train
	7½ h	13½ h
Emissions		
Transport:	460 kg CO_2	108 kg CO_2
Hotel:	280 kg CO_2 (hotel)	56 kg CO_2 (pension)
Total:	740 kg CO_2	164 kg CO_2

More than 50% of travellers reported to be interested in Italy as a destination, should Turkey not be an option. Note that travel to the airport was included with 1 hour of time, and check-in procedures as well as waiting times with 2 hours. Yet another hour was included for baggage claim and travel to the final destination.

Source: Various websites, including www.bahn.de, www.expedia.com, www.viamichelin.de, www.atmosfair.de, UNWTO-UNEP-WMO (2008)

Table 39.2 Substitution of destination and change of transport mode: New Zealand

	Original choice: New Zealand	New choice: Spain
One way flight distance from Frankfurt:	18,250 km	2,900 km
Length of stay:	21 days	21 days
Travel time (hours):	aircraft	train & taxi
	28 h	24 h
Emissions		
Transport:	4,050 kg CO_2	132 kg CO_2
Hotel:	85 kg CO_2 (pension)	168 kg CO_2 (hotel)
Total:	4,135 kg CO_2	300 kg CO_2

1) More than 70% of travellers reported that Spain would be their first choice as an alternative destination, should New Zealand not be available. Note that travel to the airport was included with 1 hour, and check-in procedures as well as waiting times with 2 hours. Yet another hour was included for baggage claim and travel to the final destination.

Source: Various websites, including www.bahn.de, www.expedia.com, www.viamichelin.de, www.atmosfair.de, Gössling (2010); UNWTO-UNEP-WMO (2008)

Calculations indicate that there is a huge potential to reduce per-trip contributions to climate change, if tourists can be convinced to choose closer destinations and less energy-intensive transport modes. Specifically the trip to New Zealand replaced by a trip to Spain indicates the importance of distance/transport mode choices in overall emissions. In this case, more than an order of magnitude higher for the New Zealand trip, even though the trip to Spain included a stay in more energy-intense accommodation. In absolute terms, the trip to New Zealand entails emissions in the order of average global per capita per year emissions (4.3 t CO_2), notably not considering the radiative forcing (RF) effects of aviation (see Chapter 17). Travel time, usually a deterrent for tourists, is also shorter for the trip to Spain, even though it is unclear how the perception of distance influences the perception of travel times. Likewise, it is unknown whether tourists could be convinced to choose different destinations, even though destination choice is to some degree influenced by marketing and trends.

Post-carbon travel

As indicated, it is possible to considerably reduce emissions from tourism through changing destination and transport choices. In the future, if tourism is to make a contribution to emission reductions in line with those postulated by the global community (i.e. a massive decline from current emission levels in the order of 60–80% by mid-century) travel may ultimately have to become carbon neutral (for a conceptualization of the concept see Gössling 2009). In the medium term, tourism products could be developed that fulfil the requirements of what might be termed 'pro-climate travel' (i.e. journeys that, on balance, contribute to net greenhouse gas emission reductions). Both carbon-neutral and pro-climate travel can only be achieved if carbon offsetting (i.e. investment in projects to reduce emissions) become part of the holiday package, and conceptually entail a range of systematic and ethical problems. For instance, it is systemically impossible to reduce emissions in non-tourism sectors to allow for continued growth in tourism in the longer term; projects to offset emissions are currently focusing on developing countries, where they are cheap; a large share of global offsetting projects focus on afforestation, with concerns regarding area availability, competition with food production, as well as the long-term viability of carbon storage in forest ecosystems (Broderick 2009; Gössling et al. 2007).

Given these considerations, two models of post-carbon travel are discussed below, both of which have originally been presented in Atmosfair (2012). Both journeys focus on Mallorca as a destination, and are currently feasible (climate-friendly travel) or may become feasible in the future (post-carbon travel).

Mallorca 2013: climate-friendly travel and accommodation

A standard trip to Mallorca causes emissions in the order of 600 kg CO_2. Activities such as scenic drives are not considered in this calculation, nor is the foodstuffs consumed by tourists. To reduce the energy intensity of the trip, tourists may arrive by train, with the train trip from Frankfurt (a starting point in the centre of Germany) to Barcelona taking 14 hours. As this is a rather long trip, a one-day stop in Barcelona may enhance its attractiveness, followed by a ferry trip to Palma (7 hours). This combined transport choice would reduce overall emissions by about 70 per cent. Staying in an eco-friendly hotel would further reduce emissions from accommodation by 50 per cent. Overall, a climate-friendly trip to Mallorca can produce lower carbon costs of about 60 per cent.

Stefan Gössling

Mallorca 2025: Post-carbon travel

Until 2025, considerable changes in travel behaviour and technological developments could be implemented to reduce emissions, many of these feasible already today. For instance, it is possible to run train systems using only renewable energy (e.g. from wind, sun and water), as exemplified by Swedish railways, which calculate lifecycle emissions as low as 2.1 g CO_2 per 1,000 pkm (load factor: 50%). To travel to/from stations/ports, travellers can rely on electro-mobility (i.e. cars or trams powered by electricity from renewable sources). In the example, the 200 km trip by ferry from Barcelona to Palma de Mallorca would take 24 hours. As an auxiliary engine would have to be used sometimes, low emissions of about 60 kg CO_2 per passenger may be produced for a return journey (see Table 39.3). By 2025, some of these may be avoided by using more efficient machines, biofuel, fuel cells and solar panels. In the destination, hotels can potentially be built as low-energy or even plus-energy structures. In such a scenario, the hotel produces more energy than it consumes, which helps to de-carbonize the destination, feeding its excess power into the grid. As even the food consumed in the destination is locally sourced, with a high number of vegetarian alternatives offered, food-related emissions are lowered in comparison to 'at home' emissions. For instance, one German citizen causes average embedded emissions of 4 kg CO_2 per day (1.55 t CO_2 per year) as a result of food consumption (Atmosfair 2012). If food was locally sourced, emissions from food consumption could be halved (Gössling et al. 2011), helping to de-carbonize food systems. If travellers also pay for a carbon offset of 100 kg CO_2, which by 2025, is offered at a price of about €5 by credible offset providers, the tourism trip contributes to the removal of 80 kg CO_2 from the atmosphere, while also inducing systemic changes towards a low-carbon economy.

While pro-climate travel as a form of post-carbon tourism is thus theoretically feasible, it is obvious that a number of problems cannot be addressed. This includes, for instance, the issue of long-haul air travel: aircraft are difficult to replace through other transport modes. For longer distances, compensation also becomes costly and systemic limits are more rapidly reached. Yet, given the enormous discrepancy between emission reduction targets in the tourism sector and current trajectories (Scott et al. 2010; Gössling et al. 2013), offsetting as a strategy for a considerable share of tourism emissions may be unavoidable, in light of the political inaction on tourism emissions (Gössling 2013). Whether post-carbon travel will become a reality is thus highly uncertain: Notions of 'carbon-neutral destinations' (Gössling 2009) have all too often remained greenwash, with little evidence that any absolute reductions in emissions have been achieved. Consequently, pro-climate travel developments currently depend on whether tour operators and tourists want to implement climatically sustainable forms of travel.

Table 39.3 Post-carbon trip to Mallorca by 2020

Aspect of trip	Emissions (kg CO_2), considering lifecycle
Travel to/from railway station with electric car	< 1 kg CO_2
Train travel to/from port (based on renewable electricity)	< 1 kg CO_2
Sailing to/from destination (auxiliary engine working on hydrogen-basis, partial use of biofuels)	20 kg CO_2
Plus-energy hotel (generating more electricity than needed by hotel)	−50 kg CO_2
Food (local, 14 days)	30 kg CO_2
Activities	20 kg CO_2
Offset	−100 kg CO_2
Total:	− 80 kg CO_2

Conclusion

An enormous gap exists between the recommendations of the international scientific community researching climate change on how to stabilize and reduce emissions of greenhouse gases (cf. IPCC 2007) and political initiatives to achieve such reductions. In tourism, this gap is even expected to widen due to rapid growth in the sector and difficulties in reducing emissions in aviation, the most emission-intense sub-sector (Gössling *et al.* 2013; see also Chapter 17). There is consequently a need to define low-carbon and post-carbon forms of tourism, and to raise awareness among tour operators and tourists as to how to implement such tourism. Specifically, any such approach needs to address the role of high-intensity travellers as well as the disproportionally high climate impact of the small share of long-haul travel.

Low-carbon tourism has been defined in this chapter as any tourism that causes, on a per-trip basis, lower emissions than global, national or regional averages. If a larger share of such tourism can be developed, this will reduce overall emissions in a scenario of stable arrival numbers. Post-carbon tourism needs to achieve even more, as such tourism would have to be virtually without impact on the climate system. Pending currently unknown technological breakthroughs, this can only be achieved if carbon offsetting becomes a more regular part of tourism. If there is over-compensation of emissions, tourism can help to achieve more rapid emission reductions in other economic sectors – perhaps it may even turn into a form of pro-climate tourism. Systemic limitations must be considered as well: if offsetting a greater amount of emissions than caused by a journey could solve the problem, this might imply that the more energy we use for tourism, the better it would be for the climate system. Ultimately, fundamental changes in the tourism system are thus unavoidable.

Key Reading

Dickinson, J.E. and Lumsdon, L. (2010) *Slow Travel and Tourism*, London: Earthscan.

Gössling, S. (2010) *Carbon Management in Tourism: Mitigating the Impacts on Climate Change*, London: Routledge.

Gössling, S., Scott, D. and Hall, C.M. (2014) 'Inter-market variability in CO_2 emission-intensities in tourism: Implications for destination marketing and carbon management', *Tourism Management*, 46: 203–12

Scott, D., Hall, C.M. and Gössling, S. (2012) *Tourism and Climate Change: Impacts, Mitigation and Adaptation*, London: Routledge.

References

Amelung, B. and Lamers, M. (2007) 'Estimating the greenhouse gas emissions from Antarctic tourism', *Tourism in Marine Environments*, 4(2–3), 121–133.

Atmosfair (2012) 'Das Reiseverhalten der Deutschen 2020: Wege zur Emissionsreduktion im Tourismus im Einklang mit der deutschen Klimapolitik', *Atmosfair*, Berlin, Germany.

Broderick, J. (2009) 'Voluntary carbon offsets: A contribution to sustainable tourism?', in S. Gössling, C.M. Hall and D.B. Weaver (eds) *Sustainable Tourism Futures: Perspectives on Systems, Restructuring and Innovations*, London: Routledge.

de Bruijn, K., Dirven, R., Eijgelaar, E. and Peeters, P. (2008) *Reizen op grote voet 2005. De milieube-lasting van vakanties van Nederlanders. Een pilot-project in samenwerking met NBTC-NIPO Research*. Breda: NHTV University for Applied Sciences.

—— (2010) *Travelling Large in 2008: The Carbon Footprint of Dutch Holidaymakers in 2008 and the Development since 2002,* Breda, the Netherlands: NHTV Breda University of Applied Sciences. NRIT Research and NBTC–NIPO Research.

Dickinson, J. and Lumsdon, L. (2010) *Slow Travel and Tourism,* London: Earthscan.

Dubois, G. and Ceron, J.P. (2009) 'Carbon labelling and restructuring travel systems: Involving travel agencies in climate change mitigation', in S. Gössling, C.M. Hall and D.B. Weaver (eds) *Sustainable Tourism Futures: Perspectives on Systems, Restructuring and Innovations,* London: Routledge.

Eijgelaar, E., Thaper, C. and Peeters, P. (2010) 'Antarctic cruise tourism: The paradoxes of ambassadorship, "last chance tourism" and greenhouse gas emissions', *Journal of Sustainable Tourism,* 18: 337–54.

Gössling, S. (2009) 'Carbon neutral destinations: A conceptual analysis', *Journal of Sustainable Tourism,* 17: 17–37.

—— (2010) *Carbon Management in Tourism: Mitigating the Impacts on Climate Change,* London: Routledge.

—— (2013) 'National emissions from tourism: An overlooked policy challenge?', *Energy Policy,* 59: 433–42.

Gössling, S., Peeters, P. and Scott, D. (2008) 'Consequences of climate policy for international tourist arrivals in developing countries', *Third World Quarterly,* 29: 873–901.

Gössling, S., Scott, D. and Hall, C.M. (2013) 'Challenges of tourism in a low-carbon economy', *Wiley Interdisciplinary Reviews Climate Change,* 4(6): 525–38.

Gössling, S., Broderick, J., Upham, P., Peeters, P., Strasdas, W., Ceron, J.-P. and Dubois, G. (2007) 'Voluntary carbon offsetting schemes for aviation: Efficiency and credibility', *Journal of Sustainable Tourism,* 15: 223–48.

Gössling, S., Garrod, B., Aall, C., Hille, J. and Peeters, P. (2011) 'Food management in tourism. Reducing tourism's carbon "foodprint"', *Tourism Management,* 32: 534–43.

Gössling, S., Hultman, J., Haglund, L., Källgren, H. and Revahl, M. (2009) 'Voluntary carbon offsetting by Swedish Air Travellers: Towards the co-creation of environmental value?', *Current Issues in Tourism,* 12: 1–19.

Intergovernmental Panel on Climate Change (IPCC) (2007) *Fourth Assessment Report: Climate Change 2007, Working Group I,* Cambridge: Cambridge University Press.

International Air Transport Association (IATA) (2013) *Homepage.* Available at: www.iata.org (accessed 5 February 2013).

Peeters, P., Gössling, S. and Lane, B. (2009) 'Moving towards low-carbon tourism: New opportunities for destinations and tour operators', in S. Gössling, C.M. Hall and D.B. Weaver (eds) *Sustainable Tourism Futures: Perspectives on Systems, Restructuring and Innovations,* London: Routledge.

Peeters, P.M., van Egmond, T. and Visser, N. (2004) *European Tourism, Transport and Environment,* Breda: NHTV Breda University of Applied Sciences, Centre for Sustainable Tourism and Transport.

REAP Tourism (2013) *Introducing REAP Tourism.* Available at: www.resource-accounting.org.uk/reap-tourism (accessed 10 June 2013).

Scott, D., Peeters, P. and Gössling, S. (2010) 'Can tourism deliver its "aspirational"emission reduction targets?', *Journal of Sustainable Tourism,* 18: 393–408.

United Nations World Tourism Organization (UNWTO), United Nations Environment Programme (UNEP) and World Meteorological Organization (WMO) (2008) *Climate Change and Tourism: Responding to Global Challenges,* Madrid: UNWTO.

40

Slow travel

Janet E. Dickinson

> **Slow travel** A form of tourism involving shorter origin to destination travel, longer stays, an emphasis on taking time to enjoy the travel experience and low-carbon consumption.
>
> **Slow tourism** A term frequently used interchangeably with slow travel but typically focused on destination-orientated tourist experiences.

Introduction

The term 'slow' typically has a negative connotation with respect to travel and transport. It implies delays, periods of waiting, consuming time and not being able to travel far. In many respects the idea of slow travel seems wrong and, from an etymological perspective, it may not be a promising descriptor to encourage a form of sustainable tourism. Where 'slow' has prefixed other things, such as food or cities (e.g. Cittáslow), the implication is more positive, and who can deny the appeal of slow sex? In comparison to slow travel, slow tourism has more positive connotations implying taking time out and relaxation which reflects people's desire to step outside the hectic, clock-bound existence of day-to-day life (Elsrud 1998; Richards 1998; Stein 2012). Yet, conceptually, there is little to separate slow travel and slow tourism and in much of the emerging literature and grassroots 'slow' communities the terms are synonymous. However, slow travel and slow tourism have been interpreted as many different things by different people. This chapter is titled 'slow travel' predominantly due to the author's heritage in using this term; however, slow tourism is also explored given its similarly widespread use. The aim of the chapter is to analyse the varied interpretations of slow travel and the potential it has to bring about more sustainable tourism. The chapter begins with some context surrounding the emergence of slow travel from the wider slow movement. It goes on to analyse both the participant and academic-led heritage of the slow travel concept. Finally the chapter addresses the contribution that slow travel might make to sustainable tourism. A case study illustrates how slow travel might be applied on the Mediterranean island of Corsica to demonstrate the significant challenges involved.

It is difficult to trace the exact origin of slow travel as the concept emerged over a period of time in a variety of contexts. At a simplistic level, the 'slow' in slow travel reflects the slower speed of the preferred modes of transport (i.e. the avoidance of air and car travel). The prefix 'slow' can also be traced to the wider slow movement that is rooted in a philosophy that challenges the speed with which many things are undertaken in contemporary Western society (Andrews 2006; Honoré 2004). The slow movement is centred on three core ideas: doing things at the right speed; changing attitudes towards time and the use of it; seeking quality over quantity (Peters 2006). Time is a central concept within slow travel and presents a conceptual challenge to the 'faster is better' perspective that was, until recently, especially prevalent within travel models. Recent work in the transport field has, however, challenged this perspective (Holley *et al.* 2008). Beyond time concerns, slow travel also values quality over quantity and reflects lifestyle practices associated with sustainable living.

Neither slow travel nor slow tourism have been definitively defined though a number of authors have presented interpretations. Dickinson and Lumsdon (2010: 190) describe a set of principles of slow travel:

- A reduction of resources in the supply of tourism.
- A reduction in the CO_2 emissions from tourism, especially in relation to the transport element.
- An increase in travel cost to reflect the reality of carbon intensity in tourism.
- A renaissance of travel (i.e. the journey) as part of the tourist experience.
- Time spent well is associated with experience and relaxation rather than speed.
- The experience is as much about locality, diversity and culture, as well as slow food.

However, they acknowledge that this is only one interpretation. At a broad level, application of the term slow tourism tends to focus at the destination level (see e.g. Timms & Conway 2011). However, academic use of the term 'slow travel' tends to take a more holistic view and focuses on the origin to destination travel component of tourism as well as the destination experience and travel around the destination (Buckley 2011; Dickinson & Lumsdon 2010).

Given the book's focus, a key concern is whether slow travel offers a sustainable development pathway for tourism. This largely depends how the concept is interpreted and operationalised and almost all interpretations of slow travel raise significant issues relative to sustainable development, as do other forms of tourism. There is a significant danger of greenwashing, with slow travel being misappropriated, and also little more than a nod to social equity. However, of even more concern, is that the concept may be ill-suited to the task of bringing about more sustainable tourism development, even in some of its most benign and beneficial guises.

In tracing the heritage of slow travel there appear to be two roots. First, a grassroots movement led by participants, social networks and small travel industry operators. Second, academic research has explored the concept and attempted to set out the core ingredients or to analyse the slow travel experience. The following sections analyse these two perspectives and their divergent understandings.

Participants' interpretation of slow travel

It is important to first acknowledge that slow travel participants do not necessarily see themselves as slow travellers. When Dickinson *et al.* (2011) recruited slow travellers to participate in a study, while they found participants to meet their criteria, these tourists had not previously thought of themselves as slow travellers. Most had an affinity for a particular style of holiday which they had pursued for many years. To this end, slow travel is a relatively new label to collectively categorise forms of tourism that have existed for many years, such as cycle tourism or coach tours. However, a plethora of travel industry operators have emerged that utilise the 'slow' label picking up on people's desire to take quality 'time out' and a market for slow food experiences. The media has also identified slow travel and, in the late 2000s, a series of articles populated the travel sections of newspapers written by journalists often pursuing an alternative lifestyle through extended travel. For example, Ed Gillespie reported in the UK *Observer* newspaper on his round the world trip avoiding air travel.

Within those participating in slow travel there are a diversity of experiences pursued and expectations. In broad terms there are two competing interpretations. One focuses on emersion in destination experiences involving long stays and engagement with people and place. This interpretation makes little or no reference to travel, especially the travel to reach the destination. This is a predominantly North American interpretation often associated with small tour operations that promote long-stay European vacations and rental accommodation. These trips embed air travel and as such offer little in the way of a climate change mitigation strategy aside from encouraging longer stays. Slow Travel Thailand offers a variation of this that plays on the perception of Thai lifestyle as slow by suggesting that the 'Thai way of life is slow in origin; we live slowly in accordance with the time and with the seasons, the true speed of life'. Tourism Thailand uses the term 'slow travel' to promote the opportunity to stay in non-mainstream, unique cultural and natural environments that offer relatively high-quality tourism offerings (Tourism Thailand 2013). Their directions to destinations assume car travel and the target market appears to be long-haul Western visitors.

The second interpretation focuses on the overland travel experience, both travel to and around the destination. In this interpretation, air and sometimes car travel is avoided in favour of train, coach, bus, foot and cycle. Here, participants see the act of travelling as a key component of the tourist experience. This is a more European interpretation of the concept. Communities pursuing this version of slow travel do not entirely reject air or car travel but there is discussion of alternatives and assumption that low-carbon travel modes will be used if available. Related to this, Dickinson *et al.* (2011) observed a continuum of commitment to environmental values within slow travellers describing those most committed to reducing the carbon footprint of their travel as 'hard' slow travellers, and others, for whom a low-carbon footprint was an added benefit, as 'soft' slow travellers.

In both instances, slow travel is associated with the quality of the experience and has been criticised as a middle-class phenomena accessible to those with the wealth and time (Fullagar *et al.* 2012). Inevitably, such a group has the power to make choices. In some instances, slow travel is an additional holiday and one that might be taken with a 'good conscience' or to gain cultural capital (Fullager *et al.* 2012). While it is easy to see this as an elitist group exerting their power to choose, it does illustrate a positive move towards more ethical purchasing decisions, though it could also be seen as a form of compensation culture whereby people justify high-impact tourism by more sustainable options for a second or third annual holiday.

Slow travel is also wrapped up in identity issues for many participants, especially with respect to mode of transport. There are strong identity associations with cycling and with train travel. There are significant identity challenges linked to air travel since this implies status (Thurlow & Jaworski 2006). Conversely, slow travel is not necessarily a choice for many people. At a global level, many people have little option but to use 'slow' forms of transport. Even in developed countries there are inequities, for example, scheduled coach travel tends to be the domain of lower socio-economic groups and it is unlikely to be a preferred form of travel.

Academic interpretations of slow travel

Inevitably, the academic analysis of slow travel has followed that of the grassroots movement in so far as studies can be categorised to those that take an holistic view of the concept, including travel to the destination (Buckley 2011; Dickinson & Lumsdon 2010; Lumsdon & McGrath 2011) and those that focus more specifically on destination provision and experience (Conway & Timms 2010). Typically, the former studies adopt the term slow travel, while studies with a more destination-orientated focus use the term slow tourism. Based on volume of studies, slow travel appears to be the dominant term but several authors use both terms (see e.g. Fullagar *et al.* 2012). The majority of studies take, as their starting point, the participant's experience and the practice of slow travel (see e.g. Tiyce & Wilson 2012); however, some are derived from a more provision-orientated perspective. Given that participants do not necessarily self-define themselves as slow travellers, there has also been a degree of academic influence in shaping the concept. For instance, in order to identify and recruit slow travel participants, Dickinson (2008) used the following working definition: 'Holiday travel involving shorter trips (distance) and longer stays (time) where air transport is rejected in favour of more environmentally benign forms of overland transport which become incorporated as part of the holiday experience.' Similarly Buckley (2011: 329) used the following description of slow travel in his analysis of tourists' responses to higher airfares: 'travelling to fewer destinations but staying longer at each'.

Dickinson and Buckley are both clearly aligned to an holistic view of slow travel and illustrate how the majority of academic analysis views slow travel as a means to an end, usually sustainable tourism. For example, Conway and Timms see slow tourism as an option for the Caribbean to move away from mass tourism that lacks authenticity and brings little benefit to the local population. Here slow tourism is analysed as an alternative tourism strategy that avoids standardisation, embraces local distinctiveness and enhances local control, therefore Conway and Timms use slow tourism to address social equity elements of sustainable tourism. Research has also explored the potential of slow travel as a climate change mitigation and adaptation strategy. For example, Dickinson and Lumsdon (2010) start from the industry challenge of re-shaping tourism such that people can still enjoy their leisure time but, at the same time, for the supply sector to avoid contributing to the worst scenarios of climate change. Buckley (2011) explores slow travel as a response to increased air travel costs through a shift to longer stays. In their analysis of time, Dickinson and Peeters (2014) explore a similar scenario relative to new packages of time becoming available in the contemporary network society; however, they are less optimistic this will reduce climate change impacts. While Lumsdon and McGrath (2011: 276) align slow travel with sustainable tourism, their grounded theory study makes no initial assumption that this is the case. In their conclusion, slow travel is defined as follows:

> Slow travel is a sociocultural phenomenon, focusing on holidaymaking but also on day leisure visits, where use of personal time is appreciated differently. Slowness is valued, and the journey is integral to the whole experience. The mode of transport and the activities undertaken at a destination enhance the richness of the experience through slowness. Whilst the journey is the thing and can be the destination in its own right, the experience of locality counts for much, as does reduced duration or distance of travel.

Time

Given the centrality of time to slow travel, the growing literature on temporality in tourism is pertinent. Time is intrinsic to the tourist experience in several respects. Tourism is a space to step out of time (Elsrud 1998), albeit one that remains to some degree constrained (Dickinson *et al.* 2013) and people experience time in multiple ways (Adam 1995). Tourists also seek out different times as destinations have distinctive temporal rhythms; some destinations represent times past as they appear to have a slower pace to life. Time is, therefore, part of the sense of place of a destination (Edensor 2010) and, to some extent, becomes a tourist commodity. Slowing down and being a tourist at the 'right' pace appears to be intrinsic to slow travel. By slowing down, the basic physics of travel frame the slow travel experience. By using a slower mode of transport (e.g. switching from air to train travel) slow travellers limit the distance that can be travelled. In this way, temporal realities govern elements of slow travel. Germann Mols (2009) suggests that there appears to be some moral superiority in being able to take time, as not everyone can do this; hence the issue presents social equity issues.

Transport accessibility plays an important role in tourism development models. Given that the amount of time allocated to travel has changed little in recent decades (Metz 2008), in order to travel greater distances, people must use faster modes of trnsport, typically air travel (Dickinson & Peeters 2014). Increased speed is associated with higher energy intensity (Poumanyvong *et al.* 2012). If slow travel is to play a role in climate change mitigation, then transport mode is a critical component; air and car travel must be reduced. To achieve this, more distant destinations become untenable unless people have the time to get there.

There are other temporal issues that influence mode of transport. For instance, car use is associated with temporal flexibility and convenience (Dickinson *et al.* 2013). Public transport, however, is spatially and temporally restricted. While tourists seek to step out of time they inevitably encounter a variety of temporal control points as their holiday is structured by transport schedules, attraction opening hours and meal times (Dickinson & Peeters 2014). In this situation, the car is a 'time shifting' device (Southerton *et al.* 2001) which enables users to negotiate space-time constraints on their own terms. For example, a tourist is less constrained by the local shop closing early as it is feasible to drive to the late-opening supermarket in a nearby town. Cars also enable tourists to respond to immediate needs or desires of the group such as a child's boredom or the urgent need for food. When slow travel is demonstrated through choice of particular modes of transport, this has implications for the negotiation of time. A coach tour will structure time to a rigid schedule and, while someone using public transport, such as buses and trains has more flexibility, they are still tied to transport schedules. Cycle tourists have a high degree of independence, but little capacity to deal with space-time challenges should they occur. Obviously, such limitations apply to any tourist, especially those on a package, and it is questionable to what extent anyone achieves 'time out' within tourism.

There is also the use of time during travel which was, until recently, viewed as wasted time (Holley *et al.* 2008). Recent studies have questioned this and there is recognition of the value of travel time as a space for social interaction and as a time for work or contemplative activities (Holley *et al.* 2008). This has re-cast travel time as a positive utility rather than a disutility. Of interest here is the increasing integration of work and leisure time (Buckley 2011; Dickinson & Peeters 2014). This raises the possibility of tourists able to travel for longer duration trips by remote working (Buckley 2011).

The contribution to sustainable tourism

Whether slow travel makes a useful contribution to sustainable tourism depends on how it is defined and operationalised. While slow travel is normally situated within the discourse of sustainable tourism, Dickinson and Lumsdon (2010) have developed a conceptual framework aligned to sustainable tourism) its contribution remains ambiguous. It is easy to appropriate the term for what appears to be sustainable tourism ends, where the impact on the natural environment (e.g. through travel-induced greenhouse gas emissions) remains high. This reflects the wider problems of operationalising sustainable tourism, which is a much-abused concept. In reality, much of the wider sustainable tourism offering is far from sustainable, being based on a limited interpretation of sustainable development.

Sustainable development revolves around three concepts: safeguarding long-term ecological systems; satisfying basic needs; and promoting inter- and intra-generational equity (Holden 2007). If this were to be realistically applied to tourism then: (a) most of the Western world would need to have much less of it and the developing world vast amounts more to achieve any degree of equity; and (b) tourism would need to be re-envisioned with radically reduced travel needs to reduce greenhouse gas emissions and safeguard long-term ecological systems. In many respects sustainable tourism only offers opportunities to satisfy basic needs and its ability to achieve this for local people is questioned in many tourism contexts (Nawijn *et al.* 2008). It is, therefore, important to approach sustainable tourism with some degree of scepticism. What, then, might slow travel offer as a sustainable development pathway for tourism?

The most optimistic scenario for slow travel is presented by Dickinson and Lumsdon (2010). They envisage a much less resource-intensive industry with reduced travel, and hence CO_2 emissions, where destinations focus on local tourism markets and tourists travel to and around destinations by low-carbon transport modes that are embedded into the tourist experience. Based on this model they suggest three scenarios:

- the current slow travel niche market, favoured by a select group of the middle class, grows at a modest rate with some wider diffusion;
- mainstream slow travel destinations emerge to exploit short-haul tourism based on low-carbon travel and good local transport infrastructure. The Alpine Pearl resorts are attempting to follow this pathway (Matos 2004); and
- a paradigm shift brings about a change in the production and consumption of tourism such that slow travel principles are applied to all types of tourism.

Each scenario nudges tourism further down a more sustainable development pathway that begins to seriously address environmental impacts associated with the transport component of tourism whilst maintaining tourism development opportunities for appropriate destinations. However, not all destinations will be suitable for this slow travel model, especially remote destinations with distant markets. While global travel under this framework is still feasible, it is for a select few who are relatively free of time and cost constraints. While Dickinson and Peeters (2014) suggest there may be some growth in this market, due to changing technology and working practices, this is only one potential outcome for this group and other less sustainable pathways may be followed.

There are other significant obstacles for the more optimistic scenarios of slow travel. Recent research draws attention to the role of personal identity in tourism travel and the role played by relationships (Hibbert *et al.* 2013) in generating obligations, opportunities and inclinations (Stradling & Anable 2008) that drive global travel. Much of this tourism would not be possible within a slow travel model.

In a more widespread, pessimistic scenario, slow travel is interpreted as a tool to enhance the quality of destination offerings. It promotes longer stays and engagement with culture and the natural environment. While this is positive in the wider scale of things, and offers good opportunities to destinations with appropriate features to exploit, it fails to address some of the most significant environmental problems of tourism by ignoring how tourists travel to destinations and in many instances promoting long-haul flights. Here, slow travel may represent sustainable tourism at the destination level, but not beyond. It is also clear that slow travel is seen as an opportunity to dress tourism up as sustainable.

Slow travel is a relatively new concept and, given the variety of interpretations, it is too early to tell whether it will bring about more sustainable tourism practice. If it evolves beyond a destination–centred approach then there is good potential for the industry to embrace slow travel as a climate change mitigation and adaptation strategy. As the tourism industry faces more challenges to address its external impacts, slow travel will be one of many options; however, it will not be suitable for all destinations and markets.

Case Study

Corsica by train, ferry, bus and on foot

Corsica is a French island in the Mediterranean with a unique natural environment and distinctive culture and food that is derived from both French and Italian influences. The island offers a diversity of natural habitats ideal for tourism from mountains to rich marine environments providing a variety of tourism opportunities. Though not purposefully positioned as a slow travel destination there is considerable potential for slow travel in Corsica and it features in blogs and articles of a number of online slow travel communities.

Walking the GR20, considered one of the most demanding of the French long-distance footpaths, is a popular activity that has attracted increasing attention from the Corsican tourism industry. The route can be completed in three weeks, depending on ability and a variety of shorter alternative routes have been developed to complement the GR20. The tourism industry supporting the route is dominated by small businesses run by local people, in common with much of the tourism provision on Corsica. Local produce is readily available and there is ample opportunity for visitors to engage with the natural and cultural environment while adjusting to the rhythm and pace of a laid-back Mediterranean region.

The island is served by one train line and a network of local buses. Given the mountainous topography, trains and buses are slow, as they negotiate a tortuous route, and services are irregular. This significantly limits the scope to move around the island, though this is, in many respects, a positive feature for slow travel as it is hard to get anywhere fast. However, the difficulties encountered when negotiating public transport around the island tend to direct people to car use; this is the dominant mode of transport on the island for tourists. That said, most long-distance walkers will be dependent on public transport to reach the start and end points of routes, but beyond walkers, very few tourists venture onto public transport aside from the scenic train ride across the centre of the island. However, for those with initiative it is perfectly possible to negotiate regions of the island without a car and, given the relatively difficult driving conditions (roads are narrow with precipitous drops), this is an opportunity that might be developed.

Another obstacle to slow travel is access to the island. The visitor base is dominated by mainland French, Italians and northern Europeans. Access is either by air or ferry, with ferry travel dominated by car users. This fails to meet the criteria of the more holistic interpretation of slow travel and generates a significant carbon footprint when travel to destination is taken into account. Based on the visitor market, alternative travel options exist, especially high-speed train travel (TGV) to the French access ports. The difficulty is switching tourists who feel dependent on the car for a range of holiday needs, such as camping equipment and flexible travel options when on the island. In this way the tourism practice on Corsica has become deeply embedded with car travel.

Key Reading

Dickinson, J.E. and Lumsdon, L. (2010) *Slow Travel and Tourism*, London: Earthscan.

Fullagar, S., Markwell, K. and Wilson, E. (eds) (2012) *Slow Tourism: Experiences and Mobilities*, Bristol: Channel View Publications.

Germann Molz, J.G. (2009) 'Representing pace in tourism mobilities: Staycations, slow travel and *The Amazing Race*', *Journal of Tourism and Cultural Change*, 7: 270–86.

Lumsdon, L.M. and McGrath, P. (2011) 'Developing a conceptual framework for slow travel: A grounded theory approach', *Journal of Sustainable Tourism*, 19: 265–79.

References

Adam, B. (1995) *Timewatch: The Social Analysis of Time*, Cambridge: Polity Press.

Andrews, C. (2006) *Slow is Beautiful*, Gabriola Island: New Society Publishers.

Buckley, R. (2011) 'Tourism under climate change: Will slow travel supersede short breaks?', *AMBIO*, 40: 328–31.

Conway, D. and Timms, B. F. (2010) 'Re-branding alternative tourism in the Caribbean: The case for "slow tourism"', *Tourism and Hospitality Research*, 10(4), 329–344.

Dickinson, J. (2008) *Travelling slowly: An Exploration of the Discourse of Holiday Travel*. Paper presented at Universities' Transport Studies Group Annual Conference, Portsmouth, January 2008.

Dickinson, J.E. and Lumsdon, L. (2010) *Slow Travel and Tourism*, London: Earthscan.

Dickinson, J.E. and Peeters, P. (2014) 'Time, tourism consumption and sustainable development', *International Journal of Tourism Research*, 16(1): 11–21.

Dickinson, J.E., Lumsdon, L. and Robbins, D. (2011) 'Slow travel: Issues for tourism and climate change', *Journal of Sustainable Tourism*, 19: 281–300.

Dickinson, J.E., Filimonau, V., Cherrett, T., Davies, N., Norgate, S., Speed, C. and Winstanley, C. (2013) 'Understanding temporal rhythms and destination travel behaviour: The potential for sustainable travel', *Journal of Sustainable Tourism*, 21(7): 1070–90.

Edensor, T. (2010) 'Introduction: Thinking about rhythm and space', in T. Edensor (ed.) *Geographies of Rhythm: Nature, Place, Mobilities and Bodies*, Farnham: Ashgate.

Elsrud, T. (1998) 'Time creation in traveling: The taking and making of time among women backpackers', *Time and Society*, 7: 309–34.

Fullagar, S., Markwell, K. and Wilson, E. (eds) (2012) *Slow Tourism: Experiences and Mobilities*, Bristol: Channel View.

Germann Molz, J.G. (2009) 'Representing pace in tourism mobilities: Staycations, slow travel and *The Amazing Race*', *Journal of Tourism and Cultural Change*, 7: 270–86.

Hibbert, J., Dickinson, J.E., Gössling, S. and Curtin, S. (2013) 'Identity and tourism mobility: An exploration of the attitude-behaviour gap', *Journal of Sustainable Tourism*, 21(7): 999–1016.

Holden, E. (2007) *Achieving Sustainable Mobility: Everyday and Leisure-time Travel in the EU*, Aldershot: Ashgate.

Holley, D., Jain, J. and Lyons, G. (2008) 'Understanding business travel time and its place in the working day', *Time and Society*, 17: 27–46.

Honoré, C. (2004) *In Praise of Slowness: How a Worldwide Movement is Challenging the Cult of Speed*, San Francisco: Harper.

Lumsdon, L.M. and McGrath, P. (2011) 'Developing a conceptual framework for slow travel: A grounded theory approach', *Journal of Sustainable Tourism*, 19: 265–79.

Matos, W. (2004) 'Can slow travel bring new life to the Alpine regions', in K. Weiermair and C. Mathies (eds) *The Tourism and Leisure Industry*, New York: Haworth.

Metz, D. (2008) *The Limits to Travel*, London: Earthscan.

Nawijn, J., Peeters, P. and Van der Sterren, J. (2008) 'The ST-EP programme and least developed countries: Is tourism the best alternative?', in P.M. Burns and M. Novelli (eds) *Tourism Development: Growth, Myths and Inequalities*, Wallingford: CABI.

Peters, P. (2006) *Time, Innovation and Mobilities: Travel in Technological Cultures,* London: Taylor & Francis.

Poumanyvong, P., Kaneko, S. and Dhakal, S. (2012). 'Impacts of urbanization on national transport and road energy use: Evidence from low, middle and high income countries', *Energy Policy*, 46: 268–77.

Richards, G. (1998) 'Time for a holiday? Social rights and international tourism consumption', *Time and Society*, 7: 145–60.

Southerton, D., Shove, E. and Warde, A. (2001) '*Harried and Hurried: Time Shortage and the Co-ordination of Everyday Life*', Manchester: Centre for Research on Innovation and Computing, University of Manchester.

Stein, K. (2012) 'Time off: The social experience of time on vacation', *Qualitative Sociology*, 35: 335–53.

Stradling, S. and Anable, J. (2008) 'Individual transport patterns', in R. Knowles, J. Shaw and I. Docherty (eds) *Transport Geographies: Mobilities, Flows and Spaces*, Oxford: Blackwell Publishing.

Thurlow, C. and Jaworski, A. (2006) 'The alchemy of the upwardly mobile: Symbolic capital and the stylization of elites in frequent–flyer programmes', *Discourse and Society*, 17: 99–135.

Timms, B.F. and Conway, D. (2011) 'Slow tourism at the Caribbean's geographical margins', *Tourism Geographies*, 10: 1–23.

Tiyce, M. and Wilson, E. (2012) 'Wandering Australia: Independent travellers and slow journeys through time and space', in S. Fullagar, K. Markwell and E. Wilson (eds) *Slow Tourism: Experiences and Mobilities*, Bristol: Channel View Publications.

Tourism Thailand (2013) *Slow Travel Thailand*. Available at: http://inter.tourismthailand.org/fileadmin/upload_img/Home_news/file/special-slow-travel.pdf (accessed 29 March 2013).

41

Tourism and sustainability

Towards a green(er) tourism economy?

C. Michael Hall, Stefan Gössling and Daniel Scott

Sustainable development is 'development that meets the needs of the present without compromising the ability of future generations to meet their own needs' (World Commission on Environment and Development (WCED) 1987: 49).

Sustainable tourism is a sub-set of sustainable development. It is a tourism system that encourages qualitative development, with a focus on quality of life and well-being measures, but not aggregate quantitative growth to the detriment of natural capital.

Introduction

> Industrialization defined the eighteenth century, imperialism the nineteenth century, and the 'endless horizon' of science the twentieth century. Sustainable development will become the defining issue of the twenty-first century. Yet, despite its importance, sustainable development is ill-defined and poorly understood.
>
> *(Harrison 2000: 1)*

This chapter examines the difficulties in achieving sustainable tourism, including the emerging relationship between tourism and 'green growth'. As noted in Chapter 1, sustainable tourism and sustainable development are more cited in academic and policy works than ever before, but tourism and arguably human use of the planet's resources overall are less sustainable than ever (Le Blanc 2009; see also Chapter 3). This concluding chapter therefore seeks to highlight the contested nature of sustainability, especially in relation to its different dimensions, the key barriers that limit its implementation, and posit significant future issues.

The essentially contested concept of sustainability

The terms 'sustainability' and 'sustainable development' are some of the most widely used in the economic, planning and policy lexicon. As noted in Chapter 1 and throughout this volume, sustainable development is usually defined in terms of the report of the World Commission on Environment and Development (WCED 1987), commonly known as the Brundtland Report, where 'sustainable development is development that meets the needs of the present without compromising the ability of future generations to meet their own needs' (WCED 1987: 49). However, as discussed in Chapter 2, the notion of sustainable development has been around much longer.

Debate over the 'wise use' of natural resources has been a major issue since the mid-nineteenth century. Hall (1998) suggested that sustainability is an 'essentially contested concept' (Gaillie 1955–56), a concept the use and application of which is inherently a matter of dispute. The reason for this is the degree to which the concept is used to refer to a 'balance' or 'wise' use in the way in which natural resources are exploited, or solutions to managing natural resource problems are approached. The appropriateness of such an approach and the very way in which appropriate or 'wise use' is defined will depend on the values and ideologies of various interests and stakeholders. Indeed, the history of natural resource management since the middle of the nineteenth century suggests that sustainable development is another term which has emerged in an attempt to reconcile conflicting value positions with regard to the environment and the perception that there is an environmental or natural resource crisis which requires solution (see Chapter 2).

In its modern form, the concept of sustainability arguably first came to public attention with the publication of the World Conservation Strategy (WCS) in 1980 (IUCN 1980). The WCS was prepared by the IUCN with the assistance of the UNEP, WWF, the FAO and UNESCO in conjunction with government agencies, non-government organizations (NGOs) and individual experts from over 100 countries. The WCS was a strategy for the conservation of the Earth's living resources in the face of major international environmental problems such as deforestation, desertification, ecosystem degradation and loss, loss of biodiversity, land use change, pollution and soil erosion. However, unlike present-day tourism concerns (Scott *et al.* 2012), climate change was only a relatively minor consideration with the WCS stating: 'There is also a need for better climatic data, for clarification of the relative roles of human and natural influences on climate, and for improved understanding of the impact of climate change on human activities' (IUCN 1980: s.17.10). Although the warnings in the document were clear:

> The most acute climatic problem…is carbon dioxide accumulation, as a result of the burning of fossil fuels, deforestation and changes in land use. At present rates of increase, the atmospheric concentration of carbon dioxide may produce a significant warming of the lower atmosphere before the middle of the next century, particularly in the polar regions. This warming would probably change temperature patterns throughout most of the world, benefitting some regions and damaging others, possibly severely.
>
> *(IUCN 1980: s.17.9)*

The WCS defined conservation as 'the management of human use of the biosphere so that it may yield the greatest sustainable benefit to present generations while maintaining its potential to meet the needs and aspirations of future generations' (IUCN 1980: s.1.6). The WCS had three specific objectives (IUCN 1980: s.1.7):

- to maintain essential ecological processes and life-support systems (such as soil regeneration and protection, the recycling of nutrients, and the cleansing of waters), on which human survival and development depend;

- to preserve genetic diversity (the range of genetic material found in the world's organisms), on which depend the breeding programmes necessary for the protection and improvement of cultivated plants and domesticated animals, as well as much scientific advance, technical innovation, and the security of the many industries that use living resources; and
- to ensure the sustainable utilization of species and ecosystems (notably fish and other wildlife, forest and grazing lands), which support millions of rural communities as well as major industries.

The notion of sustainable development espoused in the WCS emphasized the relationship between economic development and the conservation and sustenance of natural resources. In many ways there was nothing new in this idea as it had been at the core of much of the conservation debate for decades (see Chapter 2). However, what was extremely significant was the manner in which the report highlighted the global scale of environmental problems and their interrelationships, emphasizing the significance of the environmental–economic development relationship in the relationship between the developed and less developed countries (i.e. the North–South debate), and provided a basis for some government and private sector response, albeit limited, to the challenges identified in the report. The WCS was arguably the first report that put global-scale environmental change onto the public agenda. Notably, tourism and recreation were clearly recognized as significant influences on land and resource use throughout the strategy.

The WCS was also important in that it represented the halfway mark between the 1972 United Nations Stockholm Conference on the Human Environment that established the UNEP, and the 1992 UN Conference on Environment and Development (UNCED) in Rio de Janeiro (often referred to as 'the Rio Summit'). In addition to assisting in the development and promotion of the WCS, the UNEP promoted the idea of the creation of a World Commission on Environment and Development (WCED) at its ten-year review conference in 1982. In 1983, the Commission was created as an independent commission reporting directly to the United Nations Assembly with Gro Harlem Brundtland, then Parliamentary Leader of the Norwegian Labour Party, being appointed as its chair. Although the term sustainability was also used in a 1981 book by Lester Brown of the Worldwatch Institute, *Building a Sustainable Society*; the *Gaia Atlas* by Myers (1984); and Clark and Munn (1986), *Ecologically Sustainable Development of the Biosphere*, it was not until the publication of the report of the WCED in 1987, *Our Common Future*, commonly referred to as 'the Brundtland Report' that sustainable development entered into the popular lexicon, including in tourism. Indeed, as many chapters of this volume indicate, the WCED approach to sustainable development continues to dominate much work on tourism and sustainability.

However, even though the notion of sustainable development became widely adopted by the early 1990s it was also soon recognized that there were significant issues with respect to definition (Robinson *et al.* 1990), especially with respect to the relationship between development and economic growth (Redclift 1987; Sachs 1993). As the then Prime Minister of the United Kingdom, John Major, noted in his Foreword to *Sustainable Development: The UK Strategy*: 'Sustainable development is difficult to define. But the goal of sustainable development can guide future strategy' (HMSO 1994: 3). The fact that there are a number of ways in which sustainability can be defined may have even become one of the reasons why it has become so widely adopted by different stakeholders (Lele 1991; Gössling, Hall & Weaver 2009). Nevertheless, as Hall (2011a) notes, and as highlighted in the review in Chapter 3, despite the rapid acceptance of the concept in policy terms and a wealth of conferences, reports and academic publications, tourism is objectively further from being sustainable than ever.

As this book has outlined, tourism is a substantial contributor to the decline in the Earth's natural capital. As several chapters have noted, these effects are interrelated and are part of tourism's broader role within global environmental change. Yet, at the same time, the economic role of tourism, especially with respect to the continued growth of international and domestic tourism, continues to be celebrated in the context of one of the world's largest industries that employs well over 230 million people worldwide and generates over 9 per cent of global GDP (UNWTO 2014). However, the growing contribution of tourism to environmental change while simultaneously being promoted as a means of economic development suggests that sustainable tourism development is a significant policy problem and maybe even a policy failure (Hall 2011a). Such issues are clearly important for understanding the relationships between tourism and sustainability as they raise fundamental questions not only about the strategies that suggest that tourism can continue to grow while emissions and environmental and social impacts are reduced (a decoupling for which no evidence yet exists), but also the broader context of governance, implementation, effectiveness and desired outcomes and how the results of all the sustainable tourism research that has been noted in the previous chapters are utilized.

Sustainability as a policy problem

The growing contribution of tourism to environmental change, including climate change, while it is simultaneously being promoted as a means of economic growth suggests that sustainable tourism development is a significant policy problem (Hall 2011a). That is an issue that requires resolutions which pose a challenge for governance of selecting the optimum set of policy actions and their implementation (Dovers 1995). The difference between the goals of sustainable tourism and the actualities of tourism's impacts at various scales has been referred to as an implementation gap or deficit (Hjalager 1996; Treuren & Lane 2003; Hall 2009a). Understanding such policy failures and gaps and identifying the means by which they may be closed is an essential part of the process of policy learning. Policy failure can be said to have occurred if policy has failed to achieve an objective or perceived set of outcomes. 'Learning is the process in which information becomes knowledge. Governance allows for mutual, interactive learning in image formation' (Kooiman 2003: 33). If we are to avoid policy failure with respect to the measures proposed for tourism emissions mitigation or the development of a post-Kyoto agreement, for example, it therefore becomes vital that we understand why policies succeed or fail.

Sustainability is a 'meta' or 'wicked' policy problem that has led to new institutional arrangements and policy settings at international, national and local scales (Hall 2008, 2011a; see also Chapter 1). Sustainable tourism is a sub-set of this broader policy arena with its own specific set of institutions and policy actors at various scales as well as being a sub-set of tourism policy overall. Sustainability problems are recognized as posing different challenges in comparison with many other policy problems (e.g. education, taxation, health) because of their attributes that affect both how policies are framed and how the policy response is informed (see Tables 41.1 and 41.2). The analogy with a mathematical problem is actually very appropriate (Dovers 1995) as, particularly in the case of tourism's role in sustainability, there is a clearly defined problem to be 'worked out'. This is categorically different from more general notions of sustainability that are based on biophysical or environmental subdivisions, or the looser notion of environmental 'issues'. From such a perspective, sustainability can be understood as a system property and sustainable development as policy activity aimed at enhancing that property, whether it be in general (Dovers 1996), or in the specific case of the tourism system (Hall & Lew 2009) as discussed throughout this book.

Table 41.1 Policy framing and response attributes with respect to sustainability problems

Attributes	Descriptors
Policy framing	1 Spatial scale of cause or effect
	2 Magnitude of possible impacts on natural systems and/or human systems
	3 Temporal scale of possible impacts: timing and/or longevity
	4 Reversibility
	5 Mensurability of factors and processes
	6 Degree of complexity and connectivity
Response framing	7 Nature of cause(s): discrete, fundamental, systemic
	8 Perceived relevance to the polity
	9 Tractability: availability and acceptability of means
	10 Level and basis of public concern
	11 Existence of policy goals

Source: After Dovers (1996); Hall & Lew (2009); Hall (2011a)

Table 41.2 The policy attributes of sustainability

Temporality	Natural systems function over timescales that are often vastly greater than those which determine political and policy cycles.
Spatiality	Sustainability and environmental problems tend to be cross-boundary in nature and for some types of problems, such as climate change, global in scale. One of the most significant spatial problems in sustainability is the mismatch between government and ecological/resources boundaries which greatly complicates management.
Limits	The concept of sustainability suggests that there are limits to exploitation of natural capital because of its capacity for renewal.
Cumulative	Most anthropogenic impacts are cumulative rather than discrete. This is particular important in the case of atmospheric emissions.
Irreversibility	Some natural capital or environmental assets cannot be renewed once they have gone, such as a species, or are not easily substitutable. In some cases, such as soil or ozone, the timescale for renewal is well outside the normal parameters of policy cycles.
Complexity and connectivity	Sustainability problems are interconnected, meaning that issues such as climate change and biodiversity conservation cannot be easily separated in scientific terms although they often are in policy-making and institutional arrangements. Furthermore, solutions to sustainability problems impact on social and economic policy.
Uncertainty	Some aspects of sustainability are characterized by 'pervasive uncertainty' making it difficult to judge the efficacy, implications and socio-economic impacts of policy measures.
Ethical issues	Although ethical questions are integral to all policy choices sustainability is complicated by the centrality of generational and intergenerational equity to the concept as well as the rights of non-human species.
Inherent capacities of political and economic systems to respond to sustainability issues	This is both a systemic and institutional issue as well as a problem with the role of individual agencies and policy-making/regulatory bodies. It may well be that political and economic systems do not function in a way that adequately responds to major environmental problems.

Source: After Dovers (1996); Hall & Lew (2009); Hall (2011a)

That the various elements of sustainability affect the capacity of public policy-making to provide effective sustainable tourism outcomes has long been recognized (e.g. Butler 1991; Wheeller 1993). Yet there appears relatively little advance in making the sustainability of tourism more tractable to solution outside of specific businesses or locations. Global-scale sustainability for tourism remains elusive (Buckley 2012; see also Chapter 3). Several reasons as to why this has occurred can be advanced. First, the relationship between tourism and sustainable development is often treated in an overly simplistic fashion that while perhaps appealing to some academics, practitioners and policy makers fails to manage policy complexity. For example, the classic planning and implementation model of (a) set goals and policy intervention measures, (b) implement, (c) monitor and track performance, (d) learn from process and revise goals and intervention measures, is extremely useful for dealing with adaptation, mitigation and emissions accounting at a discrete micro (enterprise or destination)-policy level (Hall 2008), but is inadequate as a policy tool as the scale of policy problems and therefore the range of interests and potential ways of framing tourism and sustainability problems increases (Hall 2011a).

Second, it is possible that policy-making is continually seeking to 'catch up' with the issue of sustainability because environmental change, as well as associated economic, social and political change, is occurring faster than responses in policy systems. Indeed, the sheer complexity of sustainability issues and sustainable tourism potentially requires a 'whole of government' response that lies outside of the usual jurisdiction of tourism-specific governance (Hall 2008). This may be an issue of spatial scale, in that a government body may have limited or even no jurisdictional authority over a policy problem, or may be an issue of means with respect to the existence of operational policy processes, technologies and/or institutional arrangements. Or perhaps, the policy capacity to respond to issues of sustainable tourism may reflect the political acceptability of any solution (i.e. increases in tax, greater regulation, restrictions in access to some environments, and/or concern over travel lifestyle change) (Hall 2011a). These issues were illustrated in Table 1.4 (see Chapter 1). Indeed, Table 1.4 suggested that the larger the scale, the more the sustainability of tourism is affected by what is occurring outside of the tourism policy domain including the activities of many tourism businesses. Such a situation, if correct, therefore poses particular challenges for destination and regional governance and sustainability which is, by definition, spatially constrained as well as to the position of the tourism industry within broader governance and policy network contexts. In addition, it also possibly suggests that if sustainable tourism policy only focuses on micro-scale solutions then it may be inherently doomed to fail (Hall 2011a). So is this the reason for the failure of sustainable tourism approaches to reduce tourism's impacts?

Framing sustainable tourism

If sustainability is regarded as a meta-policy problem, then clearly there is a need to reconsider the very notion of sustainable development that is being utilized. The widely used WCED (1987) definition is based on the intergenerational equity principle, which stipulates that no avoidable environmental burdens should be inherited by future generations. However, it is also strongly anthropocentric. In contrast, sustainable development can be defined from a more ecocentric perspective: 'Improving the quality of human life, while living within the carrying capacity of supporting ecosystems' (IUCN et al. 1991: 10). This latter approach recognizes that the capacity of the environment to improve living conditions for people is actually limited. This may contrast strongly with perspectives that suggest that economic growth is not environmentally bound and that there are limits to both economic growth and natural capital. However, what notion of sustainable development will actually achieve these goals?

Hall (2011a) has argued that there are three main formulations of sustainable tourism development: economic sustainability, balanced sustainability and a third approach that is grounded in ecological economics and is often termed a degrowth or steady–state perspective (see also Chapter 2). These approaches can be imagined as occurring on a continuum that stresses the significance of natural capital as the economic foundation of human society. The elements of these approaches are outlined in Table 41.3.

Table 41.3 Three approaches to sustainability

Approach to Sustainability	Policy characteristics
Economic: Seeks to portray the sustainability issue primarily in terms of a single type of impact, usually economic impact (though may have a long-term economic growth perspective [if lucky]). The tourism system is defined in primarily economic terms.	• Sustainability is portrayed in relatively crude economic terms, though may include mid- to long-term perspectives on ROI of economic capital. • Focus on contribution to economic growth, GDP, as well as on visitor numbers and expenditure. • A 'trickle-down' approach to promoting the benefits of tourism for host communities. • Insufficient attention given to opportunity costs or long-term effects. The loss of natural capital is not costed and is usually regarded as a public good. • Substantial emphasis given to the use of 'sustainable tourism' to enhance international and domestic profile and image. • Also a strong focus on deregulation, destination competitiveness, free trade and self-regulation.
Balanced/Green growth approaches: Seeks to 'balance' economic impacts with environmental and social ones (also historically referred to as economic conservation). The tourism system does include economic, social and environmental elements but these are supposedly given equal weight in system management.	• Attention to and promotion of 'triple-bottom line' of economic, environmental and social dimensions of tourism. Although Economic growth, GDP and visitor numbers remain as core indicators of development. • Multiple-evaluation and assessment. Usually accompanied by decision to go ahead anyway because of perceived economic benefits. Although in theory all three dimensions are considered. • Focus on efficiency and technological solutions to the sustainability problem. • Promotion of the relative per-capita improvements of tourism with respect to sustainability rather than absolute contribution. • Relatively little comment on equity dimension of sustainability. When noted it is usually in the context of encouraging tourists from developed countries to travel to LDCs (Pro-poor tourism) not with respect to reducing consumption in developed countries and increasing consumption in LDCs, i.e. it does not challenge the economic (or political) status quo. • Concurrent with one-dimensional approach.
Steady-state: Sustainability is understood as being grounded in the constraints of natural capital/natural systems. It includes some aspects of sustained yield together with a more fundamental notion of environmental conservation (also referred to as degrowth). Tourism system is recognized as being dependent on natural capital.	• Grounded in ecological economics. • Looks to develop a steady-state approach, related to sustainable consumption, that pays attention to systemic effects of tourism. • Examines opportunity costs and does not regard economic growth as a good indicator of development. • Use of a broader set of economic, social and environmental indicators as part of a quality of life approach. • Reduce, reuse, recycle and regulate (also including tax and charge for running down and damage to natural capital). • In some cases international tourism might not even be considered as a development option.

Economic sustainability

An economic sustainability approach is one in which sustainability is primarily seen as being 'environmental' and development as 'economic' (and to a lesser extent 'social') and the concept of sustainable tourism or sustainable tourism development aims to mitigate the paradox between them (Hall 2011a). Baeten (2000) argues that as portrayed via government and supranational institutions the concept of sustainable development suggests that contemporary economic development paradigms are able to cope with environmental crisis without fundamentally affecting existing economic relationships. This approach is conveyed at various scales of governance (Czech 2008), but is perhaps most widely identifiable in the work of extremely influential supranational organizations in international general and tourism policy networks such as the World Economic Forum (2009a, b), and the WTTC (2003, 2009).

Balanced sustainability

The so-called 'balanced sustainability' approach is an extension of the economic anthropocentrism of economic sustainability. Balanced sustainability is also the approach that is most visible in public policy-making and is arguably the dominant approach in academic discourse on sustainable tourism. In the case of UNWTO policy recommendations, as well as those of many other supranational, national and destination governance bodies, one of the cornerstones of the sustainable tourism policy paradigm is that of 'balance' (Hall 2010a). For example, according to the then UNWTO Secretary-General Francesco Frangialli, the UNWTO is 'committed to seek balanced and equitable policies to encourage both responsible energy related consumption as well as anti-poverty operational patterns. This can and must lead to truly sustainable growth within the framework of the Millennium Development Goals' (UNWTO 2007). The UNEP and UNWTO (2005) argue that the concept of sustainable development has 'evolved' since the 1987 Brundtland definition, although do not explain how this conclusion was arrived at.

> Three dimensions or 'pillars' of sustainable development are now recognized and underlined. These are:
>
> - Economic sustainability, which means generating prosperity at different levels of society and addressing the cost effectiveness of all economic activity. Crucially, it is about the viability of enterprises and activities and their ability to be maintained in the long term.
> - Social sustainability, which means respecting human rights and equal opportunities for all in society. It requires an equitable distribution of benefits, with a focus on alleviating poverty. There is an emphasis on local communities, maintaining and strengthening their life support systems, recognizing and respecting different cultures and avoiding any form of exploitation.
> - Environmental sustainability, which means conserving and managing resources, especially those that are not renewable or are precious in terms of life support. It requires action to minimize pollution of air, land and water, and to conserve biological diversity and natural heritage.
>
> It is important to appreciate that these three pillars are in many ways interdependent and can be both mutually reinforcing or in competition. *Delivering sustainable development means striking a balance between them.*
>
> *(UNEP & UNWTO 2005: 9) (our emphasis)*

Yet the continuing contribution of a growing tourism industry to global and environmental change raises a clear question as to whether sustainable tourism can actually be achieved via a 'balanced' approach that continues to promote economic growth. Forecasts of improvements in emissions reduction from tourism, for example, rely on technological efficiencies and solutions rather than any substantial rethink about how to decouple tourism development from longer-distance travel. Indeed, taxation measures that lead to higher costs for long-distance travel are usually strongly opposed by affected governments and businesses alike (Gössling et al. 2014). The notion that you can promote tourism as a means of alleviating poverty in developing countries while simultaneously reducing tourism's contribution to climate change is also increasingly criticized (Hall 2007, 2010a; Gössling, Hall & Weaver 2009). The calls for a balanced approach to sustainability from institutions, industry groups and academics therefore obviously raises questions with respect to what balance actually means with respect to the maintenance of natural capital (Hall 2011a).

Green growth and the green economy

The notion of a green economy as it would be presently understood has existed since at least the 1980s (Miles 1985; Jacobs 1991). For example, as a response to the WCED (1987), Pearce et al. (1989) provided a 'blueprint for a green economy' as part of an extension of the concept of sustainable development to the UK. A number of works have also used the term to describe 'green capitalism' or market-based approaches to environmental problems and/or the development of new green and ethical markets (Patridge 1987; Henderson & Seth 2006), although others have provided more fundamental critiques (Jacobs 1991; Milani 2000) or alternative economic structures (Galtung 1990; Seyfang 2009). However, as discussed in more detail below, current discourse was stimulated by the interrelated responses of various NGOs, green parties and institutions to the unemployment and economic issues created by the global financial crisis from 2008 on. These can be broadly categorized as belong to a 'green new deal' approach in that they are marked by substantial state intervention in environmental infrastructure and development as a means of kickstarting the economy in a manner reminiscent of the Great Depression New Deal (Hall 2014a).

Two think-tank reports were seminal to contemporary green economy/growth thinking, a July 2008 report published by the UK New Economics Foundation (Elliott et al. 2008) and a September 2008 report sponsored by the Center for American Progress (Pollin et al. 2008). The latter report outlined a $100 billion 'green economic recovery' programme to stimulate the US economy 'and leave it in a better position for sustainable prosperity' (Pollin et al. 2008: 1). The proposal was to invest in six green infrastructure investment areas (building retrofitting, mass transit/freight rail, smart grid, wind power, solar power, advanced biofuels) in order to transition to a low-carbon economy 'to create new green jobs – particularly in the struggling construction and manufacturing sectors' (Pollin et al. 2008: 1), a proposal that it was claimed would promote 'sustainable economic growth'. Elliott et al. (2008) called for a Keynesian style 'new green deal' in order to respond to the 'triple crunch' (credit-fuelled financial crisis, accelerating climate change, and soaring energy prices underpinned by peak oil) that the world was facing. Two main initiatives were outlined. First, a re-regulation of national and international financial systems and major changes to taxation systems. Second, a sustained investment and deployment programme in energy conservation and renewable energies, coupled with effective demand management.

Both the Elliott et al. (2008) and Pollin et al. (2008) reports coincided with the economic concerns at the time over the global financial and economic crisis (Hall 2010b). In late 2008, the UNEP (2008; Steiner & Sukhdev 2010) launched an inquiry into how a 'green economy' model could be seeded at this critical time as part of a 'global green new deal' (GGND) in order to stimulate a sustainable recovery. Promoted as an 'initiative to get the global markets back to work' (UNEP 2008), according to Pavan Sukhdev, a senior banker from Deutsche Bank seconded to UNEP. 'Investments will soon be pouring back into the global economy – the question is whether they go into the old, extractive, short-term economy of yesterday or a new green economy that will deal with multiple challenges while generating multiple economic opportunities for the poor and the well-off alike' (UNEP 2008).

The sectors initially identified by the UNEP as likely to generate the biggest transition in terms of economic returns, environmental sustainability, and job creation were:

- clean energy and clean technologies including recycling;
- rural energy, including renewables and sustainable biomass;
- sustainable agriculture, including organic agriculture;
- ecosystem infrastructure;
- reduced emissions from deforestation and forest degradation (REDD); and
- sustainable cities including planning, transportation and green building.

The publication of a UNEP policy brief in March 2009 provided further impetus in the development of the green economy concept with the three broad objectives of a GGND:

1   Make a major contribution to reviving the world economy, saving and creating jobs, and protecting vulnerable groups.
2   Reduce carbon dependency and ecosystem degradation, putting economies on a path to clean and stable development.
3   Further sustainable and inclusive growth, achievement of the MDGs, and end extreme poverty by 2015 (UNEP 2009a: 5).

However, by April 2010, Edward Barbier, one of the architects of the GGND commented, 'most national recovery plans have missed this opportunity to invest in the planet while saving the economy' (Barbier 2010: 832). This was, in part, because the G20 countries had not invested a recommended expenditure of 1 per cent of GDP on green initiatives (only China and South Korea had exceeded this target), nor had they removed resource depleting energy, agriculture and fishing subsidies, advanced far on the taxing and trading of carbon emissions, or substantially aided the world's poor (Barbier 2010). Nevertheless, despite such setbacks the notion of a green economy has become firmly embedded in the discourse of sustainability, with the UNEP (2011a) *Green Economy Report* providing the new institutional orthodoxy of the significance of sustainable/green growth that has already influenced tourism studies (Reddy and Wilkes 2014), if not the tourism industry.

According to the UNEP (2011a: 16) the green economy is 'one that results in improved human well-being and social equity, while reducing environmental risks and ecological scarcities'. Such a definition is as broad as that of the WCED's on sustainable development discussed above. However, like the concept of sustainable development, the acceptability – and potential weakness – of the green economy concept probably lies in its generality. In contrast to the neoliberal policies that pervade global governance, including with respect to tourism (Hall 2011b), the UNEP (2011a) argue that market instruments alone cannot manage environmental externalities and that therefore substantial government intervention is warranted to both develop green technologies and regulate activities that harm the environment. The UNEP also suggest, 'The concept of a "green economy" does not *replace* sustainable development, but there is now a growing recognition that achieving sustainability rests almost entirely on getting the economy right' (UNEP 2011b: 2). Although Khor (2011: 6) warns: 'if the green economy concept gains prominence, while the sustainable development concept recedes, there may be a loss of the use of the holistic sustainable development approach'.

So what does getting the economy right mean? First, there remains a continued commitment to growth, albeit 'sustainable' and 'green'. Second, the UNEP (2011a) maintain that while there are a variety of causes for several concurrent crises that have unfolded since 2000: climate, biodiversity, fuel, food, water, growing unequal distribution of wealth both between (North–South) and within countries, and the global financial system, 'at a fundamental level they all share a common feature: the gross misallocation of capital' (UNEP 2011a: 14). However, the trajectories of socio-technical systems with limited focus on more environmentally benign investment areas were set well before 2000. As Perez-Carmona (2013: 110) suggests, 'An alternative fundamental reason would be that ecological and related social problems exist because of the metabolism of the industrial economy, and the economic policy of perpetual economic growth largely driven by the search of profits and rents in a non-growing planet.' Third, for how long can improvements in MRE efficiency be sustained? Is it possible to have a completely, or even substantially, dematerialized economy in real terms? (Hall 2014a). This is where the notion of green growth runs up against 'Jevon's paradox' (Polimeni et al. 2008; Santarius 2012).

On the rebound

In *The Coal Question* (1865) William Stanley Jevons, noted that, paradoxically, efficiency improvements in the use of coal result not in savings of coal but in increased coal consumption, because technical progress boosts the demand for energy. In contemporary studies of efficiency and productivity the paradox is referred to as a 'rebound effect' which 'describes the increased demand that is caused or at least enabled by one or a number of productivity increases' (Santarius 2012: 5). This means that *efficiency does not equal savings*. Such an observation has enormous issues for tourism given emphasis on technological efficiencies in reducing emissions and energy consumption. 'Tourism in a green economy refers to tourism activities that can be maintained, or sustained, indefinitely in their social, economic, cultural, and environmental contexts: "sustainable tourism". Sustainable tourism…aspires to be more energy efficient and more "climate sound" (e.g. by using renewable energy); consume less water; minimise waste' (UNEP 2011a: 416).

There are several rebound effects that can potentially affect the potential of green growth to limit the decline of natural capital (see Table 41.4). Three types of rebound effects are generally identified (Santarius 2012). First, the direct rebound effect, indicated by increased demand for the same product or service. For example, the switch from a six-litre to a three-litre car may result in additional journeys being made in the three-litre car (Gilbert & Perl 2008). Second, indirect rebound effects, expressed in increased demand for different products or services: The savings made by the change from a six-litre to a three-litre car may be used for other consumption and may result in consumers taking more holidays by air. Third, structural or macroeconomic rebound effects: Because more consumers drive three-litre cars, overall demand for petrol is lower, causing relative prices to fall and creating an incentive for increased demand for energy-using products in other sectors. The level of a rebound effect is generally defined as the percentage of an efficiency-boosting measure/technology that is offset by a rise in demand. According to Santarius (2012: 4), 'in the long term and on average, combined rebound effects of at least 50% must be assumed…energy efficiency improvements in an economic system will on average yield half the theoretical savings potential of efficiency technologies and measures, and in some cases the saving that is achieved will be even less than this'.

Table 41.4 Rebound effects

Financial rebound effects	Increases in energy efficiency result in an income gain and therefore encourage new consumption, e.g. the income effect may be triggered if petrol costs fall by 50% when a driver switches from a six-litre to a three-litre car and releases money for increased energy use in other areas – whether for additional journeys or for other goods and services that also consume energy.
Material rebound	The manufacture and use of more efficient technologies can be accompanied by increased use of energy, e.g. to produce efficient building insulation products or to develop new infrastructure and markets for energy-efficient products.
Psychological rebound	The shift to energy-efficient technologies can boost the symbolic meaning of these goods and services, e.g. increases in the driving distance of 'environmentally friendly' cars as compared with their previous vehicle.
Cross-factor rebound	Increasing the productivity of labour or capital can increase the demand for energy, e.g. through mechanization and automation that uses energy or if the use of energy-efficient technology leads to time savings.

Source: Jenkins (2011); Santorius (2012); Hall (2013a)

Rebound effects do not appear to have been considered in any forecasts of potential efficiency gains in the tourism industry with respect to either energy consumption or emissions (Jenkins *et al.* 2011; Hall 2014a). No studies have been directly conducted on rebound effects, specifically in relation to tourism, although Sorrell (2007) observed that increased consumption of air travel and tourism would potentially be driven by increases in macroeconomic efficiency gains, while Hall (2009b, 2010a, 2014a) cautioned as to the impacts of an efficiency focus in relation to sustainable tourism consumption. Barker (2009) modelled the rebound effects resulting from the global energy efficiency measures incorporated into the IPCC's (2007) Fourth Assessment Report and estimated that for transport there would be a worldwide direct rebound of 9.1 per cent in 2020 and 9.1 per cent in 2030, and a macroeconomic rebound of 26.9 per cent in 2020 and 43.1 per cent in 2030, thus leading to a total economy-wide rebound of 36.0 per cent in 2020 and 52.2 per cent in 2030. This compares with an estimated rebound for all sectors of 31 per cent of the projected energy savings potential by 2020, rising to 52 per cent by 2030 (Barker 2009). If this scale of rebound were applied to tourism then, even allowing for the estimated greater use of low–carbon fuels, the potential increase in tourism-related emissions would likely be over 200 per cent by 2030 (Hall *et al.* 2013). This means that, by 2030, the impacts of forecast energy efficiencies on proposed tourism emissions reduction will potentially be more than halved and that the reduction in the potential gains in energy efficiencies over the period to 2035 cut by more than 35 per cent (Gössling *et al.* 2013).

The UNEP (2011a: 438) propose that in a BAU scenario 2011–50, tourism growth will imply increases in energy consumption (111%), greenhouse gas emissions (105%), water consumption (150%), and solid waste disposal (252%). Even in the optimistic greener investment scenario the tourism-related drawdown of natural capital still increases:

> The tourism sector can grow steadily in the coming decades (exceeding the BAU scenario by 7 per cent in terms of the sector GDP) while saving significant amounts of resources and enhancing its sustainability. The green investment scenario is expected to undercut the corresponding BAU scenario by 18 per cent for water consumption, 44 per cent for energy supply and demand, 52 per cent for CO_2 emissions.
>
> *(UNEP 2011a: 438)*

Significantly, the UNEP (2011a) figures do not consider rebound effects although elsewhere, for example with respect to maritime and aviation emissions, the report notes, 'Aviation emissions are projected to increase exponentially in the next few decades, fuelled by income growth and reductions in the price of air travel' (2011a: 383). While behavioural responses and rebound affects are recognized (UNEP 2011a: 257, 267, 357, 360, 461, 474, 479, 481), together with fragmented governance, lack of affordability, investment, negative tradeoffs, consumer preference, vested interests, and risk aversion (UNEP 2011a: 473), as barriers to the green economy, the UNEP (2011a), rather optimistically, appear to suggest that such savings can be put into further energy saving consumption. However, in tourism, the significance of the rebound effect, as well as some of the other barriers, remains generally unacknowledged (Hall 2014a).

The industry response to green economy issues, such as climate change, suggests that technical solutions that promote greater energy efficiency are the primary means to address emissions. However, as stressed above, absolute emission reductions are unlikely, as growth in transport volumes and infrastructure outweighs efficiency gains (Scott *et al.* 2010), and potentially large rebound effects (Arvesen *et al.* 2011; Santarius 2012) have not been accounted for in the tourism sector (Gössling *et al.* 2013).

Furthermore, even if new technologies and energy sources do become available, this does not mean that 'old' carbon-intensive energy sources stop being used. Instead, they will almost certainly run in parallel as investment costs are paid off and, unless their costs are prohibitive, will be exploited in less well-regulated pollution regimes (Hoffmann 2011; Hall *et al.* 2013a). The optimism of a green growth paradigm based on MRE efficiency and major changes in the energy mix to renewables yet providing for continued increases in visitor numbers (Cabrini 2012; UNEP 2011a) is therefore extremely problematic given the constraints of arithmetic of growth and efficiency limits, governance and market limits, and systemic limits (Hoffmann 2011; Hall 2014a) (see Table 41.5). There are then significant limits of containment (Santarius 2012): Efficiency standards harbour the greatest risk of evoking rebound effects. Real income gains and falls in market prices that arise from efficiency increases can theoretically be absorbed by ecotaxes. However, this would require a complex taxation scheme with sector- and product-specific tax rates, which is difficult to implement (e.g. the EU travel tax). Finally, in theory, rebound effects cannot arise if resource use is limited by caps that provide absolute upper limits on consumption/waste. However, unless caps are introduced globally, rebound effects can still occur via international trade and increased imports, including tourism (Hall 2014a).

Steady-state sustainability and the conservation of natural capital

> Pleonexia, the insatiable desire for more, was regarded in the time of Aristotle as a human failing, an obstacle to achieving the 'good life'. In the present day it is a failing of the tourism industry in terms of its focus on growth without full consideration of the effects on natural capital....in the case of tourism, more does not mean better, and growth does not mean development.
>
> *(Hall 2010a: 140–41)*

The concept of green growth raises the fundamental difference between sustainable growth and sustainable development (Hall 2014a), a theme that underlies many of the chapters in this volume. Growth refers to the quantitative increase in economic output, whereas development refers to an increase in the quality of output *without* an increase in MRE use (Hall 2010a, 2011a). Given the role of rebound effects and the interconnectedness of growth and MRE consumption,

Table 41.5 Key weaknesses of the green growth paradigm

Arithmetic of growth and efficiency limits

Dominance of the prevailing growth paradigm in policy-making and advice

Enhanced MRE efficiency will encourage 'rebound effects' (Jevon's paradox)

Much of the MRE efficiency that has been gained in developed countries has been achieved by
outsourcing very intense MRE production to developing countries

Technically challenging to completely replace fossil fuel with renewables, especially as old and new
technologies exist on parallel energy paths for considerable time periods

The relative scarcity of conventional oil, which is especially important for transport, means that it is
likely to experience increased prices but extreme price explosions are unlikely

Continued absolute increase from tourism sector (as well as other sectors such as agriculture) at a
rate exceeding efficiency gains

Population growth, and hence consumption growth, including mobility consumption, are forecast
to continue

Governance and market constraints

Governance via market-based instruments has been problematic

International governance regimes for the environment are incoherent

Level of public debt complicates structural change

Externalization of costs as fundamental part of the capitalist market economy

Need for appropriate indicators

Political willingness to use carrots, e.g. subsidies, but not sticks, e.g. increased regulation

Colossal de-carbonization of the economy and society will only be achieved if current consumption
patterns, methods and lifestyles are also subject to profound change

Systemic limits

Biophysical limits, including those entangled with growing emissions, pollution, and global
environmental change

The capitalist economic system is predicated upon growth, capitalism rests upon the perpetual
search for surplus value (profit), and functions poorly in a contracting economy (with the
exception of short-term cyclical crises)

Source: Hoffmann (2011); Hall (2011a, 2013a, 2013b); Jenkins *et al.* (2011); Santarius (2012)

'Energy-efficient technological improvements as the solution for the world's energy and environmental problems will not work. Rather energy-efficient technology improvements are counter-productive, promoting energy consumption. Yet energy efficiency improvements continue to be promoted as a panacea' (Polimeni *et al.* 2008: 169). Yet this is not to suggest that MRE-efficient technologies should not be advanced. Rather it depends on their context and the overall nature of consumption, not only within tourism but the transfer of consumption between tourism and other aspects of what individuals consume within specific socio-technical systems (i.e. what people consume in all aspects of their lives, not just when they are tourists). As Polimeni *et al.* (2008: 169), note: 'If individual energy consumption behaviours are significantly altered to reduce consumption and this behaviour is unwavering, then energy efficient technologies can further reduce energy consumption.'

So what is to be done? As Polimeni *et al.* (2008) argue, and what others have been suggesting in the debate over growth and the environment since the 1960s (Daly 1991; Latouche 2009; see also Chapter 2) is that a sufficiency approach that looks to limit consumption patterns to bio-physical constraints is required. As long as economic growth is the goal, whether green or not, 'technological progress will not result in biodiversity conservation; rather, an expansion of the human niche and the consumption of more natural resources will result' (Czech 2006: 1563).

The problem with the notion of 'balance' is that, as suggested above, while perhaps conceptually attractive at first sight, it underplays key questions of what is being balanced for whose benefit, and devalues the importance of the natural capital that, from an ecological understanding of sustainability, actually underpins economic growth and social and economic well-being. Natural capital includes all natural assets; humans can modify and reduce it, and can enhance its reproduction, but humans cannot create it and, therefore, it is non-substitutable. The Brundtland Report did not refer to natural capital although it did note 'the planet's ecological capital' (WCED 1987: 5).

Pearce *et al.* (1989: 1) defined natural capital stock as 'the stock of all environmental and natural resource assets, from oil in the ground to the quality of soil and groundwater, from the stock of fish in the ocean to the capacity of the globe to recycle and absorb carbon'. The natural capital stock is usually divided into three categories (Roseland 2000): non-renewable resources or natural capital (NNC), such as oil and gas resources; the finite capacity of the natural system to produce renewable resources or natural capital (RNC), such as food, water, timber as ecosystem goods, as well as ecosystem services such as erosion control; and the capacity of natural systems to absorb anthropogenic emissions and pollutants without negative externalities on present or future generations. More than just a metaphor (Jabareen 2004), the natural capital concept underlies ecological economic approaches to understanding tourism and sustainability, even if it is often not fully acknowledged. From a neoclassical perspective an economy is sustainable if the value of economic output is non-declining over time. From an ecological economic perspective, sustainability is not only an economic problem but also a problem of maintaining essential, irreplaceable, and non-substitutable natural capital that is beyond the confines of market exchange (Gowdy 2000). Therefore, total income is a combination of traditional marketed economic goods and services and non-marketed ecosystem goods and services.

According to Costanza and Daly (1992), the concept of sustainability is implicit in the definition of income so natural income must be sustainable as, from this perspective, any consumption that requires the running down of natural capital, for example as a result of missions from tourism consumption, cannot be counted as income. Therefore, they conclude that the constancy of total natural capital (TNC) is the cornerstone of sustainable development.

$$TNC = RNC + NNC$$

The notion of 'balance' is therefore likely to be very different between a balanced sustainability approach and one that promotes the need to conserve natural capital, given that constancy of total natural capital is the key idea in steady-state sustainable development (Costanza and Daly 1992). A key focus of a steady-state approach is the potential incompatibility between economic growth and sustainability. Economic growth is simply an increase in the production and consumption of goods and services. It entails increasing population and/or per capita consumption, whereas consumption refers to the consumption of materials and energy by firms, households and governments. This focus on growth and consumption is reflected in Daly's (2008: 2) comments in a report to the UK Sustainable Development Commission:

> The growth economy is failing. In other words, the quantitative expansion of the economic subsystem increases environmental and social costs faster than production benefits, making us poorer not richer, at least in high-consumption countries. Given the laws of diminishing marginal utility and increasing marginal costs, this should not have been unexpected...It is hard to know for sure that growth now increases costs faster than benefits since we do not

bother to separate costs from benefits in our national accounts. Instead we lump them together as 'activity' in the calculation of GDP.

Daly (2008), therefore, emphasized that a distinction needs to be made between growth and development. This distinction is clearly significant when considering the potential growth in aviation and tourism and the implications for climate change in the context of sustainable tourism. Growth refers to the quantitative increase in economic output, whereas development refers to an increase in the quality of output without an increase in material and energy use (Hall 2011a, 2014a).

While neoclassical economists emphasize relative limitation (scarcity pricing), ecological economists stress Malthusian, general limitation. For the latter, substitution can solve relative allocation but cannot solve general limitation which can only be avoided if economic activity proceeds within appropriate cyclical resource transformations – a steady state (Khalil 1997). Hall (2009a) argues that sustainable tourism needs to be understood from a steady-state economic perspective that explicitly recognizes the extent to which economic development, including tourism, is dependent on the stock of natural capital. According to Hall (2009a) steady-state tourism is a tourism system that encourages qualitative development but not aggregate quantitative growth to the detriment of natural capital. A steady-state economy, including at the destination level, can therefore be defined in terms of 'a constant flow of throughput at a sustainable (low) level, with population and capital stock free to adjust to whatever size can be maintained by the constant throughput beginning with depletion and ending with pollution' (Daly 2008: 3).

In order to reduce its demands on natural capital, tourism therefore needs to become part of a circular economy rather than a linear one, so that inputs of virgin raw material and energy and outputs in the form of emissions and waste requiring disposal are reduced. Such a change is often categorized as sustainable consumption (Cooper 2005; Jackson 2005) (see Figure 41.1). As Boulding (1945, 1949) recognized with respect to the nature of consumption and production relationships over 60 years ago:

> There is a very general assumption in economics that income (or out-go) is the proper measure of economic welfare, and that the more income and out-goings we have, the better. In fact, almost the reverse is the case. Income consists of the value of production: out-going is the value of consumption. I shall argue that it is the capital stock from which we derive satisfactions, not from the additions to it (production) or the subtractions from it (consumption): that consumption, far from being a desideratum, is a deplorable property of the capital stock which necessitates the equally deplorable activities of production: and that the objective of economic policy should not be to maximize consumption or production, but rather to minimize it (i.e. to enable us to maintain our capital stock with as little consumption or production as possible). It is not the increase of consumption or production which makes us rich, but the increase in capital, and any invention which enables us to enjoy a given capital stock with a smaller amount of consumption and production, out-going or income, is so much gain
>
> *(Boulding 1949: 79–80).*

Therefore, with respect to sustainability, any investment that enables humanity to reduce the volume of throughput needed to maintain a given level of welfare can be considered an indirect investment in natural capital (Daly 1996).

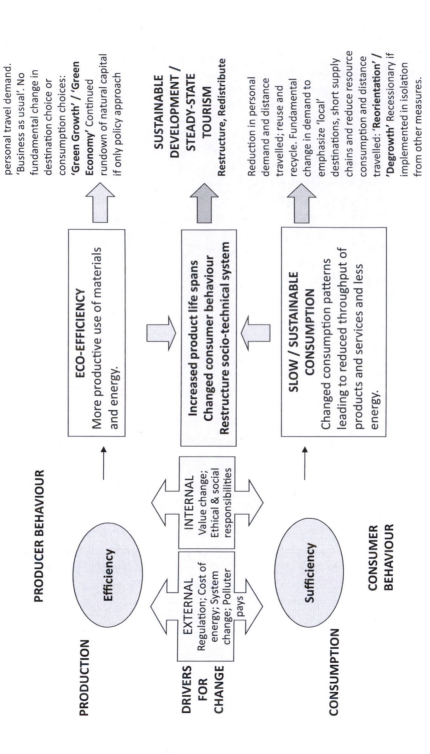

Figure 41.1 Efficiency and sufficiency in sustainable tourism development

Source: After Hall (2009b)

Economic sufficiency and degrowth

The steady-state approach to sustainability focuses on economic sufficiency as well as economic efficiency. It is the sufficiency or behavioural dimension that distinguishes the perspective from the standard view of sustainability, although the WCED (1987) did also argue that there needed to be a change in Western lifestyles if global sustainable development was to be achieved. The sufficiency approach aims to slow the rate and amount of consumption via a mix of market and regulatory mechanisms. The focus on time in much of the sufficiency literature has meant the approach is often related to the notion of 'slow' consumption as well as the concept of 'décroissance', 'degrowth' or 'slow tourism' that recently entered the lexicon of green economics (Flipo & Schneider 2008; Hall 2009a, 2011a; Dickinson & Lumsdon 2010; Martínez-Alier *et al.* 2010). Degrowth is not a theory of contraction equivalent to theories of growth, instead it is a term created by critics of growth theory that seeks to provide an alternative to the dominant doctrines of 'economism' in which growth is the ultimate good by positing the development of a non-growth form of sustainable economics bounded by the limits of humankind's ecological footprint on natural resources as part of a post-development society (Latouche 2009). Degrowth is therefore not so much connected to downsizing per se but to the notion of 'right-sizing', 'appropriate growth' and the creation of a steady state economy (Hall 2009a). Components of which include:

- reducing the global ecological footprint (including the carbon footprint) to a sustainable level;
- in countries where the per capita footprint is greater than the sustainable global level, reducing to this level within a reasonable timeframe;
- increasing consumption by those in severe poverty as quickly as possible, in a sustainable way, to a level adequate for a decent life, following locally determined poverty-reduction paths rather than externally imposed development policies; and
- increasing economic activity in some cases; but redistribution of income and wealth both within and between countries as a more essential part of poverty reduction (Flipo & Schneider 2008).

Elements of such an approach in tourism policy terms include (Hall 2010a, 2014a):

- the development of voluntary and mandated environmental standards at various scales of governance;
- the adoption of cradle-to-cradle lifecycle analysis in determining tourism infrastructure and product life spans;
- relocalization schemes that reinforce the potential economic, social and environmental benefits of consuming, producing and travelling locally;
- ethical consumption measures that focus on living better by consuming less and the satisfaction of non-material needs; and
- taxation and other measures that reflect the full environmental cost of travel and tourism development.

An alternative conceptualization of sustainable tourism development can be found in Figure 41.1. This is an approach grounded in ecological economics and suggests, for the reasons noted above with respect to efficiency-oriented green economy approaches, that sustainability also requires attention to sufficiency (i.e. that behaviour and system change are essential if tourism's contribution

– or humanity's for that matter – to the drawdown of natural capital is to be attended to). This also means paying attention to the problematic fixation with economic growth, what Georgescu-Roegen (1971) termed 'growth mania', including in tourism (Hall 2014a).

Daly's (1991) concept of an ontological steady state as:

> an economy with constant stocks of people and artefacts, maintained at some desired, sufficient levels by low rates of maintenance 'throughput', that is, by the lowest feasible flows of matter and energy from the first stage of production (depletion of low entropy materials from the environment) to the last stage of consumption (pollution of the environment with high entropy wastes and exotic materials).
>
> *(Daly 1991: 16)*

provides the basis for defining steady-state tourism as a tourism system that encourages qualitative development, with a focus on quality of life and social and ecological well-being measures, but not aggregate quantitative growth to the detriment of natural capital (Hall 2009b). The problem with tourism is that the larger something has grown, the greater, *ceteris paribus*, are its maintenance costs. More new production, more throughput, is required just to keep the larger stock constant (Daly 1996: 68). Given that central role of service in contemporary economies, it is significant to note that Daly (1991) emphasized the straightforward maxim that service is the ultimate benefit of economic activity and should be maximized while throughput is the ultimate cost of this service and should be minimized. Indeed, Latouche's (2009) recommendations for degrowth, or rightsizing the economy, of restructure, redistribute, reduce, reuse and recycle, are all entailed in Daly's (1991) stock-service throughput notion and are useful and stimulating keywords for implementing it (Kerschner 2010).

Yet changing consumption and concomitant lifestyles, particularly in respect of tourism, is a socio-political issue, not just an economic and environmental one, factoring in equity within and between societies (Khor 2011). There can be no presumption that growth alone increases welfare, rather welfare is an issue of distribution of wealth (Hall 2014a). If progressive taxes and appropriate regulation and state intervention were necessary for the functioning of the welfare state as a response to the socio-economic shocks of the Second World War and the preceding depression, then similar socio-technical system change is surely required for the current environmental shock. This is particularly important because of the limited capacities for changing individual behaviours via social marketing or nudging in the required time period to avoid disastrous climate change (Hall 2013b, 2014b). As Vermeulen (2009: 25) argues, the focus of responses to overconsumption needs to be on 'structures as a whole, rather than their individual actions. Short-term solutions may rely on improving efficiencies within existing modes of production and consumption (reformist changes). In the longer term, however, what is needed is a rethink of how and what we consume (transformist changes).'

Green growth and the green economy is therefore an incremental reform of a socio-economic system unsustainably geared towards economic growth (Hall 2014a). It is not a major shift in policy paradigm (Hall 2011a). It is not just a case of tourism getting more efficient. It is shifting consumption around spatially and temporally and reducing its overall emissions and MRE consumption. Tourism needs to adopt the polluter pays principle, and shift to shorter trips and, in some cases, less frequent travel and longer stays (Peeters & Landré 2011). This will mean that many destinations and sectors will actually benefit. The exception being aviation, which for too long has avoided the environmental costs of its activities. As Chapter 2 indicated, there is a long legacy of alternative tourism seeking to describe more sustainable forms of tourism. Perhaps some may think that to this we should now add another – Utopian tourism – for what is called for is a fundamental transformation not only of tourism mobility but the socio-technical system within which it resides (Hall 2013a, 2014a). But what other choice is there?

Changing policy paradigms and Institutions

Change is not easy in politics. It is even harder when it comes to the environment. It is therefore important to recognize how policy change occurs. Three different orders of change can be recognized (Hall 2011a). First order change is likely to be characterized by incremental, routinized, satisficing behaviour that is based around government officials and policy experts that leads to a change in the 'levels (or settings) of the basic instruments of...policy' (Hall, P. 1993: 279). Second order change is characterized by the selection of new policy instruments and techniques and policy settings due to previous policy experience but the overarching policy goals remain the same. Second order change is therefore more strategic in form although officials and policy experts still remain relatively isolated from external political pressures. According to Greener (2001: 139) this order of change is extremely significant for policy learning given that a change in an indicator or a policy instrument may also be a 'symptom of possible future paradigm change, or at least present paradigm dissatisfaction'. Indeed, the selection of policy indicators is not a neutral device (Callon 1998). As Majone (1989: 116–17) stressed, 'policy instruments are seldom ideologically neutral...distributionally neutral...[and]... cannot be neatly separated from goals' and instead tend to reflect the values of the policy paradigms within which they are selected.

Third order change, or a policy paradigm shift, takes place when a new goal hierarchy is adopted by policy makers because the coherence of existing policy paradigm(s) has been undermined, 'Where experiment and perceived policy failure has resulted in discrepancies or inconsistencies appearing which cannot be explained within the existing paradigm' (Greener 2001: 135) and set of institutional norms that support particular kinds of values and goals (Bernstein 2002). In situations where existing institutions and policies cease to be relevant to policy problems, policy failure may also lead the state to search for policy advice outside of previous internal and external sources, as in academia, think tanks and non-government organizations (Pierre & Peters 2000). Therefore, the promotion of sympathetic individuals to key positions within government agencies, changes in the composition of advisory bodies, and the development of new sets of institutional arrangements are necessary for paradigm shifts to be sustained (Hall 2011a). In the UK the establishment of the Sustainable Development Commission in 2000 as an independent advisory body on sustainable development was regarded by some as an indication of a change in direction on sustainability thinking. However, in March 2011, the new Conservative-Liberal Democratic coalition government closed it down, its website and closing communiqué stating:

> The Sustainable Development Commission, which closed on 31 March 2011, held government to account to ensure the needs of society, the economy and the environment were properly balanced in the decisions it made and the way it ran itself. This is an archive site.
>
> ...more than twenty years after the Brundtland Commission, governments still struggle to place sustainable development at the heart of what they do. It is not as if politicians and civil servants don't care – there are a great many who have devoted their careers to tackling issues of the environment, fairness and a sustainable economy. Yet we still seem to find it hard to treat the future as if it really is as important as the present, and seek to tackle each problem separately from the others.
>
> *(Sustainable Development Commission 2011)*

When a new hierarchy of policy goals is being adopted, the framework of ideas that becomes dominant is not necessarily the most technically coherent (Hall 2011a). Instead, with respect to the idea of political learning and its relationship to paradigm change, it will be the one whose supporters are best politically able to implement it despite opposition. Thereby, highlighting some of the response framing attributes of sustainability noted in Table 41.3. As Greener (2001: 136) stressed in what is a salient point with respect to environmental policy, especially with respect to climate change: 'Politicians have the most influence over the final choice of goals, but they must mobilise popular support within the media and public to carry the electorate with them.'

One potential driver for change in policy paradigms is the influence of exogenous shocks or 'crises' on the wider public of policy (Hall, P. 1993; Hall 2010b). Greener, along with Hall (1993), emphasized that, 'The oil price and currency shocks of the early 1970s helped create hostile economic conditions which made it possible for advocates of monetarism to question the ability of Keynesians to run the economy' (Greener 2001: 136). In the same way, the combined pressures of climate change and peak oil as well as other elements of environmental change might contribute to a policy paradigm change with respect to sustainability and sustainable tourism. Nevertheless, policy change can also occur without conceptual shifts, new indicators and institutional arrangements can be developed without the problem actually being 'solved' (Hall 2011a).

Arguably this has already happened with respect to the articulation of an alternative development paradigm. In the late 1960s and early 1970s as a result of oil and other environmental shocks substantial concerns were expressed with respect to an overconcentration in government policies on economic growth without consideration of the limits of natural resources (e.g. Mishan 1967; Meadows *et al.* 1972; Daly 1972). These were also discussed with respect to the implications of tourism and travel. For example, in an article entitled 'slow is beautiful' Gleditsch (1975: 91) noted, 'the severe environmental problems involved in an unlimited or uncontrolled further growth in aviation' as well as the uneven structure of personal mobility. According to Gleditsch (1975: 79), 'The concept of "overdevelopment" is relevant in this context. The historical movement in many industrialized countries has been from undernourishment to excessive caloric intake. Similarly, mobility may become too high, both from a personal and a social perspective'. In a prescient observation of what would now be described as the 'hypermobile' (Gössling *et al.* 2009), Gleditsch (1975: 91) 'hypothesized…that topdogs will secure a disproportionately high share of the advantages and a disproportionately low share of the disadvantages of any new transportation system.…With resources such as education and income, topdogs are in a position to make use of new transportation technology – and avoid its cost.'

The above comments suggest that the alternative policy paradigm for sustainable tourism is a continuation of previous critiques of a public policy focus on economic growth at the expense of environmental and social concerns. But they also suggest that, some 40 years on, an alternative policy paradigm has failed to make significant policy headway. The degree of policy failure with respect to conservation of natural capital is considerable but it has not yet been matched by an accompanying conceptual policy change that removes the focus on economic growth and the market. The national and global institutional arrangements that surround sustainable development and tourism and climate change remain wedded to assumptions based on the compatibility between the environment and economic growth and acceptance of market forces (Hall 2011a, 2014a). While this is the case, the implementation of steady-state approaches remains problematic (Gareau 2008). As Bernstein (2002: 2) notes, 'the institutions that have developed in response to global environmental problems support particular kinds of values and goals, with important implications for the constraints and opportunities to combat the world's most serious environmental problems'.

Indeed, far too much attention has been given to the assumption that a well-designed institution is 'good' because it facilitates cooperation and network development rather than a focus on norms and institutionalization as first and necessary steps in the assessment of what kind of changes institutional arrangements are promoting and their potential outcomes (Hall 2011a). Such an approach, which is widespread in tourism studies (Hall 2011b), has only reinforced limited and incremental change rather than conceptual policy learning and paradigm change.

> ...the consequence is that liberal environmentalism has resulted in enabling certain kinds of responses to global environmental problems consistent with it, such as possibilities for the privatization of environmental governance in some areas or the increasing use of market mechanisms. But at the same time it has made trade offs much more difficult because it denies that they may be necessary among values of efficiency, economic growth, corporate freedom, and environmental protection.
>
> *(Bernstein 2002: 14)*

Case Study

Carbon offsetting and CSR in the aviation industry

According to the International Air Transport Association (IATA 2012) aviation carried some 2.8 billion passengers and 48 million metric tons of cargo and helped generate 56.6 million jobs and US$2.2 trillion in economic activity during 2011. IATA forecast that by 2030, 82 million jobs and US$6.9 trillion in economic activity will depend on air transport. However, aviation emissions are a significant contributor to climate change (see Chapter 3). During flight, aircraft engines emit carbon dioxide, oxides of nitrogen, oxides of sulphur, water vapour, hydrocarbons, particles consisting mainly of sulphate from sulphur oxides, and soot (Capoccitti, Khare & Mildenberger 2010). According to the International Air Transport Association (IATA 2008), aviation is responsible for 2–3 per cent of global CO_2. However, compared with road and rail transport, emissions from air travel are particularly harmful because they are released in the upper troposphere and lower stratosphere and have substantial radiative forcing (RF) potential compared with that of carbon dioxide emissions alone (Sausen *et al.* 2005). Given forecast aviation growth, by 2050 aircraft could account for up to 15 per cent of the global warming impact from all human activities (Capoccitti, Khare & Mildenberger 2010). There is, therefore, substantial focus by both IATA (2012) and some individual airlines to find ways to reduce the emissions contribution of the aviation sector. This case study discusses the changing nature and extent of corporate responsibility communications by investigating the narrative disclosures of non-financial information on websites and reports of IATA member airlines between 2009 and 2013 to highlight progress with respect to improved sustainability.

The aviation sector is arguing for a range of technological, management and behavioural measures to seek to achieve its emissions reduction targets. CSR reporting and the availability of voluntary carbon offsetting opportunities are a significant part of seeking to encourage more sustainable corporate and consumer behaviour in the aviation sector (Lynes and Andrachuk 2008). Sustainability for airlines in this context means to achieve a synthesis growth of responsibility and profitability (Cowper-Smith & De Grosbois 2011).

Three reporting standards have become widely adopted by the aviation industry:

- United Nations Global Compact: a strategic policy initiative for businesses that are committed to aligning their operations and strategies with ten universally accepted principles in the areas of human rights, labour, environment and corruption.
- ISO 26000:2010: this standard offers guidance on socially responsible behaviour and possible actions; it does not contain requirements and, therefore, in contrast to ISO management system standards, it is not certifiable.
- Global Reporting Initiative: this non-profit organization produces a sustainability reporting framework, which guides an organizational report to give information about economic, environmental, social and governance performance (GRI 2013).

Voluntary offsetting schemes have grown rapidly since 2000 due to the interest of companies, organizations and individuals to offset their emissions even in the absence of regulatory demands (Gössling 2011). Six principles of carbon offsetting are identified by IATA (2008) (see Table 41.6): complementarity, additionality, verification, registration, traceability and guarantee, to help people and organizations gain confidence in the purchase and use of carbon offsets and to ensure the quality of offset programmes. However, there has been no comprehensive study of the extent to which such programmes have been taken up by the industry.

Table 41.6 Principles of carbon offsetting

Principles	Definitions
Complementarity	Offsets and trading should be seen as part of wider efforts to reduce emissions alongside technological and operational improvements in fuel efficiency.
Additionality	CO_2 reduction of removal used as an offset should be additional to business as usual activity as a method to ensure the environmental integrity of offsets.
Verification	Records of aircraft CO_2 emissions from operations covered by the offset programme must be maintained and be externally verified by an independent third party.
Registration	CO_2 reductions from offset projects should be recorded through a central registry, with the amounts purchased progressively subtracted from the total determined for that particular project.
Traceability	The receipt issued to the customer should clearly indicate that the credit has been/will be retired as a result of the purchase and cannot be resold.
Guarantee	If the purchased reduction in CO_2 will be achieved at some future date, then a guarantee that an alternative and equivalent offset will be made if the project fails should be provided.

Therefore, this case study profiles research undertaken to ascertain how available information on CSR and offsetting is to consumers on IATA airline member websites, and the nature of that information. In 2013, there were 238 IATA member airlines representing 84% of total air traffic influence in the aviation industry (IATA 2012); 235 members are included in the present study. Websites were examined because of their significance as interfaces with the travelling public including not only company and airline information but also their use as a direct booking facility. Website design is an important factor that influences customer access to particular information and, therefore, potentially their behaviour. In 2013, just over half of airline websites examined, 51.06 per cent (120 out of 235), provide a search bar on their homepage. The results of the analysis are illustrated in Table 41.7.

Table 41.7 IATA airlines CSR reporting and carbon offsetting

	2009	%	2013	%
Number of IATA member airlines examined	224		235	
Corporate Responsibility – Social Statement	86	38.4%	119	50.6%
Corporate Responsibility – Environmental Statement	66	29.5%	96	40.9%
Climate Change – Technology Developments	63	28.1%	62	26.4%
Climate Change – Infrastructure Developments	46	20.5%	62	26.4%
Climate Change – Efficient Operations	46	20.5%	62	26.4%
Climate Change – Economic Measures	43	19.1%	62	26.4%
Carbon Calculator available online	32	14.2%	38	16.1%
Carbon Offsetting – Personal	29	12.9%	34	14.5%
Carbon Offsetting – Corporate	8	3.5%	12	5.1%
Available when booking online	21	9.4%	34	14.5%
Able to use frequent flyer points to offset	8	3.5%	8	3.4%

This study indicates for those airline companies who reported their performance, most environmental information is derived from the non-financial information section contained in their formal annual and corporate social reports. In the aviation field, regional and domestic airlines are unlikely to provide non-financial information on their websites; among airlines without social CSR statements 70 per cent (82 out of 116) are domestic airlines. This situation perhaps reflects Soderstrom's (2013) suggestion that unless it fits specifically into their competitive strategies, smaller organizations should not provide comprehensive and fully assured sustainability reports due to the cost of compliance.

In 2013, 119 (50%, 119 out of 235) member airlines provide statements about social policies or actions, and 96 (40%, 96 out of 235) provide information about their environmental policies, of which 62 airlines (26%) have adopted the IATA's Four Pillar Strategy (Technology Development, Infrastructure Improvements, Efficient Operations, and Economics Measures) as a means of framing their environmental actions to address climate change. However, the increase in the extent of environmental reporting between 2009 and 2013 is significantly greater than the adoption of carbon offsetting measures.

Carbon offsetting is an immediate, direct and pragmatic means to encourage action to limit climate change impacts, at least in the short term and has the ability to alter customers' opinion and behaviour. Carbon offsetting information is usually included under 'Environmental Initiatives' or 'Environment and Climate' sections on websites. Information related to carbon offsetting is usually of no more than one page. In 2009, 34 airlines (15%) had carbon offsetting information on their websites or in their formal reports; 51 (22%) have statements regarding carbon neutrality on their websites or their formal reports referring to their commitments to the Carbon Neutral Growth 2020 (CNG2020) strategies established by IATA which means they are looking to limit their carbon emission from 2020 onwards. Of these airlines one-third (17) did not give their customers the opportunities to offset their carbon footprint even though the companies have committed themselves to carbon-neutral aviation in the future. A slight increase in carbon offsetting opportunities had been provided by airlines in the four years between 2009 and 2013. In 2013, 39 airlines (16%) had carbon offsetting information available on either their websites or in their formal reports; 62 (26%) of them have carbon neutral statements on their websites or their formal reports. Of these, 23 did not give their customers the opportunities to offset their carbon footprint.

C. Michael Hall, Bolin Zhou and Sandra Wilson

Conclusion

This chapter has sought to illustrate how sustainability can be treated as a policy issue at various geographic and temporal scales and the tremendous difficulties that exist in framing tourism and sustainability as a policy issue. Just as importantly, it has highlighted how such debates do not occur in a policy vacuum. Indeed, a key point of the chapter is that the policy settings that seek to deal with tourism and sustainable development are inherently political. Even the selection of indicators and policy instruments has a political dimension.

The three main approaches to sustainable tourism development identified at the start of the book were returned to and then examined through a more critical lens in the context of the green growth agenda. The latter is extremely significant as the chapter suggests that a policy paradigm that continues to favour economic growth and the primary use of indicators such as contribution to GDP is inherently destined to further draw down the Earth's natural capital. However, there are substantial issues facing the acceptance of a steady-state approach given that it challenges policy on a whole range of different scales as well as interests in the policy–making process (Hall 2011a). In particular, the approach questions an overreliance on efficiency and technology as a solution to climate and environmental change issues and instead suggests that these need to be utilized within the context of a sustainable consumption framework that is grounded in sufficiency. Explicitly addressing 'the moral and cultural issues raised by the predominant emphasis in economic thinking on individual preferences, self-interest and competitive growth' (Ekins 1993: 286) also means considering how tourism business, policy (and research) promulgates 'growthism', overconsumption and industry orthodoxies as part of 'good [BAU] practice'. As Daly (1991) suggests, steady-state economics is concerned as much with 'moral growth' as it is with biophysical equilibrium.

Nevertheless, Hall (2014a) suggests that a final sting in the sustainable tale awaits and goes to issues beyond the immediate domain of tourism. A steady-state economy inevitably requires stabilization or degrowth of the number of humans. We cannot continue to forever expand the potential tourist market. Humanity's carrying capacity is defined by the maximum sustainable impact (I) of our society. Impact (I) in turn is given by the equation

$$I = PAT$$

P = population size, A = affluence (consumption), T = pollution and environmental damage generated by technology per good consumed (Daily & Ehrlich 1992).

The reduction of (A) by sufficiency as well as that of (T) by sustainable behaviour and technological progress cannot proceed indefinitely (Polimeni *et al.* 2008), so will inevitably continue to grow if population is not stabilized or reduced (Kerschner 2010). The future is not definite, however. To identify problems is to make possible their change (Hall 2014a). The challenge is now to go beyond their identification to actually instigate transformational change.

Key Reading

Jackson, T. (2009) *Prosperity Without Growth*. London: Earthscan.

Khor, M. (2011) *Risks and Uses of the Green Economy Concept of Sustainable Development, Poverty and Equity*. Research Paper No. 40, Geneva: South Centre.

Santarius, T. (2012) *Green Growth Unravelled – How Rebound Effects Baffle Sustainability Targets When the Economy Keeps Growing*. Berlin: Wuppertal Institute for Climate, Environment and Energy.

References

Arvesen, A., Bright, R.M. and Hertwich, E.G. (2011) 'Considering only first-order effects? How simplifications lead to unrealistic technology optimism in climate change mitigation', *Energy Policy*, 39(11), 7448–7454.

Baeten, G. (2000) 'The tragedy of the highway: Empowerment, disempowerment and the politics of sustainability discourses and practices', *European Planning Studies*, 8: 69–86.

Barbier, E. (2010) 'How is the global green new deal going?' *Nature*, 8 April, 464: 832–33.

Barker, T. (2009) 'The macroeconomic rebound effect and the world economy', *Energy Efficiency*, 2: 411–27.

Bernstein, S. (2002) 'Liberal environmentalism and global environmental governance', *Global Environmental Politics*, 2(3): 1–16.

Boulding, K.E. (1945) 'The consumption concept in economic theory', *American Economic Review*, 35(2): 1–14.

—— (1949–50) 'Income or welfare', *Review of Economic Studies*, 17(2): 77–86.

Brown, L. (1981) *Building a Sustainable Society*, New York: W.W. Norton.

Buckley, R. (2012) 'Sustainable tourism: Research and reality', *Annals of Tourism Research*, 39: 528–46.

Butler, R.W. (1991) 'Tourism, environment and sustainable development', *Environmental Conservation*, 18: 201–9.

Cabrini L. (2012) 'Tourism in the UN Green Economy Report', in UNWTO High-level Regional Conference on Green Tourism, Chiang Mai, Thailand, 2012, asiapacific.unwto.org/sites/all/files/… /2012may_chiangmai_lc_0.pdf (accessed 14 November 2012).

Callon, M. (1998) 'Introduction: The embeddedness of economic markets in economics', in M. Callon (ed.) *The Laws of the Markets*. Oxford: Blackwell.

Capoccitti, S., Khare, A. and Mildenberger, U. (2010) 'Aviation industry – Mitigating climate change impacts through technology and policy', *Journal of Technology Management & Innovation*, 5(2), 66–75.

Clark, W. and Munn, R.E. (eds) (1986) *Ecologically Sustainable Development of the Biosphere*. New York: Cambridge University Press.

Cooper, T. (2005) 'Slower consumption reflections on product life spans and the "throwaway society"', *Journal of Industrial Ecology*, 9(1–2): 51–67.

Costanza, R. and Daly, H. (1992) 'Natural capital and sustainable development', *Conservation Biology*, 6(1): 37–46.

Cowper-Smith, A. and De Grosbois, D. (2011) 'The adoption of corporate social responsibility practices in the airline industry', *Journal of Sustainable Tourism*, 19(1), 59–77.

Czech, B. (2006) 'If Rome is burning, why are we fiddling?' *Conservation Biology*, 20(6): 1563–65.

—— (2008) 'Prospects for reconciling the conflict between economic growth and biodiversity conservation with technological progress', *Conservation Biology*, 22: 1389–98.

Daily, G.C. and Ehrlich, P.R. (1992) 'Population, sustainability, and earth's carrying capacity', *BioScience*, 42: 761–71.

Daly, H.E. (1972) 'In defense of a steady-state economy', *American Journal of Agricultural Economics*, 54: 945–54.

—— (1991) *Steady-state Economics*, 2nd edn, Washington DC: Island Press.

—— (1996) *Beyond Growth*. Boston: Beacon Press.

—— (2008) *A Steady-State Economy*. London: Sustainable Development Commission.

Dickinson, J.E. and Lumsdon, L. (2010) *Slow Travel and Tourism*, London: Earthscan.

Dovers, S. (1995) 'A framework for scaling and framing policy problems in sustainability', *Ecological Economics*, 12: 93–106.

—— (1996) 'Sustainability: Demands on policy', *Journal of Public Policy*, 16: 303–18.

Ekins, P. (1993) '"Limits to growth" and "sustainable development": Grappling with ecological realities', *Ecological Economics*, 8: 269–88.

Elliott, L., Hines, C., Juniper, T., Leggett, J., Lucas, C., Murphy, R., Pettifor, A., Secrett, C. and Simms, A. (2008) *Green New Deal. Joined-up Policies to Solve the Triple Crunch of the Credit Crisis, Climate Change and High Oil Prices. The first report of the Green New Deal Group*. London: New Economics Foundation.

Flipo, F. and Schneider, F. (2008) *Proceedings of the First International Conference on Economic De-growth for Ecological Sustainability and Social Equity*, Paris, 18–19 April 2008. Paris.

Gallie, W.B. (1955–56) 'Essentially contested concepts', *Proceedings of the Aristotelian Society*, 56: 167–98.

Galtung, J. (1990) 'The Green Movement: A socio-historical explanation', in M. Albrow and E. King (eds) *Globalization, Knowledge and Society: Readings from International Sociology*. London: Sage.

Gareau, B.J. (2008) 'Dangerous holes in global environmental governance: The roles of neoliberal discourse, science, and California agriculture in the Montreal Protocol', *Antipode*, 40: 120–30.

Georgescu-Roegen, N. (1971) *The Entropy Law and the Economic Process*. Cambridge MA: Harvard University Press.

—— (1977) 'The steady state and ecological salvation: A thermodynamic analysis', *Bioscience*, 27: 266–70.

Gilbert, R. and Perl, A. (2008) *Transport Revolutions: Moving People and Freight Without Oil*. London: Earthscan.

Gleditsch, N.P. (1975) 'Slow is beautiful: The stratification of personal mobility, with special reference to international aviation', *Acta Sociologica*, 18(1): 76–94.

Global Reporting Initiative (2013). G4: Sustainability Reporting Guidelines. Retrieved from https://www.globalreporting.org/resourcelibrary/GRIG4-Part1-Reporting-Principles-and-Standard-Disclosures.pdf

Gössling, S. (2011) *Carbon management in tourism: Mitigating the impacts on climate change*. London: Routledge.

Gössling, S., Hall, C.M. and Weaver, D. (2009) *Sustainable Tourism Futures: Perspectives on Systems, Restructuring and Innovations*. New York: Routledge.

Gössling, S., Ceron, J.-P., Dubois, G. and Hall, C.M. (2009) 'Hypermobile travellers', in Gössling, S. and Upham, P. (eds) *Climate Change and Aviation*. London: Earthscan.

Gössling, S., Scott, D. and Hall, C.M. (2013) 'Challenges of tourism in a low-carbon economy', *WIRES Climate Change*, DOI: 10.1002/wcc.243

—— (2014). 'Inter-market variability in CO_2 emission-intensities in tourism: Implications for destination marketing and carbon management', *Tourism Management*, in press.

Gowdy, J.M. (2000) 'Terms and concepts in ecological economics', *Wildlife Society Bulletin*, 28(1): 26–33.

Greener, I. (2001) 'Social learning and macroeconomic policy in Britain', *Journal of Public Policy*, 21: 133–52.

Hall, C.M. (1998) 'Historical antecedents of sustainable development and ecotourism: New labels on old bottles?' in C.M. Hall and A. Lew (eds) *Sustainable Tourism Development: Geographical Perspectives*. London: Addison-Wesley Longman.

—— (2007) 'Pro-poor tourism: Do "tourism exchanges benefit primarily the countries of the South"?' *Current Issues in Tourism*, 10: 111–18.

—— (2008) *Tourism Planning*, Harlow: Pearson.

—— (2009a) 'Archetypal approaches to implementation and their implications for tourism policy', *Tourism Recreation Research*, 34(3): 235–45.

—— (2009b) 'Degrowing tourism: Décroissance, sustainable consumption and steady-state tourism', *Anatolia*, 20: 46–61.

—— (2010a) 'Changing paradigms and global change: From sustainable to steady-state tourism', *Tourism Recreation Research*, 35(2): 131–45.

—— (2010b) 'Crisis events in tourism: Subjects of crisis in tourism', *Current Issues in Tourism*, 13(5): 401–17.

—— (2011a) 'Policy learning and policy failure in sustainable tourism governance: From first and second to third order change?' *Journal of Sustainable Tourism*, 19(4–5): 649–71.

—— (2011b) 'A typology of governance and its implications for tourism policy analysis', *Journal of Sustainable Tourism*, 19: 437–57.

—— (2013a) 'Green growth and tourism for a sustainable future: "We just need to put the right policies in place", or, the lunatics have taken over the asylum', presented at *International Critical Tourism Studies Conference V*, Sarajevo, Bosnia & Herzegovina, 26 June.

—— (2013b) 'Framing behavioural approaches to understanding and governing sustainable tourism consumption: Beyond neoliberalism, "nudging" and "green growth"?' *Journal of Sustainable Tourism*, DOI: 10.1080/09669582.2013.815764

—— (2014a) 'Economic greenwash: On the absurdity of tourism and green growth', in V. Reddy and K. Wilkes (eds) *Tourism in the Green Economy*, London: Earthscan.

—— (2014b) *Tourism and Social Marketing*. Abingdon: Routledge

Hall, C.M. and Lew, A.A. (eds) (1998) *Sustainable Tourism: A Geographical Perspective*. London: Addison Wesley Longman.

Hall, C.M. and Lew, A.A. (2009) *Understanding and Managing Tourism Impacts: An Integrated Approach*. London: Routledge.

Hall, C.M., Scott, D. and Gössling, S. (2013) 'The primacy of climate change for sustainable international tourism', *Sustainable Development*, 21(2): 112–21.

Hall, P.A. (1993) 'Policy paradigms, social learning, and the state: The case of economic policymaking in Britain', *Comparative Politics*, 25: 275–96.

Harrison, N.E. (2000) *Constructing Sustainable Development*. Albany: State University of New York Press.

Henderson, H. with Seth, S. (2006) *Ethical Markets: Growing the Green Economy*. White River Junction: Chelsea Green Publishing.

Hjalager, A. (1996) 'Tourism and the environment: The innovation connection', *Journal of Sustainable Tourism*, 4: 201–18.

Hoffmann, U. (2011) *Some Reflections on Climate Change, Green Growth Illusions and Development Space*, UNCTAD Discussion Paper 205. Geneva: UNCTAD.

HMSO (1994) *Sustainable Development: The UK Strategy*, Cm2426, London: HMSO.

IATA (2008) Aviation carbon offset programme. IATA guidelines and toolkit. Retrieved from: www.iata.org/whatwedo/environment/Documents/carbon-offset-guidelines-may2008.pdf

—— (2012) IATA annual review. International Air Transport Association. Retrieved from: www.iata.org/about/Documents/annual-review-2012.pdf.

Intergovernmental Panel on Climate Change (IPCC) (2007) *Climate Change 2007: Impacts, Adaptation and Vulnerability, Contribution of Working Group II to the Fourth Assessment Report*. Cambridge: Cambridge University Press.

International Union for the Conservation of Nature and Natural Resources (IUCN) (1980) *World Conservation Strategy*, The IUCN with the advice, cooperation and financial assistance of the United Nations Environment Education Program and the World Wildlife Fund and in collaboration with the Food and Agricultural Organization of the United Nations and the United Nations Educational, Scientific and Cultural Organization, Morges: IUCN.

IUCN, UNEP and WWF (1991) *Caring for the Earth: A Strategy for Sustainable Living*. Gland: IUCN, UNEP, WWF.

Jabereen, Y. (2004) 'A knowledge map for describing variegated and conflict domains of sustainable development', *Journal of Environmental Planning and Management*, 47(4): 623–42.

Jackson, T. (2005) 'Live better by consuming less? Is there a "double dividend" in sustainable consumption', *Journal of Industrial Ecology*, 9(1–2): 19–36.

Jacobs, M. (1991) *The Green Economy: Environment, Sustainable Development and the Politics of the Future.* London: Pluto Press.

Jevons, W. S. (1865) *The Coal Question: An Inquiry Concerning the Progress of the Nation, and the Probable Exhaustion of the Coal-mines.* London: Macmillan.

Jenkins, J., Nordhaus, T. and Shellenberger, M. (2011) *Energy Emergence: Rebound and Backfire as Emergent Phenomena.* Oakland: Breakthrough Institute.

Kerschner, C. (2010) 'Economic de-growth vs. steady-state economy', *Journal of Cleaner Production,* 18: 544–51.

Khalil, E.L. (1997) 'Production and environmental resources: A prelude to an evolutionary framework', *Southern Economic Journal,* 63(4): 929–46.

Khor, M. (2011) *Risks and Uses of the Green Economy Concept of Sustainable Development, Poverty and Equity.* Research Paper No. 40, Geneva: South Centre.

Kooiman, J. (2003) *Governing as Governance.* London: Sage.

Latouche, S. (2009) *Farewell to Growth.* Cambridge: Polity Press.

Le Blanc, D. (2009) 'Climate change and sustainable development revisited: Implementation challenges', *Natural Resources Forum,* 33(4): 259–61.

Lele, S.M. (1991) 'Sustainable development: A critical review', *World Development,* 19: 607–21.

Lynes, J.K., & Andrachuk, M. (2008) ,Motivations for corporate social and environmenatal responsibility: A case study of Scandinavian Airlines', *Journal of International Management, 14*(4), 377–390.

Majone, G. (1989) *Evidence, Argument and Persuasion in the Policy Process.* New Haven: Yale University Press.

Martínez-Alier, J., Pascual, U., Vivien, F-D. and Zaccai, E. (2010) 'Sustainable de-growth: Mapping the context, criticisms and future prospects of an emergent paradigm', *Ecological Economics,* 69: 1741–47.

Meadows, D.H., Meadow, D.L., Randers, J. and Behrens, W.W. (1972) *The Limits to Growth: Report to the Club of Rome.* New York: Universe Books.

Milani, B. (2000) *Designing the Green Economy: The Postindustrial Alternative to Corporate Globalization.* Lanham: Rowman & Littlefield.

Miles, I. (1985) 'The new post-industrial state', *Futures,* 17: 588–617.

Mishan, E.J. (1967) *The Costs of Economic Growth.* New York: Frederick A. Praeger.

Myers, N. (1984) *Gaia: An Atlas of Planet Management.* New York: Anchor/Doubleday.

Patridge, M. (1987) 'Building a sustainable green economy: Ethical investment, ethical work', in A. Hutton (ed.) *Green Politics in Australia.* Sydney: Angus and Robertson.

Pearce, D.W., Markandya, A. and Barbier, E.B. (eds.) (1989) *Blueprint for a Green Economy.* London: Earthscan.

Peeters, P. and Landré, M. (2011) 'The emerging global tourism geography – an environmental sustainability perspective', *Sustainability,* 4: 42–71.

Perez-Carmona, A. (2013) 'Growth: A discussion of the margins of economic and ecological thought', in L. Meuleman (ed.) *Transgovernance: Advancing Sustainable Governance.* Dortrecht: Springer.

Pierre, J. and Peters, G.B. (2000) *Governance, Politics and the State.* London: Palgrave Macmillan.

Polimeni, J.M., Mayumi, K., Giampietro, M. and Alcott, B. (2008) *The Jevons Paradox and the Myth of Resource Efficiency Improvements.* London: Earthscan.

Pollin, R., Garrett-Peltier, H., Heintz, J. and Scharber, H. (2008) *Green Recovery: A Program to Create Good Jobs and Start Building a Low-Carbon Economy.* Prepared under commission with the Center for American Progress. Amherst: Political Economy Research Institute, University of Massachusetts.

Redclift, M. (1987) *Sustainable Development:Exploring the Contradictions.* London: Methuen.

Reddy, V. and Wilkes, K. (eds) (2014) *Tourism in the Green Economy.* London: Earthscan.

Robinson, J.B., Francis, G., Legge, R. and Lerner, S. (1990) 'Defining a sustainable society: values, principles and definitions', *Alternatives: Perspectives on Society, Technology and Environment,* 17(2): 36–46.

Roseland, M. (2000) 'Sustainable community development: Integrating environmental, economic, and social objectives', *Progress in Planning,* 54(2): 73–132.

Sachs, W. (ed.) (1993) *Global Ecology: A New Arena of Political Conflict,* Halifax: Fernwood Publications.

Santarius, T. (2012) *Green Growth Unravelled – How Rebound Effects Baffle Sustainability Targets When the Economy Keeps Growing.* Berlin: Wuppertal Institute for Climate, Environment and Energy.

Sausen, R., Isaksen, I., Grewe, V., Hauglustaine, D., Lee, D.S., Myhre, G., Köhler, M.O., Pitari, G., Schumann, U., Stordal, F. and Zerefos, C. (2005) Aviation radiative forcing in 2000: An update on IPCC (1999). *Meteorologische Zeitschrift, 14*(4), 555–561.

Scott, D., Gössling, S. and Hall, C.M. (2012) 'International tourism and climate change', *WIRES Climate Change*, 3(3): 213–32.

Scott, D., Peeters, P. and Gössling, S. (2010) 'Can tourism deliver its "aspirational" emission reduction targets?' *Journal of Sustainable Tourism*, 18: 393–408.

Seyfang, G. (2009) *The New Economics of Sustainable Consumption: Seeds of Change*. London: Palgrave Macmillan.

Soderstrom, N. (2013) 'Sustainability reporting: Past, present, and trends for the future', *Insights*, *13*(1), 31–37.

Sorrell, S. (2007) *The Rebound Effect: An Assessment of the Evidence for Economy-Wide Energy Savings from Improved Energy Efficiency*. London: UK Energy Research Centre.

Steiner, A. and Sukhdev, P. (2010) 'Foreword', in E. Barbier, *Global Green New Deal: Rethinking the Economic Recovery*. Cambridge University Press, Cambridge.

Sustainable Development Commission (2011) *What Next for Sustainable Development?* Available at: www.sd-commission.org.uk/presslist.php/119/what-next-for-sustainable-development (accessed 1 April 2011).

Treuren, G. and Lane, D. (2003) 'The tourism planning process in the context of organized interests, industry structure, state capacity, accumulation and sustainability', *Current Issues in Tourism*, 6(1): 1–22.

United Nations Environment Programme (2008) 'Global Green New Deal' – Environmentally-Focused Investment Historic Opportunity for 21st Century Prosperity and Job Generation. UNEP Launches Green Economy Initiative to Get the Global Markets Back to Work. London/Nairobi, 22 October. Available at: www.unep.org/Documents.Multilingual/Default.asp?DocumentID=548&ArticleID=5957 (accessed 1 April 2013).

—— (2009) *Global Green New Deal. Policy Brief*. Geneva: UNEP.

—— (2011a) *Towards a Green Economy: Pathways to Sustainable Development and Poverty Eradication*. Nairobi: UNEP.

—— (2011b) *Towards a Green Economy: Pathways to Sustainable Development and Poverty Eradication – A Synthesis for Policy Makers*. Nairobi: UNEP.

United Nations Environment Programme and the World Tourism Organization (2005) *Making Tourism More Sustainable: A Guide for Policy Makers*. Paris: UNEP.

United Nations World Tourism Organization (2007) *Tourism Will Contribute to Solutions for Global Climate Change and Poverty Challenges*, Press release, UNWTO Press and Communications Department, 8 March, Berlin/Madrid.

—— (2014) *Tourism Highlights 2014 Edition*. Madrid: UNWTO.

Vermeulen, S.J. (2009) *Sustainable Consumption: A Fairer Deal for Poor Consumers*. Environment and Poverty Times, No. 6, September. Arendal: UNEP and GRID.

Wheeller, B. (1993) 'Sustaining the ego', *Journal of Sustainable Tourism*, 1: 121–29.

World Commission for Environment and Development (WCED) (1987) *Our Common Future: The Brundtland Report*. Oxford: Oxford University Press.

World Economic Forum (2009a) *Towards a Low Carbon Travel & Tourism Sector*. Davos: WEF.

—— (2009b) *The Travel & Tourism Competitiveness Report 2009: Managing in a Time of Turbulence*. Davos: World Economic Forum.

World Travel and Tourism Council (WTTC) (2003) *Blueprint for New Tourism*. London. WTTC.

—— (2009) *Leading the Challenge*. Available at: www.wttc.org/bin/pdf/original pdf file/climate change final.pdf (accessed 2 January 2010).

Index

Note: page numbers in **bold** type refer to Tables; those in *italic* type refer to Figures.